CONTENTS

INTRODUCTION

Edexcel has revised the structure of the HND/HNC qualifications in Business, and its Guidelines covering the content of each Unit. These changes are effective from September 2004. This book has been **written specifically to cover the revised Guidelines** and provides concise yet comprehensive coverage.

The HNC and HND qualifications in Business have always been very demanding. The suggested content, set out by Edexcel in Guidelines for each unit, includes topics which are normally covered at degree level. Students therefore need books which get straight to the core of these topics, and which build upon the student's existing knowledge and experience. BPP's series of Course Books have been designed to meet that need.

This book has been written specifically for specialist Units 21 to 24. These units form the endorsed title route in Human Resource Management. The book covers the Edexcel guidelines and suggested content in full, and includes the following features.

- The Edexcel guidelines

- A study guide explaining the key features of the book and how to get the most from your studies

- A glossary and index

- Assignments

Each chapter contains:

- An introduction and study objectives

- Summary diagrams and signposts, to guide you through the chapter

- Numerous activities, topics for discussion, definitions and examples, all designed to bring the subject to life and enable students to apply their learning to practical situations

- A chapter roundup, a quick quiz with answers and answers to activities

BPP Professional Education are the leading providers of targeted texts for professional qualifications. Our customers need to study effectively. They cannot afford to waste time. They expect clear, concise and highly-focused study material. This series of Course Books for HNC and HND Business has been designed and produced to fulfil those needs.

BPP Professional Education
2004

Other titles in this series:

Mandatory units

Unit 1	Marketing
Unit 2	Managing Financial Resources and Decisions
Unit 3	Organisations and Behaviour
Unit 4	Business Environment
Unit 5	Common Law 1
Unit 6	Business Decision Making
Unit 7	Business Strategy
Unit 8	Research Project

Endorsed title routes

Units 9-12	Finance
Units 13-16	Management
Units 17-20	Marketing
Units 21-24	Human Resource Management
Units 25-28	Law

For more information, or to place an order, please call 020 8740 2211, or fill in the order form at the back of this book.

If you would like to send in your comments on this book, please turn to the review form on the last page.

EDEXCEL GUIDELINES FOR UNIT 21: HUMAN RESOURCES MANAGEMENT

Description of the Unit

This unit provides an introduction to the concepts and practices of human resources management within the United Kingdom. The aim of the unit is to provide an understanding of the human resources management role and function within the key areas of resourcing, reward, development and relations.

Summary of learning outcomes

Outcomes and assessment criteria

Outcomes	Assessment criteria
	To achieve each outcome a learner must demonstrate an ability to:
1 Investigate the traditional view of **personnel management and the new approach of human resource management**	• distinguish between 'personnel management' and 'human resource management' and discuss the historical development and changing context in which they operate • assess the role, tasks and activities of the human resource practitioner • evaluate the role and responsibilities of line managers in human resource practices
2 Evaluate the **procedures and practices used for recruiting and selecting suitable employees**	• analyse the need for human resource planning, the information required and the stages involved in this process • compare the structured process for recruitment in two organisations and evaluate the methods and media that can be used • evaluate the interview as a selection technique and discuss a range of alternative selection methods available • evaluate selection practices and procedures in two organisations comparing these to 'best practice'
3 Establish the effectiveness of **principles and procedures for monitoring and rewarding the employee**	• evaluate the process of job evaluation and the main factors determining pay • identify a range of rewards systems, eg performance-related pay and its benefits and limitations

BPP
PROFESSIONAL EDUCATION

Outcomes	Assessment criteria
	To achieve each outcome a learner must demonstrate an ability to:
	• explain the link between motivational theory and reward
	• explore organisational approaches to monitoring performance
4 Explore **rights and procedures** on exit from an organisation	• evaluate exit procedures used by two organisations, comparing these to best practice
	• analyse selection criteria for redundancy

Content

Covered in chapter(s)

1 **Personnel management and the new approach of human resources management**

The nature and development of personnel management and human resource management: historical development of personnel management; the change in context which has led to the term human resources management

1, 8

The roles and tasks of the human resources management function: the range of tasks and activities of the human resource management practitioner, eg recruitment and selection, payroll administration and reward management, training and development and performance management and employee relations; the changing roles of human resource specialists, eg the move from reactive/welfare to proactive/ strategic and increasing requirement to work in partnership with the business; the involvement of line managers in human resource practices, eg selection, disciplinary handling, absence management, coaching and appraising

1

2 **Procedures and practices used for recruiting and selecting suitable employees**

Human resource planning: definition, purpose, processes and stages involved; the types of data needed as a basis for human resource planning; limiting factors, eg supply and demand for labour

2

The systematic approach to recruitment: recruitment policies, recruitment procedure, job analysis, job description, personnel specification, recruitment methods and media including design of application form

3

The systematic approach to selection: aims and objectives of the selection process; the interview – advantages and disadvantages, interviewer skills and questioning techniques; alternative selection methods to supplement the interview, eg assessment centres, psychological testing, work simulations, references

4

	Covered in chapter(s)

The legislative framework and benchmark evidence guiding the recruitment and selection process: reference to Sex Discrimination Act (1975), Race Relations Act (1976), Equal Pay Act (1970), Disability Discrimination Act (1995); exploration of a range of organisational approaches to recruitment and selection highlighting 'best practice'

3, 4, 5

3   **Principles and procedures for monitoring and rewarding the employee**

Reward management: the process of job evaluation and the main factors determining pay, different types of reward systems, the relationship between motivation theories and reward, approaches to monitoring and managing performance

5, 6

4   **Exit rights and procedures**

Tribunals: role, composition, powers and procedure

7, 11

Dismissal: wrongful, unfair, justified

Termination of employment: resignation, retirement, termination of contract

Redundancy: definition, procedure, selection, redeployment, retraining

Management of exit: procedures, notice, counselling, training

Guidance

Delivery

Learners' understanding of human resources management can be developed through the use of a variety of learning methods including lectures, discussions, seminars, videos, role plays, case studies and learner-led presentations.

Investigations of human resources management policies and practices within organisations and talks from human resources management practitioners can both develop understanding and provide support for the knowledge and skill base established within the unit.

Assessment

Evidence of outcomes may be assessed as follows:

- use of presentations as a context for conveying understanding of human resource management issues; learners could use their own experiences and commercial contacts as a basis for collection and analysis of human resource management policies and practices

- use of role plays to simulate interview practice

- case studies to assess learners' understanding of human resource management issues, eg disciplinary and grievance handling, reward systems, training interventions

- written assignments to test knowledge and understanding

Links

The unit is part of the HN Human Resource Management pathway and forms a direct link with other human resource units in the programme such as *Unit 3: Organisations and Behaviour, Unit 22: Managing Human Resources Issues, Unit 23: Human Resource Development* and *Unit 24: Employee Relations.*

Links are also to be found within *Unit 25: English Legal System,* which covers employment protection legislation.

The unit covers some of the underpinning knowledge and understanding for the following units of the NVQ in Operational Personnel Level 4:

- Mandatory units
- Area A – Resourcing and Retention

Resources

Sufficient library resources should be available to enable learners to achieve this unit. Texts that are particularly relevant are:

Armstrong M – *A Handbook of Human Resources Practice* (Kogan Page, 2001)

Business Basics Human Resource Management – 2nd Ed (London, BPP Publishing, 1997)

Corbridge M and Pilbeam S – *Employment Resourcing* (FT Prentice Hall, 1998)

Dransfield R, Howkins S, Hudson F and Davies W– *Human Resource Management for Higher Awards* (Heinemann, 1996)

Foot M and Hook C – *Introducing Human Resource Management* – 3rd Ed (Harlow, FT: Prentice Hall, 2002)

Torrington D, Hall L and Taylor S – *Human Resource Management* – 5th Ed (Harlow, FT: Prentice Hall, 2002)

Journals/Newspapers

- *People Management*
- *Personnel Review*
- *Personnel Today*
- *Human Resource Management Journal*
- *Training*
- Any quality broadsheet newspapers – eg *The Guardian*

Videos

Companies such as Video Arts and Melrose produce a variety of videos which may be useful in covering human resource management topics. Television current affairs programmes can also provide a useful additional resource.

Websites

- www.acas.org.uk — Advisory, Conciliation and Arbitration Service
- www.bized.ac.uk — which provides business case studies appropriate for educational purposes
- www.cipd.co.uk — Chartered Institute of Personnel and Development website with a range of learning resources

- www.compactlaw.co.uk   Employment questions and answers
- www.cre.org.uk   Commission for Racial Equality
- www.drc-gb.org.uk   Disability Rights Commission
- www.dti.gov.uk   Department of Trade and Industry
- www.employment-studies.co.uk   Institute for Employment Studies
- www.eoc.org.uk   Equal Opportunities Commission
- www.guardian.co.uk   Provides links to news items and reports
- www.hse.gov.uk   Health and Safety Executive
- www.incomesdata.co.uk   up-to-date intelligence on employment issues (Incomes Data Service)
- www.peoplemanagement.co.uk   bi-monthly journal of the Chartered Institute of Personnel and Development
- www.personneltoday.com   Relevant articles and statistics
- www.trainingjournal.com   Relevant articles on current training and development topics

For recruitment and selection learners could access websites such as:

- www.bbc.co.uk/jobs
- www.jobability.com
- www.monster.co.uk
- www.totaljobs.com

EDEXCEL GUIDELINES FOR UNIT 22: MANAGING HUMAN RESOURCES ISSUES

Description of the Unit

The aim of this unit is to build upon the knowledge and understanding developed in the human resource management unit.

A broader and wider perspective is developed in relation to the application of human resource management practices. A comparative approach is also introduced to consider HRM policy and practice in a global context.

Summary of learning outcomes

Outcomes and assessment criteria

Outcomes	Assessment criteria
	To achieve each outcome a learner must demonstrate the ability to:
1 Examine the **differing perspectives of human resource management**	• explain Guest's model of hard-soft, loose-tight dimensions of HRM • review the differences between Storey's definitions of HRM and personnel and IR practices • analyse HRM from a strategic perspective and its implications for the role of the line manager and employees
2 Review ways of developing **flexibility within the workplace**	• review and explain a model of flexibility and show how this might be applied in practice • describe the need for flexibility and the types of flexibility which may be developed by an organisation and give examples of how they can be implemented • evaluate the advantages and disadvantages of flexible working practices from both the employee and the employer perspective
3 Determine the need for **equal opportunities within the workplace**	• describe the forms of discrimination that take place • review how the legislative framework and any proposed changes relating to discrimination in the workplace can be applied by an organisation • explain a range of current initiatives and practices which focus on equal opportunities in employment

Links

The unit has particular links with the other units in the *Human Resource Management* pathway. It also has links with NVQ Level 4 in Personnel.

Resources

Suggested reading

Sufficient library resources should be available to enable learners to achieve this unit. Texts that are particularly relevant are:

Armstrong M – *A Handbook of Human Resources Practice* (Kogan Page, 2001)

Business Basics Human Resource Management – 2ⁿᵈ Ed (London, BPP Publishing, 1997)

Corbridge M and Pilbeam S – *Employment Resourcing* (FT Prentice Hall, 1998)

Dransfield R, Howkins S, Hudson F and Davies W– *Human Resource Management for Higher Awards* (Heinemann, 1996)

Foot M and Hook C – *Introducing Human Resource Management* – 3ʳᵈ Ed (Harlow, FT: Prentice Hall, 2002)

Torrington D, Hall L and Taylor S – *Human Resource Management* – 5ᵗʰ Ed (Harlow, FT: Prentice Hall, 2002)

Newspapers/Newspapers

- *People Management*
- *Personnel Review*
- *Personnel Today*
- *Human Resource Management Journal*
- *Training*
- *The Economist*
- Any quality broadsheet newspapers – eg *The Guardian*

Videos

Companies such as Video Arts and Melrose produce a variety of videos, which may be useful in covering human resource management topics. Television current affairs programmes can also provide a useful additional resource.

Websites

www.acas.org.uk	Advisory, Conciliation and Arbitration Service
www.bized.ac.uk	which provides business case studies appropriate for educational purposes
www.cipd.co.uk	Chartered Institute of Personnel and Development website with a range of learning resources
www.compactlaw.co.uk	Employment questions and answers
www.cre.org.uk	Commission for Racial Equality
www.drc-gb.org.uk	Disability Rights Commission
www.dti.gov.uk	Department of Trade and Industry

- www.employment-studies.co.uk   Institute for Employment Studies
- www.eoc.org.uk   Equal Opportunities Commission
- www.incomesdata.co.uk   up-to-date intelligence on employment issues (Incomes Data Service)
- www.guardian.co.uk   Provides links to news items and reports
- www.hse.gov.uk   Health and Safety Executive
- www.ilo.org   International Labour Organisation
- www.isma.org.uk   International Stress Management Association (UK)
- www.peoplemanagement.co.uk   bi-monthly journal of the Chartered Institute of Personnel and Development
- www.personneltoday.com   Relevant articles and statistics
- www.successunlimited.co.uk   Site on bullying in the workplace
- www.trainingjournal.com   Relevant articles on current training and development topics
- www.wfpma.com.br   A journal with articles on international aspects of managing people at work
- www.wto.org   World Trade Organisation

EDEXCEL GUIDELINES FOR UNIT 23: HUMAN RESOURCES DEVELOPMENT

Description of the Unit

This unit will develop students' understanding of the nature and role of training and employee development. The unit provides an introduction to the range of government initiatives aimed at developing skills within the labour market. It explores how people learn as well as developing a systematic approach to the design and delivery of training. Consideration is given as to how to measure the effectiveness of training and development in practice.

Summary of learning outcomes

Outcomes and assessment criteria

Outcomes	Assessment criteria To achieve each outcome a learner must demonstrate the ability to:
1 Explore a range of **differing learning theories and learning styles**	• differentiate between different learning styles • analyse learning theories and explain their contribution to the planning and design of learning events • explain the implications of the learning curve and the importance of ensuring the transfer of learning to the workplace
2 Critically evaluate the **planning and design of training and development**	• explain how training contributes to the achievement of business objectives and the role of a training and development policy • explain and describe a systematic approach to training and development using a model and outline each stage of the training cycle • critically evaluate the factors to take into account when planning a training and development event • evaluate an organisation's approach to training
3 Explore the **role and purpose of evaluation and evaluation techniques**	• examine the importance of evaluation and how it can help to market the contribution of training and development to the business • explore the way that evaluation needs to be on-going and systematically planned for at each stage of the training cycle

Outcomes	Assessment criteria
	To achieve each outcome a learner must demonstrate the ability to:
	• review the key stakeholders in the evaluation process and the roles that they play
	• compare and contrast a range of evaluation techniques and the pros and cons of these
	• analyse the contribution of evaluation models and the difficulties that these can pose in practice
4 Examine a range of **government-led initiatives** aimed at developing skills in the labour market	• analyse the context influencing the role of government in training and development and the growing emphasis on lifelong learning and continuous development
	• review the development of NVQs, MCI and the competency movement
	• examine a range of contemporary training initiatives introduced by the UK government

Content

Covered in chapter(s)

1 **Learning theories and learning styles**

Learning theories and learning styles: activists, reflectors, theorists, pragmatists (Honey and Mumford 1982), and Kolb's (1979) learning style inventory; learning theories, eg behaviourist, cognitive; impact of the learning curve and transfer of learning to the work place; impact of learning theories and styles when planning and designing a learning event

13

2 **The planning and design of training and development**

The systematic approach: the role of training and development policy within the organisation, identification of training and development needs, setting training objectives, planning issues, eg numbers, location, content, internal/external trainers, administration; designing and using a range of training and development methods, eg advantages and disadvantages of a range of on- and off-the-job methods, eg 'sitting next to Nellie', mentoring, coaching, action learning, assignments, projects, shadowing, secondments, training courses, seminars, e-learning and outdoor development; delivery of the learning event

14

Covered in chapter(s)

3 **The role and purpose of evaluation and evaluation techniques**

The 'what, why, when and who' of evaluation: exploration of what evaluation involves and what can be measured, the importance of evaluating learning events and measuring the contribution, the need for continuous evaluation at every stage in the training cycle, the key stakeholders in the evaluation process and their roles within it

14

A range of evaluation techniques: eg 'Happy Sheets', pre/post tests, and the benefits and limitations of these; different evaluation models and the difficulties that these pose in practice, eg Kirkpatrick, CIRO

14

4 **Government-led initiatives**

General and vocational training schemes and initiatives: context influencing government approaches to training and development in the UK; development of NVQs, MCI and the competency movement; national training targets and the role of the Qualifications and Curriculum Authority (QCA); specific initiatives, eg modern apprenticeship schemes, Investors in People, New Deal, University for Industry – learndirect, Learning and Skills Councils, Connexions

15

Guidance

Delivery

Learners' understanding of human resources development can be developed through the use of a variety of learning methods including lectures, discussions, seminars, videos, role plays, case studies and learner-led presentations.

Investigations of human resource development practices within organisations and talks from training and development practitioners can both develop understanding and provide support for the knowledge and skill base established within the unit.

Assessment

Evidence of outcomes may be assessed as follows:

- use of presentations as a means of demonstrating understanding of how to design and deliver a learning event. Learners could use their own experience and commercial contacts as a basis for collection and analysis of human resource development practices

- case studies and the review of current journal articles to assess learners' understanding of human resource development issues, eg e-learning, outdoor development and evaluation

- written assignments to test knowledge and understanding

Links

The unit has particular links with the other units in the *Human Resource Management* pathway. It also has links with NVQ Level 4 in Personnel.

Resources

Suggested reading

Sufficient library resources should be available to enable learners to achieve this unit. Texts that are particularly relevant are:

Barrington H and Reid M A – *Training Interventions* – 6th Ed (CIPD, 1999)

Moorby E – *How to Succeed in Employee Development* – 2nd Ed (McGraw-Hill, 1996)

Redman T and Wilkinson A – *Contemporary Human Resource Management* – (Harlow, FT: Prentice Hall, 2001)

Foot M and Hook C – *Introducing Human Resource Management* – 3rd Ed (Harlow, FT: Prentice Hall, 2002)

Newspapers/Newspapers

- *People Management*
- *Personnel Review*
- *Personnel Today*
- *Training*
- Any quality broadsheet newspapers – eg *The Guardian*

Videos

Companies such as Video Arts and Melrose produce a variety of videos, which may be useful in covering human resource development topics. Television current affairs programmes can also provide a useful additional resource.

Websites

www.bized.ac.uk	which provides business case studies appropriate for educational purposes
www.cipd.co.uk	Chartered Institute of Personnel and Development website with a range of learning resources
www.dfes.gov.uk	Department for Education and Skills
www.dti.gov.uk	Department of Trade and Industry
www.guardian.co.uk	Provides links to news items and reports
www.hse.gov.uk	Health and Safety Executive
www.iipuk.co.uk	Investors in People UK
www.incomesdata.co.uk	up-to-date intelligence on employment issues (Incomes Data Service)
www.learndirect.co.uk	UfI learndirect
www.lsc.gov.uk	The Learning and Skills Council
www.newdeal.gov.uk	New Deal
www.nto-nc.org	The National Training Organisational National Council
www.peoplemanagement.co.uk	bi-monthly journal of the Chartered Institute of Personnel and Development

- www.personneltoday.com   Relevant articles and statistics
- www.qca.org.uk   Qualifications and Curriculum Authority
- www.trainingjournal.com   Relevant articles on current training and development topics

BPP
PROFESSIONAL EDUCATION

EDEXCEL GUIDELINES FOR UNIT 24: EMPLOYEE RELATIONS

Description of the Unit

The main aim of this unit is to provide a general introduction to employee relations and develop knowledge and understanding of the changes which have taken place over the years with respect to the employment relationship in the UK. The unit considers the nature of industrial conflict and the resolution of collective disputes. The processes of collective bargaining and negotiation are also explored.

Summary of learning outcomes

Outcomes and assessment criteria

Outcomes	Assessment criteria
	To achieve each outcome a learner must demonstrate the ability to:
1　Explore the **context of employee relations against a changing background**	• explain the unitary and pluralistic frames of reference • review the development of trade unions and nature of industrial relations • determine the role of a trade union and its contribution to effective employee relations • differentiate the roles taken by the main actors in employee relations
2　Examine the nature of **industrial conflict and the resolution of collective disputes**	• explain the ideological framework of industrial relations • investigate the different types of collective dispute • review dispute procedures and the resolution of conflict • critically evaluate the effectiveness of dispute procedures in resolving conflict in a given situation
3　Explore the processes of **collective bargaining and negotiation**	• explore the nature and scope of collective bargaining • describe the processes of negotiation • prepare and apply negotiation strategy for a given situation
4　Investigate the concept of **employee participation and involvement**	• investigate the effectiveness of arrangements made by two organisations to involve their employees in decision-making

Outcomes	Assessment criteria
	To achieve each outcome a learner must demonstrate the ability to:
	• analyse the influence of the EU on democracy in the UK • distinguish between industrial relations and employee relations • assess the effectiveness of employee involvement techniques • establish the impact of human resource management on employee relations

Content

Covered in chapter(s)

1 **The context of employee relations**

The role of the trade union: types of trade union, the Trade Union Congress, employer associations, trade union representatives   16

The history and development of trade unions: the rise of trade unionism, trade unions and the law, the changing political and economic context and its relevance to industrial relations   16

The main actors in employee relations: workers and their organisations, managers and their organisations, government agencies concerned with the workplace and work community   16

The unitarist and pluralistic frames of reference: review of the differing perspectives taken by the stakeholders in employee relations   16

2 **Industrial conflict and the resolution of collective disputes**

The nature of industrial conflict: ideological framework, conflict and co-operation   17

Different types of dispute: collective disputes, strike action, strike statistics, ballots, no-strike agreements   17

Resolving conflict: dispute procedures, arbitration and the role of the Advisory, Conciliation and Arbitration Service (ACAS)   17

3 **Collective bargaining and negotiation**

The nature and scope of collective bargaining: role of shop stewards, union officials, employer associations and management   17

The collective bargaining process: institutional agreements for collective bargaining, local workplace bargaining, single-table bargaining   17

Negotiation processes: negotiation strategy, preparation for negotiation, conducting the case-settlement, disclosure of information   17

4 **Employee participation and involvement**

Consultation and employee participation: different forms of employee consultation and participation, joint consultation committees, upward-downward forms of communication   18

	Covered in chapter(s)
Industrial democracy and employee participation: European Works Councils (European Objectives), the social dimensions of the European Union and supervisory boards, national cultural differences towards democracy and employee participation	18
Employee involvement techniques: sharing information, consultation, financial participation, commitment to quality, developing the individual, involvement of other stakeholders	18
Empowerment: devolution of responsibility/authority to line managers/employees, the role of human resource management, approach to employee relations (link to unitarist and pluralist perspectives)	18

Guidance

Delivery

Learners' understanding of employee relations can be developed through the use of a variety of learning methods including lectures, discussions, seminars, videos, role plays, case studies and learner-led presentations.

Investigations of employee relations policies and practices within organisations and talks from union officials and human resource management practitioners can both develop understanding and provide support for the knowledge and skill base established within the unit.

Assessment

Evidence of outcomes may be assessed as follows:

- use of presentations as a context for conveying understanding of employee relations
- use of role plays for exploring the processes of collective bargaining and negotiation
- case studies to assess learners' understanding of the nature of industrial conflict and the resolution of collective action
- written assignments to test knowledge and understanding

Links

This unit is part of the HN Personnel pathway and forms a direct link with other personnel units in the programme: *Unit 3: Organisations and Behaviour, Unit 21: Human Resource Management, Unit 22: Managing Human Resources Issues* and *Unit 23: Human Resource Development.*

Links may also be found with *Unit 4: Organisations, Competition and Environment, Unit 6: Business Decision Making, Unit 26: English Legal System* and *Unit 39: Quality Management.*

This unit covers some of the underpinning knowledge and understanding for units of the NVQ in Personnel at Level 4.

Resources

Sufficient library resources should be available to enable learners to achieve this unit. Texts that are particularly relevant are:

Blyton P and Turnbull P – *The Dynamics of Employee Relations* – 2nd Ed (Palgrave, 1998)

Farnham D – *Employee Relations in Context* – 2nd Ed (London, CIPD, 2000)

Gennard J and Judge G C – *Employee Relations* – 3rd Ed (London, CIPD, 2002)

Newspapers/Newspapers

- *British Journal of Industrial Relations*
- *Employment Gazette*
- *Industrial Relations Journal*
- *Industrial Relations Review and Report*
- *People Management*
- *Personnel Review*
- *Personnel Today*
- *European Journal of Industrial Relations*
- *Labour History Review*
- *Labour Research*
- Any quality broadsheet newspapers – eg *The Guardian*

Videos

Companies such as Video Arts and Melrose produce a variety of videos, which may be useful in covering employee relations topics. Television current affairs programmes can also provide a useful additional resource.

Websites

- www.acas.org.uk — Advisory, Conciliation and Arbitration Service
- www.bized.ac.uk — which provides business case studies appropriate for educational purposes
- www.cac.gov.uk — Central Arbitration Committee
- www.cbi.org.uk — Confederation of British Industry
- www.compactlaw.co.uk — Employment questions and answers
- www.cre.org.uk — Commission for Racial Equality
- www.drc-gb.org.uk — Disability Rights Commission
- www.dti.gov.uk — Department of Trade and Industry
- www.employment-studies.co.uk — Institute for Employment Studies
- www.eoc.org.uk — Equal Opportunities Commission
- www.ets.gov.uk — Employment Tribunal Service
- www.gftu.org.uk — General Federation of Trade Unions
- www.guardian.co.uk — Provides links to news items and reports
- www.hse.gov.uk — Health and Safety Executive

- www.icftu.org   International Confederation of Free Trade Unions
- www.incomesdata.co.uk   up-to-date intelligence on employment issues (Incomes Data Service)
- www.labournet.net   Discussion forum for various employment issues
- www.lowpay.gov.uk   Low Pay Commission
- www.peoplemanagement.co.uk   bi-monthly journal of the Chartered Institute of Personnel and Development
- www.personneltoday.com   Relevant articles and statistics
- www.tuc.org.uk   Trades Union Congress

PART A

UNIT 21: HUMAN RESOURCES MANAGEMENT

Chapter 1:
PERSONNEL MANAGEMENT AND HRM

Introduction

It can be argued that people are an organisation's most important resource: after all, organisations are made up of people, and the way money, technology, information and other resources are used depends on human decisions. So it is generally recognised that the success of any business is greatly influenced by the calibre and attitude of the people who work for it.

It is therefore also commonly recognised that *someone* in every organisation will need to be responsible for the many matters that arise in connection with the recruitment, selection, training, motivation, payment and movement of staff through the organisation, as well as compliance with the various laws relating to employment. This is traditionally the role of the personnel function.

However, as the pace of social and technological change has quickened, there has been a growing recognition that thought must be given to managing the vital human resource at an earlier stage and at a higher level of organisational planning than has previously been the case. This has encouraged a longer-term, more proactive and strategic approach to people management, known as 'Human Resource Management' or HRM. In this chapter, we trace the development of this approach, while in Chapter 8, we explore its implications further, as an introduction to the various HR issues covered in Unit 22.

Your objectives

In this chapter you will learn about the following.

(a) The historical development of personnel management

(b) The shift towards 'human resource management' as an alternative approach

(c) The role and tasks of the human resource management (HRM) function

(d) The involvement of line managers in human resource practices

1 THE NATURE OF PERSONNEL MANAGEMENT

1.1 The nature of personnel management

The main professional body for personnel managers in the UK is the Chartered Institute of Personnel and Development (CIPD). The CIPD (formerly known as the Institute of Personnel Management) defined the function of personnel management as follows.

Definition

'Personnel management is that part of management concerned with people at work and with their relationships within an enterprise...'

'[Personnel management's] aim is to bring together, and develop into an effective organisation, the men and women who make up an enterprise, having regard for the well-being of the individual and of working groups, to enable them to make their best contribution to its success.

'In particular, personnel management is concerned with the development and application of policies governing:

- Human resources planning, recruitment, selection, placement and termination

- Education and training; career development

- Terms of employment, methods and standards of remuneration

- Working conditions and employee services

- Formal and informal communication and consultation both through the representatives of employers and employees and at all levels throughout the enterprise

- Negotiation and application of agreement on wages and working conditions; procedures for the avoidance and settlement of disputes.

'Personnel management must also be concerned with the human and social implication of change in internal organisation and methods of working, and of economic and social changes in the community.'

This statement highlights a number of useful – and potentially controversial – ideas about personnel management.

(a) It is centrally concerned with **people and relationships**. It is founded on attempts to understand and manage human behaviour: we will encounter some of these attempts – in the form of theories of learning, motivation and so on – in later chapters of this Course Book. It also involves a moral or ethical dimension: the employment relationship has 'human and social implications', raising issues of human dignity, fairness and corporate social responsibility.

(b) It embraces not only 'soft' values to do with the well-being of people at work, but also 'hard' values to do with the **success of the enterprise**: the role of people and relationships in fostering efficiency, effectiveness and contribution. (These 'soft' and 'hard' perspectives, and HRM's role in seeking a 'fit' between them, are discussed in Part B of this Course Book.)

(c) It is a '**part of management**'. Organisation of the personnel function may require a specialist department or departments, but it has been suggested that a separate function need not exist: *all* managers in an organisation needs to achieve results through the efforts of other people, and must therefore manage the employment relationship.

Activity 1 (30 minutes)

Check out the websites of two or three Professional HR associations, such as:

www.cipd.co.uk   Chartered Institute of Personnel & Development (UK)

www.shrm.org   Society for Human Resource Management (USA)

www.jshrm.org   Japan Society for Human Resource Management

Browse through their home and mission statement pages, noting any useful definitions of 'personnel management' and 'Human Resource Management', and any statements of the philosophy underlying these concepts. How (and why) are people seen as important to the success of business? What cultural differences (if any) can you notice? What kinds of activity are seen as part of the personnel/HR professional's role?

---

2 THE HISTORICAL DEVELOPMENT OF PERSONNEL MANAGEMENT

Tyson & Fell (1986) suggest that personnel management has its roots in four traditions, arising from developments in the employment environment over the last 150 years.

- The welfare tradition
- The industrial relations tradition
- The control of labour tradition
- The professional tradition

2.1 The personnel practitioner as welfare worker

It is generally agreed that the personnel function can be traced back to the benevolent attempts by some employers in the latter half of the nineteenth century to improve the working conditions and circumstances of workers, who had been hard hit by the first wave of industrialisation and urbanisation. Victorian entrepreneurs in the UK like Rowntree, Cadbury and Lever initiated programmes providing such facilities as company housing, basic health care, canteens and education for workers' families, managed on behalf of the employer by 'industrial welfare workers'.

There was a dual motivation for these measures.

(a) They reflected a wider programme of **social reform and philanthropy,** led by political and religious movements of the day. Groups such as the Quakers, who in the USA were leaders in the abolition of slavery, strove to integrate successful business performance with the social, moral and spiritual betterment of their workers. (This may seem unduly paternalistic today, but at the time brought much-needed improvements in the quality of working life and the legal protection of workers.)

(b) Improved health and education, and the appreciation of their beneficiaries, secured an on-going pool of **suitable and willing labour** for the employer. Cadbury considered welfare and efficiency as 'two sides of the same coin' at his model factory at Bournville.

Both motivations were highlighted when the British government attempted to recruit troops for the Crimean and Boer wars: so many volunteers were prevented from enlisting by medical deficiencies that there was an outcry about the health of the nation's labour force.

Nevertheless, the **welfare tradition** of personnel management arose from the time when much of the work and responsibility of the personnel officer was directed to the benefit of the employees, rather than to the strategic concerns of the enterprise and its management. Personnel management was in a sense the 'soft' or person-centred part or side of management. In specialised areas of personnel management today, such as occupational health, employee assistance schemes, workplace counselling services and so on, elements of this tradition persist with some force. However, as we will see below, the personnel officer is not in any formal sense the representative of the workforce: (s)he is paid to be part of the organisation's management team, as both representative and adviser.

2.2 The personnel practitioner as industrial relations negotiator

From the mid 19th century, the newly industrialised workers were also becoming increasingly organised. The legalisation of trade unions in 1871 raised the need for systematic frameworks for negotiation, conflict resolution and the management of relations between labour and management.

The increasingly active role taken by labour organisations was reflected in political recognition. The Labour Party was formed in 1900 (as the Labour Representation Committee, renamed in 1906), largely out of, and funded by, the trades union movement.

The industrial relations tradition of personnel management arose in response to the growing power of trade unions through to the 1960s and '70s, when much of the work and responsibility of the personnel officer involved mediating between the sides in industrial disputes, facilitating collective bargaining and negotiation and ensuring compliance with industrial relations law and regulation.

Elements of this tradition may persist in the modern era in the perceptions of personnel officers and other parties to negotiations, conflict resolution, discipline and grievance procedures and so on. The 'diplomatic' role of personnel may also pose a dilemma of dual allegiance – particularly where there is lack of trust in the relationship between the personnel function and other members of the management team.

> **Activity 2** **(20 minutes)**
>
> Whose 'side' is the personnel practitioner on? From your own experience or current knowledge of what a personnel officer does, suggest three examples of the conflict which might exist between his or her position as a member of the management team and his or her special relationship with the workforce, and discuss what you feel are the issues involved. Where would *you* stand on these issues?

2.3 The personnel practitioner as bureaucrat

Meanwhile, in the boom following the industrial revolution, businesses had been growing larger and more complex. The control of labour tradition of personnel management arose in response to the increasing pace of organisational growth and change. The primary responsibility of the personnel officer came to be seen as supporting management by standardising, monitoring and controlling the range and complexity of workplace activity. This involved a range of activities such as: job allocation and performance monitoring; time-keeping and control of absenteeism; recording sick leave and holidays; administering pay and benefits, training and promotion; devising rules, regulations and compliance checklists; preparing workforce-related reports and returns and so on.

This is an essentially bureaucratic tradition, which is still evident in many personnel departments. It has been perpetuated, in part, by the ambiguity of personnel's perceived role and authority in the management team: where a department lacks direct positional or 'line' authority, the application of rules, regulations, procedures and forms is one of the key methods of exercising influence.

2.4 The personnel practitioner as professional

The latter half of the 20th century saw a period of intense legislation in all areas of employment: health and safety, employment protection, equal opportunities and so on. (This has continued in the early 2000s, largely driven by the requirement to implement European social policy and EU directives.)

The increasing complexity of legislation and regulation, together with the development of increasingly sophisticated behavioural and managerial theory, fostered specialism within the personnel function. The need for a specialised body of knowledge – drawing on law, economics, administrative management and the social sciences (sociology, psychology and so on) led to the establishment of a scheme of education and qualification, and the professionalisation of the work of the personnel practitioner.

Personnel management became recognised as a discipline in its own right, broadly applicable to all fields of employment. The Institute of Personnel Management made determined efforts to establish personnel management as a profession, through a programme of learning and examinations leading to qualification; opportunities for professional communication and networking; and requirements for continuing professional development.

According to the CIPD's *Code of Professional Practice in Personnel Management*, the personnel practitioner has three principle areas of responsibility.

- 'A personnel manager's primary responsibility is to his **employer**.'

- He will 'resolve the conflict which must sometimes exist between his position as a member of the **management team** and his special relationship with the **workforce** in general and with individual **employees**.'

- He will 'use his best endeavours to enhance the standing... of his **profession**' in dealing with other bodies.

EXAMPLE

TEAM PLAYERS WITH ENERGY AND VISION

Resource manager

You will have overall management for the movement of resources within projects, be an active member in negotiations with departmental heads and project managers, have close links with other offices in order to utilise international resources, be responsible for defining yearly recruitment targets and identify detailed skill sets within each competence.

You must have 2+ years of resource or project-management experience. New media knowledge is desirable as well as knowledge of other European languages.

Training adviser

You will co-ordinate all aspects of the training cycle from identifying training needs to drawing up and implementing plans, sourcing external providers in order to develop enthusiastic and passionate employees. Working alongside department heads, HR and recruitment, you will be driving the development strategy together with the company.

You must be CIPD-qualified (full or part) with at least two years' experience in a training environment.

HR officer

You will be an integral part of this dynamic company by providing the day-to-day HR function, defining resource requirements, tracking employees, ensuring appraisal objectives are met, assisting with the induction process.

You need to be CIPD part qualified, have good time management skills, computer literacy and excellent communication skills.

(Recruitment advertisements in *People Management*, September 2000)

Activity 3 (20 minutes)

Analyse the recruitment advertisements shown in the example above, in terms of the four 'traditions' of personnel management discussed above. What elements of each tradition can be seen, if any? What key words stand out as foreign to these traditions, and what do they suggest about the organisation, its environment and the role of personnel management within it?

2.5 A shift in perception of the personnel management role

By the 1950s, the personnel function appeared to have developed as 'a collection of incidental techniques without much internal cohesion': 'partly a file clerk's job, partly a housekeeping job, partly a social worker's job and partly "fire-fighting" to head off union trouble or to settle it.' (Drucker, 1955).

Nick Georgiades (*Personnel Management,* February 1990) proposed a different set of job titles:

- The **administrative handmaiden** – writing job descriptions, processing forms and so on

- The **policeman** – ensuring that both management and staff obey the rules, and keeping a watchful eye on absenteeism, sickness and punctuality

- The **toilet flusher** – administering downsizing policies (cutting staff numbers)

- The **sanitary engineer** – ensuring that there is an awareness of the unhealthy psychological conditions under which many people work

Despite the ironic tone, such classifications reflect the perception of personnel management as an essentially reactive – even defensive – role: avoiding or settling industrial disputes, preventing accidents and ill-health (and their associated costs) and so on.

Figure 1.1 illustrates this traditional perception of the role of the personnel function in the organisation.

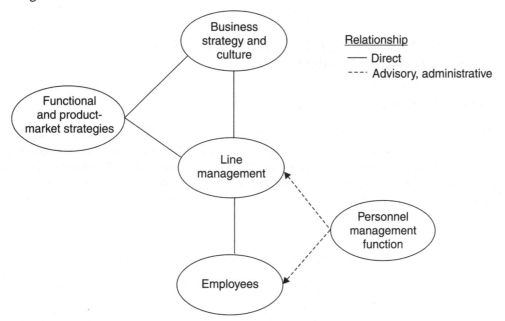

Figure 1.1 The personnel function in the organisation

The profession was becoming increasingly aware, however, that as long as personnel policy and practice were divorced from the strategy of the business, and failed to be proactive and constructive, personnel management would continue to be perceived by line management as having little to do with the 'real' world of business management and the 'bottom line' (profitability). Personnel specialists were commanding scant respect as business managers, and their influence continued to be limited to areas of little strategic impact.

A typical call, from the professional literature of the 1980s and '90s, was:

'The real requirement is **proactive** and **constructive**, rather than **defensive** and **reactive**. To discharge their true role, personnel managers must anticipate the needs of the organisation in the short and the long term. They must develop the policies to produce solutions to anticipated problems resulting from the external and internal environment, whilst influencing and creating the attitudes amongst employees needed for the enterprise's survival and success.' (Livy, 1988)

FOR DISCUSSION

'People may be regarded as a vital resource – at least plenty of lip service is paid to this concept by company chairmen in their annual statement – but many managers find it difficult to appreciate where the personnel department fits in, except in the simplest terms as a procurement (recruitment) and fire-fighting function.'

Role-play a discussion between the company CEO or line manager (in a field of your choice: say, Marketing or IT) and the personnel manager: what is the personnel function really *for*, from their respective points of view?

We have highlighted some of the key sources of discontent with the role of the traditional personnel function: its reactive/defensive (rather than proactive/ constructive) nature, and its perceived irrelevance to the strategic and performance concerns of the business. We will now look at some further factors which prompted a re-evaluation of the role of personnel management, and the emergence of the new term 'human resource management'.

3   THE DEVELOPMENT OF HUMAN RESOURCE MANAGEMENT (HRM)

3.1   Context for a shift in perspective

Throughout the 20th century, new models and theories of **organisation and management** had been emerging to reflect the accelerating page of change in the business environment, the diversity and expectations of workers and consumers, and the increasing sophistication of work psychology. The commitment, involvement and flexibility of the workforce was increasingly recognised as a key to organisational survival, challenging the personnel function to become involved in concerns of broader relevance to the business and its objectives:

- The management of change and changing organisational forms

- Quality issues as a key to competitive performance and employee commitment

- Planning for the long-term challenges of falling birthrates and skill shortages in the pool of available labour

- Creating attractive 'employer brands' in the labour marketplace

- Empowering workers; facilitating team-working and flexible working methods

- Managing increasing diversity in the workforce

- Creating and adapting organisational culture.

Intensifying business competition was likewise demanding that personnel management justify itself in terms of **contribution** to the organisation's goals for growth, competitive gain and the improvement of bottom line performance. The payroll costs of many organisations today are of such magnitude (30-80% of total expenses) that 'senior managers must be concerned with human resources' (Kramar, McGraw and Shuler, 1997).

In the **social environment**, advances in education, technological skills and general affluence raised employee expectations of the quality of working life and awareness of their rights within the employment relationship. The need to compete in innovative, technology- and quality-sensitive markets put a premium on skilled knowledge workers, altering the balance of power in the employment relationship. Coercive and controlling psychological contracts of employment are no longer the norm (other than in very stable markets and/or areas of high unemployment): employees expect to have access to influence, responsibility and information related to their work. There has been a shift from compliance to commitment as the core of the psychological contract.

Definition

> A **psychological contract** is the set of values that determines what an organisation expects of its employees, and what they expect of it, in the employment relationship.

Politically, the UK government of the 1980s encouraged a shift away from trade union power and collective bargaining, instead emphasising entrepreneurialism, individualism and a 'unitary' perspective (discussed in detail in Part D of this Course Book) which assumed that management and employees shared a common interest in the success of the enterprise. It seemed possible that industrial conflict and collective negotiation could be pre-empted – and ultimately replaced – by pro-active people-focused personnel strategies such as participation and information-sharing.

Meanwhile, the popularity of the American anecdotal literature focusing on 'excellence' (for example, *In Search of Excellence* by Peters and Waterman) associated the success of high-performing companies with enlightened, people-focused management practices. 'All the **value** of this company is in its people. If you burnt down all of our plants and we just kept our people and information files, we would soon be as strong as ever. Take away our people and we might never recover.' (Tom Watson, former president of IBM, quoted in Peters and Waterman, 1982)

This represented a conceptual shift away from regarding employees as a cost to be managed and controlled, and towards regarding them as an asset to be nurtured and developed. A former IBM President, Barry Curnow, further noted in the late 1990s that: 'We've moved through periods when money has been in short supply and when technology has been in short supply. Now it's the people who are in short supply. So personnel directors are better placed than ever before to make a real difference – a bottom line difference. The **scarce resource**, which is the people resource, is the one that makes an impact at the margin, that makes one firm competitive over another.'

A variety of research studies have attempted to support the anecdotal evidence with hard data. Although the link to **business performance** is by no means clear cut, there is broad agreement that a greater use of 'human resource practices' (notably those focused on securing employee skills, motivation/commitment and flexible working) is associated with positive employee attitudes, higher levels of productivity and higher quality of service.

3.2 The emergence of Human Resource Management (HRM)

Definition

> **Human Resource Management (HRM)** may be defined as: 'a strategic approach to managing employment relations which emphasises that leveraging people's capabilities is critical to achieving sustainable competitive advantage, this being achieved through a distinctive set of integrated employment policies, programmes and practices.' (Bratton & Gold, 2003)

As this definition suggests, the term HRM is often associated with both:

- An orientation towards **personnel management**, viewing its role as proactive, system-wide interventions, linking HRM with strategic planning and cultural change; and

- An orientation towards the **employment relationship**, embracing distinctive people-centred values such as trust, commitment, involvement and collaboration.

The term Human Resource Management (HRM) gained recognition in the USA in early 1980s as a label for the way certain blue-chip companies such as IBM, Xerox and Hewlett Packard were managing their people. The terms and its implications were subsequently explored by UK writers including David Guest, Karen Legge and John Storey, in the late 1980s and early 1990s. Despite heated debate about the nature, impact and morality of HRM (discussed briefly in Paragraph 3.5 below), the term has had widespread adoption in the last few years, and many of its underlying assumptions are now being incorporated into personnel management policy and practice.

3.3 Characteristics of HRM

The main features of HRM may be summed up as follows (Armstrong 2000, 2003).

(a) The attempt to achieve **strategic 'fit'** or integration between HR and business planning: HR policy should be formulated at the strategic level, and directly related to the organisation's competitive and value-adding objectives. (This may be called 'vertical' integration.)

(b) The development of coherent, mutually-supporting **HR policies and practices**: the strategic management of people will be reflected in all areas and systems of HRM. (This may be called 'horizontal' integration.)

(c) An orientation towards **commitment**: securing employee identification with the organisation's goals and values, not mere compliance with directives. This is often associated with management practices such as flexibility, teambuilding, empowerment, involvement and the creation of strong cultural values.

(d) The treatment of people as **assets** rather than costs: regarding employees 'as a source of competitive advantage and as human capital to be invested in through the provision of learning and development opportunities'. This is often associated with a strong emphasis on the delivery of quality and customer satisfaction, and on rewarding performance, competence, contribution and added value.

(e) A unitarist approach to **employee relations,** which assumes that there need be no inherent conflict of interest between employers and employees. This is often reflected in a shift from collective/representative to more individual employee relations.

(f)   The responsibility of **line management** for delivery of HRM objectives.

EXAMPLE

'The **Selfridges** story is one of reinvention and growth, in which people management has played a vital role in creating a highly successful retail chain... One of the [new management] team's first critical choices was to decide what sort of retailer it should be – and how its people management should support that identity.

'Selfridges now markets itself as the "house of Brands", with its own strong image based on that presumption. In transforming its employment culture to complement the change, it adopted a series of new HR initiatives. It conducted culture surveys, organised focus groups and replaced its old Hay job evaluation scheme with a broadbanding pay arrangement. The Trafford Park store in Manchester... put great emphasis on communication, training and development.

'Behind all these innovations, Selfridges made an explicit effort to model the underlying stakeholder values required in its dealings with customers, employees, the local community, suppliers and other stakeholders. These values were expressed under four goals: to be "aspirational, friendly, accessible and bold"...

'Staff turnover, particularly in the first few years [of the Manchester store] was high... but the company did cut it from 78% in 2000 to 40% in 2001. There is a heavy reliance on part-time staff, making it more expensive to develop a sophisticated HR system, and another complication is that a large number of the sales associates are concession staff. The values matrix includes the statement "My concession staff are treated well and made to feel welcome". In practice, this means that they join the Selfridges sales teams, take the same training and are included in company communications...

'Staff at Selfridges displayed one of the highest levels of commitment out of the 12 organisations in our research. The factors they particularly linked to job satisfaction, motivation and commitment were challenging work; job security; teamwork; career opportunities; appraisal; and, most of all, communication, involvement and the way their managers managed.'

(Purcell *et al*, 2003)

Guest (1989) defines the four key policy goals of HRM as follows.

(a)   **Strategic integration** – 'the ability of organisations to integrate HRM issues into their strategic plans, to ensure that the various aspects of HRM cohere and for line managers to incorporate an HRM perspective into their decision-making.'

(b)   **High commitment** – people must be managed in a way that ensures both their genuine 'behavioural' commitment to pursuing the goals of the organisation and their 'attitudinal' commitment, reflected in strong identification with the enterprise.

(c)   **Flexibility** – HRM policies must be structured to allow maximum flexibility for the organisation, so it can respond to ever-changing business needs: for example, by encouraging functional versatility in employees and by creating 'an adaptable organisational structure with the capacity to manage innovation'.

(d) **High quality** – the notion of quality must run through everything the organisation does, 'including the management of employees and investment in high-quality employees, which in turn will bear directly on the quality of the goods and services provided.'

3.4   Personnel management or HRM?

The main conceptual difference between HRM and personnel management is, arguably, its focus on strategic integration. This can be illustrated as follows: Figure 1.2. Compare this model with that shown in Figure 1.1.

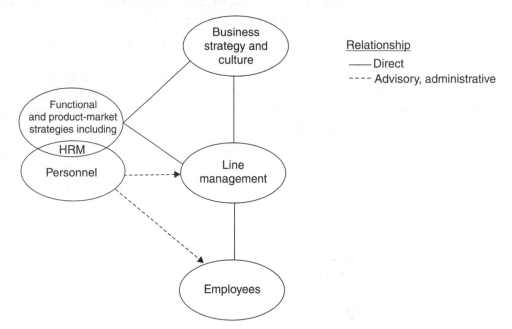

Figure 1.2 HRM: the strategic integration of personnel management

The 'new assumptions' underpinning the 'HRM transformation' have been summarised as follows (Beer and Spector, 1985).

Old assumptions (personnel management)	New assumptions (HRM)
Reactive, piecemeal interventions in response to specific problems	Proactive, system-wide interventions, with emphasis on fit, linking HRM with strategic planning and cultural change
People are a variable cost	People are social capital, capable of development
Self interest dominates, conflict between stakeholders (pluralist perspective)	Co-incidence of interest between stakeholders can be developed (unitary perspective)
Seeks power advantages for bargaining and confrontation	Seeks power equalisation for trust and collaboration
Control of information flow to enhance efficiency, power	Open channels of communication to build trust, commitment
Relationship orientation	Goal orientation
Control from the top	Participation and informed choice

However, some commentators (Armstrong, 2003; Guest, 1989; Legge 1989) have suggested that that there are more similarities than differences between personnel management and HRM – and that HRM should perhaps been seen rather as a particular orientation to personnel management than an alternative approach.

We will discuss other differences between personnel management and HRM – and different perspectives on HRM itself – in Chapter 8, where the ambiguities of the approach are explored in more detail, as part of Unit 22.

Activity 4   **(30 minutes)**

Think of the business context(s) you are familiar with, or arrange to conduct a brief informal or telephone interview with any personal contacts you may have in the HR/Personnel field.

(a)   What label is given to the personnel management function in the organisation?

(b)   Is the term 'HRM' used – and if so, what is it understood to mean?

(c)   If the name 'HRM' was adopted in place of 'Personnel Management' (or something similar), how was this reflected in changes of philosophy, policy and practice?

(d)   Why do you think the name of the function might matter?

3.5   On-going debate about 'HRM'

The concept and terminology of HRM have fuelled on-going debate among academics and practitioners.

- **Is HRM (in practice) really different from 'personnel management'?** The terms are often used interchangeably. One point of view is that 'HRM' is a term which practitioners have seized upon and applied to themselves, in the interests of their individual and professional status – whether or not they are in fact doing anything more than traditional personnel management: 'old wine in new bottles'. Another point of view, however, is that by continually focusing debate on the nature of the employment relationship and its role in business performance, HRM – whatever terminology is used – has helpfully altered both the orientation and practice of management and the expectation and experience of working life.

- **Is HRM a fair and ethical way to manage people?** One viewpoint is that HRM policies are merely a more subtle, psychologically-based form of manipulation than authoritarian or bureaucratic control. Another reservation is that acknowledging the importance of people in business success may simply be a more acceptable 'spin' on using or exploiting employees as a means to an end. 'Sadly, in a world of intensified competition and scarce resources, it seems inevitable that, as employees are used as a means to an end, there will be some who will miss out.' (Legge, 1998) On the other hand, 'it could be argued that if organisations exist to achieve ends, which they clearly do, and if those ends can only be achieved through people, which is clearly the case, the concern of managements for commitment and performance from those people is not unnatural... What matters is *how* managements treat people as ends and *what* managements provide in return.' (Armstrong, 2000)

- **Does it really make a difference to organisational performance?** Recent major research for the CIPD by Purcell, Kinnie and Hutchinson (2003) argues that 'organisations that support their employees by developing effective policies based on ability, motivation and opportunity will create higher levels of organisational commitment, motivation and job satisfaction', which in turn 'give (employees) the chance to help make their team, section and company better'. However, research has also shown 'a disjunction between rhetoric and reality... between HRM theory and HRM practice; between what the HR function says it is doing and that practice as perceived by employees; and between what senior management believes to be the role of the HR function, and the role it actually plays' (Gratton *et al*, 1999)

FOR DISCUSSION

Set up a discussion or debate about any one of the three questions cited above, and justify the alternative points of view given (or your own viewpoints on the questions).

Having explored the nature of personnel management and HRM, we can now gather together some ideas on what personnel/HR practitioners typically do in practice, and how they operate within the organisation.

4 THE ROLE OF THE HRM FUNCTION

4.1 Tasks and activities of the human resource practitioner

The range of tasks and activities commonly carried out by human resource practitioners include the following.

Organisation	• *Organisational design:* structuring the organisation, by grouping activities, assigning accountabilities and establishing communication and authority relationships
	• *Organisational development:* planning and implementing interventions in the organisation's social processes to improve effectiveness through techniques such as structural change, team-building, process consultancy, interpersonal skill development and role negotiation.
	• *Job/role design and definition:* structuring the content and size of jobs (for efficient task performance, flexibility and worker satisfaction) and defining their component tasks, conditions and competency requirements (for recruitment, appraisal, reward and a number of other HR processes)
	• *Flexible working:* planning and implementing flexible structures and procedures to maximise the efficiency and adaptability of the organisation

NOTES

Human resource planning and resourcing	<ul><li>*Human resource planning:* forecasting the organisation's future requirements for labour, skills and competence, and planning to meet them through subsidiary plans for recruitment, deployment, development, retention and so on</li><li>*Recruitment:* Attracting employment applications from the number, type and calibre of people required by the HR plan</li><li>*Selection:* Assessing and selecting suitable employees from applicants</li><li>*Retention:* Planning rewards and incentives to control labour turnover and retain high quality staff</li><li>*Exit management:* managing the termination of contracts, retirements, resignations, dismissals and redundancies, in such a way as to comply with legal requirements and minimise human and organisation costs</li></ul>
Performance management	<ul><li>*Objective and competence requirement setting:* developing and agreeing frameworks of organisational, unit and individual goals to direct and motivate performance</li><li>*Performance monitoring and appraisal:* on-going monitoring and periodic assessment of performance within agreed requirements</li><li>*Discipline handling:* managing informal and formal processes to confront employee behaviour or performance which falls below organisational rules and standards</li><li>*Grievance handling:* managing informal and formal processes to address individual employee grievances or complaints</li><li>*Identifying learning and development needs:* as part of continuous improvement of performance</li></ul>
Reward management	<ul><li>*Pay systems:* developing and managing salary structures, systems and scales that are equitable, fair and compliant with equal pay legislation.</li><li>*Performance pay systems:* developing and managing ways of relating pay progression or bonuses to results, attainments (eg competence or skill), effort and other measures of performance</li><li>*Benefit schemes:* developing and managing employee entitlements (eg pensions, maternity and sick pay, annual leave) and 'fringe' benefits (eg allowances and services)</li><li>*Non-financial rewards:* building non-monetary rewards (such as recognition, challenge, personal development) into job design and management style, as part of a 'total reward' package</li></ul>
Human resource development	<ul><li>*Learning organisation:* creating a culture and systems to support individual and organisational learning, information gathering and sharing and so on</li><li>*Education and training:* planning, implementing and evaluating on- and off-the-job learning opportunities and programmes to meet identified gaps in the skills required by the HR plan</li></ul>

Human resource development cont'd	• *Personal development:* facilitating individual learning plans and opportunities, beyond the immediate job (eg for general employability)
	• *Career management:* identifying potential and planning career development opportunities; succession and promotion planning; guiding and mentoring individuals in career planning
	• *Managerial development:* providing education, training and opportunities to develop managerial competencies and support enhanced contribution
Health, safety and welfare	• *Occupational health and safety:* monitoring and managing work environments, practices and culture to ensure that employees are protected from health hazards and accidents; complying with relevant legislation; actively promoting health and fitness to improve the wellbeing and performance of staff
	• *Welfare services:* providing services such as catering or recreational facilities, individual counselling and support (eg for illness, forthcoming redundancy or retirement, personal health problems)
Employee relations	• *Industrial relations:* managing informal and formal relationships with employee representatives (trade unions and staff associations); collective bargaining on terms and conditions; resolving collective disputes; implementing consultative committees and partnership agreements
	• *Employee communication:* informing employees about matters relevant to their work or of interest or concern to them
	• *Employee voice:* creating consultation opportunities for employees to contribute to decision-making in matters affecting them and their work
HR services	• *Managing the employment relationship:* contract management
	• *HR policies and procedures:* developing and administering guidelines and systems for all the above, to guide line managers and employees
	• *HR information systems:* developing and operating paper- or computer-based employee files, management information, statistical reports and returns and so on, while complying with Data Protection legislation

Graham and Bennett (1998) classify these activities into three dimensions of management:

(a) The **utilisation of people at work**: recruitment, selection, transfer, promotion, separation, appraisal, training and development

(b) The **motivation of people at work**: job design, remuneration, fringe benefits, consultation, participation, negotiation and justice

(c) The **protection of people at work**: working conditions, welfare services, safety, implementation of appropriate legislation.

If this seems too employee-centred a classification, it must be added that the overall objective of these dimensions of management is maintained or enhanced **business performance.**

We will be covering many of these tasks and activities in detail, in the following chapters of this Course Book.

Another way of thinking about what HR practitioners do is to consider the various **processes** that are involved in performing the various activities and tasks listed above.

Armstrong (2003), for example, identifies a broad set of processes underpinning the HRM approach.

(a)   **Strategic HRM** – 'defining intentions and plans for the development of HRM practices, and ensuring that HR strategies are integrated with the business strategy and one another'.

(b)   **Policy making** – formulating and implementing HR policies which set guidelines on how personnel issues should be handled.

(c)   **Competency, job and role analysis** – developing content and competency frameworks to support various activities such as organisation and job design, recruitment, appraisal, training and reward.

(d)   **Change management** – advising on and facilitating the process of change in organisational structures and systems.

(e)   **Knowledge management** – developing systems for obtaining and sharing knowledge, to foster organisational learning, innovation and performance.

Activity 5   **(no time limit)**

Use whatever online, work or personal contact sources you have at your disposal to obtain a copy of a job or role description of a personnel/HR manager. Such a document may be available – without breaching organisational confidentiality – as part of a job application package, on a careers/recruitment website, on a corporate Internet or intranet site, or via your own business contacts.

Assess:

(a)   the objectives/outcomes of the role, as stated in the description

(b)   the tasks, activities and responsibilities set out in the description

(c)   any relationships with other roles in the organisation which are mentioned

---

4.2   Roles of HR/personnel management

Personnel/HR practitioners generally fulfil a range of roles.

(a)   **Guidance role** – offering specialist recommendations and policy frameworks to guide line management decisions: for example, in regard to emerging HR issues, and the consistent and effective implementation of HR procedures.

(b)   **Advisory role** – offering specialist information and perspectives to line managers (and individual employees) on employment matters. Managers, for example, may be advised on training options, legislative provisions or how to handle specific people problems. Employees may be advised on their legal rights or development options, or counselled in relation to work or personal problems.

(c) **Service role** – providing services to a range of internal customers. This includes administrative services (in areas such as payroll administration, employee records, reports and returns) and delivery of HRM programmes (recruitment and selection, training, health and welfare and so on).

(d) **Control/auditing role** –analysing personnel indices (such as wage costs or labour turnover), monitoring performance, carrying out benchmarking or a local government review, say. This role has traditionally caused conflict with line managers, who felt they were being 'policed' – but line managers' discretion must be balanced with the need for consistency in applying HR policy, compliance with legal obligations, and ensuring that the strategic aims of HRM are being met.

(e) **Planning/organising role** – for example, in human resource forecasting and planning, developing flexible working methods and so on.

At a more strategic and proactive level of HRM, HR practitioners may also take on role as:

(a) **Strategists**: helping to fulfil the business objectives of the organisation through strategic management of the human resource *and* influencing business planning by highlighting the human resource implications of objectives and strategies.

(b) **Business partners**: sharing responsibility with senior and line management for the success of the enterprise, through the identification and exploitation of opportunities and the seeking of competitive advantage.

(c) **Internal management consultants**: working alongside line managers in analysing business processes and systems, diagnosing and exploring problems, recommending solutions that the 'client' can own and implement, or implementing solutions and delivering services.

4.3 Shared responsibility for HRM

Definitions

> **Centralisation** and **decentralisation** refer to the degree to which the authority to make decisions is held centrally by a particular group of people *or* delegated and spread to a number of individuals and groups within the organisation.

Centralised control over personnel management generally implies the existence of a personnel officer or department with authority over all personnel management tasks in the organisation.

De-centralised control over personnel management generally implies the delegation to line managers and team leaders of the authority for personnel management tasks affecting their own staff and activities.

In practice, there is a need for a mix of both, in order to gain the benefits of co-ordination and consistency as well as flair and flexibility.

FOR DISCUSSION

'Managers, if one listens to the psychologists, will have to have insights into all kinds of people. They will have to be in command of all kinds of psychological techniques. They will have to understand an infinity of individual personality structures, individual psychological needs, and individual psychological problems... But most managers find it hard enough to know all they need to know about their own immediate area of expertise, be it heat-treating or cost accounting or scheduling.' (Drucker, 1955)

What does this say about the respective roles of line managers and HR specialists in managing people at work?

As the role of the personnel management function has become more strategic/proactive, rather than welfare/administrative/reactive, the following areas have commonly been retained as the responsibility of the HR function.

(a) **Strategic issues**, such as change management programmes and human resources planning, and all aspects of HR at the strategic level, including the formulating and communication of organisational policy. This ensures that the impact of human factors on strategic plans (and vice versa) is taken into account.

(b) **Organisation-wide** communication and employee relations management. Centralisation has the advantage both of special expertise and a wider organisational viewpoint.

(c) Provision of **specialist services** and **advice/consultancy**, where up-to-date specialist knowledge or input, or extra-departmental perspective, is required.

(d) **Researching and auditing** of HR systems. This helps to co-ordinate and control HR functions across the organisation, to ensure that line departments are complying with policy and that policies are effective and relevant to the needs of line departments.

Such centralised functions create a coherent and integrated framework of policies, plans, systems and rules, developed by HR specialists, which help to maintain consistent practice and minimise redundant problem-solving and 're-inventing the wheel' by line managers. Within such a framework, a number of aspects of personnel management could be devolved to line departments.

Activity 6   **(30 minutes)**

You are a sales manager in Mpower Ltd, an organisation which develops and markets software and services for Internet users: web page design, Internet connection, browser programmes and so on. You are responsible for a team of 12 salespeople who work more or less 'independently' from home and 'on the road' and who service a remote rural area with a widely dispersed population.

What personnel management tasks would you wish to be *your* responsibility? What areas would you wish to have specialised or centralised help with? What other options might you consider?

(You might like to do this activity with a fellow student who can take the role of Mpower's head office HR manager. See what conflicts of interest come up, and how they might be resolved.)

4.4 The role and responsibilities of line managers in human resource practices

Most commentators observe a trend toward greater decentralisation of personnel management roles, in line with 'slimmer' head office staffs, flatter management structures and the fostering of flexibility by giving greater autonomy to local business units.

The increase in the white-collar 'knowledge-based' workforce, with its mobility and higher expectations, has also supported a move toward individualism in career development, reward negotiation and other areas, which may be more flexibly managed by line managers and team leaders than by centralised personnel departments.

Meanwhile, the sophistication of computerised personnel information and administrative systems has facilitated HR decision-making, on a day-to-day basis, by line managers.

The responsibility of line managers for delivering HR outcomes is a distinctive feature of the HRM approach. Legge (1989) suggests that

- While personnel management is an activity aimed primarily at non-managers, HRM is more concerned with the activities of *all* managerial staff.

- While personnel management seeks to *influence* line management, HRM is more of an integrated line management activity.

EXAMPLE

'A key finding [of recent CIPD-funded research into 12 organisations to investigate how effective HRM creates competitive advantage] was the role of line managers in bringing HR policies to life... Their managerial behaviour – in implementing HR policies; in showing leadership by involving staff and responding to their suggestions; and in controlling quality, timekeeping and absence – makes a real difference to employees' attitudes...

'Looking at the information from our employee interviews, we found that there were frequent and statistically significant associations between people's approval of their managers' leadership style and a range of HR policies and practices. The way in which managers brought these HR policies to life and exercised leadership was strongly related to positive employee views on such areas as involvement, worker-management relations, communication, openness, coaching and guidance, performance appraisal, reward and recognition, training, job influence and quality control.

'Three of the case-study organisations made significant changes to the roles and competence profiles of their line managers after our first-year survey. One of these was Selfridges, where performance has continued to improve. We found similar remarkable results at the Royal United Hospital at Bath. Despite difficulties at the top of the organisation, at ward level a new manager was appointed, a revised appraisal scheme was implemented and a stronger focus on work-life balance was achieved. Employee attitudes improved markedly and what once had been a retention blackspot ended the second year with no job vacancies.

'This was also true at Clerical Medical, now the life insurance arm of HBOS. We asked a manager in charge of a department that had achieved great progress which HR policies he had found most helpful. His answer was instructive: "It is the quality of team leaders that's important. If they take a close interest in people, it makes a big difference."

(Purcell *et al*, 2003)

Even in a traditional personnel management model, line managers would often have responsibility for activities immediately concerned with the manager-team relationship, such as:

- Selection of department/team members: formulation of selection criteria (in line with HR-prepared frameworks); interviewing and selection.

- Discipline and grievance handling: informal conflict resolution, counselling, initial stages of disciplinary action (complaint investigation, interviews)

- Absence management: monitoring time-keeping and absenteeism; record keeping

- Performance management: agreeing performance criteria and targets; monitoring performance and giving feedback; identifying learning needs and opportunities; instructing, coaching, counselling and mentoring; employee appraisal reporting and interviewing; motivation (as a leadership process)

- Employee relations: immediate employee communication (upward and downward); managing team participation and involvement; reinforcing cultural values through management style and so on.

Definition

> **Devolution** is a term used to describe the shift of responsibilities away from personnel specialists, back towards line management.

Connock (1991) suggests that devolution is not a loss for HR specialists, but will allow them to concentrate on more value-adding areas: forecasting the strategic implications of HR issues (and vice versa), formulating guidance on more complex matters and so on.

FOR DISCUSSION

Which 'side' do you naturally relate to: the line managers trying to get things done but hedged in by personnel rules and policies – or the HR manager having to beat his or her head against a brick wall to convince line managers of hard-won insights into people at work? Do you feel that as a line manager, you would be glad of expert help with complex people issues? Or as an HR manager, would you be glad that line managers are prepared to get on with their jobs, leaving you to more 'global' perceptions of the organisation's needs?

Set up a discussion between line and 'staff/advisory' functions: 'Why should we/you listen to the personnel department?'

4.5 Outsourcing HR tasks

The *IPD Guide to Outsourcing* (IPD 1998), notes that the need for organisational flexibility has supported 'the concept of the core organisation which focuses its in-house expertise on its primary function and purchases any necessary support from a range of sources in its periphery'. We will discuss the 'core-periphery' model in Chapter 9 of this

Course Book, but for now, it may be sufficient to note that a number of HR activities may be regarded as 'peripheral' or complementary to the primary functions of the business, and outsourced to external consultants or service providers.

The main areas identified by the IPD as amenable to effective outsourcing include:

- Training

- Recruitment

- Health and safety monitoring and advice (and related health and fitness promotion and services, if provided)

- Employee welfare and counselling

- Payroll management (and related benefit schemes, pensions administration and so on)

- Legal advice

Activity 7	**(15 minutes)**

Why might it be beneficial to outsource the particular activities listed above? What sort of external service providers would be suitable to take on each activity?

In addition, the HR function may have *de facto* responsibility for a range of ancillary activities – such as on-site catering, security, office/facility management, child care, company care fleet management and so on – which could be more effectively outsourced to external specialists.

The advantages and disadvantages of outsourcing may be summarised as follows.

Advantages	Disadvantages
• HR costs are reduced by downsizing the HR function and potentially cheaper provision of services by specialists	• External advisers/providers must be carefully chosen, contracted and managed, in order to maintain standards and organisational values
• HR specialists are freed up to focus on core value-adding and business-specific tasks and knowledge	• External advisers/providers may lack understanding or flexibility to be able to tailor their offering to reflect the organisation's objectives, culture or brand
• Specialist knowledge and expertise may be easier to buy in than to develop within the organisation	• Outsourcing may be carried out for short-term cost saving without defining which activities are (or may become) 'core' to the business or role of HRM in the organisation
• External specialists may have access to infrastructure development (eg website or application software, purpose-built facilities) that the business lacks	• The horizontal integration and consistency of application across the range of HR policy and practice may be lost
• The objectivity of external service/advice providers may improve the quality of solutions and their acceptability to members of the organisation	

4.6 Summary

As we have suggested, HRM is perhaps most helpfully seen as a broadly distributed organisational competence or orientation, rather than a 'function' in the sense of a department of specialists. The HR function may be thought of as the integration of people management systems throughout the organisation, rather than a particular set of roles and activities.

The diagram on the following page (Figure 1.3), loosely based on the work of Shuler *et al* (1995) may be read from the bottom up (following the classical planning hierarchy) or from the top down (from a functional perspective).

5 EVALUATING THE HR FUNCTION

5.1 The problem of evaluation

If HRM is to be taken seriously at a strategic level as a contributor to bottom line business performance, it must be subject to evaluation. However, there are considerable difficulties attached to the evaluation of the personnel function.

(a) While some performance-based criteria (profitability, productivity, error reduction, compliance and so on) are relatively easy to measure and compare, having to do with units and monetary values, others are not (for example, innovation or flexibility)

(b) Effective personnel management should, over the long term, measurably impact on improved business performance. However:

   (i) Its short-term activities may not show such effects

   (ii) It is difficult to attribute these effects to HR activity alone: organisational performance involves many other variables, including technology, management effectiveness, market conditions, competitor initiatives and so on

(c) Subjective criteria such as the quality of working life, employee motivation, team spirit, openness to change, job satisfaction, the quality of employee relations and so on are notoriously difficult to measure, let alone to attach monetary values to, as a means of comparison

(d) Benchmarking, or standard-setting on the basis of best practice in other organisations, is difficult because of the wide differences in the environmental and internal variables affecting different organisations

(e) Personnel management itself is a wide-ranging activity, and therefore requires a wide range of criteria for evaluation

5.2 Cost-benefit analysis

Despite these difficulties, there are certain criteria, both quantitative and qualitative, which allow HR managers to demonstrate their effectiveness in the way that other managers do: by cost-benefit analysis. Assessing the costs of their activities against the benefits resulting from them, HR managers can determine:

(a) Whether the costs are justified by equal or greater benefits

(b) Whether costs and/or benefits are increasing or decreasing over time

(c) How the costs and/or benefits compare to competitor or benchmark organisations

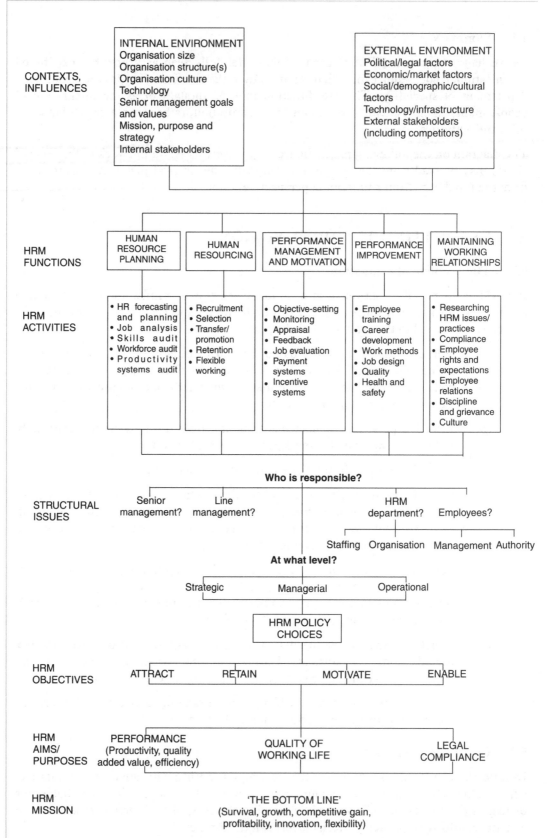

Figure 1.3: **HRM** in context

> **Activity 8**   **(15 minutes)**
>
> Before we proceed, see if you can brainstorm ten examples each of benefit criteria and cost criteria relevant to personnel management.

You may have noted that benefit criteria – such as 'legal compliance' or 'improved productivity' – may apply to all HRM activities, while costs tend to be more specific to each activity: the cost of training, for example, which might include training resources, teacher payroll, coaches' and trainees' time in lost production and so on. Costs are more easily measurable, because they have a monetary value attached, but benefit criteria can usually be given a monetary value, if required: 'reduced accidents and illness', for example, can be expressed as a saving of the potential costs of lost production, benefits and compensation payments, training of replacement workers and so on.

5.3 Quantitative measures

Quantitative or statistical indices of the HR function's activities may be available in relation to areas such as the following.

(a) Staff turnover/labour wastage (or labour stability) ratios

(b) Absenteeism rates

(c) Unit labour costs (useful in comparison to previous periods and/or competing businesses)

(d) Incidences of grievance procedures, disciplinary procedures, appeals to industrial tribunals, compensation claims, proceedings for non-compliance and so on

(e) Number of days production (and associated costs) lost through accidents, sickness, industrial disputes and so on

(f) Number of applications attracted by recruitment methods and/or lead time to recruit an employee

(g) Number of selected recruits remaining in the job, achieving performance targets, achieving promotion and so on

(h) Number of staff (including HR staff) achieving professional or other qualifications, or undertaking training programmes

(i) Success of training (and other) programmes in achieving their objectives

(j) Number of requests for information handled by the HR department, lead time in responding to requests, ability to answer technical personnel questions on demand and so on

(k) The costs of any and all of the above

We will look at means of evaluating specific HR activities, such as recruitment and training, in relevant chapters.

5.4 Qualitative measures

Qualitative, or subjective, criteria may be harder to measure, but may be equally important in the field of HRM. Examples include the following.

(a) Employee motivation, team spirit, job satisfaction, acceptance of change and so on – as gauged by attitude surveys, interviews, psychological testing and other tools of behavioural science, as well as presumed observed effects on productivity, communication, absenteeism and so on

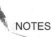
    (b)   The extent to which HR proposals, policies, documentation and so on are accepted by line managers – as suggested by implementation rates, questions and objections

    (c)   The perception of the HR function's value, service, expertise, quality of advice, professionalism and so on by its internal customers: senior management, line managers and employees

5.5 The Four Cs

The Four Cs model was developed by researchers at the Harvard Business School as a means of investigating HRM issues (Beer *et al*, 1984). It suggests that the effectiveness of the outcomes of HRM should be evaluated under four headings.

    (a)   **Commitment** – that is, employees' identification with the organisation, loyalty and personal motivation in their work. This, like the qualitative criteria mentioned above, may be assessed through methods such as attitude surveys, exit interviews and analysis of presumed effects (such as absenteeism and labour turnover).

    (b)   **Competence** – that is, employees' skills and abilities, training needs and potential for performance improvement and career development. This may be measured through skill audits, competency testing and performance management systems.

    (c)   **Congruence** – that is, the harmonisation of the goals, values and efforts of management and employees (or at least the *perception* by employees that they have a mutual vision and purpose, to mutual benefit). This may be estimated by the quality of employee/industrial relations, the incidence of grievance and disciplinary action, conflict and communication and so on.

    (d)   **Cost-effectiveness** – that is, efficiency, whereby HRM objectives are met and benefits obtained at the lowest input cost.

The Harvard model does not solve the problems of the accurate measurement of qualitative criteria; nor of the incompatibility of varying criteria (cost-effectiveness achieved by downsizing, for example, might not encourage commitment or congruence); nor of the sheer variety of HR activity and contexts (since there are organisations and areas of organisational activity in which low-skilled monotonous jobs and authoritarian management styles, for example, are still possible and indeed appropriate). However, it does offer a simple framework for thinking about HR effectiveness.

Activity 9   **(30 minutes)**

Think about your own work organisation, or an organisation you know well.

(a)   How would you go about assessing the effectiveness of its HRM, according to the Four Cs model?

(b)   Without doing a detailed assessment, how do you estimate it would rate on each of the Four Cs?

Chapter roundup

- The personnel function may take different forms in different organisations. Traditionally, it has been regarded as a primarily administrative, reactive, problem-handling function, concerned with hiring and firing, employee welfare and industrial relations.

- Four traditions colour perceptions of personnel management: the welfare tradition, the industrial relations tradition, the control of labour tradition and the professional tradition.

- Human Resource Management (HRM) is a concept which seeks to recognise employees as an asset to be nurtured, rather than a cost to be controlled, and which views the sourcing, deploying and developing of these human resources as a key integrated element of business strategy.

- HRM developed out of influences such as: the increased complexity of business processes and their dependence on employee flexibility and commitment; the need for competitive advantage; the increased power and expectations of highly-skilled knowledge workers; and the identification of human relations policy as the key to management effectiveness and business 'excellence'.

- Key areas of HR/personnel management activity include: organisation; human resource planning and resourcing; performance management; reward management; human resource development; health, safety and welfare; employee relations; HR services

- One of the distinctive characteristics of an HRM orientation is the devolution of responsibility for delivering HRM outcomes to line management. In practice, strategic, specialised and organisation-wide activities are often centralised under the control of an HRM function, while day-to-day aspects of people management are often devolved to line managers, who are able to manage the employment relationship in a more individualised and flexible way. A further option is the outsourcing of peripheral HR functions.

- The HR function can only establish credibility by systematic evaluation of its activities in the light of business objectives.

Quick quiz

1   List the four 'traditions' of personnel management.

2   To what groups of people does the HR practitioner have responsibilities?

3   List a number of factors which contributed to the shift towards an HRM orientation.

4   What are the main features of HRM?

5   What, according to Guest, are the four key policy goals of HRM?

6   List eight broad areas into which HR activities may be grouped.

7   List the possible roles of personnel/HR practitioners.

8   What is the role of line managers in delivering HR outcomes?

9   Summarise the arguments for and against outsourcing HR activities?

10   What are the Four Cs of the Harvard model?

Answers to quick quiz

1 Welfare, industrial relations, control of labour, professional (para 2)

2 To the employer, to the workforce (in part), to the profession (para 2.4)

3 Dissatisfaction with the reactive role of personnel management; developments in organisation/management theory; competition putting pressure on contribution; social changes raising employee expectations of the psychological contract; political support for pro-active employee relations; focus on the value of people as a scarce resource and source of value. (para 2.5, 3.1)

4 Strategic fit; integrated HR policies and practices; commitment orientation; people as assets; unitarist employee relations; involvement of line managers. (para 3.3)

5 Strategic integration, high commitment, flexibility, high quality (para 3.3)

6 Organisation; HR planning and resourcing; performance management; reward management; human resource development; health, safety and welfare; employee relations; HR services. (para 4.1)

7 Guidance, advice, service, control/auditing, planning/auditing, strategy, business partnership, internal consultancy. (para 4.2)

8 Delivering HR policies to employees (explicit in HRM orientation); interpersonal processes of team management and motivation; specific devolved personnel management tasks at the interface between the employer and the team (eg team selection, individual discipline, absence management, motivation). (para 4.4)

9 See Paragraph 4.5 for a complete answer

10 Commitment, congruence, competence, cost-effectiveness (para 5.5)

Answers to activities

1 There is no suggested answer to this activity: it is intended to stimulate your awareness of:

(a) some of the research sources available to you in exploring this topic further

(b) the variety of ways in which HRM concepts are expressed

(c) cultural, legal and other variations in HRM principles and practices in different parts of the world.

2 Examples of conflicts of interest might include the following.

(a) The need for downsizing or delayering for organisational efficiency. The workforce may well see this as a betrayal, yet it is part of resource management to know when to liquidate assets: organisational survival may even depend on increased efficiency/flexibility or cost reduction.

(b) The negotiation of reward packages. As a member of management, you may wish to minimise increases in the cost of labour, or rationalise them in some other way. The workforce perceives pay rises as a 'right' or as an indication of the value the organisation puts on its services, and may be disappointed.

(c) Disciplinary procedures. The interests of management may best be served by 'clamping down' on absenteeism, poor time-keeping and so on in order to keep general discipline and efficiency – but the workforce, or particular individuals, will often feel that rules are unfair or unfairly applied.

Broadly, these are issues of the way power is used in organisations. The personnel function can go a long way to minimising the potential hurt and conflict caused by applying and communicating the decisions of management fairly and sensitively.

3   *Welfare tradition*: very little sign of such an orientation in the job descriptions – except perhaps in the HR officer's responsibility for 'assisting with the induction process': even this seems more likely to be performance-oriented rather than for the psychological comfort of the recruits.

Industrial relations tradition: very little of this either, in the traditional sense. The word 'negotiations' crops up (Resource Manager), but more in the sense of collaborative responsibility for project resourcing. The phrase 'enthusiastic and passionate employees' (Training Advisor) suggests a unitarist perspective on the employment relationship: no inherent conflict anticipated.

Control of labour tradition: targets, competence frameworks, plans, co-ordination, the 'tracking' (monitoring) of employees against appraisal objectives, the requirement for computer literacy: this suggests the presence of administrative control systems in the organisation. However, these elements are tempered with more 'dynamic' elements.

Professional tradition: the Training Advisor and HR officer are required to have CIPD qualifications and the Training Advisor additionally requires specific specialist experience. However, more general managerial skills and experience are also mentioned: time management, languages, communication and so on.

Non-traditional concepts: the key word seems to be integration. 'In negotiation with departmental heads and project managers... links with other offices... overall management...' (Resource Manager). 'Driving the development strategy together with the company' (Training Adviser). 'Integral part' (HR Officer).

4   Terminology clearly matters to some of the people who perform the function, for their own sense of self-esteem and the status of their profession. An important consideration is whether the employees view the idea of themselves as 'resources' positively or negatively, and whether practice justifies the more 'enlightened' sounding title, or is indeed viewed cynically as the same 'old wine' in 'fancy new bottles'. Adoption of the title may be a sign of conflict and power struggles within the organisation (with HR trying to boost its status, credibility and influence) or it may enhance the organisation's reputation or 'brand' as an employer in the labour market.

5   This is a research activity. The methodology fits well with the guidelines on fulfilling the Assessment Criteria: keep written evidence of your information search.

6   The answer to this activity is personal to you. However, the case scenario suggests some areas for consideration.

(a)   As sales manager, you are responsible for staff who have particular needs: notably for motivation, encouragement and supervision while 'on the road'. You need to think about whether team-building would be best served by *your* maintaining contact with them on HR matters (such as appraisal, reward, training) or through a (possibly anonymous) personnel department. On the other hand, you might like some expert briefing on how to manage 'virtual teams', on problems suffered by team members (eg suffering isolation or stress) and so on.

(b) You have quite specific requirements for your staff. They need to be technically aware (in order to advise customers), highly knowledgeable about the company's products, proactive sales people (since the customers are dispersed, and likely to be a bit traditional – although ideal candidates for the products). You might feel, given the difficulties of team building, that you would like to retain responsibility for selection and training – or you may prefer a more organisation-wide perspective: perhaps it would be good to have centrally selected/trained people who are close to the product and its technical possibilities – and then train them in sales?

These are just some suggestions to show you how widely and deeply an organisation needs to think through these issues.

7 *Training:* specialist facilities/equipment/resources, specialist knowledge of learning techniques, suitable for 'off-the-job' training. Providers: eg colleges, training companies, online campuses, publishers of books and software

Recruitment: specialist techniques (eg in psychometric testing), networks of contacts, savings in advertising media buying, online facilities (e-recruitment), removes routine pre-screening etc. Providers: eg recruitment consultants, e-recruitment sites, Job Centres, careers officers

Health/safety: specialist knowledge of law/regulation, removes perception of 'policing' from team leaders, special facilities (medical testing, fitness etc). Service providers: consultants, fitness/medical facilities

Welfare/counselling: specialist training, access to networks/referrals, removes 'personal' issues from workplace. Providers: counsellors, welfare agencies, Employee Assistance providers

Payroll/benefits/pensions: specialist software/knowledge, removes routine peripheral tasks, avoids legal responsibility for financial advice. Providers: specialist agencies, financial service providers

Legal advice: specialist knowledge, removes 'policing' on compliance from the HR department. Providers: law firms

8 Some examples are as follows.

(a) Benefit criteria: increased productivity, increased quality/reduced error/wastage, reduced absenteeism, reduced labour turnover, increased job satisfaction, legal compliance, reduced accidents/ illness, reduced employee stress, increased job involvement, increased innovation, reduced costs of fines, reduced grievance/ disciplinary actions, reduced industrial disputes, enhanced response to recruitment, enhanced community goodwill

(b) Cost criteria: costs of health and safety activity, training, recruitment, consultancy, remuneration, HR department training, welfare provision, computerisation, HR salaries, ergonomic improvements, compliance

9 Suggested methodologies include attitude surveys, questionnaires, observation, interviews (eg exit interviews, counselling interviews, appraisal interviews), and analysis of the presumed effects of more or less 'C' factors (positive or negative labour stability, absenteeism rates, incidence of conflict and so on).

In terms of the evaluation of your chosen organisation's HRM function, you are on your own! Do attempt this exercise, however, even if it is just a brief mental survey of your college, your favourite fast food outlet or whatever. This will get you thinking not just about how to evaluate the success of HRM policy and practice, but about how HRM goes about fostering, maintaining and increasing the 'C' factors in the organisation.

Assignment 1

Class One Insurance Services

Background

Class One Insurance Services is a small but growing business specialising in household and commercial insurance. It has developed over the years by acquisition and merger but now wishes to consolidate its current base. Around 200 employees work in three divisions and at headquarters. The headquarters is based in East London, sharing premises with the Motor Insurance division. The Home Insurance division is based in Borehamwood, Hertfordshire while the Personal Insurance division runs from offices in Basildon, Essex.

Staffing

The company is staffed as follows:

Headquarters: Managing director, other directors, office manager, personnel officer and 50 administrative and clerical staff.

Motor insurance: Divisional director plus 30 specialist and administrative staff, 35 telephone enquiry and sales clerks, 25 sales representatives.

Home insurance: Divisional manager plus 20 specialist and administrative staff, 15 telephone sales clerks, 12 sales representatives, office manager.

Personal insurance: Divisional manager plus 5 administrative staff, 12 telephone enquiry and sales clerks, 10 sales representatives.

Business and personnel factors

The state of business and personnel factors in each of the firm's main units are as follows:

Head office: In order to achieve greater integration, the directors have increased headquarters' role in developing financial and administrative procedures for the whole organisation. A full-time personnel officer has just been appointed. Administrative and clerical staff are mostly local people and staff turnover is very low. Salaries are reasonable without being generous.

Cont'd

Assignment 1 *cont...*

Motor insurance:	This division is maintaining its market position but at an increasing cost to the company. Salaries are modest, but generous commission payments can be earned by sales staff. Staff turnover is high among this group. Administrative staff are paid at competitive rates and staff turnover here is low. Although morale appears high, there is a feeling of the division being in a state of flux, with people leaving and joining on a weekly basis.
Home insurance:	Business is just being maintained in the face of fierce competition from the main building societies. Wages are high in comparison to other sections of the company. The workforce is stable and the employees are generally older than in other divisions. Most employees are members of MSF trade union
Personal insurance:	Business is expanding and the division has increased its market share in the Essex region. Salaries are lower than in other divisions, but staff turnover is also lower (except on the sales side). All staff are members of MSF.

Your task

You are the newly appointed personnel offer at headquarters, with a responsibility for staff in all divisions. Your task is to identify the problems which are likely to face you over the first six months in the job. Then take a longer term view, say over the next 1-2 years, and identify which aspects of personnel management should receive your special attention.

Chapter 2:
HUMAN RESOURCE PLANNING

Introduction

As we saw in Chapter 1, human beings are one of the resources that a business must obtain and manage in pursuit of its objectives. Human resource (or 'manpower') planning is the task of assessing and anticipating the skill, knowledge and labour time requirements of the organisation, and initiating action to fulfil or 'source' those requirements. If the organisation (or a particular area of its activity) is declining, it may need to plan a reduction or redeployment of the labour force. If it is growing, or moving into new areas of activity, it will need to find and tap into a source of suitably skilled labour.

It may already have occurred to you that this cannot be as easy as it sounds! External factors – particular over the long term – create fluctuations in the demand for and supply of labour. So do internal factors, such as individual and team productivity, training, and labour turnover through retirements, resignations, maternity leaves and so on.

If anything, as we shall see, the uncertainties of human resource planning make it even more important – and certainly, it becomes more important to approach it systematically. In this chapter, we consider how this can be done. In the chapters that follow, we look at external and internal sources of labour.

Your objectives

In this chapter you will learn about the following.

- (a) The purpose of human resource planning
- (b) The processes and stages involved in human resource planning
- (c) The need for human resource planning and the difficulties involved in accurately predicting manpower requirements
- (d) Limiting factors in the external environment, and changes in the external environment, which influence the human resource planning process

1 HUMAN RESOURCE PLANNING

1.1 Manpower planning and HRP

Definition

> **Human resource planning** (sometimes still known as 'manpower planning') may be defined as 'a strategy for the acquisition, utilisation, improvement and retention of the human resources required by the enterprise in pursuit of its objectives.'

The traditional 'manpower planning' process may be broadly outlined as follows.

- Forecast *demand* for specific skills, competences or grades of employee.

- Forecast *supply* of these skills, competences or grades, both within and outside the organisation.

- Plan to remove any *discrepancy* between demand and supply. If there is a shortage of labour, for example, you would need to reduce demand (say, through improved productivity), or improve supply (through training and retention of current staff, or recruitment from outside, for example).

This traditional model has, in the light of HRM, come to seem too narrow in two key respects.

(a) It is heavily reliant on calculations of employee numbers, with insufficient attention to skills and competences (Taylor 1998).

(b) It is sufficiently integrated with other key factors in the management of the human resource: motivation and productivity; organisational culture and systems; job and organisation design; and so on.

(c) It is based on matching people with 'jobs', in an era when traditional job designs are being eroded by the emphasis on functional, temporal and numerical flexibility in the workforce.

Liff (2000) notes that 'there has been a shift from reconciling numbers of employees available with predictable, stable jobs, towards a greater concern with skills, their development and deployment'.

(a) **Recruiting** the required number and type/quality of staff

(b) **Retaining** the required number and type/quality of staff – and therefore letting go those who are not required (by natural labour turnover and/or by planned downsizing)

(c) **Utilising** staff in the most efficient and effective manner: increasing productivity, introducing multi-skilling and other forms of flexibility and so on

(d) **Improving** the skills, capabilities and motivation of staff, so that they become a more flexible resource capable of fulfilling new requirements

It is arguable that forecasting staff and skill requirements has become more *difficult* in recent times because of the increasing uncertainty and rate of change in the business environment. However, it has also arguably become more *necessary*, because the risks of 'getting it wrong' are correspondingly greater.

Human resource planning (HRP) is a form of **risk management**. It involves realistically appraising the present and anticipating the future (as far as possible) in order to get the **right people** into the **right jobs** at the **right time** (manpower planning) *and* managing employee behaviour, organisational culture and systems in order to maximise the human resource in response to anticipated opportunities and threats.

Activity 1 **(15 minutes)**

We have noted that the supply (and demand) of skilled human resources is subject to a number of factors outside and within the organisation. Suggest three possible reasons why a business might find itself experiencing a shortage of a particular skill/type of employee.

1.2   HRP and corporate planning

As suggested in Chapter 1, human resources are one element of the overall corporate strategy or plan, and the two are mutually inter-dependent. If the corporate plan envisages a cut in output, for example, or the closure of a particular plant, then the human resource plan will need to consider redeployment of staff, redundancies and so on. If the corporate plan specifies a move into a new product market, the human resource plan will have to source the required labour from outside or within the organisation, through recruitment or training.

In turn, the availability of labour resources can act as a constraint on, or spur to, the achievement of corporate goals. If there are skill shortages and employees cannot be recruited, plans for expansion may have to be curtailed. The availability of multi-skilled or expert teams, on the other hand, my inspire innovative strategies for growth and change.

Lam and Schaubroeck (cited in Torrington *et al*, 2002) argue that HR planning is critical to organisation strategy, because it is able to identify:

- *Shortfalls in organisational capability* (skills, knowledge, people) which would *prevent* the corporate plan from being implemented successfully

- *Surpluses in organisational capability* which might *shape* the corporate plan by suggesting opportunities to capitalise on currently under-utilised resources

- *Poor utilisation of people* in the organisation, which would highlight the need to add value through *revised HR practices*

Some people might still argue that proactive forward planning to meet human resource requirements is a waste of time, especially for small to medium-sized businesses. Why does it have to be so complicated? Surely, if you are short of staff, you hire some – or train or promote some of your existing staff? And if business declines and you find yourself with superfluous staff, you make some redundancies? In fact, it is not quite so simple. We will suggest why.

1.3 Why is HRP necessary?

An attempt to look beyond the present and short-term future, and to prepare for contingencies, is increasingly important. Some manifestations of this are outlined below.

> 'Manpower planning has maintained its imperatives for several reasons: (i) a growing awareness of the need to look into the future, (ii) a desire to exercise control over as many variables as possible which influence business success or failure, (iii) the development of techniques which make such planning possible.'
>
> Livy (1988)

(a) Jobs often require experience and skills which cannot easily be bought in the market place, and the more complex the organisation, the more difficult it will be to supply or replace highly specialised staff quickly. The need will have to be anticipated in time to initiate the required development programmes.

(b) Employment protection legislation and general expectations of 'social responsibility' in organisations make downsizing, redeploying and relocating staff a slow and costly process.

(c) Rapid technological change is leading to a requirement for manpower which is both more highly skilled and more adaptable. Labour flexibility is a major issue, and means that the career and retraining **potential** of staff are at least as important as their actual qualifications and skills. 'Trainability' as a major criteria for selection is one of the most popular innovations of HRM.

(d) The scope and variety of markets, competition and labour resources are continually increased by environmental factors such as on-going progress towards full European union, the globalisation of business and the explosive growth of e-commerce.

(e) Computer technology has made available techniques which facilitate the monitoring and planning of human resources over fairly long time spans: manipulation of employment statistics, trend analysis, 'modelling' and so on.

Armstrong (2003) sums up the aims of HRP as follows.

- To attract and retain the number of people required, with the skills, expertise and competencies required

- To anticipate potential surpluses or shortfalls which will need to be adjusted

- To develop a well-trained and flexible workforce which will support organisational adaptation to external changes and demands

- To reduce dependence on external recruitment to meet key skill shortages (by formulating retention and development strategies)

- To improve the utilisation of people (most notably by developing flexible working systems).

Activity 2	(15 minutes)

To what extent would HRP be possible and desirable for:

(a) A company designing, manufacturing and selling personal computers?
(b) A large local authority?
(c) An international airline?

1.4 A contingency approach to HRP

We have suggested that **long-range, detailed human resource planning** is necessary as a form of risk management, preparing businesses for foreseeable contingencies. However, Kane and Stanton (1994) have suggested that HRP should itself be viewed in a more flexible or contingent way, in response to variables in the organisation's internal and external environments.

There has been some disillusionment about the feasibility and value of long-range, detailed HR planning, given the rapidly evolving and uncertain business environment and the kinds of highly flexible organisational structures and cultures that have been designed to respond to it.

(a) The trend in *organisation and job design* is towards functional feasibility (multi-skilling), team working, decentralisation (or empowerment) and flexibly-structured workforces (discussed later in this Course Book) to facilitate flexible deployment of labour. Peters (1994) cites successful US businesses like McKinsey, CNN and Titeflex as examples of 'unglued' structures made up of small, functionally versatile units that come together and disband constantly, according to task requirements; that find their own customers, set up their own networks and generate their own projects; that continuously re-educate themselves to meet new demands. Such structures are entirely flat, output/customer-focused, business-generating, information-seeking, continuously learning and shifting. They sweep aside traditional barriers to innovation, customer service and creative problem-solving – but also effectively abolish 'jobs' and predictability of labour utilisation.

(b) Within flexible structures and markets, where manipulating information – not making things – is the primary business activity, the traditional concepts of 'job' and 'career' are being eroded. Bridges (1995) sees a workforce made up of 'vendor workers' who sell their services to a variety of clients and work for them on a project basis. Peters (1994) similarly notes that workers must become adept at 'résumé management', the development and marketing of a skill portfolio. This fundamentally changes the nature of 'job vacancies' and of the labour pool.

(c) With new emphasis on continuous improvement, customer service and product innovation, organisations are striving to be more adaptive, visionary, fluid in their structures and holistic in their thinking. The *'learning organisation'* embraces learning at all levels and in all areas, focusing on the process of learning and adapting to what is learned: HRP is thus an opportunity to explore different scenarios without pre-conceived requirements or solutions.

In such environments, a different, less prescriptive approach to HRP may be required. Recent literature suggests three broad alternatives.

(a) **The staff replacement approach.** Staff are recruited or promoted to fill a vacancy as and when it occurs – if it is still required – with little formal planning. While this is essentially reactive, and does not provide for much change in the knowledge and skill base of the organisation, it allows a degree of flexibility on an ad hoc basis. Organisations or organisational units with relatively stable environments and a very small organisation may have little difficulty filling vacancies as they arise while in volatile environments and organisations with high staff mobility and turnover, it may be recognised that longer range projections of labour requirements are in any case meaningless.

(b) **Short-term Human Resource Strategy.** In environments where long-term forecasting of future requirements is quickly rendered obsolete by change and uncertainty, yet the ability to adapt the skills and knowledge of the workforce is required, a short-term strategic model may be more suitable. This approach has a 'key issues' orientation: HR and line managers collaborate to determine what the organisation's key HR issues are in the short term, emphasising flexibility and speed of response to emerging threats and opportunities. HR plans are thus more likely to be:

- focused on short-term action planning and implementation
- based on simpler data analysis
- owned by line managers.

(c) **Vision-driven Human Resource Development.** This approach is long-term in its orientation, but is driven by organisational vision, mission and core values, rather than detailed staffing forecasts and targets. Such an approach is often employed where a major cultural shift is required, calling for corresponding shifts in employee attitudes, skills and behaviours.

The process of choosing the appropriate approach may be shown as follows (adapted from Kane and Stanton (1994): Figure 2.1.

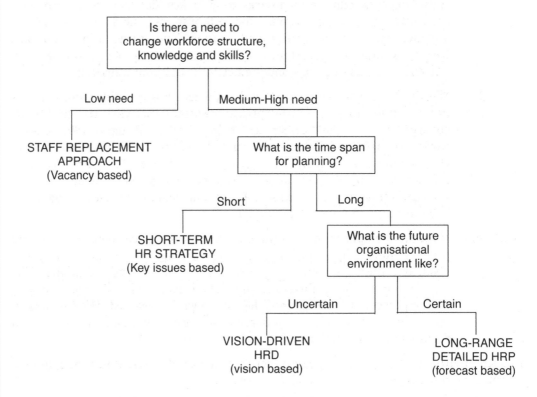

Figure 2.1: Approaches to human resource planning

Let us now look at the manpower planning process in more detail. We have already suggested that it is a form of 'supply and demand management', aiming to minimise the risk of either surplus (and therefore inefficiency) or shortage (and therefore ineffectiveness) of the labour resource. We shall now see how that works in practice.

2 THE PROCESS OF HRP

2.1 Forecasting demand

The **demand** for labour, competencies and productivity levels may be forecast by considering several factors.

(a) The **objectives** of the organisation, and the long and short-term plans in operation to achieve those objectives. Where plans are changed, the effect of the changes must be estimated: proposed expansion, contraction, innovation or diversification of the organisation's activities will affect the demand for labour in general or for particular skills. This may be estimated by market research, competitive analysis, trends in technological advances and so on, (although sudden changes in market conditions complicate the process: the effect of global terrorism on defence spending, for example).

(b) **Manpower utilisation** – how much labour will be required, given the expected productivity or work rate of different types of employee and the expected volume of business activity. Productivity in turn will depend on a range of factors, such as capital expenditure, technology, work organisation, employee motivation, management style and negotiated productivity deals.

(c) **The cost of labour** – including overtime, training, benefits and so on – and therefore what financial constraints there are on the organisation's manpower or skill levels.

(d) **Environmental factors** and trends in technology and markets that will require organisational change in response to emerging demands, threats or opportunities. Economic recession and developments in ICT (information and communications technology) have recently encouraged downsizing and delayering. At the same time, ICT developments have created new markets and products, creating demand for new skills (such as website design).

EXAMPLE

NatWest: an integrated approach to HR planning

'The knowledge and skills of the workforce are crucial and difficult to change quickly, so it is important to plan ahead to identify the skills required to deliver business plans (demand) compared with those that are currently available (supply), to find out where potential skill gaps may lie and how these might be filled.'

NatWest has approached this process as follows.

(a) Demand for skills was assessed through a systematic, top-down approach, driven from the corporate centre. The central HR function held a series of meetings with line managers and HR leaders in each of five core businesses to consider the implications of their strategic plan in the light of their existing skills mix.

(b) A shared model was developed, which highlighted likely demand for skills, and provided an initial perspective on potential skill gaps, as a basis for exploring ways of filling gaps, and discussing the specific concerns of each business.

(c) A bottom-up skills audit was then implemented, to validate the findings of the top-down analysis, and to give a 'better feel' for the likely future supply of skills.

(i) Because of the size and variety of the workforce, NatWest 'needed to establish a common language between businesses to describe skills', and chose a broad-based 'job family' approach. An agreed set of job families (such as 'project manager') was drawn up: each family included characteristic competency profiles for different levels of staff. Gaining agreement on the families and profiles was the major challenge of the exercise, given 'the need to establish a common language and framework, while still recognising differences of interpretation between businesses'.

(ii) A range of different auditing techniques were used, such as sampling the performance of staff from each of the job families.

(d) Recognising the importance of flexibility to environmental factors, NatWest devolved responsibility for assessing demand for skills back to line managers in individual businesses, based on their own job family frameworks, tailored to their particular business environments. However, 'there is still a need to take an overview of the results of the business' analysis, to build an organisational picture of the changes in core or generic skills.'

(e) Such broad-based thinking has led to HR plans such as the introduction of annualised-hours contracts, thought to be the biggest arrangement of its kind for employees in a retail environment. The 'Hours by Design' system is based on what cover is required, which hours staff want to work and how long branches are open: managers set out the expected workflow demands and the staffing levels these require, and employees work out staffing rosters four weeks in advance. In effect, this is on-going human resource planning at the micro-level.

(Bottomley, 1998)

Activity 3 (30 minutes)

Bratton and Gold (2003) note that many HR departments practice 'e-HR': using the Internet and related ICT systems (including internal networks or intranets) to support their activities.

(a) How might e-HR be used in HR planning?

(b) What other sources of information can you brainstorm, that might be used in supply and demand forecasting for HRP?

2.2 Forecasting supply

The available **supply** of labour, competencies and productivity levels may be forecast by considering the following factors.

(a) The competencies, skills, trainability, flexibility and current productivity level of the existing work force.

(b) The structure of the existing workforce in terms of age distribution, skills, hours of work, rates of pay and so on.

(c) The likelihood of changes to the productivity, size and structure of the workforce. Such changes may come through:

(i) Wastage (turnover through resignations and retirements), promotions and transfers, absenteeism and other staff movements; this will require information on:

- The age structure of staff (forthcoming retirement or family start-up)

- Labour turnover for a comparable period

- The promotion potential and ambitions of staff

(ii) Employee trainability, morale and motivation, which may influence productivity and flexibility

(iii) Organisational, technological, cultural, managerial and other changes which may positively or negatively affect employee productivity, loyalty and so on

(d) The present and potential future supply of relevant skilled labour in the environment – that is, the **external labour market**. The HR planner will have to assess and monitor factors such as:

(i) Skill availability: nationally and locally and also internationally (for example, within the European Union)

(ii) Changes in skill availability, due to education and training initiatives (or lack of these)

(iii) Competitor activity which may absorb more or less of the available skill pool

(iv) Demographic changes: areas of population growth and decline, the proportion of younger or older people in the workforce in a particular region, the number of women in the workforce and so on

(v) Wage and salary rates in the market for particular jobs. ('Supply' implies **availability**: labour resources may become more or less affordable by the organisation.)

FOR DISCUSSION

Select an organisation you are familiar with. Is its need for labour growing, shrinking, or perhaps moving into new skill areas? What , if anything, is the organisation doing about this? What other key strategic issues is the organisation facing – and what challenges do they present for human resource management?

2.3 Closing the gap between demand and supply

Shortfalls or surpluses of labour/skills/productivity which emerge may be dealt with in various ways, in accordance with the organisation's specific HR and business objectives and policies (for example, equal opportunities), cultural values (for example about encouraging commitment, quality focus or developing people within the organisation) and available structures and technologies. Detailed action programmes may be drawn up for the following strategies.

Shortfalls **may be met by:**

Internal transfers and promotions, training and development (including individual career management and succession/promotion planning)

External recruitment or improvement of recruitment methods (eg diversity programmes to encourage more applicants)

The extension of temporary contracts, or the contracts of those about to retire

Reducing labour turnover, by reviewing possible causes (including pay and conditions), improving induction/socialisation measures

The use of freelance/temporary/agency staff to cover fluctuating demand

Outsourcing appropriate activities to external contractors

The development of flexible (or otherwise more productive) working methods and structures: multi-skilling, project structures, delayering

Productivity bargaining encouraging overtime working or offering bonuses and incentives to increase productivity

Review and adjustment of corporate culture, management style and organisation to increase productivity

New technology (increasing productivity, and/or reducing the need for human labour)

Adjustment of corporate objectives: contracting in recognition of the constraints

Surplus **may be met by:**

Running down manning levels by natural wastage or 'accelerated wastage' (see below)

Restricting or 'freezing' recruitment

Redundancies (voluntary and/or compulsory)

Early retirement incentives

Short-contract and flexible-hours (eg annual hours contracts) to cover fluctuating demand

Eliminating overtime and 'peripheral' workforce groups (freelance and temporary workers)

Retraining and/or redeployment of staff to other areas of skill/productivity shortage. This may involve diversification by the organisation, to utilise existing skills/knowledge; retraining of employees in newly-needed skill areas; and/or multi-skilling, so that the workforce can be flexibly deployed in areas of labour shortage as and when they emerge

Definition

Accelerated wastage involves **encouraging** labour turnover, by withholding or retaining incentives to loyalty, for example by pay freezes or barriers to promotion.

Bear in mind that there are also **external constraints** on HR planners in considering any or all of the above: UK legislation and EU directives, regulations and court rulings, the employer brand or reputation and other factors must be taken into account when planning to hire, 'fire', or alter working terms and conditions.

Note that the sources of labour are both internal (the current workforce and its future potential) and external (people in the 'labour pool'). We will discuss the external labour market and the internal labour market (and related issues of promotion and succession) in Chapter 3. Another key issue of HRP– flexibility – is discussed in detail in Part B of this Course Book. We will now look at a major factor in forecasting the internal supply of labour: turnover and retention.

3 LABOUR TURNOVER AND RETENTION

3.1 Measuring labour turnover

Definition

> **Labour turnover** is the number of employees leaving an organisation and being replaced. The rate of turnover is often expressed as the number of people leaving as a percentage of the average number of people employed, in a given period. The term 'natural wastage' is used to describe a 'normal' flow of people out of an organisation through retirement, career or job change, relocation, illness and so on.

There are different ways of measuring labour turnover. Most simply, actual gross numbers of people leaving may provide a basis for recruitment/replacement – but the statistic does not say anything about whether or not these people need replacing. To measure labour turnover in a more systematic and useful way, an index such as the following may be used.

(a) **Crude labour turnover rate** (*the BIM Index, British Institute of Management,* 1949)

Here we express turnover as a percentage of the number of people employed.

$$\frac{\text{Number of leavers in a period}}{\text{Average number of people employed in the period}} \times 100 = \% \ turnover$$

This is normally quoted as an annual rate and may be used to measure turnover per organisation, department or group of employees. The **advantage** of this index is that it can alert HR planners to unusually high percentages of the workforce leaving – compared with the HR plan, or with the industry average, say – which would suggest that something is wrong, or that more effort is needed to retain employees. The **disadvantage** of this index is that it does not indicate *who* is leaving the department or organisation: even a high turnover rate may not reflect any real instability if the core of experienced staff consistently remains. (In fact, most wastage occurs among young people and those in the early stages of their employment in an organisation: stability tends to increase with length of service.)

(b) **Labour stability**

Here we try to eliminate short-term employees from our analysis, thus obtaining a better picture of the significant movements in the workforce.

$$\frac{\text{Number of employees with one or more years' service}}{\text{Number of employees employed at the beginning of the year}} \times 100\% = \% \ stability$$

Particularly in times of rapid expansion, organisations should keep an eye on stability, as a meaningful measure.

(c)   The labour stability index ignores new starts during the year and does not consider actual length of service, which may be added to the measurement via **length of service analysis**, or **survival rate analysis**. Here, the organisation calculates the proportion of employees who are engaged within a certain period who are still with the firm after various periods of time. There may be a survival rate of 70% after two years, for example, but only 50% in year three: the distribution of losses might be plotted on a survival curve to indicate trends.

Activity 4   (20 minutes)

Suppose a company has 20 employees at the beginning of 2004, and 100 at the end of the year. Disliking the expansion, 18 of the original experienced labour force resign.

Calculate:

(a)   The crude labour turnover rate
(b)   The stability rate

Comment on the significance of your results.

3.2   Causes of labour turnover

Some reasons for leaving will be largely unavoidable, or unforeseeable. '**Natural wastage**' occurs through:

(a)   Illness or accident (although transfer to lighter duties, excusing the employee from shiftwork or other accommodations might be possible)

(b)   A move from the locality for domestic, social or logistical reasons

(c)   Changes to the family situation, for example, when an individual changes job or gives up work to accommodate child-rearing responsibilities

(d)   Retirement

(e)   Career change

Activity 5   (15 minutes)

Suggest a number of factors that might contribute to labour turnover, which might broadly be grouped under the heading of 'job dissatisfaction'.

Which of these factors would be sufficient to make you leave an organisation: (a) in a market where you were reasonably sure of finding other employment and (b) in a market where other employment was scarce?

Other causes of labour turnover, however, may be to do with the organisation, management, terms and conditions and so on: in other words **job dissatisfaction**.

Labour turnover is also influenced by the following factors.

(a) **The economic climate and the state of the jobs market.** When unemployment is high and jobs are hard to find, labour turnover will be much lower.

(b) **The age structure and length of service of the work force.** An ageing workforce will have many people approaching retirement. However, it has been found in most companies that labour turnover is highest among:

   (i) Young people, especially unmarried people with no family responsibilities

   (ii) People who have been in the employment of the company for only a short time

   The employment life cycle usually shows a decision point shortly after joining, when things are still new and perhaps difficult. This is called the 'first induction crisis'. There is then a period of mutual accommodation and adjustment between employer and employee (called the 'differential transit' period): in the settling of areas of conflict, there may be further turnover. A second (less significant) induction crisis occurs as both parties come to terms with the new status quo. Finally, the period of 'settled connection' begins, and the likelihood of leaving is much less.

So far, you may have got the impression that 'labour turnover' equals 'instability', and that, since it is caused by job dissatisfaction, it must be a bad thing for the organisation. But remember: earlier in this Chapter we noted that an organisation may from time to time have a surplus of labour or particular skills, which it would like to be able to 'lose' through natural wastage instead of costly redundancies. So should organisations fight to retain employees – or not?

3.3 Is turnover a 'bad thing'?

The following table puts labour turnover in perspective.

Potential advantages of labour turnover	*Potential disadvantages of labour turnover*
(a) Opportunities to inject 'new blood' into the organisation: new people bringing new ideas and outlooks, new skills and experience in different situations.	(a) Broken continuity of culture and succession, where continuity could offer stability and predictability, which may be beneficial to efficiency.
(b) Balance in the age structure of the workforce. Absence of labour turnover would create an increasingly aged workforce, often accompanied by an increasing wage/salary cost.	(b) There is bound to be an hiatus while a replacement is found and brought 'on line' to the level of expertise of the previous job-holder.
(c) The creation of opportunities for promotion and succession which offers an important incentive to more junior employees.	(c) Morale problems. Turnover may be perceived by other employees as a symptom of job dissatisfaction, causing the problem to escalate.
(d) The ability to cope with labour surpluses, in some grades of job, without having to make redundancies.	(d) The costs of turnover, including:
	(i) **Replacement costs:** recruiting, selecting and training; loss of output or efficiency

Potential advantages of labour turnover	Potential disadvantages of labour turnover
	(ii) **Preventive costs:** the cost of retaining staff, through pay, benefits and welfare provisions, maintaining working conditions or whatever

It is common to hear that turnover is bad when it is high – but this cannot be assessed in isolation. What is an acceptable rate of turnover and what is excessive? There is no fixed percentage rate of turnover which is the borderline between acceptable and unacceptable. Labour turnover rates *may* be a signal that something is wrong when:

(a) They are higher than the turnover rates in another similar department of the organisation; for example, if the labour turnover rate is higher at branch A than at branches B, C and D in the same area, something might be wrong at branch A

(b) They are higher than they were in previous years or months; in other words, the situation might be deteriorating

(c) The costs of labour turnover are estimated and are considered too high – although they will be relative to the costs of *preventing* high turnover by offering employees incentives to stay.

Otherwise, the organisation may live with high rates because they are the norm for a particular industry or job, because the organisation culture accepts constant turnover, or because the cost of keeping employees is greater than the cost of replacing them.

EXAMPLE

The CIPD's 2003 *Labour Turnover Survey* showed a steep reduction in the average UK employer's turnover from 26% in 2000 to 16.1% in 2003.

'Charles Cotton, CIPD adviser, reward and employment conditions, said the reduction was down to a number of factors – but particularly efforts by firms to address retention issues.

' "The low economic growth being experienced in the UK at the moment is creating much more uncertainty, and could meant people are more reluctant to leave their jobs … But it is also the case that staff retention strategies put in place by many firms, such as better reward packages and career opportunities, are starting to have an impact."

'The survey, of more than 600 HR professionals, also revealed that the average cost to an organisation of an employee leaving now stood at more than £4,300. The average cost of losing an employee from a managerial position is more than £6,800.

'Cotton warned that more firms should be calculating this cost to their business, as only 12 per cent of respondents said they currently did so.

' "In sectors where firms invest large amounts of time and money in giving employees the skills they need to do the job, they must be aware of the cost to the business of losing employees." '

(Watkins, 2003)

So, if an organisation does decide that it needs to control or reduce its labour turnover rate, what can it do?

3.4 Retention planning

A systematic **investigation** into the causes of unusually or undesirably high turnover will have to be made, using various methods.

(a) Information given in **exit interviews** with leaving staff, which should be the first step after an employee announces his/her intention to leave. (It must be recognised, however, that the reasons given for leaving may not be complete, true, or those that would be most useful to the organisation. People may say they are 'going to a better job', while the real reason for the move is dissatisfaction with the level of interest in the current job.)

(b) **Attitude surveys,** to gauge the general climate of the organisation, and the response of the workforce as a whole to working conditions, management style and so on. Such surveys are notoriously unreliable, however.

(c) Information gathered on the number of (interrelated) **variables** which can be *assumed* to correlate with labour turnover – such as an ageing workforce, higher rates of pay outside the organisation and so on.

The causes of turnover should be addressed by HR planning, where it is practical and cost-effective to do so.

(a) If particular managers' practices or styles are creating significant dissatisfaction, performance improvement measures may be implemented.

(b) Coherent policies may be introduced (or more consistently applied) with regard to training and development and promotion from within the organisation.

(c) Induction or orientation programmes for new recruits should address the issues that cause problems at the 'first induction crisis' stage.

(d) Selection programmes should be reviewed to ensure that future recruits are made aware of (and ideally are compatible with) the demands of the job and culture of the organisation.

(e) Problems with working conditions should be solved – especially if they also concern health and safety.

(f) Pay levels and structures may be reviewed in the light of perceived fairness and/or market rates.

FOR DISCUSSION

'Accelerated wastage' is the practice of allowing (or using) job dissatisfaction to encourage people to leave in higher numbers than they would by 'natural wastage', in order to reduce a labour surplus.

How do you respond to this concept? Do you think it has a place in an ethical HRM policy? How would you justify it?

The apparently simple 'supply and demand' equation discussed in Section 2 above makes manpower planning look scientific – but there are so many 'messy' human factors involved in HRP that its feasibility and reliability have been questioned. This raises the further question of how the success and value of HRP can be measured by the organisation. We will look at some of these issues below.

4 EVALUATING HRP

4.1 How reliable is HRP?

Human resource planning is regarded as a scientific, statistical exercise, but it is important to remember that statistics in themselves are limited in value.

Forecasting is not an exact science. Few exponents of even the most sophisticated techniques would claim that they are wholly accurate, although:

(a) The element of guesswork has been substantially reduced by the use of computer models to test various assumptions and to indicate trends

(b) The general principles can still be applied to indicate problems and stimulate control action

---

Activity 6   **(15 minutes)**

Given that HR planners are human beings, and so are the 'HRs' themselves, what might be the major limitations on the reliability or objectivity of statistical methods in HR planning?

Statistical methods can be used to create a more accurate model of the future than simple subjective estimates. Computerisation has greatly enhanced the speed, ease and accuracy with which they can be applied, and many PC-based HR software packages are now available. (If you are curious, you might like to check out www.softwaresource.co.uk, a site established by the CIPD to provide information on HR software suppliers and products.) Even so, there are a number of assumptions involved, and the results are purely **quantitative** – for example, numbers of staff required – where **qualitative** information may be required for meaningful decision-making: the effects of change, re-staffing or management style on the culture of the organisation and individual/group behaviour and so on.

Where end products are measurable, **work-study techniques** can offer a reasonably accurate forecast of staffing requirements. In service sectors and 'knowledge work', however, end products and output may not be easily subject to standard-setting. For example, the number of telephone calls, interviews, customers served, or ideas generated is likely to fluctuate widely with the flow of business and the nature of particular transactions.

Definition

Work study methods break down and measure the elements of a given task in order to define the standard number of staff hours per unit of output.

Managerial estimates form the simplest and cheapest method of assessment. As such, they may be the most appropriate – and are the most common – method for small organisations. At the best of times, however, this method has the disadvantage of a high degree of subjectivity, and although this can be controlled to an extent (by requiring managers to support their estimates with reasons and to reconcile their estimates with those of senior management), it is a source of potential risk.

A measure of flexibility will need to be built into any HR plan, so that it can be adapted to suit likely or even unforeseen contingencies. Above all, it should not be seen or communicated as an inflexible plan, as if it were based on certainty.

> 'Clearly, the more precise the information available, the greater the probability that manpower plans will be accurate. But, in practice, they are subject to many imponderable factors, some completely outside an organisation's control... international trade, general technological advances, population movements, the human acceptance of or resistance to change, and the quality of leadership and its impact on morale. The environment, then, is uncertain, and so are the people whose activities are being planned. Manpower plans must therefore be accepted as being continuous, under constant review, and ever-changing. Since they concern people, they must also be negotiable.'
>
> *Cuming* (1993)

4.2 Is HRP working?

Definition

A **human resource audit** is an investigation designed to:

(a) Give a picture of the current structure, size and productivity of the organisation's labour force

(b) Check the HR plans, systems, policies and procedures have been and are being carried out

---

The best test of the accuracy and effectiveness of HRP is to check whether the reality has in fact conformed to the forecasts and plans: a basic system of control.

(a) Actual staffing levels and trends should be checked against budgets.

   (i) If HR planners have allowed for reductions in staffing levels through natural wastage, it is important to ensure that such wastage is allowed to happen. (It is a natural tendency for managers to seek replacements for any staff losses, even those which have been budgeted for.)

   (ii) The budgets themselves may be (or may have become) inappropriate. The HR plan must constantly be reviewed and revised in the light of changes and actual events (unanticipated).

(b) Personnel records should be checked to identify that each change (promotion, transfer, redundancy, recruitment, etc) has been properly approved, in line with the HR plan.

   This process may uncover:

   (i) Inadequate authorisation of particular types of change; for example, it may be common to transfer employees within the same department without proper approval or reference to the overall staffing plan

   (ii) Unauthorised or unnecessary use of agency or temporary personnel

(c) Staff utilisation should be reviewed: how efficiently is the human resource employed? This process may uncover a need for some fundamental change (such as a complete restructuring of work practices). Apart from the satisfaction and development of employees, it should be clear that under-utilisation of a skill category is an inefficient use of the organisation's resources.

4.3 Is HRP cost-effective?

Although the labour costs in many manufacturing companies are falling as a proportion of total cost, as more expensive technology is used, human resources costs are still significant and may form a large proportion of total costs in labour-intensive industries such as services.

The organisation should therefore assess the **cost** effect of any HR plan – recruitment drive, training initiative or indeed downsizing exercise – in proportion to the **expected benefits** to be derived from it.

Definition

> A **cost-benefit analysis** is a comparison of the cost of an actual or proposed measure with an evaluation or estimate of the benefits gained from it. This will indicate whether the measure has been, or is likely to be, cost-effective – or 'worthwhile'.

There are a number of reasons why a cost-benefit analysis of the HR plan might be useful.

(a) It emphasises the total cost of the plan, including wages and related costs, in relation to gains in efficiency or effectiveness.

(b) It allows costs of the plan to be compared with other options. For example, once the cost of recruitment has been evaluated in relation to gains in productivity, the organisation can assess the merits of alternative plans such as:

   (i) Contracting out the services or production to outsiders (eg getting a catering firm to run a canteen)

   (ii) Buying capital equipment or altering work processes in other ways to enhance productivity

(c) It emphasises that **cost-effectiveness** – not cost-minimalisation – is the aim. For example, temporary or part-time workers may be 'cheaper' for the organisation – but if long-term gains in stability, expertise, management succession and motivated output are lost (compared with employing full-time, permanent staff), this would be a false economy.

FOR DISCUSSION

Do a cost-benefit analysis of your HND qualification. Is education and training an investment – and if so, for whom?

It should be clear that HRP, at the stage of closing the gap between supply and demand, actually involves planning in a number of areas of personnel management. We will end this chapter with a summary of the Human Resource Plan.

5 THE HUMAN RESOURCE PLAN

Once the analysis of human resource requirements has been carried out, and the various options for fulfilling them considered, the **human resource plan** will be drawn up. This may be done at a strategic level (and indeed, as we saw in section 1.2 above, it will have strategic impact). It will also involve tactical plans and action plans for various measures, according to the strategy that has been chosen. Typical elements might include the following.

(a) **The resourcing plan**: approaches to obtaining skills/people within the organisation, and by external recruitment

(b) **Internal resource plan**: availability of skills within the organisation; plans to promote/redeploy/develop

(c) **The recruitment plan**: numbers and types of people, and when required; sources of candidates; the recruitment programme; desired 'employer brand' and/or recruitment incentives

(d) **The training plan**: numbers of trainees required and/or existing staff who need training; training programme

(e) **The re-development plan**: programmes for transferring or retraining employees

(f) **The flexibility plan**: plans to use part-time workers, jobsharing, homeworking, outsourcing, flexible hour arrangements and so on.

(g) **The productivity plan**: programmes for improving productivity, or reducing manpower costs; setting productivity targets

(h) **The downsizing plan**: natural wastage forecasts; where and when redundancies are to occur; policies for selection and declaration of redundancies; redevelopment, retraining or relocation of employees; policy on redundancy payments, union consultation and so on

(i) **The retention plan**: actions to reduce avoidable labour wastage

The plan should include budgets, targets and standards. It should allocate responsibilities for implementation and control (reporting, monitoring achievement against plan).

NOTES

Chapter roundup

- HRP is a strategy for the acquisition or reduction, utilisation, improvement and retention of an enterprise's human resources in response to the requirement of the organisation's strategic plan.

- A systematic approach to HRP would be as shown in the diagram below.

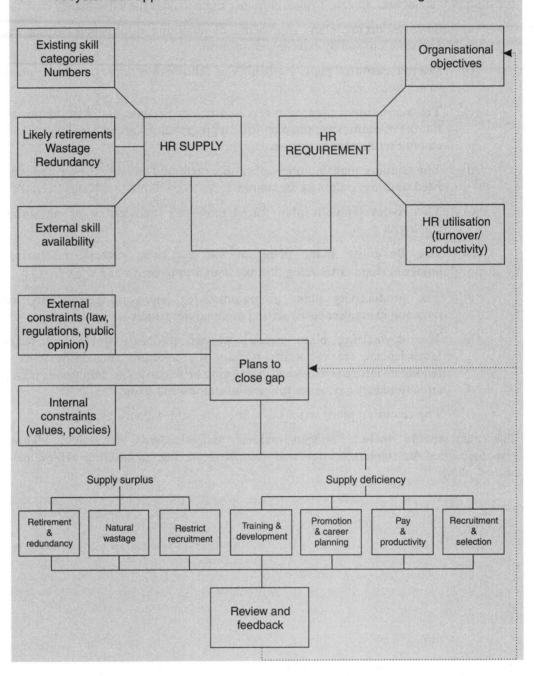

Quick quiz

1 List the elements of human resource planning.

2 Outline the items commonly contained in an organisation's corporate or strategic plan as they affect HRP.

3 List the reasons why human resource planning has increased in importance in recent years.

4   List three basic approaches to HRP in a changing environment

5   Outline the three major stages involved in the human resource planning process.

6   What are the major areas of information required by the human resource planner?

7   How is labour turnover measured?

8   What are the **advantages** of labour turnover?

9   List three methods used in forecasting for HRP.

10   What is meant by the human resource audit?

Answers to quick quiz

1   Recruitment, retention, utilisation, improvement and downsizing of staff.
                                                        (see paragraph 1.1)

2   Predicted financial situation; intended product markets and market share; desired output and productivity; changes in location; employee numbers.
                                                        (para 1.2)

3   Difficulty in replacing specialised staff; employment protection legislation; rapid technological change; need for effective utilisation of staff; national skills shortages in certain areas; international competition; computer technology.   (para 1.3)

4   The staff replacement approach; short-term; HR strategy; vision-driven HRD approach.   (para 1.4)

5   Forecasting demand; forecasting supply; closing the gap between demand and supply.   (section 2)

6   Organisational objectives; staff utilisation; labour costs; environmental factors; staff turnover; production levels.   (para 2.1)

7   Crude labour turnover rate; labour stability index; survival rate analysis.

                                                        (para 3.1)

8   Opportunities for 'new blood'; balanced age structure; promotion/ succession opportunities; reduction of labour surplus.   (para 3.3)

9   Statistical methods; work study; managerial estimates.   (para 4.1)

10   The process whereby an organisation ensures that its human resource planning systems work, and that the plans they incorporate are properly implemented.   (para 4.2)

Answers to activities

1   A skill shortage might be caused by:

      (a)   long-term declines in education and training, or in population (nationally or in the local area)

      (b)   the immediate effects of a competitor entering the market or area and employing some of the pool of skilled labour

      (c)   increases in demand for the product or service for which the skill is required; or the relocation, resignation or demotivation of key skilled people – for all sorts of personal and circumstantial reasons

NOTES

2   (a)   The computer company is operating in an extremely volatile and changing market, which will present HRP difficulties. The technology, and associated skills, are constantly changing, along with competitive pressures: an innovative competitor could 'steal' the market. This is also a highly-skilled business, however, with skill shortages in the labour market, and long training times: despite the difficulties, long-term planning will be important.

        (b)   Some years ago, the local authority would have represented a fairly stable (not to say 'ponderous') bureaucratic structure, with fairly rigid, predictable HR plans. Reductions in funding, and the contracting out of services, have made HRP more difficult and desirable: workforce reduction and flexibility, and the use of HRP to change organisational culture, will be key issues.

        (c)   The airline is a business which is potentially volatile, and sensitive to barely controllable factors such as price wars. Political/terrorist action, industrial action, airspace restrictions, crashes affecting image and so on. At the same time it is dependent on several categories of employees (airline pilots, aerospace engineers) who are scarce and have long training cycles: planning ahead for selection and retention will be crucial.

3   (a)   The Internet is a rich source of statistical, environmental, benchmarking and other relevant information for HRP. Internal corporate databases (possibly integrated into Human Resource Information Systems) should provide data on current skills, workforce structure, productivity and so on. Expert and decision-support software is also available for manpower and 'Enterprise Resource Planning' (ERP). (You may like to do a web search on 'ERP' or 'Human Resource Planning' and check out some of the resources for yourself.)

        (b)   This may be useful as the beginnings of a research/information database. There are many potential sources of labour and environmental information. Just a few suggestions:

- CIPD and other HR journals (and their websites)

- News media

- Employment and industry journals (*Employment Gazette, Employment Digest,* specific industry journals, *Industrial Relations Review, Labour Market Quarterly*)

- Government statistical publications (census information, *Social Trends*)

- Publications, websites and contacts of relevant bodies: trade unions, trade associations, employers' associations, training bodies and so on.

- Competitors and other employers (websites, annual reports and accounts, personal contacts)

4   At the end of 2004, the company works out that it has:

BIM Index: $\dfrac{18\ \text{leavers}}{60\ (\text{average})\ \text{employees}} \times 100 = 30\%$ *turnover*

This is not uncommon, and would cause no undue worries. However:

Stability index: $\dfrac{2 \text{ year servers}}{20} \times 100 = 10\%$ *stability*

Only 10% of the labour force is stable (and therefore offering the benefits of experience and acclimatisation to the work and culture of the organisation). A crude turnover rate has disguised the significance of what has happened.

5 Common factors include the following.

   (a) **Incompatibilities with the organisation climate or culture, or its style of leadership**. An organisation might be formal and bureaucratic, where employees are expected to work according to prescribed rules and procedures. Other organisations are more flexible, and allow more scope for individual expression and creativity. Individuals will prefer – and stay with – one system or the other.

   (b) **Unsatisfactory pay and conditions of employment.** If these are not good enough according to people's needs (or in comparison with others), people will leave to find better terms elsewhere, or will use this as a catalyst to express their discontent in other areas.

   (c) **Poor physical working conditions.** If working conditions are uncomfortable, unclean, unsafe, or noisy, say, people will be more inclined to leave.

   (d) **Lack of career prospects and access to training.** If the chances of advancement before a certain age are low, an ambitious employee is likely to consider leaving to find a job where promotion is likely to come more quickly. The same may be true where an employee wants training for a qualification or skill development, and opportunities are limited in his/her current job.

The second part to this Activity is personal to you.

6 (a) Statistics are not the only element of the planning process, and are subject to interpretation and managerial judgements that are largely qualitative and even highly speculative (involving future growth, say, or potential for innovation).

   (b) Trends in statistics are the product of social processes, which are not readily quantifiable or predictable. Staff leave for various social reasons in (unpredictable) individual cases, to get married, relocate or whatever. The growth of the temporary and freelance workforce is a social trend, as are the buying patterns which dictate demand for goods and services.

Assignment 2   **(2 hours)**

Human Resource Planning at Quick-Send Ltd

Scenario

Quick-Send Ltd is a mail-order clothing company. They currently employ just over 200 people in their warehouse and packing section.

The need to be more competitive and productive has led to the planned introduction of new technology, and an update of the system and procedures used to process and despatch orders.

The personnel department at Quick-Send is currently carrying out its annual human resource planning exercise.

Table 1 shows the current age profile of staff (Year X).

Table 2 shows the number of orders dealt with over the year (Year X), the number of staff employed to deal with these orders, and the ratio of staff to orders – in other words, how many orders a single staff member will be expected to deal with.

Table 3 shows the predicted number of orders for the next five years, together with the new ratios proposed, which take into account the introduction of new technology and new systems.

Annual labour turnover for this group of staff is currently 5% and is predicted to stay at this level for each of the next five years.

TABLE 1	
Current age profile of staff in Warehouse and Packaging	
Age range	*Staff numbers*
Under 20	10
20–25	22
26–30	30
31–35	22
36–40	16
41–45	9
46–50	14
51–55	43
56–60	31
Over 60	20
Total	217

Cont'd

Assignment 2 cont'd

TABLE 2		
Current orders, staff numbers and ratio (Year X)		Ratios
	Number of staff	Staff : orders
Number of orders	217	1:1,705
370,000		

TABLE 3			
Estimated orders and ratios for each of next five years			
Year	Estimated orders	Number of staff	Estimated ratio
X + 1	380,000		1:2,000
X + 2	400,000		1:2,500
X + 3	500,000		1:2,500
X + 4	600,000		1:2,600
X + 5	640,000		1:2,700

Task

You are a personnel officer at Quick-Send

Produce a report for the attention of the Managing Director, covering the following:

1 (a) Decide upon the most appropriate illustration of the current age profile in Table 1.

(b) Analyse the age profile and comment on the implications such a profile has for the resourcing of the department in the future.

2 (a) Using the ratios given in Table 3, calculate the estimated number of total staff numbers required in Warehouse and Packaging for each of the next five years.

(b) Calculate the estimated surplus/shortage of staff numbers for each year.

3 What human resource implications has the plan got for Quick-Send?

What action would you advise the company to take in order to meet their planned numbers for the next five years?

Chapter 3:
THE SYSTEMATIC APPROACH TO RECRUITMENT

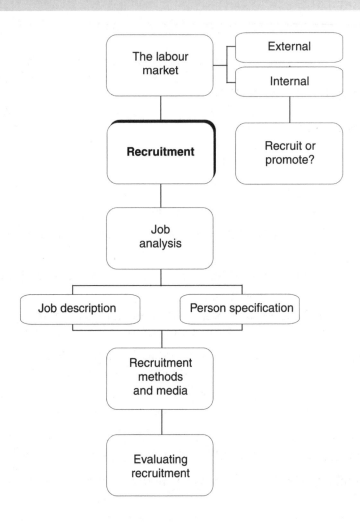

Introduction

In Chapter 2 we noted that there were sources of labour supply both **inside** the organisation and in its **environment**. In this chapter, we look briefly at the labour market (external and internal) and at some of the issues affecting the resourcing and recruitment plan.

The process whereby an organisation goes into the labour market and communicates opportunities and information, seeking to attract the quantity and quality of potential employees it requires to fulfil its human resource plan is called **recruitment**. This chapter outlines a systematic approach to this task.

The process of deciding which of the candidates attracted by recruitment are suitable and/or unsuitable for the organisation's need is called **selection**: this will be discussed in Chapter 4.

Your objectives

In this chapter you will learn about the following.

(a)   The structured approach to recruitment (highlighting 'best practice')

(b)   Recruitment policies and procedures, including job analysis, job description and person specification

(c)   Recruitment methods and media, including job advertisements, application forms and e-recruitment (e-recruitment is part of Unit 22)

(d)   The legislative framework and benchmark evidence guiding recruitment policy and practice

1   THE LABOUR MARKET

1.1   The labour market

Definition

> The **labour market** is the sphere in which labour is 'bought' and 'sold', and in which market concepts such as supply and demand and price operate with regard to human resources.

The **labour market** has changed dramatically in the last few decades. Writers on manpower planning (as it was then called) in the 1970s suggested that a 'seller's market' had been established, as technology increased the skills and therefore scarcity value of employees in certain jobs, and as the scale of state benefits blunted the fear of unemployment: the initiative seemed to be with the employee, or with organised groups of employees.

The decline of manufacturing, the increase of women in employment and the more general application of technology, among other factors, have changed that situation. A 'buyer's market' for labour now gives employers considerable power, with a large pool of available labour created by unemployment and non-career labour.

On the other hand, even in conditions of high overall employment, particular skill shortages still exist and may indeed be more acute because of economic pressures on education and training. Engineers and software designers, among other specialist and highly trained groups, are the target of fierce competition among employers, forcing a re-evaluation of recruitment and retention policies.

We will be discussing the labour market in other contexts in this Course Book: as a spin to flexibility (in Chapter 9) and as a globalised phenomenon (in Chapter 12).

Here we will note some of the key labour market trends that may affect the recruitment plan.

1.2   Key labour market trends in the UK

The following have been identified (Torrington *et al*, 2002) as the three major trends in the UK labour market as a whole:

- Demographic trends
- Diversity
- Skills and qualifications

Demographic trends

Definition

> **Demography** is an analysis of statistics on birth and death rates, the age structure of populations, ethnic groups within communities, population movements and so on.

(a) The *number of people who are economically active* in the UK is currently increasing, principally because more women are entering the paid workforce and spending more of their lives in paid work (both before and after having children) than in the past. Over the long term, however, the proportion of the population that is available for work is expected to shrink: birth-rates have been falling, and life-expectancy has been lengthening, creating an increasing retired population in proportion to those of working age.

(b) As a result, the *age profile of the workforce* is also changing: the population as a whole is getting older, with fewer young people entering the workforce (especially as a greater proportion of them remain longer in full-time education).

> **Activity 1** (10 minutes)
>
> What can you see as the main implications for employers of the demographic changes identified above, in terms of challenges in attracting and retaining quality workers?

Diversity

The workforce is becoming more diverse in its make-up, in several respects.

(a) *Gender diversity.* Increased female participation in the workforce has been a significant social trend since the Second World War. The employment rate for women of working age is currently just under 70%. Although a majority of managerial posts are still occupied by men, and there is a continued gender gap in overall pay levels, there has been an increase in the representation of women at senior levels, and representation in the workforce as a whole is no longer dominated by men (approximately 52% male, 48% female in the UK according to the most recent Workplace Employee Relations Survey). There is still significant segregation in terms of the types of work performed, with particular areas of work dominated by either men or women. Women currently account for over 80% of part-time workers in the UK, which is in itself a growth sector.

(b) *Ethnic diversity.* Representation of ethnic minorities has increased in the UK workforce. The Workplace Employee Relations Survey suggests that over

50% of workplaces now employ someone from an ethnic minority – compared to only 30% in 1980.

Major implications for employee resourcing include:

- The need to take account of anti-discrimination legislation and best practice in recruitment (discussed further in Paragraph 2.4 below). As well as legal protection for groups which are currently under-represented in the workplace, heightened sensitivity to such matters means that positive equal opportunity policies play an important part in building an employer brand which will enable organisations to attract quality labour.

- The need to take account of the needs of increasingly diverse family shapes and circumstances, in order to attract and retain people. Legislation has begun to address the needs of dual income families (eg parental leave and time off for emergencies) but proactive HR initiatives – such as career breaks and childcare support - contribute importantly to a 'family-friendly' employer brand.

Other issues in the management of diversity will be covered in detail in Chapter 10 of this Course Book (Unit 22).

Skills and qualifications

There has been a steady decline in the demand for skills in the manufacturing and agricultural sectors, and a corresponding growth in managerial and professional occupations and in service industries. A new premium has been placed on interpersonal skills (such as team-working, customer service and communication) and on personal skills (such as flexibility, time-management and self-motivation).

Since the early 1990s, there has been an increase in the number of *graduates* entering the labour market. However:

(a) the number of 'graduate jobs', despite strong demand, has not kept pace with the increase in supply (Bratton & Gold, 2003), making it difficult for new graduates to find employment on advantageous terms;

(b) there remain specific skill shortages, creating difficulties for recruiters in filling vacancies. 'There are still too few people with high-level IT and scientific qualifications entering the labour market and far too many people lacking basic numeracy and literacy skills' (Torrington *et al*, 2002), despite on-going policy initiatives (discussed in Chapter 16 of this Course Book) to improve the skill base.

The implications for recruiters may be:

- the need to compete more aggressively for skilled candidates

- the need to re-define jobs to maximise the use of rarer skills

- the need to recruit (or relocate work) overseas

- the need to 'lower' recruitment requirements for specific skills and qualifications and invest in employee training and development in the required skills

FOR DISCUSSION

Select an organisation or business sector that you know well, and identify the key issues facing human resourcing in that organisation or sector.

(Alternatively, you may wish to interview a contact in business, and write a report on the recruitment issues in his or her firm.)

Activity 2	(45 minutes)

Outline a simple HRP procedure (refer to Section 2 of Chapter 2 if you need to) which will take into account demographic and educational trends.

When forecasting the supply of labour and skills available to the organisation to meet the demands of its activities and objectives, the HR planner must take into account:

- *the current skill base, size and structure of its existing workforce*
- *the potential for change in that skill base, size and structure.*

This constitutes an **internal labour market**

1.3 Internal sources of labour

If the organisation faces a demand for a particular skill, that demand may be satisfied from within the existing labour force by:

(a) **Retaining** skilled individuals, against the flow of labour turnover

(b) **Transferring** or deploying individuals with the relevant skills from their current job to the job where those skills can more effectively be utilised

(c) **Training and developing** individuals in the required skills and abilities

(d) **Exploiting its contacts** with present employees, friends and family of employees, and former external applicants, who might be referred (and to en extent, pre-appraised) for vacancies

If the organisation experiences **fluctuating** demand for a particular skill or for numbers of workers, it may need to approach the above strategies somewhat differently, in order to be able to deploy labour flexibly. If a retail business requires extra sales people in the pre-Christmas period, for example, or a factory requires trained specialists in a particular field only at certain stages of a project – or in the event of problems – what do they do? Train, retain and transfer sufficient people for the busiest scenario? You should be able to see that this would be costly and inefficient – and unlikely to enhance the credibility of the HR planner! This is in essence what **labour flexibility** – in terms of numbers and skills deployed – is about.

Retention was discussed in Chapter 2. Training and development are covered in detail in Part C of this Course Book (Unit 23). Flexibility is discussed in Chapter 9 (Unit 22). Here we will briefly discuss **promotion** *as a form of internal 'recruitment'.*

1.4 Promotion

Definition

> **Succession** is the act, process or right by which one person 'succeeds to' or takes over the office or post of another person. (Under an hereditary monarchy, for example, the heir of the King or Queen succeeds by right to the throne when it become vacant. In a business organisation, there may be a policy whereby a 'successor' is developed to replace a more senior manager who retires or leaves.)

Promotion and succession policies are a vital part of the human resource plan, as a form of risk management associated with the internal supply of labour. The planned development of staff (not just skills training, but experience and growth in responsibility) is essential to ensure the **continuity** of performance in the organisation. This is particularly so for **management** planning. The departure of a senior manager with no planned or 'groomed' successor could leave a gap in the organisation structure: the lead time for training and developing a suitable replacement may be very long.

A comprehensive **promotion programme**, as part of the overall HR plan will include:

(a) Establishing the relative significance of jobs by analysis, description and classification, so that the line and consequences of promotion are made clear

(b) Establishing methods of assessing staff and their potential for fulfilling the requirements of more senior positions

(c) Planning in advance for training where necessary to enhance potential and develop specific skills

(d) Policy with regard to internal promotion or external recruitment and training

A coherent **promotion policy** may vary to include provisions such as the following.

(a) All promotions, as far as possible, and all things being equal, are to be made from within the firm. (For the argument for this, see our answer to Activity 4.)

(b) Merit and ability (systematically appraised) should be the principal basis of promotion, rather than seniority (age or years of service).

(c) Vacancies should be advertised and open to all employees.

(d) There should be full opportunities for all employees to be promoted to the highest grades.

(e) Personnel and appraisal records should be kept and up-dated regularly.

(f) Training should be offered to encourage and develop employees of ability and ambition in advance of promotion.

(g) Scales of pay, areas of responsibility, duties and privileges of each post and so on should be clearly communicated so that employees know what promotion means – in other words, what they are being promoted *to*.

Activity 3   **(15 minutes)**

What problems with line/departmental managers can you foresee for a Personnel Manager who attempts to implement a policy such as the one outlined above?

1.5 Internal or external recruitment?

Promotion is useful from the firm's point of view, in establishing a management succession, filling more senior positions with proven, experienced and loyal employees. It is also one of the main forms of reward the organisation can offer its employees.

The decision of whether to promote from within or fill a position from outside will hinge on many factors. If there is simply no-one available on the current staff with the expertise or ability required (say, if the organisation is venturing into new areas of activity, or changing its methods by computerisation), the recruitment manager will obviously have to seek qualified people outside. If there is time, a person of particular

Activity 4   **(15 minutes)**

Outline what you think would be the **advantages** of promoting from within the organisation, instead of recruiting someone from outside. What would be the main **disadvantages**?

potential in the organisation could be trained in the necessary skills, but that will require an analysis of the costs as compared to the possible (and probably less quantifiable) benefits.

2 RECRUITMENT

Definition

Recruitment is the part of the human resourcing process concerned with finding the applicants: it is a positive action by management, going into the labour market, communicating opportunities and information, and encouraging applications from suitable candidates.

2.1 A systematic approach

The overall aim of the recruitment process in an organisation is to obtain the quantity and quality of candidates required to fulfil the objectives of the organisation.

A systematic approach to recruitment will involve the following stages.

(a) Detailed **human resource planning** defining what resources the organisation needs to meet its objectives.

(b) **Job analysis,** so that for any given job or role there is a definition of the skills, knowledge and attributes required to perform the job.

    (i) A **job description**: a statement of the component tasks, duties, objectives and standards

    (ii) A **person specification**: a reworking of the job description in terms of the kind of person needed to perform the job

(iii) Some other appropriate definition of the requirement, such as a *competence definition.*

If such documents exist, they may need to be updated or confirmed.

(c) An identification of vacancies, from the requirements of the human resource plan or by a **job requisition** from a department, branch or office which has a vacancy, and subsequent approval or **authorisation** for engagement. Seeking authorisation to refill a vacancy is a means of ensuring that the need for recruitment, and the criteria for recruitment, are in line with departmental and organisational requirements, timely and cost-effective. It may also provide an opportunity to review other options, such as redeploying existing staff, restructuring tasks, allowing natural wastage and so on.

(d) Evaluation of the **sources of staff,** which again should be forecast in the human resource plan. Internal and external sources, and media (**job advertisement** or other means) for reaching both, will be considered.

(e) Preparation and publication of **information** (ie advertising copy), which will:

(i) Attract the attention and interest of potentially suitable candidates

(ii) Give a favourable (but accurate) impression of the job and the organisation

(iii) Equip those interested to make an attractive and relevant application (how and to whom to apply, desired skills, qualifications and so on)

(f) **Processing applications** prior to the selection process. This may include:

(i) Screening replies at the end of the specified period for application
(ii) Short-listing candidates for initial consideration
(iii) Advising applicants of the progress of their application
(iv) Drawing up a programme for the selection process which follows

---

Activity 5 **(30 minutes)**

Which features of the recruitment process suggest that it might be most efficient and effective if *centralised* within the personnel function, rather than delegated to line managers in their own departments? (Refer back to Chapter 1 if you need some hints.) Suggest five advantages of centralised recruitment.

Movements towards flexibility and multi-skilling have encouraged a slightly different approach, which is oriented more towards 'fitting the job to the person' than 'fitting the person to the job'. In a highly innovative market, technological environment or organisational culture, for example, rigid job descriptions would not be suitable. In order to 'thrive on chaos' (Peters, 1989), organisations should be able to look at the skills and attributes of the people they employ, and those of gifted outsiders, and ask: 'What needs doing, that this person would do best?' In a relatively informal environment, where all-round knowledge/skills and experience are highly valued and suitable external labour resources are scarce (say, in management consultancy), this approach would give much-needed flexibility. The organisation would try to recruit excellent, flexible, motivated and multi-skilled personnel, without reference to any specific job, as defined by a job description. They would form an available 'resource' for any tasks or requirement that arose.

NOTES

However, the 'selection' approach ('fitting the person to the job') is still by far the most common, and is suitable for most organisations with fairly defined goals and structures.

2.2 Recruitment policy and best practice

Detailed procedures for recruitment should only be devised and implemented within the context of a coherent **policy**, or code of conduct.

A typical recruitment policy might deal with:

(a)   Internal advertisement of vacancies

(b)   Efficient and courteous processing of applications

(c)   Fair and accurate provision of information to potential recruits

(d)   Selection of candidates on the basis of qualification, without discrimination on any grounds

In 1994, the Institute of Personnel and Development issued a Recruitment Code that seeks to establish a model of good practice for recruitment.

Recruitment Code

1   Job advertisements should state clearly the form of reply desired, in particular, whether this should be by a formal application form or by curriculum vitae. Preferences should also be stated if handwritten replies are required.

2   An acknowledgement of reply should be made promptly to each applicant by the employing organisation or its agent. If it is likely to take some time before acknowledgements are made, this should be made clear in the advertisement.

3   Applicants should be informed of the progress of the selection procedures, what these will be (eg group selection, aptitude tests etc), the steps and time involved and the policy regarding expenses.

4   Detailed personal information (eg religion, medical history, place of birth, family background etc) should not be called for unless it is relevant to the selection process.

5   Before applying for references, potential employers must secure the permission of the applicant.

6   Applications must be treated as confidential.

7   The code also recommends certain courtesies and obligations on the part of the applicants.

Detailed **procedures** should be devised in order to make recruitment activity systematic and consistent throughout the organisation (especially where it is decentralised in the hands of line managers). Apart from the personnel resourcing requirements which need to be effectively and efficiently met, there is a **marketing** aspect to recruitment, as one 'interface' between the organisation and the outside world: applicants who feel they have been unfairly treated, or recruits who leave because they feel they have been misled, do not enhance the organisation's reputation in the labour market or the world at large.

> **Activity 6** (1 hour)
>
> Find out, if you do not already know, what are the recruitment and selection procedures in your organisation, and who is responsible for each stage. The procedures manual should set this out, or you may need to ask someone in the personnel department.
>
> Get hold of and examine some of the documentation your organisation uses. We show specimens in this chapter, but practice and terminology varies, so your own 'house style' will be invaluable. Try to find the job description for your job; the personnel specification for your job (if any); the application form(s) of the organisation; an interview assessment form (if any); and any benchmarking information used to define 'best practice' and policy.

2.3 Influences on recruitment policy

Recruitment policy will be influenced by the following considerations.

(a) The organisation's image in the community, market-place and labour market: its 'employer brand' or image and identity as an employer. Recruitment advertising, in particular, is a public relations exercise: it must reflect the organisation's values and professionalism – and, where appropriate, its marketing message (quality, products/services and so on)

(b) The human resource plan and subsidiary plans

(c) Fairness, courtesy and professionalism in dealing with applicant, as defined by 'best practice' benchmark evidence.

(d) Legislation and regulations affecting:

   (i) Terms and conditions able to be offered to (or imposed on) potential employees (for example, minimal wage, working hours, holiday entitlements)

   (ii) Equal opportunities – the prevention of direct and indirect discrimination by:

- The wording and placing of recruitment advertisements which imply or tend towards a preference for a particular group

- Indicating or implying **intention to discriminate** in internal planning, advertising or instructions to recruitment agencies

- Failing to state that the organisation is an equal opportunity employer

This will be discussed further below.

   (iii) Labour mobility – for example, discrimination on the basis of nationality or national origin against candidates from the European Economic Area

(e) The cultural values of the organisation, as well as national culture. These are often reflected in the attributes considered essential or desirable in candidates: the importance attached to educational, vocational or professional qualifications; value attached to youth or maturity (and/or associated attributes); identification with the organisation's self-image (responsible, fun, fast-paced, flexible or whatever).

2.4   The legislative framework on recruitment

We will be discussing *equal opportunity* and the *management of diversity* in detail in Chapter 10 of this Course Book, as one of the key HRM issues specified by Unit 22. The key points in relation to recruitment, however, are as follows.

Sex and race

- The *Sex Discrimination Act 1975* (amended 1986) makes it unlawful to discriminate – directly or indirectly – between the sexes in recruitment policy, job advertisements and application forms. This includes discrimination on the grounds of change of sex and marital status.

- The *Race Relations Act 1976* (amended 1996) makes similar provisions in regard to colour, race, nationality or ethnic or national origin.

Direct discrimination occurs when one group is treated less favourably than another. This may be implied by job titles and terminology in recruitment documentation. Recruiters should avoid terms potentially perceived as sexist, such as 'salesman': alternatives include unisex/neutral terms such as 'sales representative' or amplifications such as 'salesman or saleswoman'. Similarly, references to the sex of the desired candidate should be avoided by the use of terms such as 'the applicant', 'the candidate' or 'man or woman', 'he or she' and so on. Armstrong (2003) suggests that, in regard to the Race Relations Act, 'as long as race is never mentioned or implied in an advertisement, you should have no problem in keeping within the law'.

Indirect discrimination occurs when requirements or conditions are imposed, which have a disproportionate affect on a particular group. For example, a requirement that applicants be over six feet tall would prohibit more women than men from applying. The employer must, if challenged, justify the conditions on non-racial or non-sexual grounds.

There are, however, strictly defined exceptions which justify stated preference for a particular group.

- (a) 'Genuine occupational qualifications' in relation to women, which include reasons of physiology (*not* 'strength'), decency/privacy, special welfare consideration and international law or customs which would prevent women operating effectively in a foreign context.

- (b) Special welfare considerations and authenticity criteria (eg in dramatic or photographic roles), in the case of ethnic minorities.

Disability

The *Disability Discrimination Act 1995* makes it unlawful to discriminate against a disabled person in deciding whom to interview or whom to employ or in the terms of an employment offer.

A disabled person is defined as a person who has a physical or mental impairment that has a substantial and long-term (more than 12 months) effect on his ability to carry out normal day-to-day tasks. (This effect may include: mobility; manual dexterity or physical co-ordination; and lack of ability to lift, speak, hear, see, remember, concentrate, learn or understand.)

Other discrimination issues

A number of other current and forthcoming measures are relevant to recruitment.

Under the *Employment Equality Regulations 2003*, it is now unlawful for employers to discriminate on the basis of:

- *sexual orientation:* whether people are (or are perceived to be) gay, lesbian or bisexual

- *religious belief*

Under EU Directive 'Article 13', provisions against discrimination of the basis of *age* will be enacted in UK law by 2006. Currently, a 1999 voluntary Code of Practice sets the standard of 'reasonable behaviour' for use by tribunals. The Code of Practice on Age Diversity in Employment suggests that recruiters should:

- recruit on the basis of skills and abilities;

- refrain from using age limits or phrases that imply restrictions (such as 'newly qualified' or 'recent graduate') in job advertisements.

EXAMPLE: BARCLAYS BANKS ON OLDER STAFF

'Barclays Bank is planning to raise its maximum recruitment age to 70 this year, after successfully extending it to 65-year olds.

'Karen Caddick, head of HR policy at Barclays, said the decision to recruit older workers had been driven by demand. "There are many workers in the financial sector industry who want to keep working longer," she said. "Many employees do not want to retire, while others feel that they cannot afford to do so … All we are doing is playing catch-up as people live longer and are able to work for longer. We are gaining and keeping some of our most experienced people with this policy."

(Roberts, 2003 (a))

FOR DISCUSSION

'For those employers who ignore or fail to comply with the legislation, the consequences will be severe,' says [employment lawyer] Richard Lister.

'Damage can also be inflicted on a company's reputation, according to [diversity manager for financial services group, HBOS] Jones. "Forget about legal claims: it is about treating people with respect."

'It's also about the war for talent. Employers will also miss out on a talented and diverse workforce and lose their competitive edge if they ignore this legislation, believes Dinah Warman, CAP adviser, diversity. "These new legal obligations will help employers stamp out the kinds of prejudices that stop organisations from accessing the talent they need and that keep talented people out of the job," she said.'

(Higginbottom, 2003)

What are the HRM values behind each of these three statements? You might like to take each of the three positions and argue them against opposing or resistant viewpoints.

We will now discuss some of the recruitment procedures listed in Paragraph 2.1 in more detail.

3 JOB ANALYSIS

Definitions

> **Job analysis** is 'the determination of the essential characteristics of a job', the process of examining a job to identify its component parts and the circumstances in which it is performed (*British Standards Institute*).
>
> The product of the analysis is usually a **job specification** - a detailed statement of the activities (mental and physical) involved in the job, and other relevant factors in the social and physical environment.

3.1 Uses of job analysis

Job analysis, and the job specification resulting from it, may be used by managers:

(a) In recruitment and selection - for a detailed description of the vacant job to provide a source of information for the preparation of job descriptions and personnel specifications

(b) For appraisal - to assess how well an employee has fulfilled the requirements of the job

(c) In devising training programmes - to assess the knowledge and skills necessary in a job

(d) In establishing rates of pay - this will be discussed later in connection with job evaluation

(e) In eliminating risks - identifying hazards in the job

(f) In re-organisation of the organisational structure - by reappraising the purpose and necessity of jobs and their relationship to each other

3.2 Content of job analysis

Information which should be elicited from a job appraisal is both task-oriented information, and also worker-oriented information, including:

(a) **Initial requirements of the employee:** aptitudes, qualifications, experience, training required; personality and attitudinal considerations

(b) **Duties and responsibilities of the job:** physical aspects; mental effort; routine or requiring initiative; difficult and/or disagreeable features; degree of independence of discretion; responsibilities for staff, materials, equipment or cash etc; component tasks (where, when, how frequently, how carried out); standards of output and/or accuracy required; relative value of tasks and how they fit together

(c) **Environment and conditions of the job:** physical surroundings, with notable features such as temperature or noise; hazards; remuneration; other conditions such as hours, shifts, benefits, holidays; career prospects; provision of employee services - canteens, protective clothing etc

(d) **Social factors of the job:** size of the department; teamwork or isolation; sort of people dealt with - senior management, the public; amount of supervision; job status

3.3 Methods of job analysis

Opportunities for analyses occur when jobs fall vacant, when salaries are reviewed, or when targets are being set, and the personnel department should take advantage of such opportunities to review and revise existing job specifications.

Job analysis can be carried out by:

(a) **Observation of working practice,** where jobs are relatively routine and repetitive. The analyst watches and records the job holder's activity, task times and performance standards, working conditions and so on. A proforma question sheet listing the factors to be recorded would normally be used, incorporating range statements (circumstances in which each task is carried out and standards to which competence is required) and rating scales

(b) **Questionnaires and interviews,** for jobs with longer task cycles and invisible work (planning, relationship management and so on). The job holder would be asked to explain, describe and quantify (as far as possible) the job. His or her supervisor or manager, and other third parties, may be asked to complete the same exercise.

(c) **Diaries, time sheets and other self-recording techniques.** The job holder may be asked periodically to record activity, or may include **critical incidents** highlighting key aspects of the job.

Activity 7 **(15 minutes)**

The fact that a job analysis is being carried out may cause some concern among employees: they may fear that standards will be raised, rates cut, or that the job may be found to be redundant or require rationalisation.

How might the analyst need to carry out his or her work in order to gain their confidence?

4 JOB DESCRIPTION

Definition

A **job description** is a broad description of a job or position at a given time (since jobs are dynamic, subject to change and variation). 'It is a written statement of those facts which are important regarding the duties, responsibilities, and their organisational and operational interrelationships.' (Livy, 1988)

4.1 Uses of job description

In **recruitment,** a job description can be used:

(a) To decide what skills (technical, human, conceptual, design or whatever) and qualifications are required of the job holder. When formulating recruitment advertisements, and interviewing an applicant for the job, the interviewer can use the resulting job specification to match the candidate against the job.

(b) To assess whether the job will efficiently utilise the abilities and provide scope for the aspirations of the prospective job holder

(c) To determine a rate of pay which is fair for the job, if this has not already been decided by some other means

4.2 The contents of a job description

A job description should be clear and to the point, and so ought not to be lengthy. Typically, a job description would show the following.

(a) **Job title** and department and job code number; the person to whom the job holder is responsible; possibly, the grading of the job.

(b) **Job summary** - showing in a few paragraphs the major functions and tools, machinery and special equipment used; possibly also a small organisation chart.

(c) **Job content** - list of the sequence of operations that constitute the job, noting main levels of difficulty. In the case of management work there should be a list of the main duties of the job, indicating frequency of performance - typically between 5 and 15 main duties should be listed. This includes the degree of initiative involved, and the nature of responsibility (for other people, machinery and/or other resources).

(d) The extent (and limits) of the jobholder's authority and responsibility.

(e) Statement showing relation of job to other closely associated jobs, including superior and subordinate positions and liaison required with other departments.

(f) Working hours, basis of pay and benefits, and conditions of employment, including location, special pressures, social isolation, physical conditions, or health hazards.

(g) Opportunities for training, transfer and promotion.

(h) Possibly, also, objectives and expected results, which will be compared against actual performance during employee appraisal - although this may be done as a separate exercise, as part of the appraisal process.

EXAMPLE

MIDWEST BANK PLC

1	Job title:	Clerk (Grade 2)
2	Branch:	All branches and administrative offices
3	Job summary:	To provide clerical support to activities within the bank
4	Job content:	Typical duties will include:

    (a) Cashier's duties
    (b) Processing of branch clearing
    (c) Processing of standing orders
    (d) Support to branch management

cont'd ...

5   *Reporting structure*:

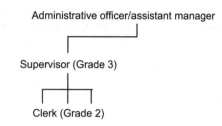

Administrative officer/assistant manager

Supervisor (Grade 3)

Clerk (Grade 2)

6   *Experience/Education*: Experience not required, minimum 3 GCSEs or equivalent.

7   *Training to be provided*: Initial on-the-job training plus regular formal courses and training.

8   *Hours*: 38 hours per week

9   *Objectives and appraisal*: Annual appraisal in line with objectives above.

10 *Salary*: Refer to separate standard salary structure.

Job description prepared by: Head office personnel department

4.3 Limitations of job descriptions

Townsend (1985) suggested that job descriptions are of limited use.

(a)   They are only suited for jobs where the work is largely repetitive and therefore performed by low-grade employees: once the element of judgement comes into a job description it becomes a straitjacket.

(b)   Management jobs are likely to be constantly changing as external influences impact upon them, so a job description is constantly out of date.

(c)   Job descriptions encourage demarcation disputes, where people adhere strictly to the contents of the job description, rather than responding flexibly to task or organisational requirements: this in turn leads to costly overmanning practices.

Where job descriptions are used, it should be remembered that:

(a)   A job description is like a photograph, an image 'frozen' at one point in time

(b)   A job description needs constant and negotiated revision

(c)   A job description should be secondary in importance to a customer requirement, quality improvement or problems solved

5   PERSON SPECIFICATION

Definition

A **person specification** (or 'personnel specification') identifies the type of person the organisation should be trying to recruit for a given position: their character, aptitudes, educational or other qualifications, aspirations in their career and other attributes.

Professor Alec Rodger was a pioneer of the systematic approach to recruitment and selection in the UK. He suggested that:

> If matching *[ie of demands of the job and the person who is to perform it]* is to be done satisfactorily, the requirements of an occupation (or job) must be described in the same terms as the aptitudes of the people who are being considered for it.

This was the basis for the formulation of the person specification as a way of matching people to jobs on the basis of comparative sets of data: defining job requirements and personal suitability along the same lines.

5.1 Models for person specification

The *Seven Point Plan* (Rodger, 1970) draws the selector's attention to seven points about the candidate:

(a) Physical attributes (such as neat appearance, ability to speak clearly and without impediment)

(b) Attainment (including educational qualifications)

(c) General intelligence

(d) Special aptitudes (such as neat work, speed and accuracy)

(e) Interests (practical and social)

(f) Disposition (or manner: friendly, helpful and so on)

(g) Background circumstances

Munro Fraser's *Five Point Pattern of Personality* (1971) draws the selector's attention to:

(a) Impact on others, including physical attributes, speech and manner

(b) Acquired knowledge or qualifications, including education, training and work experience. (Most person specifications include achievements in education, because there appears to be a strong correlation between management potential and higher education.)

(c) Innate ability, including mental agility, aptitude for learning

(d) Motivation: individual goals, demonstrated effort and success at achieving them

(e) Adjustment: emotional stability, tolerance of stress, human relations skills

Note that the person specification includes job requirements in terms of a candidate's:

(a) Capacities - what (s)he is *capable* of
(b) Inclinations - what (s)he *will* do

In other words, behavioural versatility must be accounted for by considering not only the individual's mental and physical attributes, but attitudes, values, beliefs, goals and circumstances - all of which will influence the individual's likely response to work demands.

Each feature in the specification may helpfully be classified as:

(a) **Essential** - for instance, honesty in a cashier is essential whilst a special aptitude for conceptual thought is not

(b) **Desirable** - for instance, a reasonably pleasant manner should ensure satisfactory standards in a person dealing with the public

(c) **Contra-indicated** - some features are actively disadvantageous, such as an inability to work in a team when acting as project leader

EXAMPLE

PERSON SPECIFICATION: CUSTOMER ACCOUNTS MANAGER

	ESSENTIAL	DESIRABLE	CONTRA-INDICATED
Physical attributes	Clear speech Well-groomed Good health	Age 25-40	Age under 25 Chronic ill-health and absence
Attainments	2 'A' levels GCSE Maths and English Thorough knowledge of retail environment	Degree (any discipline) Marketing training 2 years' experience in supervisory post	No experience of supervision or retail environment
Intelligence	High verbal intelligence		
Aptitudes	Facility with numbers Attention to detail and accuracy Social skills for customer relations	Analytical abilities (problem solving) Understanding of systems and IT	No mathematical ability Low tolerance of technology
Interests	Social: team activity		Time-consuming hobbies 'Solo' interests only
Disposition	Team player Persuasive Tolerance of pressure and change	Initiative	Anti-social Low tolerance of responsibility
Circumstances	Able to work late, take work home	Located in area of office	

5.2   Limitations of personnel specifications

As our example suggests, a wide number of variables may be included in a person specification. If it is not used flexibly, however, and the specification fails to evolve as business and employment conditions change, it may swiftly lose its relevance. For example:

(a)   Attainments are often focused on educational achievements, since there has traditionally been a strong correlation between management potential and higher education. However, graduate recruitment is now in crisis, as more people enter higher education, with more diverse educational backgrounds, and more diverse educational standards.

(b)   'Physical attributes' and 'background circumstances' may suggest criteria which can now be interpreted as discriminatory, to the disabled (in the case of a speech impairment, say) or to women (for example, the ability of women with family responsibilities to undertake full-time employment).

(c) The category of 'general intelligence' has traditionally been based on 'IQ', a narrow definition of intelligence as mental dexterity. It is now accepted that there are at least seven different intelligences, not least of which are emotional, intuitive, practical and interpersonal intelligence, which are key factors in the new fluid, horizontal business world.

FOR DISCUSSION

'Forget loyalty and conformity. We can't afford narrow-skill people' (Rosabeth Moss Kanter). What does this say about the concept of the desirable **disposition** for an employee? What kind of characteristics may now take the place of loyalty and conformity as desirable attributes for success and contribution in today's business environment (or in an industry or occupation of your choice)?

5.3 Competency frameworks

Definition

> **Competency** may be defined as 'the set of behaviour patterns that the incumbent needs to bring to a position in order to perform its tasks and functions with competence'. (Woodruffe, 1992)

Competency frameworks, definitions or profiles may be based on key success factors in a given business or sector (through benchmarking exercises or definitions formulated by standard-setting lead bodies). They may also be developed within organisations, linked to their own strategic objectives, cultural values and task requirements.

They are more readily adaptable to changing circumstances and requirements, since they are non-prescriptive about task specifics. Bridges (1994) suggests a 'portfolio' of competencies embracing skills in selling, negotiating and time management, as well as more specific task-related skills. Competencies can be made applicable to employees at all levels of the organisation hierarchy (although the specific behaviours expected will vary), which also helps to create an integrated organisation culture based on central values and attributes.

Competency frameworks have a range of applications beyond recruitment: in employee appraisal, training and development, and in providing a benchmark for rewards and promotion. However, they are particularly useful as a basis for recruitment and selection (Wood & Payne, 1998) in:

(a) Underpinning a range of recruitment and selection tools: advertisements, application forms, interviews and selection tests

(b) Increasing the predictive validity of selection (the accuracy of predictions about a candidate's suitability and job performance)

(c) Ensuring a close watch between the candidate's attributes and the demands of the job, in the particular organisational context.

Armstrong (2003) suggests that competencies can provide the most effective means of identifying suitable candidates, as long as the competencies:

- Focus on areas which candidates are likely to have demonstrated in their academic or working life

- Are likely to predict successful job performance

- Can be assessed in a targeted, behaviour/event focused interview (or using other selection techniques)

Activity 8   **(5 minutes)**

Think of an example of competencies which fulfil each of the criteria for effective competency profiles just given above.

---

6 RECRUITMENT METHODS AND MEDIA

6.1 External recruitment

A number of methods are available to organisations to contact (and attract) potential candidates. These can be summarised as follows.

Method	*Evaluation*	
(a) **Unsolicited requests:** Write-ins or walk-ins (Media: word-of mouth, recommendation, previous recruitment advertising, general employer branding)	**Advantages:**	Inexpensive. Pre-selected for enthusiasm, initiative Open **walk-in** policy may encourage application where job difficult to fill
	Disadvantages:	Needs control and systematic application handling
(b) **Existing contacts;** Previous (re-employable) employees; retirees; career break; previous applicants of suitable general quality held on file.	**Advantages:**	work behaviour/attributes known; may be amenable to part-time, temporary or flexible working
	Disadvantages:	Needs systematic database management
(c) **Referrals:** Registers of members seeking employment, kept eg by trade unions and professional bodies	**Advantages:**	Pre-selection at low cost
	Disadvantages:	Indirectly discriminative
(d) **Agencies** **Job Centres:** Network of agencies provided by central government: particularly for manual and junior positions in admin/clerical/retail	**Advantages:**	Free Local and national Socially responsible (not-for-profit)
	Disadvantages:	Register limited to unemployed Require relationship/selection management
Resettlement Services: Finding civilian positions for armed forces personnel at end of service	**Advantages:**	Can be highly trained/experienced
	Disadvantages:	Inexperience in civilian culture?

Method	Evaluation	
Careers Services: Placing graduates of schools and training institutions	**Advantages:**	Potential for young unsocialised recruits Potential for preview through work placements Financial incentives (government schemes such as YT, Apex) Potential for strong relationship – selection preference, curriculum influence
	Disadvantages	Recruits may lack experience Administration of work-experience Possible indirect discrimination
Employment Agencies: Wide range of specialising agencies; temporary agencies for one-off requirements and short-term cover (eg of maternity or sick leave)	**Advantages:**	May undertake pre-screening Temp agencies facilitate flexible working
	Disadvantages:	Quality can vary Cost
(e) **Consultancies** **Selection consultants:** Recruit and select for positions; may cover clerical/admin staff, specialist staff (media, financial etc), or managerial	**Advantages:**	Reduces administration for employer Specialist selection skills Wide-ranging contacts
	Disadvantages:	Cost May lack awareness of organisation's culture, values, detailed criteria Excludes internal applicants Lack of accountability
Outplacement consultants: Registers, retraining etc to help redundant and early-retired employees	**Advantages:**	Perceived socially responsible Provide some training
	Disadvantages:	Quality varies
Search consultants: 'Head hunters'. Networking to track highly employable individuals: candidates proactively approached	**Advantages:**	Selects for high employability net-working, exploration opportunity
	Disadvantages:	Cost Limited range Organisation may be victim as well as beneficiary!
(f) **Direct to source:** Schools, colleges, universities (Media: advertisement, 'milk-round' presentation)	**Advantages:**	Networking relationships Opportunities to preview via work placement, 'gap' year etc Access to graduates in desirable (scarce) disciplines
	Disadvantages:	Local catchment area Tends to be annual 'season' Recruits lack experience Potential for indirect discrimination
(g) **The Internet:** Wide range of recruitment databases	**Advantages:**	IT-literate users Pre-selection through employer information database World-wide catchment
	Disadvantages:	Difficulty of verification Competition

> **Activity 9**   **(1 hour)**
>
> We have already mentioned some of the 'media' by which an organisation can advertise or make known its staffing needs by the methods listed above. Brainstorm as a full list as you can of advertising/information media relevant to recruitment. For each of the media you mention, add any advantages or disadvantages you can think of.

E-recruitment is one of the 'topical HR issues' cited in the content for Unit 22. We will cover it, in context, here.

6.2   E-recruitment

E- (or Internet) recruiting has exploded in recent years, having been used mainly for IT jobs in the early stages of Internet adoption. The Internet can be used:

- To 'post' or advertise vacancies, either on the employer's own website (or intranet, for internal advertising) or on specialist online recruitment sites.

- To provide information about the employer, recruitment policies and jobs (often available on the employer's own website, as well as recruiter databases).

- To allow database searches, matching employers' requirements and job seekers' CVs.

- To facilitate communication (via e-mail) between enquirers/applicants and employers.

- To complete recruitment applications electronically (online application forms, computerised screening of essential matching criteria, online psychometric tests and so on).

The key advantages of e-recruitment are:

(a) Its ability to reach a wide and geographically dispersed (even global) audience of potential candidates.

(b) Its cost-effectiveness, compared to traditional forms of advertising.

(c) Its ability to offer more information (for self-selection) about the organisation and the job, potentially in a more attractive (interactive, multi-media) format.

(d) Its demonstration of basic computer literacy (where desired) by applicants.

(e) Electronic support for application, CV matching, short-listing and so on – more swiftly and cost-effectively than by human agency.

(f) The provision of application information for use in Human Resource Information Systems, eg to analyse applications received, monitor equal opportunities and so on.

However, many applications through e-recruitment are irrelevant (especially if the organisation only wants to recruit locally or nationally) or ill-prepared (since it takes so little effort to e-mail a prepared CV). Screening and short-listing software relies heavily on matching keywords, and can disqualify suitable candidates on this basis. Despite the increasing take-up of Internet technology, e-recruitment may still screen out otherwise suitable applicants for whom it is not the preferred job-seeking tool: there are still security concerns about transmitting personal data via the web.

EXAMPLE

'Is the HR function really taking online recruitment and its accompanying technology to heart? Are recruitment managers genuinely enthusiastic about the savings and quality increases it can lead to? Or, with half of all FT500 firms having no corporate website recruitment, is there another side to the story?

'Ask many of the top companies in the UK, and they are enthusiastic about online recruitment. They say they have their current vacancies online, they have e-mail links, they may even have online forms and a system to scan them. It is, they say, a cheap and easy method of gathering more applications from a wider pool.

'Yet the first major benchmarking study of the top 500 companies' own online recruitment efforts show that the effects permeate no further. Only a tiny fraction of those that recruit online back this up with fully automated recruitment systems to manage the process … Is it the money? Or the real ability of the tools to deliver? Or something deeper …

' "We expected a big spread in the levels of performance – but not this big," says Colin Farrow, managing director of consultancy The Driver Is, which … combed each FT500 site to find if it fulfilled nine simple recruitment criteria …

' "The overriding criterion was 'as a user – what would I expect to find?' We were not looking for leading-edge technology," Farrow insists, "just assistance and information – an existing career profile, an impression of working there. These are indicators of above-average empathy with the user." …

'One firm that can feel proud of its recruitment website is engineering services provider Amec. Coming joint first in the corporate website benchmarking study, the site offers taster job profiles, latest jobs and help during studies and internships.'

The nine criteria; How e-savvy is your firm?

☐	Are current vacancies listed?
☐	Can people apply online?
☐	Can potential candidates see an existing employee's career profile?
☐	Are company business principles referred to?
☐	Can people register for e-mail alerts?
☐	Do they actually receive e-mail alerts?
☐	Is there a graduate section?
☐	Is there an 'experience of hires' section?
☐	Are HR contacts featured?

Welch (2003)

For more results of the benchmarking study by The Driver Is, visit:

www.ukcorporatewebrankings.com

Activity 10 (1 hour)

Use the Internet to appraise the e-recruitment strategies of two or more firms, using the checklist suggested by the benchmarking study cited above.

(a) Start with your own organisation. Check its own website recruitment (if any).

(b) Browse the sites of Amec, or any other top companies you are interested in.

(c) Browse the 'jobs' or 'careers' channels of your preferred Internet portal (Yahoo! or MSN, say), or the specialist jobs agencies/sites advertised.

6.3 The recruitment advertisement

The object of recruitment advertising is to home in on the target market of labour, and to attract interest in the organisation and the job.

In a way, it is already part of the **selection** process. The advertisement will be placed where suitable people are likely to see it (say, internally only - immediately pre-selecting members of the organisation - or in a specialist journal, pre-selecting those specialists). It will be worded in a way that further weeds out people who would not be suitable for the job (or for whom the job would not be suitable). Be aware however, that some such forms of pre-selection may be construed as discriminatory if it disadvantages some groups more than others. (Advertising internally only, where the current workforce is overwhelmingly male, may be construed as indirectly discriminatory to women, for example.)

The way in which a job is advertised will depend on the type of organisation and the type of job.

A factory is likely to advertise a vacancy for an unskilled worker in a different way to a company advertising for a CIPD-qualified person for a senior HR position. Managerial jobs may merit national advertisement, whereas semi- or un-skilled jobs may only warrant local coverage, depending on the supply of suitable candidates in the local area. Specific skills may be most appropriately reached through trade, technical or professional journals.

The advertisement, based on information set out in the job description, job and person specifications and recruitment policy, should contain information about:

(a) The organisation: its main business and location, at least

(b) The job: title, main duties and responsibilities and special features

(c) Conditions: special factors affecting the job

(d) Qualifications and experience (required, and preferred); other attributes, aptitudes and/or knowledge required

(e) Rewards: salary, (**negotiable**, if appropriate) benefits, opportunities for training, career development, and so on

(f) Application: how to apply, to whom, and by what date

The advertisement should encourage a degree of **self-selection,** so that the target population begins to narrow itself down. (The information contained in the advertisement should deter unsuitable applicants as well as encourage potentially suitable ones.) It should also reflect the desired image of the organisation in the outside world: its employer brand.

NOTES

AT MILTON KEYNES
'NO' ISN'T A WORD WE LIKE TO USE

We'd much rather give the thumbs up to new ideas and new innovations. And in our forward-thinking HR department, that's exactly what we're doing.

It's all part of the Council's wider aims to change the way local government operates. Embracing new legislation and bringing our services closer to internal and external clients alike, we're adopting a real business focus - and shaping some bold plans for the future. If you're MCIPD qualified, have a record of continued professional development and you're aware of the wider issues confronting a Council like ours, they're plans you could share in.

HUMAN RESOURCES OFFICER - OPERATIONS

£22,194 - £26,091 REF: RO1331

You'll be part of our central HR operation, ensuring that all our services run smoothly and effectively - as well as contributing to the overall development of the department. We'll also look to you to provide Council-wide advice on everything from employment legislation to HR procedure, calling on at least 3 years' generalist human resources experience, a background in trade union liaison and proven communication skills. Requests for full/part-time or term-time only are welcome.

HUMAN RESOURCES OFFICER - EMPLOYEE RELATIONS

£22,194 - £26,091 REF: RO1332

You'll be reviewing, developing and undertaking briefings on HR policies; advising managers and HR colleagues on policies and employment legislation; trade union consultation; reviewing and monitoring the Occupational Health contract. You will have at least 3 years' human resources experience.

CLOSING DATE: 16 OCTOBER 2000.

Further information and application forms are available by telephoning (01908) 253344 or 253462 (answerphone service available 24 hours per day) or by writing to HR Recruitment Team, Milton Keynes Council, Saxon Court, 502 Avebury Boulevard, Milton Keynes MK9 3HS. Minicom (01908) 252727 (office hours only) or e-mail: Helen.Davey@milton-keynes.gov.uk

PLEASE QUOTE THE APPROPRIATE REFERENCE.

MILTON KEYNES
COUNCIL

The Council is an Equal Opportunities Employer. Applications are invited from candidates with the necessary attributes regardless of gender, colour, ethnic origin, nationality, creed, disability or sexual orientation. Many Council jobs are suitable for job sharing.

The aim of the recruitment process is applications by suitably qualified candidates. What form might an application take, in order for it to be fed into the selection process?

6.4 Applications

Applications for a particular advertised (or unadvertised) vacancy, or for employment in the organisation as and when vacancies arise, may be received in various forms.

(a) **Unsolicited letter, e-mail, 'walk-in' or other enquiry**. This would normally be responded to with a request for the following.

(b) **Application form**

  (i) For lower-level, relatively standardised jobs, for which a high volume of applicants is expected, this may be a brief, directly targeted form (focusing on qualifications and experience considered essential to the job) in order to facilitate ruthless weeding out of unsuitable applicants, and requiring minimal discretion, self-expression and time in both completion and interpretation.

  (ii) For managerial, specialist or culturally-driven jobs, a more complex application form or package may be used, in order to elicit more complex responses: biographical/psychological ('biodata') questionnaires, guided self-expression, samples for hand-writing analysis, preliminary testing (an account of job problem-solving, or response to case-study scenarios, say) and so on. Such in-depth tools for pre-selection save time and effort at the interview stage, but are time-consuming to prepare and analyse, and should be subjected to cost-benefit considerations.

(c) **Curriculum vitae (CV)** or **résumé**, usually accompanied by a **covering letter** drawing the recruiter's attention to specific vacancy – or organisation - relevant aspects of the applicants' CV. The CV is essentially a brief, systematic summary of the applicant's qualifications, previous work experience and relevant skills/interests/requirements, plus details of individuals willing to vouch for his or her performance, character and employability (**referees**).

The application form or CV will be used to find out relevant information about the applicant, in order to decide, at the initial sifting stage:

(a) Whether the applicant is obviously unsuitable for the job or

(b) Whether the applicant might be of the right calibre, and worth inviting to interview

The application form will be designed by the organisation, and if it is to be useful in the sifting process, it should fulfil the following criteria.

(a) It should ask questions which will elicit information about the applicant and which can be directly compared with the requirements of the job. For example, if the personnel specification requires a minimum of 2 'A' Level passes the application form should ask for details of the applicant's educational qualifications. It should likewise discourage irrelevant and unnecessarily lengthy responses.

(b) For managerial, interpersonal and culturally-driven jobs – requiring particular values, orientations and attributes – it should also give applicants the opportunity to write about themselves, their career ambitions or why they want the job. It might be possible to obtain some information about their:

  (i) Organisational abilities
  (ii) Intelligence
  (iii) Ability to express themselves in writing
  (iv) Motivation
  (v) Self-image and values

(c)   It should convey a professional, accurate and favourable impression of the organisation, a public relations and employer branding tool.

(d)   It should elicit any information required to enable the organisation subsequently to monitor and evaluate the success of its recruitment procedures (in regard to numbers of female, minority and disabled applicants, number of applications per source and so on).

An example of a basic application form is given on the next page.

Activity 11   **(20 minutes)**

Suggest four other ways in which an application form could be **badly** designed (both in appearance and content). You may be able to do this from personal experience.

6.5   Internal recruitment

Internal advertising of vacancies may be a requirement for some organisations, under agreements negotiated with trade unions. Advertising media include noticeboards (paper and electronic – for example via corporate intranet), in-house journals, memoranda to supervisors/managers soliciting recommendations and observation and word-of-mouth (the **grapevine**).

Methods of **internal recruitment** include:

(a)   Advertising for self-applicants

(b)   Soliciting recommendations from supervisors/managers, training officers and so on

(c)   Soliciting referrals by existing employees to family, friends and contacts

(d)   Formal succession, promotion and transfer planning

Most of these methods incur little extra cost, being based on existing or easily accessible information about the candidate's abilities, attitudes and so on.

7   EVALUATING RECRUITMENT

An evaluation of recruitment and selection procedures will aim to determine whether the procedures succeeded in getting a *suitable* person into a job, at the *time* when the person was required and at an acceptable cost. At a more strategic level, it determines whether recruitment and selection procedures are succeeding in achieving the organisation's overall manpower plan.

Connock (1991) suggests that auditing the recruitment process can occur at four levels.

(a)   **Performance indicators** should be established for each stage of the process. Data can be collected about actual performance and compared with the standards. As Connock says 'Significant variations from the established standards will need to be individually investigated, and remedial action initiated if necessary. Remedial action might include extra staffing for the recruitment section if turn-round times are not being met. One of the major causes of candidate demotivation is a slow turn round of applications'.

NOTES

AOK PLC		Page 1
APPLICATION FORM		

Post applied for ….

PERSONAL DETAILS

Surname Mr/ Mrs/ Miss/Ms

First name

Address

Post code

Telephone   (Daytime)   (Evenings)

Date of birth

Nationality

Marital status

Dependants

Education (latest first)

Date		Institution	Exams passed/qualifications
From	To		

TRAINING AND OTHER SKILLS

Please give details of any specialised training courses you have attended.

Please note down other skills such as languages (and degree of fluency), driving licence (with endorsements if any), keyboard skills (familiarity with software package).

Page 2

Unit 21: Human Resources Management

EMPLOYMENT

Dates		Employer name and address	Title and duties
From	To		

Current salary and benefits …

INTERESTS

Please describe your leisure/hobby/sporting interests.

YOUR COMMENTS

Why do you think you are suitable for the job advertised?

ADDITIONAL INFORMATION

Do you have any permanent health problems? If so, please give details.

When would you be able to start work?

REFERENCES

Please give two references. One should be a former employer.

Name   Name
Address   Address

Position   Position

Signed   Date

(b) **Cost-effectiveness** of the various methods used should be measured. It may be that a certain advertising medium is too costly for the number of worthwhile responses it generates. Advertising in the national press, for example, may generate a large number of responses, but few of the required quality; meanwhile an insertion in a professional journal may, with a smaller circulation, generate a higher proportion of potentially suitable candidates.

Activity 12   **(20 minutes)**

What kind of information would you need to record in order to appraise the cost-effectiveness of a recruitment method/medium? Aim to end up with a meaningful figure for the cost per person appointed (and actually entering employment).

(c) **Monitoring the make up of the workforce** and the impact on its constitution of new recruits is essential as part of an equal opportunities policy. This will identify areas where certain groups are under-represented, for example women, disabled people or ethnic minorities. The reasons for this should be investigated and eliminated.

(d) Finally, Connock suggests conducting an **attitude survey** amongst staff who have been recruited to find out whether they were satisfied with the various stages of their recruitment and selection – did they feel that the job advertisement they responded to gave them a fair idea of the nature of the job, were they frustrated by the length of time they had to wait for a decision and so on.

Other methods of evaluating recruitment and selection include *'benchmarking'* – comparing the organisation's systems with known example of good practice used in other organisations.

Where a personnel department has adopted the notion of the 'internal customer', it can seek the views of its customers (line managers) and users (job applicants).

Some specific **performance indicators** for evaluating recruitment procedures are as follows.

(a) Total numbers of applications received
(b) Time taken to locate applicants
(c) Cost per applicant
(d) Time taken to process applications/per application
(e) Number of female/minority/disabled applicants
(f) Number of qualified applicants (matching advertised criteria)
(g) Number of qualified female/minority/disabled applicants

These basically assess the effectiveness and cost-efficiency of recruitment advertising, equal opportunities policy in recruitment and recruitment administration. Post-entry criteria – such as number of offers extended per source/method or in relation to applications received, cost and time of training recruits, subsequent job performance and length of service of recruits and so on – may only be applied after the selection process. However, they also reflect on recruitment retrospectively.

Chapter roundup

- The labour market consists of potential employees, both internal and external to the organisation.

- Demographic trends have important implications for personnel management, especially the falling number of young people in the workforce, the rising number of female and older workers, and national/regional education trends.

- Recruitment is concerned with defining job requirements and attracting suitable applicants. Selection is concerned with fitting the person to the job.

- The essential points in this chapter can be summarised in diagrammatic form.

Cont...

Quick quiz

1 Why is the shift towards an ageing population important for HRP?

2 Suggest two ways in which recruiters can avoid discrimination on the basis of (a) sex and (b) age.

3 List three methods by which job analysis may be carried out.

4 What is a job description?

5 What three criteria make 'competencies' effective in guiding recruitment and selection?

6 List five methods of recruitment of candidates from the external job market.

7 What are the *drawbacks* of e-recruitment?

8 List four methods of receiving applications.

9 List four methods by which vacancies could be filled from the internal labour pool.

10 List three methods by which recruitment procedures may be evaluated.

Answers to quick quiz

1 Because the workforce will reflect the proportion of older workers, and because of the corresponding decline in the number of young people available to work. (see paragraph 1.2)

2 (a) Avoid sexist terms. Avoid unjustifiable (indirectly discriminatory) requirements.

   (b) Avoid stating age limits. Avoid implying restrictions (eg 'recent graduate'). (para 2.4)

3 Observation, questionnaire/interview, diaries/self-recording (para 3.3)

4 A broad description of the purpose, scope, duties and responsibilities of a particular job. (para 4)

5 Focusing on demonstrable areas; likely to predict job performance; readily assessable. (para 5.3)

6 Agencies, consultancies, Internet, direct to source, existing contacts.
   (para 6.1)

7 Irrelevant and ill-prepared applications. Difficulty of accurate screening. Lack of take up by potentially suitable applicants. (para 6.2)

8 CV; application form; unsolicited enquiry; web application. (para 6.4)

9 Retention, transfer or redeployment, training and development, promotion, exploiting employee contracts and/or flexible working methods. (para 6.5)

10 By determining key performance indicators and monitoring performance against them; by measuring cost-effectiveness; by monitoring the make-up of the workforce; by conducting attitude surveys; by benchmarking.
   (section 7)

Answers to activities

1   (a)   The falling number of younger workers will make it increasingly difficult to recruit and retain skilled younger people, with intense competition – particularly among organisations that have traditionally recruited school leavers and new graduates. Organisations will either have to revise strategies to compete for younger workers – or change their resourcing policies and culture to accept older workers.

(b)   In the UK, the ratio of people 65+ to those of working age is 21 : 100. By 2030, this is anticipated to be 25+ : 100, adding to the difficulties of the state to provide pensions for the retired population. Employers are likely to find the provision of occupational pension benefits an increasingly important tool in attracting and retaining employees.

2   Connock (1991) suggests six steps by which organisations can cope with these demographic and educational trends.

(1)   Establish what labour market the organisation is in (eg young people, part-time workers).

(2)   Discover the organisation's catchment areas (ie location of potential recruits).

(3)   Discern the supply side trends in the catchment area labour force. (For example, how many school leavers are expected? What is the rate of growth/decline of local population?)

(4)   Examine education trends in the location.

(5)   Assess the demand from other employers for the skills you need. (For example, if there is a large concentration of, say, electronics companies in the region, then they will be interested in hiring people with similar skills).

(6)   Try to assess whether some of your demand can be satisfied by a supply from other sources.

3   It is often difficult to persuade departmental managers to agree to the promotion of a subordinate out of the department, especially if he/she has been selected as having particular ability: the department will be losing an able member, and will have to find, induct and train a replacement. Moreover, if the manager's resistance were made known, there would be a motivational problem to contend with. The personnel manager will have to be able to back his/her recommendation with sound policies for providing and training a replacement with as little loss of the department's efficiency as possible.

4   Where the organisation has the choice, it should consider the following points.

(a)   Management will be familiar with an internal promotee: there will be detailed appraisal information available from employee records. The outside recruit will to a greater extent be an unknown quantity – and the organisation will be taking a greater risk of unacceptable personality or performance emerging later.

(b)   A promotee has already worked within the organisation and will be familiar with its:

(i)   Culture, or philosophy; informal rules and norms as well as stated policy

(ii) Politics; power-structures and relationships

(iii) Systems and procedures

(iv) Objectives

(v) Other personnel (who will likewise be familiar with him/her)

(c) Promotion of insiders is visible proof of the organisation's willingness to develop people's careers. This may well have an encouraging and motivating effect. Outsiders may well invite resentment.

(d) Internal advertisement of vacancies contributes to the implementation of equal opportunities policies. Many women are employed in secretarial and clerical jobs from which promotion is unlikely – and relatively few are in higher-graded roles. Internal advertising could become a route for opening up opportunities for women at junior levels.

(e) On the other hand, an organisation must retain its ability to adapt, grow and change, and this may well require new blood, wider views, fresh ideas. Insiders may be too socialised into the prevailing culture to see faults or be willing to 'upset the apple cart' where necessary for the organisation's health.

5 Five from:

(a) The overall priorities and requirements of the organisation will be more clearly recognised and met, rather than the objectives of sub-systems such as individual departments.

(b) There will be a control reference point for communication, queries and applications from outside the organisation.

(c) Communication with the environment will also be more standardised, and will be more likely to reinforce the overall corporate image of the organisation.

(d) Potential can be spotted in individuals and utilised in the optimum conditions – not necessarily in the post for which the individual has applied, if he or she might be better suited to another vacant post.

(e) The volume of administration and the need for specialist knowledge (notably of changing legal and industrial relations requirements) may suggest a specialist function.

(f) Standardisation and central control should be applied to, for example, equal opportunities, pay provisions and performance standards, where fairness must be seen to operate.

6 This task is intended to develop your research skills and your awareness of HR practice in a specific organisation – starting with your own. In order to fulfil the assessment criteria for this unit, you are required to 'compare the structured process for recruitment in two organisations': this activity gets you half way there! Make it an on-going assignment to gather case study information about the recruitment policies and practices of organisations that interest you.

7 The job analyst will need to gain their confidence by:

(a) Communicating: explaining the process, methods and purpose of the appraisal

(b) Being thorough and competent in carrying out the analysis

(c) Respecting the work flow of the department, which should not be disrupted

(d) Giving feedback on the results of the appraisal, and the achievement of its objectives. If staff are asked to co-operate in developing a framework for office training, and then never hear anything more about it, they are unlikely to be responsive on a later occasion

8 Competencies:

- Likely to be demonstrated: eg leadership, initiative, ability to work with others, ability to work under (or without) supervision

- Likely to predict job performance: eg motivation to achieve, specific technical skills related to the job (numeracy, computer use)

- Assessable: eg team building (asking candidates to describe when they have successfully built a team), problem analysis (asking candidates to analyse and suggest solutions to a case study scenario), conflict resolution (asking a candidate to role play a mediator in an industrial conflict scenario)

9 Some of the media you may have come up with include the following.

(a)	Newspapers and journals (trade, professional) – ie 'Press' media	• Journals better targeted, papers offer wider local or national coverage • Wider and more targeted coverage – higher cost: cost-effectiveness must be monitored, controlled • May offer opportunity to produce own artwork – may not (control required)
(b)	Cinema, radio, TV – ie 'broadcast' media	• Can offer general marketing opportunity • Powerful all-senses effect • Expensive (especially TV) • Mass coverage (option of local) • Appeal to young audience
(c)	Posters, leaflets, notices on notice boards (+ multi-media equivalents: cassettes, videos)	• Targeting through positioning only • Can be expensive, hit-and-miss, long timescale • Content/style controlled by organisation
(d)	Exhibitions, conferences, roadshows, open-days, presentations	• If well targeted location, can reach large number of relevant people • Opportunities for non-committal networking, exploration • Immediacy of face to face communication – but also a risk • Can be expensive to organise/delegate
(e)	Websites	• Untargeted (except to IT-literate) • Controllable • Relatively low-cost • Opportunity for general marketing

10 This is a research exercise. You may like to print out some of your findings, as evidence that you have grained relevant knowledge in this area.

11 (a) Boxes too small to contain the information asked for

(b) Forms which are (or look) so lengthy or complicated that prospective applicants either complete them perfunctorily or give up (and apply to another employer instead)

(c) Illegal (eg discriminatory) or offensive questions

(d) Lack of clarity as to what (and how much) information is required

12 Connock suggests that a framework such as that shown below be used to determine the cost per person appointed for each method.

Source of application	Number of applications	Number of shortlisted candidates	Number offered job	Number commenced employment	Total cost	Cost per head appointed
Local press advert National press advert Specialist press advert Leaflet drop etc						
Total						

Activity 3 (1¹/₂ hours)

Rottenborough District Hospital

You are the Human Resources Manager at Rottenborough District Hospital, a major general hospital in Cambridgeshire. In spite of the recession you are finding it increasingly difficult as an organisation to recruit non-professional staff, namely auxiliary and care assistants. Staff recruited to these positions in the past have traditionally been women in their 30s and 40s. While your commitment to equal opportunities obviously means that you welcome applications from both sexes and all ages, you are aware that this is your target group and you must somehow make Rottenborough District Hospital a more attractive place to work in for these women.

You know that the NHS is suffering external pressures which impinge on staffing issues. For example, you are losing a considerable number of staff, both professional and non-professional, to NHS Trust status hospitals. You have also read a lot about the demographic timebomb, which leads you to believe that it won't be long before your target group becomes everybody's. Thirdly, and related to the second point, the country is faced with the task of dealing with an ageing population who will inevitably require more health care. This will have an obvious and powerful impact on any human resource planning you undertake. Indeed, you find yourself working in one of the very few growth industries in Britain: the NHS has predicted some 100,000 vacancies across the board by the turn of the century.

Your main problem, therefore, is to find ways to improve the 3Rs: the recruitment, retention and return of staff into your organisation. This is not easy because you already offer good maternity benefits, compassionate leave, sick pay, pensions and relocation packages. Write a report to your director of human resources outlining alternative ways in which you can attract, keep and encourage back your target group.

Chapter 4:
SELECTION

Introduction

As suggested in the Introduction to Chapter 3, selection is the part of the employee resourcing process which follows on from recruitment. It essentially involves the identifying of the most suitable of the potential employees attracted to the organisation by recruitment efforts. (In practice, this may be a negative process of weeding out people who are **unsuitable** for the job or organisation – or people for whom the job or organisation may be unsuitable.)

The selection of the right candidate(s) is of vital importance. No organisation wants to find that it has rejected out of hand someone who goes on to be a 'star' for another (possibly competing) organisation, any more than it wants to get 'stuck' with an employee who can't do the job and doesn't fit in – but who looked perfect in the interview! Various selection methods are used to try to reduce the risks by gathering as much relevant information about the candidate as possible, and we will evaluate some of the main approaches.

Your objectives

In this chapter you will learn about the following.

    (a)   The aims and objectives of the selection process

    (b)   The selection interview

    (c)   A range of alternative selection methods to supplement the interview

    (d)   The legislative framework and benchmark evidence guiding the selection process

NOTES

1 THE SELECTION PROCESS

1.1 The aims and objectives of selection

The overall aim of the selection process is to identify candidates who are suitable for the vacancy or wider requirements of the HR plan (eg in regard to workforce diversity).

Within this aim, there may be a number of subsidiary goals.

(a) To predict, as accurately as possible, the future or potential job performance of candidates.

(b) To compare, as validly as possible, one candidate with another, to find 'best fit' between applicants and the organisation's needs.

(c) To inform candidates, as accurately and attractively as possible, about the organisation, the job, the psychological contract of employment and likely future prospects, in order to:

   (i) facilitate self-selection by the candidates

   (ii) facilitate subsequent adjustment by the successful candidate, minimising disappointment and induction crisis: supporting retention

(d) To give the best possible impression of the organisation as a potential employer: creating a brand as 'employer of choice' in an industry or sector, or in competition with other potential employers candidates may be considering.

(e) To comply with legislation, policy and organisational values in regard to equal opportunity, fair treatment and professionalism in dealing with candidates.

(f) To provide information for other HRM processes, such as employee induction and development, or the evaluation of the selection process itself.

1.2 A systematic approach to selection

A typical selection system will include the following basic procedures.

(a) Take any **initial steps** required. If the decision to interview or reject cannot be made immediately, a standard letter of acknowledgement might be sent, as a courtesy, to each applicant. It may be that the job advertisement required applicants to write to the personnel manager with personal details and to request an application form: this would then be sent to applicants for completion and return.

(b) Set each application against **key criteria** in the job advertisement and specification. Critical factors may include age, qualifications, experience or whatever.

(c) **Sort applications** into 'possible', 'unsuitable' and 'marginal'.

(d) 'Possibles' will then be more closely scrutinised, and a **shortlist for interview** drawn up. Ideally, this should be done by both the HR specialist and the prospective manager of the successful candidate, who will have more immediate knowledge of the type of person that will fit into the culture and activities of his department.

(e) Invite candidates for **interviews** (requiring them to complete an application form, if this has not been done at an earlier stage). Again, if large numbers of interviewees are involved, standard letters should be used (pre-printed, or prepared on a word processor using the direct mail facility).

(f)   Interview potentially qualified candidates.

(g)   Reinforce interviews with **selection testing** if suitable.

(h)   Check the **references** of short-listed candidates.

(i)   Institute **follow-up procedures** for successful applicants.

   (i)   Make an **offer of employment**, negotiating terms and conditions if appropriate.

   (ii)   Draw up a **contract** or **written particulars of employment**.

   (iii)   Arrange **work permits** and related issues of residency, if required by cross-border recruitment.

   (iv)   Plan initial **induction** into the organisation and provide preparatory information if required.

(j)   Review un-interviewed 'possibles', and 'marginals', and put potential future candidates on **hold** or in reserve

(k)   Send standard letters to **unsuccessful applicants**, informing them simply that they have not been successful.

   (i)   'Rejects' should be briefly, but tactfully, dismissed: 'Thank you for your interest in the post of ... We have given your application careful consideration. I regret to inform you, however, that we have decided not to ask you to attend for an interview. The standard of application was very high...'.

   (ii)   Reserves will be sent a holding letter: 'We will keep your details on file, and should any suitable vacancy arise in future...'.

1.3   The legal framework on selection

Discrimination

Detailed provisions in regard to equal opportunities will be discussed in Part B of this Course Book, since it is an area of relevance throughout the HR policy and practice. However, in regard to selection, you should be aware of the following.

(a)   **Application forms** should include no questions which are not work-related (such as marital or domestic details) unless they are asked of all applicants/groups.

Medical references should not be required exclusively from older applicants (according to a 1999 Code of Practice on Age Diversity in Employment).

(b)   **Interview procedures** and documentation should be carefully controlled to avoid discrimination. For example:

   (i)   a non work-related question must be asked of all candidates, if any, and even then, should not imply discriminatory intent (by asking only women about care of dependants, or about hormonal influences on moods, say)

   (ii)   at least one representative of both sexes and all races of applicants should be invited for interview

(iii)   detailed notes of proceedings, criteria and decisions should be made in order to furnish justification in the event of a claim of discrimination

(c)   **Selection tests** should demonstrably avoid favouring particular groups (although this is a contentious area, as we will see in Paragraph 3.3 below).

Remember, as discussed in Chapter 3, that current UK legislation outlaws discrimination on the grounds of sex, or change of sex, sexual orientation and marital status; colour, rate, nationality, ethnic or national origin; disability; and religious belief. In addition, there is a voluntary Code of Practice seeking to discourage discrimination on the basis of age.

In the selection context, there is also legislation protecting offenders whose convictions have been 'spent' after a period of time (which varies according to the severity of the offence). Under the *Rehabilitation of Offenders Act 1974*, such an offender is not obliged to disclose the nature of his or her offence, nor details of the conviction. Failure to disclose a previous conviction (eg answering 'no' to a question in a selection interview) is not justifiable grounds for non-engagement (or subsequent dismissal). Exceptions include life imprisonment, prison sentences over 30 months, and convictions for doctors, lawyers, teachers, accountants and police officers.

The Police Act 1997 makes it easier for recruiters to screen out applicants with unspent convictions by making available 'conviction certificates'.

Activity 1	**(15 minutes)**

The following is a classic IQ test 'odd man out' question from an old '11+' paper.

'Which is the odd man out?

MEASLES, STEAMER, LEAVE, OMELETTE, COURAGE.'

(a)   What is the answer?

(b)   How might this question discriminate against certain tested groups?

Privacy and data protection

The gathering of data in the application and selection process is also a sensitive area. The Data Protection Act 1998 came into force in March 2000 and is being implemented in stages up to 2007 – but retrospectively, to affect all record systems set up on or after 24 October 1998. Major provisions include:

(a)   The right of employees to access their personnel files, to be informed of the purpose for which data is being collected about them and to approve the use of that data for other purposes)

(b)   Requirements for the adequacy, up-to-dateness and security of information (particularly if it is to be exported outside the European Economic Area)

(c)   Additional safeguards on the collection of data about race, ethnic origin, religious or political beliefs, union membership, health, sexual orientation or criminal activities (except for the purposes of monitoring racial equality).

EXAMPLE

A US employer that required applicants to answer intimate personal questions in a pre-employment psychological examination agrees to pay more than $2 million to settle a lawsuit over the test.

The employer, which operates a chain of retail stores in California, administered the test to about 2,500 applicants for security jobs. The test's 'true or false?' questions included the following.

* I have never indulged in any unusual sexual practices
* I have often wished I was a girl
* I am very strongly attracted by members of my own sex
* I believe my sins are unpardonable
* I feel sure there is only one true religion

'Before settling the suit, the employer argued that the test was necessary to screen out applicants who are emotionally unstable, unreliable, undependable, and not inclined to follow directions or established rules, as well as applicants with addictive or violent tendencies who might put customers or other employees at risk.'

(From *Bulletin to Management*, 1993, cited by Shuler, 1995)

FOR DISCUSSION

Aside from the actual outcome of the case example cited above, how far do you think a test of this kind is:

(a)   useful or effective (and with what intention)? and
(b)   ethically reprehensible (and on what grounds)?

To the extent that the employer's concerns are genuine, what other means of screening might or should they employ?

We will now go on to outline some of the methods by which selection of/between applicants can be made.

1.4   Selection methods

Various techniques are available, depending on the policy and criteria of selection in each case.

(a)   **Interviews**. These may be variously structured (one-to-one, panel, sequential), and using various criteria of job relevance (application details, skills and competences, critical incident/situational questions) and scoring methods (general impressions, criteria ratings). As the most **popular** of methods, interviews will be considered in detail below.

(b)   **Evaluation of education and experience**, comparing application data to job requirements.

(c)   **Selection testing**. Written tests of ability and aptitude (cognitive and/or mechanical), personality and so on are increasingly used, alongside work sample tests (such as typing tests) which simulate job related activities. Tests are also discussed in more detail below.

(d) **Background and reference checks,** in order to verify application claims as to qualifications, previous employment record and reasons for leaving and so on. References will be discussed in Section 5 of this chapter.

(e) **Biodata analysis.** Biodata (biographical data) is gathered via multiple choice questions on family background, life experiences, attitudes and preferences. The results are compared against an 'ideal' profile based on correlations with effective job performance.

(f) **Handwritten analysis,** or graphology. Handwriting is said to indicate up to 300 character traits of the individual. There is no scientific evidence of its predictive accuracy, but it is popular in Europe and to a lesser extent in the USA and Australia. (In general, handwritten covering letters are requested as a useful general indicator of orderly thinking, presentation and so on.)

(g) **Group selection methods,** or *assessment centres*, allowing the assessment of team-working, leadership, problem-solving and communication skills through the use of group discussions, role plays, business games and 'in-tray' simulations. These are discussed below.

(h) **Physical/medical testing.** Medical examinations are often one of the final steps in selection, to ensure fitness for work (and avoid compensation claims for pre-existing injuries or conditions). Specific tests – for example, testing for HIV/AIDS (subject to strict policy guidelines, and mindful of discrimination), drug and/or alcohol abuse or genetic sensitivity to workplace chemicals – may also be used for particular job categories: privacy and data protection principles will apply.

Activity 2 **(20 minutes)**

How accurate do you think these methods are?

A number of studies (surveyed in Arnold *et al*, 1995) to show how **popular** and how **effective** various techniques are. **Effectiveness** is measured according to the '**predictive validity**' scale, which ranges from 1 (the technique unfailingly predicts candidates' subsequent job performance) to 0 (the technique is no better than random chance at predicting candidates' subsequent job performance). **Popularity** is measured by the % of surveyed companies that use the technique.

(a) Rank the following techniques in order from most popular to least popular, from what you might anticipate.

(b) For each, add a number between 0.00 and 1.00 to indicate what you think their predictive validity might be.

Techniques: Personality tests, references, work sampling, interviews, assessment centres, cognitive tests, graphology, biodata.

We will now look at each of the three major techniques in turn.

2 SELECTION INTERVIEWS

2.1 Types of interview

Individual or **one-to-one interviews** are the most common selection method. They offer the advantages of direct face-to-face communication, and opportunity to establish

rapport between the candidate and interviewer: each has to give his attention solely to the other, and there is potentially a relaxed atmosphere, if the interviewer is willing to establish an informal style.

The disadvantage of a one-to-one interview is the scope it allows for a biased or superficial decision.

(a) The candidate may be able to disguise lack of knowledge in a specialist area of which the interviewer himself knows little.

(b) The interviewer's perception may be selective or distorted (see Paragraph 2.4 below), and his lack of objectivity may go unnoticed and unchecked, since he is the sole arbiter.

(c) The greater opportunity for personal rapport with the candidate may cause a weakening of the interviewer's objective judgement: he may favour someone he got on with over someone who was unresponsive but better-qualified. Again, there will be no cross-check with another interviewer.

Panel interviews are designed to overcome the above disadvantages. A panel may consist of two or three people who together interview a single candidate: most commonly, a personnel manager and the departmental manager who will have responsibility for the successful candidate. This may be more daunting for the candidate (depending on the tone and conduct of the interview) but it has several advantages.

(a) The personnel and line specialists gather the information they need about the candidate at the same time, cutting down on the subsequent information-sharing stage, and making a separate subsequent interview with one or the other unnecessary.

(b) The questions each specialist wants to put to the interviewee (related to their own field of activity and expertise) will be included, and the answers will be assessed by the specialist concerned: each will also be able to give the interviewee the information he wants, both about the employment aspects of the position, and about the departmental task-related aspects.

(c) The interviewers can discuss their joint assessment of the candidate's abilities, and their impressions of his behaviour and personality at the interview. They can thus gain a more complete picture, and can modify any hasty or superficial judgements. Personal bias is more likely to be guarded against, and checked if it does emerge.

Large formal panels, or **selection boards,** may also be convened where there are a number of individuals or groups with an interest in the selection. This has the advantage of allowing a number of people to see the candidate, and to share information about him at a single meeting: similarly, they can compare their assessments on the spot, without a subsequent effort at liaison and communication.

Offsetting these administrative advantages, however, there are severe drawbacks to the effectiveness of the selection board as a means of assessment.

(a) Questions tend to be more varied, and more random, since there is no single guiding force behind the interview strategy. The candidate may have trouble switching from one topic to another so quickly, especially if questions are not led up to, and not clearly put - as may happen if they are unplanned. Candidates are also seldom allowed to expand their answers, and so may not be able to do justice to themselves.

(b) If there is a dominating member of the board, the interview may have greater continuity - but he may also 'force' the judgements of other members, and his prejudices may be allowed to dominate the assessment.

(c)   Some candidates may not perform well in a formal, artificial situation such as a board interview, and may find such a situation extremely stressful. The interview will thus not show the best qualities of someone who might nevertheless be highly effective in the work context and in the face of work-related pressures.

(d)   The pressures of a board interview favour individuals who are confident, and who project an immediate and strong image: those who are articulate, dress well and so on. First impressions of such a candidate may cover underlying faults or shortcomings, while a quiet, overawed candidate may be dismissed, despite his strengths in other areas.

Activity 3   **(20 minutes)**

'In some cases, the option of sequential interviewing may be open to managers. Instead of, say, four people on a panel spending an hour with each of four candidates, the members might each spend an hour alone with each candidate. The panel could then take its selection decision in the light of the information obtained at the separate interviews.'

Rees (1991)

Weigh up the pros and cons of 'sequential interviewing'.

2.2   Preparing interviews

In brief, the factors to be considered with regard to conducting selection interviews are:

(a)   The impression of the organisation given by the interview arrangements

(b)   The psychological effects of the location of the interview, seating arrangements and manner of the interviewer(s)

(c)   The extent to which the candidate can be encouraged to talk freely (by asking open questions) and honestly (by asking probing questions), in accordance with the organisation's need for information

(d)   The opportunity for the candidate to learn about the job and organisation

(e)   The control of bias or hasty judgement by the interviewer

The interview is a two way process, but the interviewer must have a clear idea of what the interview is setting out to achieve, and must be in sufficient control of the interview to make sure that every candidate is asked questions which cover the same ground and obtain all the information required.

The agenda and questions will be based on:

(a)   The job description (or competence profile), and what abilities are required of the job holder

(b)   The personnel specification: the interviewer must be able to judge whether the applicant matches up to the personal qualities required from the job holder

(c)   The application form, and/or the candidate's CV and covering letter

(d)   More culture – or vision-focused criteria (such as flexibility or creativity), if a job-based approach is not appropriate

The interview process should be efficiently run to make a favourable impression on the candidates and to avoid unnecessary stress (unless ability to handle pressure is a selection criterion!). The interview room should be free from distraction and interruption.

Activity 4　　　　　　　　　　　　　　　　　　　　**(30 minutes)**

Think back to a selection interview you have had, for a job, school or place at your university/college.

(a) What sort of interview did you have: one-to-one, panel, formal or informal?

(b) What impression of the organisation did you get from the whole process?

(c) How well-conducted was the interview, looking back on it?

(d) What efforts (if any) were made to put you at your ease?

2.3 Interviewer skills and questioning techniques

'Interviews are so common that they are often taken for granted. People view interviews as simply conversations during which information is gathered. While interviews are similar to conversations, there are important differences. An interview is a specialised form of conversation conducted for a specific task-related purpose.' (Whetton & Cameron, 2002).

Whetton & Cameron identify the following key skills for interviewers.

(a) Creating effective questions, arising out of a clear purpose and agenda, with the aim of eliciting the information required.

(b) Creating an appropriate climate for information sharing, using supportive communication techniques, such as:

- rapport building, establishing trust and relationship

- active listening, using attentive body language and responsive verbal behaviours (eg summarising, clarifying)

- introducing the interview in a way that establishes a positive tone and orients the candidate as to how the interview will be conducted.

(c) Using question types intentionally, in order to control the pace and direction of the interview, remaining responsive to the replies given by the candidate. (This is discussed further below.)

(d) Using and interpreting non-verbal cues, or 'body language' (dress, posture, eye contact, gestures, facial expressions).

(e) Being willing, and able, to identify shallow or unconvincing responses, and to probe and challenge when necessary: in other words, critically evaluating the candidate's responses.

(f) Being alert to the influence of first impressions, stereotypes and other forms of potential bias.

EXAMPLE

Whetton & Cameron (2002) cite a six-step process used by a major firm (un-named) outlining an effective interview process.

"*PEOPLE*-oriented Selection Interview Process"

P   = Prepare

    1   Review application, CV and other background information
    2   Prepare both general and individual-specific questions
    3   Prepare suitable physical arrangements

E   = Establish Rapport

    1   Try to make applicant comfortable
    2   Convey genuine interest
    3   Communicate supportive attitude with voice and names

O   = Obtain Information

    1   Ask questions
    2   Probe
    3   Listen carefully
    4   Observe the person (dress, mannerisms, body language)

P   = Provide Information

    1   Describe current and future job opportunities
    2   Sell positive features of firm
    3   Respond to applicant's questions

L   = Lead to Close

    1   Clarify responses
    2   Provide an opportunity for final applicant input
    3   Explain what happens next

E   = Evaluate

    1   Assess match between technical qualifications and job requirements
    2   Judge personal qualities (leadership, maturity, team orientation)
    3   Make a recommendation

A variety of question styles may be used, to different effects.

(a)   **Open questions** or open-ended questions ('Who...? What...? Where...? When...? Why...?') force interviewees to put together their own responses in complete sentences. This encourages the interviewee to talk, keeps the interview flowing, and is most revealing ('Why do you want to be in Personnel?')

(b)   **Probing questions** are similar to open questions in their phrasing but aim to discover the deeper significance of the candidate's experience or achievements. (If a candidate claimed to have had 'years of relevant experience', in a covering letter, the interviewer might need to ask 'How many years?', or 'Which particular jobs or positions do you consider relevant and how?')

(c) **Closed questions** are the opposite, inviting only 'yes' or 'no' answers: ('Did you...?', 'Have you...?'). A closed question has the following effects.

    (i) It elicits answers only to the question asked by the interviewer. This may be useful where there are small points to be established ('Did you pass your exam?') but there may be other questions and issues that he has not anticipated but will emerge if the interviewee is given the chance to express himself ('How did you think your studies went?').

    (ii) It does not allow the interviewee to express his personality, so that interaction can take place on a deeper level.

    (iii) It makes it easier for interviewees to conceal things ('You never *asked* me....').

    (iv) It makes the interviewer work very hard.

(d) **Multiple questions** are just that: two or more questions are asked at once. ('Tell me about your last job? How did your knowledge of HRM help you there, and do you think you are up-to-date or will you need to spend time studying?') This type of question can be used to encourage the candidate to talk at some length, but not to stray too far from the point. It might also test the candidate's ability to listen and handle large amounts of information, but should be used judiciously in this case.

(e) **Problem solving or situational questions** present the candidate with a situation and ask him to explain how he would deal with it or how he has dealt with it in the past. ('How would you motivate your staff to do a task that they did not want to do?' or 'Can you tell us about a time when you were successful about setting a goal and achieving it?') Such questions are used to establish whether the candidate will be able to deal with the sort of problems that are likely to arise in the job, or whether he has sufficient technical knowledge. The interviewer is after specific behavioural information. Whetten and Cameron (2002) suggest asking negative questions as well as positive ('Now tell us about a time you failed to meet a goal you set. How could you have done better?') in order to expose hidden bias.

(f) **Leading questions** lead the interviewee to give a certain reply. ('We are looking for somebody who likes detailed figure work. How much do you enjoy dealing with numbers?' or 'Don't you agree that...?'. 'Surely...?')

The danger with this type of question is that the interviewee will give the answer that he thinks the interviewer wants to hear, but it might legitimately be used to deal with a highly reticent or nervous candidate, simply to encourage him to talk.

NOTES

Activity 5   **(20 minutes)**

Identify the type of question used in the following examples, and discuss the opportunities and constraints they offer the interviewee who must answer them.

(a) 'So you're interested in a business studies degree, are you, Jo?'

(b) 'Surely you're not interested in business studies, Jo?'

(c) 'How about a really useful qualification like a Business Studies degree Jo? Would you consider that?'

(d) 'Why are you interested in a Business studies degree, Jo?'

(e) 'Why particularly Business Studies, Jo?'

Candidates should be given the opportunity to ask questions. Indeed, well-prepared candidates should go into an interview knowing what questions they may want to ask. Their choice of questions might well have some influence on how the interviewers finally assess them. Moreover, there is information that the candidate will need to know about the organisation and the job, and about:

(a) Terms and conditions of employment (although negotiations about detailed terms may not take place until a provisional offer has been made) and

(b) The next step in the selection process - whether there are further interviews, when a decision might be made, or which references might be taken up

Having said all this, why did interviews score so badly on the predictive validity scale? (See our answer to Activity 2, if you have not already done so.) Despite their popularity, they have a number of limitations...

2.4 Limitations of interviews

Interviews are criticised because they fail to provide accurate predictions of how a person will perform in the job. The main reasons why this might be so are as follows.

(a) *Limited scope.* An interview is necessarily too brief to 'get to know' candidates in the kind of depth required to make an accurate prediction of their behaviour in any given situation.

(b) *Limited relevance.* Interviews that lack structure and specific reference to the competence and attribute requirements of the job may fail to elicit information that will be relevant in assessing the candidate's likely future performance in the job and compatibility with the organisation.

(c) *Artificiality.* An interview is an artificial situation: candidates may be 'on their best behaviour' or, conversely, so nervous that they do not do themselves justice. Neither situation reflects what the person is 'really like'.

(d) *Errors of judgement* by interviewers. These might be:

    (i) The **halo effect** - a tendency for people to make an initial general judgement about a person based on a single obvious attribute, such as being neatly dressed, or well-spoken, which will colour later perceptions.

    (ii) **Contagious bias** - a process whereby an interviewer changes the behaviour of the applicant by suggestion. The applicant might be led by the wording of questions or non-verbal cues from the interviewer, and change what he is doing or saying in response

 (iii) **Incorrect assessment** of qualitative factors such as motivation, honesty or integrity. Abstract qualities are very difficult to assess in an interview

 (iv) **Logical error**. For example, an interviewer might place too much emphasis on isolated strengths or weaknesses or draw unwarranted conclusions from facts (confusing career mobility with disloyalty, say).

(e) *Lack of skill and experience by interviewers.* For example:

- Inability to take control of the direction and length of the interview

- A reluctance to probe into facts and challenge statements where necessary

3 SELECTION TESTING

3.1 Types of tests

In many job selection procedures, an interview is now supplemented by some form of selection test. The interviewers must be certain that the results of such tests are reliable, and that a candidate who scores well in a test will be more likely to succeed in the job. The test will have no value unless there is a direct relationship between ability in the test and ability in the job.

Cushway (1994) lists six criteria which such tests should satisfy.

 ' 1 A sensitive measuring instrument that discriminates between subjects.
 2 Standardised, so that an individual score can be related to others.
 3 Reliable, in that it always measures the same thing.
 4 Valid, in that the test measures what it is designed to measure.
 5 Acceptable to the candidate.
 6 Non-discriminatory.'

The science of measuring mental capacities and processes is called 'psychometrics'; hence the term 'psychometric testing'. There are five types of test commonly used in practice.

Intelligence or cognitive ability tests

These are tests of **general** cognitive ability typically test memory, ability to think quickly (perceptual speed, verbal fluency and logically (inductive reasoning), and problem solving skills. Reliance on such criteria has shown steady increase, perhaps because of uncertainty in UK employers' minds about the validity of A-level and GCSE results, the wide variation in degree classes between higher educational institutions and the difficulties of comparing international qualifications.

Most people have experience of IQ tests and so forth, and few would dispute their validity as good measures of **general** intellectual performance currently.

Aptitude tests

Aptitude tests are designed to predict an individual's potential for performing a job or learning new skills. There are various accepted areas of aptitude, as follows.

(a)   Reasoning - verbal, numerical and abstract/visual: (eg accuracy and speed in arithmetical calculations, naming or making words, identifying shapes)

(b)   Spatio-visual ability - practical intelligence, non-verbal ability and creative ability (eg ability to solve mechanical puzzles)

(c)   Perceptual speed and accuracy - clerical ability (identifying non-identical pairs of numbers)

(d)   'Manual' or 'psycho-motor' ability - mechanical, manual, musical and athletic: ability to respond accurately and rapidly to stimuli (eg pressing lighted buttons) using controlled muscular adjustments and/or finger dexterity

With a few possible exceptions most of the areas of aptitude mentioned above are fairly easily measurable and so long as it is possible to determine what particular aptitudes are required for a job it is likely that aptitude tests will be useful for selection.

Personality tests

Personality tests may measure a variety of characteristics, such as applicants' skill in dealing with other people, ambition, motivation or emotional stability. Probably the best known example is the 16PF, originally developed by Cattell in 1950. This was described as follows in *Personnel Management* (February 1994).

> The 16PF comprises 16 scales, each of which measures a factor that influences the way a person behaves.
>
> The factors are functionally different underlying personality characteristics, and each is associated with not just one single piece of behaviour but rather is the source of a relatively broad range of behaviours. For this reason the factors themselves are referred to as source traits and the behaviours associated with them are called surface traits.
>
> The advantage of measuring source traits, as the 16PF does, is that you end up with a much richer understanding of the person because you are not just describing what can be seen but also the characteristics underlying what can be seen.
>
> The 16PF analyses how a person is likely to behave generally, including, for example, contributions likely to be made to particular work contexts, aspects of the work environment to which the person is likely to be more or less suited, and how best to manage the person.

Other examples include the Myers-Briggs Type Indicator (mostly intended for self-development purposes), the Minnesota Multiphasic Personality Inventory (MMPI) and the FIRO-B personality profile. The validity of such tests has been much debated, but it seems that some have been shown by research to be valid predictors of job performance, so long as they are used and interpreted properly. A test may indicate that a candidate is introverted, has creative ability and is pragmatic, but this is only of use if this combination of characteristics can be linked to success or failure in the type of work for which the candidate is being considered.

You may like to visit the website of the BTPA (British Test Publishers Association) at www.btpa.org.uk, if you are interested in this area.

Proficiency tests

Proficiency tests are perhaps the most closely related to an assessor's objectives, because they measure ability to do the work involved. An applicant for an audio typist's job, for example, might be given a dictation tape and asked to type it. This is a type of **attainment** test, in that it is designed to measure abilities or skills already acquired by the candidate.

Activity 6 **(30 minutes)**

What kind of work sample or proficiency tests would you devise for the following categories of employee? For each, state whether your test is a physical, verbal or mental test.

(a)   Administrative assistants
(b)   Construction supervisors
(c)   Pilots
(d)   Magazine editors
(e)   Telephone operators

EXAMPLE

'A government agency has adopted innovative recruitment techniques by using psychometric tests to measure how well candidates fit in with the public-sector culture.

'And other public-sector organisations could soon follow suit, after the *Environment Agency* revealed the move had dramatically reduced staff turnover rates.

'The agency overhauled its recruitment for environmental officers, following retention problems. Candidates are now sent to assessment centres specifically to evaluate whether they have the "personality and qualities to work in the public sector" ...

' "Understanding the public-sector ethos is being increasingly recognised as important and as necessary to getting the right skills ... It is certainly harder to train people in those behavioural attributes than it is to train them in the technical side." '

Watkins (2003)(b)

3.2   Limitations of psychometric testing

Psychometric testing has grown in popularity in recent years, but you should be aware of certain drawbacks.

(a)   There is not always a direct (let alone predictive) relationship between ability in the test and ability in the job: the job situation is very different from artificial test conditions.

(b)   The interpretation of test results is a skilled task, for which training and experience is essential. It is also highly subjective (particularly in the case of personality tests), which belies the apparent scientific nature of the approach.

(c)   Additional difficulties are experienced with particular kinds of test. For example:

(i)   An aptitude test measuring arithmetical ability would need to be constantly revised or its content might become known to later applicants

(ii)   Personality tests can often give misleading results because applicants seem able to guess which answers will be looked at most favourably

(iii)   It is difficult to design intelligence tests which give a fair chance to people from different cultures and social groups and which test the *kind* of intelligence that the organisation wants from its employees:

the ability to score highly in IQ tests does not necessarily correlate with desirable traits such as mature judgement or creativity, merely mental agility. In addition, 'practice makes perfect': most tests are subject to coaching and practice effects.

(d)   It is difficult to exclude discrimination and bias from tests. Many tests (including personality tests) are tackled less successfully by women than by men, or by immigrants than by locally-born applicants because of the particular aspects chosen for testing. This may make their use indirectly discriminatory.

The most recent edition of the 16PF test, for example has been scrutinised by expert psychologists 'to exclude certain types of content, such as dated material, content that might lead to bias, material that might be unacceptable in an organisational setting and anything considered to be strongly socially desirable or undesirable.

FOR DISCUSSION

'Among the qualities which neither the interview nor intelligence tests are able to assess accurately are the candidate's ability to get on with and influence his colleagues, to display qualities of spontaneous leadership and to produce ideas in a real-life situation.'

(Plumbley, 1991)

Why might this be a drawback? What can be done about it?

4   GROUP SELECTION METHODS

4.1   Techniques in group selection

Group selection methods or **assessment centres** might be used by an organisation as the final stage of a selection process for management jobs. They consist of a series of tests, interviews and group situations over a period of two days, involving a small number of candidates (typically six to eight) for a job.

Group selection methods are appropriate for assessing the following.

(a)   **Social skills** such as sensitivity to the views and opinions of others, reaction to disagreement and criticism, and the ability to influence and persuade others

(b)   **Intellectual skills** such as the consideration of the merits and demerits of other arguments put forward and the ability to think clearly (particularly at short notice), situational problem-solving and so on

(c)   **Attitudes**, such as political, racial or religious views, and attitude to authority, particularly where these may be relevant to a potential employee's efficiency at work

Typical techniques used in group selection include:

(a)   Group **role-play** exercises, in which they can explore (and hopefully display) interpersonal skills and/or work through simulated managerial tasks

(b)   **Case studies**, where candidates' analytical and problem-solving abilities are tested in working through described situations/problems, as well as their interpersonal skills, in taking part in (or leading) group discussions of the case study

(c)   **'In-tray' exercises,** simulating a typical work-load to be managed

(d)   **Leaderless discussion groups** (LDGs), allowing leadership skills and issues to emerge freely

Often what are termed 'leaderless group activities' will be conducted. Such activities can be used to assess the leadership potential of job applicants in uncertain situations with no formal power structure. The group of applicants are presented with a topic for discussion, and are normally advised that they are expected to reach a conclusion within a defined period of time. The topic may be related to the job in question, and may either be of a problem-solving nature ('Should product X be developed given the following marketing and financial information?') or of a more general nature ('Is capital punishment an effective deterrent?'). The contribution made by individual candidates will be scored according to factors such as assertiveness, quality of thought and expression, analytical skill, and the ability to lead the group towards a decision.

Another method of assessment involves giving candidates a typical job problem to solve individually in a set time, at the end of which each candidate has to set out his solution to the problem to the other members of the group, and defend his views against the group's criticisms.

EXAMPLE

The *Dixons Group* uses an assessment centre as part of its selection process to pick 20 people to join its executive development programme ach year.

'50 people were invited to the event, which included tests of verbal and numerical reasoning, the Myers-Briggs Type Indicator and FIRO-B tests, individual presentations and group exercises.'

In 2004, the company plans to introduce selection interviewing prior to short-listing people for the assessment centre. 'This should increase the effectiveness of the selection process, and allow us to run a centre for fewer potential delegates.'

(Upton, 2000)

4.2   Purposes of group selection

Group sessions might be thought useful because:

(a)   They give the organisation's selectors a longer opportunity to study the candidates.

(b)   They reveal more than application forms, interviews and tests alone about the ability of candidates to persuade others, negotiate with others, and explain ideas to others and also to investigate problems efficiently. These are typically management skills.

(c)   They reveal more about how the candidates' personalities and attributes will affect the work team and his own performance. Stamina, social interaction with others (ability to co-operate and compete), intelligence, energy, self confidence or outside interests will not necessarily be meaningful in themselves (as analysed from written tests), but may be shown to affect performance in the work context.

(d)   They achieve some measure of comparability between candidates.

(e)   The pooled judgement of the panel of assessors is likely to be more accurate than the judgement of a single interviewer.

(f)   They provide information in situations where little historical information is known about the candidate in relation to the qualities to be assessed (such as when the candidate is an undergraduate or school leaver).

Since they are very suitable for selection of potential managers who have little or no previous experience and two days to spare for the sessions, group selection methods are often used for selecting university graduates for management trainee jobs.

We will now look at some of the later considerations in the selection process, bringing the candidate through to a contract of employment.

Activity 7   **(1 hour)**

Think back to your own selection for your first job with your organisation. What procedures did you have to go through? What sort of interview did you have: was it well-conducted, looking back on it now? Did you have to take any tests?

Find out who does the selection interviewing in your office, what guidelines are laid down for them, and what training they get in interview technique.

Find out what selection tests (if any) are used in your organisation, and for what kinds of jobs.

---

5   FOLLOW UP PROCEDURES

5.1   Checking references

References provide further confidential information about the prospective employee. This may be of varying value, as the reliability of all but the most factual information must be in question. A reference should contain:

(a)   Straightforward factual information confirming the nature of the applicant's previous job(s), period of employment, pay, and circumstances of leaving.

(b)   Opinions about the applicant's personality and other attributes. These should obviously be treated with some caution. Allowances should be made for prejudice (favourable or unfavourable), charity (withholding detrimental remarks), and possibly fear of being actionable for libel (although references are privileged, as long as they are factually correct and devoid of malice).

At least two **employer** references are desirable, providing necessary factual information, and comparison of personal views. **Personal** references tell the prospective employer little more than that the applicant has a friend or two.

Written references save time, especially if a standardised letter or form has been pre-prepared. A simple letter inviting the previous employer to reply with the basic information and judgement required may suffice. (If the recruiting officer wishes for a more detailed appraisal of the applicant's suitability, brief details of the post in question may be supplied but the previous employer's opinion will still be an ill-informed and subjective judgement.) A standard form to be completed by the referee may be more acceptable, and might pose a set of simple questions about:

(a)   Job title
(b)   Main duties and responsibilities

(c) Period of employment

(d) Pay/salary

(e) Attendance record

If a judgement of character and suitability is desired, it might be most tellingly formulated as the question: 'Would you re-employ this individual? (If not, why not?)'

Telephone references may be time-saving, if standard reference letters or forms are not available. They may also elicit a more honest opinion than a carefully prepared written statement. For this reasons, a telephone call may also be made to check or confirm a poor or grudging reference which the recruiter suspects may be prejudiced.

Note that when **giving** references, caution is also required.

A landmark legal judgement in *Spring v Guardian Assurance plc 1995*, decided that an employer owes a duty of care to employees in relation to giving a reference, and in obtaining the information upon which the reference is based.

On the other hand, an employer could face civil liability from a company which suffered economic loss as a result of hiring an employee on the basis of a false complimentary reference.

Activity 8   **(20 minutes)**

(a) At the end of a recent selection process one candidate was, in the view of everyone involved, outstanding. However, you have just received a very bad reference from her current employer. What do you do?

(b) For fun, rephrase the following comments in the way that you might expect to see them appear in a letter of reference.

    (i) Mr Smith is habitually late

    (ii) Remains immature

    (iii) Socially unskilled with clients

    (iv) Is rather dull

5.2 The offer of employment

Assuming that the 'right' candidate has by now been identified, an offer of employment can be made. Time may be sensitive, so it is common for an oral offer to be made, with a negotiated period for consideration and acceptance: this can then be followed up with a written offer, if appropriate.

(a) All terms, conditions and circumstances of the offer must at this point be clearly stated.

(b) Any provisos ('subject to... satisfactory references, medical examination, negotiation of contract terms', or whatever) must also be clearly set out.

(c) Negotiable aspects of the offer and timetables for acceptance should be set out, in order to control the closing stages of the process.

The organisation should be prepared for its offer to be rejected at this stage. Applicants may have received and accepted other offers. They may not have been attracted by their first-hand view of the organisation, and may have changed their mind about applying; they may only have been testing the water in applying in the first place, gauging the market for their skills and experience for future reference, or seeking a position of strength from which to bargain with their present employers. A small number of eligible applicants should therefore be kept in reserve.

5.3 Contracts of employment

Once the offer of employment has been confirmed and accepted, the contract of employment can be prepared and offered.

A contract of employment may be written, oral or a mixture of the two. At the one extreme, it may be a document drawn up by solicitors and signed by both parties; at the other extreme it may consist of a handshake and a 'See you on Monday'. Senior personnel may sign a contract specially drafted to include terms on confidentiality and restraint of trade. Other employees may sign a standard form contract, exchange letters with the new employer or supply agreed terms orally at interview. Each of these situations, subject to the requirements (outlined below) as to written particulars, will form a valid contract of employment, as long as there is agreement on essential terms such as hours and wages.

Written particulars of employment

Although the contract need not be made in writing, the employer must give an employee (who works at least eight hours a week) a written statement of certain particulars of his or her employment, within two months of the beginning of employment (*Employment Rights Act 1996*)

The statement should identify the following.

(a)   The names of **employer** and **employee**

(b)   The **date** on which employment began

(c)   Whether any service with a previous employer forms part of the employee's **continuous period** of employment

(d)   **Pay**

(e)   **Hours** of work

(f)   Any **holiday** and **holiday pay** entitlement

(g)   **Sick leave** and **sick pay** entitlement (if any)

(h)   **Pensions** and pension **schemes**

(i)   Length of **notice** of termination to be given on either side (or the **expiry** date if employed for a fixed term)

(j)   The **title** of the job which the employee is employed to do

(k)   Details of **disciplinary procedures** and **grievance procedures,** works rules, union of staff association membership

(l)   Rules on **health and safety at work** (by custom only)

It is sufficient to refer to separate booklets or notices (on pension schemes, disciplinary/grievance procedures and so on) where the relevant details can be found: not all the information needs to go in the written statement!

The purpose of these rules is to ensure that the employee has precise information of the terms on which he is employed. Some employers invite the employee to countersign and return a second copy of the particular as evidence that he has received them. But the statement is not the contract itself – it is merely written evidence, so if the particulars are found to contain an error, that does not bind either party to the erroneous terms: the true agreed terms of the 'contract' prevail.

6 EVALUATING THE PROCESS

6.1 Evaluating selection

Much the same method can be used to evaluate selection as recruitment: see Paragraph 7 of Chapter 3.

Selection procedures can further be evaluated by determining whether selection decisions seem to have been 'correct' in the light of subsequent job performance, cultural impact and service longevity of the successful candidate.

(a) If tests were used to assess likely potential to perform certain tasks, the retained test results can be compared against actual performance in the job. Regular discrepancies may suggest that the tests are flawed.

(b) Similar comparisons may be made using interview ratings and notes. Interviewers who consistently fall short in the accuracy of their judgements should be trained accordingly.

Other performance criteria for evaluating selection procedures include:

(a) Number of candidates (and/or minority/female/disabled candidates) interviewed in relation to applications

(b) Number of offers made in relation to number of interviews (especially to minority/female/disabled candidates)

(c) Number of acceptances in relation to offers made

(d) Number of successful applicants subsequently appraised as competent in the job

(e) Lead time for successful applicants to be trained to competence

(f) Number of starters still employed after 1 year (2 years etc)

(g) Cost of selection methods per starter employed 1 year later

Chapter roundup

- The contents of this chapter may again be summarised in diagrammatic form.

Quick quiz

1   What are the aims of selection?

2   A job selection interview has several aims. If you were conducting one, though, you should **not** be concerned with:

A   Comparing the application against the job/personnel specification
B   Getting as much information as possible about the applicant
C   Giving the applicant information about the job and organisation
D   Making the applicant feel he has been treated fairly

3   What are the stages of the systematic approach to selection?

4   What are two key legal issues in selection?

5   What can be done to improve the effectiveness of selection interviews?

6   Amon Leigh-Hewman is interviewing a candidate for a vacancy in his firm. He asks a question about the candidate's views on a work-related issue. The candidate starts to answer, and sees to his horror that Amon in pursing his lips and shaking his head slightly to himself. 'Of course, that's what some people say', continues the candidate, 'but I myself...' Amon smiles. His next question is 'Don't you think that...?

Amon is getting a distorted view of the candidate because of:

A   The halo effect
B   Contagious bias
C   Stereotyping
D   Logical error

7   Selection tests such as IQ tests and personality tests may not be effective in getting the right person for the job for several reasons. Which of the following criticisms is false, though?

A   Test results can be influenced by practice and coaching rather than genuine ability

B   Subjects are able (and tend) to deliberately falsify results

C   Tests do not eliminate bias and subjectivity

D   Test are generally less accurate predictors of success than interviews

8   List four main types of selection testing.

9   What is an 'assessment centre'?

10   What types of information should an employer reference contain about the candidate?

Answers to quick quiz

1   Filling vacancies with best person; informing applicants (to facilitate self-selection and adjustment); creating employer brand; upholding values of fairness and professionalism.   (see paragraph 1.1)

2   B. Information needs to be relevant   (para 2.1)

3   Set key criteria; compare applications (forms, CV) against criteria; sort and shortlist; acknowledge all responses; invite candidates to interview/selection testing or other methods; check references; issue offer of employment; draw up contract; obtain work permits (if necessary); plan induction; send standard letters to 'rejects' and 'reserves'.   (para 1.2)

4   Discrimination/equal opportunity and privacy/data protection   (para 1.3)

5   Planning; relevant criteria; interviewer training and appraisal; structured style of questioning; awareness of potential for bias.   (para 2.2-2.3)

6   B   (para 2.4)

7   D. Interviews are generally less accurate.   (para 3.1)

8   Cognitive, aptitude, personality, proficiency.   (para 3.1)

9   A group selection process, using a series of tests, interviews and group situations and exercises over a period of two days, typically involving 6-8 candidates for a job.   (para 4.1)

10   Factual information confirming the nature of the applicant's previous job, period of employment, pay and circumstances of leaving. Opinions (cautious) about the applicant's attributes and employability.   (para 5.1)

Answers to activities

1   (a)   'Steamer'. (The others share national connotations: German measles, French leave, Spanish omelette, Dutch courage.)

     (b)   The answer presupposes a knowledge of expressions which are rooted in a European context and, in some cases, are old-fashioned and dependent on a middle-class upbringing and education.

2

Method	% use	Predictive validity
Interviews	92	0.17
References	74	0.13
Work sampling	18	0.57
Assessment centres	14	0.40
Personality tests	13	0.40
Cognitive tests	11	0.54
Biodata	4	0.40
Graphology	3	0.00

The results (Smith & Abrahamsen, 1994) show a pattern of employers relying *most* heavily on the least *valid* selection methods for their recruitment purposes. Interviews, in particular, seem not much better than tossing a coin.

3   Rees suggests the following points. You may not agree with all of them.

     (a)   The method need take no more time for the organisation: in fact single interviews may turn out to take less than an hour.

     (b)   Candidates would have to spend more time being interviewed but 'might not mind this if they felt it was a more effective method of selection'.

     (c)   It is normally easier to create rapport and coax information out of a person when you are seeing him alone.

     (d)   However, inexperienced interviewers will be far more 'exposed' than they would have been in a panel interview. They may prefer merely to observe.

     (e)   The method is liable to create more argument about the final decision: the interviewee may be flagging by the end of the session and give a totally different impression to different interviewers.

4   This is personal to your experience: it will help you develop the evidence to show your competence in investigating selection procedures in organisations.

5   (a)   Closed. (the only answer is 'yes' or 'no', unless Jo is prepared to expand on it, at his or her own initiative.)

       (b)   Leading. (Even if Jo was interested, (s)he would get the message that 'yes' would not be what the interviewer wanted, or expected, to hear.

       (c)   Leading closed multiple! ('Really useful' leads Jo to think that the 'correct' answer will be 'yes': there is not much opportunity for any other answer, without expanding on it unasked.)

       (d)   Open. (Jo has to explain, in his or her own words.)

       (e)   Probing. (Jo has to defend his or her decision.)

6   Here are some suggestions:

		Test
(a)	Admin assistants	Word-processing on specific equipment (physical)
		Dictation (physical)
		Filing (physical)
		Letter proof-reading/correction (mental)
		Telephone answering (verbal)
(b)	Construction supervisors	Plan error recognition (mental)
(c)	Pilots	Rudder control, direction control (physical)
		Navigational reading (mental)
		Radio procedures (verbal)
(d)	Magazine editors	Writing headlines (mental)
		Proof-reading/correction (mental)
		Page-layout (mental/physical)
(e)	Telephone operators	Switchboard handling (physical/mental)
		Role play in-coming calls (verbal)

7   This is another investigation opportunity: use these same questions/skills on another organisation that you know, know someone in, or read about. Develop your findings into evidence for Assessment Criteria 21:2

8   (a)   It is quite possible that her current employer is desperate to retain her. Disregard the reference, or question the referee by telephone, and seek another reference from a previous employer if possible.

       (b)   The phrases given are 'translations' by Adrian Furnham, (*Financial Times,* December 1991) of the following.

           (i)   'Mr Smith was occasionally a little lax in time keeping'
           (ii)   'Clearly growing out of earlier irresponsibility'
           (iii)   'At her best with close friends'
           (iv)   'Got a well deserved lower second'

Assignment 4 (2 hours)

Task one

Use your knowledge of recruitment methods and media to locate and select a **job advertisement** which contains a reasonable amount of detail about the activities and culture of the employing organisation and about the job and candidate requirements.

Task two

From the information available, draft an interview agenda suitable for the job, which might be used as a structure for a personnel officer sorting applications and guiding a selection interview. Consider what information you would need to gather *and* give.

Task three

With the collaboration of a fellow student, colleague or family member, conduct a role-play interview, in which you are the interviewer ($^1/_2$ hour maximum).

Task four

Debrief. Discuss with your role-play partner (and observers, if any) how each of you felt the interview went; what information did not effectively come out of the interview; whether the interview was sufficient to make a decision; what further selection methods (if any) would be helpful; whether bias, discrimination or invasion of privacy were evident at any stage.

Chapter 5:
REWARD MANAGEMENT

Introduction

'**Reward management** is concerned with the formulation and implementation of strategies and policies that aim to reward people fairly, equitably and consistently in accordance with their value to the organisation. It deals with the design, implementation and maintenance of reward practices that are geared to the improvement of organisational, team and individual performance.' (Armstrong, 2003)

Reward management strategies are designed to:

- Support the achievement of business objectives, by helping to ensure that the organisation can attract, retain and motivate competent and committed employees

- Reflect the behaviours and outcomes that are valued by the organisation, by seeking to reward people according to the value they are perceived to add to the business.

In this chapter, we will look briefly at the role of reward in the context of motivation theories (a topic of which you may already be aware from your studies in *Unit 3: Organisations and Behaviour*). We will then go on to explore some key aspects of reward management: how the value of work is determined (by job evaluation) and other determinants affecting pay. We will also look at a variety of financial and non-financial reward systems, as part of the 'total reward' concept.

This chapter discusses several ways in which people can be rewarded differentially according to their *performance*. This theme will be explored further in Chapter 6, where we cover the monitoring of performance – partly for the purposes of allocating rewards.

Your objectives

In this chapter, you will learn about the following.

(a) The relationship between motivation theory and reward

(b) The process of job evaluation

(c) The main factors determining pay levels

(d) Different types of reward systems, including performance-related pay

(e) Flexible benefits (Unit 22)

1   MOTIVATION AND REWARD

1.1 What is motivation?

The word 'motivation' is commonly used in different contexts to mean:

(a) The mental process of choosing desired outcomes, deciding how to go about them, assessing whether the likelihood of success warrants the amount of effort that will be necessary, and setting in motion the required behaviours. This is sometimes called 'intrinsic motivation', as it arises from factors and processes within the individual.

(b) The social process by which the behaviour of an individual is influenced by others. 'Motivation' in this sense usually applies to the attempts of organisations to maintain or increase workers' effort and commitment by using rewards and punishments. This is sometimes called 'extrinsic motivation', as it arises from actions done to or for the individual by others.

Theories of motivation are often categorised as 'content theories' and 'process theories'

Content theories assume that human beings have an innate package of motives (needs or desired outcomes) which they take action to pursue. They ask: '*What* motivates people?' Maslow's need theory and Herzberg's two-factor theory are two of the most important approaches of this type.

Process theories explore the psychological process through which outcomes become desirable and are pursued by individuals. They ask: '*How* are people motivated?' This approach assumes that people are able to select their goals and choose the paths towards them, by a conscious or unconscious process of calculation. Expectancy theory is a key example.

We will look briefly at these key motivational theories in turn, highlighting the nature of 'rewards' in each.

1.2 Need theory

Need theories suggest that individuals have certain innate needs. When a need is unsatisfied, the individual experiences tension – and acts in pursuit of goals that will satisfy the need.

Abraham Maslow (1954) developed the original and most famous need theory. He argued that Man has five innate needs, which he suggested could be arranged in a 'hierarchy of relative pre-potency': Figure 5.1.

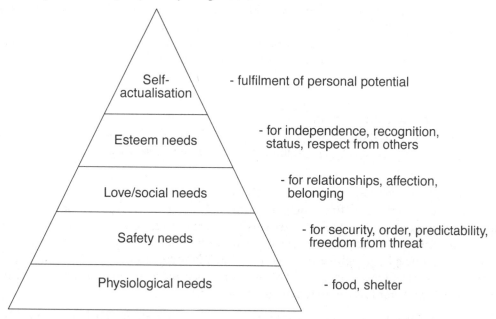

Figure 5.1: Maslow's Hierarchy of Needs

Each level of need is dominant until satisfied: only then does the next level of need become a motivating factor. Maslow regarded self-actualisation as the ultimate human goal: 'the desire to become more and more what one is, to become everything that one is capable of becoming'. It can never be satisfied in full.

Maslow's hierarchy is simple and intuitively attractive: you are unlikely to worry about respect if you are starving! However, it is only a theory, and not derived specifically from work psychology. Empirical verification of the hierarchy is hard to come by. Individuals may select any number of specific goals to satisfy their needs: for example, esteem needs may be satisfied by promotion, or a pay increase – or neither, depending on the individual's values and vocation. Research has also suggested that the hierarchy reflects UK and US cultural values, which may not transfer to other contexts.

Nevertheless, the hierarchy underpins later recognition that people can be motivated at work by **rewards which offer satisfaction of their 'higher order needs'**: esteem (competence, achievement, independence, confidence and their reflection in the perception of others: recognition, appreciation, status, respect) and self-actualisation (challenge, personal development, fulfilment).

1.3 Two factor theory

Frederick Herzberg (1966) interviewed Pittsburgh engineers and accountants about 'critical incidents' which made them feel good or bad about their work. He identified two basic need categories of individuals at work:

- The **need to avoid unpleasantness,** associated with fair treatment in compensation, supervision, working conditions and administrative practices. These needs are satisfied by what Herzberg called '**hygiene' factors**: they may minimise dissatisfaction and poor job performance, but have little ability to motivate the individual to higher levels of job satisfaction or extra performance. Hygiene factors are essentially extrinsic rewards, deriving from factors in the environment or context of work, and offering satisfaction of lower-level needs.

- The **need to develop in one's occupation**, as a source of personal growth, associated with factors such as advancement, recognition, responsibility, challenge and achievement. These needs are satisfied by what Herzberg called '**motivator**' **factors**, which are seen to be effective in motivating the individual to more positive attitudes, and greater effort and performance. Motivator factors are essentially intrinsic rewards, deriving from factors inherent in the content of the work itself, and offering psychological satisfaction of higher-level needs.

The two-factor model has been criticised as being based on an inadequately small sample size and a limited cultural context. In particular, the impact of job satisfaction on work performance has proved difficult to verify and measure: 'A satisfied worker is not necessarily a high producer, and a high producer is not necessarily a satisfied worker.' (Armstrong, 2003)

However, Herzberg's key assertion that 'dissatisfaction arises from environment factors: satisfaction can only arise from the job' confirmed the growing recognition of the **value of intrinsic rewards** – as opposed to extrinsic rewards – as motivating factors. Herzberg's work focused on job-design, as a means of building challenge, scope and interest into jobs: his concept of **job enrichment** ('the planned process of up-grading the responsibility, challenge and content of the work') became a cornerstone of the quality of working life and employee empowerment movements.

Today's '**total reward**' **concept** recognises that a reward system offering a mix of both extrinsic *and* intrinsic rewards is likely to be the most effective way of motivating employees.

Definition

Reward refers to 'all of the monetary, non-monetary and psychological payments that an organisation provides for its employees in exchange for the work they perform.' (Bratton & Gold, 2003)

Activity 1 (30 minutes)

What 'intrinsic' or internal satisfactions and rewards do you value in your own job (as opposed to the 'extrinsic' or external things the organisation can give you, like pay, comfortable working environment or likeable management)? Why do you work? What do you get out of your work that you most value? What would you miss most if you didn't work?

Try putting each of these satisfactions into (a) Maslow's categories of needs and (b) Herzberg's categories of hygiene and motivator factors.

Did you have any hesitation about where to put 'pay' in these categories? If so, why?

1.4 Expectancy theory

The expectancy theory of motivation basically states that the strength of an individual's motivation to do something will be influenced by:

- The perceived link between individual effort, performance and particular outcomes (Will reward follow effort?) and

- The importance of those outcomes to the individual (Will the reward make the effort worthwhile?)

Vroom (1964) suggested a formula by which motivation could be assessed and measured, based on an expectancy theory model. In its simplest form it may be expressed as:

Force or strength of motivation to do x	=	**V**alence (Strength of the individual's preference for outcome y)	x	**E**xpectancy (Individual's perception of the likelihood that doing x will result in outcome y)

Valence is represented as a positive or negative number, or zero – since outcomes (or rewards) may be desired, avoided or considered with indifference. Expectancy is expressed as a probability (in the perception of the individual): any number between 0 (no chance) and 1 (certainty).

So, for example, an employee may have a high expectation that behaviour x (say, increased productivity) will result in outcome y (say, promotion) – because of a performance contract, perhaps – so E = 1. However, if she is indifferent to that outcome (say, because she doesn't want the responsibility), V = 0 (or less) and she will not be motivated to increase her productivity. Similarly, if the employee has a great desire for promotion – but doesn't believe that more productive behaviour will secure it for her (say, because she has been passed over previously), E = 0 and she will still not be highly motivated.

This model helps to explain why performance incentives and rewards work most effectively when:

- **The link between effort and reward is clear**. (This is a key criterion in designing performance-based pay schemes – but would also apply to the giving of non-financial rewards such as praise and recognition, for example.)

- **Intended results and goals are made clear**, and especially when individuals share in setting goals (so that their expectation of being able to earn the rewards is taken into account)

- **The reward is perceived to be worth the effort**. (This is part of the rationale for flexible benefit schemes, allowing employees to choose from a menu of incentives and rewards.)

FOR DISCUSSION

How might reward systems in the broadest sense – including a range of HRM policies and practices – increase (a) the 'valence' or importance of rewards to employees and (b) the 'expectancy' of employees that increased productivity and commitment will result in being rewarded?

What kinds of HRM policies and practices might have the opposite effect?

1.5 Pay as a motivator

Monetary reward has a central, but ambiguous, role in motivation theory. It is not mentioned explicitly in any need list, but it can offer the satisfaction of many of the various needs. According to Herzberg, it is the most important of the hygiene factors:

valuable not only in its power to be converted into a wide range of other satisfactions, but also as a consistent measure of worth or value, allowing employees to compare themselves with other individuals or occupational groups. However, it is still only a hygiene factor: it gets taken for granted, and often becomes a source of dissatisfaction (particularly by comparison with others) rather than satisfaction.

Individuals may have needs unrelated to money, to which the pay system of the organisation is irrelevant or even conflicting (eg overtime bonuses conflicting with the need for work-life balance). Although the size of their income will affect their standard of living, most people tend not to be concerned to *maximise* their earnings. They may like to earn more but are probably more concerned to:

(a)   earn enough to meet their needs and aspirations

(b)   know that their pay is fair in comparison with the pay of others in comparable groups both inside and outside the organisation. This is sometimes known as the principle of distributive equity (Adams, 1963): it has been highlighted in recent decades by expectation and legislation in regard to equal pay for men and women (discussed later in the Chapter).

'Instrumentality' is the concept that people will do one thing in order to achieve or bring about another. An 'instrumental orientation to work' is an attitude that sees work purely as a means to other ends: in other words, people basically work for money. This assumption has its roots in scientific management, pioneered by Frederick Taylor in the early 20th century. By redesigning jobs into routine, repetitive and highly controlled tasks, 'Taylorism' created an environment which essentially lacked intrinsic rewards – leaving workers only the possibility of extrinsic motivation through higher pay for higher productivity (Huczynski & Buchanan, 2001).

The 'Affluent Worker' research of Goldthorpe, Lockwood *et al* (1968) illustrated an instrumental orientation to work in highly-paid Luton car assembly workers, who experienced their work as routine and dead-end. The researchers concluded that they had made a rational decision to enter employment offering high monetary reward rather than intrinsic interest. However, the research also suggested that people will seek a suitable balance of:

(a)   the rewards that are important to them; and
(b)   the deprivations they feel able to put up with in order to earn them.

Even those with an instrumental orientation to work have limits to their purely financial aspirations, and will cease to be motivated by money if the deprivations required to earn it – in terms of long working hours, poor conditions and so on – become too great.

Pay should be seen as only one of several intrinsic and extrinsic rewards offered by work. If it is used to motivate, it can only do so in a wider context of the job and other rewards. The significance in motivation theory of high-order needs, intrinsic rewards and subjective factors (such as expectancy and valance) suggest that HR managers need to:

- Develop reward systems which offer both financial and non-financial rewards, rather than relying on simplistic assumptions of instrumentality

- Support job re-design, employee involvement and on-going development planning which offer intrinsic satisfactions (particularly in the area of potential self-actualisation)

- Support an organisational and managerial culture which consistently values and expresses appreciation for employee contribution.

We will return to the influence of rewards on performance in section 4 of this Chapter. First, we will look in more detail at 'pay' and how pay levels are determined.

2 JOB EVALUATION

Definition

> **Job evaluation** is the process of analysing and assessing the content, worth or size of jobs within an organisation, in order to rank and group them as a basis for an equitable remuneration system.

2.1 The purpose and aims of job evaluation

Job evaluation is intended to create a rational and fair framework for job gradings and the pay decisions arising from them. It aims to:

(a) Assess the value of jobs to the organisation in relation to one another

(b) Support the development of job gradings and pay structures that are objective, balanced and equitable

(c) Ensure that the organisation is able to give (and demonstrate that it gives) equal pay for work of equal value, as required by law

2.2 Arguments for and against formal job evaluation

Formal job evaluation fell out of favour in the 1980s, being seen as too bureaucratic and inflexible for business environments which increasingly emphasised flexibility and reward for individual performance. However, a renewed focus on equity – and specifically, on equal pay – has encouraged widespread adoption of formal job evaluation schemes in recent years. 'Non-discriminatory job evaluation should lead to a payment system which is transparent and within which work of equal value receives equal pay regardless of sex' (Equal Opportunities Commission, 2000) or indeed any other grounds of discrimination.

The arguments for and against job evaluation may be summarised as follows.

Advantages	Disadvantages/limitations
• Job evaluation can offer a systematic approach to determining job values and relativities, without which it is difficult to justify the equity of pay differentials.	• Job evaluation can be bureaucratic, inflexible and time-consuming.
• Job evaluation offers a framework for consistent on-going decision-making about job grades and rates of pay.	• Job evaluation can inhibit the development of a flexible, 'high-involvement' workplace (Bratton & Gold, 2003), because it adds 'rigidity' to the job and the pay structure, and imparts a 'top-down' ethos.
• A properly designed and applied job evaluation process is more likely to be *felt* to be fair and equitable by employees than informal approaches.	• Job evaluation ratings can be gender biased, eg if job factors to be valued are based on jobs dominated by men.
• An analytical job evaluation scheme is the only acceptable defence in equal pay cases, as a means of achieving equal pay for work of equal value.	• Job evaluation is at best 'systematic' rather than 'scientific': there is an element of subjective judgement.
	• Job evaluated salary structures get out-of-date, unless attention is given to periodic review and maintenance.

In general, the criticisms focus on badly designed or applied job evaluation, rather than the concept of job evaluation itself.

Activity 2   **(1 hour)**

Do you feel your salary is fair for the job you do, and in relation to others? (Remember, job evaluation concerns the content, size and value of the *job* to your organisation – not on how much you put into it or how well you perform it.) Do you know how your job is evaluated? Do you know how your salary is worked out? What could the organisation do to make the system (a) clearer and (b) fairer?

Either answer these questions yourself, or ask them of an employed person who is willing to be interviewed by you on this topic.

2.3 The process of job evaluation

The process of job evaluation covers four basic steps.

Step 1.   **Select compensable factors**

Compensable factors represent the aspects of jobs for which the organisation is willing to pay. Armstrong (2003) suggests that effective factors should:

(a) Apply equally well to different types of work (including specialists and generalists, lower level and higher level jobs, and jobs performed by men and women)

(b) Refer to relevant and important differences between jobs, in order to allow comparison for ranking purposes

(c) Be understandable by, and acceptable to, all those who will be covered by the scheme

Examples of compensable factors include: knowledge and skills, judgement and decision-making, freedom to act and responsibility for financial resources.

Step 2.   **Gather data on jobs**

Some information for evaluation may already be available in the form **of job descriptions,** or may have to be gathered by **job analysis** (see Chapter 3).

Step 3.   **Evaluate jobs**

There are two basic types of job evaluation scheme.

(a) **Non-analytical schemes** make largely subjective judgements about the whole job, its difficulty, and its importance to the organisation relative to other jobs.

(b) **Analytical schemes** systematically analyse how far compensable factors are present in each job, in order to arrive at appropriate weightings and rankings.

These methods will be discussed further below.

Step 4. **Assign specific pay values to the job**

The output of a job evaluation scheme is a **pay structure:** a ranking or hierarchy of jobs in terms of their relative value to the organisation. The organisation must then make policy decisions to assign pay values to jobs or job grades within the structure. This is generally done with reference to market rates of pay, how the organisation's pay levels compare with those of its competitors, and how aggressively it must compete to attract and retain quality labour. (This will be discussed in Section 3 below.)

2.4 Job evaluation schemes

Non-analytical schemes

Job classification is most common non-analytical approach. The organisation decides what grades of pay there should be and defines the requirements of each grade. Jobs are allocated to an appropriate grade by matching job descriptions to grade definitions: the job is not broken down into its component elements.

Job ranking compares whole jobs with one another and ranks them in accordance with their relative importance or contribution to the organisation. Having established a hierarchy of jobs, they can be divided into groups for grading purposes.

Analytical schemes

Points rating is currently the most popular method of formal job evaluation. It begins with the definition of about 8 – 12 compensable factors: these will vary according to the type of organisation and can be adapted to its changing needs and key values.

A number of *points* is allocated to each compensable factor, as a maximum score, across a range of '*degrees*' which reflect the level and importance (or weighting) of the factors within a job.

A comprehensive *points rating chart* is therefore established, covering a range of factors and degrees which can be applied to a variety of specific jobs. An example of such a chart is shown in Figure 5.2.

Each *job* is then examined, analysed factor by factor according to the points rating chart, and a points score is awarded for each factor, up to the maximum allowed. The total points score for each job provides the basis for ranking the jobs in order of importance, for establishing a pay structure and for pricing the pay structure. An example of a job evaluation form for points rating is shown in Figure 5.3.

Factor comparison involves the selection of key *benchmark jobs*, for which the rate of pay is considered to be fair (perhaps in comparison with similar jobs in other organisations).

Each of these jobs is analysed, using compensable factors, to decide how much of the total salary is being paid for each factor. So if technical skill is 50% of a benchmark job paying £12,000, the *factor pay rate* for technical skill (within that job) is £6,000. When this has been done for every benchmark job, the various factor pay rates are correlated, to formulate a ranking and pay scale for each factor.

	Compensable factor	DEGREE (Weighting)				
		1	2	3	4	5
G E N E R A L	Job knowledge	10	25	50	70	-
	Practical experience	15	30	50	70	-
	Physical effort	5	10	15	-	-
	Complexity	15	20	25	30	-
	Judgement/initiative	15	20	30	40	50
	Job conditions	5	10	15	-	-
	Contact with peers	5	10	20	40	-
	Contact with clients	10	20	30	40	50
	Attention to detail	5	10	15	20	-
	Potential for error	5	10	20	40	-
	Confidential data	5	10	15	20	30
	.....	...	...	...	...	...
S U P E V I S O R Y	Nature of supervision	5	10	20	-	-
	Scope of supervision	10	15	25	-	-
	Resource allocation	10	15	25	30	-
	Trust	15	20	30	40	50
	Management reporting	10	15	25	30	-
	Quality	15	30	90	50	60
	.....	...	...	...	...	...

Degree definitions

- **Job knowledge**

1. Maintain basic procedures; operate and maintain basic machinery; undertake range of tasks under supervision; comply with rules and policies.

2. Administer a routine area of work, under supervision; operate and maintain basic machinery to proficient standard; understand purpose of rules and policies and be able to identify compliance issues.

3. Supervise a small number of staff in routine and non-routine tasks; be responsible for checking of working; manage own routine and non-routine workload; control maintenance of range of machinery and compliance with rules and policies, including coaching/briefing of staff; certificate-level qualification in job-related area

4. Supervise staff in routine and non-routine tasks; manage quality and customer service issues; plan and co-ordinate own and section workload; systematic view of rules and procedures, with ability to propose improvements; diploma-level qualification in job-related area

5. -

Figure 5.2: Points rating chart (excerpt)

Each **job** is then examined, analysed factor by factor according to the value chart, and a points score awarded for each factor, up to the maximum allowed. The total points score for each job is found by adding up its points score for each factor. The total points scored for each job provides the basis for ranking the jobs in order of importance, for grading jobs, if required, and for fixing a salary structure.

Job evaluation form

Key job code _____   Department _____

Job type _____   Job holder studied _____

Date _____   Employee number _____

Task number

Description

Factor	Rating			Comments
	Points	Weighting	Total	

Skills and knowledge
    Education/qualifications
    Experience
    Dexterity				

Skills sub-total				
Initiative				

Responsibility
    People
    Equipment
    Resources				

Responsibility sub-total				

Effort
    Mental
    Physical				

Effort sub-total				

Communication
    Oral
    Written				

Communication sub-total				
Interpersonal skills				

Conditions of work
    Hazards
    Isolation
    Monotony				

Conditions sub-total				
TOTAL				
RANKING				
COMMENTS				

Figure 5.3: Points rating form

Other (non-benchmark) jobs are then evaluated factor by factor, to build up a *job value*. For example, an analysis for a clerical job might be:

Factor	Proportion of job		Pay rate for factor (as established by analysis of benchmark jobs)	Job value £
Technical skills	50%	×	£12,000 pa	6,000
Mental ability	25%	×	£16,000 pa	4,000
Responsibility for others	15%	×	£10,000 pa	1,500
Other responsibilities	10%	×	£5,000 pa	500
				12,000

The Equal Pay (Amendment) Regulations 1984 clearly state that job evaluations must use analytical methods in order to demonstrate that the organisation is offering equal pay for work of equal value. They must examine 'the demands on a worker under various headings (for instance, effort, skill, decision)'.

Activity 3	**(30 minutes)**

Can you see how an element of subjectivity may remain even in 'analytical' methods?

(a)   Suggest *three* ways in which such methods would remain subjective to an extent.

(b)   Why is objectivity desirable?

2.5   Comparison of job evaluation methods

The strengths and weaknesses of the job evaluation schemes discussed above can be summarised as follows.

Method	Strengths	Weaknesses
Job ranking	• Simple to use • Simple to explain to employees	• Non-analytical: no defence in an equal pay case • No defined criteria for evaluation for consistency • Does not measure differences between jobs
Job classification	• Simple to use and explain • Some criteria for judgements are provided in grade definitions	• Non-analytical: no defence in an equal pay case • Grade definitions tend to be generalised: difficult to place complex jobs or compare jobs with each other
Points rating	• Analytical method: should aid objectivity and consistency of pay structure • Provide a defence against equal value claims	• Can be complex and time-consuming • The selection of factors, points scoring and weighting remain subjective judgements, despite appearance of precision

Method	Strengths	Weaknesses
	• Factors selected can be suited to the particular types of job being evaluated • Use of degrees and point allocations gives great flexibility • Output is a rank order of jobs, without determining the money value of the job: this allows other factors to be taken into consideration in job grading and pricing	• Factors and weightings can be discriminatory, invalidating the defensibility of the analytical method • Depends heavily on effective job analysis
Factor comparison	• Analytical method: compares jobs on a factor by factor basis • Avoids spurious precision of points rating • Can be used in benchmarking exercises: comparing roles in different job categories	• Involves assumptions based on existing pay rates for benchmark jobs • No defined criteria to aid evaluators' judgements • Best suited to situations where the range of jobs is limited and of a fairly simple nature • Not easy to explain to employees

FOR DISCUSSION

The 'transparency' or openness of the job evaluation exercise is critical to its effectiveness. Why might employees and their representatives be suspicious, or feel threatened, by a job evaluation programme (particularly if it is being introduced for the first time)? What kinds of information and messages will the HR manager want to give them in order to support effective job evaluation and preserve employee relations? (You may like to role play this as a discussion between staff, union representatives and an HR manager.)

Job evaluation only determines a job's relative worth to the organisation, by ranking. It does not reflect its monetary worth to the organisation. We will now consider a number of other factors influencing the pricing of the pay structure.

3 OTHER FACTORS DETERMINING PAY

3.1 Market rates of pay

In order to arrive at pay rates which support recruitment, retention and motivation, a pay structure should be a combination of:

- The results of job evaluation, based on relative worth of jobs to the organisation and internal equity *and*

- The results of market pay analysis, based on the 'absolute' worth of jobs to the organisation and competitiveness in the labour market.

The concept of the market rate is not exact: different employers will pay a range of rates for similar job titles – particularly in the case of managerial jobs, whose scope and nature will vary according to context and culture. However, most organisations use **pay surveys** of key or 'benchmark' jobs to get a broad indication of the 'going rate' of pay for a job. Sources of information on market rates include:

- Published surveys

- Surveys carried out by HR specialists or commissioned from management consultants

- Business network or 'club' surveys, where organisations exchange pay information on a regular basis

- General market monitoring and intelligence: recruitment advertising, government statistics, recruitment consultancies and so on.

Market rate information on benchmark jobs can be used to add monetary values to 'similar' jobs within the organisation's job-evaluated rankings. Other jobs can then be placed on the pay scale according to their relative positions in the ranking, and priced accordingly.

Activity 4   **(30 minutes)**

You may like to check out some of the sources of published pay surveys available online, such as the UK New Earnings Survey (www.statistics.gov.uk) or www.salariesreview.com.

(a) How reliable do you think each of the sources of market rate data listed in Paragraph 3.1 would be?

(b) How would you go about 'job matching': comparing the jobs cited in market rate data with jobs in your own organisation, as 'like with like' in terms of the type and size of the job and the type of organisation?

The market rate of pay will vary with supply/demand factors such as:

(a) The relative scarcity of particular skills in the particular market from which the organisation draws its labour

(b) The sensitivity of employees to pay levels or differentials. Pay may or may not act as an incentive to change employers, depending on the availability of work elsewhere, the employee's loyalty and the non-financial rewards offered by the organisation or the job.

Market rates of pay will have most influence on pay structures where there is a standard pattern of supply and demand in the open labour market. If an organisation's rates fall below the benchmark rates in the local or national labour market from which it recruits, it may have trouble attracting and holding employees. Management has three basic policy choices:

- To **lead** the competition: often used for key or scarce skills, or to establish a leading employer brand as part of the organisation's competitive strategy

- To **match** what other employers are paying: the least-risk approach

- To **lag** behind the market: may be cost-effective where vacancies can be easily filled in the local labour market (minimising direct competition with other employers)

Activity 5	**(45 minutes)**

What are the arguments *for* and *against* an organisation's offering above-market rates of pay?

Other factors which may distort or dilute the effect of the forces of supply and demand on labour pricing (in addition to job-evaluated equity criteria) include:

(a) **Affordability:** the organisation's ability to pay the market rate

(b) The **culture and value systems** of the organisation, which will influence the attitude of management towards the market rate, and whether age, length of service, motivation, employee aspirations and/or other factors are taken into account in the determination of pay, rather than fluctuations in supply and demand. (You may note from some of the International Comparison Examples in this chapter that national cultural differences also influences salary strategy.)

(c) The bargaining strength of trade unions (where applicable) in **collective bargaining** negotiations. Pay scales, differentials and minimum rates may be negotiated at plant, local or national level.

(d) **Government intervention**, including incomes policies and anti-inflationary measures (limiting the size of pay increases by pay controls). UK governments have often used control of public sector pay to influence general pay trends. We will look further at the legal framework on pay in Paragraph 3.3 below.

EXAMPLE: INTERNATIONAL COMPARISONS

Reward policy in Germany is highly collectivised. Each union (organised on broad industry lines) negotiates with the employers' federation on a state by state basis – allowing for the relative prosperity of the region. Companies (such as Volkswagen) which are not part of a trade association may negotiate separately with the relevant trade union. Many HR managers will therefore not be involved in wage negotiation at all, but will implement the agreement locally.

The system of industrial democracy known as 'co-determination' gives a plant-level works council the right to co-determine company policy on matters including how wages and salaries are to be paid (method, time), the use of incentives (bonus schemes, piece work, performance-related pay) and so on. Traditionally popular elements of reward systems include holiday and long-service bonuses, suggestion schemes, incentive/merit pay (for manual grades) and profit sharing (for managerial grades), with employee share ownership schemes attracting tax incentives.

3.2 Individual performance

Job evaluated pay structures are generally designed to allow increasing rewards for seniority (eg by using incremented rates for age or length of service), competence (eg by applying competence-based bands) and/or performance (eg by applying merit or contribution bands). The *incentive* role of pay in motivating employees to higher levels of performance may also be built into the reward system through separate bonus schemes, performance-related pay, employee share ownership schemes and so on. We will discuss these aspects in detail later in the Chapter.

3.3 Legal provisions on pay

Key provisions on pay levels in the UK concern the minimum wage and equal pay.

National Minimum Wage Regulations 1999

In 1999, the UK government accepted the findings of the Low Pay Commission and introduced a national minimum wage.

(a)	Over the age of 21:	£3.70 per hour (from October 2000)
(b)	18-21 year olds:	£3.20 per hour (from June 2000)

16-17 year olds on formal apprenticeships, casual workers, agency workers and homeworkers are excluded. In general, where there is no express agreement, an employee is legally entitled to 'reasonable remuneration'.

Equal Pay Act 1970 and amendments

The Equal Pay Act was the first major attempt 'to prevent discrimination as regards terms and conditions of employment between men and women.' Women were entitled to claim equal pay and conditions of service for:

- Jobs rated as equivalent under a job evaluation scheme and

- Work that was 'the same as or broadly similar' to the work of a man in the same establishment, where job evaluation was not used.

The Equal Pay (Amendment) Regulations 1984 established the right to equal pay and conditions for work of equal value (that is, not necessarily 'similar' work, but work of equivalent evaluation). If job evaluation was not used in an organisation, the employee could apply to an Industrial (now Employment) Tribunal for a (legally enforceable) order to have an evaluation carried out by an independent expert.

The Equal Opportunities Commission issued a 1997 Code of Practice on Equal Pay, covering pay systems, methods of identifying discrimination, job evaluation recommendations and a model policy on equal pay.

Its *Good Practice Guide: Job evaluation schemes free of sex bias* (EOC, 2000) further sets out detailed requirements to ensure that job evaluation schemes select compensable factors which reflect jobs undertaken by women as well as those undertaken by men – and then evaluate them fairly.

FOR DISCUSSION

Why do you think there has been increasing sensitivity in recent years to the issue of equal pay?

Why is it important for business organisations to take this into account?

NOTES

We will now look briefly at reward systems and how they can be structured.

4 REWARD SYSTEMS

Definition

A **reward system** is 'the mix of extrinsic and intrinsic rewards provided by the employer... [It] also consists of the integrated policies, processes, practices and administrative procedures for implementing the system within the framework of the human resources (HR) strategy and the total organisational system.' (Bratton & Gold, 2003)

4.1 Objectives of the reward system

The key objectives of any reward system can be summed up as follows.

(a) **Recruiting and retaining quality labour** in line with the human resource plan. External competitiveness with market rates may be the strongest influence on recruitment, while internal equity may be the strongest influence on retention.

(b) **Motivating individual and team performance**, to maximise return on investment from the human resource. There are various forms of reward system which link reward to performance (discussed below).

(c) **Supporting organisational culture**, by conveying messages about the values, behaviours and outcomes that the organisation prizes and is willing to pay for.

(d) **Supporting flexibility**, by responding to changing organisational skill and performance requirements.

4.2 Components of the reward system

Three broad reward components can be identified within the reward system.

(a) **Direct or base pay**: a fixed salary or wage that constitutes a standard rate for the job, as defined by market pricing and job evaluation. This amount is paid at intervals of a week or month and reflects 'hours of work': the amount of *time* spent at the workplace or on the job. It is appropriate as a basic pay component in jobs where output or effort are less meaningful or measurable (for example, where monitoring, supervising and cognitive activity is concerned). It also provides a relatively consistent and predictable basic income. Pay *progression* (increases in basic pay over time) may be related to age or length of service, or to performance-related criteria such as competence or skill attainment.

The key advantages of direct pay are that it is easy to implement and administer; it is generally felt to be fair (especially if established by job evaluation); and it helps to establish mutual commitment in the psychological contract of employment.

(b) **Performance or variable pay**: a method or component of payment directly linked to work-related behaviour, such as performance or attainments. There are various types of variable pay, including:

PROFESSIONAL EDUCATION

(i)   *Incentive pay*, which is offered prior to setting performance targets

    (ii)   *Merit pay*, offered for outstanding past performance in a job

    (iii)   *Payment by results (PBR)*, which links pay directly to the quantity of output produced by the individual (or team): piecework, commission (usually a percentage of sales value generated) or output- or target-based bonuses

    (iv)   *Performance-related pay (PRP)*, offering additional payments for individual or team performance according to a range of possible performance criteria (quality, customer service, teamworking, innovation and so on)

    (v)   *Organisation performance pay*, based on the profitability of the firm: eg value added schemes, profit-sharing schemes and employee shareholding

The key advantage of such rewards (in theory) is that they motivate employees to higher levels of performance; foster a culture in which performance, competence and contribution (and specific criteria such as teamworking or innovation) are valued; and fulfil the desire for equity. However, as we noted in Section 1 of this Chapter, the assumption that people are motivated and managed solely by pay is simplistic.

(c)   **Indirect pay or 'benefits'**: non-cash items or services. These may include 'deferred pay' in the form of pension contributions, legal entitlements (for example, to sick pay, maternity pay, maternity/paternity leave, and annual leave), and so-called 'fringe' benefits such as company cars, housing assistance, medical insurance and allowances.

4.3   The 'total reward' concept

The sum of the components discussed above is known as **'total remuneration'**. The concept of **'total reward'** is based on the premise that monetary payments are not the only, or necessarily the most effective, form of reward and that financial and non-financial rewards should be linked together as an integrated reward package: Figure 5.4.

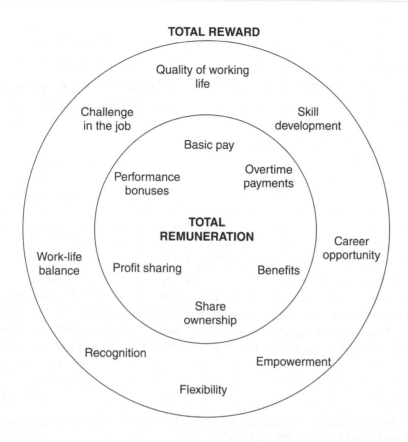

Figure 5.4: Total reward package

A total reward orientation seeks to integrate reward strategy both vertically (with business strategy) and horizontally (with a range of other HRM strategies).

Armstrong (2003) cites a study by WorldatWork which suggests the following benefits of a total reward approach:

- *Increased flexibility:* tailoring rewards to changing circumstances

- *Recruitment and retention:* offering employees the 'total value' of the employment package (and monitoring its true cost to the organisation)

- *Potential for low-cost reward solutions*

- *Heightened visibility in tight labour markets:* offering valued rewards

We will now look at each of the three components of the total remuneration package in turn.

5 BASIC PAY

5.1 Salary and wage systems

The terms 'wages' and 'salaries' are sometimes used interchangeably to refer to monetary rewards, but there are traditional distinctions between them.

Wages	Salaries
• Manual/'blue collar' workers – historically on short contract terms	• White-collar workers – historically with greater security of tenure
• Paid weekly	• Paid monthly, as a proportion of an annual fixed sum
• Based on a weekly or hourly rate for time/output	• Related to seniority, qualifications, performance, with progression over time
• Premium rates paid for overtime	• Overtime not usually paid

In the UK and US, wage payment systems are increasingly being replaced by salaries as part of **single status** schemes. These represent an attempt to harmonise the payment systems operating in an organisation, mainly by removing the distinction between the treatment of manual and white-collar staff. Such agreements 'represent more than just a change of payment systems and an improvement in manual workers' conditions of work. The employers involved were consciously attempting to change the relationships between workers and management. They wanted to encourage responsibility, pride in work and co-operation, and hoped thereby to increase efficiency.' (Lupton, 1974)

> **Activity 6** **(10 minutes)**
>
> What advantages and disadvantages for the organisation and its workers can you see from single status schemes?

EXAMPLE: INTERNATIONAL COMPARISON

In the US, non-unionism and a strong internal labour market have encouraged individualised and independent pay policy. Internalised wage structures sheltered employees in large US firms from external labour market forces, allowing a high degree of employment security, coupled with above-market pay and benefits (with profit sharing and employee share ownership schemes adding up to 50% to the value of rewards). Observers note, however, that this is changing with downsizing and flexible working: wages are becoming more sensitive to local external conditions, and differentials are no longer driven by seniority or length of service. US firms are increasingly emphasising individual performance factors in remuneration, and are reducing their pension obligations to employees. The culture of employment in the US, minimising artificial status distinctions between managerial and non-managerial grades, supports salaried status for all staff.

5.2 Salary systems

Armstrong (1998) identifies the main objectives in designing a coherent salary structure as being 'to provide for internal **equity** in grading and paying staff and to maintain **competitive rates** of pay' and notes that 'neither of those objectives can be achieved if a chaotic set of rates exists which have evolved over the years and is altered at whim or because of a panic reaction to difficulties in recruitment or retention.' We have already discussed job evaluation and market rate analysis in Sections 2 and 3 of this Chapter.

A salary system generally consists of:

- A **grade structure,** consisting of a hierarchy of bands or levels ('grades') to which are allocated groups of jobs that are broadly comparable in value: Figure 5.5.

- A **pay structure**, defining pay ranges or scales for each grade, allowing scope for *pay progression* or increases according to length of service and performance.

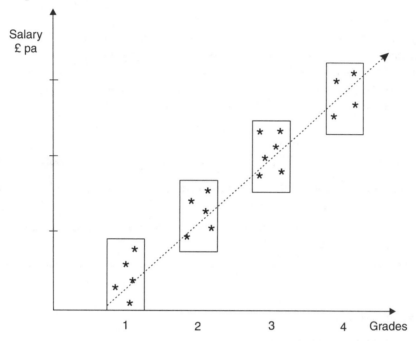

Figure 5.5: Grade structure

The grade structure will require careful design, because of the consequences for promotions and transfers between grades.

(a) Differentials between pay ranges should recognise increases in job value between one grade and another, in order to avoid arguments about grading in borderline cases.

(b) The range of each grade should be wide enough to allow for progression: people in similarly-graded jobs may perform differently and should be rewarded accordingly.

(c) There should be some overlap, in recognition that an experienced person performing well in a given job may be of more value than a new or poor performer in the next grade up.

Progression or pay increases within a grade may be achieved by fixed increments linked to age or length of service (common in the public sector) or by various forms of performance-related increases.

Flexibility will be required: changes in job content or market rates should prompt re-grading. Individual growth in competence should also be allowed for: in the case of an individual whose performance is outstanding, but for whom there are no immediate openings for promotion, discretionary payment above the grade maximum may be made.

Narrow-graded structures used to be the norm. They consist of typically 8 to 12 narrow grades, each with a range of 20-40%. Such a structure is easy to manage and explain to employees, and enables close control over pay pricing and progression. It allows flexibility, but also maintains equity by specifying narrow pay scales for closely grouped (similarly evaluated) jobs. However it reflects a tall, hierarchical organisation structure (which may or may not still exist). If grades are too narrow, people will constantly seek to upgrade, creating grade 'drift'.

A popular alternative approach is a **broad-banded structure**. This typically includes as few as 4-6 grades or 'bands', each spanning the pay range previously covered by a number of grades, with a range of 50-100%. Wide bands allow rates of pay to be adapted more flexibly to market rate fluctuations and individual performance, and offers rewards for lateral career development and competence development (since in today's flatter organisations, there may not be many levels available for 'vertical' promotion). Broad-banding reduces the bureaucratic rigidity of more narrow-graded structures, and fits more flexible organisations. However, it is also harder to manage than a narrow graded structure. Wide bands build up exaggerated expectations of pay rises, which are controlled in practice. Because jobs of widely different value are included within bands, and market rates are used to place jobs within bands, there may also be equal pay issues.

Activity 7	(No time limit)

(a) Is there a salary policy and structure in your organisation? Find out and record their salient details.

(b) If you had trouble finding out, what does this say about the political aspects of salary administration?

5.3 Wage systems

A typical wage structure will include:

(a) A basic (time or piecework) rate; *plus*

(b) Overtime premium rates for work done outside normal hours

(c) Shift pay premium rates for employees who work unusual or socially disruptive hours or shift patterns: this is a form of *compensatory* pay

(d) Compensatory payments for abnormal working conditions (eg 'danger money', 'dirt money', 'wet money'), although these may be built into basic rates during job evaluation

(e) Allowances (eg to employees living in high cost-of-living areas like London)

(f) Merit or length-of-service bonuses

(g) Payment by results bonuses and incentives (discussed below).

6 PERFORMANCE PAY

6.1 Effective performance pay systems

Effective performance (or 'contingent') pay systems should fulfil the following criteria.

- Targets and standards of performance required to earn the rewards must be made clear to the people involved.

- The formulae used to calculate rewards, and any conditions that apply, should be easily understood.

- The rewards should be – and perceived to be – significant enough to make the effort worthwhile (perhaps 10% of basic salary)

- Rewards should be related to performance indicators over which people have control or influence, through their own behaviour or decision-making.

- There should not be a lengthy time lag between performance and reward.

6.2 Payment by results

Payment by results (PBR) is based on work study techniques, establishing what output per hour/day (or time taken to produce a unit of output) should be: it is an approach traditionally applied to manual work, which has a steady and measurable flow of task and output.

There has been a decline in PBR systems in recent years, as quality and flexibility issues (among others) have made output quantity a less valuable measurement criterion. Team-based PBR, in particular, was subject to inequity (due to necessary fluctuations in output between members) and the whole system was a source of shopfloor conflict around measurement, rate fixing and output norms.

6.3 Performance-related pay (PRP)

Individual performance-related pay (IPRP) relates monetary bonuses and/or the rate and extent of pay progression (increases in basic pay over time, within the pay brackets attached to job grades) to the performance of individuals, assessed according to defined criteria.

For managerial and other salaried jobs, a form of **performance management** is usually applied so that:

(a)   Key results can be identified and agreed, for which merit awards will be paid

(b)   The exact conditions and amounts of awards can be made clear to employees

(c)   Performance indicators can be regularly monitored and evaluated, in order to establish when targets have been reached and awards earned

For service and other departments, a PRP scheme may involve **bonuses** for achievement of key results, or **points schemes**, where points are awarded for performance on various criteria (efficiency, cost savings, quality of service and so on) and a certain points total (or the highest points total in the unit, if a competitive system is used) wins cash or other awards.

PRP is not appropriate for all organisations. It requires an individualistic, performance-oriented culture, where individuals have an instrumental orientation to work, are able to control the outcomes of their work, and are supported by systematic performance management (goal setting, feedback and objective results measurement). (Torrington *et al*, 2002)

Advantages of IPRP	Disadvantages/limitations of IPRP
• Encourages the setting, clarification and communication of key task behaviours and performance criteria	• Based on over-simplistic belief in instrumentality: not all employees motivated by financial incentives
• Encourages the monitoring, gathering and sharing of feedback on current performance	• Fosters instrumentality: creates a culture where employees expect to be rewarded for everything

Advantages of IPRP	Disadvantages/limitations of IPRP
• Integrates organisational and individual priorities and objectives	• Fosters a manipulative management culture based on 'carrot and stick' rather than intrinsic rewards
• Promotes a results-focused culture and behaviours: flexibility, customer service, quality and 'entrepreneurial' thinking	• Undermines teamworking by focusing on individual effort
• Reduces the need for other types of managerial control (direct supervision, technology), fostering self-motivation	• May focus on quantitative outputs, at the expense of quality
• Attracts and retains people who expect to be rewarded for delivering results	• May focus on established ways of doing things, inhibiting creativity and innovation
• Provides a concrete means of rewarding performance	• May focus on short-term productivity gains rather than long-term strategic goals
	• May frustrate employees, where they are not able to control all factors in their performance
	• Relies heavily on effective performance management for objective performance definition and assessment

FOR DISCUSSION

'Managers who insist that the job won't get done right without rewards have failed to offer a convincing argument for behavioural manipulation. Promising a reward to someone who appears unmotivated is a bit like offering salt water to someone who is thirsty. Bribes in the workplace simply can't work.' (Kohn, cited by Torrington *et al*, 2002)

Do incentives only secure temporary compliance – or can they change underlying attitudes?

EXAMPLE: INTERNATIONAL COMPARISON

A key feature of employment in Japan is the seniority system, which links reward with length of service rather than with job or performance factors. This is a subtler distinction than it may appear, since length of service is equated with commitment, skill development and status. 'It is a scale of 'person-related' payments – as opposed to 'job related' payments... an intricate set of rules, based on the exponential principle that the higher you go, the faster you rise, designed to give recognition to both seniority and merit. The seniority principle requires that everybody goes up a notch every year' (Dore, cited by Beardwell and Holden, 1997). This concept of 'performance related pay' is very different from the Western concept of performance as individual achievement: it reflects the complexity of the relationship between the individual, the organisation, the job and socio-cultural values of status, commitment and belonging.

6.4 Suggestion schemes

Another variant on performance-based pay is the **suggestion scheme**, where payments or non-cash prizes are offered to staff to come up with workable ideas on improving efficiency or quality, new marketing initiatives or solutions to production problems. The theory is that there is in any case motivational value in getting staff involved in problem-solving and planning, and that staff are often in the best position to provide practical and creative solutions to their work problems or the customer's needs – but that an added incentive will help to overcome any reluctance on the part of staff to put forward ideas (because it is seen as risky, or doing management's job for them, or whatever).

Wherever possible, the size of the payment should be related to the savings or value added as a result of the suggestion – either as a lump sum or percentage. Payments are often also made for a 'good try' – an idea which is rejected but considered to show initiative, effort and judgement on the part of the employee.

Suggestion schemes usually apply only to lower grades of staff, on the grounds that thinking up improvements is part of the manager's job, but with the increase of worker empowerment and 'bottom up' quality initiatives, they are becoming more widespread in various forms.

6.5 Team-based pay

Group incentives schemes typically offer a bonus for a group (equally, or proportionately in the earnings or status of individuals) which achieves or exceeds specified targets. Offering bonuses to a whole team may be appropriate for tasks where individual contributions cannot be isolated, workers have little control over their individual output because tasks depend on each other, or where team-building is particularly required.

The advantage of team reward is to enhance team-spirit and co-operation as well as to provide performance incentives – but it may also create pressures within the group, if some individuals are seen to be 'not pulling their weight'.

Long-term, large-group bonus schemes may be applied plant- or organisation-wide. **Gain sharing** schemes allocate additional awards when there has been an increase in profits or a decrease in costs.

(a) **Value-added** schemes, for example, work on the basis that improvements in productivity (indicated by a fall in the ratio of employment costs to sales revenue) increases value added, and the benefit can be shared between employers and employees on an agreed formula.

(b) **Scanlon plans** pay frequent, plant-wide bonuses, based on improvements in productivity and reduction in labour costs which are brought about through collective bargaining and the participation of employee representatives.

Profit-sharing schemes offer employees current or deferred bonuses (paid in cash or shares) based on company profits. The formula for determining the amounts may vary, but in recent years, a straightforward distribution of a percentage of profits above a given target has given way to a value-added concept.

The link between individual effort and profitability is recognised to be remote, so profit sharing does not constitute a direct incentive. However, it is based on the belief that all employees can contribute to profitability, and that their contribution should be recognised. It may foster profit-consciousness and commitment to the future prosperity of the organisation. The greatest effect on productivity arising from the scheme may in fact arise from its use as a focal point for discussion with employees about the relationship between their performance and results, and areas and targets for improvement.

NOTES

An **employee stock plan** or **employee share ownership scheme** (such as an *All Employee Share Ownership Plan* or *Savings-Related Share Option Scheme)* allows employees to acquire shares in their employing company. The key advantage of such systems may be to encourage employees to take 'ownership' of the long-term success of the business – although the notorious collapse of the Enron Corporation, in the United States, has highlighted the extent to which this may be a double-edged sword.

Activity 8	**(15 minutes)**

Are you motivated by monetary incentives? At what point would the offer of more money cease to motivate you to longer hours, greater efforts (or whatever)? Try and identify three likely problems with, or limitations of, cash/monetary incentives.

6.6 Non-cash incentives

Incentive and recognition schemes are increasingly focused not on cash, but on non-cash awards. Traditionally aimed at sales people, non-cash gifts and incentives are now widely used to add interest to quality and suggestion schemes, enabling managers to recognise staff contribution flexibly, informally and at relatively low cost. Incentive awards include vouchers, air miles, the choice of gift from a catalogue, travel experiences and so on.

EXAMPLES

A recent article in *People Management* (Tulip, 2003 (a)) suggests that incentive schemes need to be up-to-the-minute, fresh and flexible if they are to be effective.

'An incentive scheme has to be achievable, but people also have to be rewarded with the sort of things they want. Call centre workers, for example, tend to be a young market, often making a first home, and so tend to select electrical merchandise or kitchen goods. These are less likely to incentivise high-flyers, older workers and managers, who typically go for an "experience", whether that be a holiday or something more extreme.'

A wide range of fresh ideas for incentives is highlighted, including:

- Experience-based incentives (particularly effective as rewards for successful teams or team-based projects) such as snowboarding or dolphin watching events. The latest trend is to use learning and training in skills, sports and hobbies. ('If you are learning something, you are keeping your 'skills to learn' alive, and probably gaining skills that can be transferred back into the workplace.')

- New variations on the gift vouchers traditionally backed by major retailers such as Marks & Spencer and John Lewis Partnership: the trend is towards vouchers offering a wider range of opportunities eg those offered by the Virgin brand (from CDs to hot air ballooning).

- New variations on the gift catalogue, notably web-based incentive sites: 'We can set up a virtual shopping site, tailored to the needs of a company, so that the experience is just like personal shopping, only without having to pay.' (www.LongService.com)

Such schemes can be regarded by some staff as manipulative, irrelevant or just plain gimmicky. However, they can be effective as team-building exercises and as part of a total reward programme.

FOR DISCUSSION

Which of the non-cash incentive examples mentioned above do you think would be a good investment for the organisation, and why? Which would you, as an employee, find most attractive? (Explore any personal and cultural differences in the answers from your discussion group.)

7 INDIRECT PAY

7.1 Benefits

Employee benefits consist of items or awards which are supplementary to normal pay. Some – such as pension provisions and sick pay, maternity/paternity leave and maternity pay – are legal entitlements, so the common term 'fringe' benefits is perhaps misleading. Other benefits are more in the nature of optional extras, and as such may be part of the total remuneration package.

Discretionary benefits which may be offered include the following.

(a) **Extended holiday entitlement**. This is a benefit which is often taken for granted, but it was only recently (Working Time Regulations 1998) that any formal entitlement to annual leave was formulated.

(b) **Company cars** are a highly-regarded benefit in the UK, especially among managerial staff (despite the reduction in tax incentives over the years) and those whose work requires extensive road travel.

(c) **Employee assistance**, for example with transport (loans or discounted purchase of annual season tickets) or housing (allowances for transferred or relocated staff, bridging loans or preferential mortgage terms)

(d) **Insurance** – including life and private medical/dental insurance.

(e) **Catering services** – eg subsidised food and drink at the workplace, or luncheon vouchers.

(f) **Recreational facilities** – the subsidy or organisation of social and sports clubs, or provision of facilities such as a gymnasium.

(g) **Allowances** for telephone costs, professional subscriptions or work-related reading matter.

(h) **Discounts or preferential terms** on the organisation's own products/services.

(i) **Educational programmes** – in-house study opportunities, or sponsorship of external study (not necessarily work-related).

(j) **Family-friendly policies** such as workplace crèche, term-time hours contracts, career break schemes and generous maternity/paternity terms.

Activity 9	(15 minutes)

Which, of all the benefits mentioned, would you think were the most important to people?

You might like to check out websites such as www.benefitslinks.com or www.benefits.org for more information in this area.

7.2 Objectives of benefit packages

There are a number of reasons why organisations offer benefit packages.

(a) To attract and retain staff by the generosity and/or relevance of benefits offered, and by facilitating career longevity and work-life balance (eg by allowing career breaks and sabbaticals, flexible work hours and so on)

(b) To encourage commitment to (and consumption of) the organisation's own products (eg by offering employees discounted rates)

(c) To demonstrate corporate social responsibility (CSR) by giving above-statutory levels of sick pay, paternity leave, pension provisions, employee assistance and so on

(d) To promote desirable behaviours and values in employees (for example, by subsidising clothing, fitness programmes or learning/training experiences)

(e) To offer rewards of perceived high value to employees, ideally with discounted or marginal cost to the employer

Flexibility is a key trend in benefit programmes: this is mentioned as a 'topical HR issue' in the content requirements for Unit 22. We will discuss it, in context, here.

7.3 Flexible benefits

Increasing recognition that individuals have different needs and wants has led to the development of flexible benefit ('flex') or 'cafeteria' benefit programmes (CBP). A range of benefits with different values are on offer, and employees can choose from among them up to their budget, as allocated to a personal benefit account: the most common allowance for flexible benefits is 5-10% of basic salary.

This is not a new concept, having been accepted practice for some time in America, where there has been a relative lack of state-sponsored welfare benefits. However, Tulip (2003 (b)) reports the following results of a market review.

(a) Hewitt, Bacon & Woodrow's 2003 survey (*Employer Attitudes to Flexible Benefits*) looked at 400 organisations, of which 70% had either implemented or were considering flex. A fifth of those that had implemented flex did so in 2002, doubling the annual rate compared with the previous year.

(b) The greatest uptake is in the middle market level. 'The biggest firms often have complex, multinational structures and while general philosophies and concepts ('we support healthcare') can be applied across borders, it is difficult to reproduce the same degree of flex in different administrations... Smaller companies can do this sort of thing quicker, and the messages that flex aims to promote does not get diluted by layers of management.' However, the economics of flex become marginal when applied to fewer than 100 employees, unless they are exceptionally high earning.

(c) Although more than 45% of employers in the HBW survey have paper-based flex schemes, the Internet is increasingly recognised as an important tool, 'both in communicating the merits and values of the benefit scheme and in shifting part of the administrative burden on to the employees themselves as 'self-service'.' New technologies may also support the outsourcing of the design, maintenance and management of flexible benefit schemes.

EXAMPLE

'The benefits most commonly offered in flexible form, according the HBW survey, are private medical insurance, holiday arrangements and life assurance. Coming up strongly, however, are the more unusual benefits of home computer purchase and childcare vouchers, followed by travel insurance and retail vouchers. Certainly, this range is broadly offered by companies leading the way in total reward packages, such as AstraZeneca, a finalist in the CIPD PM Award 2002.

'Only 22% [of employees], mostly young people with a first mortgage, trade all their allowance for cash.'

(Tulip (2003 (b))

The advantages claimed for flexible benefits are, broadly, that:

(a) Choice allows employees to select benefits to meet their individual needs, increasing their appreciation of the benefit (especially where state-funded provision for sickness and retirement are increasingly uncertain)

(b) Choice supports the management of diversity, in meeting the needs of a diverse workforce (in terms of age, culture and personal preferences)

(c) Choices such as additional holidays, learning accounts, home PCs and childcare vouchers support (and are supported by) UK government initiatives in regard to work-life balance and skill development

(d) The organisation only pays for the most highly-desired benefits, allowing it to capitalise cost-effectively on any motivational value accruing from them

(e) The system can help to reduce the total cost of compensation and specific future cost increases, through: savings on national insurance; better control of benefit spend; reduced premium costs for health and life insurance (which tend to be brokered less aggressively than in conventional schemes); and even reduction in payroll costs, if employees take more holiday.

However, it should also be noted that there are significant start up and administrative costs involved in flex schemes. There are also risks for the employer, especially in dealing with long-term financial benefits: the choice of benefits must be clearly the responsibility of the employee, and any financial advice (eg on life insurance or pensions) must be given by the benefit provider – not the employing organisation. The distinction between fixed benefits (laid down in the contract of employment) and variable benefits (linked to individual service or performance) must be made clear, to avoid benefits becoming taken for granted. In addition, the link between benefits and performance has still not been proved.

FOR DISCUSSION

Do flexible benefits meet the real needs of employees – or are they a way for the organisation to try to buy commitment more cheaply?

Chapter roundup

- Reward management is concerned with the formulation and implementation of strategies and policies that aim to reward people fairly, equitably and consistently in accordance with their value to the organisation.

- Need theories of motivation (Maslow, Herzberg) suggest that intrinsic rewards (as well as extrinsic rewards) must be included in reward strategy. Process theories of motivation (Vroom) highlight the need for flexibility, clear communication and careful design of reward systems to support the motivation calculation. Instrumentality underpins monetary reward systems, but it is recognised that there are limitations to financial incentives.

- Job evaluation is the process of analysing and assessing the content of jobs, in order to place them in an acceptable rank order which can then be used as a basis for a remuneration system. Job evaluation methods may be non-analytical (job ranking, job classification) or analytical (points rating, factor comparison): only analytical methods provide a defence in equal pay claims.

- Other factors in determining pay levels include market rate analysis (using pay surveys), affordability, organisation strategy and culture, government intervention, collective bargaining, the need to offer performance incentives and rewards, and legal provisions on minimum wage and equal pay.

- Total remuneration includes basic (or direct) pay, performance (or contingent) pay and indirect pay (or benefits). Total reward is a wider concept still, embracing a range of intrinsic rewards available from the job.

- Salary structures are commonly graded, with a range (or scale) or salaries within each grade.

- Incentives may be built into graded salary systems on a limited basis. In addition, many organisations operate incentive or performance-related pay schemes, including IPRP, suggestion schemes, gain sharing schemes and profit-sharing.

- A range of benefits may be offered to employees in addition to basic entitlements. Flexible benefits have become particularly popular in the UK in recent years.

Quick quiz

1   Explain the formula $F = E \times V$ in terms of motivational theory.

2   What is 'instrumentality' and what is its relevance to reward management?

3   Outline the advantages and disadvantages of job evaluation.

4   List the four basic steps in job evaluation.

5   List four sources of information on market rates of pay.

6   What are the implications of the Equal Pay Act for setting pay levels?

7   Define a 'grade structure' and a 'pay structure' in a salary system.

8   What are the advantages and disadvantages of performance-related pay?

9   List three options for organisation-wide performance rewards.

10   What are the advantages of flexible benefits?

Answers to quick quiz

1   Force of motivation to do x = valence (important of outcome y) x expectancy (perceived probability that doing x will lead to y.
                                                                    (see paragraph 1.4)

2   The concept that people will do something as a means to an end: eg work for money. Lies behind monetary/extrinsic reward systems, but is simplistic: instrumentality is not universal or straightforward as a motivating factor.   (para 1.5)

3   For a full answer, see the table in paragraph 2.2

4   Select compensable factors, gather data on jobs, evaluate jobs (using non-analytical or analytical methods), assign pay values to jobs.
                                                                    (para 2.3)

5   Published surveys; special surveys; business network/club surveys; general marketing monitoring and intelligence.   (para 3.1)

6   Women are entitled to claim equal pay for work of equal value. This should be justified by analytical job evaluation, which uses both non-gender-biased compensable factors and non-gender-biased evaluation
                                                                    (para 3.3)

7   Grade structure: a hierarchy of bands or levels ('grades') to which are allocated groups of jobs that are in the same value range.

     Pay structure: pay ranges or scales for each grade, allowing scope for pay progression within the grade.   (para 5.2)

8   For a full answer, see paragraph 6.3.

9   Gain sharing schemes, profit-sharing, employee share ownership.
                                                                    (para 6.5)

10   For a full answer, see paragraph 7.3

Answers to activities

1   The answers to this activity will be personal to you, and should clarify your thinking about need theories and rewards. The issue of pay will be discussed in Paragraph 1.5 of the chapter.

2   Again, the answer to this activity will be personal to you, but remember to draw out the relevant learning. *Your* subjective experience of job evaluation (your own sense of the fairness of your salary *and* the transparency and perceived fairness of your organisation's job evaluation scheme) should highlight some of the issues for HR managers. You will

also be building up your 'case study' file of examples of HR practices in the real world.

3   (a)   Subjectivity may take the following forms.

(i)   The factors for analysis are themselves qualitative, not easy to define and measure. Mental ability and initiative are observable in job holders, but not easily quantifiable as an element of the job itself.

(ii)   Assessment of the importance and difficulty of a job cannot objectively be divorced from the context of the organisation and job holder. The relative importance of a job is a function of the culture and politics of the organisation, the nature of the business and not least the personal power of the individual in the job. The difficulty of the job depends on the ability of the job holder and the favourability or otherwise of the environment/technology/work methods/management.

(iii)   The selection of factors and the assignment of monetary values to factors remain subjective judgements.

(b)   It is undoubtedly desirable to achieve objectivity, to reduce the resentment commonly felt at the apparent arbitrariness of pay decisions. If job evaluation were truly objective, it would be possible to justify differentials on a rational basis, the organisation would have a balanced and economical pay structure based on contribution, and employers would be safe from accusations of unfair pay decisions.

4   (a)   Published surveys are quick and relatively inexpensive – but may not be relevant to the organisation's jobs, and may be out of date.

Special surveys may be time-consuming and costly, but they directly compare jobs in the market place with jobs in the firm.

Network/club surveys are a cost-effective way of accessing surveys, and are regularly updated.

Recruitment ads and consultancies may be misleading: the job descriptions are unlikely to be sufficient to match jobs accurately, and salaries offered/cited may not be reflected in practice.

(b)   Job matching may be done by using job titles, but this is likely to be very misleading. Job descriptions are likely to offer greater accuracy in identifying directly comparable jobs: the fuller the description, the greater the comparability. Comparing full job evaluations of different jobs would be most valuable – if such data were available (eg through commissioned or published surveys).

5   One may list the general arguments for paying over market rate as follows.

(a)   The offer of a notably higher remuneration package than market rate may be assumed to generate greater interest in the labour market. The organisation will therefore have a wider field of selection for the given labour category, and will be more likely to have access to the most skilled/experienced individuals. If the organisation establishes a reputation as a 'wage leader' it may generate a consistent supply of high-calibre labour.

(b)   There may be benefits of high pay offers for employee loyalty, and better performance resulting from the (theoretically) higher calibre and motivation of the workforce.

(c)   Even if a cheap supply of labour were available, and the employer could get away with paying a low rate, its ideology or ethical code of an organisation may make reluctant to do so. A socially responsible employer may wish to avoid the exploitation of labour groups, such as immigrants, who may not be aware of general market rates.

(d)   An employer might adopt a socially responsible position not purely for ethical reasons but to maintain a respected image and good relations with government, interest groups, employee representatives and the general public (potential customers/ consumers).

(e)   Survival and immediate profit-maximisation are not necessarily the highest objective of any organisation. Employers in growth markets, or hoping to diversify into new markets, cannot afford a low-calibre, high-turnover workforce. Notably innovative organisations can be seen to be offering higher than market rate on salaries (eg Mars) or remuneration packages including profit-related bonuses (eg Sainsbury's): moreover, their financial performance bears out their view that pay is an investment. To an extent, this pay strategy stems from the culture or value system of the organisation, the importance it attaches to loyalty, innovation and initiative, and its willingness to pay more to attract and retain such higher-level attributes: quantity may not be the prime employment criterion.

On the other hand, there are substantial cost savings in paying lower rates. It cannot be assumed that high remuneration inevitably leads to higher motivation and better performance. Not everybody has an instrumental orientation to work: money may not be the prime incentive - and pay is often a source of dissatisfaction rather than satisfaction, whatever its level.

If the organisation's ability to maintain high rewards in the future is in doubt, management ought also to be aware that the disappointment and culture shock of reversing a high-remuneration policy is very great.

6   Single status schemes can save an organisation administrative and overtime costs, and may improve employee flexibility and industrial relations. For manual workers, there are clear advantages in receiving a wider range of benefits and an annual salary (which at least improves their borrowing position).

However, there may be an increase in labour costs overall. For the workers, too, there is a drawback, in monthly – instead of weekly – payments. There is also a perceived loss of status for salaried workers, in the achievement of parity by previous wage-earners: this may affect their morale, although the organisation culture will have a lot to do with whether harmonisation is perceived as threatening or equitable and exciting.

7   If you are not employed in a work organisation, ask a salaried acquaintance. Do not neglect to think about part (b) of this activity: research has shown that in the absence of information about salaries, people become dissatisfied by what they **think** they are earning in relation to others. Some people seem genuinely not to want to know how

their salary is determined, as long as it progresses year on year: what might the consequences of such an attitude be for loyalty, motivation and the salary bill of the organisation?

8   There are a number of difficulties associated with incentive schemes based on monetary reward.

(a)   Increased earnings simply may not be an incentive to some individuals. An individual who already enjoys a good income may be more concerned with increasing his leisure time, for example.

(b)   Workers are unlikely to be in complete control of results. External factors, such as the general economic climate, interest rates and exchange rates may play a part in **profitability** in particular. In these cases, the relationship between an individual's efforts and his reward may be indistinct.

(c)   Greater specialisation in production processes means that particular employees cannot be specifically credited with the success of their particular products. This may lead to frustration amongst employees who think their own profitable work is being adversely affected by inefficiencies elsewhere in the organisation.

(d)   Even if employees *are* motivated by money, the effects may not be altogether desirable. An instrumental orientation may encourage self-interested performance at the expense of teamwork: it may encourage attention to output at the expense of quality, and the lowering of standards and targets (in order to make bonuses more accessible).

Workers remain suspicious that if they achieve high levels of output and earnings, management will alter the basis of the incentive rates to reduce future earnings. Work groups therefore tend to restrict output to a level that they feel is 'fair' and 'safe'.

9   In a survey of 2,000 people in full-time employment in France, Britain, Germany and Italy, it was discovered that:

(a)   Most workers think a staff restaurant is a more important benefit than a company car (84% of workers, in 'cuisine-conscious' France!)

(b)   Company cars were also rated less important than pensions or private health insurance

See also the example in Paragraph 7.3.

Assignment 5 (1½ hours)

Ad Hoc Ltd is a small firm which manufactures highly fashionable computer mouse devices for sale through selected dealerships (such as Dixons and Apple Centres). It employs a 500-strong diverse team of:

(a) Designers, responsible for creating new models and 'packages' in response to user trends and endorsements (eg by Apple Macintosh)

(b) Customer support workers, responsible for responding to end-users installation and software inquiries via a 24-hour hotline and subscription Technical Support programme

(c) Technical hardware/software designers, carrying out technical research and product planning and development. These individuals are encouraged to spend 15% of work time on their own technical projects and interest (following the model of US giant 3M, which used this as a device to encourage innovation)

(d) Manufacturing controllers/co-ordinators who liase with management and staff at the technical manufacturing facility which Ad Hoc contracts to do its component manufacturing, assembly and packing

(e) Sales staff, responsible for selling on to dealerships, negotiation of promotions in-store, stock control and replenishment, and dealer relations and

(f) Support staff, including technical writers (for instruction manual development and related collaborative publishing projects), HR, finance and administrative departments

Addison Hoc, the young general manager and founder of the company, has strong attitudes about the kind of freewheeling, entrepreneurial, flexible, innovative organisation he wants to develop. Jobs are considered fluid and cross-department collaborations and 'deals' – like those with external partners – are encouraged. Individuals have always negotiated their remuneration packages on a one-to-one basis with the general manger and HR manger.

As a result, there is a wide-ranging disparity in the structure and amount of rewards. Recently, this has begun to cause problems. Salary costs have been spiralling: differentials are all over the place, to the disgruntlement of several senior staff members; commissions on sales frequently push sales salaries above those of the technical designers; and now, several female staff in the customer support department have threatened to bring appeals against the company, because they feel they are being paid less than the men in sales support.

Addison Hoc has been advised by his lawyers that he may need to consider introducing some form of job evaluation scheme, in order to prevent equal pay claims.

As HR manager, you have been asked your opinion: is job evolution worth doing? You will give a presentation to the senior management team.

Task

(a) Prepare notes, weighing up the pros and cons of job evaluation

(b) Anticipate objections on the basis of the cons, so that you can suggest how the scheme could be made to work effectively at Ad Hoc.

Chapter 6:
MONITORING AND MANAGING PERFORMANCE

Introduction

The process of monitoring individual and group performance, and giving helpful feedback for improvement, is generally called **performance appraisal**. The purpose of appraisal was traditionally regarded as constructive criticism of the employee by his or her manager, but nowadays it tends to be more about:

(a) Helping the employee to overcome any problems or obstacles to performance

(b) Identifying where an employee's potential for improved performance and greater challenge could be better fulfilled

(c) Setting goals and priorities for further monitoring and development

Your objectives

In this chapter you will learn about the following.

(a) Organisational approaches to monitoring performance, including appraisal and performance management

(b) The role, purpose and types of appraisal (Unit 22)

(c) 360 degree feedback (Unit 22)

(d) Skills in appraisal and giving feedback (Unit 22)

(e) Performance management interventions including discipline, grievance and counselling

1 THE PURPOSE OF APPRAISAL

Definition

> **Performance appraisal** is the process whereby an individual's performance is reviewed against previously agreed goals, and where new goals are agreed which will develop the individual and improve performance over the forthcoming review period.

1.1 Role of appraisal

Monitoring and evaluating the performance of individuals and groups is an essential part of human resource management. It has several uses.

(a) Identifying the current level of performance to provide a basis for informing, training and developing team members to a higher level of competence

(b) Identifying problems or areas where improvement is needed in order to meet acceptable standards of performance

(c) Identifying people whose performance suggests that they might be suitable for promotion in future

(d) Measuring the individual's or team's level of performance against specific standards, to provide a basis for reward above the basic pay rate (productivity or results-related bonuses, competence-related increments, merit awards and so on)

(e) Measuring the performance of new team members against the organisation's (and team's) expectations, as a means of assessing whether selection procedures have been successful

(f) Improving communication about work tasks between managers and team members, as a result of discussing the assessment

(g) In the process of defining what performance should be, establishing what key results and standards must be reached for the unit to reach its objectives

It may be argued that a particular, deliberate stock-taking exercise is unnecessary, since managers are constantly monitoring and making judgements about their subordinates and (theoretically) giving their subordinates feedback information from day to day.

1.2 Why have a formal appraisal system?

It must be recognised that, if no system of formal appraisal is in place:

(a) Managers may obtain random impressions of subordinates' performance (perhaps from their more noticeable successes and failures), but not a coherent, complete and objective picture

(b) Managers may have a fair idea of their subordinates' shortcomings – but may not have devoted time and attention to the matter of improvement and development

(c) Different managers may be applying a different set of criteria, and varying standards of objectivity and judgement, which undermines the value of appraisal for comparison and equitable reward decisions, as well as its credibility in the eyes of employees

(d) Managers rarely give their subordinates adequate feedback on their performance. Most people dislike giving criticism as much as receiving it

Definition

A **criterion** (plural: criteria) is a factor or standard by which something can be judged or decided. For example, 'meeting output targets' is one criterion for judging work performance.

| **Activity 1** | **(15 minutes)** |

List four disadvantages to the employee of not having an appraisal system.

1.3 The systematic approach to appraisal

A typical system would therefore involve:

(a) Identification of **criteria** for assessment

(b) The preparation of an **appraisal report**

(c) An **appraisal interview,** for an exchange of views about the results of the assessment, targets for improvement, solutions to problems and so on

(d) The preparation and implementation of **action plans** to achieve improvements and changes agreed

(e) **Follow-up:** monitoring the progress of the action plan

This can be summarised in diagrammatic form as follows.

Figure 6.1: Appraisal as a control system

We will now look at each stage in turn.

2 APPRAISAL PROCEDURES AND TECHNIQUES

2.1 What should be monitored and assessed?

Assessments must be related to a common set of standards, so that comparisons can be made between individuals. On the other hand, they should be related to *meaningful performance criteria* which take account of the critical variables in each job.

> **Activity 2** (20 minutes)
>
> Think of some criteria which you would want to use in assessment of some jobs – but which would not be applicable in others.

There is also the important question of whether you assess **personality** or **performance**. Personal qualities like reliability or outgoingness have often been used as criteria for judging people. However, they are not necessarily relevant to job performance: you can be naturally outgoing, but still not good at communicating with customers, if your product knowledge or attitude is poor. Also, personality judgements are notoriously vague and unreliable: words like 'loyalty' and 'ambition' are full of ambiguity and moral connotations.

In practical terms, this has encouraged the use of competence or results-based appraisals, where performance is measured against specific, job-related performance criteria.

Most large organisations have a system in place, with pre-printed assessment forms setting out all the relevant criteria and the range of possible judgements. (We reproduce such a form later in this chapter). Even so, a team manager should critically evaluate such schemes to ensure that the criteria for assessment are relevant to his or her team and task – and that they remain so over time, as the team and task change.

Relevant criteria for assessment might be based on the following.

(a) **Job analysis:** the process of examining a job, to identify its component tasks and skill requirements, and the circumstances in which it is performed (discussed in Chapter 3).

(b) **Job descriptions:** general descriptions of a job or position at a given time, including its purpose and scope, duties and responsibilities, relationship with other jobs, and perhaps specific objectives and expected results. A job description offers a guide to what competences, responsibilities and results might be monitored and assessed.

(c) **Departmental or team plans, performance standards and targets.** These are the most clear-cut of all. If the plan specifies completion of a certain number of tasks, or production of a certain number of units, to a particular quality standard, assessment can be focused on whether (or how far) those targets have been achieved.

(d) **Individually negotiated goals and standards** for performance and/or improvement. This is a feature of 'performance management', discussed in Section 4 of this Chapter.

Let us now look at some of the performance monitoring and reporting methods used in organisations.

2.2 Monitoring and reporting methods

Overall assessment

The manager writes in narrative form his or her judgements about the appraisee. There will be no guaranteed consistency of the criteria and areas of assessment, and managers may not be able to convey clear, effective judgements in writing.

Guided assessment

Assessors are required to comment on a number of specified characteristics and performance elements, with guidelines as to how terms such as 'application', 'integrity' and 'adaptability' are to be interpreted in the work context. This is a more precise, but still rather vague method.

Grading

Grading adds a comparative frame of reference to the general guidelines, whereby managers are asked to select one of a number of defined levels or degrees to which an individual displays a given characteristic. These are also known as rating scales, and have been much used in standard appraisal forms. (See Figure 6.4 on the following page.)

Numerical values may be added to gradings to give rating scores. Alternatively a less precise graphic scale may be used to indicate general position on a plus/minus scale, as in Figure 6.2.

Factor: job knowledge

Figure 6.2: graphics scale

Behavioural incident methods

These concentrate on employee behaviour, which is measured against typical behaviour in each job, as defined by common **'critical incidents'** of successful and unsuccessful job behaviour reported by managers. The analysis is carried out for **key tasks,** which are identified as critical to success in the job and for which specific standards of performance *must* be reached. This makes scales highly relevant to job performance, and facilitates objective assessment because ratings are described in behavioural terms.

The behavioural equivalent of the graphic scale for a manager's key task of 'marketing initiative' might appear as follows: Figure 6.3.

| Produces no new ideas for marketing. Appears apathetic to competitive challenge | Produces ideas when urged by head office. Ideas not clearly thought out nor enthusiastically applied | Produces ideas when urged by head office and gives full commitment to new programmes | Spontaneously generates new ideas for marketing and champions them through head office approval. Ideas related to identified needs and effective in practice |

Figure 6.3: Critical incident scale

Performance Classification

Outstanding performance is characterised by high ability which leaves little or nothing to be desired.

Personnel rated as such are those who regularly make significant contributions to the organisation which are above the requirements of their position. Unusual and challenging assignments are consistently well handled.

Excellent performance is marked by above-average ability, with little supervision required.

Satisfactory Plus performance indicates fully adequate ability, without the need for excessive supervision.

Personnel with this ratings are able to give proper consideration to normal assignments, which are generally well-handled. They will meet the requirements of the position. '**Satisfactory plus**' performers may include those who lack the experience at their current level to demonstrate above-average ability.

Marginal performance is in instances where the ability demonstrated does not fully meet the requirements of the position, with excessive supervision and direction normally required.

Employees rated as such will show specific deficiencies in their performance which prevent them from performing at an acceptable level.

Unsatisfactory performance indicates an ability which falls clearly below the minimum requirements of the position.

'**Unsatisfactory**' performers will demonstrate market deficiencies in most of the major aspects of their responsibilities, and considerable improvement is required to permit retention of the employee in his current position.

Personal Characteristic Ratings

1.- Needs considerable improvement - substantial improvement required to meet acceptable standards.

2.- Needs improvement - some improvement required to meet acceptable standards

3.- Normal - meets acceptable standards

4.- Above normal - exceeds normally acceptable standards in most instances.

5.- Exceptional - displays rare and unusual personal characteristics.

4168B/1

Personnel Appraisal: Employees in Salary Grades 5-8

Date of review	Time on position		S.G.	Age		Name
	Yrs	Mths		Yrs	Mths	

| Period of Review | Position Title | | | | Area | |

Important : Read guide notes carefully before proceeding with the following sections

Section One	Performance Factors						Section Two	Performance Characteristics					
	N/A	U	M	SP	E	O		1	2	3	4	5	6
Administrative Skills							Initiative						
Communications - Written							Persistence						
Communications - Oral							Ability to work with others						
Problem Analysis							Adaptability						
Decision making							Persuasiveness						
Delegation							Self-confidence						
Quantity of Work							Judgement						
Development of Personnel							Leadership						
Development of Quality Improvements							Creativity						

Section Three Highlight Performance Factors and particular strengths/weaknesses of employee which significantly affect Job Performance

| Overall Performance Rating (Taking into account ratings given) | |

Prepared by: Signature _____ Date _____ Position Title _____

| | IR Review Initial |

Section Four Comments by reviewing authority

Signature _____ Date _____ Position Title _____ Date _____

Section Five Supervisor's Notes on Counselling Interview

Signature _____ Date _____ Position Title _____

Section Six Employees Reactions and Comment

Signature _____ Date _____

Figure 6.4: Standard appraisal form

Results-orientated schemes

All the above techniques may be used with more or less results-orientated criteria. A wholly results-orientated approach sets out to review performance against specific targets and standards of performance, which are agreed in advance by a manager and subordinate together.

Key advantages of such an approach include the following.

(a) The subordinate is more involved in appraisal, and performance, because (s)he is able to evaluate progress in achieving clear, jointly-agreed measures.

(b) The manager is relived of the 'critic' role and becomes more of a 'counsellor', jointly defining solutions to performance issues.

(c) Clear and known targets are beneficial in motivation, especially in maximising the effectiveness of financial incentives.

(d) The emphasis of appraisal becomes forward-looking (offering incentive), rather than purely retrospective (offering compensation).

FOR DISCUSSION

Which of the above reporting methods would you consider:

(a) Fairest
(b) Most easily justified to the person being appraised
(c) Most suitable for determining performance pay awards?

In introducing 'performance management', we have raised the possibility that an employee might be involved in monitoring and evaluating his or her own performance. We will look at some of the sources of assessment feedback other than the appraisee's immediate boss.

2.3 Sources of performance feedback

Organisations have begun to recognise that the employee's immediate boss is not the only (or necessarily the best) person to assess his or her performance. Other options include:

(a) The employee him or herself (self appraisal)
(b) Peers and co-workers (peer appraisal)
(c) Subordinates (upwards appraisal)
(d) Or a combination of the above (360 degree feedback)

Self-appraisal

Self-appraisal allows individuals to carry out a self-evaluation as a major input to the appraisal process.

Advantages

(a) It **saves the manager time** as the employee identifies the areas of competence which are relevant to the job and his/her relative strengths.

(b) It offers **increased responsibility** to the individual which may improve motivation.

(c)   This reconciles the goals of the individual and the organisation.

(d)   It may overcome the problem of needing skilled appraisers, thus cutting training costs and reducing the managerial role in appraisal.

(e)   In giving the responsibility to an individual, the scheme may offer more **flexibility** in terms of timing, with individuals undertaking ongoing self-evaluation.

Disadvantages

(a)   People are often not the best judges of their own performance.

(b)   People may deliberately over- (or under-) estimate their performance, in order to gain approval or reward – or to conform to group norms.

Upward appraisal

A notable modern trend, adopted in the UK by companies such as BP and British Airways , is **upward** appraisal, whereby employees are rated not by their superiors but by their subordinates. The followers appraise the leader.

The advantages of this method might be as follows.

(a)   Subordinates tend to know their superior (particularly in the area of leadership skills) better than anyone.

(b)   Multiple ratings (from a group of subordinates) has greater statistical validity than a single view.

(c)   Subordinates' ratings may have more impact, because it is less usual to receive such feedback.

(d)   Upward appraisal encourages subordinates to give feedback and raise problems they may have with their boss, which otherwise would be too difficult or risky for them

(e)   It supports upward communication in general, which may have knock-on benefits for creativity, problem-solving and employee relations.

Activity 3   **(15 minutes)**

Imagine you had to do an upward appraisal on your boss, parent or teacher. Suggest the two major problems that might be experienced with upward appraisal.

Customer appraisal

In some companies part of the employee's appraisal process must take the form of feedback from 'customers' (internal or external). This may be taken further into an influence on remuneration (at Rank-Xerox, 30% of a manager's annual bonus is conditional upon satisfactory levels of 'customer' feedback). This is a valuable development in that customers are the best judges of customer service, which the appraisee's boss may not see.

360 degree feedback

360 degree feedback (also known as 'multi-rater instruments' and 'multi-source assessment') is the most radical recognition of multiple 'stakeholders' in an individual's

performance. According to Peter Ward (who introduced the system at Tesco back in 1987):

> Traditional performance measurement systems have rarely operated on more than one or two dimensions. However, 360-degree feedback is designed to enable all the stake-holders in a person's performance to comment and give feedback. This includes the current (and perhaps previous) boss (including temporary supervisors), peers and co-workers, subordinates and even external customers. Finally, the employee's own self-assessment is added and compared.

Information is usually collected (anonymously) through questionnaires, either on paper or online.

The advantages of 360 degree feedback are as follows.

(a)　It offers the opportunity to build up a rounded picture of an employee's performance: the more relevant parties contribute, the more complete the picture.

(b)　Multiple appraisal may reduce or at least balance the element of subjectivity which inevitably enters appraisal of one individual by another, particularly where there are interpersonal or political issues between the individual and his immediate superior.

(c)　360 degree feedback increases the amount and openness of task and performance-related communication in the organisation, especially where inter-departmental colleagues are asked to participate. This in turn can lead to:

　　(i)　Increased awareness and integration of overall and sub-unit objectives

　　(ii)　Increased integration of plans for learning and performance improvement

　　(iii)　Cross-fertilisation of ideas on performance and objectives, which may elicit innovations and creative solutions to problems

(d)　The element of upward appraisal (of superior by subordinate) can overcome barriers to upward communication, and can encourage improvement of leadership through a better appreciation of the experience of the followers.

(e)　It takes into account feedback from customers (external and internal) that is particularly valuable in:

　　(i)　Encouraging and monitoring the customer care orientation of the organisation as a whole - in line with modern thinking about business processes, quality management and so on

　　(ii)　Showing a commitment to respond meaningfully to customer feedback

　　(iii)　Focusing areas of an employee's performance that are recognised to have real impact on the business

　　(iv)　Encouraging the 'internal customer' concept within the organisation, as an aid to co-ordination

(f)　The extensive information-gathering process, and feedback from key performance areas and contacts, signals the seriousness with which appraisal is regarded by the organisation, reinforcing commitment to performance management and improvement.

The approach has a number of disadvantages, however.

(a)   Subjectivity is not eliminated by the process: a number of subjective viewpoints is arguably no fairer than just one.

(b)   Suspicion and hostility may be aroused by being judged by one's peers: the appraiser may hesitate to give a critical appraisal that may be construed as 'disloyal'.

(c)   Upward appraisal is notoriously difficult: there may be fears of reprisal by the superior for a critical appraisal, or vindictive appraisal for political reasons. Superiors may find it hard to adjust to learning from their subordinates.

(d)   It is not easy to define performance criteria that will be meaningful and measurable for each appraiser, nor to weight the evaluations of the different appraisers, nor to reconcile or prioritise contradictory evaluations by different appraisers.

(e)   There is extra organisation, paperwork and evaluation to be done. This has cost implications, as well as behavioural ones: some parties to the appraisal process may resent extra work.

EXAMPLE

W H Smith (reported by Mike Thatcher, *People Management*, 21 March 1996), decided to supplement their existing upwards appraisal system (introduced 1990), covering 1,200 managers, with 360 degree appraisal. The personnel function was chosen.

'Between eight and fifteen people filled in forms covering each manager's competences and personal objectives. The appraisers were asked to rate them on a scale of one to five and give anecdotal examples to support the marks. The forms were sent to an independent third party for collating.

Ainley is pleased with the results, which have sharpened the developmental aspects of W H Smiths standard appraisal meetings. But there have been problems: a minimum of eight people commenting on 15 managers means at least 120 forms - a significant increase in administration; many appraisers found it difficult to comment on the individual manager's objectives; and there was a reluctance to back up ratings with anecdotal comments.

The second trial involving senior IT managers has just finished and the results are currently being evaluated. This time, the processing has been done in house to save costs, whilst a computerised system is being developed to cut down on the bureaucracy.

Ainley is now considering extending 360 degree appraisal to the rest of the organisation.'

Activity 4 (20 minutes)

Peter Ward gives an example of the kinds of questionnaire that might be used as the instrument of 360-degree feedback. 'A skill area like "communicating", for example, might be defined as "the ability to express oneself clearly and to listen effectively to others". Typical comments would include "Presents ideas or information in a well-organised manner" (followed by rating scale); or: "Allows you to finish what you have to say".'

Rate yourself on the two comments mentioned here, on a scale of 1–10. Get a group of friends, fellow-students, even a tutor or parent, to write down, **anonymously**, on a piece of paper **their** rating for you on the same two comments. Keep them in an envelope, unseen, until you have a few.

Compare them with your self-rating. If you dare... What drawbacks did you (and your respondents) find to such an approach?

Having reported on an individual's performance – whether in a written narrative comment, or on a prepared appraisal form – a manager must discuss the content of the report with the individual concerned.

2.4 The appraisal interview

There are basically three ways of approaching appraisal interviews (Maier, 1958).

(a) The **tell and sell** method. The manager tells the subordinate how (s)he has been assessed, and then tries to 'sell' (gain acceptance of) the evaluation and any improvement plans. This requires unusual human relations skills, in order to convey feedback in a constructive manner, and to motivate behavioural change.

(b) The **tell and listen** method. The manager tells the subordinate how (s)he has been assessed, and then invites comments. The manager therefore no longer dominates the interview throughout, and there is greater opportunity for counselling as opposed to pure direction. The employee is encouraged to participate in the assessment and the working out of improvement targets and methods. Change in the employee may not be the sole key to improvement, and the manager may receive helpful feedback about job design, methods, environment or supervision.

(c) The **problem-solving** approach. The manager abandons the role of critic altogether, and becomes a counsellor and helper. The discussion is centred not on assessment of past performance, but on future solutions to the employee's work problems. The employee is encouraged to recognise the problems, think solutions through, and commit himself to improvement. This approach is more involving and satisfying to the employee and may also stimulate creative problem-solving.

EXAMPLE

A survey of appraisal interviews given to 252 officers in a UK government department found that:

(a) Interviewers have difficulty with negative performance feedback (criticism), and tend to avoid it if possible

(b) Negative performance feedback (criticism) is, however, more likely to bring forth positive post-appraisal action, and is favourably received by appraisees, who feel it is the most useful function of the whole process, if handled frankly and constructively

(c) The most common fault of interviewers is talking too much

The survey recorded the preference of appraisees for a 'problem-solving' style of participative interview, over a one-sided 'tell and sell' style.

Many organisations waste the opportunity represented by appraisal for **upward communication**. If an organisation is development-focused, it should harness the aspirations and abilities of its employees by asking positive and thought-provoking questions such as: Could any changes be made in your job which might result in improved performance? Have you any skills, knowledge, or aptitudes which could be made better use of in the organisation?

2.5 Follow-up

After the appraisal interview, the manager may complete his or her report with an overall assessment and/or the jointly-reached conclusion of the interview, with recommendations for follow-up action. This may take the following forms.

(a) Informing appraisees of the results of the appraisal, if this has not been central to the review interview.

(b) Carrying out agreed actions on reward, training, problem-solving and so on

(c) Monitoring the appraisee's progress and checking that (s)he has carried out agreed actions or improvements

(d) Taking necessary steps to help the appraisee to attain improvement objectives, by guidance, providing feedback, upgrading equipment, altering work methods or whatever

Activity 5 (5 minutes)

What would happen if there was no follow up action?

2.6 Skills in giving feedback

Giving feedback on performance is a key leadership skill. Many people find receiving positive feedback (compliments, praise) just as hard to receive as negative feedback. However, the purpose of feedback is to help people learn by increasing their awareness of what they do, how they do it and its impact on other people. There are two main types of feedback, both of which are valuable in enhancing performance and development.

(a) *Motivational feedback* is used to reward and reinforce positive behaviours, progress performance by praising and encouraging the individual. Its purpose is to increase *confidence*.

(b) *Developmental feedback* is given when a particular area of performance needs to be changed and how this might be done. Its purpose is to increase *competence*.

'Constructive' feedback is designed to widen options and increase development. It does *not* mean giving only positive or 'encouraging' feedback about what a person did well: feedback about undesirable behaviours and their effects, given skilfully, is in many ways more useful.

The following are some brief guidelines on giving constructive developmental feedback.

(a) **Pick the time**. Feedback should be given close to the event, so that what happened is fresh in the mind – but with sensitivity as to the appropriate time, especially in the case of negative feedback. Emotions may be running high: feedback is best given calmly. There may be other people present: feedback is best given confidentially.

(b) **Start with positives**. People will more readily accept that criticism is objective and constructive if it is balanced with praise for positive aspects of their behaviour or performance.

(c) **Focus on the behaviour.** Feedback needs to refer clearly to behaviours, actions and results – *not* the person or their personality. ('Tough on the problem, soft on the person' is a good general rule.) Behavioural change may seem encouragingly possible, where personality change is discouragingly difficult. Feedback should identify the behaviours of concern: *not* 'you are lazy' but 'you have spent today dealing with personal matters on the telephone but have not completed the work you were given yesterday'.

(d) **Be precise**. Feedback needs to be specific, avoiding vague and global statements: *not* 'your timekeeping is disappointing' or 'you are always late' but 'on two occasions this week you have been more than five minutes late for meetings'.

(e) **Maintain objectivity.** Try to focus on observed behaviours, avoiding inferences and assumptions: *not* 'you obviously didn't like that client very much', but 'your manner and tone of voice with that client seemed very abrupt: you interrupted him twice'.

(f) **Gain co-operation**. It is often easier to identify your own mistakes than to have someone else point them out. Try asking people first how *they* think they acted or handled a particular situation: you may find that, in giving feedback, you are able to confirm what they are already aware of. This encourages collaborative problem-solving.

(g) **Don't tackle everything at once**! Give the person one or two priority areas to deal with at a time.

(h) **Close with encouragement**. Balance negative feedback with positive encouragement that change is possible and will be supported.

FOR DISCUSSION

Consider a situation in the past when you had to give feedback to someone about their performance or behaviour.

(a) How did you feel about it?

(b) What do you think makes giving (i) positive feedback on good performance and (ii) negative feedback on poor performance difficult for you (and others)?

In theory, systematic appraisal schemes may seem fair to the individual and worthwhile for the organisation, but in practice the system often goes wrong. Let's see how, and what can be done.

3 PROBLEMS WITH APPRAISAL SCHEMES

3.1 Problems in practice

Lockett (1992) lists a number of reasons why appraisal may not always be effective in practice.

Appraisal barriers	Comment
Appraisal as confrontation	Many people dread appraisals, or use them 'as a sort of show down, a good sorting out or a clearing of the air.' In this kind of climate: • There is a lack of agreement on performance levels. • The feedback is subjective - in other words the manager is biased, allows personality differences to get in the way of actual performance etc. • The feedback is badly delivered. • Appraisals are 'based on yesterday's performance not on the whole year'. • There is lack of attention to appraisee's development aspirations.
Appraisal as judgement	The appraisal 'is seen as a one-sided process in which the manager acts as judge, jury and counsel for the prosecution'. This puts the subordinate on the defensive. Instead, the process of performance management 'needs to be jointly operated in order to retain the commitment and develop the self-awareness of the individual.'
Appraisal as chat	The appraisal is conducted as if it were a friendly chat 'without ... purpose or outcome ... Many managers, embarrassed by the need to give feedback and set stretching targets, reduce the appraisal to a few mumbled "well dones!" and leave the interview with a briefcase of unresolved issues.'
Appraisal as bureaucracy	Appraisal is a form-filling exercise, to satisfy the personnel department. Its underlying purpose, improving individual and organisational performance, is forgotten.
Appraisal as unfinished business	Appraisal should be part of a continuing future-focused process of performance management, not a way of 'wrapping up' the past year's performance issues.

Unit 21: Human Resources Management

Appraisal barriers	Comment
Appraisal as annual event	Many targets set at annual appraisal meetings become irrelevant or out-of-date. Feedback, goal adjustment and improvement planning should be a continuous process.

Activity 6 (15 minutes)

What would you anticipate the effects of appraisal on employee motivation to be?

3.2 Evaluating appraisal

The appraisal scheme should itself be assessed (and regularly re-assessed), according to the following general criteria.

(a) **Relevance**

☐ Does the system have a useful purpose, relevant to the needs of the organisation and the individual?

☐ Is the purpose clearly expressed and widely understood by all concerned, both appraisers and appraisees?

☐ Are the appraisal criteria relevant to the purposes of the system?

(b) **Fairness**

☐ Is there reasonable standardisation of criteria and objectivity throughout the organisation?

☐ Has attention been given to the potential for direct or indirect discrimination in the criteria and methods of appraisal?

(c) **Serious intent**

☐ Are managers committed to the system – or is it just something the personnel department thrusts upon them?

☐ Who does the interviewing, and are they properly trained in interviewing and assessment techniques?

☐ Is reasonable time and attention given to the interviews – or is it a question of 'getting them over with'?

☐ Is there a genuine demonstrable link between performance and reward or opportunity for development?

(d) **Co-operation**

☐ Is the appraisal a participative, problem-solving activity – or a tool of management control?

☐ Is the appraisee given time and encouragement to prepare for the appraisal, so that he can make a constructive contribution?

☐ Does a jointly-agreed, concrete conclusion emerge from the process?

(e) **Efficiency**

☐ Is all the above achieved with a justifiable investment of time and cost?

Activity 7 **(2 hours)**

Look up the procedures manual of your organisation, and read through your appraisal procedures. Also get hold of any documentation related to them; the appraisal report form and notes, in particular.

How effective do you think your appraisal procedures are? Measure them against the criteria given above. How do you **feel** about appraisal interviews?

If you can get hold of an appraisal report form, have a go at filling one out for yourself - a good exercise in self-awareness!

---

4 PERFORMANCE MANAGEMENT

4.1 What is performance management?

Definition

Performance management is a form of management by objectives in which there is a dual emphasis: on setting key accountabilities, objectives, measures, priorities and time scales for the following review period *and* appraising performance at the end of the period.

Torrington *et al* (2002) summarise a typical performance management system as follows: Figure 6.5.

Figure 6.5: Typical performance management system

4.2 Why performance management?

'In the late 1980s the emphasis moved from performance appraisal to performance management. Whilst setting clear and measurable objectives was always a major part of earlier schemes, the emphasis was more on the appraisal of past performances'. (Connock, 1991)

Connock suggests four reasons for this shift in emphasis.

(a) Competitive pressures mean that if organisations do not improve they will not survive.

(b) It is now widely realised that strategic objectives can be more effectively implemented by linking them to individual objectives.

(c) The new focus on quality in many companies mean that quality standards have to be set or refined and this has fed through to the performance management processes.

(d) Performance-related pay is being used more and more widely. If it is to be used effectively, 'clear objectives, measures and time scales are necessary from which judgements about the individual's contribution can be made'.

There are a number of advantages to performance development.

(a) Performance management separates performance appraisal from performance-related pay awards. This takes some of the fear and inhibition out of the appraisal part of the process.

(b) Objective-setting gives employees the security and satisfaction of both understanding their jobs and knowing exactly what is expected of them. (A 1995 report by the Audit Commission, entitled '*Calling the Tune*', showed that local authorities who operated a comprehensive performance management system also scored highly in staff attitude surveys on 'know how' and 'feel good' factors. In other words, objective-setting and appraisal help staff to feel that they understand more about their work, and 'feel good' about it.)

(c) Joint-objective setting and a developmental approach are positive and participatory, encouraging regular and frequent dialogue between managers and individuals or teams, with a shared results focus, and helping employees' to accept and 'own' - commit to - change and improvement.

(d) Performance management focuses on future performance planning and improvement rather than retrospective performance appraisal, so it contributes to an output, customer and flexibility focus.

However, it should also be noted that the system depends on the integration of goal-setting, development planning, appraisal and reward planning activities – and this appears (Torrington *et al*, 2002) not to be widespread in organisations using it. Performance management is also not immune to the problems of appraisal: inconsistent use of ratings, appraiser bias, lack of training by line managers implementing the scheme and so on.

FOR DISCUSSION

Armstrong (2003) describes the purpose of performance management as follows.

'Performance management is a means of getting better results from the organisation, teams and individuals by understanding and managing performance within an agreed framework of planned goals, standards and competence requirements. It is a process for establishing shared understanding about what *is* to be achieved, and an approach to managing and developing people in a way which increases the probability that it *will* be achieved in the short and long term. It is owned and driven by line management.'

How is this different from performance appraisal? What are its implications for the HR function: recruitment, reward, training and development and its own role?

How does this work in practice?

4.3 Performance management activities

There are four key performance management activities.

- Preparation of performance agreements (also known as performance control)

- Preparation of performance and development plans

- Management of performance throughout the year

- Provision of performance reviews

Preparation of performance agreements or contracts

These set out the individual's or team's objectives, how performance will be measured (ie the performance measures to be used), the knowledge, skills and behaviour needed to achieve the objectives and the organisation's core values.

Objectives may be either:

(a) Work/operational (results to be achieved or contribution to be made to the accomplishment of team, departmental and/or organisational objectives) or

(b) Developmental (personal or learning objectives)

The following points should be borne in mind when performance measures are established.

(a) Measures used should be objective and capable of being assessed
(b) Appropriate data should be readily available
(c) If possible, existing measures should be used or adapted
(d) Measures should relate to results and not to effort
(e) Those results should be within the individual's control

Discussions between managers and individuals should ensure that individuals fully understand what is expected of them and that if they fulfil those expectations they will be regarded as having performed well.

The organisation's core values might cover quality, customer service, equal opportunities and so on.

Preparation of performance and development plans

These set out detailed performance and personal development needs and action plans to address them, in order to meet individual objectives.

Management of performance throughout the year

This involves the **continuous process** of providing feedback on performance, conducting informal progress reviews and dealing with performance problems as necessary. This may include the planning and implementation of:

(a) Training interventions, to address competence gaps or other shortfalls (or opportunities).

(b) Disciplinary action, to improve individual behaviours and attitudes.

(c) Counselling interventions, to guide individuals in defining and solving problems.

We will discuss training in detail in Section C of this Course Book. We will discuss some of the other problem-solving interventions below.

Provision of performance reviews

Performance reviews involve both taking a view of an individual's progress to date *and* reaching an agreement about what should be done in the future. The performance review provides the means by which:

(a) Results can be **measured** against targets

(b) The employee can be given **feedback**

(c) An **agreement can be reached** on on-going development needs and future performance targets

(d) The **link** between results and performance-related pay can be made

We will now look at some of the standard performance management information that may be required. The area of individual performance management is vast, and covered by a vast literature on management and leadership. In this Course Book, we are focusing on the role of HR practitioners: disciplinary and grievance handling, performance counselling and training/development planning are key tasks in this area. We cover training in detail in Part C of the Course Book (Unit 23), so we will discuss the remaining aspects briefly here.

5 DISCIPLINE

Definition

> **Discipline** can be considered as: 'a condition in an enterprise in which there is orderliness in which the members of the enterprise behave sensibly and conduct themselves according to the standards of acceptable behaviour as related to the goals of the organisation'.

'Negative' discipline is the threat of sanctions designed to make employees choose to behave in a desirable way, although this need not be a wholly negative matter. Disciplinary action may be **punitive** (punishing an offence), **deterrent** (warning people not to behave in that way) or **reformative** (calling attention to the nature of the offence so that it will not happen again). Its goal is nevertheless always to improve the future behaviour of the employee and other members of the organisation.

5.1 Types of disciplinary situations

There are many types of disciplinary situations which require attention by the manager. The most frequently occurring are:

(a) Excessive absenteeism (not coming to work, perhaps giving the excuse of ill health)

(b) Excessive lateness in arriving at work

(c) Defective and/or inadequate work performance

(d) Poor attitudes which influence the work of others or which reflect on the public image of the firm

---

Activity 8   **(15 minutes)**

Suggest five more reasons for management taking disciplinary action. (You might be able to draw on your own experience at work, school or college.)

In addition, managers might be confronted with disciplinary problems stemming from employee behaviour **off** the job: abuse of alcohol or drugs, or involvement in some form of law-breaking activity. If off-the-job conduct has an impact upon performance **on** the job, the manager must be prepared to deal with it.

5.2 Model disciplinary procedure

Many enterprises have accepted the idea of **progressive discipline**, which provides for increasing severity of the penalty with each repeated offence: a bit like the yellow card (warning), red card (sent off) system used in football. The following are the suggested steps of progressive disciplinary action.

(a) **The informal talk**

The manager simply discusses with the employee his or her behaviour in relation to the standards expected by the organisation, and tries to get a recognition that such behaviour is unacceptable, with a commitment that it will not be repeated.

(b) **Oral warning or reprimand**

The manager emphasises the undesirability of repeated violations, and warns the offender that it could lead to more serious penalties.

(c) **Written or official warning**

A written warning is a formal matter, and becomes a permanent part of the employee's record. (It may also serve as evidence in case of protest against the later dismissal of a repeated offender.)

(d) **Suspension without pay**

Disciplinary lay-offs may extend over several days or weeks, and may only be used if provided for in the contract of employment.

(e) **Dismissal**

This should be reserved for the most serious offences. For the organisation it involves waste of a labour resource, and potential loss of morale in the work team.

Under the Employment Act 2002, regulations have been developed to encourage the internal resolution of workplace disputes by introducing minimum internal discipline and grievance procedures. The regulations (effective from 1 October 2004) require a standard three step procedure:

- The parties must put the issue in writing

- The parties must meet to discuss the issue (accompanied by a trade union or staff association representative if desired)

- An appeal must be held if required

Steps must be taken without unreasonable delay; the timing and location of meetings must be reasonable; parties must be able to explain their cases; and the employer's representative at appeals should be more senior than the representative who attended the first meeting.

Failure to complete this basic procedure will make any subsequent dismissal of the employee on disciplinary grounds unfair.

This is a statutory minimum requirement. Employers should still take notice of the guidance given by the ACAS (Advisory, Conciliation and Arbitration Service) Code of Practice 2002. (This is also due to be revised: watch this space!)

Good disciplinary procedures should:

- Be in writing

- Specify to whom they apply

- Be non-discriminatory

- Provide for matters to be dealt with without undue delay

- Provide for proceedings, witness statements and records to be kept confidential

- Indicate the disciplinary actions which may be taken

- Specify the levels of management which have the authority to take the various forms of disciplinary action

- Provide for workers to be informed of the complaints against them and where possible all relevant evidence before any hearing

- Provide workers with an opportunity to state their case before decisions are reached

- Provide workers with the right to be accompanied

- Ensure that, except for gross misconduct, no worker is dismissed for a first breach of discipline

- Ensure that disciplinary action is not taken until the case has been carefully investigated

- Ensure that workers are given an explanation for any penalty imposed

- Provide a right of appeal – normally to a more senior manager – and specify the procedure to be followed

---

FOR DISCUSSION

How (a) accessible and (b) clear are the rules and policies of your college: do people really know what they are and are not supposed to do? Have a look at the student regulations. How easy is it to see them – or were you referred elsewhere? Are they well-indexed and cross-referenced, and in language that all students will understand?

How (a) accessible and (b) clear are the disciplinary procedures? Who is responsible for discipline?

The crucial interpersonal event in disciplinary action will be the interview. The following advice takes into account both procedural guidelines and interpersonal issues.

5.3 Disciplinary interviews

Preparation for the disciplinary interview will include the following.

(a) Gathering facts about the alleged infringement.

(b) Determination of the organisation's position: how valuable is the employee, potentially? How serious are his offences/lack of progress? How far is the organisation prepared to go to help him improve or discipline him further?

(c) Identification of the aims of the interview: punishment? deterrent to others? problem-solving? Specific standards for future behaviour/performance need to be determined.

(d) Notification of the employee concerned, with time to prepare for the disciplinary interview. (The Employment Relations Act 1999 provides that employees involved in 'serious cases' may be represented by a fellow employee or trade union representative.

The disciplinary interview will then proceed as follows.

Step 1. The manager will explain the purpose of the interview.

Step 2. The charges against the employee will be delivered, clearly, unambiguously and without personal emotion.

Step 3. The manager will explain the organisation's position with regard to the issues involved: disappointment, concern, need for improvement, impact on others. This can be done frankly - but tactfully, with as positive an emphasis as possible on the employee's capacity and responsibility to improve.

Step 4. The organisation's expectations with regard to future behaviour/performance should be made clear.

Step 5. The employee should be given the opportunity to comment, explain, justify or deny. If he is to approach the following stage of the interview in a positive way, he must not be made to feel 'hounded' or hard done by.

Step 6. The organisation's expectations should be reiterated, or new standards of behaviour set for the employee.

   (i)   They should be specific and quantifiable, performance related and realistic.

   (ii) They should be related to a practical but reasonably short time period. A date should be set to review his progress.

   (iii) The manager agrees on measures to help the employee should that be necessary. It would demonstrate a positive approach if, for example, a mentor were appointed from his work group to help him check his work. If his poor performance is genuinely the result of some difficulty or distress outside work, other help (temporary leave, counselling or financial aid) may be appropriate.

Step 7. The manager should explain the reasons behind any penalties imposed on the employee, including the entry in his personnel record of the formal warning. He should also explain how the warning can be removed from the record, and what standards must be achieved within a specified timescale. There should be a clear warning of the consequences of failure to meet improvement targets.

Step 8. The manager should explain the organisation's appeals procedures: if the employee feels he has been unfairly treated, there should be a right of appeal to a higher manager.

Step 9. Once it has been established that the employee understands all the above, the manager should summarise the proceedings briefly.

Records of the interview will be kept for the employee's personnel file, and for the formal follow-up review and any further action necessary.

6   GRIEVANCE

Definition

A **grievance** occurs when an individual feels that (s)he is being wrongly treated by a colleague or supervisor: picked on, unfairly appraised or blocked for promotion, or discriminated against on grounds of race or sex.

6.1   Purpose of a grievance procedure

When an individual has a grievance he should be able to pursue it and ask to have the problem resolved. Some grievances should be capable of solution informally by the individual's manager. However, if an informal solution is not possible, there should be a formal grievance procedure:

(a)   To allow objective grievance handling – including 'cooling off' periods and independent case investigation and arbitration

(b)   To protect employees from victimisation – particularly where a grievance involves their immediate superiors

(c)   To provide legal protection for both parties, in the event of a dispute resulting in claims before an Employment Tribunal

(d)   To encourage grievance airing – which is an important source of feedback to management on employee problems and dissatisfactions

(e)   To require full and fair investigation of grievances, enabling the employer-employee relationship to be respected and preserved, despite problems

6.2   Grievance procedures

Formal grievance procedures, like disciplinary procedures, should be set out in **writing** and made available to all staff. These procedures should do the following things.

(a) State what **grades of employee** are entitled to pursue a particular type of grievance.

(b) **Distinguish between individual grievances and collective grievances** (which might be pursued through industrial relations processes).

(c) State the **rights of the employee** for each type of grievance: what actions and remedies may be claimed.

(d) State what the **procedures for pursuing a grievance** should be. They will typically involve appeal in the first instance to the line manager (or next level up, if the line manager is the subject of the complaint). If the matter cannot be resolved, the case will be referred to specified higher authorities. The assistance of the HR department may be required.

(e) Allow for the employee to be accompanied by a trade union or staff association representative or other colleague.

(f) **State time limits** for initiating certain grievance procedures and subsequent stages of them, such as appeals and communication of outcomes.

(g) **Require written records** of all meetings concerned with the case to be made and distributed to all the participants.

(h) Provide for right of appeal, and specify the appeals procedure.

As with disciplinary action, the focus of conflict resolution will be in an interview between the manager and the subordinate.

6.3 Grievance interviews

The dynamics of a grievance interview are broadly similar to a disciplinary interview, except that it is the **subordinate** who primarily wants a positive result or improvement in someone else's behaviour.

Prior to the interview, the manager should have some idea of the complaint and its possible source. The meeting itself can then proceed through the following stages.

Step 1. **Exploration**. What is the problem: the background, the facts, the causes (obvious and hidden)? At this stage the manager should simply try to gather as much information as possible, without attempting to suggest solutions or interpretations: the situation must be seen to be open.

Step 2. **Consideration**. The manager should:

- Check the facts

- Analyse the causes – the problem of which the complaint may be only a symptom

- Evaluate options for responding to the complaint, and the implication of any response made

It may be that information can be given to clear up a misunderstanding, or the employee will withdraw his complaint – having 'got it off his chest'. However, the meeting may have to be adjourned (say, for 48 hours) while the manager gets extra information and considers extra options.

Step 3. **Reply**. The manager, having reached and reviewed various conclusions, reconvenes the meeting to convey (and justify, if required) his or her decision, hear counter-arguments and appeals. The outcome (agreed or disagreed) should be recorded in writing.

NOTES

7   PERFORMANCE COUNSELLING

Where problems are identified in an individual's performance – whether through annual appraisal or on-going monitoring – a line manager may need to intervene.

7.1   Reasons for poor performance

Not all performance problems will be disciplinary in nature, or due to training/competence gaps. Other factors the manager may need to consider include:

(a)   Job changes which have left the job-holder less suited for the work

(b)   Personality factors or clashes with team members

(c)   Factors outside the work situation (eg marital or financial problems)

(d)   Problems with job design, work layout, management style and other factors outside the individual's own control

7.2   Performance counselling process

A basic three-step process for dealing with poor performers may be as follows.

In order to deal with the issue, the following four-step process could be implemented.

(a)   Counsel the individual through a basic problem-solving process.

   (i)   **The facts.** The manager should help the individual to accept and define the problem, through constructive feedback and supportive questioning.

   (ii)   **The causes.** The individual and the manager should explore and agree on the causes of the problem. A collaborative, problem-solving orientation is needed.

   (iii)   **The remedies.** The individual and the manager should explore and agree on the remedies to the problem. Some of these might relate to the individual, such as presentation, or completion of work by deadlines. The manager might have to take responsibility for some remedial action.

(b)   Ensure the individual understands the consequences of persistent poor performance, where relevant; this might involve invoking the firm's disciplinary procedures.

(c)   Set and agree clear improvement targets and action plans.

(d)   Agree a period of time over which performance is expected to improve.

(e)   Support the individual with agreed follow-up action: training, coaching, specialist counselling and so on.

NOTES

Workplace counselling, and the skills involved, will be considered further in Chapter 11 of this Course Book.

Chapter roundup

- Performance appraisal is the process whereby an individual's performance is reviewed against previously agreed goals, and where new goals are agreed which will develop the individual and improve performance over the forthcoming review period.

- Trends in appraisal include: the use of behavioural and results-oriented appraisal criteria; the use of multiple sources of feedback; and a problem-solving approach to interviewing.

- 360° feedback is designed to enable all the stakeholders in a person's performance to comment and give feedback.

- Performance management is a recent approach which emphasises *both* defining the knowledge, skills, behaviours and standards required to produce the desired results *and* the appraisal and comparison of performance against objectives for the purposes of on-going performance improvement. It is a forward-looking, on-going and collaborative approach.

- Performance management interventions which may be required to address identified problems in an individual's performance include:

  o disciplinary action, to address problems of behaviour or attitude: a model procedure is set out in the ACAS Code of Practice

  o grievance procedures, to address workplace conflicts

  o performance counselling, to investigate and collaboratively attempt to solve a range of performance problems

  o training and development planning (discussed in Part C of this Course Book)

Quick quiz

1 What are the purposes of appraisal?

2 What bases or criteria of assessment might an appraisal system use?

3 What is 360-degree feedback?

4 What follow-up should there be after an appraisal?

5 Distinguish between motivational and developmental feedback.

6 What kinds of criticism might be levelled at appraisal schemes by a manager who thought they were a waste of time?

7 How can appraisal be made more positive and empowering to employees?

8 What is the difference between performance appraisal and performance management?

9 What are the four key performance management stages?

10 Distinguish between discipline and grievance.

Answers to quick quiz

1   Identifying performance levels, improvements needed and promotion prospects; deciding on rewards; assessing team work and encouraging, communication between manager and employee.   (see paragraph 1.1)

2   Job analysis, job description, plans, targets and standards.   (para 2.1)

3   Appraisal by all the stakeholders in a person's performance.   (para 2.3)

4   Appraisees should be informed of the results, agreed activities should be taken, progress should be monitored and whatever resources or changes are needed should be provided or implemented.   (para 2.5)

5   Motivational: used to reward and reinforce positive behaviour, increase confidence.

   Developmental: given in order to guide and motivate change and improvement, to increase competence.   (para 2.6)

6   The manager may say that he or she has better things to do with his or her time, that appraisals have no relevance to the job and there is no reliable follow-up action, and that they involve too much paperwork.

   (para 3.1)

7   Ensure the scheme is relevant, fair, taken seriously and co-operative.
   (para 3.2)

8   Appraisal is a backward-looking performance review. Performance management is a forward-looking results-orientated scheme.   (para 4.1)

9   Preparation of performance agreements or contracts, preparation of performance/development plans; on-going management of performance; performance reviews.   (para 4.3)

10   Discipline is the 'downward' process whereby a manager addresses the behaviours or performance of an employee which do not meet the firm's standards. Grievance is the 'upward' process by which employees can appeal to higher authority to address problems or conflicts affecting them.   (sections 5 and 6)

Answers to activities

1   Disadvantages to the individual of not having an appraisal system include the following. The individual is not aware of progress or shortcomings, is unable to judge whether s/he would be considered for promotion, is unable to identify or correct weaknesses by training and there is a lack of communication with the manager.

2   You will have come up with your own examples of criteria to assess some jobs but not others. You might have identified such things as:

(a)   Numerical ability (applicable to accounts staff, say, more than to customer contact staff or other non-numerical functions)

(b)   Ability to drive safely (essential for transport workers – not for desk-bound ones)

(c)   Report-writing (not applicable to manual labour, say)

(d)   Creativity and initiative (desirable in areas involving design and problem-solving not routine or repetitive jobs in mass production or bureaucratic organisations)

3   Problems with upward appraisal include fear of reprisals or vindictiveness (or extra form-processing). Some bosses in strong positions might feel able to refuse to act on results, even if a consensus of staff suggested that they should change their ways.

4   Drawbacks to 360-degree appraisal include:

   (a)   Respondents' reluctance to give negative feedback to a boss – or friend

   (b)   The suspicion that management is passing the buck for negative feedback, getting people to 'rat' on their friends

   (c)   The feeling that the appraisee is being picked on, if positive feedback is not carefully balanced with the negative

5   If follow-up action is not taken, employees will feel that appraisal is all talk and just a waste of time, and that improvement action on their side will not be appreciated or worthwhile.

6   The effects of appraisal on motivation are a tricky issue.

   (a)   Feedback on performance is regarded as vital in motivation, because it enables an employee to make calculations about the amount of effort required in future to achieve objectives and rewards. Even negative feedback can have this effect – and is more likely to spur the employee on to post-appraisal action.

   (b)   Agreement of challenging but attainable targets for performance or improvement also motivates employees by clarifying goals and the value (and 'cost' in terms of effort) of incentives offered.

   (c)   A positive approach to appraisal allows employees to solve their work problems and apply creative thinking to their jobs.

   However, people rarely react well to criticism – especially at work, where they may feel that their reward or even job security is on the line. In addition, much depends on the self-esteem of the appraisee. If s(he) has a high self-image, (s)he may be impervious to criticism. If s(he) has a low self-image, (s)he may be depressed rather than motivated by criticism.

7   This research activity, if you tackle it systematically and record your answers (or prepare them as a presentation), will help you to gather evidence of your competence in Assessment Criteria 21.3

8   Reasons for disciplinary action might include:

   (a)   Breaking rules regarding rest periods and other time schedules, such as leaving work to go home early.

   (b)   Improper personal appearance or dress.

   (c)   Breaking safety rules, such as failing to observe fire regulations, failing to wear protective clothing and so on.

   (d)   Other violations of rules, regulations and procedures, such as smoking in a non-smoking office, or abuse of expenses claims.

   (e)   Open insubordination: refusal to carry out a legitimate order.

   (f)   Fighting, sexual harassment, racial abuse or other forms of unacceptable conflict.

9   Assuming you did do something about your grievance, you probably found there were various stages of the procedure. Hopefully the first and

second stages were sufficient to solve the problem, but you may have felt that the procedure was too cumbersome or long-winded.

Assignment 6   (1¹/₂ hours)

Biotherm plc

You are the Personnel Director for Biotherm PLC, a detergent and washing powder manufacturer based in Bootle, Merseyside. You have a staff of nine reporting to you, from junior clerks to senior managers, and you are just preparing for the annual round of appraisal interviews. One of your senior personnel officers, Alan Heath, has become a real problem child of late. You have never particularly warmed to this individual; he never really seems part of the team, his attendance record is poor and he never works beyond contracted hours. You know that Alan is not especially fit and healthy, but you rather feel he is playing on his physical condition.

You would describe yourself as a 'person-oriented' leader, although you acknowledge that with difficult staff you tend to become *laissez faire*. This has been the case with Alan: you have never tackled him on his absence record (29 days sickness in the past year) nor on his desire to work to contract. Apart from yourself, he is the only person with extensive and detailed knowledge of employment law, which is valuable in your organisational environment. You secretly admit that this is the main reason for your reticence in handling him: in spite of his difficult demeanour you would be lost without him.

However, you must now grasp the nettle and deal with the situation at his appraisal interview. Prepare a plan for the interview which not only reviews his past performance but also proposes a set of acceptable objectives for the forthcoming year. Remember that your meeting should not, if possible, degenerate into a disciplinary case! Your plan should be organised according to the following headings:

—   Assessment of performance

—   How to improve current performance

—   How to motivate Alan Heath

—   How to assess him for promotability

—   How to tackle unsatisfactory performance areas

Throughout this plan, you should anticipate questions, issues and objectives which he will raise, and resolve how to deal with them.

Chapter 7:
EXIT RIGHTS AND PROCEDURES

Introduction

So far, this Course Book has covered some of the processes by which the human resource is managed as it moves into and through or within the organisation. In this chapter, we look at some of the ways in which it must be managed on its way **out** of the organisation.

The exit of employees from the organisation requires careful management because of:

(a)　The need for compliance with the legal framework on employment protection (particularly in regard to dismissal and redundancy)

(b)　The need for sensitivity to the human issues involved (since the employment relationship, work and competence are so central to people's sense of their role and value in life)

(c)　The need for the organisation to gather feedback from voluntarily departing employees (resigners or early retirers) in order to identify retention problems

We will consider these aspects in the context of each type of exit.

As you read through this Course Book, which covers the law and regulations on various employment-related issues, remember: 'The law is a floor'. It sets minimum standards below which no organisational practice may fall without penalties. It does not set out 'best practice'. Personnel managers should ask themselves 'What *must* we do?' (compliance) – but also 'What *should* we do and what *can* we do to enhance business performance *and* employee satisfaction?'

Your objectives

In this chapter you will learn about the following.

(a) The role and operation of Employment Tribunals

(b) Various form so termination of employment: resignation, retirement and termination of employment

(c) Wrongful, unfair and justified dismissal of employees

(d) The nature and procedures of redundancy

(e) Issues in the equitable and responsible management of exit

1 TERMINATION OF EMPLOYMENT

1.1 Termination of the employment contract

As we discussed in Chapter 4, the formation of a contract signals the beginning of an employment relationship. That relationship is **finite**: it comes to an end.

Contracts of employment can be 'terminated' in the following ways.

(a) **By performance**

The employee does what he or she was hired to do, and the employer gives the agreed payment or consideration: the contract is fulfilled. This is common in fixed-term contracts and contracts for specific services. (It may also be said to apply in the case of retirement, where there is an agreed age at which employment ends.)

(b) **By mutual agreement**

Both parties can agree that they are entitled to terminate the contract at any time, say in the event of 'irreconcilable differences'.

(c) **By notice**

One party can terminate the contract, but must give adequate notice or warning to the other. This happens in the case of:

(i) Resignation by the employee
(ii) Dismissal of the employee
(iii) Redundancy

There are strict rules on the periods of notice which must be given to protect both parties: we will cover them in this chapter.

(d) **Breach of contract**

If one party 'breaks' or fails to fulfil the terms of the contract, the other party has the option of considering the contract to have been terminated. (In addition, he or she may seek legal remedies to compensate for, or minimise the effects of, the breach.) Failure by the employer to pay the agreed wage, or gross misconduct by the employee, would be in breach of the implied terms of the employment contract, for example.

(e) **Frustration**

A contract is 'frustrated' when it is prevented from being fulfilled – for example, because of the death, illness or imprisonment of one of the parties.

Activity 1 (20 minutes)

(a) Alan countersigns his employment contract and written statement with Sheerbrow Ltd but after two weeks is told that the holiday entitlement of four weeks per annum as stated in the particulars should have read three weeks, as was originally agreed. What can he do?

(b) Anita was engaged for a two-year period as sub-editor of a newspaper. Six months later, however, the publishers sold the newspaper and ceased to publish it. What has happened to Anita's contract?

(c) Ambrose attended a selection interview for a job due to begin on September 1. The interviewer said he was impressed with Ambrose's CV; he felt that Ambrose was an ideal candidate, and he would get back to him as soon as possible after the selection process was finished. Owing to confusion in the personnel department, no-one subsequently contacted Ambrose. Ambrose turned up to work on September 1, and (owing to further confusion in the personnel department) put in a day's work before it was realised that he was not, in fact, the successful candidate! The company told Ambrose to leave, and refused to pay him for the day's work. What can Ambrose do?

We will now go on to look at the HR department's role in managing the termination of employment contracts, looking in particular at the legislative and managerial frameworks that influence policy in this area. We will start by looking at employee-side reasons for leaving: retirement and resignation

1.2 Retirement

The average age of the working population has been steadily increasing, with higher standards of living and health care. The problems of older workers, and the difficulties of adjusting to retirement, are therefore commanding more attention. The time at which an individual will experience difficulties in obtaining or retaining jobs because of age will obviously vary according to the individual, his/her lifestyle and occupation, and the attitudes of his/her society and employers.

There are two basic approaches to retirement policy

(a) **Flexible retirement,** whereby a stated retirement age is a minimum age at which the contract can be ended for retirement purposes: fit and capable employees are allowed to continue to work after this age.

(b) **Fixed retirement,** whereby retirement is enforced at the stated age.

Organisations currently set their own normal retirement ages, beyond which employees are not entitled to sue for unfair dismissal: these are often set some years below the statutory pension age (SPA). The DTI has launched a consultation paper to alter this. The UK has to implement EU directives by 2006, outlining discrimination on the basis of age – including at the time of retirement. A recent CIPD survey (*Age, Pensions and Retirement,* 2003) suggests that, of employees in their fifties, 31% want to work beyond the age of 60, and 80% do not want to retire formally. Soon it will be unlawful to insist that they do.

There are various arguments for delaying or enforcing the retirement of older workers.

Disadvantages of retaining older workers	Advantages of retaining older workers
• There is resistance to late retirement from younger workers, because it is felt that promotion opportunities are being blocked.	• Older workers are still capable of non-strenuous work, and may be particularly valuable in jobs requiring mature judgement, conscientiousness, attention to detail or experience.
• Younger employees with family responsibilities have a greater need for job security: in the event of downsizing, workers nearing retirement should be selected first for redundancy.	• They may make a great contribution to the training and coaching of more junior staff.
• The age structure of an organisation may become unbalanced for future work requirements: there may have to be an injection of 'younger blood'.	• There is some evidence that older workers create greater labour stability. • An organisation may perceive age to be an equal opportunity/ discrimination issue: this is due to be enacted in UK law in the next few years.
• Engaging staff above middle age can be costly for the organisation: the cost of providing pensions rises according to the age at which the employee joins a superannuation scheme.	• There may be specific skill shortages among young people which necessitate the recruitment and retention of older workers.
• Individual mental and/or physical shortcomings may render an older individual unfit to carry out his or her duties efficiently.	• The government wishes to support people remaining economically active, in order to defuse pressures on pension provision from the aging population.

How far any of the above factors apply will depend to a large extent on the individual concerned, the type of work involved, the state of the local labour market and government intervention on retirement ages and pension eligibility. Retirement policies, and age limits on particular posts will have to be clearly communicated; and decisions regarding particular cases discussed confidentially and tactfully with the individual concerned. Written confirmation of the decision to retire an employee should likewise be tactful, with expressions of regret and appreciation as appropriate. Whatever is done should be done carefully, because the way an organisation treats its retiring workers sends powerful messages to its other employees, and the labour market.

Social responsibility also dictates that the needs of older workers be taken into account. Ball (2003) notes that retirement is hard for people, because:

(a) Many people have insufficient non-state retirement income than they planned, because of the poor performance of pension funds in recent years

(b) Work has a team/social element, which means a lot to people

(c) Work is a primary source of identity – particularly for managers, who have worked longer and longer hours over the past decade

(d) The norm is still to go from full-time work to total retirement (rather than preparing people through flexible or part-time working).

NOTES

Activity 2   **(10 minutes)**

Employers can give not only financial assistance to retiring employees, but also practical help and advice. Suggest three ways in which the HR department could help older employees.

It should be noted that the Sex Discrimination Act 1986 introduced an equal retirement age for men and women. **Employers** setting a compulsory retirement age must apply it to men and women alike: women made to retire earlier than male colleagues can claim both discrimination and unfair dismissal. At present the State retirement age (the age at which the individual is entitled to a State pension) is 65 for men and 60 for women.

EXAMPLE

The NHS has introduced a flexible retirement policy, made available to GPs in November 2002:

'This sits within a suite of flexible working policies designed to help improve productivity, developed by Debbie Mellor, head of employment. It encourages highly trained, highly skilled staff – who would otherwise leave – to remain within the service or return later, on flexible contracts …

'Unsurprisingly, Mellor says initial feedback suggests the intrinsic reward of the job features highly in doctors' motivations to say on. "You don't go into the NHS simply to make lots of money like in the City. Many [doctors] feel their contribution to patient care can continue to offer great benefits to local communities and they are keen to remain active and use their skills for as long as possible. As one of them put it: 'There's only so much golf you can play'."

'Mellor says performance management is paramount. "[Training] co-ordinators are in place to ensure that the pathway back to practice fits with an individual's training and development requirements." Alan Trickett, 67, is about to return as a GP after four years of retirement and says: "We live in an age of audit in every professional walk of life and we [doctors] should be no different." He cites cheaper, non-branded drugs as an area he must swot up on. "One of the most important aspects of being a GP is listening very carefully to patients and I think that is something which can often improve with age," he says.'

(Ball, 2003)

You may like to check out www.agepositive.gov.uk for more information.

1.3 Resignation

Definition

Resignation is the process by which an employee gives notice of his or her intention to terminate the employment contract.

Employees may resign for any number of reasons, personal or occupational. Some or all of these reasons may well be a reflection on the structure, management style, culture or personnel policies of the organisation itself. Management should attempt to find the real

BPP
PROFESSIONAL EDUCATION

reasons why an employee is leaving in an **exit interview,** which may provide helpful feedback on its policies and practices: note, however, that there is no legal requirement for the employee to give reasons for leaving.

The principal aspect of any policy formulated to deal with resignations must be the length to which the organisation will go to try to dissuade a person from leaving. In some cases, the organisation may decide to simply let the person go, but when an employee has been trained at considerable cost to the firm, is particularly well qualified and experienced, or has knowledge of information and methods that should not fall into the hands of competitors, the organisation may try to keep him or her. Particular sources of employee dissatisfaction (eg salary) *may* sometimes be resolved, but there are dangers in setting precedents by giving special treatment.

Various arrangements will have to be made when an employee decides to leave. There will have to be co-operation and full exchange of information between the HR function and the leaver's immediate superior, so that procedures can begin when notice is given of an intended departure.

(a)   If attempts to make the employee stay have been unsuccessful, the exit interview will have to be arranged.

(b)   The period of notice required for the employee to leave should be set out in his/her contract of employment, but some leeway may be negotiated on this, for example if the employee wishes to take up another position immediately. The statutory minimum notice period (Employment Rights Act 1996) is one week.

(c)   Details of the departure have to be notified to the wages clerk, pension fund officer, social secretary, security officer and so on, so that the appropriate paperwork and other procedures can be completed by his/her date of leaving. The organisation may have a departure checklist to ensure that all procedures are completed.

(d)   The departmental head and/or supervisor should complete a leaving report form: an overall assessment of the employee's performance in the organisation. This can then be used to provide references to his/her future employer(s).

It should be noted that during the notice period, all terms and conditions of the employment contract still apply: the employee still owes the employer duties of fidelity, obedience and care, while the employer still owes the employee duties of trust, care and provision of work. If there is any doubt that this kind of relationship will be possible during the notice period, due to the circumstances or feelings, surrounding the resignation, it may be advisable to let the employee leave immediately with pay in lieu of notice: this may prevent loss of morale in the team from a disgruntled employee's behaviour, and indeed possible sabotage of work or customer relations by the outgoing employee, gathering of information for use by the new (competing) employer and so on.

Activity 3	(30 minutes)

Brainstorm:

(a)   Some reasons for resigning from a job

(b)   Some procedures that might be included on an Employee Departure Checklist

Of course, not everybody leaves their organisation on a 'voluntary' basis. Where employees are required to leave employment, there is a clearer need to protect their rights and livelihoods against injustice or exploitation by employers. After all, people may be 'resources' and 'assets' – but they are not 'things'. This is where employment protection legislation comes into force. We will start by looking at the key bodies enforcing employee rights.

2 EMPLOYMENT TRIBUNALS

Definition

> **Employment tribunals** are independent judicial bodies which arbitrate in employment matters including unfair dismissal, employment protection and claims in relation to sexual/racial discrimination and equal pay.

2.1 The composition of tribunals

The composition of an employment tribunal is governed by the Employment Tribunals Act (ETA) 1996. A tribunal usually has three members:

- a legally-qualified chairperson (solicitor or barrister)
- an employer representative
- an employee representative (usually from a trade union)

2.2 The powers of tribunals

Tribunals have powers to hear disputes or claims, and to:

(a)   Order the disclosure and inspection of documents, or otherwise demand information relevant to the claim

(b)   Set timescales for compliance with information requests

(c)   Strike out applications and/or award costs, if a party does not comply with a directive order, or conducts proceedings in a disruptive or abusive fashion

(d)   Make legally binding decisions and orders (eg to reinstate an employee who has been unfairly dismissed) and award compensation payments, within the boundaries of employment legislation.

In effect, the tribunal is a court, with jurisdiction in a wide range of matters derived from relevant statutory provisions.

The *Employment Appeal Tribunal (EAT)* hears appeals on the decisions of Employment Tribunals, but only on matters of law – not disputed facts of the case.

2.3 Tribunal procedures

A case is initiated when an employee presents an application, specifying the persons against whom relief is sought and the grounds on which it is sought.

The application is registered, and a copy is sent to the respondent in the case, and to ACAS. Either party to the case (or the tribunal itself) may then require:

(a)   That the case go through mediation and/or arbitration by ACAS

(b)   That a preliminary hearing may be held to consider the merits of the case before proceeding to a full hearing

(c)   That the other party provide further or better particulars of any facts or contentions relevant to the claim, so that both parties are clear in advance what the nature of the case is. The tribunal may enforce this with orders for the disclosure and inspection of documents.

If the case proceeds to a full hearing, both parties must gather witnesses and documentation to support their case. Employees may be represented by a lawyer, trade union representative or other person of their choice: if they do not have a representative, the tribunal will assist them as far as possible (without bias) to comply with proper procedure.

At the hearing, witnesses are heard, or witness statements read out, and may be cross-examined by the other side and questioned by the tribunal.

Tribunal members then withdraw to consider their decision. If the employee is successful, further submissions may be made in regard to compensation or other forms of relief to be awarded.

2.4   Watch this space

The Employment Act 2002 contains a number of changes in relation to Employment Tribunals, due for implementation during 2004. These include:

- Providing for swifter, more efficient delivery of Tribunal services (including the redrafting of standard forms; the mandatory use of standard forms; the issuing of practice directors to ensure consistency of approach)

- Encouraging internal resolution of workplace disputes, by strengthening disciplinary and grievance procedures

- Paving the way to introduce a 'stay of proceedings' to allow conciliation by ACAS

Activity 4

You are the Personnel Assistant of a small company. The Personnel Manager comes to you with a copy of an 'ET1' form (an originating application) by a former employee, sent to the Employment Tribunal claiming unfair dismissal, and an 'ET3' form (a blank 'notice of appearance' form) which he has 21 days to complete.

'I have no idea what this means!' he says. 'Why have these been sent to me? What happens now?'

Write a memo with your answer.

3   DISMISSAL

3.1   Dismissal

An individual can be legally dismissed in three ways.

- His or her employment is terminated with notice, or without notice (eg where someone is dismissed summarily for gross misconduct).

- He or she is employed under a fixed-term contract which comes to an end and is not renewed on the same terms.

- He or she resigns (with or without notice) because of 'conduct [on the part of the employer] which is a significant breach of the contract of employment or which shows that the employer no longer intends to be bound by one or more of the essential terms of the contract' *(Western Excavating v Sharp 1978)*. This is known as 'constructive dismissal'.

Dismissal with notice

The Employment Rights Act sets out detailed requirements to:

(a) The statutory minimum period of notice that must be given (depending on length of service and contract terms)

(b) Rights to waive notice periods, or accept payment in lieu

(c) Rights to explanation of reasons for dismissal

(d) Definitions of 'length of service' and 'continuous employment' (which quality employees for many of the rights established by the Act) in regard to hours of work, periods of absence and transfer of the undertaking

Dismissal without notice

In most cases, the statutory and/or contractual minimum notice of dismissal must be given to the employee. However, rare circumstances may justify 'summary' dismissal without notice. The law protecting employees from unfair dismissal (discussed below) requires that summary dismissal be limited to cases of serious breach of contract, such as:

(a) Gross misconduct by the employee: theft, violence, serious refusal to obey reasonable instruction, endangerment of other staff

(b) Serious neglect of duties, or absence from work without permission or good cause

(c) Serious breaches of trust or conflicts of interest affecting the organisation's business

Even then, with the onus on employers to justify fair dismissal, an organisation may prefer to use temporary suspension and other disciplinary measures, or dismissal by notice (with pay in lieu of notice if the employee must be removed immediately from the workplace).

FOR DISCUSSION

Debate for and against the proposition.

'An employer should have the right to fire incompetent, incompatible and dishonest employees without costly restrictions and red tape.'

Dismissal is clearly a bit of a political, legal and interpersonal minefield! Fortunately there are two relatively clear definitions of circumstances in which an employee cannot legally be dismissed.

3.2 Wrongful dismissal

A claim for **wrongful dismissal** is open to employees at **common law**, if they can show they were dismissed in *breach of contract* (for example, with less than the required notice) and that he or she thereby suffered loss. He/she may then be able to claim damages compensating for the amount lost: accrued wages, payment for an entitlement to notice, or the balance of wages due under a fixed-term contract. In practice, such claims are less common now that **unfair** dismissal provisions offer wider remedies, but the common law remedy is still useful for those who cannot claim unfair dismissal (for example, because they have not been continuously employed for long enough to qualify).

Wrongful dismissal claims are taken to Employment Tribunals if they are for less than £25,000, and to the county court for larger sums.

Wrongful dismissal is compensated under common law – but only to the amount lost by the employee. Employment protection legislation has widened the scope of protection and increased the range of remedies available. The concept of 'unfair dismissal' is an extremely important element of this legislation.

3.3 Unfair dismissal

Under the Employment Rights Act 1996 (and 1999 amendments) an employee currently has the right not to be unfairly dismissed if (s)he:

(a) Is under the normal retiring age applicable to his/her job, or under 65 (likely to be extended under forthcoming age discrimination legislation)

(b) Has been continuously employed for 12 months (whether full-time or part-time) (ERA 1999)

(c) Lodges a claim with the tribunal office within three months of the date of dismissal

Dismissal will *automatically* be deemed justified or unfair in the following cases.

Dismissal is justified where related to:	Dismissal is unfair where related to:
(a) **Redundancy** (provided that the selection for redundancy was fair).	(a) **Redundancy** where the selection is deemed unfair.
(b) **Legal impediment** – eg loss of driving licence or lack of work permit	(b) **Trade union membership** (actual or proposed) and activities, or **refusal** to join a trade union.
(c) Incapability (including ill health) or lack of **qualifications**.	(c) **Pregnancy**, maternity, or exercising rights to time off for dependant care or parental leave.
(d) **Misconduct**, provided that minimum disciplinary procedures have been followed (Employment Act 2002).	(d) **Spent conviction** under the Rehabilitation of Offenders Act 1974.
(e) Some other '**substantial**' **reason**: for example, the employee marries a competitor, or refuses to accept a reorganisation made in the interests of the business and with the agreement of other employees.	(e) **Transfer of the undertaking** (unless there are ETO – 'economic, technical or organisational' – reasons justifying it).

Dismissal is justified where related to:	Dismissal is unfair where related to:
	(f) **Assertion of a statutory right** (eg under Equal Pay, Working Time Regulations or Minimum Wage provisions).
	(g) **Participation in official industrial action**, within the first eight weeks (Employment Relations Act 1999).
	(h) **Refusal to work on a Sunday** (shop or betting workers).
	(i) **Disclosure of information believed to expose malpractice, injustice or health and safety dangers** ('whistle blowing') – under the Public Interest Disclosure Act 1998.
	(j) Carrying out **duties as a safety representative** or **pension fund trustee**.
	(k) **Discrimination** (on grounds of sex, marital status, sex change, race, disability or part-time status).

3.4 Remedies for unfair dismissal

An employee who believes (s)he has been unfairly dismissed may present a complaint to an Employment Tribunal, within three months of dismissal.

Before a case comes to tribunal, ACAS will often try to help the parties reach a settlement, rather than proceed to a full tribunal hearing.

In order to defend such a claim successfully, the employer must show:

(a) That the real or principal reason for the dismissal was one of the justifiable reasons listed above, or was otherwise a '**substantial reason** of a kind such as to justify the dismissal of an employee' (rather than some lesser action) and

(b) That it was '*reasonable*' to dismiss in all the circumstances of the case (including any mitigating circumstances on behalf of the employee)

(c) That a '*fair procedure*' was followed, eg in regard to warnings, investigation, appeals, acting in good faith and attempting lesser disciplinary measures where relevant and possible.

Points (b) and (c) highlight the importance of HR policy and practice – particularly disciplinary and grievance procedures (discussed in Chapter 6).

Activity 5 (20 minutes)

All other criteria being met, would the following cases be fair or unfair?

(a) Bernie is a van-driver for a carrier firm. After a number of driving infringements in his own car and in his own time – ie not on the job – Bernie has lost his driving licence. The carrier firm dismisses him.

(b) Berenice is a shop manageress, but after an period when it has been observed that she leaves the shop dirty and untidy, fails to maintain cash registers and does not put stock away, the chain of shops dismisses her.

(c) Bernadette worked in telecommunications. The global economy and internet usage requires increased staffing at night, and the company proposes a change in its shift-working, which is accepted by the trade union following a vote. Bernadette refuses to work night shifts. She is dismissed.

(d) Benedict has noticed that he is not getting an itemised pay statement, and believes that he is entitled to one by law. The personnel department is evasive. Benedict consults the union representatives, who press the question. The personnel department stalls. Benedict starts putting up posters and holding meetings. He is told to stop 'being a trouble maker'. He refuses, and continues lobbying his colleagues. He is dismissed for persistent trouble-making.

The Conciliation Officer or Employment Tribunal to whom a complaint of unfair dismissal is made may order various remedies including:

(a) **Re-instatement** - giving the employee his old job back

(b) **Re-engagement** - giving him a job comparable to his old one

(c) **Compensation** - this may consist of:

    (i) A **basic award** based on age and length of service. (If the employee is also entitled to redundancy pay, the lesser is set off against the greater amount.)

    (ii) A **compensatory award** (taking account of the basic award) for any additional loss (earnings, expenses, benefits) on common law principles of damages for breach of contract

    (iii) A **punitive additional award** if the employer does not comply with an order for re-instatement or re-engagement, and in cases of sex and race discrimination.

    (iv) A **special award** in the case of health and safety, trade union membership or activity.

In deciding whether to exercise its powers to order re-instatement or re-engagement the Tribunal must take into account whether the complainant wishes to be reinstated, whether it is practicable for the employer to comply with such an order and, if the complainant contributed to any extent to his dismissal, whether it would be just to make such an order. Such orders are very infrequent.

Compensation payments may also be reduced if the ex-employee is deemed to have contributed to his or her own dismissal or loss. So, for example, an employee may be found to have been unfairly dismissed on grounds of poor work performance because no warnings were given – but the poor performance will still be taken into account.

The Employment Relations Act 1999 raised the ceiling for unfair dismissal awards to £50,000. It also provided that there should be **no** limit on compensation payouts for employees dismissed as 'whistleblowers'.

3.5 Dismissal procedures

Procedures for dismissal should include the following.

(a) Ensuring that **standards** of performance and conduct are set, clearly defined and communicated to all employees

(b) **Warning** employees where a gap is perceived between standard and performance, or where other legal impediments or 'substantial reasons' are foreseen to arise

(c) Giving a clearly defined and reasonable **period for improvement** or adjustment - with help and training where necessary, and clear improvement targets

(d) Ensuring that **disciplinary procedures** (including appeal procedures, rights to representation and so on) are made clear and meticulously followed – especially once minimum statutory requirements come into force in October 2004

(e) Implementing fair and transparent procedures for **redundancy**, particularly in regard to selection

(f) **Evaluating all decisions** and actions in the light of policy, legislation and the requirement to 'act reasonably' at all times

One of the fair and justified reasons for dismissal (listed earlier) is 'redundancy' – provided that selection of employees for redundancy is fair. We will now go on to look at redundancy in detail.

4 REDUNDANCY

Definition

Redundancy is defined by the Employment Rights Act 1996 as dismissal:

(a) By reason that the employer has ceased (or intends to cease) to carry on the business for the purposes of which the employee was employed

(b) By reason that the employer has ceased (or intends to cease) to carry on the business in the place where the employee was employed

(c) By reason that the requirements of the business for employees to carry out work of a particular kind have ceased or diminished, or are expected to

(d) For reasons 'not related to the individual concerned.' (The Trade Union Reform and Employment Rights Act 1993 says that all such dismissals shall be presumed to be for redundancy, for the purposes of statutory consultation with trade unions – though not for redundancy pay. This complies with the EU directive on collective redundancy.)

4.1 Causes of redundancy

In simple terms, 'redundancy occurs when the employer closes down completely, moves premises, requires fewer people for particular jobs or requires no people for particular jobs' (Gennard & Judge, 2003).

There has been increasing redundancy for many decades, due to:

(a) Adverse trading conditions, especially in recessionary phases of the economy. This affects particular sectors (such as the manufacturing industry in the 1960s and '70s) and the whole economy (as in the UK in the 1970s and '80s). In recent years, though the UK economy has been perceived to be relatively strong and stable, there have been high-profile 'downturns' – such as the 'dot.com' collapse or the post-9/11 downturn in air travel.

(b) Increased global competition across business sectors. Many organisations have 'delayered' (eliminated excess layers of management and supervision), or 'downsized' (reduced their labour force) in order to reduce labour costs. Armstrong (2003) notes that productivity and added-value objectives has increased the use of indices such as added value per £ of employment cost to measure business performance and drive business process re-engineering.

(c) The introduction of technology has reduced shop floor labour in unskilled and semi-skilled jobs, and permitted increased outsourcing of functions and replacement of customer service and other skilled jobs (notably through the use of e-business and e-commerce via the Internet).

Redundancies are therefore a fact of life for HR practitioners, and an important element in the *change management* role of HRM.

FOR DISCUSSION

'Organisations are becoming mean as well as lean.'

(Armstrong, 2003)

How far is this true in your experience?

Why might an orgnisation wish to minimise redundancies or minimse their impact on employees, above statutory requirements?

4.2 HR responsibilities in regard to redundancy

The HRM function will have to:

(a) Establish a redundancy policy which clarifies the psychological contract, balancing the organisation's commitment to maintain employment with clear recognition of the need to ensure the economic viability of the business.

(b) Develop appropriate redundancy procedures

(c) Conduct advance HR planning (see Chapter 2) in order to achieve downsizing as far as possible without involuntary redundancy

(d) Advise on and/or implement other methods of avoiding or minimising involuntary redundancy

(e)   Advise on and/or take part in managing redundancy (in regard to consultation, outplacement, counselling, payment and other measures)

We will look at some of these matters in turn.

Activity 6   **(5 minutes)**

(a)   A's job is abolished, and A is transferred to B's job, and B is dismissed. Is this a case of redundancy?

(b)   An employer wishes to alter employees' contract terms in order to harmonise terms following a merger. It decides to do this by dismissing all employees and re-employing them all on new terms: no one effectively ceases to be employed, since everyone accepts the new terms. Has there been a redundancy?

4.3   Minimising involuntary redundancies

Unemployment can represent not only an economic threat to lifestyle, but a source of insecurity, loss of self-esteem, extreme stress and hopelessness. On grounds of social responsibility, therefore, (quite apart from the costs of involuntary redundancy to the firm) the HR function should attempt to minimise involuntary redundancy as far as possible. This can be done by:

(a)   Advance manpower planning, so that foreseen seasonal or other contractions in demand for labour can be taken into account, and natural wastage can be allowed to downsize the organisation.

(b)   Adjusting HR plans to ban non-essential recruitment; reduce overtime working; develop job-sharing (people alternating or splitting days of work in the same job); encourage short-contract working; restrict the use of sub-contracted, temporary and casual staff; and, if necessary, implement temporary layoffs.

(c)   Encouraging *voluntary redundancy*. People may be induced to volunteer to leave by offering financial incentives (above statutory redundancy pay), offering outplacement training or counselling (to help them find work elsewhere) and so on. A key disadvantage of this approach is that the volunteers may be people the organisation wants to keep: loyalty incentives may have to be offered to retain them.

(d)   Retraining and redeployment programmes. This may be a solution where alternative jobs are available, employees have some of the skills (or at least aptitudes) required and retraining facilities are available. The organisation may use outplacement agencies, or liaison with other employers in the same industry, supply chain or area, with a view to securing redeployment within a network of organisations.

(e)   Encouraging *early retirement*, or insisting on the retirement of employees over the normal retirement age. This may be felt to be fair, if careers are seen to 'wind down' in any case but may not be appropriate in a high loyalty/seniority culture such as that pertaining in Japan. It may also be a factor, in terms of social responsibility, that mature-aged employees will have greater difficulty in finding new employment if they wish to do so.

NOTES

Most claims for unfair dismissal in respect of redundancy are for **unfair selection** *and* **lack of consultation:** *we will look at these two areas next.*

4.4 Selection for compulsory redundancy

There are two basic approaches for selection for redundancy, which have proved acceptable to tribunals and trade unions.

(a) The least contentious and easiest method may be *'Last in, first out' (LIFO):* newcomers are dismissed before long-serving employees. This may be deemed 'reasonable' by Tribunals, but in the case of *Blatchfords v Berger and Others* (2001, cited in Gennard & Judge, 2003) the Employment Appeal Tribunal stated: 'It cannot be said with certainty either that selection on the basis of LIFO would always be reasonable or that no reasonable employer today would adopt LIFO as the sole criterion'. The method may be construed as indirectly discriminatory, if the recruitment of women and ethnic minorities is recent, for example. LIFO may sound fair (especially in a loyalty/seniority culture of employment) – but it may also mean that the organisation loses its youngest employees, those with the most up-to-date skills, or employees of particular merit.

(b) *Point score systems* are an alternative favourably viewed by tribunals. These allow *retention by merit* – retaining good performers and dismissing less effective ones – while supporting the objectivity of the process.

   (i) Clear criteria should be chosen, and ideally agreed in advance with trade unions. They may be based on aspects such as attendance records, disciplinary records, competence assessments, range of work experience and other objectively measurable factors.

   (ii) Each employee is scored on each criteria to build up a points score.

   (iii) Managers implementing the system should have clear definitions of criteria; points available for different degrees of fulfilment of each criterion (eg 1-10); and weighting of criteria to reflect their relative importance and value to the organisation (eg × 1-5).

   (iv) Once all scores have been calculated, employees with the lowest scores are selected for redundancy.

From the organisation's point of view, selection criteria should ensure that the skills needed for organisational survival and regrowth are not lost through redundancy, and if possible that the best people are retained in the most value-added jobs.

Employees who are employed on special projects or who have special skills required by the organisation may need to be removed from the pool prior to selection, or this should be provided for in the selection criteria.

4.5 Employee rights and redundancy procedures

Armstrong (2003) notes that redundancy procedures have three key aims:

* To treat employees as fairly as possible
* To reduce hardship as much as possible and
* To protect management's ability to run the business effectively

In addition, any procedure must take into account the employee's legal rights in redundancy situations. Many large organisations provide services and benefits well in excess of the statutory minimum with regard to consultation periods, terms, notice periods, counselling and aid with job search and so on.

EXAMPLE: THE BODY SHOP

'How does a firm that prides itself on its ethical approach to its "employees, customers, franchisees, suppliers and shareholders" negotiate the process of making redundancies?'

'At the start of 1999, (the Body Shop) found itself in the potentially embarrassing situation of having to cut jobs in order to press ahead with restructuring and fight off competition from cheap suppliers ... An ethical employer cannot be seen to hand out redundancy notices without any thought for the people involved...

'The entrepreneurs' club was set up to try and reduce the impact of impending redundancies on the local area. As well as loans, it also provided coaching and mentoring, opportunities for networking and access to an IT business centre. Other new businesses set up by former staff included a payroll consultancy, a glass-staining business and a video and music soundtracking company...

'Mark Barrett, head of HR at Body Shop International, says ... "We're a young company. People leaving the Body Shop were well thought of, and so found it easier to get new roles ..."

'About 40 per cent of the redundancies were voluntary, although Barrett believes some of those who were made compulsorily redundant were also happy to leave. Outplacement support was provided ...

'Special treatment was given to staff aged over 50. This was partly a result of pressure from the consultation and representation committee, made up of employee representatives (the firm is non-unionised). People over 50 who had not found a job by the end of their redundancy period were entitled to an extra 25% on top of their original redundancy payment – although only 4 out of the eligible 25 applied for any additional cash. Employees leaving the firm were also offered £1,000 to spend on training ... matched by a further £1,000 from Sussex Enterprise, a local training and enterprise council.

'Only 37 out of the 200 staff show jobs were made redundant did not take up the training grant. It was later decided to extend the £1,000 offer to people who weren't leaving ... "There was a feeling at the time that people were leaving and being well supported, but that maybe those who were staying were not being given the same backing" ...

'Staff in the service centre (where the redundancies occurred) felt under pressure because of the length of time it took to decide who was going to be made redundant. Barrett admits that the consultations, which took up to three months in some cases, went on too long. Some managers failed to tell people what was happening ... These criticisms were initially made by ... a consultant on employee surveys who was asked to evaluate the consultation exercise.

'In an attempt to improve communication, the firm introduced a monthly newsletter for all employees, along with fortnightly meetings with managers from the service centre, so that people could be kept better informed ...

'An employee attitude survey, carried out among 390 staff who stayed at BSI and 220 who left or transferred to other parts of the Body Shop, clearly demonstrates some of the problems that occurred ... Leavers were the most dissatisfied with the support they received from the HR department, while employees who stayed also highlighted communications with managers as an area of concern ... 61% of those who took compulsory redundancy were satisfied with the outplacement support ... More than two thirds of all leavers said that they had enjoyed their time at the Body Shop and would consider working for the company again.'

Neil Merrick, *People Management*, 26 October 2000

> **Activity 7** (1½ hours)
>
> Use your research skills to find one or more further accounts (written or oral) of a redundancy situation: HR journals, quality press and acquaintances who have experienced redundancy are good sources. The **redundancy policy** of a business organisation, including selection criteria and ethical aims, will also be useful if you can gain access to one (or more).

Consultation

From a social responsibility point of view, it is obviously desirable to consult with employee representatives and to give warning of impending redundancies and methods of selection as early as possible.

The Employment Protection Act 1975 obliged employers to consult with recognised trade unions on redundancy. Amendments made in the Trade Union Reform and Employment Rights Act 1993 added the requirement that consultation should include ways of avoiding dismissals. Further amendments made in the Collective Redundancies and Transfer of Undertakings (Protection of Employment) (Amendment) Regulations 1995 addressed the need to consult with elected employee representatives, where there is no recognised trade union for the purposes of collective bargaining. Forthcoming legislation under the European Directive on Information and Consultation of Workers at National Level will broaden employee rights to information and consultation on decisions likely to affect them: see Chapter 18.

In the case of collective redundancies, affecting 20 or more employees, the employer must consult with 'appropriate representatives'. If there is no recognised trade union in the workplace, employers are bound to make suitable arrangements for the fair election (by secret ballot) of employee representatives from among the affected workforce.

Consultation about proposed redundancies must begin 'at the earliest opportunity', defined as:

(a) A minimum of 90 days before the first dismissal, if 100 or more employees are to be dismissed at any one establishment

(b) A minimum of 30 days before the first dismissal of 20–99 employees

These rules are applied to the total number involved and cannot be evaded by making essential dismissals in small instalments.

Prior to consultation, employees or their representatives must have been provided with information about: the reason for redundancies; numbers to be dismissed; proposed methods of selection for redundancy; timescale and methods of the redundancy programme; and method to be used in calculating redundancy pay (eg if not the statutory formula). The consultation period is not deemed to have started until sufficient information is provided on all these matters.

Consultation must be 'genuine', with the intention of reaching agreement with the employee representatives. It has to explore:

(a) Ways of avoiding dismissals where possible
(b) Ways of reducing the numbers to be dismissed and
(c) Ways of minimising the impact on those who must be dismissed

Failure to comply with consultation requirements entitles the union to bring a complaint before the industrial tribunal. If conciliation (facilitated by ACAS) is not possible, the tribunal will hear the complaint. If the complaint is upheld, the tribunal may postpone dismissal and order consultation to take place, or may make a 'protective award' of pay to employees concerned, based on the number of redundancies and the period over which they are carried out.

FOR DISCUSSION

'The obligation on the employer is only to consult before proposals become fixed decisions. The likely outcome of the consultation is that the employer's proposal will be implemented either unaltered or altered in a way that the employer finds acceptable.' (Dalganna & Davies, 2003)

What do you think is the purpose and importance of consultation?

Redundancy pay

Redundant employees are entitled to compensation, in the form of **redundancy pay**:

 (a) For loss of security

 (b) To encourage them to accept redundancy without damage to employee relations

The employee may not be entitled to redundancy pay if the employer has made an offer of 'suitable' alternative employment and the employee has unreasonably rejected it.

The statutory minimum entitlement is half a week's pay for each year of employment under the age of 22; one week's pay for each year of employment between 22 and 40; and one-and-a-half weeks' pay for each year of employment above the age of 41. In practice this is often supplemented by voluntary payments by the employer.

Other employee rights

Redundant employees also have:

 (a) The right to 'reasonable' time off with pay to look for another job or arrange training

 (b) The right to accept alternative work offered by the employer for an agreed trail period, and to refuse that work (if unsuitable) at the end of the trial period without prejudice to the right of redundancy pay

4.6 Compassionate exit management

A number of measures may be taken to alleviate the consequences of redundancy for employees.

 (a) *Informing employees* who are to be dismissed of their selection should be managed with as much sensitivity as possible. This is generally done by what is called a *'release interview'*. The interview is generally conducted by a line manager, but an HR specialist may also be present, in order to explain the basis of selection, the employee's entitlements and organisational support services that will be offered. Managers should be given training and/or guidance in how to handle the difficult situation sensitively. They should also be given information about any special circumstances that might make the employee react particularly badly.

 (b) *Counselling* may be offered to employees, to aid their readjustment and job search. (Counselling is discussed in Chapter 11 of this Course Book.) The employee will be guided in reinforcing his or her sense of employability, redefining career objectives, devising strategies for job search, and working through personal issues (including anger and grief) around job loss.

(c) *Outplacement services* may be offered, often through external consultancies, to help redundant employees to find alternative work. The HR department or consultancy may offer services such as:

(i) Seeking specific job opportunities in the local area

(ii) Training employees in CV preparation, selection interview techniques and application filling

(iii) Helping employees to draw up skill or competence inventories, personal success/attainment inventories and other aids to applications

(iv) Carrying out psychometric assessments and helping employees to set career and job objectives

(v) Matching of employee details to advertised vacancies or network opportunities

(vi) Helping the employee to plan a focused job-search campaign

(d) *Information* on job, self-employment and retaining opportunities and funding should be made available. Individuals should be made aware of the role and accessibility of the Department of Employment's facilities, and private sector services for careers counselling, recruitment, CV preparation and so on.

Activity 8   **(30 minutes)**

Conduct a web search and develop your own source list of organisations and websites that provide outplacement support.

The impact of redundancy is also felt by those who were *not* selected.

'Survivors' may suffer guilt and anxiety, insecurity about their own job security and a loss of reciprocal loyalty to the organisation: they may tend to identify more closely with fellow workers and less with the organisation as an 'impersonal' entity. Efforts will have to be made to reinforce survivors' loyalty and morale by acknowledging their worth to the employer – particularly since, despite the concept underlying 'redundancy', remaining workers may in fact have to shoulder an increased workload in downsized organisations.

Definition

The **survivor syndrome** has been coined as a term for a psychological state which involves long-term anxiety about job loss, increased loyalty to co-workers and reduced loyalty to the employer.

'Survivor syndrome' can lead to increased labour turnover, deliberately restricted output, risk-averse behaviour (suppression of feedback, new ideas, innovation) and industrial conflict.

Management's motives and intentions must be transparent and true, and fairness (even generosity, if possible) demonstrated. Positive values (better chances of corporate survival and success, 'heroism' of the lean-mean workforce, the value of retained employees) must be sold.

EXAMPLE: THE ROYAL MAIL

'Having made a loss after tax of £940 million in 2001-02, the Royal Mail announced one of the biggest restructures in British corporate history. In 2002 around 30,000 redundancies were announced and more have been made since then.

'Andrew Kinder was, until recently, principal welfare co-ordinator and chartered occupational psychologist for the Royal Mail, and now provides the same services of agency Schlumberger Sema. Describing the impact of such large-scale change on Royal Mail staff, he says: "Many individuals find it hard to cope, some feeling that they have to work harder to secure their futures, others feeling deep concerns about why they kept their jobs. Royal Mail is committed to addressing these issues not only because they could have a negative effect on productivity but also because the organisation takes its legal duty of care to individuals very seriously. Reorganisations like this happen and we as humans can't control change but we can control how we respond to it. Counselling is one of the key aspects of the firm's efforts to empower employees to cope with change."

'Pauline Leech, head of information services in the Royal Mail's property division, has taken advantage of Kinder's counselling services. "The team in which I work has been going through so much change that we felt it would be useful to bring in a counsellor," she says. "Andrew ran a session helping us to develop a number of coping strategies. We talked about our feelings and behaviour, completed a questionnaire and discussed responses to situations. A drama triangle, involving three people playing the role of victim, persecutor and rescuer, was very interesting and gave an insight into different approaches to the same situation. It gave us good insight into the pressure felt by colleagues. For me it helped to know that the firm cared enough to offer this support." '

(Blyth, 2003)

NOTES

Chapter roundup

- Exit from employment takes several forms, voluntary and involuntary, including:

  ○ Retirement: termination of contract at a fixed, statutory or negotiated retirement age

  ○ Resignation: voluntary termination by notice on the part of the employee

  ○ Dismissal: termination, with or without notice, on the part of the employer, or (constructive dismissal) on the part of the employee where (s)he is entitled to assume that the employer has terminated the contract by breach

  ○ Redundancy; dismissal by reason of the ending of the work for which the employee was contracted

- Employment protection legislation and regulations set out employee rights with regard to:

  (a) Notice periods to be given for dismissal

  (b) Valid reasons for dismissal

  (c) Remedies in the event of dismissal being judged 'unfair'

  (d) Consultation with employee representatives over proposed redundancies

  (e) Redundancy pay

  (f) Time off to prepare for redundancy

  (g) Trial periods prior to acceptance of alternative employment

- In addition to statutory requirements, exit has ethical and employee relations implications. Attention is commonly given to:

  (a) Learning from resignations by means of exit interviews

  (b) Socially responsible polices surrounding progressive discipline, dismissal and redundancy

  (c) The motivation of 'surviving' employees

Quick quiz

1 In what five basic ways may a contract (including a contract of employment) be terminated?

2 What are the arguments for enforcing retirement?

3 What procedures should be carried out when an employee resigns from the organisation?

4 Who are the members of an Employment Tribunal?

5 What is the difference between wrongful dismissal and unfair dismissal?

6 What reasons may an employer rely on in seeking to show that a dismissal was fair?

7 When is dismissal called 'redundancy'?

8 What measures can be used to avoid compulsory redundancies?

9   What are two potentially justifiable methods of selecting employees for redundancy?

10   Explain the term 'survivor syndrome'.

Answers to quick quiz

1   Performance, mutual agreement, notice, breach or frustration.

(see paragraph 1.1)

2   To open up promotion opportunities; to offer security to younger employees; to inject 'young blood'; to save money; to enhance efficiency.

(para 1.2)

3   Persuade to stay (if appropriate); exit interview; negotiate notice period; notify key people; complete performance assessment.   (para 1.3)

4   A legally-qualified chairperson, employer representative and employee representation.   (para 2.1)

5   Wrongful dismissal is where there are insufficient reasons to justify dismissal, whereas unfair dismissal is where law and internal policies have been breached.   (paras 3.2, 3.3)

6   Redundancy; legal impediment; non-capability; misconduct; some other substantial reason.   (para 3.3)

7   Cessation of the business; cessation of the business in a particular location; cessation of the need for work of a particular kind.   (para 4)

8   A full answer is provided in paragraph 4.3.

9   LIFO and point score systems.   (para 4.4)

10   A psychological state suffered by employees who have survived redundancy programmes, characterised by long-term anxiety, increased loyalty to co-workers and decreased commitment to the organisation.

(para 4.6)

Answers to activities

1   (a)   Alan's only option is to require Sheerbrow Ltd to provide him with an amended copy of the particulars (within one month). The written particulars are merely evidence of the employment contract's terms – they do not represent the contract itself, so an amendment of an error cannot be said to be a breach.

(b)   The publisher has breached the contract, because of the **express** contract terms of two year's work in a particular post: the employer also had the implied duty to supply the work, and failed to do so.

(c)   Ambrose cannot claim that the company is in breach of contract for failure to provide work, or pay for work done, because no contract existed in the first place! There was no offer made – although Ambrose 'accepted' what he **thought** was an offer, by turning up to work.

2   (a)   The burden of work in late years can be eased by shortening hours or a transfer to lighter duties.

(b)   The final stage of employee training and development may take the form of courses, commonly run by local technical colleges, intended to prepare employees for the transition to retirement and non-work.

(c) The organisation may have, or may be able to put employees in touch with, social/leisure clubs and other facilities for easing the shock of retirement.

3 (a) Reasons for leaving are many and various, but some of the ones you may have thought of are: relocation to another city/area; dissatisfaction with work conditions (or location, or workmates or scope for responsibility or any number of work-related factors); finding another (preferred) job; being head-hunted; change of career (or return to full-time education, or move to self-employment, or change of domestic circumstances/family responsibilities); clash of culture/values with the employer; ill-health; to pre-empt dismissal in order to save face.

(b) Procedures may include: return of keys, security passes and so on; handing of files to department head; completion or transfer of work-in-progress; removal of personal data/passwords from computer files; collection of final pay and leaving information; removal of personal effects.

4 Full material for your answer is provided in Paragraph 2.3 of this chapter.

5 (a) Bernie was fairly dismissed by reason of legal impediment.

(b) Berenice was fairly dismissed by reason of lack of 'capability': she is clearly incompetent compared to the standard of performance required by the job.

(c) Bernadette was fairly dismissed: failure to accept necessary reorganisation is a 'substantial' reason.

(d) Benedict was unfairly dismissed, because he was trying to enforce his employment rights in a reasonable manner.

6 (a) Yes – but it is **B** who has been made redundant.

(b) Yes – for the purposes of consultation with trade unions, since this fits the TURER '93 definition of collective redundancy: the reasons for dismissal were not related to the individuals concerned. The consultation requirements refer to 'proposals to dismiss': the employer presumably proposed to dismiss any employee who did not accept the new terms – even if this did not eventuate. The employer bound to consult – and to pay penalties if it had failed to do so. (This is based on an actual case before the EAT: *GMBV v Man Truck and Bus UK Ltd, 2000*)

7 The answer is up to you!

8 A research activity. Find out more about outplacement – *and* the kind of information employees can be steered towards.

Assignment 7 (1½ hours)

Q and R Ferries PLC

You are the newly-appointed Personnel Manager for Q and R Ferries PLC, a passenger and cargo-handling service operating out of East Anglia. Unusually for such a large company, Q and R had no personnel function until you were recruited two months ago. The culture of the company has been largely based around allowing line managers to 'do their own thing' so far as staff are concerned, provided, of course, that they work within general company guidelines and consult with department heads if in any doubt. Two claims for unfair dismissal (which have just landed on your desk) lead you to suspect that this notion of 'reasonable authority' has completely broken down.

Both claims concern sickness, though of a very different nature from each other, and both employees were dismissed under 'capability and qualifications'. In other words, the sickness record of both employees was considered sufficient grounds to question their ability to do their jobs to the required standard. Dismissal took place accordingly.

The first employee, Roger Price, was a maintenance man at Q and R's headquarters at Harwich. He had been off sick with a bad back for 3 weeks but, during this period, he was seen on a Q and R ferry doing a striptease in a karaoke evening. He was dismissed for contravention of the sick pay scheme.

The second employee, Mary Gardner, who is disabled, had been a satisfactory credit control clerk for many years. But in 1991 her health deteriorated and she was frequently absent. In 1993 she became part-time. In 1995 she was off for some time. Mrs Gardner believed she was improving, but her GP's report was that her health was not good; he considered she would not return to work in the near future. The company decided that a full time replacement was necessary. Mrs Gardner's manager did not consult with her about this because he thought it would be difficult as she believed she was improving. Instead, he wrote to her announcing his decision to terminate her employment.

Both employees have now submitted claims for unfair dismissal. Your task is to prepare a report to the Chief Executive, outlining whether you believe Q and R will win the cases, defining what you consider are the main points a tribunal will take into account when they go to trial. You must draw up a checklist of questions you wish to raise with the relevant department managers when you interview them shortly about Mr Price and Mrs Gardner.

PART B

UNIT 22: MANAGING HUMAN RESOURCES ISSUES

Chapter 8:
DIFFERING PERSPECTIVES OF HRM

Introduction

In this chapter, we explore further some of the themes already discussed in Chapters 1 and 2, highlighting the ambiguities and dualities in the role of the personnel function and some of the issues that arise from the shift to an 'HRM' orientation.

One of the key assumptions of HRM is that the employment relationship can be managed so that the needs of both organisation and employees are met, to mutual benefit. Ethical, people-friendly HR policies are intended to facilitate efficient and effective working as well as employee health, welfare and satisfaction. This dual emphasis will be reflected in the following chapters as we look at some of the major issues facing HR managers in the 21st century workplace.

Your objectives

In this chapter you will learn about the following.

(a) Guest's model of hard-soft, loose-tight dimensions of HRM

(b) Storey's model of the differences between HRM and personnel/industrial relations practices

(c) HRM from a strategic perspective and its implications for the role of the line manager and employees

(d) How HRM impacts on the success of the business

1 SOFT AND HARD HRM

In Chapter 1, we defined HRM as 'a strategic approach to managing employment relations which emphasises that leveraging people's capabilities is critical to achieving sustainable competitive advantage' (Bratton & Gold, 2003).

We have so far suggested that the role of HRM is twofold (leading to some ambiguity): both business-oriented (concerned with performance) and people-oriented (concerned with the motivation and quality of working life of employees). However, key writers on HRM (Storey, 1989, Legge, 1998; Guest, 1999) identify two distinct versions of HRM, which they characterise as 'hard' and 'soft'.

1.1 Hard HRM

Definition

> Legge (1998) defined the **'hard' model** of HRM as a process emphasising 'the close integration of human resource policies with business strategy which regards employees as a resource to be managed in the same rational way as any other resource being exploited for maximum return'.

The **hard model of HRM** may be summarised as follows.

(a) Its philosophy towards managing people is rational, quantitative and explicitly business-oriented: employees must be managed in such a way as to obtain value-adding performance, which will in turn give the organisation competitive advantage.

> The drive to adopt HRM is... based on the business case of a need to respond to an external threat from increasing competition. It is a philosophy that appeals to managements who are striving to increase competitive advantage and appreciate that to do this they must invest in human resources as well as new technology.
>
> (Guest, 1999)

(b) It regards employees as a resource of the organisation, to be managed (exploited) in as rational and strategic a manner as any other economic resource: **human capital** from which a return can be obtained by adding value, through judicious investment in performance management and employee development.

(c) It emphasises the interests, role and authority of management 'over' those of employees.

(d) It is essentially a pluralist viewpoint, which maintains that the interests of the owners and managers of a business are inherently different from those of the workers: organisations are therefore political systems, within which there is competition for scarce power and resources. Workers must be controlled in order to ensure that they perform in the organisation's interests.

Features of hard HRM include:

(a) A close matching or integration of the strategic objectives of the HR function with the business strategy of the organisation. 'Hard strategic HRM' will emphasise the yield to be obtained by investing in human resources in the interests of the business (Storey, 1989)

(b)   A focus on quantitative, business-strategic objectives and criteria for management

(c)   An emphasis on the need for performance management and other forms of managerial control.

Activity 1   **(10 minutes)**
What HRM techniques would you expect to be adopted as a result of a hard HRM approach?

1.2   Soft HRM

Definition

Legge (1998) defined the **'soft'** version of HRM as a process whereby employees are viewed as 'valued assets and as a source of competitive advantage through their commitment, adaptability and high level of skills and

---

The **soft model of HRM** may be summarised as follows.

(a)   Its philosophy towards managing people is based in the human and neo-human relations schools of management thought which emphasised the influence of socio-psychological factors (relationships, attitudes, motivation, leadership, communication) on work behaviour.

(b)   It views employees as 'means rather than objects' (Guest, 1999): 'treating employees as valued assets, a source of competitive advantage through their commitment, adaptability and high quality (of skills, performance and so on)' (Storey, 1989).

(c)   It focuses on 'mutuality', a unitarist viewpoint which assumes that the interests of management and employees can and should coincide in shared organisational goals, working as members of an integrated team. Employees are viewed as 'stakeholders' in the organisation.

The main **features of soft HRM** are:

(a)   A complementary approach to strategic HRM in relation to the business strategies of the organisation. Brewster (1999) argues that a stakeholder perspective and environmental constraints (such as EU legislation) mean that HR strategies cannot be entirely governed by business strategy. 'Soft strategic HRM' will place greater emphasis on the human relations aspect of people management, stressing security of employment, continuous development, communication, involvement and the quality of working life.

(b)   A focus on socio-psychological and cultural objectives and criteria for management.

(c)   An emphasis on the need to gain the trust and commitment of employees – not merely compliance with control mechanisms.

NOTES

> **Activity 2** **(10 minutes)**
>
> What HRM techniques would you expect to be adopted as a result of a soft HRM approach?

We will now look at two early US models of HRM which reflect the roots of the soft and hard approaches respectively.

1.3 The Michigan model

The **matching model** of HRM was developed by the Michigan School (Fombrun *et al*, 1984). It suggested that HR systems should be managed in such a way as to 'match', or be congruent with, the organisation's business strategy: an essentially hard orientation. The **human resource cycle** consists of four basic functions which are performed in all organisations to drive business performance.

(a) Selection: designed to match available human resources to jobs

(b) Performance management/appraisal: designed to match performance to objectives and standards

(c) Rewards: reinforcing short- and long-term achievements

(d) Development: matching the skill quality of the human resource to future requirements

Fombrun *et al* suggest that the HR function should be linked to line management by:

(a) Providing good HR databases

(b) Ensuring that senior mangers give HR issues as much attention as they give to other functions

(c) Measuring the contribution of the HR function at the strategic (long-term policies designed to encourage organisational 'fit' to its environment in the future), managerial (medium-term activities ensuring the acquisition, retaining and development of people) and operational (daily support of business activities) levels

1.4 The Harvard Framework

The Harvard Framework (Beer *et al*, 1984) was based on the belief that the problems of historical personnel management can only be solved

> when general managers develop a viewpoint of how they wish to see employees involved in and developed by the enterprise, and of what HRM policies and practices may achieve those goals... Today, many pressures are demanding... a longer-term perspective in managing people and consideration of people as potential assets rather than merely a variable cost.

The Harvard model was influential in emphasising the fact that:

(a) 'Human resource management involves *all* management decisions and actions that affect the nature of the relationship between the organisation and its employees'

(b) Organisations involve a variety of stakeholders who have an interest in the practice and outcomes of HR policies: there is a 'trade-off' between the interests of owners and employees, as well as other stakeholders, with a view to mutuality and commitment

(c)   Strategic HRM choices are influenced by a broad range of contextual factors, including both product-market and socio-cultural factors

(d)   Line managers are at the interface between competitive strategy and personnel policies and must take more responsibility for their alignment

The Harvard framework can be illustrated as follows (Beer *at all* 1984): Figure 8.1.

Figure 8.1 Map of the HRM territory

This is essentially a soft HRM model,

> composed of policies that promote mutuality – mutual goals, mutual influence, mutual respect, mutual rewards, mutual responsibility. The theory is that policies of mutuality will elicit commitment, which in turn will yield both better economic performance and greater human development
> (Walton, cited by Armstrong, 2003)

FOR DISCUSSION

How do you respond intuitively to the 'hard' and 'soft' versions of HRM? What words and phrases connected with each strike you as positively or negatively loaded: where do you perceptions come from? Are 'soft' and 'hard' perspectives really as different as contrasting descriptions make them seem? Does your experience of organisations suggest that they operate under **either** one **or** the other?

1.5   Hard or soft?

In practice, there are likely to be times when a hard orientation (eg in the face of the need for organisational downsizing) directly conflicts with the more developmental and paternal philosophy of the soft approach. Many organisations operate a mix of soft-hard, loose-tight systems. One way of formalising this is to segment the labour force into a 'core' of permanent employees managed via soft HRM policies, and a 'periphery' of short-contract labour used as an exploitable commodity. As Kramer, McGraw and Shuler

(1997) note, 'whether an organisation leans more towards the hard or soft version of HRM, or does not consider HRM to be relevant to its operation, depends very much on the values of the organisation.'

In addition, research (cited by Armstrong, 2003) suggests that organisations in practice implement a mix of hard and soft approaches, so that the distinction may not always be precise or helpful.

The broad 'achieve success through people' focus of HRM may therefore be approached from two different perspectives which imply very different techniques of management. These techniques have been classified, according to the amount of control each orientation assumes to be necessary to obtain job performance from workers, as 'tight' and 'loose'. Before we discuss the characteristics of tight and loose HRM, we will look at an early model of how managerial philosophy and assumptions set up the hard-soft, tight-loose continuum.

1.6 Theory X and Theory Y

The distinction between hard/tight and soft/loose management control was suggested by **Douglas McGregor,** an influential contributor to the neo-human relations school. In *The Human Side of Enterprise* (originally published in 1960), he discussed the way in which managers handle people according to the assumptions they have about them and about what kind of management style will obtain their efforts. He identified two extreme sets of assumptions (Theory X and Theory Y) and explored how management style differs according to which set of assumptions is adopted (McGregor, 1987).

(a) **Theory X** holds that human beings have an inherent dislike of work and will avoid it if they can. People prefer to be directed, wishing to avoid responsibility. They have relatively little ambition and want security above all, resisting change. They are self-interested, and make little effort to identify with the organisation's goals. They must be coerced, controlled, directed, offered rewards or threatened with punishments in order to get them to put adequate effort into the achievement of organisation objectives: this is management's responsibility.

(b) According to **Theory Y**, however, the expenditure of physical and mental effort in work is as natural as play or rest. The ordinary person does not inherently dislike work: according to the conditions, it may be a source of satisfaction or deprivation. A person will exercise self-direction and self-control in the service of objectives to which they are committed: they are not naturally passive or resistant to organisational objectives, but may have been made so by bad experience. The most significant reward that can be offered in order to obtain commitment is the satisfaction of the individual's personal growth and development needs. The average human being learns, under proper conditions, not only to accept but to seek responsibility. Management's responsibility is to create conditions and methods that will enable individuals to integrate their own and the organisation's goals.

You will have your own viewpoints on the validity of Theory X and Theory Y. In fact, McGregor intentionally polarised his theories as the extremes of a continuum along which most managers' attitudes fall at some point. However, he also recognised that the assumptions are self-perpetuating, even where the 'types' of employee described did not really exist. If people are treated according to Theory X (or Theory Y) assumptions, they will begin to act accordingly – thus confirming management in its beliefs and practices. Essentially, Theory X embodies the 'hard-tight' **control theory of management**, while Theory Y embodies the 'soft-loose' **commitment theory of management**.

Activity 3 (45 minutes)

The following was sent to the letter page of *Personnel Management*.

> Hark, I think I detect the first cuckoo of a recessionary spring on your pages ('Making time for productivity', March), with such an unashamed reassertion of Taylorism. Come on, all you personnel folk. Off with your HR nomenclature; away with all this nonsense about the 'success culture', 'employee involvement', 'maximising people power', 'establishing the right climate' and 'sharing gains' (all drawn from the CIPD's current national priorities). Get out your sticks and stopwatches, 'precisely time' those tea breaks, slash that overtime, enforce 'bell-to-bell working', put in a few more controls and 'disincentives'... Surely employee involvement is not just an illusion created by the 1980s boom which we can ignore now times are tough?

What are the characteristics of the approach to HRM which the letter identifies? Why might economic recession lead managers to adopt such an approach?

1.7 Tight and loose HRM

The distinction between tight and loose HRM may be characterised as the difference between a system based on compliance and a system based on commitment.

Definitions

Compliance means performing according to set rules and standards, according to what you are expected and asked to do.

Commitment has been defined as 'the relative strength of an individual's identification with and involvement in a particular organisation. It is characterised by at least three factors:

(a) A strong belief in and acceptance of an organisation's goals and values

(b) A willingness to exert considerable effort on behalf of the organisation

(c) A strong desire to maintain membership of the organisation

(Mowdray *et al*, 1982)

Compliance based systems of control reflect a low level of trust and challenge: performance is expected to be no less than the set standard – but also no **more**, since there is little room for creative or exceptional input or effort, which may militate against tight managerial control. Such systems may be effective and efficient: in a highly stable market environment; where the task is low-tech and low-discretion, with little need to differentiate skills or abilities and little difference between compliant and committed performance; and where the managerial prerogative of superiority and control continue to have meaning because of cultural values to do with respect and conformity (eg in latino cultures and traditional family businesses).

Commitment based systems of control reflect a high level of trust and mutuality, based on Theory Y assumptions that the work relationship can offer employees opportunities to meet their needs and aspirations as well as the organisation's needs. Such systems are effective in environments where customer demands and technologies are varied and changing, and employees are required to be flexible, creative and positive in contributing to the organisation's goals.

Unit 22: Managing Human Resources Issues

Guest (2001) set out the differences in personnel policy in a compliance-based system of control and a commitment-based system of control, as follows.

Aspects of policy	Compliance	Commitment
Psychological contract of work	'Fair day's work for a fair day's pay'	Mutual/reciprocal commitment
Behavioural references	Norms, custom and practice	Values/mission
Source of control over workers' behaviour	External (rules, instructions)	Internal (goals, values, willingness)
Employee relations	Pluralist perspective ('Us' and 'Them')	Unitarist ('Us')
	Collective	Individual
	Low trust	Trust
Organising principles/ organisational design	Formal/defined roles	Flexible roles
	Top down	Bottom-up
	Centralised control	Decentralised control (delegation, empowerment)
	Hierarchy	Flat structures
	Division of labour	Team-work/autonomy
	Managerial control	Self control
Policy goals	Administrative/efficiency	Adaptive/effectiveness
	Performance to standard	Constantly improving performance
	Minimising cost	Maximising utilisation for added value

Guest also identified these contrasting dimensions as distinguishing 'traditional industrial relations' and 'HRM' approaches.

Activity 4 (10 minutes)

Would you say you were compliant in your attitude to your studies, or committed? Think about how you approach the assignments set for you, the classes you attend and so on.

(a) What are (or would be) the benefits to you if you are/were committed rather than compliant?

(b) What are/would be the benefits to your trainers?

(c) What could (1) you and (2) your trainers do to increase your commitment to your studies?

EXAMPLE

When Levi Strauss & Co UK was beset by a loss of market share, the HR department drove the necessary change, as "managers were the key resisters to change," said Bruce Robertson, head of HR at the company.

Managers were so resistant that "it resulted in senior leadership being removed". When Robertson first saw the results of a customer survey that called service "just abysmal", "chaotic" and "totally disorganised" he said, "my blood went cold. I sent it to managers and the response at the UK head office was 'so?' ".

In 2002, Robertson and his HR team led a series of changes. "We repositioned to a more adult/adult relationship between the company and employees," he said. The old relationship had created a culture where many employees were too passive to make decisions and where "little power struggles broke out," Robertson said. He spearheaded a new way of thinking, calling for employees to respect the Levi's heritage and be "passionate about our brands".

Employees are now called upon to be committed to making things better and be more flexible and adaptable in their ways of working. "They need to be more positive. The glass needs to be half full more of the time," he said. "Be happy with us or be happy somewhere else."

Employees are encouraged to take a solutions-oriented approach, to support co-workers and be more team-focused.

(Overman, 2003)

2 STOREY'S 'IDEAL TYPE' OF HRM

2.1 Storey's definitions

Storey (1992) regarded HRM as a 'set of interrelated policies with an ideological and philosophical underpinning'. A meaningful version of HRM involves:

(a) A particular cluster of beliefs and assumptions

(b) A strategic focus to decision-making about people management

(c) A central role for line managers in delivering HR outcomes

(d) The use of 'levers' to shape the employment relationship, which can be distinguished from those used under traditional industrial relations systems

Storey put forward a theoretical 'ideal type' description of what a fully implemented model of HRM might look like, in contrast to a similarly abstracted description of the traditional personnel/industrial relations model. As you consider the differences tabulated in Figure 8.2 below, remember that this is an 'ideal': it is not meant to describe the current, typical state of affairs – since, as we have seen, the definition of HRM, and its application in practice, is by no means clear cut. The model does, however, reflect the general direction of the shift in approach in recent decades.

DIMENSION	PERSONNEL/IR APPROACH	HRM APPROACH
Beliefs and assumptions		
1 Contract	Careful delineation of written contracts	Aim to go 'beyond contract'
2 Rules	Importance of devising clear rules/mutuality	'Can do' outlook; impatience with 'rules'
3 Guide to management action	Procedures/consistency/control	'Business-need'/flexibility/commitment
4 Behaviour referent	Norms/custom and practice	Values/mission
5 Managerial task vis-à-vis labour	Monitoring	Nurturing
6 Nature of relations	Pluralist	Unitarist
7 Conflict	Institutionalised	De-emphasised
8 Standardisation	High (eg 'parity' an issue)	Low (eg 'parity' not seen as relevant)
Strategic aspects		
9 Key relations	Labour-management	Business-customer
10 Initiatives	Piecemeal	Integrated
11 Corporate plan	Marginal to	Central to
12 Speed of decision	Slow	Fast
Line Management		
13 Management role	Transactional leadership	Transformational leadership
14 Key managers	Personnel/IR specialists	General/business/line managers
15 Communication	Indirect	Direct
16 Prized management skills	Negotiation	Facilitation
Key levers (strongly-featured issues and techniques)		
17 Foci of attention for interventions	Personnel procedures	Wide ranging cultural, structural and personnel strategies
18 Selection	Separate, marginal task	Integrated, key task
19 Pay	Job evaluation (fixed grades)	Performance related
20 Job categories and grades	Many	Few
21 Conditions	Separately negotiated	Harmonisation
22 Labour management	Collective bargaining contracts	Towards individual contracts
23 Thrust of relations with union delegates	Regularised through facilities and training	Marginalised (with exception of some bargaining for change models)
24 Communication	Restricted flow	Increased flow
25 Job design	Division of labour	Teamwork
26 Conflict handling	Reach temporary truces	Manage climate and culture
27 Training and development	Controlled access to courses	Learning companies

Figure 8.2: Twenty-seven points of difference

Activity 5   **(10 minutes)**

What kinds of personnel policies and practices might:

(a)   'Institutionalise' or 'de-emphasise' conflict (point 7)?

(b)   'Restrict' or 'increase' the flow of communication (point 24)?

2.2 Implications for the line manager's role

Transactional and **transformational** leadership (referred to in Storey's model) were terms coined by Burns (1978) for two different styles of leadership.

- **Transactional leaders** see the relationship with their followers in terms of a trade: they give followers the rewards they want, in exchange for services, loyalty and compliance.

- **Transformational leaders** see their role as inspiring and motivating others to work at levels beyond mere compliance. Transformational leadership is achieved through role modelling, articulating powerful goals, team-building, high expectations, two-way communication, empowering, developing and other such processes.

Transactional leadership can arguably be mediated via HR policies and practices. Transformational leadership is an essentially interpersonal process, underscoring the role of line managers and team leaders in delivering HRM.

2.3 Implications for the worker's role

The HRM viewpoint, as outlined above, is explicitly unitarist. It implies that employees can be willingly co-opted to the business task of competition, quality enhancement and problem-solving. Tight managerial control over workers is replaced by a culture of trust: performance is assumed to be largely self-regulating within a guiding framework of inspirational leadership and shared cultural values and aspirations.

Instead of power being used from the top down to **control** workers' performance, power is used to **support** workers' performance: performance (including quality, customer satisfaction, innovation and so on) becomes the guiding force of the organisation, not the wishes of senior management.

This has implications for the personnel function, as illustrated in Figure 8.3.

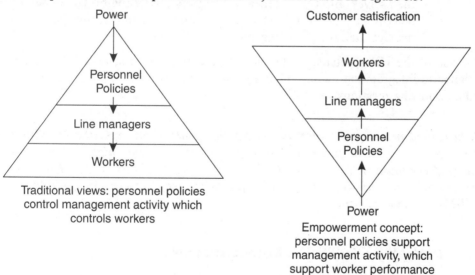

Figure 8.3: From control to empowerment

Activity 6 (10 minutes)

What might be the consequences of empowerment for personnel policy in the areas of (a) recruitment and selection and (b) training?

NOTES

2.4 Implications for HR responsibilities

One of the key features of HRM is that 'its performance and delivery are integrated into line management' (Storey, 1989).

According to Armstrong (2000) the hard HRM approach, in particular,

> is claimed to be a central, senior management-driven strategic activity that is developed, owned and delivered by management as a whole to promote the interests of the organisation that they serve. It purports to be an holistic approach concerned with the total interests of the organisation – the interests of the members of the organisation are recognised but subordinated to those of the enterprise. Hence the importance attached to strategic integration and strong cultures, which flow from top management's vision and leadership, and which require people who will be committed to the strategy, who will be adaptable to change, and who will fit the culture. By implication, as Guest (1991) says: 'HRM is too important to be left to personnel managers'.

Kramar, McGraw and Shuler (1997) note the ironic and paradoxical result:

> HRM has become more influential in company decision-making, yet has declined as a separate department within the organisation as HR tasks and decisions have been devolved to line managers. Many leading edge HR practitioners now see themselves more in an internal consultancy capacity assisting line managers to devise and implement more sophisticated ways of managing people, rather than implementing and managing those systems themselves. Such HR managers would also claim to be working towards the eventual removal of their own positions within the organisation.

HR specialists therefore increasingly share responsibility for delivering HR policy outcomes with:

(a) Top management, who shape the aims, strategy and culture of the organisation.

(b) Line managers, who take on a day-to-day leadership-oriented responsibility for people management.

(c) Employees themselves. It is no longer uncommon for employees to appraise themselves (and their peers and superiors), write their own job descriptions, determine their own performance standards and improvement goals, and manage their own learning and career development.

The role of the HR specialist is therefore to establish guiding principles and policies designed to integrate top management aims and strategy with line management activity and individual aspirations.

We suggested in Chapter 1 that four key policy goals of an authentic HRM approach are: high commitment, flexibility, strategic integration and high quality. We have discussed commitment (above), and will be covering flexibility in detail in Chapter 9. Here, we will look briefly at some models for the strategic integration of HRM, and then at HRM as a quality issue.

3 HRM AS STRATEGIC MANAGEMENT

3.1 Strategic HRM

The term 'strategic human resource management' emerged in the 1980s to describe a variety of models which attempt to explain how human resource policies can be integrated with business strategy.

Definitions

> **Strategic management** 'denotes a specific pattern of decisions and actions undertaken by the upper echelon of an organisation in order to accomplish specific outcomes and/or performance goals'.
>
> **Strategic HRM** is 'the process of linking the human resource function with the strategic objectives of the organisation in order to improve performance'.
>
> (Bratton & Gold, 2003)

Bratton & Gold (ibid) note that the term 'strategic HRM' can be seen as:

- an *outcome:* 'organisational systems designed to achieve sustainable competitive advantage through people' (Snell *et al*)

- a *process:* 'the process by which organisations seek to link the human, social and intellectual capital of their members to the strategic needs of the firm' (Bamberger & Meshoulam).

Torrington *et al* (2002) note that strategic HRM may be achieved by the integration of HRM policy goals into business strategy and line management thinking, or by the involvement of the personnel/HR function in both organisational and HR strategy development. They argue that while there is a greater likelihood of involvement in strategy when the most senior HR person is a member of the Board of Directors, Board membership does not guarantee the involvement of specialists in strategy – and is not necessarily essential to strategic involvement. In order to maximise opportunities to influence strategy, the HR function must:

(a) Use business and financial language (elements of 'hard' HR)

(b) Describe the rationale for HR activities in terms of business benefits or competitive advantage

(c) Appoint line-experienced managers into the HR function

(d) Concentrate on the priorities defined by business strategy

(e) Offer well-developed change-management skills

(f) Demonstrate an ability to think strategically, having its own mission, strategy and integrative approach (involving line management in the development of HR strategy)

EXAMPLE

Four years ago Kim Reid was running British Aerospace's youth programmes, ranging from graduate development to schools liaison. Before that she was a pensions specialist. Now she sits round a boardroom table with 11 others, helping to run one of the main business divisions of what is now BAE Systems.

Her views have fed into the business strategy for the customer solutions and support division (CS&S), a 14,000-strong business, and she has led the senior team through workshops to develop the vision and capabilities needed to support the strategy. She also chairs the group pensions committee. Reid is one of dozens of HR professionals at BAE Systems whose role has been transformed since the merger of British Aerospace and Marconi Electronic Systems in 1999.

In many ways, what the company did is a textbook example of current thinking on HR and corporate strategy – what Richard Finn, of Penna Consulting, calls 'tiering'. It split off the HR administration into a service centre, run for BAE Systems by a joint venture company called Xchanging, which was set up for the purpose. Most of the remaining HR staff became business partners (although BAE doesn't use the term as a job title), working closely with line managers in the group's dozen or so divisions. John Whelan, now the company's HR director for resourcing and development, says: "We wanted people to take on an organisation development/consultancy type of role."

(Pickard, 2003)

We will now look at some of the different approaches suggested for developing and integrating HR strategies.

According to Armstrong (2000):

> the fundamental aim of strategic HRM is to generate strategic capability by ensuring that the organisation has the skilled, committed and well-motivated employees it needs to achieve sustained competitive advantage. Its objective is to provide a sense of direction in an often turbulent environment so that the business needs of the organisation, and the individual and collective needs of its employees can be met by the development and implementation of coherent and practical HR policies.

3.2 Strategic integration or fit

The concept of strategic fit is central to strategic HRM. It suggests that to maximise competitive advantage, a firm must:

(a) Match its capabilities and resources to the opportunities and constraints of the external environment (external fit)

(b) Match the macro features of the organisation: its mission, strategy, structure, technology, products and services, culture and workforce (internal fit)

For Guest (1989), there are three aspects to strategic fit in HRM terms:

(a) Developing HR strategies that are integrated with the business strategy and support its achievement (vertical integration or fit)

(b) Developing integrated HR practices (resourcing, reward, development and so on) so that they complement and mutually reinforce one another (horizontal integration or fit), so that they consistently encourage quality, flexibility and commitment

(c) Encouraging line managers to realise and internalise the importance of human resources

As one of the key policy goals of HRM specified by Guest, strategic integration ensures that HRM 'is fully integrated into strategic planning so that HRM policies cohere both across policy areas and across hierarchies and HRM practices are used by line managers as part of their everyday work.'

3.3 Approaches to developing strategic HRM

Guest identified various types of fit, which reflect different approaches to developing HR strategies.

(a) **Fit as strategic integration.** HR strategies are congruent with, or aligned to, the thrust of business competitive strategies (for innovation, quality and cost-leadership); appropriate to the stage of the business life-cycle reached by the business (start-up, growth, maturity, decline); adapted to organisational dynamics and characteristics and so on. Employee expectations should also be aligned with strategic direction, by communication of the organisational vision, translating strategy into performance management, and developing a corresponding organisational culture.

(b) **Fit as an ideal set of practices**: ensuring that internal practices reflect '*best practice*'. The best practice approach is based on the belief that adopting certain broadly-applicable HRM practices will lead to superior organisational performance. Several sets of best practices, based on benchmarking, have been developed, including elements such as: employment security; sophisticated recruitment and selection processes; self-managed teams; high compensation contingent on performance; high-level participation processes; information sharing; coherent appraisal; skill flexibility; motivating job design (including responsibility, flexibility and development); on-going training; use of quality improvement teams; and harmonised (single status) terms and conditions (Armstrong, 2003). Armstrong himself notes that while 'these could all be regarded as "good practice" ... it is difficult to accept that they will universally constitute "best practice". What works well in one organisation will not necessarily work well in another.'

(c) **Fit as contingency**: ensuring that internal practices suit the particular (and changing) context of the firm, and its business strategy. The '**best fit**' approach (or contingency approach) is based on the belief that there is no 'one best way' or set of universal prescriptions for strategy: it all depends. Benchmarked 'good practices' must be selected and adapted to fit specific needs identified by analysis of the firm's context both external (opportunities, threats and constraints) and internal (culture, structure, technology and processes). Purcell *et al* (2003) note that the contingencies or variables in HR decision-making are so complex that it is impossible to isolate them all: the important thing is to be sensitive to changing needs and circumstances.

(d) **Fit as 'bundles'**: developing and implementing distinct **configurations** or 'bundles' of HR practices (such as quality management, performance management or competence frameworks) which can be used in multiple contexts to create coherence across a range of activities, ensuring that they complement and mutually reinforce each other. In particular, practices designed to enhance employee skills/competences should be integrated with practices designed to enhance employee motivation, since both are essential to performance. So, for example, if the overall HR strategy is to improve performance, the sourcing strategies for competence-based recruiting will be integrated with development strategies for competence-based training and rewards strategies to offer competence-related pay. Likewise, to increase motivation, strategies will need to integrate motivation-based selection criteria with development opportunities, job design and other intrinsic motivating factors.

NOTES

Activity 7   **(10 minutes)**

What do you think might be the key HR policy issues and approaches of an organisation:

(a)   Pursuing an innovation strategy
(b)   Pursuing a cost leadership strategy
(c)   In the growth stage of its life-cycle
(d)   In the decline stage of its life-cycle?

4   HRM AND BUSINESS SUCCESS

4.1   How does HRM impact on business performance?

Key research carried out by the Work and Employment Research Centre, University of Bath (Purcell *et al*, 2003) attempted to look inside 'the black box' which previously obscured the process by which people inputs are transformed into performance outputs. The researchers developed a complex 'People and Performance Model', which can be simplified as follows: Figure 8.4

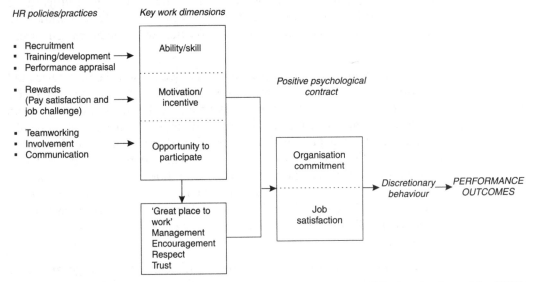

Figure 8.4: People and Performance Model (simplified and adapted by BPP)

This is primarily a behavioural model. A more strategic model was suggested by Guest *et al* (2000) as follows: Figure 8.5.

Figure 8.5: HRM and performance

> **Activity 8**   **(no time limit)**
>
> Using whichever of the above models appeals to you, analyse the link between the HR practices of an organisation you know (or know about) and its economic performance (or fulfilment of other outcomes, if it is a not-for-profit organisation). See if you can trace the effects all the way through the 'black box'.

4.2 HR vision: a quality workforce

Connock (1991) suggests that there has been a renewed focus on the need for a 'productive, trained, flexible and innovative workforce', which he sums up as 'a **quality** workforce'. He suggests that human resource managers should use vision and strategies to create and maintain this quality workforce in support of business objectives: this is the source of perceived added value for the HR function.

Connock lists what he considers the dimensions of quality for employers.

    (a)   A customer services orientation

    (b)   Taking personal responsibility for quality output

    (c)   Well trained and developed staff to meet quality requirements

    (d)   Employee involvement in all aspects of quality

    (e)   Maintaining quality standards

    (f)   Communication and recognition programmes which reinforce quality

    (g)   Searching for continuous improvement

    (h)   Knowledge of and identification with quality from staff at all levels

4.3 Human capital accounting

'Human capital' consists of the combined intelligence, knowledge, skills, abilities and energies of the people employed by a given organisation. These attributes have *value* as an organisational resource, and can have *value added* to them by investment.

- Organisations invest in human capital (through recruitment, retention, training, development, organisation and motivation) in order to enlarge their skill base, increase levels of competence, and foster knowledge acquisition and sharing. This in turn should reap returns in the form of productivity, flexibility, innovation and performance.

- Individuals invest in human capital (through acquiring skills, knowledge and experience) and reap returns in terms of higher earnings, enhanced cover (or employability) prospects, greater job satisfaction and so on.

'Human resource accounting' (or 'human asset accounting') is an attempt to quantify the financial value of human capital to the firm, as part of its market worth and asset base.

Under recommendations published in November 2003 by the DTI's Accounting for People taskforce, employers will have to report on human capital management (HCM) in their operating and financial reviews (OFRs) by 2005.

'Following wide consultation with employers, investors and other stakeholders, the taskforce has decided against a one-size-fits-all approach to HCM reporting. Instead, it has advised that employers should report on the aspects of HCM they see as key to business performance and strategy, including training, recruitment, diversity and leadership. Employers will have to show clearly how these policies affect business strategy and performance' (Higginbottom, 2003 (b)).

NOTES

EXAMPLE

'Since 2002 food company Geest has included an "Our People" section in its annual report and accounts. This includes employment profiles by sex and age, and information on appraisal, career development and graduate development structures. It includes detailed information on management development programmes. Statistics and figures are supplemented by case studies on HR initiatives, written by members of the HR department. These link the initiatives to company business strategy.

"Including this information in our reports has helped us benchmark ourselves against competitors," said Geest's group HR director, Mark Martin. He said investors were increasingly focused on the quality of training and management development: "If we are talking about business expansion then investors want to know that our people have the skills to carry that forward."

And Martin warned that it would be clear to investors where companies have merely applied a tick-box approach to human capital reporting. "Putting in disjoined information will not convince investors," he said.

(Higginbottom, 2003 (b))

The *Accounting for People* consultation paper highlighted four basic areas for Human Capital Reporting.

(a) The size and composition of the workforce – the numbers of people that the company relies on for its performance. This should include agency, contract staff and those on the payroll. Information should be produced in relation to age, gender and ethnicity.

(b) Employee motivation. As well as data on staff turnover and absentee rates, this should include information on arrangements for gathering employees' views.

(c) Staff training and development – this should include the match between the skills acquired and business objectives.

(d) Remuneration and fair employment – the organisation's approach to pay and incentives, and the means by which it satisfies itself that it does not discriminate unfairly.

FOR DISCUSSION

'The amount of information in a company's annual report about its employees, and on how the ways in which they are managed and developed add value to the business, is pathetically inadequate. Maybe there's a bland statement on people being our most important asset, a few pictures, a dozen pages on executives' rewards and perhaps total numbers employed in the notes – but that's about it. Hardly a "true and fair" view in our knowledge-, information- and service-based economy.'

(Brown & Baron, 2003)

What benefits can you see for organisations, employees and other stakeholders (shareholders, potential investors, potential employees) in having more rigorous human capital reporting?

(You might like to check out www.accountingforpeople.gov.uk for more information.)

NOTES

Chapter roundup

- While HRM is about 'success through people', there are two different orientations of this view.

  ° 'Hard' HRM emphasises the close integration of human resource policies with business strategy, and regards employees as a resource to be quanititatively measured and managed in the same rational way as any other resource being exploited for maximum returns.

  ° 'Soft' HRM views employees as valued assets and as a source of competitive advantage through their commitment, adaptability and high level of skills and performance.

- The Michigan model stressed the matching of HR policy to business strategy (hard), while the Harvard model stressed development and neutrality (soft).

- HR policies may be categorised as tight or loose according to the extent of managerial control which they assume to be necessary to achieve performance goals. Guest identifies the contrast between (tight) systems of compliance and (loose) systems of commitment.

- Storey developed an ideal type model or HRM contrasted to the traditional personnel/industrial relations model of labour management. 27 points of difference (expressed as extremes) were identified in the areas of beliefs and assumptions, strategy, the line management role and key levers used to shape the employment relationship.

- Strategic HRM is the direction of HR policy in such a way as to achieve the strategic goals of the business. HR strategy may be developed using business strategy, 'best fit', 'best practice' or 'configuration/bundling' approaches.

- There is increasing emphasis on the need to report accurately on the value of human resources and their impact on business performance, with Human Capital Reporting requirements due to be introduced in 2005. Various models have been devised to shed light on the 'black box' process whereby people inputs are transformed into performance outputs.

Quick quiz

1 What are the features of hard HRM?

2 What are the philosophical underpinnings of soft HRM?

3 What levels of management should HR be involved in, according to the Michigan model?

4 List four key ideas of the Harvard framework.

5 Distinguish between:

(a) Theory X and Theory Y
(b) Compliance and Commitment

6 What is the difference between a personnel/IR approach and an HRM approach in the dimensions of:

(a) The role of rules
(b) The nature of relations

(c) Prized managerial skills

   (d) The focus of attention for interventions

7 What does 'strategic fit' involve as applied to HRM?

8 Distinguish between a 'best fit' and 'best practice' approach to HR strategy.

9 Draw Guest's model of HRM and performance.

10 What is human capital?

Answers to quick quiz

1 Matching of HR and business strategy; focus on yield on human resources; focus on quantitative measures of management effectiveness; emphasis on the need for performance management and managerial control. (see paragraph 1.1)

2 Human relations school of management; socio-psychology; view of employees as assets/means rather than costs/objects; unitarist ideology; stakeholder perspective. (para 1.2)

3 Strategic (long-term, focus on future 'fit'), managerial (medium-term, focus on acquisition, retention and development), operational day-to-day, focus on supporting business activities. (para 1.3)

4 HRM involves all management decisions affecting the employment relationship. Organisations are made up of stakeholders and there is a trade-off between their interests. HRM is influenced by a range of contextual factors. Line managers take responsibility for aligning HR policy and competitive strategy. (para 1.4)

5 See paragraphs 1.6 and 1.7 for a full account.

6 (a) Importance of rules v 'can do' outlook creating impatience with rules

   (b) Pluralist v unitarist

   (c) Negotiation v facilitation

   (d) Personnel procedures v wide-ranging cultural, structural and personnel strategies. (para 2.1)

7 HR strategies integrated with business strategy to support its achievement (vertical fit). HR practices developed to complement and mutually reinforce one another with consistent results (horizontal fit). Line managers internalising the importance of human resources.

               (para 3.2)

8 'Best practice' assumes there are universally effective HR practices; 'best fit' assumes that 'good practices' will need to be selected and adapted to fit the external and internal context of the organisation, and remain sensitive to change. (para 3.3)

9 See paragraph 4.1., figure 8.5.

10 The combined intelligence, knowledge, skills, abilities and energies of people employed by an organisation. (para 4.3)

Answers to activities

1 **Hard**: high levels of rules, procedures and instructions, and appropriate training; strong corporate culture/values for the purposes of selection, socialisation and 'weeding out'; selection on the basis of pre-determined job criteria; close supervision and work inspection; administrative

controls on time-keeping, absence, hours worked and so on; performance management focused on monitoring of performance against imposed standards and targets; job descriptions; job evaluation based on standard measures of performance; payment by results (narrowly defined); short-term cost-benefit evaluation of HR policies; centralised control over HR functions; adversarial mechanisms for dealing with discipline, grievance and relationships with trade unions; 'need to know' communication policies; welfare to minimise costs/lost production; managerial status symbols and tiered terms and conditions.

2   **Soft**: articulation of goals and values; strong corporate culture/values for the purposes of inspiration – especially quality; flexible working methods; emphasis on teamwork; self-managed time-keeping and attendance; consultation and agreement on work targets and criteria; values- and outputs-driven criteria; consultation and agreement on issues affecting the workforce; delegation and empowerment; HR fulfilling and enabling rather than controlling role; training for development, employability, flexibility; personal development and improvement plans; employee relations based on communication and involvement; welfare based on well-being and enabled performance; reward systems and performance management based on collaboratively agreed criteria; harmonised terms and conditions.

3   The writer is describing a Theory X, tight-control approach. In a recession, organisations are likely to be faced with pressures to cut costs and improve productivity in order to remain competitive: managers may be tempted to adopt this approach towards HR issues to achieve these goals. Remember that 'loose-tight' is a continuum. According to a contingency view of strategic 'fit', there is nothing inherently right or wrong about loose or tight control strategies: the chosen approach must suit the business needs of the organisation and respond to changes in its environment.

4   This answer will be highly individual to you and your situation (which may indicate why commitment is not easy to pin down or foster in practice). Benefits to **you** (analogous to the employee) may have included enjoyment, sense of purpose, possibly extra effort resulting in better results, which in turn may lead to further satisfaction and opportunities for development. Benefits for your **trainers** (analogous to employers) may have included the same, perhaps defined in different ways: better attendance and time keeping, more creative ideas put forward to improve the course, encouragement to other students from your positive attitude, better results. Ways of **increasing commitment** may have included: clearer instructions, linking your studies to your goals in HRM, more enjoyable or challenging teaching methods and activities, and perhaps your willingness to put effort in now for rewards later.

5   Some examples you may have thought of are:

   (a) **Institutionalise conflict** through strict procedures for disciplinary action, grievance handling, appeals mechanisms, conflict resolution, negotiation with union representatives. (These are all good and helpful in the event of conflict – but they do assume that conflict is going to occur...) **De-emphasise conflict:** interpersonal conflict resolution handled on a contingency basis by management; win-win approach (assuming mutuality of interests); emphasise and reward teamworking and co-operation.

   (b) **Restrict communication:** institutionalised communication avenues (eg house journal or bulletin); managerial control over in-house communication; hierarchical, functional channels of communication; 'need to know' policies; lack of training in communication skills; centralised information storage and retrieval; discouragement of social networking among employees (by job and work environment design). **Increase communication:** training in communication; cultural reinforcement of communication (management example, reward and appraisal on communication skills); encouragement of multi-functional teamworking and/or briefings; encouragement of informal networking; focus on quality/customer overriding procedure.

6   Empowerment might influence recruitment/selection in the following ways.

(a)   Empowered workers may wish to take over responsibility for recruiting new members of their teams.

(b)   Jobs (and therefore job descriptions and selection criteria) would need to reflect new ways of working such as multi-skilling, team-working and so on.

(c)   Communication, leadership and facilitation skills would become key selection criteria for managers.

Empowerment might influence training as follows.

(a)   Training would be initiated and shaped by the job needs of empowered workers: relevant to the job, focused on areas such as responsibility, planning, teamworking and communication.

(b)   The trainer's role would be that of 'coach', reflecting the empowering/equipping philosophy towards training.

(c)   The manager may well take on the coaching/facilitating role: training will be seen to be a continuous on-the-job process and part of personal development by employees.

7   (a)   For innovation, the organisation will require creative behaviour, long-term thinking, collaborative working, willingness to take risks and tolerance of unpredictability. HR practices that may help foster these qualities include: teamworking, high communication flow, multi-skilling and flexible working; broader career/development paths allowing flexibility; longer-term, team-based performance appraisal; selection and reward for innovation values.

(b)   For cost leadership, the organisation will need a focus on output quantity (with less concern for quality), a relatively short-term outlook, and controlled/low-risk performance. HR practices that may help foster these qualities include: narrow job design and explicit job descriptions; short-term, output-focused appraisal and reward; close monitoring of employee activities; little investment in training and development; focus on cost minimisation.

(c)   In the growth stage, the organisation will require more progressive and sophisticated recruitment and selection (compared to start-up), training and development, performance management processes and reward systems, a focus on achieving high commitment and emphasis on developing stable employee relations.

(d)   In decline, the organisation may have to shift to rationalisation, down-sizing by accelerated wastage or redundancy, curtailing of

HR programmes (especially employee development) in order to cut costs, the attempt to marginalise or de-recognise trade unions.

8   This exercise is designed to help you build up case study material. It may also help you to realise how complex the relationships between all these variables are. In the 'People and Performance' model, for example, you might notice that the line management aspects (trust, respect) also *increase* the likelihood that HR policies (eg communication, teamworking, job satisfaction) will be successful. This underlines the key role of line managers in delivering HRM outcomes.

Assignment 8   **(1½ hours)**

You are the HR assistant in a chain of retail outlets. It manages its real estate, positioning and buying policies well, resulting in steady growth, but it also has a somewhat variable reputation for customer service. There is a high turnover of staff, and frequent representations from staff for better pay and conditions, which your department constantly has to handle. HR policies have been introduced to try and improve staff morale, but these tend to be piecemeal and reactive to problems. Attention has recently been paid to tighter selection criteria according to specific job descriptions, to try and recruit staff who will be more amenable to the highly developed norms, rules and procedures laid down for the floor staff. Additional training has also been offered to supervisors, so that they will be able to monitor staff behaviour and operate disciplinary measures where necessary.

The HR Manager has been trying to convince the Board of Directors that HR should be represented on the Board, and that it should completely review the role of personnel policy and practice in the organisation. 'We don't pay enough attention to the people aspects of our business – and that includes the customers as well as the staff!' she has said to you on several occasions. 'We're not doing HRM – we're doing personnel management! And it isn't working, so they think HRM makes no contribution to the bottom line. It's a vicious circle.'

The HR Manager asks you to prepare some notes for a forthcoming presentation to the Board of Directors. 'I want a good clear summary of the difference between personnel management and HRM, which will show that our current approach is not really HRM…They're still bound to say that HRM is too 'soft' and people-focused. We need to emphasise that business success is central to its aims – that there are 'hard' aspects to it as well as 'soft'… Pick out a couple of good punchy theories, will you, and do me up something that will come across well on visual aids.

Your task: summarise (a) Storey's points of difference between personnel/IR and HRM, and (b) hard and soft HRM in a format suitable for presentation (via a medium of your choice: presentation software, flip chart, overhead slides, written handouts and so on).

Chapter 9:
FLEXIBILITY WITHIN THE WORKPLACE

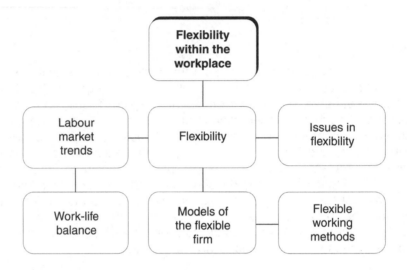

Introduction

In Chapters 2 and 3, we noted that sourcing labour requirements may be achieved from **within** the organisation as well as from the external labour market. The efficiency with which labour resources can be deployed and redeployed, at need, within the organisation depends on a measure of flexibility. Employees who are functionally versatile (or multi-skilled) and culturally flexible may be redeployed across the functional boundaries previously set by job descriptions and occupational demarcation zones. A flexible workforce may be deployed at periods of peak workloads. Given the pace of change in technologies and market places, and the 'ungluing' of traditional organisational structures to meet changing customer demands, flexibility is one of **the** Hot Topics in HRM!

Your objectives

In this chapter you will learn about the following.

    (a)   Labour market trends reinforcing the need for flexibility

    (b)   Models of the flexible firm

    (c)   Types of flexibility and flexible working methods

    (d)   The advantages and disadvantages of flexible working practices

1 FLEXIBILITY

1.1 Why flexibility?

Flexibility emerged as a major issue in the 1980s, as the Western European economies were forced to respond to change. Increased competition (particularly from the newly-industrialised Pacific Rim), international recession, uncertainty about future markets and the effects of new technology undermined historical expectations of stable economic growth. The pace and complexity of such changes has continued to increase.

(a)   Increased competition has placed emphasis on quality, innovation and reducing the unit costs of production: job design and the organisation of work must both mobilise employees' energies for quality/innovation and secure productivity.

(b)   Increased market uncertainty means that organisations need to be more adaptable to changes in demand: able to vary the size and deployment of their workforces to meet demand as effectively and efficiently as possible.

(c)   Technological change, particularly in the automation and computerisation of work processes, has eroded traditional demarcation boundaries between jobs: job design and the organisation of work must fit the new technology in order to secure its benefits for efficiency.

(d)   Demographic (and related labour market) changes have highlighted the need for flexible job and career designs, in order to meet the needs of dual income families, women and older workers for 'work life balance'. (This is discussed in more detail below.)

The need for flexibility therefore suggested three key objectives:

•   Increasing managerial ability to adapt the size and deployment of the workforce in line with changing demand and supply

•   Increasing scope for flexible working for individual employees

•   Raising the quality and/or quantity of workforce output

1.2 Labour market trends and flexibility

In Chapter 2, we discussed how HR planners need to take account of demographic and other factors in the internal and external labour markets, in order to meet the organisation's demand for skills. Specific pressures towards flexibility include the following.

(a)   **Age structure**

Social Trends shows that the number of economically active people in the age group 16-24 is falling, while those aged 25-44 is rising. As well as the resourcing implications discussed in Chapter 2, this means that an increasing proportion of the workforce may have family and child-rearing responsibilities, or care of a dependent aged relative: focus on 'work life balance' (Paragraph 1.3 below) has created the need for flexibility in working hours and place of work to support these workers.

(b)   **Diversity**

The most recent *Workplace Employee Relations Survey* data (WERS 1998) shows (Bratton & Gold, 2003) that in the UK:

•   Women's share of total employment increased to 47% (from 42% in 1980)

- The proportion of all workplaces with a low concentration of female workers (less than 25%) fell to 27% (from 36% in 1980)

- The majority of women workers are engaged in clerical, serving or cleaning work, but female participation has also increased in middle and senior management

'In the next 10 years, the workforce will grow by 1.5 million, of which 85% will be women. Some 22% of workers expect to have care responsibilities for older people within the next five years, and 78% of women with school-age children work outside the house' (Bond, 2003).

Gender diversity in the workplace, and the need to recruit and retain female workers (in order to meet both skill/labour shortages *and* equal opportunity requirements) has reinforced the focus on work life balance. Organisations need to deploy labour flexibly in order to accommodate the demands made of working mothers (and fathers, given the related trend towards shared family responsibilities and dual career families) and the desire for career breaks and return after child-rearing.

(c) **The use of non-standard contracts**

According to WERS 1998, the proportion of all employees working part time in the UK (30 hours or less per week) increased to 25% (from 21% in 1980), while subcontracting was undertaken by 90% of all workplaces. Overall, there has been a trend towards flexible labour practices, whereby firms replace full-time 'core' workers with part-time, temporary and sub-contracted labour. This represents 'a looser contractual relationship' between the firm and the worker (Atkinson, 1984).

This trend relates to increasing diversity and equal opportunity, as the majority of part-time and temporary workers are women.

(d) **Fluctuations and differences in particular labour markets**

Employers may compete for labour and skills in a number of different markets: local, national and international.

Particular factors in the local labour market (people living in the 'travel to work area' or within reasonable commuting distance) may create pressure for flexibility. For example:

- Geographical dispersion or lack of public transportation may require flexible starting hours, or work from home options.

- Local skill shortages may require the subcontracting of work.

- Different occupational structures and orientations (at local and national level) may require different approaches to the employment relationship, career management and so on. Professionally and technically qualified staff, for example, may be treated differently (as 'core' employees) from lower-skilled and high-mobility workers (who may be more flexibly contracted).

(e) **Regulation of working hours**

The *Working Time Regulations 1998* sets (currently negotiable) limits on working hours per week and entitlement to rest breaks and days. In order to cover equivalent workloads, employers may have to implement job-sharing and other flexible work patterns.

Activity 1 **(30 minutes)**

Check out www.statistics.gov.uk, or the WERS 98 website: www.dti.gov.uk/er/emar/1998wers. (Alternatively, there are government publications such as *Social Trends* or the *Department of Employment Gazette*.)

See if you can locate the following information.

- The percentage of the UK labour force in permanent employment in the current year.

- The percentage of women in the UK labour force in the current year.

- The percentage of women in part-time work in the current year.

1.3 Work life balance

Work-life balance is a concept which recognises the need for employers to support workers in achieving a balance between the demands of their work and the demands of home and family responsibilities (including the care of children, older people and sick family members).

Flexible working policies, designed to give employees options in regard to their hours and/or locations of work, have been supported in recent years by equal opportunity and family-friendly rights law.

Equal opportunities

Changes to work patterns (eg new shifts or working hours) that result in loss of earnings or dismissal of women unable to comply because of childcare responsibilities, for example, have been construed as sexual discrimination. Staff who return from maternity leave and are refused part-time work (without objective business justification) are likewise protected.

Family-friendly rights

Parental leave and reasonable time off to deal with family emergencies have been provided for in UK law for some years. The Employment Act 2002 provided for an additional package of rights introduced on 6 April 2003 (Cartwright, 2003).

(a) Any employee with 26 weeks' service, who is the parent or legal guardian of a child under six (under 18 if the child is disabled) has the right to request flexible working arrangements: to change the total numbers of hours contracted to work; when those hours are worked; and/or where the work is done.

(b) Requests must be written/emailed, and include details of the applicant's eligibility, the nature and timetable of the requested change, and consideration of the impact of the change on the business. A number of on-line resources is available to help applicants think the issues through: eg www.flexrequest.co.uk.

(c) The employer has 28 days to consider the request and approve – or at least meet with the applicant to discuss the application. Employees are entitled to be accompanied by a work colleague at any discussion.

(d) If the application is declined, the employee may appeal. Justified reasons for refusal include: the burden of extra costs; negative impact on productivity,

NOTES

quality or performance; inability to reorganise or redistribute work; or inability to recruit extra staff to make up lost hours.

(e)   If the employer refuses to consider a request, or fails to follow the statutory procedure, the employee has three months to bring a complaint before an Employment Tribunal.

'For years, best-practice organisations have taken an informal approach to fielding flexible working requests, with local line managers making decisions that best fit an individual or department, by involving other team members in the matter. In many cases, this method will continue to be the most effective in driving a flexible work culture while avoiding red tape' (Cartwright, 2003).

The UK government has stated its aim for employers to act 'in the spirit of the legislation', to attempt to help employees work in alternative ways to facilitate work-life balance. However it is also committed to reviewing the new rights in April 2005: if firms were being too quick to reject requests for 'business reasons', there may be tightening of the requirement to produce 'objective justification' for refusing (Evans, 2003). Watch this space!

For more information on work life balance, you may like to check out the TUC website (www.tuc.org.uk/changingtimes); *People Management* online (www.peoplemanagement. co.uk/work-life); or Parents at Work (www.parentsatwork.org.uk).

EXAMPLE

'Telford and Wrekin Borough Council won two Parents at Work Awards in 2003. Since introducing flexible working practices, it has been able to extend its hours of operation – and has seen dramatic reductions in staff turnover and sickness levels.

'The borough has one of the highest concentrations of single mothers in Europe and, as roughly 80 per cent of the council's workforce are female, HR supports a range of initiatives that enable mothers to return to work and generally help working parents. These include assistance with childcare costs, a workplace crèche, local shop discounts and a hot-line to a nursery for those needing emergency childcare. Most important are working hours that allow parents to combine careers with bringing up children.

'[The council] also stresses the need to help the wider community, especially the elderly and the young. For example, allowing an employee to work flexible hours so they can care for an elderly relative relives the council of some or all of the burden of caring for that person itself.

'Over the past three years, the composition of the council's workforce has changed dramatically, with 52 per cent working part-time. Many work from home, others opt for annualised hours, term-time working or a week-on, week-off working pattern. [The council's manager] believes a decentralised approach is best, with line managers handling individual requests. "We encourage managers to use their common sense and be caring in a practical way," he says.

'Managers are expected to initiate work-life balance conversations and act as a role models by looking after their own work-life balance. Senior managers are as eligible for flexible working as junior staff. To ensure consistency and fairness, managers are assessed on the work-life balance competencies in their department through a management development programme. An annual employee survey also looks at the issue, asking questions such as: "Is your manager flexible to your own personal circumstances?" ...'

(Woolnough, 2003)

PROFESSIONAL EDUCATION

Flexibility is clearly in line with the HRM approach to making the most effective and efficient use of the human resource. As we saw in Chapter 8, however, there are two ways of looking at HR issues: from a 'hard' perspective and from a 'soft' perspective. What does flexibility look like from each of these.

1.4 Hard or soft HRM?

There are two distinct orientations to flexibility, in accordance with the hard and soft views of HRM.

(a) Flexibility is a key goal of strategic HRM, with its hard emphasis on meeting business needs through efficient deployment of the labour resources. 'Hard' flexibility, in the words of Beardwell and Holden, means 'the ability to adjust the size and mix of labour inputs in response to changes in product demand so that excess labour is not carried out by the organisation'. This approach has been popularised as '**lean production**': minimising overhead labour costs by reducing jobs not directly contributing to production, and minimising the cost of directly productive labour by raising productivity.

(b) Flexibility is consistent with the soft HRM emphasis on empowerment and involvement of employees for increased commitment, motivation and development. 'Soft' flexibility means creating an adaptable workforce, by involving employees in decision-making, broadening their skills individually and through teamworking and creating a culture of continuous learning and improvement focused on outcomes rather than inputs or procedures.

1.5 Mutual benefits

Depending whether a hard or soft flexibility approach is used, flexibility may have benefits for the employing organisation and for employees. We will discuss the advantages and disadvantages of specific flexible working practices, from both points of view, as we proceed through this chapter. In general, however, the intended benefits are as follows.

(a) For the **organisation**, it offers a cost-effective, efficient way of utilising the labour resource. Under competitive pressure, technological innovation and a variety of other changes, organisations need a flexible, 'lean' workforce for efficiency, control and predictability. The stability of the organisation in a volatile environment depends on its ability to adapt swiftly to meet changes, without incurring cost penalties or suffering waste. If employee flexibility can be achieved with the co-operation of the employees and their representatives, there may be an end to demarcation disputes, costly redundancy packages and other consequences of apparently rational organisation design.

(b) From the point of view of the **employee,** the erosion of rigid specialisation, the micro-division of labour and the inflexible working week can also offer benefits. For example, a higher quality of working life; an accommodation with non-work interests and demands (work-life balance); greater job satisfaction, through variety of work; and perhaps job security and material benefits, since a versatile, mobile, flexible employee is likely to be more attractive to employers and have a higher value in the current labour market climate.

Unit 22: Managing Human Resources Issues

FOR DISCUSSION

'The concept of flexible working has been at the top of the HR agenda for some time now. It is clear that many people (particularly women) feel unable to accept the old-style pattern of "full-time" commitment to a job – without any opportunity to spend time with small children, care for older relatives or even simply take time out. Employers have responded in a number of ways: from the bare legal minimum to packages that offer enormous flexibility.

'But it's equally clear that workplaces aren't always finding it easy to put these policies into practice. A study from the Institute for Employment Studies last year, *Work-Life Balance Beyond the Rhetoric*, demonstrated that employees wanted a work pattern that offered them flexibility for other commitments; and HR managers were generally convinced that this had definite business benefits. But the same study shows that few people actually move away from conventional work patterns.

'This is mainly because they think that doing so would affect their career prospects; and many managers, even if they would like to be supportive, simply don't know how to help. In practice, long working hours and heavy workloads (and, of course, the need to bring in a full-time wage) remain the norm for many.'

(Holmström, 2003)

How might work-life, family-friendly and flexible polices be undermined by corporate culture, management style and econoimc reality?

You may have noticed from the preceding paragraph that there are a number of different types of flexibility, including not only the employer's ability to change the size of the workforce in response to demand, but the broadening of employees' skills and task variety, and the re-structuring of the working day or week. We will now summarise the flexibility approaches.

1.6   Types of flexibility

There are a number of possible approaches to flexibility.

Type of flexibility	Responding to:	Personnel management approach
• **Numerical**	Fluctuations in demand for staff numbers (seasonal, cyclical, task-related and so on)	Use of non-permanent, non-career labour: temporary staff, part-time staff, short-contract staff, consultants, sub-contractors
• **Temporal**	Fluctuations in working patterns, over 24 hours/week/year: fluctuations in demand for labour at particular times; the need for work-life balance and support for equal opportunity	Use of 'flexi-time' and variations: overtime, shift-working, annualised hours

Type of flexibility	Responding to:	Personnel management approach
• **Functional** (versatility)	Fluctuations in demand for particular skills – not necessarily related to staff numbers (since one person can be multi-skilled)	Deployment of staff across job/skill boundaries ('demarcation lines'): multi-skilling, multi-disciplinary teams, fewer or broader job descriptions
• **Financial**	The need for functional/ temporal staff to be rewarded flexibly and fairly - since 'the job' is no longer a fixed basis for reward. The need for choice (eg in incentive and benefit schemes) to raise value of rewards in a diverse workforce	Performance - and/or profit-related pay; individual pay negotiation; broad-band pay schemes; flexible benefits
• **Locational**	Opportunities presented by information and communication technology (ICT) to reduce office costs and create 'virtual' (dispersed but interconnected) teams	Use of home-working, tele-working and networking; use of ICT to facilitate mobile working (eg for sales and service staff)
• **Cultural**	The need for a change of traditional attitudes towards jobs, careers, occupational identify: the need for a culture which embraces flexibility, variety, change, entrepreneurship	Recruitment and reward systems geared to employ and advance culturally flexible and versatile people; communication of flexibility and work-life balance as key values; counselling to help overcome fear of change

---

Activity 2   **(No time limit)**

Observe staff at a local supermarket and talk to friends who might work for one of the big supermarket chains. What evidence of flexibility can you see within organisations such as these? Which 'type' of flexibility is suggested by each of your examples?

We will now look in more detail at two key models for numerical flexibility.

2 MODELS OF THE FLEXIBLE FIRM

2.1 The core and periphery model

Fluctuations in the (numerical) demand for workers may be foreseeable: regular peaks due to daily, weekly or seasonal cycles (such as lunch and dinner times at an all-day restaurant, Saturdays at supermarkets, or Easter at a chocolate factory) or irregular peaks due to organisational activity (such as a product launch). Other fluctuations may be unforeseeable: industrial action affecting competitors; events or reports in the media which stimulate or 'kill' demand for the product/service and so on.

The organisation cannot afford to employ a full-time workforce based on the best-case scenario or greatest demand. Indeed, in times of pressure to downsize the workforce (or at least, not to expand it), organisations prefer to increase their proportion of non-permanent labour, to avoid redundancies and/or seasonal layoffs.

The 'flexible firm' model (Atkinson, 1984; Atkinson & Meager, 1986). It suggested 'a reorganisation of firms' internal labour markets and their division into separate components, in which the worker's experience and the employer's expectation of him/her are increasingly differentiated'.

A model was developed which divided the workforce in 'core' and 'peripheral' groups of workers: Figure 9.1.

Figure 9.1: Atkinson's core-periphery model of the flexible firm (Atkinson, 1984)

The core

The **core** group is permanent and stable, and is based on:

(a)   The lowest number of employees required by work activity at any time throughout the year and

(b)   Core tasks which are specific to the firm and require firm-specific skills and experience

The core group offers **functional** flexibility by virtue of re- or multi-skilling: training, retraining and redeployment within core tasks.

HR implications include:

(a)   The need for training in core skills

(b)   The need to offer employment security/continuity in order to facilitate skill/experience build-up and in order to protect the firm's investment in core workers' training

(c)   The need for reward structures which reflect and support flexibility and multi-skilling by removing rigid grade or functional barriers

(d)   The need to secure the commitment of the core workforce: this would usually foster commitment-based 'soft' HRM policies

The periphery

The **peripheral** group is designed to offer numerical flexibility: the ability to meet short-term fluctuations in demand for skills which are not distinctive of the firm.

(a)   Full-time employees in areas where there is a high level of mobility and wastage/turnover (clerical/secretarial and so on), creating a relatively numerically flexible internal labour market: the first peripheral group

(b)   Workers on non-standard contracts: the second peripheral group

(c)   'Distance' workers not employed by the organisation but contracted to supply services

Core-periphery flexibility

By acting as a 'buffer' against the need to downsize the organisation in the face of fluctuating demand (Figure 9.2), the core-periphery model allows for:

(a)   Relatively 'hard' HR policies aimed at reducing labour costs, and avoiding labour excesses and shortages, applied at the periphery and

(b)   Relatively 'soft' HR policies aimed at increasing productivity and commitment, providing employment security and organisational stability, applied at the core

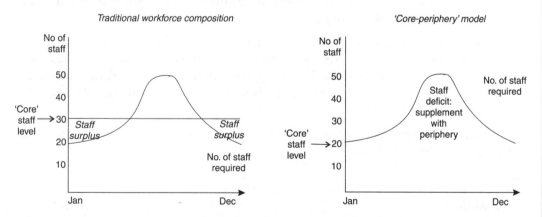

Figure 9.2: The flexible firm and HR planning

2.2   The Shamrock organisation

Handy (1989) puts forward the idea of the *shamrock* (or *clover-leaf*) organisation, giving examples such as Rank Xerox and IBM.

Mullins (1999) represents this as follows: Figure 9.3.

Figure 9.3: The Shamrock Organisation

- The *professional core* are permanently-employed people who represent the distinctive knowledge and competences of the firm. They are qualified professionals, technicians and managers. Their commitment is focused on their work and career within the organisation.

- The *flexible labour force* are temporary and part-time workers who can be brought in as and when needed – especially to meet peaks in the demand for services (since they have to be supplied in 'real time'). Their commitment is typically focused on the immediate job and work group, rather than career or the organisation. However, they are crucial in maintaining standards of service – so it is important for the firm not to treat them 'casually': they should receive fair and equitable treatment (now enshrined in employment law), adequate training and status.

- The *contractual fringe* are external providers (freelancers, consultants and sub-contractors) who are able to undertake non-core activities and/or provide specialist services, more economically than the firm could manage internally. Their commitment is typically to achieving specified results in return for fees.

These represent three distinct labour forces, each with its own type of psychological (and legal) contract with the firm.

Activity 3   **(5 minutes)**

What would you expect the key HRM issues to be in the case of each of Handy's 'leaves' discussed above?

In addition, Handy notes the 'lucky' fourth leaf of the clover: the organisation may be able to 'sub-contract' some sales, service and supply tasks – for free – to *customers*. Information and communication technology (ICT) has supported a wide range of 'self service' applications such as: Internet/phone banking and automated teller machines (ATMs); Internet/telephone reservations and ticketing, in entertainment and travel; online information services and so on – in addition to traditional self-service retail and catering outlets, self-assembly products and so on. This should allow labour savings in other 'leaves' of the organisation.

We will now look at other approaches to numerical, locational, functional and temporal flexibility.

3 FLEXIBLE WORKING METHODS

3.1 Part-time and temporary working

Definition

> Under the EU directive on part-time work, a **part-time employee** is someone with a contract or employment relationship whose normal hours of work, averaged over a period of up to a year, are less than the normal hours of comparable full-timers.

Activity 4 (45 minutes)
Why do you think there has been an increase in part-time working?
Consider the employer and employee points of view.

The thrust of legislation and court decisions has been to protect 'peripheral' employees from exploitation by 'hard' flexibility policies.

EU directives on part-time and temporary work were incorporated into UK law by regulations and a Code of Practice under the Employment Relations Act 1999. Part-time and temporary or fixed-contract employees are now entitled to the same employment and health and safety protection as permanent full-time staff.

(a) Part-timers (who work 8 hours or more per week) may not be treated less favourably because they work part time. This applies to access to training, proportional entitlement to benefits (paid holiday, sick pay and access to pensions and parental leave etc), selection for promotion, protection from unfair dismissal, rights to written particulars of employment, and so on.

(b) Obstacles to part-time work should be removed: there should be opportunities for part-time work at all levels, and for transfer between full-time, part-time and job-sharing arrangements (part-time (and temporary) workers should be informed of permanent full-time vacancies, for example).

(c) The Working Time Regulations (discussed in Chapter 11) give equal rights to part-time and temporary workers in respect of night working, minimum rest periods and Health and Safety protection services, since they are held to be particularly at risk.

(d) Temporary and fixed-contract workers are also entitled to the same social security benefits as permanent employees.

(e) Individuals engaged under temporary contracts must be informed of the reasons for their being employed on a temporary rather than a permanent contract.

NOTES

(f)   Health and safety legislation applies equally to full-time, part-time and temporary workers.

FOR DISCUSSION

Does the protection and extension of part-time and temporary workers' rights defeat the object of the core-periphery model? What does it suggest about the perceived advantages of the model to employers and its perceived disadvantages to peripheral employees?

EXAMPLE: INTERNATIONAL COMPARISONS

- Temporary work has traditionally been more highly regulated in other member states of the EU than in the UK, including the obligation to justify temporary work, provide a contract, limit the duration of the contract and provide comparable pay and conditions. Fixed-term contracts automatically became permanent in most states if they over-run. Some countries (Belgium, France, Portugal, Spain) have placed restrictions on the use of temporary workers, specifying their use only to cover absences, and for seasonal and exceptional workloads: Italy banned temp agencies, while Germany and the Netherlands specified that agency temps not work for more than six months in any one establishment. (These provisions may change as directives come into effect.)

- The USA has a free approach to part-time and temporary workers. Beardwell and Holden suggest that 'there are grounds for thinking that workers employed by temporary help agencies or contracting firms in the USA are denied the benefits of employment security, job progression and benefits such as pensions that go with internal labour markets.

3.2   Job-sharing

Job-sharing is an approach to part-time job creation in which an existing full-time position is split in two, so that two people can share it, working part-time and paid pro-rata.

3.3   Tele-working and home-working

Definition

> **Tele-working** describes the process of working from home, or from a satellite office close to home, with the aid of networked or Internet-linked computers, fax machines and other ICT applications.

Tele-working offers:

(a)   Savings on overheads, particularly premises costs, in view of rising rents in many of the major cities in the UK

(b)   The opportunity to bring into employment skilled and experienced people for whom traditional working practices have hitherto been impracticable: single parents, mothers, the disabled, carers and so on

PROFESSIONAL EDUCATION

(c)   Elimination of the need to commute - with consequent reductions in traffic congestion, fuel consumption, travel costs, pollution, commuter stress

(d)   Better work-life balance: less stress; more employment opportunities for those with family responsibilities

Tele-working may take the form of:

(a)   *Homeworking:* traditional outworkers such as home typists, market-research/ tele-sales workers etc

(b)   *Freelancing:* working for a number of different clients from a home office, or in client offices

(c)   *Mobile working:* using laptop computers, the Internet and mobile phone technology to work 'on the road' (eg field sales staff)

(d)   *Call-centre working:* working in specialist centres providing helpline services, telesales, data entry and so on

EXAMPLE: GOOD PRACTICE: SOLAGLAS

Taking flexibility to the customer

Solaglas is a UK subsidiary of French multinational glassmaker Saint-Gobain employing glaziers and installation workers. Its "Moving Forward" agreement on annualised hours with the GMB and AEEU is designed to focus its business on customer service, through flexibility in working hours. Features of the agreement include: single-status employment; annual salaries; flexible start times (between 7 am and 11 am, Monday to Saturday); computerised working for home-based glaziers using palm-tops for job allocation, progress reports and factory contact.

The benefits for the company are increased productivity, a single pay scheme, flexibility, profitability and significant reinvestment by the French parent company. Benefits for staff include enhanced terms and conditions, permanent status and greater choice in working time (of particular benefit for two men who were caring for wives with long-term illnesses). The work is also carried out at the customer's convenience.

(Bond, 2003)

Barnes (1997) suggests how teleworking might be most effectively managed.

Proper management of teleworking will go a long way to ensuring its success and reducing the fear of loss of control which is the major employer preoccupation. Some pointers for good practice are:

- Develop relationships of trust

- Have policies covering operational issues such as insurance, confidentiality, taxation (possible capital gains tax liability arising from the use of domestic property for business purpose), security and health and safety

- Use criteria when recruiting which enables the selection of those with self-discipline, good self-management skills and other attributes of effective teleworkers

- Have formal and informal channels of communication (social isolation is the major disadvantage of teleworking as reported by the workers themselves) with visits by supervisors, regular meetings at the office, use of telephone, newsletters, informal gatherings etc

- Clearly define quantitative and qualitative targets to "manage-by-results" and give thought to monitoring performance making use of electronics whenever possible

- Have performance appraisal, career management and training policies which meet the needs of teleworkers

- Be open to part-time home and part-time office working and even 'occasional' teleworking if appropriate

- Maintain the voluntary principle and have a "revolving door" policy whereby as circumstances change workers can return to full-time office working

- Evaluate outcomes against objective measures in productivity, quality of output, accommodation cost etc.

3.4 Multi-skilling

Jobs are changing from simple, well-defined tasks (set out in job descriptions) to more flexible, multi-dimensional work. This new approach recognises that:

(a) Performing a whole meaningful job is more satisfying to a worker than performing only one of its component tasks (as in 'scientific' job design)

(b) Allowing workers to see the big picture enables and encourages them to contribute information and ideas for improvements, which might not otherwise have come to light

(c) The focus on the task and overall objectives reduces the need for tight managerial control and supervision over work processes and practices

Definition

Multi-skilling is functional versatility: the opposite of specialisation, with its tendency towards rigid job descriptions and demarcation lines between one job and another. It involves the development of versatility in the labour force, so that individuals can perform more than one task if required to do so: workers are being encouraged, trained and organised to work across the boundaries of traditional jobs and crafts.

Multi-skilling has been difficult to achieve historically, because craft and occupational groups (such as trade unions) have supported demarcation in order to protect jobs and maintain special skills, standards and pay differentials. This situation is changing now that multi-skilled, flexible labour is highly prized in today's labour market.

EXAMPLE: SMITHKLINE BEECHAM

SmithKline Beecham introduced multi-skilling at its factory in Irvine in 1995 . This was accomplished across a great 'divide' of strict demarcation between **operators** (belonging to the Transport and General Workers' Union, TGWU) and **craftsmen** (represented by the Amalgamated Electrical and Engineering Union, AEEU). Further problems were posed by deeply-entrenched working practices, and the strong trade union traditions of western Scotland.

In the past, process operators faced with a blockage in the pipes (carrying materials from one stage of the process to another) have had to tell their supervisor, who would tell the engineering foreman, who would send a fitter to deal with it: meanwhile, production would grind to a halt. After multi-skilling, the job could be done by whoever was best placed to do it: craftsman or - more often - operator.

Analysis of such situations by working parties resulted in the concept of the 'best person': instead of jobs being 'owned' by particular groups, the most appropriate individual to do a particular job should be trained and skilled to do it!

'The intention was to increase efficiency across the whole site by cross-skilling electrical, mechanical and instrument engineers, while at the same time equipping operators with basic engineering, materials movement and analytical skills'.

Agreement was achieved after three years' consultation and negotiation with the unions.

The benefits of multi-skilling to the organisation are as follows.

(a) It is an efficient use of manpower.

    (i) It smoothes out fluctuations in demand for different skills or categories of worker.

    (ii) It may be possible to maintain a smaller staff, because specialists would not be needed in each skill area.

(b) It puts an end to potentially costly demarcation disputes, where one category of worker objects to others 'invading' their area of work, as defined by narrow job descriptions.

(c) On the other hand, it is less likely that a task will be left undone because it does not explicitly appear on anybody's job description.

Activity 5   **(15 minutes)**

What does multi-skilling offer the *employee*?

3.5 Flexible working groups

The basic work units of organisations have traditionally been specialised functional departments. In recent decades, organisations have moved towards small, functionally flexible working groups or teams. Teamworking allows work to be shared among a number of individuals, without the requirement for complex and lengthy co-ordination and communication mechanisms.

Teams may be:

(a) Temporally flexible: called together to achieve specific task objectives and then disbanded (project management) and/or

(b) Numerically flexible: co-opting members and advisers as different skills, attributes and expertise are required

In terms of functional flexibility, there are two basic types of flexible working groups.

(a) **Multi-disciplinary teams**, which bring together individuals with different skills and specialisms, so that their skills, experience and knowledge can be pooled or exchanged (like different pieces making up a jigsaw puzzle).

This is regarded as a useful mechanism for organisational communication and co-ordination. It is particularly useful in problem-solving and creative ideas generation, since it fosters awareness of overall objectives, allows the airing of wide-ranging organisational issues, and accesses different ideas which can 'hitchhike' or 'leapfrog' on one another.

(b) **Multi-skilled teams** which bring together a number of multi-skilled individuals who can each perform any of the group's tasks. These tasks can therefore be shared out in a more flexible way between group members, according to who is available and best placed to do a given job at the time it is required. (See the Smithkline Beecham example above.)

Activity 6 (45 minutes)

What may be the drawbacks to teamworking? (Your earlier studies in *Unit 3: Organisations and Behaviour* should furnish some ideas ...)

Finally, we will look at approaches to temporal flexibility.

3.6 Flexible contracts

Forms of flexible contracted hours of work include the following.

(a) **Overtime**: premium rates of pay for hours worked in excess of standard hours. A business may ask employees to work overtime:

(i) To increase production to meet seasonal or ad hoc peaks in demand, without increasing the labour force

(ii) To maintain production (eg machine running) despite temporary shortages of labour. (Covering colleague absence is an example of this in the service section.)

Overtime can militate **against** efficiency where it is employee-driven, as a means of increasing outcome. Salaried workers are often not paid overtime, and some businesses negotiate higher basic pay rates for wage earners in lieu of overtime.

(b) **Zero hour contracts**: no guarantee of work (or pay) is given for the week. Staff may be called upon as and when required, on a full- or part-time basis, effectively imposing self-employed status. This is obviously highly flexible from the employer's point of view, but has been identified by the National Association of Citizens' Advice Bureaux (NACAB) as potentially abusive, since it creates financial insecurity and inability to plan commitments.

(c) **Annualised hours contracts**: agreeing a number of hours' work per year, rather than per week or month. Some or all of these hours may be committed to a rota schedule or roster while additional 'bank hours' may be held in reserve for unforeseen fluctuations (such as the need to cover for absences) plus 'reserve hours' designated for specific purposes other than normal working (such as training). Intensive hours can be called on during seasonal peaks in labour demand via longer working days or shifts, with time off in periods of low demand. This offers high flexibility for the employer, with employment security for the employee, although there is the danger of overwork during peak hours.

In an annualised hours scheme, workers may be paid a basic annual salary in monthly instalments. A system of 'credits' for hours worked, hours 'on call' for work but not called, and hours spent at work but not needed (and so on) minimises the effect of fluctuations in work load and allows for positive or negative balances to be rolled over into the following year. Detailed planning of rosters, monitoring of hours and recording of credits is clearly required.

(d) **Term-time contracts**: similar to annualised-hours but allowing parents to maximise hours during school terms, so that family responsibilities can be met during holidays.

3.7 Flexi-time

There are many 'flexi-time' systems in operation providing freedom from the restriction of a '9 to 5' work-hours routine. The concept of flexi-time is that predetermined fixed times of arrival and departure at work are replaced by a working day split into two different time zones.

(a) The main part of the day is called 'core time' and is the only period when employees must be at their job (this is commonly 10.00 to 16.00 hours).

(b) The flexible time is at the beginning and the end of each day and during this time it is up to the individual to choose when he arrives and leaves. Arrival and departure times would be recorded by some form of 'clocking in' system. The total working week or month for each employee must add up to the prescribed number of hours, though he may go into 'debit' or 'credit' for hours from day to day, in some systems.

A flexi-time system can be as flexible as the company wishes.

(a) The most basic version involves flexibility only within the day, with no possibility of carrying forward debit or credit hours into other days, so if you arrive late, you work late. This type of system is used in some factories where transport difficulties make arrivals and departures difficult.

(b) Another system is flexible hours within the span of the week. Hours can be carried forward to the next day. This enables an employee to cope with a fluctuating work load without overtime and gives him some control over his work and leisure time.

(c) Finally, flexi-time may be operated by the month. Each employee will have a coded key which can also serve as an identity card, and this will be used on arrival and departure by insertion into a key acceptor, which records hours worked on a 24 hour clock.

Activity 7 (20 minutes)

Suggest three advantages to

(a) the organisation, and
(b) the worker,

of implementing a flexi-time system.

We have already covered some of the HR implications of flexible working on a method-by-method basis. Here, we will draw together some of the threads.

4 ISSUES IN FLEXIBILITY

4.1 HR issues

Some of the HR policy choices to be considered are as follows.

(a) **Recruitment and selection**. Flexibility will need to be reinforced by selection criteria, both in terms of temperament (adaptability, willingness to adopt flexible working) and skills (trainability, existing multiple skills). In return, flexible working practices may act as a boost to the recruitment and retention of staff (especially women returners, say).

(b) **Training and development**. Performance management, training needs analysis and career planning will have to be tailored to flexible working in terms of: broadening skills, fostering flexible attitudes, teamworking (where relevant: criteria may be different for isolated homeworkers), opportunities for promotion (with equal access for part-time and temporary workers).

(c) **Supervision and control**. Flexibility militates against the supervisor's traditional role as monitor/controller of performance - especially where outworking and/or self-managing teams are used. The supervisor is increasingly becoming a coach/mentor/facilitator to empowered teams and/ or a co-ordinator/facilitator ensuring that communication is maintained with distant or part-time workers. (This change in role may itself require HR interventions in training and counselling support.) Control mechanisms must be developed to retain cohesion without rigidity: performance management, communication of cultural values, commitment-based policies and so on.

(d) **Motivation and reward**. Flexible payment structures will be required to reflect multi-skilling and team-working, while detailed administrative systems will have to support flexi-time and its variants. Attention will need to be given to employee morale and esprit-de-corps, particularly where people are only part-time or external members of the team: team-building will have to be broadened to include geographically separated 'virtual' teams.

(e) **Health and safety and other compliance aspects**. The employment environment is more highly regulated than ever before in terms of the protection of flexible workers. It places planning, administrative and employee relations duties on HR departments. In addition to compliance, there are the issues of social responsibility and employer branding/reputation, which dictate that 'soft' flexibility approaches may be more favourably regarded than 'hard' approaches such as zero hours contracting.

(f) **Cultural reinforcement**. HRM will have an important role in developing a culture which accepts and celebrates flexibility in general, through integrated systems for recruiting, rewarding, promoting, developing and facilitating flexibility, change, innovation and so on.

(g) **Problem-solving**. As we have seen, there are a number of drawbacks to flexibility from the point of view of the employee. HRM as a welfare function will have the task of minimising the impact of uncertainty, fluctuating earnings, isolation and so on, through supportive systems, compensations, safeguards and benefits. There may also be negative impacts on the firm's employer brand (and ability to attract and retain staff), if it is seen to abuse or exploit flexibility.

Activity 8   **(2 hours)**

Pick an organisation that you have worked for, or are familiar with, or can find out about. How flexible is the workforce in this organisation? Is it versatile, multi-skilled and happy to work unorthodox hours or without a strict job description? What does the human resource department in this organisation do to encourage, or to discourage, flexibility of labour? (Think about job descriptions, training and development, working hours and so on.)

4.2 New psychological contracts

In our discussion of the labour market in Paragraph 1.2 of this chapter, we noted that, according to the concept of 'job shift' (Bridges, 1995), the workforce is increasingly made up of 'skill vendors' who sell their services to a variety of clients on a project basis, and who take responsibility for their own résumé management: skill development, experience, self-marketing and so on.

This amounts to the re-writing of the traditional psychological contract of employment. Many organisations are making this explicit, by spelling out the new contract, in which concepts such as 'lifetime employment' or even a 'career' within a company are no longer valid. There are compelling reasons why an organisation may wish to repudiate responsibility for the job security and career development of its employees, even where it is offering 'permanent' employment.

(a) It may wish to discourage a culture of complacent performance based on job security and the fulfilment of job descriptions, and instead encourage the perception that competitive, value-adding performance is required in order to keep one's position.

(b) It may genuinely be unable to guarantee long-term, secure employment: in making this explicit, it is being socially responsible in encouraging employees to take ownership of their careers.

(c) It may wish to establish an attractive employer brand as an honest, open and realistic employer, in a market where educated employees are cynical about unrealistic recruitment offers.

On the other hand, there are risks to such an approach.

(a) There may be some loss of morale and performance, as the effects of newly-articulated insecurity are felt.

(b) There may be some loss of skilled labour, where individuals are alienated by the implication that they are not doing enough, or made uncomfortable by the uncertainty and responsibility of having to manage their own careers.

(c) There may be some loss of skilled labour, where individuals embrace the 'skill vendor' approach and career mobility to the point where they leave the organisation in order to develop their career portfolio.

One concept arising from the de-jobbing of employment is 'employability': a term which describes a portfolio of knowledge, skills and attributes that enhances an individual's marketability in the labour pool. Companies which have spelled out the new psychological contract may offer employability training in order to be socially responsible in facilitating employees' transition (if necessary) to other employment – while simultaneously benefiting from the resulting flexibility and versatility of employable individuals. (Employability and employability training are discussed further in Chapter 14.)

EXAMPLE

People Management (28 September 2000) reported how King's Healthcare NHS Trust, London, used an innovative package of flexible working practices – called Kingsflex - to meet a serious shortage of nursing and midwifery professionals.

The Kingsflex 10-point package

- Part-time working.

- Job-sharing.

- Temporary reductions in hours for specific periods to help employees deal with special circumstances.

- Staggered working hours. Staff can determine their working patterns on a planned, weekly basis. Hours can be staggered - for example, 10am to 6pm instead of the standard 9am to 5pm - for the whole week or for one or two days.

- Annual hours. Work can be spread unevenly over the year, giving employees scope for reducing their hours during school holidays, for example.

- A phased return to work. Staff can build up the number of weekly hours over a period after an absence such as sickness or maternity leave.

- Special and parental leave. Staff can take paid time off for specific needs - fostering, for example.

- Working from home - an occasional option as long as normal work is fulfilled.

- Career breaks. Employees can take unpaid leave for up to two years in order to travel, pursue further education or fulfil their caring responsibilities.

- 'Personalised' annual leave. Individuals can buy or sell days of annual leave, adjusting their entitlement by up to 10 days and increasing or decreasing their salaries accordingly.

Although these options are open to everyone, they were recognised as offering a better work-life balance for working mothers in particular. The Trust was overall champion in the 2000 Parents at work/Employer of the year awards.

FOR DISCUSSION

'The TUC guide to work-life balance (*Changing Times*) argues that, without staff involvement and support, flexibility can mean management imposing forms of work organisation on employees who are given no opportunity to state their opinions or explain their needs. In contrast, "positive flexibility" gives people more autonomy and choice, with the employer investing in development and training and working in partnership with the workforce.'

(Bond, 2003)

What do you think are the 'exploitative' and 'positive' aspects of flexibility?

Chapter roundup

- Labour flexibility has been driven by demographic factors (notably the increased participation of women in the labour force) and the increasing focus on work-life balance. The rights of parents of small children to request flexible working arrangements have recently been enacted in law.

- Labour flexibility can be approached from a 'hard' HRM orientation (focused on reducing labour costs and unit costs of production and on minimising the organisation's exposure to 'excess' labour: an approach called 'lean production') or from a 'soft' HRM orientation (focused on enhancing the quality and adaptability of the labour resource through broadening skills and commitment).

- Flexibility may be numerical, temporal, locational and/or functional, and must be supported by cultural flexibility through integrated HRM systems. (A number of specific methods and techniques of flexibility were discussed in detail.)

- Two main models have been developed for the flexible firm: Atkinson's core-periphery model and Handy's Shamrock model.

- Flexibility poses key HR issues for recruitment and selection, training and development, control and the role of the supervisor, motivation and reward and compliance with legal requirements.

- 'Flexible working arrangements used positively can benefit employees as well as being in the interests of the business ... but abusing them could make it more difficult to recruit people and could damage competitiveness in the long run.' (CIPD).

- The nature of the 'job' and the psychological contract of employment have changed with the emphasis on flexible working.

Quick quiz

1   What are the pressures that have led organisations to develop flexible working?

2   What kinds of flexible working arrangements are parents of small children entitled to request and what are the justified grounds for refusing such a request?

3   What are the five types of flexibility?

4   Outline (a) the core-periphery model and (b) the Shamrock organisation.

5   What are the rights of part-time workers under the Employment Rights Act 1999?

6   List three advantages of teleworking.

7   What are the two basic approaches to flexible group working?

8   List five methods of allowing flexibility in working hours.

9   How does flexibility affect the supervisor's role?

10   What is 'employability'?

BPP PROFESSIONAL EDUCATION

Answers to quick quiz

1   Increased market uncertainty, increased competition, technological change, labour market demographics and the shift towards work-life balance.   (see paragraph 1.1)

2   See paragraph 1.3 for a full answer.

3   Numerical, temporal, functional, financial, locational, cultural.   (para 1.6)

4   For a full account, see paragraphs 2.1 and 2.2.

5   Rights to equal treatment in respect to access to training, selection for promotion, protection from unfair dismissal (and other statutory requirements); proportional entitlement to benefits (paid holiday, sick pay, maternity pay); access to pension schemes and parental leave, protection under all health and safety legislation.   (para 3.1)

6   Savings on overheads; employment access for home-bound workers; elimination of commuting; reduction in stress through better work/life balance.   (para 3.3)

7   Multi-disciplinary teams, multi-skilled teams.   (para 3.5)

8   Zero hours, annualised hours, overtime, flexi-time, term-time contracts.   (para 3.6)

9   Shift from monitor/controller to coach/facilitator and/or co-ordinator.   (para 4.1)

10   The development of a portfolio of knowledge, skills and experience that enhances a worker's marketability and mobility in the labour pool.   (para 4.2)

Answers to activities

1   This is a research activity, designed to get you explaining sources of information on the labour market and labour market trends. You may only have been able to find forecasts relevant to the data requested – since the gathering and analysis of statistics takes time: this should remind you that HRM is a forward-looking activity!

2   Examples of flexibility in a supermarket might include:

    (a)   Extra staff employed for Christmas (numerical)

    (b)   Adult staff with family responsibilities employed just during school term-times (numerical/temporal)

    (c)   School-age staff employed just during school holidays (numerical/temporal)

    (d)   Staff on zero hours contracts (only called in to work when needed) (numerical/temporal)

    (e)   Staff paid according to their performance (financial)

    (f)   All staff trained to use checkouts (functional)

    (g)   Staff skilled enough to work in more than one department (functional)

3   *Professional core:* recruitment of high quality core people; retention, intrinsic rewards, career management; knowledge management. Possibly also delayering or downsizing: as the core is expensive, it makes sense to keep it as small as possible. This will take careful HR

NOTES

planning, to decide what core activities are and which people belong to the core group.

Flexible labour force: HR planning, management and control of work (to maintain standards), teambuilding, equitable treatment (while controlling costs), culture management and communication.

Contractual fringe: planned outsourcing, contracting (results and standard specification), relationship management, quality control, communication.

4   Connock (1991) gives seven main reasons for the increase in part-time working.

   (a)   Employers can match working hours to operational requirements better.

   (b)   The personal circumstances of key staff can be accommodated through part-time working. This will be particularly relevant to women returners.

   (c)   The productivity of part-timers is generally higher than that of full-timers (hardly surprising, since work is undertaken in more concentrated time periods).

   (d)   The absence levels of part-timers are generally lower: domestic requirements can more easily be fitted into the free periods in the part-time schedule.

   (e)   A pool of trained employees is available for switching to full-time work, or extending working time temporarily.

   (f)   Difficulties in recruiting full-time staff have prompted organisations to recruit and train part-time staff. Women returners are more likely to be attracted to an organisation if the hours of work are suitable, which will generally mean working part-time.

   (g)   Part-time working can cut overtime costs, since it makes it possible to avoid paying premium rates.

5   The erosion of rigid specialisation and fragmented job design can offer:

   (a)   A higher degree of job satisfaction, through variety of work and a greater understanding of its purpose and importance.

   (b)   Job security and material benefits, since a versatile, flexible employee is likely to be more attractive to employers, and have a higher value in the current labour market; and

   (c)   Personal skill development.

6   (a)   Teamworking is **not suitable for all jobs**: it does not always lead to superior or faster decision-making or performance than individuals working alone.

   (b)   Teams can delay decision-making in search of consensus (although consensus decisions do offer commitment and a rounded perspective).

   (c)   Social relationships might be maintained at the expense of other aspects of performance.

   (d)   **Group norms** may **restrict individual personality** and flair.

   (e)   **Group think**, or self-maintaining consensus, may prevent consideration of alternatives or constructive criticism.

(f) **Personality clashes** and **political behaviour** can get in the way of effective working.

7   Benefits to the organisation include: improved staff morale (because of flexibility); less stressed/distracted staff (because problems outside work can be solved without the guilt attached to lateness); less absenteeism (because of the 'I'm late for work: I'd better not go at all' syndrome).

Benefits to the workers include: less frustration in rush-hour commuting; less pressure over needs like the dentist or school sports days; time to shop, socialise etc in off-peak times; satisfaction of choice.

8   This allowed some space for your own research and reflection on your own experience. Plenty of sources of information: the HRM journals regularly report on flexibility initiatives, the currency of which is constantly reviewed by fresh considerations like family-friendly policies for recruitment, EU directives on worker rights and so on.

Assignment 9 (1 hour)

Flexconsult

You are a human resources consultant for Flexconsult, a consultancy which specialised in advising businesses on the best way to utilise their labour force, and on using flexible organisation structures and mechanisms to ensure that they have a labour force capable of fluctuating numerically in response to short term and/or seasonal changes in demand for their products and services.

You have just been handed a memo by your managing partner, which reads as follows.

Flexconsult

MEMO

To: (Your name)
From: Ed Hon Cho, Managing Partner
Date: (Today)
Re: New clients briefing

The partners have just met to discuss leads to prospective new clients. We are having preliminary discussions in two weeks with:

- A seaside holiday hotel

- A manufacturer of domestic appliances and

- A firm of management consultants

We would like to go into these meetings with an initial report, just to demonstrate our understanding of the HRM/labour demand issues involved in these businesses.

Please brief the Research Team on what you think those issues are, and what flexibility measures we might initially invite each business to consider.

EHC

Task

Compile some brief notes for yourself for the briefing of the Research Team. Include the supply/demand issues and some possible flexibility mechanisms for each of the three prospective clients.

Chapter 10:
EQUAL OPPORTUNITIES WITHIN THE WORKPLACE

Introduction

In this chapter, we look at discrimination at work and the legal framework shaping personnel policy in this area. As you read, be aware that while the law defines certain 'groups' against whom discrimination is illegal, discrimination can result from bias and prejudice of any kind. An ethical and cultural framework for justice and equality is as important as legislation and codes of practice: the 'management of diversity' concept is one development of this line of thought.

You may also note that discrimination can take subtle forms - classified as 'indirect' in current legislation: 'sexual harassment' is perhaps the most high-profile example of an issue which has emerged and been recognised as a form of discrimination.

Your objectives

In this chapter you will learn about the following.

(a) Forms of discrimination in employment

(b) The legislative framework on discrimination, including proposed changes

(c) Equal opportunities practices and initiatives in the workplace

(d) The move from equal opportunity to managing diversity

1 DISCRIMINATION IN EMPLOYMENT

1.1 Equal opportunities

Definition

> **Equal opportunities** is an approach to the management of people at work based on equal access and fair treatment irrespective of gender, race, ethnicity, age, disability, sexual orientation or religious belief.

Equal opportunities employers will seek to redress imbalances based around differences, where they have no relevance to work performance. Certain aspects of equal opportunities are enshrined in law; others rely upon models of good practice and have no legislative foundation.

1.2 Women in employment

Despite the fact that women have contributed directly to the national product since medieval times - on the land and in home-based industries such as textiles - the acceptance of women in paid employment has been a slow process, which is even now having to be enforced by law.

The distribution of women in the UK workforce today is still heavily concentrated in categories such as textiles, footwear, clothing and leather, hotel and catering, retail distribution and repairs, professional and scientific services, and miscellaneous services. A significant percentage of the women employed in these categories work part-time.

Only in recent decades has there been a widespread challenge to gender segregation in employment - the idea that there are 'men's jobs' and 'women's jobs', with only a few genuinely 'unisex' categories of work.

> **Activity 1** (30 minutes)
>
> Why do you think women have been regarded as 'second-class citizens' in the work place? Consider social values, educational influences; the changing nature of work; the historical composition of the workforce and so on.

Many assumptions about women's attitudes to work, and capabilities for various types of work are being re-examined, and we will look a bit later at some of the measures being taken to remove the barriers to women in employment.

Meanwhile, pay differentials between men and women have remained an issue, despite equal pay legislation. The *New Earnings Survey* (2000) reported that across all occupations, women earned 60-70% of male earnings in the same occupational group.

1.3 Ethnic minorities in employment

The TUC (2000) reports that the level of unemployment for black and Asian communities in the UK is 13% (compared to 6% for the white population).

There is also ethnic segregation in the labour market, with a concentration of minority (male) employees in manufacturing, hotel, catering, repairs and distribution sectors.

The proportion of ethnic minority employees falls sharply at higher levels of the organisation (only 1% of senior managers in FTSE 100 companies).

> **Activity 2** (5 minutes)
>
> Have you ever felt discriminated against (at school, work or training institution)? On what grounds: your sex, colour, age, social background./ beliefs/attitudes? What was the effect of the discrimination on your plans and attitudes?

Reasons cited for adopting positive action plans on racial equality include:

(a) Good HR practice, in attracting and retaining the best people (not just ethnic minority employees, but all those who care about discrimination)

(b) Compliance with the Codes of Practice which are used by Employment Tribunals

(c) Widening the recruitment pool for access to more labour

(d) Other potential benefits to the business, through its image as a socially responsible employer, and through the loyalty of customers, particularly in geographical areas of ethnic diversity

1.4 Disabled people in employment

Definition

> **Disability** is 'a physical or mental impairment which has a substantial and long-term adverse effect on a person's ability to carry out normal day-to-day activities' (*Disability Discrimination Act 1995.*)

Disability covers a wide range of impairments, including restricted mobility, speech impediment, poor hearing or eyesight, learning disability and disfigurement. It is estimated that this applies to one in five of the working age population (Torrington *et al*, 2002). The choice of jobs for the disabled is often restricted, resulting in higher and longer unemployment rates than the general population. Jobs are concentrated in plant/ machine operative jobs, which tend to be low-paid: disabled people are under-represented in professional and managerial jobs.

Attitudes towards the disabled in the workplace have been extremely negative, tending to focus on generalised and stereotypical problems such as:

(a) Long periods off work for medical causes

(b) Accident-proneness

(c) Poor skill levels

(d) Difficulties of adjusting the work environment for wheelchair access and other disability needs

(e) Negative image to customers, who allegedly felt awkward in the presence of disabled people

(f) The 'positive' association of certain jobs with disabled workers (eg lift attendants, switchboard operators, simple assembly tasks) stereotyping disabled roles and capabilities

1.5 Older people in employment

Despite demographic and educational changes and associated skill shortages among the younger population, a certain amount of discrimination is still directed at more mature workers.

The voluntary Code of Practice on Age Diversity in Employment (1999) appears to have had some impact on the number of recruitment advertisements specifying or implying age limits (Torrington *et al*, 2002). However, there are still negative perceptions of older workers which may impact on recruitment, selection for promotion, selection for redundancy, access to training opportunities and so on.

Activity 3	**(10 minutes)**

List some reasons - perhaps based on your own experience or prejudices! - why organisations might practise age discrimination.

The fact is that older workers:

(a) Have developed experience and skills in the job that may counteract any age-related loss of performance.

(b) Tend to stay in the job, reducing turnover and associated costs, and have better attendance and disciplinary records.

(c) Do experience some loss of strength and stamina. However, this is unlikely to be relevant to performance in most modern jobs, and older workers typically understand and work within their physical limitations.

(d) Do experience some loss of mental functioning (short term memory, for example) but retain - or even gain - in other cognitive functions.

(e) Are no more likely to be flexible or inflexible in relation to learning and change than younger employees.

(f) Do not necessarily cost the organisation more, as age-based reward systems are being replaced by performance-related ones.

EXAMPLE: INTERNATIONAL COMPARISONS

In the Far-East, great value is placed on 'the wisdom of age'. In Japan, age is equated with long service, the acquisition of skill and experience, and hence the quality of the worker.

1.6 Other forms of discrimination

As we noted in our introduction to this chapter, there are many potential differences that may be used as a point of discrimination. Recent attention has particularly been drawn by legislation (see Section 2 below) in regard to:

(a) *Sexual orientation*. Gay, lesbian and bi-sexual people may experience discrimination in:

- The culture of the firm: behavioural norms and attitudes that may cause harassment, verbal abuse or isolation of 'outed' gay workers, or the need to hide sexual orientation for fear of discrimination.

- HR practices: discrimination in terms and benefits due to eligibility criteria which exclude same-sex partners, for example.

(b) *Religious belief.* Apart from direct religious (often related to ethnic) discrimination against adherents to particular faiths, there is indirect discrimination through work practices which affect some groups more than others. Dress codes, time off for religious holidays and available facilities to comply with prayer requirements, for example, have recently been highlighted as diversity issues.

EXAMPLE: OUT WITH DISCRIMINATION

'HBOS, the financial services group, is a member of Stonewall's employer champion network, which meets quarterly to discuss topical issues surrounding sexual orientation. The company has also established a joint working group from its lesbian and gay network, supported by its unions Accord and Unifi, explained Tyrone Jones, diversity manager for HBOS.

' "The group meets to support colleagues and helps ensure that discriminatory practices have no place in the organisation," he said. HBOS has equality-proofed its employment policies to ensure that staff are not disadvantaged by their sexual orientation. For example, its paternity leave applies to same-sex partners.

'In addition, the financial services group has raised awareness of sexual orientation among its staff through holding diversity roadshows, workshops and divisional diversity taskforces. "Our HR teams have received information on the impact of the new regulations and a presentation on sexual orientation is available to all staff on the company's intranet," said Jones.'

(Higginbottom, 2003 (b))

FOR DISCUSSION

What aspects of religion or belief and sexual orientation are most clearly subject to discrimination, harassment or lack of understanding in your own work or study environment?

Is the discrimination systematic/procedural – or cultural/personal?

We will now look at the laws passed to protect the rights of key disadvantaged groups, as well as some of the issues which are currently being worked out in European courts and professional Codes of Practice.

2 THE LEGISLATIVE FRAMEWORK

2.1 Sex Discrimination and Race Relations Acts

In Britain, two main pieces of legislation deal with inequality of opportunity by reason of sexual and racial discrimination.

- The Sex Discrimination Act (SDA) 1975 (amended in 1986) outlaws certain types of discrimination on the grounds of sex, marital status, maternity or pregnancy.

- The Race Relations Act (RRA) 1976 (amended 1996 and 2000) outlaws certain types of discrimination on the grounds of colour, race, nationality, or ethnic or national origin.

There are three types of discrimination, under the Acts.

Definitions

- **Direct discrimination** occurs when one interested group is treated less favourably than another (except for exempted cases).

- **Indirect discrimination** occurs when requirements or conditions are imposed, which disadvantage a significantly larger proportion of one group than another. The employer must, if challenged, justify the conditions on non-racial or non-sexual grounds.

- **Victimisation** occurs when an employer disadvantages workers because they have sought to exercise their legal rights or assisted others in doing so.

An example of *direct* discrimination would be failing to select or promote a women because she is pregnant, or a person because they are of a particular nationality or race.

An example of *indirect* discrimination would be requiring promotion candidates to be available for prolonged periods of travel (disadvantaging married employees) where this was not in practice essential to the position; or setting a high standard of written English, where this was not objectively necessary for the job.

An example of *victimisation* would be passing an employee over for promotion because (s)he had recently threatened to take the firm to an Employment Tribunal over discriminatory practices.

The obligation of non-discrimination applies to all aspects of employment, including advertisements, recruitment and selection programmes, access to training, promotion, disciplinary procedures, selection for redundancy, grounds for dismissal and retirement ages for men and women.

Activity 4 **(15 minutes)**

Suggest four examples that would constitute **indirect** discrimination on the grounds of sex.

In each of the Acts, however, there are certain exceptions, in which discrimination of a sort may be permitted.

Permissible reasons for discriminating on grounds of gender (*genuine occupational qualifications*)	Permissible reasons for discriminating on racial grounds
• Physiology (not physical strength) • Decency or privacy (closely defined) • Special welfare consideration • Provision of personal services promoting welfare or education • Legal restrictions, particularly jobs likely to involve work outside the UK, where 'laws or customs are such that the duties could not, or could not effectively, be performed by a woman'	• Dramatic performances, where the *dramatis personae* requires a person of a particular racial group • Artists or photographic models for advertising purposes, for reasons of authenticity • Personal services rendered for the **welfare** of the particular group

Activity 5   **(15 minutes)**

Think of examples of **each** of the categories of exception listed above.

The Employment Act 1989 laid down some restrictions on employing women, particularly while pregnant, to avoid exposing them to substances (lead, radiation) and work situations (aircraft) that might damage their health.

Despite these 'special cases', the legislation does *not* permit **positive discrimination** - actions which give preference to a protected person, regardless of genuine suitability and qualification for the job (eg by stating that the employer 'welcomes' applications from women or ethnic minorities).

Training may be given to particular groups exclusively, if the group has in the preceding year been substantially under-represented. It is also permissible to encourage such groups to:

(a)   Apply for jobs where such exclusive training is offered

(b)   Apply for jobs in which they are under-represented

Complaints

Complaints of discrimination may be made to an Employment Tribunal within three months of the alleged offence. If conciliation is unsuccessful, the tribunal will hear the case, with the power to award:

(a)   An order declaiming the rights of both parties

(b)   A recommendation for action to redress discriminatory practices within a specified time and

(c)   An order requiring the discriminating employer to pay compensatory damages

The **EU Reversal of Burden of Proof in Sex Discrimination Cases Directive** establishes the assumption that employers accused of sexual discrimination are guilty unless they can prove the contrary: a reversal of the previous system whereby the complainant had to prove that discrimination took place. (This has caused huge controversy in the UK: watch the business press to see how the situation develops.)

EXAMPLE

'BT has launched a female executive network as part of a drive to boost the number of women in senior management and on its board.

'Like many FTSE 100 companies, BT has no full-time female executives on its board. And while women make up 24 per cent of its workforce, they hold only 18 per cent of senior management positions.

'The first networking event was held this week and included 200 of BT's top female managers, both at executive level and just below. It was aimed at giving these senior women a chance to meet and exchange careers advice.

'There will be further events, both formal and informal, which will focus on helping women to move up through the top ranks. Senior women from outside the company will also be invited to participate in future events.

'There are a number of networks at BT, ranging from "Able To", a network for disabled employees, to "Kaleidoscope", for gay, lesbian and bisexual workers.'

(Roberts, 2003 (d))

The Equal Opportunities Commission and Commission for Racial Equality

The **Equal Opportunities Commission** and **Commission for Racial Equality** (set up under the Acts) have powers, subject to certain safeguards: to investigate alleged breach of the Acts; to serve a 'non-discrimination notice' on employers found guilty of contraventions; and to follow-up the investigation until satisfied that undertakings given (with regard to compliance and information of persons concerned) are carried out. In cases of persistent discrimination they might institute legal proceedings. Both bodies also publish **Codes of Practice** giving detailed guidance on how personnel policies can be developed to avoid discrimination, how staff should be informed and trained, how practices should be monitored and so on.

The UK government is planning to replace these specialist bodies – together with the Disability Rights Commission – with a single organisation: the *Commission for Equality and Human Rights*. The umbrella body (proposed for implementation in late 2006) will assume additional responsibility for current and forthcoming laws on sexual orientation, religious discrimination and age discrimination. It will also seek to promote equal opportunities and access to services in society as a whole.

2.2 Equal Pay Act

The Equal Pay Act 1970 was the first major attempt to tackle sexual discrimination. It was intended specifically 'to prevent discrimination as regards terms and conditions of employment between men and women'.

The Equal (Amendment) Regulations 1984 established the right to equal pay for 'work of **equal value**', so that a woman would no longer have to compare her work with that of a man in the same or broadly similar work, but could establish that her work had equal value to that of a man in the same establishment. These provisions were discussed in Chapter 5.

EXAMPLE

'Equal pay questionnaires were launched in the UK on 6 April 2003, giving employees the right to request the pay details of a named colleague, to support claims that they are being paid less because of their race or sex. However, if the comparator refuses to volunteer their pay information, employers are in danger of breaching the Data Protection Act 1998 if they reveal it.

'Len Aspel, head of employee relations at HSBC bank, says the issue of confidentiality and privacy is a concern ... "When it comes to requests on the pay of branch managers at banks of a certain size then we can quite easily give out those figures without breaching confidentiality," says Aspel. "But it becomes more difficult if they are asking for the pay of the person sitting next to them." He says that in these cases, unless the comparator agrees to share information, it will not be given until legal proceedings start ...

' "What we hope to be able to do is discuss with [the applicant] what the issues are," he says. "If we need to, we will let them know that, yes, their comparator is being paid more and explain to them the justified reasons why," he says. We may also end up revealing the person's pay."

'Aspel believes that if pay systems are already open and transparent then employees are less likely to submit pay questionnaires. "To some extent people are likely to go on fishing exercises in companies where the pay culture is very secretive," he says. "We have a very open, transparent system and carry out audits each year." '

(Roberts, 2003 (b))

2.3   Sexual harassment (Code of Conduct)

Definition

> **Sexual harassment** as set out in the 1991 EU Code of Conduct is:
>
> (a) 'Unwanted conduct of a sexual nature, or other conduct based on sex affecting the dignity of women and men at work'
>
> (b) 'Unwelcome physical, verbal or non-verbal conduct'
>
> (c) 'Conduct that denigrates or ridicules or is intimidatory or physically abusive of an employee because of his or her sex, such as derogatory or degrading abuse or insults which are gender-related and offensive comments about appearance or dress'

Compliance with the EU Code of Conduct on sexual harassment is only voluntary, and there is no specific law against sexual harassment in Europe. However, it has been ruled by the courts that proven sexual harassment is **unlawful sex discrimination**, under the Sex Discrimination Act.

Recommendations to organisations for handling sexual harassment in the EU Code of Conduct - and the CIPD statement on sexual harassment - include the following.

(a)   The issuing of a clear policy statement or corporate Code of Conduct, with communication and awareness training (especially for managers) to highlight the seriousness of the offence.

(b) The implementation of counselling procedures, giving advice to victims, and hopefully resolving problems by informal means, but - if not - also planning further proceedings.

(c) The design of complaints procedures.

(i) Informal procedures would include person-to-person reproof (a clear statement by the victim to the offender that the conduct is unwelcome) and intervention by a trusted third party.

(ii) Formal procedures should exist for confidentiality to be guaranteed, and for an investigator of the same sex as the victim to be available to follow up complaints.

(d) The implementation of disciplinary action. Rules should be defined, including protection of the complainant from further victimisation as a result of the action.

FOR DISCUSSION

Come up with some examples of what might be defined as 'sexual harassment': you may even have experienced some. Are these examples clear-cut? What issues are involved? How are your examples discriminatory? Consider how male and homosexual workers might also be harassed.

2.4 Disability Discrimination Act 1995

Previous legislation on disability focused narrowly on securing employment (on a Quota Scheme) for disabled people, without addressing the issue of discrimination. This shortcoming was addressed when the **Disability Discrimination Act 1995** came into force in December 1996.

Definition

> A **disabled person** is defined as a person who has a physical or mental impairment that has a substantial and long-term (more than 12 months) adverse effect on his ability to carry out normal day to day activities. The effect includes mobility, manual dexterity, physical co-ordination, and lack of ability to lift or speak, hear, see, remember, concentrate, learn or understand or to perceive the risk of physical danger. Severe disfigurement is included, as are progressive conditions such as HIV even though the current effect may not be substantial.

The Act contains provisions for disabled access to services, transport facilities and education and training opportunities. In the sphere of employment, it makes it unlawful for an employer with more than 20 employees to discriminate against a disabled person/employee:

(a) In deciding who to interview or who to employ or in the terms of an employment offer

(b) In the terms of employment and the opportunities for promotion, transfer, training or other benefits, or by refusing the same

(c) By dismissal or any other disadvantage

The employer also has a duty to make reasonable adjustments to working arrangements or to the physical features of premises where these constitute a disadvantage to a disabled job applicant or employee. Examples of changes to working arrangements given in the Government's Code of Practice include the following.

   (a)   Altering working hours
   (b)   Acquiring or making changes to equipment
   (c)   Allocating some duties to another employee
   (d)   Providing supervision
   (e)   Making adjustments to premises
   (f)   Assigning the employee to a different place of work
   (g)   Training
   (h)   Providing a reader or interpreter

A number of factors will be relevant in deciding whether a change is reasonable, chiefly its effectiveness, cost (both financially and in terms of disruption), and practicability in the light of the employer's resources and the availability of financial or other help.

A **Disability Rights Commission** was established to ensure that employers and disabled people are informed of their respective rights and duties.

The Government has issued a Code of Practice on disability which gives advice to employers on how to avoid disability discrimination in employment. It does not itself impose legal obligations, but will be taken into account by Employment Tribunals. The Code provides many examples of good practice, as well as general principles.

   (a)   Be flexible
   (b)   Do not make assumptions
   (c)   Consider whether expert advice is needed
   (d)   Plan ahead
   (e)   Promote equal opportunities.

Activity 6   **(30 minutes)**

What arguments would you put forward as to why an organisation should consider employing people with disabilities?

2.5   Employment Equality Regulations 2003

The Employment Equality Regulations 2003 came into force on 2 December 2003, outlawing discrimination on the basis of:

- *Religious belief*
- *Sexual orientation*

The Regulations outlaw both direct and indirect discrimination and harassment (jokes, verbal abuse or physical intimidation). They apply to private- and public-sector organisations and cover all aspects of employment, from recruitment to working conditions and terms, to dismissal. Compensation for successful claims is unlimited.

HR practitioners will therefore have to review and monitor a wide range of existing policies to ensure that staff are not being treated less favourably on grounds of religious belief or sexual orientation: for example, equalising pension and benefit entitlements for same sex partners, imposing dress codes that infringe religious customs, or handling requests for time off to celebrate religious holidays.

The HR department will need to communicate policy changes and guidelines clearly to line managers. This will also present an opportunity to raise awareness of religious and sexual orientation issues. Cultural change will be important to control jokes and other forms of harassment: the regulations make employers liable for the acts of their employees, unless they can prove that they have taken steps to prevent them – for example, with clear anti-harassment policies and supporting awareness training.

ACAS has issued guidelines for employers, and the CIPD has also released a 'change agenda'. You may like to check out www.acas.co.uk or www.cipd.co.uk/changeagendas, if you are interested in this area.

EXAMPLES

'The employers who are least likely to fall foul of the [Employment Equality (Religion or Belief) Regulations] are those with progressive HR policies. They include Croydon London Borough Council, which has moved from flexitime to a 'worksmart' system whereby staff don't have to work a core number of hours but can arrange job shares or to work from home. The move will, for example, make it easier for Muslims to choose not to work on Friday, their holy day.

'Transport for London is considering replacing bank holidays with a number of 'floating days' which will allow non-Christians to work through Christmas and Easter.

'Unilever has a casual dress policy which permits employees to wear what they like, including clothing associated with their religion, so long as this is within the bounds of reason and safety. BT has gone a step further by attaching flexible straps to its safety helmets so that Rastafarian employees can wear them above their religiously significant hats. ...

'The Royal Mail is also thinking of introducing 'quiet rooms'. As well as providing prayer space, these could be used by all staff for quiet reflection. The organisation may also install foot basins to allow Muslim staff to wash their feet in preparation for prayers, but would need to discuss this with staff first, it says.

'In its canteens, BT provides kosher and halal meals on request, although most Jewish and Muslim employees bring their own or use the company's flexible working arrangements to go out for lunch.'

(Cooper, 2003)

Activity 7	(10 minutes)

Can you see any areas of potential conflict in practice between:

(a) Religious belief and sexual orientation regulations?

(b) Anti-discrimination regulations and privacy/data protection law?

2.6   Age diversity

Discriminatory practices are not currently illegal in the UK. However, there is already some redress for employees treated unfairly on the grounds of age. Age is *not* one of the reasons for dismissal acknowledged as potentially fair under the Employment Rights Act 1996, except on grounds of ill-health. Ageism has also successfully been challenged in terms of indirect sex and race discrimination, on the grounds that fewer women are able to comply with age requirements because of childbearing, and fewer ethnic minorities because of adult immigration.

The 1999 Voluntary Code of Practice on Age Diversity in Employment currently used as guidance for Employment Tribunals, states that employers should:

    (a)   Recruit on the basis of the skills and abilities; refrain from using age limits or phrases that imply restrictions (such as 'newly qualified' or 'recent graduate') in job advertisements; refrain from asking for medical references only from older applicants

    (b)   Select on merit and use, where possible, a mixed age panel of interviewers, trained to avoid decisions based on prejudices and stereotypes

    (c)   Promote on the basis of ability, having openly advertised opportunities

    (d)   Train and develop all employees and regularly review training to avoid age being a barrier

    (e)   Base redundancy decisions on objective, job-related criteria, and ensure that retirement schemes are applied fairly. 'Last in first out' policies may be construed as discrimination to young people

The UK government is required to implement age discrimination, under EU directive, by October 2006. Draft regulations are due to be laid before Parliament by the end of 2004: watch this space! (Details of the EU directive can be found at http://europa.eu.int, and ongoing UK consultation at www.dti.gov.uk/er/equality/age.) Among key proposals are:

    (a)   Abolishing employers' mandatory retirement ages, unless they can be objectively justified. Employer will be open to claims of unfair dismissal if they dismiss older workers without establishing that they are no longer capable of discharging their duties (eg with progressive warnings, formal performance appraisal and so on).

    (b)   Banning employers from setting a retirement age below 70 (a 'default' retirement age).

FOR DISCUSSION

Will the protection of older workers demotivate – or even disadvantage – younger workers?

2.7 Temporary workers

The other item on the UK legislative agenda is implementation of the EU Agency Workers' Directive, intended to protect temp agency workers in relation to pay and working time. The employment status of agency workers is currently unresolved: the law is unclear as to whether temps are employees of their agency or the business to which they are assigned. Protection against unfair dismissal under the Employment Rights Act 1996 requires an 'employee' to have entered into a contract of employment (Bronstein, 2003).

Current rights of temporary (and part-time) workers were discussed in Chapter 9.

3 EQUAL OPPORTUNITIES IN PRACTICE

3.1 Formulating effective policies

In it often suggested that many organisations make minimal efforts to avoid discrimination. They pay lip-service to the idea, to the extent of claiming 'We are an Equal Opportunities Employer' in advertising literature or (more recently) adding the words 'religion' and 'sexual orientation' to discrimination policies. A number of measures are necessary to establish equal opportunity in reality.

Ingam (2003) suggests the following key steps in implementing a *diversity policy* taking into account all the equal opportunity requirements.

Step 1. **Analyse your business environment**

- Internally – does the diversity of the organisation reflect the population in its labour market?

- Externally – does the diversity of the workforce mirror that of the customer base?

Step 2. **Define diversity and its business benefits**

- Legal, moral and social benefits

- Business benefits: better understanding of market segments; positive employer brand; attraction and retention of talent

- Employee benefits: more representative workforce; value and respect for people; opportunity to contribute fully; enhanced creativity

Step 3. **Introduce diversity policy into corporate strategy**

- Weave diversity into corporate values and mission

Step 4. **Embed diversity into core HR processes and system**

- Review and refocus recruitment and selection, induction, reward and recognition, career management and training and development

Step 5. **Ensure leaders implement policy**

- Leaders and top management need to provide long-term commitment and resources

- Use diversity as a key factor in coaching, awareness training and development of managers

Step 6. **Involve staff at all levels**

- Educate the workforce through awareness training
- Create a 'diversity handbook'
- Set up diversity working parties and councils
- Establish mentoring schemes

Step 7. **Communicate, communicate, communicate**

- Communicate diversity policy and initiatives clearly
- Internally: updates, briefings, training, intranet pages
- Externally: to boost employer brand and recruitment

Step 8. **Understand your company's needs**

- Match resources to the size of the organisation and the scale of change required

- Consider using diversity consultants or best practice representatives to provide advice, support and training

Step 9. **Evaluate**

- Benchmark progress at regular intervals
- Internally: diversity score cards, employee climate surveys
- Externally: focus groups, customer/supplier surveys

Monitoring will be a particularly important part of the implementation process. The numbers of female, disabled and ethnic minority staff can easily be monitored using 'Equal Opportunity Monitoring Forms' filled out by employees:

(a) On entering (and applying to enter) the organisation
(b) On leaving the organisation
(c) On applying for transfers, promotions or training schemes

The Commission for racial Equality's guide on ethnic monitoring recommends that monitoring and analysis of workforce composition should be sufficiently detailed (in terms of ethnic classifications and areas checked) to indicate whether

- minority groups are concentrated in certain jobs or levels of the organisation

- minority groups are under-represented in recruitment (applications and acceptance) and in more skilled jobs and grades

- disproportionate numbers of minority employees leave the organisation

Another area of particular sensitivity is recruitment and selection. There is always a risk that a disappointed job applicant, for example, will attribute his or her lack of success to discrimination, especially if the recruiting organisation's workforce is conspicuously lacking in representatives of the same ethnic minority, sex or group.

Activity 8   **(1½ hours)**

Outline a set of anti-discrimination policy points for the recruitment manager, covering:

(a) Job advertising
(b) Use of recruitment agencies
(c) Job application forms
(d) Job interviews
(e) Selection tests
(f) Record keeping

Bear in mind the need to avoid both discrimination and **allegations of discrimination**.

3.2 Positive action approaches

In addition to responding to legislative provisions, some employers have begun voluntarily to address the underlying problems of equal opportunities, by taking active steps to encourage the recruitment, training and promotion of previously under-represented groups. The following are just some of the positive action measures that might be used.

(a) Putting equal opportunities higher on the agenda by appointing Equal Opportunities Managers (and even Directors) reporting directly to the Personnel Director.

(b)   Flexible hours, childcare, 'term-time' or annual hours contracts (to allow for school holidays), career break and return-to-work schemes to help women to combine careers with family responsibilities. Terms and conditions, however, must not be less favourable.

(c)   Fast-tracking school-leavers, as well as graduates, and posting managerial vacancies internally, giving more opportunities for movement up the ladder for groups currently over-represented at lower levels of the organisation.

(d)   Assertiveness training and business networking to support minority groups in managing their career potential.

(e)   Awareness training for managers and staff to encourage them to think about issues of discrimination, harassment and diversity.

(f)   Positive action to encourage job and training applications from minority groups: using ethnic languages and pictures showing a racial/ethnic mix of people in advertisements, for example. Another example is pre-recruitment or pre-training training for minority groups: the metropolitan police piloted a scheme of such courses, covering literacy, numeracy, current affairs, physical fitness and interpersonal skills, to allow ethnic minority applicants to compete on an equal basis for training places.

(g)   Alteration of premises to accommodate wheelchair users: supplying Braille or large-print versions of documentation; supplying computerised text-based telephones or interpreters for hearing impaired people and so on.

We have illustrated other positive action approaches in our examples throughout this chapter.

3.3   Opportunity 2000

The Opportunity 2000 campaign (led by the voluntary organisation, Business in the Community) was launched on 28 October 1991, with an initial 62 organisations - mostly household names. Each set out and published its goals for employing and promoting women during the years up to 2000. Examples include:

- **J Sainsbury**: More than 95,000 staff, about two-thirds women, are employed in more than 320 supermarkets and 60 DIY stores. At the end of last financial year 40 per cent of management were women.

  New measures included scholarships to female weekend employees who are going on to higher education to take courses in areas in which women are traditionally under-represented, such as retailing, information technology, transport studies and engineering.

- **IBM (UK)**: The computer group set four goals: 'To contribute externally to the advancement of women in the national workforce; ensure that the company takes full advantages of the economic potential of women in the workforce; encourage women employees to realise their full potential; and increase the representation of women in senior management positions.' To achieve these IBM aimed for 30 per cent of graduate intake to be female.

People Management (1995) reported on the experience of the 293 member organisations who had signed up for the initiative. The number of women directors had doubled in the previous year (from 8% to 16%), while the number of women in middle and senior management positions had also increased by some 4-5% (to 28% and 17% respectively).

3.4 Race for Opportunity

In January 1995, the Commission for Racial Equality (CRE) launched an initiative in the drive for equal opportunities with its benchmarking standard for employers, **Racial Equality Means Business**, or **Race for Opportunity**. This aims to move the issue beyond compliance with legislation, and even beyond commitment to the moral principle of equality to a recognition of its business benefits.

EXAMPLE

'Royal Mail has the worst race discrimination, harassment and bullying record in the UK, its chairman Allan Leighton has admitted. Speaking exclusively to *PM* about the launch of the Race for Opportunity (RfO) Top 100, Leighton, who also chairs this organisation, said it was his challenge to stop racial discrimination at Royal Mail.

'Royal Mail is one of more than 180 organisations that benchmark their diversity performance through RfO – a national business network focusing on race and diversity as a business agenda.

'The launch of the third annual RfO Top 100 report revealed that more organisations than ever had a clear business case for their diversity programmes.

'It found that 63 per cent reported having an explicit business agenda linked to diversity objectives, up from 45 per cent in 2002. The majority (87 per cent) had a board-level individual who championed its activities on race.

' "We are a very commercially-focused network and want everyone to benchmark," said Leighton. "The focus for each organisation is to ensure that they have progressed since the previous year."

'The report monitors organisations in four key areas: representation of ethnic minority employees, marketing to ethnic minority customers, engaging with ethnic minority businesses through supply chains and diversifying community investment.

'The top private-sector performer this year is Lloyds TSB, which reported a 30 per cent increase in sales in some branches where staffing was changed to reflect the ethnicity of customers. Top of the public sector is the Army, followed by the DTI.'

(Roberts, 2003 (c))

Perhaps it is unfair to expect legislation to change deep-seated attitudes towards individual differences. Law may only change people's behaviour; to change how we feel and what we know (ie our attitudes) requires long term education and actual experience of working with the affected groups. A new approach to the management of individual differences emerged in the USA and is beginning to capture the imagination of British employers.

4 MANAGING DIVERSITY

4.1 Diversity

Definition

> **Managing diversity** is based on the belief that the individual differences we currently focus on under equal opportunities (gender, race, age etc) are crude and irrelevant classifications of the most obvious differences between people, and should be replaced by a genuine understanding of the ways in which individuals differ.

The ways in which people are **meaningfully** different in the workplace include personality, preferred working style and individual needs and drives. These things do not necessarily correlate with racial or gender differences in any way. For example, it would be a gross oversimplification to say that all women in your organisation require assertiveness training: it may be less appropriate for many women than for some men. Thus, effective managers seek to understand the job-relevant ways in which their staff differ and should seek to manage their performance in ways which recognise those differences as far as possible. Managers need to understand the unique contribution each person - not each 'category or person' - can make to the organisation.

A 'managing diversity' orientation implies the need to be proactive in managing the needs of a diverse workforce in areas (beyond equal opportunity and discrimination) such as:

(a) Tolerance of individual differences

(b) Communicating effectively with (and motivating) culturally diverse workforces. (We will address this issue further in Chapter 12.)

(c) Managing workers with diverse family structures and responsibility

(d) Managing the adjustments to be made by the ageing workforce

(e) Managing diverse career aspirations and paths

(f) Confronting literacy, numeracy and qualifications issues in an international workforce

(g) Managing co-operative working in ethnically diverse teams

EXAMPLE

Kramer, McGraw and Schuler (1997) describe the award-winning diversity strategy of USA multi-national, Pitney Bowes.

The vision statement on diversity reads

> Pitney Bowes will provide an open, flexible and supportive work environment that values the uniqueness of each of its employees. Through leadership, communication and training programs, Pitney Bowes will aggressively promote an understanding of individual difference, including (but not limited to) age, gender, race, religion, ethnicity, disability, sexual orientation and family circumstances.

The five goals of the Pitney Bowes strategic plan on diversity and examples of the action the company has taken to achieve these are set out below.

- **Goal 1: Communications**: 'Our vision of diversity and its implications for the organisation will be clearly communicated to all of us'. Action:

  - Formed diversity councils throughout the company

  - Engaged in widespread promotional activity to promote the diversity agenda

  - Development of diversity marketing guidelines for Pitney Bowes products and services.

- **Goal 2: Education and training**: 'We will become sensitive to and demonstrate an understanding of the value of differences through education and training'. Action:

  - Provided multiple training opportunities for the stimulation of diversity awareness.

  - Identified high profile minority customers to address employees on diversity issues.

- **Goal 3: Career development:** 'We will create a culture that enables and encourages the development and upward mobility of all of us'. Action:

  - Introduced new succession planning process based on 'assessing competencies for tomorrow'

  - Published career networking directory

  - Increased opportunities for rotational assignments and cross-training

  - Increased participation in employee mentoring programme.

- **Goal 4: Recruitment and hiring**: 'We will further increase the diversity of our employees so that our organisation reflects the demographic changes in our labour force'. Action:

  - Developed new minority recruitment campaigns including new promotional material and specific recruitment from schools with diverse populations

  - Supported minority scholarships and intern programs

  - Increased funding support for external organisations promoting the diversity agenda

  - Tied management bonuses to diversity recruitment goals.

- **Goal 5: Work/life balance**: 'We will provide a flexible and supportive work environment for employees in achieving a balance of work/life issues'. Action:

  - Developed training to enhance flexible work environment for all employees
  - Expanded child care, elderly care and school referral programs
  - Supported emergency sick child care
  - Conducted employee surveys on work/life balance
  - Piloted telecommuting program.

In order to achieve the five goals of diversity, the business units at Pitney Bowes have tied the concept of diversity to management performance ratings. Part of the incentive compensation plan for the corporate management committee, for instance, includes a diversity component directly linked to the business unit's diversity action plan, and all managers are held accountable for diversity through the performance appraisal system.

4.2 Equal opportunities and management of diversity

Torrington *et al* (2002) sum up the major differences between an 'equal opportunities' approach and a 'management of diversity' approach as follows.

	Equal opportunities	Managing diversity
Purpose	Reduce discrimination	Utilise employee potential to maximum advantage
Case argued	Moral and ethical	Business objectives: improve profitability
Responsibility	HR/personnel function	All managers
Focuses on	Groups	Individuals
Benefits for employees	Improved opportunities for disadvantaged employees	Improved opportunities for all employees
Focus of management activity	Recruitment	Managing
Remedies	Changing systems and practices	Changing corporate culture

Chapter roundup

- Discrimination at work affects a number of different groups, including women and ethnic minorities, the disabled, gays and bisexuals, and people of different religious beliefs (who are protected by current legislation) and older workers (who will be protected under an EU directive to be enacted in UK law by 2006).

- Discrimination can be both direct and indirect, or by implication. Victimisation and harassment are also addressed by equal opportunities policy – although sexual harassment is currently only indirectly covered by sex discrimination law.

- Equal opportunities is concerned with access to employment and also the whole employment life cycle: training and development, appraisal, promotion, reward, employment protection and so on.

- Managing diversity means managing people according to the meaningful individual ways in which people differ, instead of crude classifications.

Quick quiz

1   List five major forms of discrimination that may occur.

2   What is meant by:

   (a)   Direct discrimination
   (b)   Indirect discrimination and
   (c)   Victimisation?

3   A woman may lawfully be turned down for promotion if she is pregnant, if she intends to take maternity leave. True or false?

4   What is sexual harassment?

5   What are the three main provisions of the Disability Discrimination Act 1995?

6   What are the Employment Equality Regulations 2003?

7   Outline a 9-step plan for implementing diversity policy.

8   What are 'Opportunity 2000' and 'Race for Opportunity'?

9   What is managing diversity?

10   How is an 'equal opportunities' approach different from a 'managing diversity' approach?

Answers to quick quiz

1   Direct and indirect discrimination (and victimisation), against women, ethnic minorities, older workers, disabled workers, gay/lesbian/bisexual workers and religious groups.   (see paragraph 1)

2   (a)   Direct discrimination is where one group is treated less favourably than another.

        (b)   Indirect discrimination is where a condition is applied which is not relevant to the job and which serves to disadvantage one group disproportionately.

        (c)   Victimisation is where an individual is penalised for seeking to assert legal rights.   (para 2.1)

3   False. Pregnancy/maternity rights are protected regardless of circumstances.   (para 2.1)

4   Sexual harassment is unwanted physical or verbal conduct with sexual connotations.   (para 2.3)

5   (a)   A 'disabled person' is defined as one who has a physical or mental impairment that has a substantial and long-term effect on his/her ability to carry out normal activity.

        (b)   It is unlawful to discriminate against a disabled person in selection, and employment terms and conditions.

        (c)   The employer must make reasonable adjustments to working arrangements and premises which disadvantage the disabled person.

    (para 2.4)

6   Anti-discrimination laws relating to religion and belief, and sexual orientation.   (para 2.5)

7   See paragraph 3.1 for a full answer.

8   National initiatives aimed at benchmarking standards for gender and racial equality.   (paras 3.3, 3.4)

9   It is an alternative to equal opportunities which seeks better performance from employees based on their individual differences in personality, style and needs, rather than cruder distinctions such as gender and ethnicity.   (para 4.1)

10   See paragraph 4.2 for a full answer.

Answers to activities

1   Reasons for discrimination against women at work include the following.

(a)   Social pressures on the woman to bear and rear children, and on the man to make a lifetime commitment to paid work as the 'breadwinner'. Employers assumed - and sometimes still assume - that women's paid work would be short term or interrupted, and that training and development was therefore hardly worthwhile.

(b)   The nature of earlier industrial work, which was physically heavy: legal restrictions were placed on women's employment in areas such as mines, night work in factories etc.

(c)   Lack of organisation of women at work and influence in trade unions (except in industries like textiles), up until 1980s.

(d)   The reinforcing of segregation at home and at school: for example, lack of encouragement to girls to study mathematical and scientific subjects.

(e)   Career ladders which fail to fast-track women. Apprenticeships, for example, are rarely held by girls. A woman graduate starting as a secretary is less likely to advance than a male graduate who starts as a management trainee. In addition, organisations like banks, which have traditionally developed staff on the assumption of a lifetime career with the one employer, have tended to assume that women are unlikely to want a lifetime career. Commitments to geographical mobility are similarly assumed to be undesirable to women.

(f)   Child-bearing and family responsibilities. Part-time work has enabled many women to continue in paid employment, but tends to apply to jobs which carry little prospect for promotion.

2   This is personal to you. Note, however, how pervasive, subtle and influential discrimination can be.

3   Organisations offer a variety of excuses for doing this:

(a)   Cost (although performance-based pay systems are taking over from age-based ones in many companies).

(b)   Fear that the pay-back period on training will be too short.

(c)   A young customer base (on the supposition of an affinity between people of a common age).

(d)   A 'young' organisational culture.

(e)   In IT recruitment, lack of relevant experience among older workers.

(f)   Stereotypes about older workers' assumed resistance to change, inability to learn (and 'unlearn') skills and reduced motivation.

(g)   'Image' - if this is the right word! Middle managers will often go for very young glamorous secretaries, particularly if they are recruiting themselves.

In addition, one of the principle reasons for discriminatory practices is that they are not currently illegal in the UK.

4   (a)   Advertising a vacancy in a primarily male environment, where women would be less likely to see it.

(b)   Offering less favourable terms to part-time workers (given that most of them are women).

NOTES

(c) Specifying age limits which would tend to exclude women who had taken time out of work for child-rearing.

(d) Asking in selection interviews about plans to have a family (since this might be to the detriment of a woman, but not a man).

5 (a) Examples of gender exception to the discrimination laws include:

    (i) Specification of a male artist's model where male anatomy is required

    (ii) Specification of a female changing room attendant for a women's lingerie shop

    (iii) Specification of a same-sex employee in a private household, where the degree of contact and knowledge of intimate details may infringe privacy

    (iv) Specification of women-only access to free breast cancer screening services

    (v) Specification of women-only access to 'well women' clinics promoting women's health, or open days at college to encourage vocational education

    (vi) Specifying a male driver in some Muslim countries

(b) Examples of ethnic minority exceptions include:

    (i) A white actress to play the part of Queen Elizabeth

    (ii) Specifying an Afro-Caribbean model for the advertisement of Afro-Caribbean cosmetic products

    (iii) Inviting ethnic minority applicants only for a training course

6 (a) Most people with disabilities have the same skills and abilities to offer as able-bodied people and are effective as employees without the need for any special help.

(b) Many other people with disabilities have as much to offer as able-bodied people, given the use of appropriate help which is readily available.

(c) When the abilities of workers with disabilities are overlooked, companies are missing out on the contribution of potentially valuable employees.

(d) Employers have obligations, along with the rest of the society, to ensure that people with disabilities are treated fairly.

(Code of Good Practice on the Employment of Disabled People, Employment Service, 1984)

7 (a) Potential conflict between religious beliefs and sexual orientation, eg if an employee is homophobic on the basis of religious belief. Policy will have to state clearly that the right not to be harassed has priority over the right to religious expression, and what this means in practice.

(b) Potential conflict between anti-discrimination law and privacy/data protection law; where questions of a potentially 'sensitive' nature may be asked to justify challenges. (The Employment Equality (Sexual Orientation) Regulations protect people who are 'perceived' to be lesbian, gay or bisexual, so they do not have to 'prove' their orientation to an Employment Tribunal.) Where employees request details of colleagues' pay, under Equal Pay Questionnaires.

8   (a)   **Advertising**

   (i)   Any wording that suggests preference for a particular group should be avoided (except for genuine occupational qualifications).

   (ii)   Employers must not indicate or imply any 'intention to discriminate'.

   (iii)   Recruitment literature should state that the organisation is an Equal Opportunities Employer.

   (iv)   The placing of advertisements only where the readership is predominantly of one race or sex is construed as indirect discrimination.

   (b)   **Recruitment agencies.** Instructions to an agency should not suggest any preference.

   (c)   **Application forms**. These should include no questions which are not work-related (such as domestic details) and which only one group is asked to complete.

   (d)   **Interviews**

   (i)   Any non-work-related question must be asked of all interviewees, if any. Even then, some types of question may be construed as discriminatory. (You cannot, for example, ask only women about plans to have a family or care of dependants, or ask - in the worst case - about 'the pill' or PMT.)

   (ii)   It may be advisable to have a witness at interviews, or at least to take detailed notes, in the event that a claim of discrimination is made.

   (e)   **Selection tests**. These must be wholly relevant, and should not favour any particular group. (Even personality tests have shown to favour white male applicants.)

   (f)   **Records**. Reasons for rejection, and interview notes, should be carefully recorded, so that in the event of investigation the details will be available.

Assignment 10 (1½ hours)

Glamour Products

You have recently been appointed as Personnel and Training Officer at Glamour Products, which employs 250 staff manufacturing cosmetics at its plant in the West Midlands. Your post is a new initiative for this very 'traditional' company, and it is your first job since leaving university and qualifying as Grad.CIPD. so you are very much 'on probation'.

Previously, staff management was the responsibility of line managers and supervisors, who seem to resent your appointment. You do have the goodwill of the Managing Director, however, who has sent the following memorandum to you. You found it in your post this morning.

MEMO

To: P Jones (Personnel and Training Officer)
From: G Bull (Managing Director)
Date: 1 June 2004
Re: **Equal Opportunities Training**

Please arrange a short training course within the next two weeks on equal opportunities for all our 18 supervisors. Book the Works Canteen.

As you've probably discovered, they are a good bunch of blokes, but a bit conservative. Most of them have worked for us for most of their lives. But the recent complaints we've been receiving alleging racial discrimination are embarrassing, and have given rise to some adverse publicity in the local press, probably whipped up by troublemakers.

Relations with the ethnic minority workforce have been pretty good until recently, so we don't need the paraphernalia of an Equal Opportunities policy etc. But Patel's ET case alleging unfair dismissal on grounds of race - though preposterous - is bad news, not least because it gives the Union ammunition to fire at us, after we defeated them over pay last year. I want to get the shop stewards off our backs by showing we're putting a stop to any alleged race problems.

The main objectives of the course must be to get the supervisors to realise they've got to be more diplomatic, and obey the letter of the law. Make it clear to them they can't use 'racist' language, even in light-hearted banter.

I'll leave this with you, but I want a draft programme for approval quickly. I'll be at HQ in Dagenham all this week. Fax your proposals to me by Thursday, with any comments you want to make.

Task

Draft your reply to the Managing Director's memo.

Chapter 11:
WELFARE, HEALTH AND SAFETY

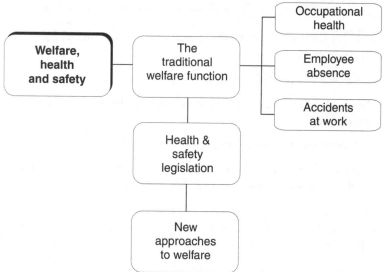

Introduction

Health, safety and well-being at work may be considered important for several reasons.

(a)   Employees should be protected from needless pain and suffering (obvious - we hope!)

(b)   Employers have legal obligations to take reasonable measures to protect the health and safety of their employees.

(c)   Accidents, illness and other causes of employee absence and/or impaired performance cost the employer money.

(d)   A business's image in the market place (to which it sells goods and services and from which it recruits labour and purchases other resources) may suffer if its health and safety record is bad.

This chapter looks at the law and best practice relating to health and safety at work, as well as broader welfare issues.

Your objectives

In this chapter you will learn about the following.

(a)   The traditional welfare function

(b)   Occupational health practices and policies

(c)   The management of employee absence and absenteeism

(d)   Accidents at work

(e)   Health and safety legislation and the role of the Health and Safety Commission

(f)   New approaches to welfare, ergonomics, substance abuse, stress, HIV/AIDS and workplace counselling

1 THE TRADITIONAL WELFARE FUNCTION

1.1 What is welfare?

Definition

> **Welfare** is 'a state of faring or doing well, freedom from calamity, enjoyment of health'. In HRM terms, this implies 'efforts to improve conditions of living for a group of employees or workers'.

In Chapter 1 of this Course Book, we described how the personnel/HR function grew out of industrial welfare work.

Employers might want to provide welfare:

(a) Because of a genuine sense of corporate social responsibility towards employees

(b) To improve the morale and loyalty of employees

(c) Because work (and non-work) problems impact on the 'steady state' performance of employees

(d) Because other companies and organisations are offering similar services/benefits, and they need to do the same in order to attract and retain the calibre of staff they require

FOR DISCUSSION

Staff spend at least half their waking time at work or in getting to it or leaving it. They know they contribute to the organisation when they are reasonably free from worry, and they feel, perhaps inarticulately, that when they are in trouble they are due to get something back from the organisation. People are entitled to be treated as full human beings with personal needs, hopes and anxieties; they are employed as **people**, they bring themselves to work, not just their hands, and they cannot readily leave their troubles at home.

(Martin, 1967)

Is this a 'soft' or a 'hard' HRM view? Is it a convincing argument for welfare?

A case can, however, be made *against* the provision of discretionary welfare.

(a) Welfare is provided for by the state: why should other organisations duplicate services?

(b) Welfare is irrelevant or even counter to the strategic objectives of the business (notably, profit maximisation).

(c) Welfare services have not been shown to increase loyalty or motivation: they are largely taken for granted, and as such are more likely to be a source of disappointment and dissatisfaction at any shortcomings than a source of satisfaction. Even gratitude/or appreciation is not a prime motivator. Any positive effects are hard to measure: the whole concept is relentlessly 'soft'.

(d) The non-work affairs and interests of employees are not the business of employers. If this attitude prevails in some situations (so that if the employee commits an offence outside work, this is not sufficient grounds for dismissal) it should prevail in others.

(e) Business organisations are not equipped to deal with welfare issues. Line managers are not trained to do so, and cannot devote sufficient time to follow-up. Centralising welfare responsibilities places a burden on HR specialists who are struggling to get away from the 'nursemaid' role and into strategic management.

Welfare may not demonstrably have a *positive* effect on morale and productivity - but anxiety, stress and distress invariably have a *negative* effect which should be alleviated where possible in the interests of effectiveness. In other words, welfare is a hygiene factor.

The more recent orientation of HRM towards welfare is that the health of the individual (in the broadest sense) represents the health of the organisation: if employees can be proactively helped not just to avoid accidents and illnesses, but to become more resilient to stress, healthier, physically fitter, mentally more flexible, emotionally more stable, they are more likely to perform at a consistent and high level on behalf of the organisation. We will examine this orientation and its implications in Section 4 below. Here, we will look at some of the concerns of traditional welfare.

1.2 Occupational health

Occupational health programmes are concerned largely with the effects of the working environment on workers. This may involve:

(a) Identifying substances, conditions or processes which are actually or potentially hazardous, and in what circumstances

(b) Identifying the effect of methods and processes of work on the human body and mind

(c) Exercising control over the working environment and substances used in the course of work, so as to minimise risk

Thus, occupational health is concerned with toxic substances (such as lead oxide, chlorine, asbestos, and radiation) and with protective measures against all of these, as well as less obvious sources of ill health at work, including noise, fatigue and physical and mental stress (excessive demands on the body and mind). Increasingly, it is also concerned with personal substance abuse (such as smoking and alcoholism) and other fitness and mental well-being factors that might have a direct or indirect affect on the workplace and work performance. We will discuss these factors in Section 4 below.

Activity 1   **(30 minutes)**

What aspects of your work or study environment (if any) do you think are:

(a) A hindrance to your work?
(b) A source of stress or dissatisfaction?
(c) A hazard to your health?

Some of the key 'traditional' causes of ill-health at work, and the regulations applying to them, are as follows:

(a) **Noise**

Industrial hearing impairment has long been recognised as a problem for factory workers and machine operators, but the stressful and distracting effects of noise have more recently been identified. Continuous loud noise can be protected against by sound-proofing and personal ear protection. Sound-proofing (eg acoustic hoods over noisy office printers) and broadcast 'white noise' (soft, constant, featureless sound) are often used in office environments to reduce noise irritation. (Noise at Work Regulation 1989)

(b)   **General environmental 'hygiene'**

The Workplace (Health, Safety and Welfare) Regulations 1992 provides for health and hygiene in areas such as the following.

(i)   **Ventilation**. Air should be fresh or purified.

(ii)   **Temperature** levels must be 'reasonable' inside buildings during working hours: not less than 16°C where people are seated, or 13°C if moving about.

(iii)   **Lighting** should be suitable and sufficient, and natural if practicable. Windows should be clear and unobstructed.

(iv)   **Cleaning and decoration**. Premises must be kept clean.

(v)   **Space**. Each person should have at least 11 cubic metres of space.

(vi)   **Sanitary conveniences and washing facilities** must be suitable and sufficient: properly ventilated and lit, properly cleaned, separate for men and women - and enough of them to avoid undue delay!

(vii) **Drinking water** should be available in adequate supply, with suitable drinking vessels.

(viii) **Rest facilities and eating facilities** must be provided unless the employees' work stations are suitable.

(ix)   **First aid** equipment should be provided, under the charge of a responsible person who should be trained in first aid.

(c)   **Hazardous substances and work-related diseases**

Procedures will need to be in place for: warning signs and labels identifying toxic or hazardous chemicals and other substances; training of staff in handling and storing substances and in first aid treatment and reporting mechanisms in the event of exposure; secure storage of substances; protective clothing and equipment for handling substances and so on. (Control of Substances Hazardous to Health Regulations 1994.) Hazards include not only burning, blinding, respiratory dysfunction, poisoning and other 'immediate' effects of substances, but also **work-related diseases**.

(d)   **Manual handling operations**

Back injuries due to the incorrect lifting and carrying of heavy objects accounts for more than a quarter of the accidents reported each year in the UK. Employers should, as far as is reasonably practical, avoid the need for employees to undertake risky manual handling activity. All remaining operations must be assessed, and steps taken to reduce risks to the lowest level reasonably practicable: providing properly maintained equipment and procedures (back braces, conveyer belts etc) and training in their use. (Manual Handling Operations Regulations 1992)

(e)   **Use of computer workstations**

The workstation has become one of the potentially toxic hazards of the workplace. If you have ever worked for a long period at a VDU you may personally have experienced some discomfort: back ache, stiffness, eyestrain and muscular disorders are common effects. Referred to collectively as 'Repetitive Strain Injury' or RSI, they now account for more than half of all work-related injuries in the USA and have reached epidemic proportions in Australia. Problems are due both to the ergonomics of the workstation and to working practices: poor posture, insufficient breaks for movement and so on. The Health and Safety (Display Screen Equipment) Regulations 1992 provide for the adaptation of computer workstations and equipment so that: VDU screens do not flicker, are free from glare and are able to swivel and tilt; radiation is reduced to negligible levels; and desk, chair and keyboard arrangement allows for forearm rest and adjustment for improved posture. Additional policies should emphasise education in posture, stretching exercises and so on, and the provision of regular work breaks or changes in activity for VDU users.

(f) **Pregnancy/maternity**

Pregnant women, those who have recently given birth and those who are breastfeeding are traditionally recognised as a special at-risk group by occupational health regulation and policy. The EC directive on pregnancy and maternity was incorporated into the Management of Health and Safety at Work (Amendment) Regulations 1994.

Provisions include: risk assessment; adjustment or offers of alternative work to reduce the risk; suspension on full pay as a last resort.

Activity 2 (30 minutes)

Reassess your appraisal of the health of your workplace in answer to Activity 1 above, in the light of the specific issues and provisions discussed. Were any of the health hazards mentioned new to you - or easily overlooked in the course of work? If so, what does this say about the need for occupational health policies?

Occupational health policy

There will be several elements to occupational health policy in any given area.

(a) Hazard minimisation: removing hazards where possible. Assessing and reducing employees' exposure to risk.

(b) Information about hazards: education, warning signs and labels, consultation with employees and safety experts.

(c) Equipment; protective clothing, ergonomically-designed work-stations, sound-proofing, safety equipment, maintenance.

(d) Training in the use of equipment: systems and procedures for safe and healthy working, compulsory use of safety/protective equipment and clothing.

(e) Employee responsibilities: to co-operate with health and safety policies, use systems responsibly, inform the employer of conditions placing them at risk, inform the employer or health and safety officer of identified hazards.

(f) Monitoring of occupational health: reporting of illness and injury, identification of emerging health issues.

NOTES

'Ill-health' and 'injury' are obviously closely related, and occupational health policies would consider issues relating to both. We will consider accidents as a particular workplace risk, in Section 2 of this chapter.

1.3 Absenteeism and employee absence

Employee absence

Ill-health and injury are major causes of long- and short-term employee absence from work. A 2002 Investors in People survey suggested that such absences cost UK business more than £11 billion a year. The CBI suggested in the same year that 166 million working days are lost as 'sick days'.

Only 14% of respondents to a recent CBI survey believed that all short-term sickness absence was genuine. There has been an increase in stress-related illnesses, and short-term absence due to ill health shows an upward trend in non-manual workers, especially those in government agencies. This suggests that absence may also be a cultural issue, influenced by factors such as management practices, work organisation, job design, motivation and employee relations. Since **statutory sick pay** is payable for the first eight weeks of absence through illness (reclaimed by the employer from national insurance payments), it has been claimed that workers frequently see sickness absence as a paid entitlement to be 'used up' in much the same way as holiday entitlement.

Some other reasons for absence are covered by employment protection legislation, such as pregnancy, redundancy preparation and trade union activities.

The Employment Relations Act 1999 provides for:

(a) 'Ordinary' *maternity leave* of 18 weeks plus 'additional' maternity leave (a further 29 weeks, after a qualifying period of one year's service).

(b) *Paternity leave*, whereby prospective fathers may take unpaid leave to be present at the birth of their child.

(c) *Right of return*, following maternity and paternity leave, to the same job on equivalent terms, provided that written notice of intention to return has been given prior to the absence.

(d) *Parental leave*, whereby parents, adoptive parents and legal guardians with one year's continuous service have the right to 13 weeks' unpaid leave during a child's first five years in order to care for that child. The time off in any one year is limited to four weeks, and leave has to be taken in blocks of at least one week.

(e) 'Reasonable' time off, unpaid, to deal with 'family emergencies' involving a dependent, including sickness, accident, death or serious problems at a child's school.

As we suggested in Chapter 10, many companies are now pursuing 'family friendly' policies over and above the statutory minimum.

Absence procedure

An absence procedure should do the following.

(a) Require all employees to notify their manager as soon as possible on the first day of absence, giving as much information as possible about the nature and likely duration of the absence.

(b) Require all employees absent with prior consent to complete an absence form on their return to work.

(c)   Require a medical certificate to be provided (where relevant) for absences of seven days or more.

(d)   Discuss absences with employees and keep in touch with them, alerting them to the possibility of disciplinary action where appropriate.

(e)   Ensure access to medical information and check this is up to date, prior to any disciplinary action being considered.

(f)   Require the employee to notify management in the event of infectious or dangerous illness (so that other staff can be checked or warned).

(g)   Look for suitable alternative work within the organisation for employees no longer able to perform their duties, and consider requests for flexible working where this might help.

(h)   Check employees' entitlements to relevant benefits.

EXAMPLE

The state government of New South Wales, Australia, has found a radical way of cutting 'sickies' (sick days) among ferry deckhands, with a deal which obliges fellow team-members to work extra shifts - unpaid - to cover for absent colleagues! Introduced as part of a wages package, the agreement is based on the 'mateship concept', applying peer pressure within the team. A recent report by Morgan and Banks revealed that most Australians took an average of six days' sick leave a year - with 12.4% admitting none of their 'sickies' were genuine! The new State Transit deal, however, has seen the average number of sick days per employee per year plunge from 13.13 to 5.56.

(Australian *Daily Telegraph*, 6 June 1999)

'Absence' raises issues such as ill-health and injury and domestic problems. What might the organisation do to help its employees in such times?

1.4   Welfare benefits and services

Some of the key issues (from the traditional welfare perspective) are as follows.

(a)   **Pension schemes**

Many firms set up occupational pension schemes for their employees, with various levels of employer and employee contributions.

Tight controls have been placed over the operation of pension funds, particularly with regard to the accountability of trustees, fund managers, auditors and advisers (Social Security Act 1985; Pensions Act 1995). Employees in occupational schemes which are contracted out of the State Earnings-Related Pension Scheme (SERPS) lose their future entitlements under the state scheme: occupational schemes are required to ensure that they provide adequate benefits, however, and are potentially much more generous than the state scheme.

(b)   **Sick pay**

Statutory Sick Pay provides a basic income to employees who are incapable of attending their normal place of work due to illness. Employers are responsible for the first four weeks of SSP, after which they can claim payments back from the State through reduced National Insurance contributions.

Employers may also wish to offer discretionary Occupational Sick Pay, for example by maintaining full salary payment for a defined period of time. In order to minimise abuse of OSP, HR practitioners and line managers will need to monitor absence rates and periods carefully.

For motivational reasons, claims of sickness might be taken on trust as far as possible (unless there is positive proof of malingering). An illness or diagnosis may be confirmed by referring the employee to a company-approved doctor - but disciplinary action cannot be taken against an employee who refuses to be examined (unless there is a contractual agreement).

Welfare calls and visits may also be made during prolonged absence, in order to identify financial or practical help that may be offered, alleviate anxiety, offer counselling and so on.

(c) **Maternity**

Maternity leave and health and safety provisions for pregnant workers have already been discussed above.

Statutory maternity pay is payable at any time from the 11th week before the estimated week of confinement (EWC), for 18 weeks. If a woman is absent with a pregnancy-related illness, statutory (or occupational) sick pay will apply until the 6th week before the EWC, at which time statutory maternity pay is triggered.

(d) **Domestic problems**

Situations such as marital breakdown or bereavement are essentially private, but their effects are likely to carry over into the workplace. The Employment Relations Act 1999 provides for what used to be called 'compassionate leave' (unpaid) to deal with 'family emergencies', but organisations may develop a policy on:

(i) What constitutes 'reasonable' time off
(ii) Whether time off will be paid to some degree
(iii) Whether additional welfare interventions will be offered

Welfare services may include: access to the firm's own counsellors or referral to other support organisations; help with financial, legal and funeral arrangements arising from bereavement; and so on.

(e) **Retirement/redundancy**

As discussed in Chapter 7, retirement and redundancy may be regarded as major adjustment crises in the lives of employees, and a variety of counselling, training and other services may be offered.

Activity 3 (45 minutes)

Does your college or workplace have provision for welfare services? What are they? How well publicised are they? Ask for information, if it is not available in the Student/Employee Handbook or on notice boards. List the issues which are highlighted by the counselling or welfare programme

We will now look at a major health and safety issue: workplace accidents.

2 ACCIDENTS AT WORK

2.1 Incidence of industrial accident

Newspapers frequently quote statistics showing large number of employee hours lost through accident and the associated cost to business. Torrington *et al* (2002) cite IRS figures of 1.3 million workers taken ill in the UK as a result of their work, resulting in the loss of 24.3 million working days at a total annual cost to employers of £2.5 billion. However, it should be noted that:

(a) Accident rates vary substantially by industry. (In the year to April 2000, 218 people died as a result of accidents sustained at work: 75 deaths occurred in the construction industry alone.)

(b) Small and large organisations have lower incidence rates than medium-sized organisations (perhaps because supervision is closer in small organisations and investment in safety/accident prevention staff and systems is greater in large ones).

(c) Working conditions (outdoor v indoor) and tools and technology (heavy machinery v PC) have the greatest impact on incident rates, followed by …

(d) The 'accident proneness' of individual workers. There are suggestions that some people are more prone to accidents than others (due to poor vision, stress, depression, alertness, immaturity and so on). However, accident proneness is also related to the working patterns, responsibility and safety-awareness of individual employees: horseplay, practical jokes, cutting corners on safety measures and so on are frequent causes of accident.

(e) Death by homicide is, in fact, the biggest cause of death in the workplace in the USA (Filipczale, 1993).

EXAMPLE

Deaths at work down by 10 per cent

Workplace deaths fell 10 per cent last year, bringing the proportion of fatalities to its lowest since the Health and Safety Commission (HSC) was launched nearly 30 years ago.

HSC statistics revealed that 226 people died in accidents at work in 2002/03 – 25 fewer than the previous year. That figure, together with employment growth, means fatal accidents declined to 0.79 per hundred thousand workers. This is around a third of the rate in 1981, the commission said. Chairman Bill Callaghan said, "The statistics give some grounds for optimism, but no room for complacency."

People Management, 11 September 2003

> **Activity 4**   **(10 minutes)**
>
> A scene from everyday life is shown below: Figure 11.1. Note down anything that strikes you as being dangerous about this working environment.

Figure 11.1: Unsafe work practices!

Apart from obviously dangerous equipment in factories, construction sites and even offices, there are many hazards to be found in the modern working environment. Many accidents could be avoided by the simple application of common sense and consideration by employer and employee, and by safety consciousness encouraged or enforced by a widely acceptable and well published **safety policy**.

2.2 Cost of accidents

The **cost** of accidents to the employer consists of:

(a) Time lost by the injured employee

(b) Time lost by other employees whose work is interrupted by the accident

(c) Time lost by supervision, management and technical staff as a result of the accident

(d) A proportion of the cost of first aid materials, or even medical staff

(e) The cost of disruption to operations at work

(f) The cost of any damage and repairs and modification to the equipment

(g) The cost of any compensation payments or fines resulting from legal action

(h) The costs associated with increased insurance premiums

(i) Reduced output from the injured employee on return to work

(j) The cost of possible reduced morale, increased absenteeism, increased labour turnover among employees

(k) The cost of recruiting and training a replacement for the injured worker

An employer may also be liable to an employee in tort if the employee is injured as a result of either:

(a) The employer's failure to take reasonable care in providing safe premises and plant, a safe system of work and competent fellow employees, or

(b) The employer's breach of a statutory duty - say, to fence dangerous machinery. Although the injured employee's damages may be reduced if the injury was partly a consequence of his/her own contributory negligence, due allowance is made for ordinary human failings, such as inattentiveness, tiredness and so on.

2.3 Accident prevention

The prevention of accidents requires integrated HR-led policies and practices, including attention to workplace design, communication of health and safety rules and values, training and so on. Some of the steps which might be taken to reduce the frequency and severity of accidents are as follows.

(a) Developing safety awareness among staff and workers and encouraging departmental pride in a good safety record.

(b) Developing effective consultative participation between management, workers and unions so that safety and health rules can be accepted and followed.

(c) Giving adequate instruction in safety rules and measures as part of the training of new and transferred workers, or where working methods or speeds of operation are changed.

(d) Minimising specific hazards. Materials handling, a major cause of accidents, should be minimised and designed as far as possible for safe working and operation.

(e) Building and equipment maintenance - apart from making sound job repairs, temporary expedients to keep production going should not prejudice safety.

(f) Safety inspections – carried out as a comprehensive audit, working through a checklist; or by using random spot checks or regular checks of particular risk points. Checklists used in the inspection process should identify corrective action to be taken, and allocate responsibility for that action.

(g) Compliance with legislation and industry/work environment codes of practice.

2.4 Accident reporting

An accident report is a management tool, designed to:

(a) Identify problems and
(b) Indicate corrective action

Recurring accidents may suggest the need for special investigation, but only more serious incidents will have to be followed-up in depth. Follow-up should be clearly aimed at preventing recurrence - not placing blame.

The drawing below (Figure 11.2) shows the format of a **typical accident book** which should by law be kept by any organisation which employs more than 10 people. (The one used by your organisation may be laid out differently, or it might consist of loose-leaf sheets.)

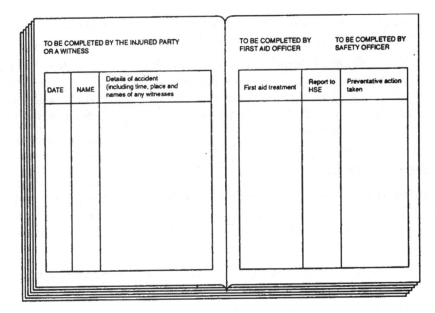

Figure 11.2: Accident Book

The **Reporting of Injuries, Diseases and Dangerous Occurrences Regulations 1995 (RIDDOR 95)** require employers to do the following.

(a) Notify the environmental health authority or the Health and Safety Executive **immediately** if one of the following occurs.

  (i) There is an accident connected with work and either an employee or self-employed person working on the premises is killed or suffers a major injury (including as a result of physical violence) or a member of the public is killed or taken to hospital.

  (ii) There is a dangerous occurrence.

(b) Send a completed **Accident report form** (see next page) to do the following.

  (i) Confirm within ten days a telephone report of an accident or dangerous occurrence (as described in (a) above).

  (ii) Notify, within ten days of the accident, any injury which stops someone doing their normal job for more than three days.

  (iii) Report certain work-related diseases.

Definitions

> **Major injuries** include things like fractures other than to fingers, thumbs or toes, amputation, temporary or permanent loss of sight and any other injury which results in the person being admitted to hospital for more than 24 hours.
>
> **Dangerous occurrences** are 'near misses' that might well have caused major injuries. They include the collapse of a load bearing part of a lift, electrical short circuit or overload causing fire or explosion, the malfunction of breathing apparatus while in use or during testing immediately before use, and many others.
>
> **Notifiable diseases** include certain poisonings, occupational asthma, asbestos, hepatitis and many others.

The standard for the notification of injuries and dangerous occurrences is reproduced below: Figure 11.3.

HSE
Health & Safety
Executive

Health and Safety at Work etc Act 1974
The Reporting of Injuries, Diseases and Dangerous Occurrences Regulations 1995

Report of an injury or dangerous occurrence

Filling in this form
This form must be filled in by an employer or other responsible person.

Part A

About you

1 What is your full name?

2 What is your job title?

3 What is your telephone number?

About your organisation

4 What is the name of your organisation?

5 What is its address and postcode?

6 What type of work does your organisation do?

Part B

About the incident

1 On what date did the incident happen?

/   /

2 At what time did the incident happen?
(Please use the 24-hour clock eg 0600)

3 Did the incident happen at the above address?

Yes   Go to question 4

No   Where did the incident happen?

    elsewhere in your organisation - give the name, address and postcode

    at someone else's premises - give the name, address and postcode

    in a public place - give the details of where it happened

If you do not know the postcode, what is the name of the local authority?

4 In which department, or where on the premises, did the incident happen?

Part C

About the injured person

If you are reporting a dangerous occurrence, go to Part F.
If more than one person was injured in the same incident, please attach the details asked for in Part C and Part D for each injured person.

1 What is their full name?

2 What is their home address and postcode?

3 What is their home phone number?

4 How old are they?

5 Are they

    male?

    female?

6 What is their job title?

7 Was the injured person (tick only one box)

    one of your employees?

    on a training scheme? Give details:

    on work experience?

    employed by someone else? Give details of the employer:

    self-employed and at work?

    a member of the public?

Part D

About the injury

1 What was the injury? (eg fracture, laceration)

2 What part of the body was injured?

NOTES

3 Was the injury (tick the one box that applies)

☐ a fatality?

☐ a major injury or condition? (see accompanying notes)

☐ an injury to an employee or self-employed person which prevented them doing their normal work for more than 3 days?

☐ an injury to a member of the public which meant they had to be taken from the scene of the accident to a hospital for treatment?

4 Did the injured person (tick all the boxes that apply)

☐ became unconscious?

☐ need resuscitation?

☐ remain in hospital for more than 24 hours?

☐ none of the above?

Part E

About the kind of accident

Please tick the one box that best describes what happened, then go to part G.

☐ Contact with moving machinery or material being machined

☐ Hit by a moving, flying or falling object

☐ Hit by a moving vehicle

☐ Hit by something fixed or stationary

☐ Injured while handling, lifting or carrying

☐ Slipped, tripped or fell on the same level

☐ Fell from a height
How high was the fall?

☐ [_____] metres

☐ Trapped by something collapsing

☐ Drowned or asphyxiated

☐ Exposed to, or in contact with, a harmful substance

☐ Exposed to fire

☐ Exposed to an explosion

☐ Contact with electricity or an electrical discharge

☐ Injured by an animal

☐ Physically assaulted by a person

☐ Another kind of accident (describe it in part G)

Part F

Dangerous occurrences

Enter the number of the dangerous occurrence you are reporting. (The numbers are given in the Regulations and in the notes which accompany this form.)

[_____]

Part G

Describing what happened

Give as much detail as you can. For instance
- the name of any substance involved
- the name and type of any machinery involved
- the events that led to the incident
- the part played by any people.

If it was a personal injury, give details of what the person was doing. Describe any action that has since been taken to prevent a similar incident. Use a separate piece of paper if you need to.

[____]

Part H

Your signature

[_____]

Date

[__ / __ / __]

Where to send the form
Please send it to the Enforcing Authority for the place where it happened. If you do not know the Enforcing Authority, send it to the nearest HSE office.

For official use
Client number   Location number   Event number

[_____] [_____] [_____]   ☐ INV REP ☐ Y ☐ N

Figure 11.3: Riddor Report Form

Activity 5	(30 minutes)

Invent (or *carefully* role-play) your own scenario for a typical (or unusual) workplace accident causing injury. Invent as many relevant details as you can. Now complete the specimen RIDDOR report reproduced here.

We will now look at some of the main legislation on Health and Safety at work. Much of it is refreshingly practical, with lots of measures to be taken and procedures to be put in place: we will only be able to summarise. Like other legal provisions we have discussed in this Course Book, the 'law is a floor': remember that these are minimum standards - not 'best practice'! Best practice among employers is likely to be:

- *more scrupulous in enforcing safeguards*

- *more committed to providing consultation, information and training on health and safety, and*

- *more wide-ranging in its attempt to promote positive health and well being and a culture of safety*

3 HEALTH AND SAFETY LEGISLATION

3.1 The legal framework

In 1972, a Royal Commission on Safety and Health at Work reported that unnecessarily large numbers of days are lost each year through industrial accidents, injuries and diseases, because of the 'attitudes, capabilities and performance of people and the efficiency of the organisational systems within which they work'. Since then, major legislation has been brought into effect in the UK, most notably:

(a) Health and Safety at Work Act 1974

(b) Regulations and Codes of Practice implementing EU directives on Health and Safety, including:

    (i) The Workplace (Health, Safety and Welfare, Regulations 1992

    (ii) Management of Health and Safety at Work Regulations 1992

    (iii) The Health and Safety (Consultation with Employees) Regulations 1996

Be aware that the framework for policy and practice in specific areas of health and safety is extensive and detailed!

3.2 Health and safety responsibilities

In the UK, the *Health and Safety at Work Act 1974* provides for the introduction of a system of approved Codes of Practice, prepared in consultation with industry. Thus an employee, whatever his/her employment, should fund that his/her work is covered by an appropriate code of practice.

Employers also have specific duties under the 1974 Act.

- All systems (work practices) must be safe.

- The work environment must be safe and healthy (well-lit, warm, ventilated and hygienic).

- All plant and equipment must be kept up to the necessary standard.

The Workplace (Health, Safety and Welfare) Regulations 1992 define specific safety requirements in regard to a range of hazards: machinery and equipment; falls and falling objects; floors, passages and stairs; doors and windows; fire prevention and so on.

The **employee** also has a duty under the 1974 Act.

- To take reasonable care to avoid injury to himself/herself and others

- To co-operate with his or her employers to help them comply with their legal obligations (including enforcing safety rules)

3.3 On-going risk management

Information, instruction, training and supervision should be directed towards safe working practices. Under the Management of Health and Safety at Work Regulations 1992, employers must:

- Carry out **risk assessment,** generally in writing, of all work hazards on a continuous basis.

- Introduce **controls** to reduce risks.

- Assess the **risks to anyone else** affected by their work activities (such as suppliers, customers, visitors)

- **Share hazard and risk information** with other employers, including those on adjoining premises, other site occupiers and all subcontractors coming onto the premises

- **Revise safety policies** in the light of the above – or initiate safety policies if none were in place previously

- Identify **employees who are especially at risk** (such as pregnant women or night shift workers)

- Provide up-to-date and appropriate **training in safety matters**

- Provide **information to employees** (including part-time and temporary workers) about health and safety

- Employ **competent health and safety advisers**

Employees also have specific responsibilities to:

- Use all equipment, safety devices, etc, provided by your employer **properly** and in accordance with the instructions and training received

- **Inform** your employer, or another employee with specific responsibility for health and safety, of any perceived shortcoming in safety arrangements or any serious and immediate dangers to health and safety.

Activity 6   **(no time limit)**

Consider the health and safety programme at your place of work (or study).

(a) How well *aware* are you of any rules, procedures and information regarding health and safety? (Who is responsible for *making* you more aware of such matters?)

(b) How well do the organisation's rules, procedures and information comply with the requirements of the Regulations?

3.4 Information and consultation

Under the Safety Representatives and Safety Committees Regulations 1977 and the Health and Safety (Consultation with Employees) Regulations 1996, employers must consult all of their employees on health and safety matters (such as the planning of health and safety training, any change in equipment or procedures which may substantially affect their health and safety at work or the health and safety consequences of introducing new technology). This involves giving information to employees *and* listening to and taking account of what they say before any health and safety decisions are taken.

EXAMPLE: INTERNATIONAL COMPARISONS

'Developing countries are often so in need of economic development that they may accept any industry, even those that have the potential for significant harm ... Health hazards are still ignored: by having lax safety standards, developing countries can lure large multinational firms to their shores.'

(Kramer, McGraw Shuler, 1997)

3.5 Health and Safety authorities

The **Health and Safety Commission** was set up under the Health and Safety at Work Act 1974 to develop health and safety policies. It is made up of representatives of employers, employees, local government and relevant professional bodies. Responsibility for communicating, monitoring and enforcing the Commission's policies and relevant legislation falls to the Health and Safety Executive, which has powers of inspection and enforcement by:

(a) **Prohibition notice** requiring the shut down of hazardous processes until remedial action has been taken

(b) **Improvement notice** requiring compliance with a statutory provision within a certain time (subject to appeal to an industrial tribunal)

(c) **Seizure** of hazardous articles for destruction or rendering harmless, and /or

(d) **Prosecution** of offenders, who are liable to fine and even imprisonment in serious cases

3.6 Health and safety policy

There will be several elements to a health and safety policy, whatever the specific needs and hazards of a particular workplace.

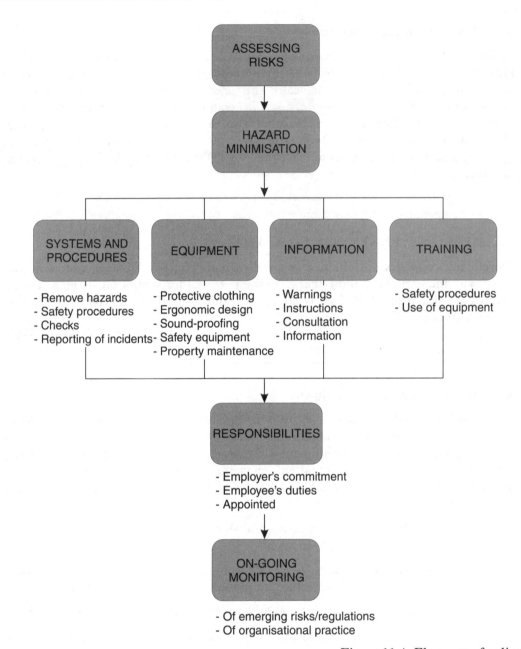

Figure 11.4: Elements of policy

The following is an **example of a Policy Statement** released by the former Department of Environment, Transport and the Regions (DETR), which used to have responsibility for the Health and Safety Commission (HSC) and the Health and Safety Executive (HSE). (In 2002, this responsibility was taken over by the Department for Work and Pensions.)

Health and safety policy statement

This Health and Safety Policy Statement is to be observed by staff throughout the Department (including the Agencies and Government Offices). It reflects the importance I attach to the health, safety and welfare of all staff and others who may be affected by our activities. That includes contractors and visitors to our premises.

I expect all managers to give similar importance to these issues in their operational area and when determining local priorities, plans and resource allocation. I also recognise the valuable role played by Safety Representatives appointed by Trade Unions.

---

1   **Objectives.** The Department will meet all current and proposed legal requirements in the Health and Safety at Work Act 1974 and relevant subordinate legislation. This will be achieved through effective risk assessment and the implementation of appropriate measures for the prevention or control of risks at work. The Department will promote continuous improvement in health and safety performance to become an exemplar of good practice. Regular feedback on progress will be provided.

2   **Systems.** The Department will put systems and procedures in place designed to ensure a safe system of work. As far as reasonably practicable, all equipment, vehicles, plant, premises, other work sites and work practices will be safe and free from any hazards to health and that employees, the public and other affected by our operations are not exposed to undue risk.

3   **Communication/Co-operation.** The policy will be brought to the attention of all employees and contractors. Legally all employees must co-operate in establishing and maintaining safe and healthy working conditions and avoid any actions which may adversely affect the health, safety and welfare of themselves, their colleagues, contractors or visitors. Consultation on Departmental health and safety issues will be undertaken...

4   **Monitoring and Auditing.** The Department will monitor and audit health and safety management systems and performance. An annual report on health and safety will be produced reflecting the Department's progress, forward plans and innovative initiatives.

5   **Review.** The policy will be continuously reviewed. A full review, including related management arrangements and performance, will be held in three years time, or earlier, following any major change in health and safety legislation or our organisation.

This policy is fully endorsed by the Board and will be implemented by management throughout the Department. Roles and responsibilities will be clearly defined to ensure effective communication, provision of information, training, and systems for reporting to those with delegated responsibilities.

Activity 7

Underline or highlight the key words and phrases in the above example of a Policy Statement, which seem to you to reflect the most important aspects of health and safety policy, as described so far.

This will help you to know what to look for when you appraise the health and safety policies of your own organisation.

FOR DISCUSSION

Safety policy must be implemented in detailed practice (such as fire drills and equipment checking) but it is less likely to be consistently observed if senior managers fail to set a good example, to discipline breaches of policy, or to reward health and safety suggestions. The aim is to create a culture in which health and safety are key values.

What are the cultural values in your nation, local community and organisation that:

(a)   Promote health and safety?
(b)   Promote risk-taking and ill-health?

NOTES

Activity 8   **(15 minutes)**

Since we have broadened our awareness of what constitutes threat to health and safety, take some time to think about what other issues personnel policies might cover? Suggest five areas for consideration. (If you are currently employed, check you organisation's manual on health and safety.)

3.7 Working hours

You should be aware that working hours are also a health and safety issue, under the Working Time Regulations 1998 (implementing the EU Working Time Directive).

(a) Working hours are limited to 48 hours per week, averaged over a standard reference period of 17 weeks (or 26 weeks, where continuity of work is necessary, as in health or essential services, 24-hour production or seasonal work). This **can** be extended to a year by collective workplace agreement - to preserve annual hours schemes, for example.

(b) An employee may agree individually, in writing, to work more than 48 hours per week, and a record of hours should be retained in case the Health and Safety Commission requires it.

(c) All employees are entitled to a daily rest of 11 consecutive hours in every 24, and a 24-hour rest in every seven days (averaged over 2 weeks) - subject to adjustment by collective agreement.

(d) If the working day exceeds six hours, the employee is entitled to a minimum of 20 minutes' break.

*Now let's look at the 'new' welfare role of **HRM**, and some of the hazards of the new workplace.*

4   NEW APPROACHES TO WELFARE

4.1   A shift in perspective

HRM specialists have tried to distance themselves from the traditional welfare tag with its legalistic/reactive and paternalistic associations.

The new orientation to welfare activities is based on the recognition that healthy and focused individuals are likely to perform better at work, to be more flexible (physically, mentally and emotionally) and adaptable to change: in short, that it is possible to take a business-strategic view of employee health and well-being.

The new model of welfare is therefore:

(a) **Pro-active** in its attempt to address potential health and safety issues, rather than reacting to regulation, complaint or crisis

(b) **Positive** in its attempt to promote health and well-being rather than focusing solely on ill-health, injury and crisis

(c) **Holistic** in its definition of health and well-being, including emotional and even spiritual factors

(d) **Wide-ranging** in its attention to diverse issues, rather than being led by legislative agendas

Goss (1994) summarised this new perspective as 'tough love': a hard-soft policy aimed at offering benefits and services which employees need and value, 'linked strategically with the needs of the organisation by enhancing performance'.

Issues in the new welfare model include:

(a) Work-life balance and the management of stress

(b) Ergonomics

(c) Promotion of positive health and fitness, and the management of substance abuse

(d) Confrontation of emerging health issues (such as HIV/AIDS) and other sources of distress

(e) Workplace counselling

(f) Employee Assistance Programmes (EAPs)

We will discuss each of these issues, briefly, in turn.

4.2 Work-life balance and control of stress

Overwork is frequently associated with poor diet, lack of exercise, inadequate relaxation, stress and relationship difficulties.

Despite the desire to increase productivity or enhance performance, many companies are realising that increasing workloads and working hours is in fact counter-productive, potentially encouraging absenteeism, ill-health, accidents and poor-quality work.

Elements in a work-life balance programme may include:

(a) In-house or consultant-led awareness training: clarification of values and priorities and so on

(b) In-house or consultant-led skills training: in time-management, delegation, work organisation, relaxation techniques and, say,

(c) Flexible working arrangements to allow time for family and social activities within the working week (as discussed in Chapter 9)

Stress and stress management

Stress is a term which is often loosely used to describe feelings of tension - usually associated with too much, or overly demanding, work. In fact, stress is the product of demands made on an individual's physical **and mental** energies: monotony and feelings of failure or insecurity are sources of stress, as much as the conventionally-considered factors of pressure, overwork and so on.

It is worth remembering, too, that demands on an individual's energies may be stimulating as well as harmful: many people, especially those suited to managerial jobs, work well under pressure, and even require some form of stress to bring out their best performance. (It is excessive stress that can be damaging: this may be called **strain.**) This is why we talk about the management of stress, not about its elimination: it is a question of keeping stress to helpful proportions and avenues.

Harmful stress can be identified in symptoms such as nervous tension, irritability, sensitivity, sleeplessness, withdrawal (reluctance to communicate, absenteeism), depression, substance abuse and a variety of physical symptoms (such as skin and digestive disorders, tension headaches). Some symptoms of stress - say, absenteeism -

may or may not be **correctly** identified with stress: there are many other possible causes of such problems, both at work (lack of motivation) and outside (personal problems).

All these things can, however, adversely affect performance, which is why stress management has become a major workplace issue. The Health and Safety Executive estimated in 2003 that stress accounts for more than 13 million of the working days lost through sickness each year.

Stress can be caused or aggravated by:

(a) **Personality**. Competitive, sensitive and insecure people feel stress more acutely

(b) Ambiguity or conflict in the **roles** required of an individual

(c) Insecurity, risk and change

(d) Management style including:

    (i) Unpredictability
    (ii) Destruction of workers' self esteem
    (iii) Setting up win/lose situations

Activity 9   **(30 minutes)**

What sources of stress are there in your own lifestyle? Are you aware of the symptoms of stress in yourself? What do you do (if anything) to control your stress?

Greater **awareness** of the nature and control of stress is a feature of the modern work environment. **Stress management techniques** are increasingly taught and encouraged by organisations, and include:

(a) Counselling

(b) Time off or regular rest breaks

(c) Relaxation techniques (breathing exercises, mediation)

(d) Physical exercise and self-expression as a safety valve for tension

(e) Delegation and planning (to avoid work-loan related stress)

(f) Assertiveness (to control stress related to insecurity in personal relations)

In addition, **job** training can increase the individual's sense of competence and security and **ecological** control can be brought to bear on the problem of stress, creating conditions in which stress is less likely to be a problem: well designed jobs and environments, and an organisation culture built on meaningful work, mutual support, communication and teamwork.

Other causes of 'dis-ease' at work

Workplace intimidation, harassment and physical violence have been the subject of recent studies, suggesting that *bullying* is every bit as prevalent - and painful - in the workplace as it is in the school playground!

Policies should take into account victim-side factors (grievance procedures, confidentiality, counselling, transfer) and perpetrator-side factors (disciplinary procedures, counselling, transfer, cultural change): see the sexual harassment guidelines in Chapter 10 for a good model.

If you are interested in this area, check out www.bullyonline.org or www.cipd.co.uk.

Activity 10 (15 minutes)

Brainstorm a list of behaviours you would consider 'bullying' in the workplace.

The HSE's report *Beacons of Excellence in Stress Management* outlines a 'good practice model' for reducing stress: see www.peoplemanagement.co.uk/stressbusters, or www.hse.gov.uk/stress.

EXAMPLES

- Rolls-Royce uses an intranet questionnaire to survey staff on aspects of their work that may be causing stress. In addition, senior managers have attended one-day training courses aimed at raising awareness of stress-related problems.

- Somerset County Council is training managers to monitor and detect stress factors before they "manifest themselves as stress-related illness or absence".

- GlaxoSmithKline has opened "Well-being" centres in its offices where staff can go to relax and many employees are now working flexitime or partly from home. To make that process easier, the firm has opened "drop-in" centres that home workers can visit to use office facilities. Responsibility for preventing and managing workplace stress is held by a specially created Employee Health Management group.

(Watkins 2003 (c))

EXAMPLE: INTERNATIONAL COMPARISON

In extreme cases, stress is a killer. The Japanese, who work longer hours than people in the US and the UK, experience **karoshi** (death from overwork). This is a documented ailment in which people develop illnesses and die from high stress and the pressures of overtime. **Karoshi** was officially registered as a fatal illness in 1989.

4.3 Ergonomics

Definition

Ergonomics (Greek: **ergos** (work) + **nomos** (natural laws) is the scientific study of the relationship between Man and his working environment. This sphere of scientific research explores the demands that can arise from a working environment and the capabilities of people to meet these demands.

Ergonomics supports the design of machines and working conditions which function well and are best suited to the capacities and health requirements of the human body. In old people's homes and hospitals, for example, switches are placed according to measurements of chair height and arm reach. In the same way, computer consoles and controls, office furniture, factory layout and so on can be designed so that the individual expends minimal energy and experiences minimal physical strain in any given task.

More recently ergonomics has developed into a field that embraces the whole range of psychological factors that affect people at work. Apart from purely mechanical considerations - in what position should a worker be sitting in order to exert maximum force over a long period of time without physical strain or fatigue? - the ergonomist must now take into account the increasing problems of the worker as information processor. The perceptual limitations of the worker can also be measured, and systems designed which do not make unreasonable demands on the worker's attention span or capacity to absorb information - for example, the use of sound signals to attract attention to visual displays or equipment.

4.4 Promoting positive health and fitness

Approaches to health promotion include the following.

(a) **Health monitoring and awareness campaigns**

Employees may be given regular health checks under occupational health regulations (hearing and eye tests, for example): this may be extended to heart and cholesterol checks, general fitness checks, skin cancer checks and so on, as part of a campaign to increase health awareness. Campaigns may be run to educate employees on nutritional guidelines, smoking and substance abuse hazards, the need for exercise and so on.

(b) **Nutritional support**

The link between motivation and health is well-documented. Employers can encourage healthy eating habits through education programmes and through access to nutritionally balanced food in staff canteens, voucher schemes linked to health food outlets or products, sponsorship of weight-loss (or gain) programmes and so on.

(c) **Anti-smoking programmes**

Many organisations now operate smoke-free workplaces or separate smoking areas, following a 2000 HSC Code of Practice on preventing passive smoking. However, there is still a need to promote and support 'quit' campaigns because of smokers' health and time/environment in 'popping out (or elsewhere) for a smoke'. Information packs are available from health agencies, and incentives and encouragement may be offered.

(d) **Fitness promotion**

Sedentary occupations erode physical strength, stamina and flexibility, interfere with sleep patterns and metabolic rate, reduce alertness and contribute to the long-term consequences of all the above in stress, heart disease and other serious ailments. Fitness promotion in the workplace may range from educating employees in basic stretching exercises during work breaks to extensive facilities, accessed via discounted membership at health clubs and sports centres. In radical cases (considered the norm in Japan), whole staff exercise may be held at the start of each day.

EXAMPLE

'Companies have long offered healthcare and private medical insurance (PMI) schemes as part of employee benefits packages. But many have now switched focus from cure to prevention.

'In January, Standard Life teamed up with health management firm vielife to create a package that combines PMI with health management programmes. Employees have access to a personalised, private online portal with email advice on topics including sleep, stress, nutrition and fitness.

'As for fitness, the British Heart Foundation (BHF) is so concerned about the predominance of 'desk potatoes' it has launched a workplace health activity toolkit to provide employers with ideas to increase staff activity levels and thus avoid ill health, stress and low morale. According to the BHF, physical activity programmes at work reduce absenteeism by up to 20 per cent and physically active employees take 27 per cent fewer days of sick leave than their less active colleagues. The Foundation recommends at least 30 minutes of moderately intense exercise, such as brisk walking, swimming or cycling, at least five times a week.

'Nicki Cooper, BHF head of education, says, "Researchers have found that employees who are more physically active can better manage stressful situations at work. These employees are also more likely to have less sick days for back problems and other health issues, making them more productive long-term employees." '

(Persaud, 2003)

4.5 Substance abuse

Substance abuse has become a major work-place issue.

> Binge drinking is costing UK employers £6.4 billion a year – with up to 17 million working days lost annually as a result of alcohol-related absences.

Cabinet Strategy Unit, 2003

> The less quantifiable costs associated with alcohol misuse in terms of accidents at work are likely to inflate the figure significantly. Employees with alcohol problems also pay heavily in terms of their own health and, in extreme cases, their jobs.

IRS Employment Trends 517

Most estimates place the numbers of drug users slightly below these levels, taking into account the sheer variety of prescription and non-prescription drugs used, and the difficulties of gathering user information (given the illegality of most drug use).

Alcohol policy

Alcohol may be part of the culture of the workplace. Studies have found that:

(a) Workers who suffer from job stress and organisational frustration frequently turn to alcohol as a tool for unwinding.

(b) Organisations continue to encourage social drinking, despite the known effects of physical/psychological dependency. Company celebrations frequently revolve around alcohol, and little concern is shown for the heavy drinker until his or her work is adversely affected, which may not be for some time after the onset of dependency.

Activity 11	**(30 minutes)**

What would you expect to be the symptoms of alcohol abuse that might alert a supervisor or manager to the problem?

NOTES

Most alcohol policies embrace the following areas.

(a) **Positive aims and objectives** - including statistics on alcohol-related harm and affirmation of successful treatment.

(b) **Restrictions on alcohol possession or consumption**. These may be:

    (i) A total ban on alcohol consumption on and/or off the premises during the working hours

    (ii) Restriction of alcohol consumption to certain areas of the premises (say, visitors' dining rooms or a licensed canteen) and/or hours (usually special occasions)

    (iii) Selective restrictions on certain employees - usually for health and safety reasons

(c) **The links between the policy and disciplinary procedure**. This is a sensitive area. Violent or illegal behaviour under the influence of alcohol would clearly trigger disciplinary action. Instances of random drunkenness and bad behaviour are usually treated under the heading of 'gross misconduct'. Deterioration in work performance or behaviour may, however, be better handled under the terms of the counselling and referral provisions of the alcohol policy - unless counselling and treatment are refused or ineffective. These fine lines will need to be clearly set out.

(d) **Policy on testing**. Employers must be clear that the benefits of testing justify the privacy intrusion.

Draft guidelines from the information commissioner (December 2003) ban the blanket testing of employees for alcohol (and drugs) and restrict tests to jobs that pose safety risks, such as operating dangerous machinery. Performance and conduct issues are unlikely to be justifiable reasons for testing – unless employers suspect use where it breaches the employee's contract, or where it might cause 'substantial damage' to the employer's reputation.

(e) **Confidentiality** of all measures undertaken in relation to alcohol problems of individual employees.

(f) **The roles of line and other managers in identifying and helping individuals with alcohol problems**. There should be detailed provisions on dealing with the problem drinker at work, from the initial identification of deteriorating work performance to assessing appropriate treatments and how to deal with the return to work.

(g) **Internal and external counselling services available**. Counselling is one of the central objectives of most alcohol policies. They should specify provisions for time off for counselling, the right of the individual to return to his job, any 'rehabilitation' requirements and a period of monitoring.

Drugs policy

Drug abuse policies are much more difficult to implement because:

(a) A significant number of workers may be legitimate short- or long-term users of prescription drugs and over the counter medicines which may impair performance in various ways (for example, by causing drowsiness)

(b) The illegality of the use of many drugs makes it difficult to gather information, and places drug use firmly within disciplinary as well as welfare policy frameworks

(c) Harm minimisation approaches (restricted use, risk avoidance and so on) may be interpreted as condoning drug use, although they do address the major workplace issues of safety risk and impaired performance

(d) It is difficult to distinguish fairly between 'acceptable' recreational drug use (of ecstasy or cannabis, say) and 'hard' drug use

(e) Random drug testing is fraught with industrial relations and legal issues (for example, under the Human Rights Act 1998), particularly since there are major problems of test reliability and privacy

Counselling, harm-minimisation (avoiding heavy machinery, driving and so on if affected) and voluntary supported rehabilitation programmes may be used judiciously as the basis of a policy. Entry into a company treatment programme should not be compulsory, where an employee can show that (s)he is undertaking independent treatment. The disciplinary issues will (as with alcohol) have to be worked out in detail.

FOR DISCUSSION

- Alcohol and drug use are a private matter.
- Zero tolerance is the only approach to stopping alcohol and drug abuse.

Debate these two propositions, from the perspective of HR policy.

4.6 HIV/AIDS

The fear and prejudice surrounding the Acquired Immune Deficiency Syndrome and the Human Immunodeficiency Virus require positive policy commitments from employers. Guidelines on policy, followed by many major employers, include the following.

(a) People with AIDS or who are HIV positive are entitled to the same employment rights and quality of working life as people with other serious diseases.

(b) Employment policies should be based on the scientific evidence that people with AIDS or HIV do not pose a risk of transmitting the virus through normal workplace contact.

(c) Employers should provide all workers with up-to-date, sensitively-handled information about AIDS/HIV, safe practices and risk reduction.

(d) Employers must protect the confidentiality of employees' medical histories, test results and so on.

(e) Employers should not require HIV screening ('AIDS testing') as part of general pre-employment or workplace physical examinations; nor should particular groups (eg gay men) be unfairly targeted for screening (discriminatory practice).

(f) Education and counselling programmes are considered helpful, but should not replace rigorous equal opportunities policies.

The Health and Safety Executive has issued a booklet (*AIDS and the Workplace*, 1990) with policy guidelines.

EXAMPLE

The Body Shop runs an education and counselling programme on HIV and AIDS. Its purpose is to give support to HIV-positive employees and employees with HIV-positive partners, and to prevent fear and discrimination by other employees, while promoting safe practices.

We have already suggested 'counselling' as part of many welfare policies. We will now go on to discuss counselling itself.

4.7   Workplace counselling

Definition

> '**Counselling** can be defined as a purposeful relationship in which one person helps another to help himself. It is a way of relating and responding to another person so that that person is helped to explore his thoughts, feelings and behaviour with the aim of reaching a clearer understanding. The clearer understanding may be of himself or of a problem, or of the one in relation to the other.' (Rees, 1996)

> **Activity 12**   **(10 minutes)**
>
> Suggest five situations, already mentioned in this Course Book, in which workplace counselling may be helpful.

The CIPD's 1994 *Statement on Counselling in the Workplace* makes it clear that effective counselling is not merely a matter of pastoral care for individuals, but is very much in the organisation's interests.

(a)   Appropriate use of counselling tools can prevent under performance, reduce labour turnover and absenteeism and increase commitment from employees. Unhappy employees are far more likely to seek employment elsewhere.

(b)   Effective counselling demonstrates an organisation's commitment to and concern for its employees and so is liable to improve loyalty and enthusiasm among the workforce.

(c)   The development of employees is of value to the organisation, and counselling can give employees the confidence and encouragement necessary to take responsibility for self and career development.

(d)   Workplace counselling recognises that the organisation may be contributing to the employees' problems and therefore it provides an opportunity to reassess organisational policy and practice.

The counselling process has three stages.

(a)   **Recognition and understanding**. Often it is the employee who takes the initiative, but managers should be aware that the problem raised initially may be just the tip of the iceberg. (*Personnel Management Plus*, February 1993, cited a case where an employee came forward with a problem about pension contributions, and mentioned, as he was about to leave 'By the way – my wife wants a divorce'.)

(b) **Empowering**. This means enabling the employee to recognise their own problem or situation and encouraging them to express it.

(c) **Resourcing**. The problem must then be managed, and this includes the decision as to who is best able to act as counsellor. A specialist or outside resource may be better than the employee's manager.

Confidentiality is central to the counselling process. There will be situations when an employee cannot be completely open unless he is sure that his comments will be treated confidentially. However, certain information, once obtained by the organisation (for example, about fraud or sexual harassment) calls for action. In spite of the drawbacks, therefore, the CIPD statement is clear that employees must be made aware when their comments will be passed on to the relevant authority, and when they will be treated completely confidentially.

The CIPD checklist below contains much useful advice for meeting and interviewing people generally, not merely in counselling situations.

Counselling checklist

Preparation

- Choose a place to talk which is quiet, free from interruption and not open to view

- Research as much as you can before the meeting and have any necessary papers readily available

- Make sure you know whether the need for counselling has been properly identified or whether you will have to carefully probe to establish if a problem exists

- Allow sufficient time for the session. (If you know you must end at a particular time, inform the individual of this)

- Decide if it is necessary for the individual's department head to be aware of the counselling and its purpose

- Give the individual the option of being accompanied by a supportive colleague

- If you are approaching the individual following information received from a colleague, decide in advance the extent to which you can reveal your source

- Consider how you are going to introduce and discuss your perceptions of the situation

- Be prepared for the individual to have different expectations of the discussion, eg the individual may expect you to solve the problem - rather than come to terms with it himself/herself

- Understand that the individual's view of the facts of the situation will be more important than the facts themselves and that their behaviour may not reflect their true feelings

Format of discussion

- Welcome the individual and clarify the general purpose of the meeting

- Assure the individual that matters of confidentiality will be treated as such

- The individual may be reticent through fear of being considered somewhat of a risk in future and you will need to give appropriate reassurances in this regard

- Be ready to prompt or encourage the individual to move into areas he/she might be hesitant about

- Encourage the individual to look more deeply into statements

- Ask the individual to clarify statements you do not quite understand

- Try to take the initiative in probing important areas which may be embarrassing/ emotional to the individual and which you both might prefer to avoid

---

- Recognise that some issues may be so important to the individual that they will have to be discussed over and over again, even though this may seem repetitious to you

- If you sense that the individual is becoming defensive, try to identify the reason and relax the pressure by changing your approach

- Occasionally summarise the conversation as it goes along, reflecting back in your own words (not paraphrasing) what you understand the individual to say

- Sometimes emotions may be more important than the words being spoken, so it may be necessary to reflect back what you see the individual feeling

- At the close of the meeting, clarify any decisions reached and agree what follow-up support would be helpful

Overcoming dangers

- If you take notes at an inappropriate moment, you may set up a barrier between yourself and the individual

- Realise you may not like the individual and be on guard against this

- Recognise that repeating problems does not solve them

- Be careful to avoid taking sides

- Overcome internal and external distractions. Concentrate on the individual and try to understand the situation with him/her

- The greater the perceived level of listening, the more likely the individual will be to accept comments and contributions from you

- Resist the temptation to talk about your own problems, even though these may seem similar to those of the individual

Source: CIPD (1994)

4.8 Employee assistance programmes (EAPs)

Recognising the difficulty of providing an effective counselling service in-house and also the special skills involved, a notable modern trend is to use outsiders for employee support.

Companies such as EAR, Focus, and ICAS provide Employee Assistance Programmes (EAPs), offering a 24-hour telephone line with instant access to a trained counsellor. Meetings can be face-to-face if the employee wants, and their immediate families are also covered by the scheme. The providers offer thorough briefing on the scheme for all employees, and management information and consultancy for the employers.

An article in *People Management* (12 October, 2000) laid out how to get the best from an EAP.

What to look for in an EAP

- Effective promotion of services

- Easy access - normally through a round-the-clock operations centre

- Expert consultation and training for managers, HR and occupational health professionals

- Confidential, appropriate and timely assessment of problems

- 'Brief-focused' professional counselling

- Referrals to long-term treatment

- Follow-up and monitoring of employees who access clinical services

- Crisis support after critical incidents

Dos and don'ts for the HR manager

Do   use the programme yourself

press for a dedicated EAP account manager

insist that complaints are fully investigated

check take-up figures each year

check the capabilities of the operations centre

check up on clinical procedures, counsellors' qualifications and supervision processes

intervene quickly during critical incidents and bigger crises

encourage managers and supervisors to use the EAP

Don't   expect your EAP provider to be proactive on all of these issues

imagine that your firm is receiving a high-quality EAP - verify it yourself.

Chapter roundup

- The traditional welfare function was legalistic/reactive or paternalist in its orientation, and regarded as entirely 'soft'. The new welfare model, while meeting its legal obligations (in traditional health and safety and welfare benefits and services) is more positive, pro-active, holistic, flexible and strategic in aiming to improve employee performance.

- Occupational health and safety are key areas of legislation and regulation. The Health and Safety at Work Act and regulations implementing EU directives cover many areas of policy and practice.

- The modern workplace contains many potential hazards and particular attention must be given to accident prevention and reporting.

- Issues in the new welfare model include: work-life balance and stress management; ergonomics; positive health promotion; and meeting emerging health issues such as substance abuse and HIV/AIDS.

- Counselling in the workplace and Employee Assistance Programmes are two ways of accessing help.

Quick quiz

1   Give reasons for the importance of health and safety at work.

2   What are the health risks associated with VDU use?

3   What does the cost of accidents to an employer consist of?

4   What preventative action could be taken to reduce the possibility of illness or accidents at the workplace?

5   What are the duties placed on an employee by the Health and Safety at Work Act 1974?

6   What additional duties have been placed on employers by recent regulations?

7   What are the major work-related causes of stress?

8   What is ergonomics?

9   What might be the components of an HIV/AIDS policy?

10   What is an Employee Assistance Programme?

Answers to quick quiz

1. To protect employees from pain and suffering; legal obligations; the cost of workplace accidents; to improve the company's image.

   (see introduction)

2. Various manifestations of RSI. (para 1.2)

3. Time lost by employees and management; cost of first aid and staff; cost of disrupted work. (para 2.2)

4. Safety consciousness; consultation and participation; adequate instruction; minimal materials handling; safety devices on machines; good maintenance; codes of practice. (para 2.3)

5. To take reasonable care of self and others; to allow employers to carry out their duties. (para 3.2)

6. Risk assessment; risk control; information on risks and hazards; revise and initiate safety policies; identify 'at risk' employees; training; competence of advisers; consultation with employees. (para 3.3)

7. Job demands; role conflict; role ambiguity; role overload and underload; responsibility for others; lack of social support; non-participation in decision making. (para 4.2)

8. The study of the relationship between Man and his working environment. (para 4.3)

9. Equal opportunities for employees with HIV/AIDS; emphasis on low risk of infection; education on safe practices; counselling of employees with HIV (or HIV positive partners). (para 4.6)

10. A contract for counselling services with an external service provider. (para 4.8)

Answers to activities

1,2 Your own environment and experience - but the text in paragraph 1.2 should give you some ideas. If you spot any hazards: make a report and submit it to the relevant person in authority!

3. Again, your own research: learn to use the real-life resources you have available to you!

4. You should have spotted the following hazards

   (a) Heavy object on high shelf
   (b) Standing on swivel chair
   (c) Lifting heavy object incorrectly
   (d) Open drawers blocking passageway
   (e) Trailing wires
   (f) Electric bar fire
   (g) Smouldering cigarette unattended
   (h) Overfull waste bin
   (i) Overloaded socket
   (j) Carrying too many cups of hot liquid
   (k) Dangerous invoice 'spike'

   If you can see others, you are probably right.

5. Up to you: have fun!

6. Your own research: do think the questions through, once you have gathered your data!

7   How about: risk assessment; feedback; systems and procedures; attention of all employees and contractors; monitor and audit; full review.

8   Some areas you might have thought of include:

(a)   Alcohol on the premises
(b)   Drug taking (including prescription drugs) on the premises
(c)   Horse play and practical jokes
(d)   Noise (or 'acoustic shock'), particularly from headset use.
(e)   Workplace behaviour: running, throwing things, etc
(f)   Tiredness (dangerous objects, dust, slippery objects etc)

9   Your own experience. Be as honest as you can. If you aren't doing much to control your stress, consider doing some further research on the list of techniques following the Activity.

10   Some suggestions are: shouting, swearing; persistent public criticism; ridicule and name-calling; threats; physical intimidation (use of threatening body language or actual violence); sexual harassment; racial vilification; victimisation in applying work rules; deliberately allocating difficult or unpleasant tasks to an individual; sabotaging the individual's work complaining to other staff or supervisors about the individual; multiple grievance or disciplinary actions and so on.

11   Symptoms typically include: avoidance of supervisors and workmates; uncharacteristic aggression, mood swings and variations in work pace; sloppy appearance, signs of hangover; hand tremors, gastric upsets, insomnia; financial difficulties and relationship problems; bizarre excuses for work deficiencies; increased accidents and absences for ill health. (Similar symptoms apply to drug abuse, with the addition of: dilated or contracted pupils in the eyes; sudden 'nodding off'; slurred speech; uncontrolled laughter or tears; sloppy appearance and unsteady movements but without the smell of alcohol).

12   The need for workplace counselling can arise in many different situations, including the following.

(a)   During appraisal

(b)   In grievance or disciplinary situations

(c)   Following change, such as promotion or relocation

(d)   On redundancy or dismissal

(e)   As a result of domestic or personal difficulties, alcoholism, drug abuse, HIV/AIDS

(f)   In cases of sexual harassment or violence at work

Assignment 11   **(1½ hours)**

Duntoiling Nursing Homes

You are the personnel officer for Duntoiling Nursing and Retirement Homes PLC, a chain of residential complexes for senior citizens in the West Midlands region. Recently, Gareth Cheeseman, the bullish, entrepreneurial director, sent a brief memorandum to all staff informing them that all premises now constitute 'No Smoking' areas for patients, visitors and staff alike. Notices to this effect have gone up round the homes. Duntoiling is also declaring its 'No Smoking' policy in recruitment advertisements.

The abruptness with which Cheeseman introduced this policy is now causing problems. It seems that some staff are continuing to smoke 'behind closed doors', and visitors and patients are flouting the ban in the corridors and toilets. Staff rebuking them have been subject to verbal abuse. Some staff also complain of suffering from stress because they cannot give up the craving.

The crunch came last week, when one supervisor issued a formal oral warning to a member of his staff caught 'red-handed' smoking in her office, and stated that if she repeated the offence she would be dismissed. The employee in question resigned in a fit of pique and is now claiming constructive dismissal, with union support.

Cheeseman has asked you to brief him on what action needs to be taken:

(a) To deal with the disciplinary case and
(b) To ensure that the policy is complied with in the future

What advice will you give? Present your answer in the form of a memorandum to Gareth Cheeseman.

Chapter 12:
INTERNATIONAL HRM

Introduction

We have already made some international comparisons in the context of specific HR policies and practices, in earlier chapters: similar comparisons will be made in Parts C and D of this Course Book with reference to employment development and employee relations. The key point, however, is that there are very many complex differences in the culture, law and practice relating to HRM from nation to nation.

In this chapter, we draw together the threads of an international perspective on HRM.

We begin by considering the implications of **cross-national transfer of people**: the impact of globalisation on the labour market and human resource planning, policy and practice.

We then go on to consider the implications of **cross-national transfer of HRM values and practices**: the extent to which there is (or should be) convergence or divergence.

Finally, we look at the ways in which **national cultures** differ, and the implications of this for the management of **diversity** in the workplace, following on from our discussion in Chapter 10.

This is clearly a vast area of study. We recommend that you use this brief overview to identify your own areas of interest and to guide you in follow-up reading (in the Press, International HR journals and so on).

Your objectives

In this chapter you will learn about the following.

- (a) The impact of globalisation on human resource planning and policy
- (b) The HRM implications of European Union
- (c) Areas of convergence and divergence in international HRM
- (d) The impact of different national cultures, and ways of managing a culturally diverse workforce

1   INTERNATIONAL HRM

> **International HRM** is 'the process of employing and developing people in international organisations... It means working across national boundaries to formulate and implement... strategies, policies and practices which can be applied to an international workforce.' (Armstrong, 2003)

Definition

1.1   The global employment context

People are increasingly likely to work in an organisation that has multinational or multiethnic elements, whether based in their own national culture, or in another culture at home or abroad. In some respects, a global labour market has developed in recent decades, because of such factors as:

- Domestic skill/education shortages, encouraging international recruitment – which in turn has been facilitated by social policy harmonisation (eg freedom of labour movement within the European Economic Area)

- The emergence, with political change, of new markets in areas such as Eastern Europe, South-east Asia and China.

- The development of integrated trading blocs such as NAFTA (North American Free Trade Agreement), the European Union, and the World Trade Organisation

- The 'shrinking' of the world through Information and Communication Technology (ICT) developments and travel. There is now talk of 'virtual organisations' scattered geographically around the globe, in which people work together via e-mail, the Internet, video-conferencing and so on.

- The pressures of globalised competition. Under the ethos of globalisation, local markets are considered too small to justify the costs of developing and marketing new products. This has encouraged the growth of multinational corporations operating outside national boundaries, and an increase in international mergers, acquisitions, joint ventures and strategic alliances.

At the same time, however, geo-political 'chunking' (the separatist aspirations of political/ethnic/religious movements, as in the Balkan states) is creating new and more culturally complex markets.

> **Activity 1**   **(15 minutes)**
>
> What **barriers** to a common, global employment environment can you foresee? What, for example, might prevent a UK organisation from recruiting in China?

1.2   Characteristics and challenges of cross-national HRM

Torrington (1994) suggests that international personnel management has seven key characteristics.

1. **Cosmopolitan**. People who cope well with cross-national management tend to be culturally flexible, multi-lingual and geographically mobile

2. **Culture**. Cross-national management faces major diversity in terms of cultural backgrounds and values

3. **Compensation**. There are complex issues in the remuneration of people working outside their country of origin, and of ensuring a balance of equity and market rate across different national labour markets.

4. **Communication**. The flow of information and network of relationships must be maintained between geographically dispersed units of the business.

5. **Co-ordination**. Formal and informal methods must be used to ensure integration of the direction and effort.

6. **Competence**. Cross-national (and cross-cultural) working requires the definition, resourcing and development of a wider set of competences than intra-national working.

7. **Consultancy**. Where local requirements outstrip business competence in a given unit, there is a greater need to bring in expertise (from local partners or consultants, or from the parent company if the requirement is to transfer particular policies or practices from the 'home' nation).

Torrington suggests that international HRM is in many ways qualitatively similar to HRM within the borders of a single country – but on a wider scale, involving greater variety and complexity. However, Armstrong (2003) argues that international HRM is likely to be significantly more demanding than intra-national management for four reasons.

(a) **The complexity of the workforce mix**. International organisations may include 'home' country nationals working in subsidiaries abroad, as well as foreign nationals working in the 'home' country or a third 'host' country (eg Europeans working for a UK-owned firm in the US). This particularly impacts on HRM because of the legal complexities of labour mobility.

(b) **The management of diversity**. Different nations vary (as we see throughout this chapter) on a number of key dimensions, including cultural values and norms, social systems and legal requirements.

(c) **The need for communication**. International co-ordination poses huge information and communication challenges. In the field of HRM, face-to-face communication is particularly important – and not easily substituted.

(d) **Resourcing 'world-wide capabilities'**. International operations must recruit and retain people with the skills to deal with the complexities of cross-border and cross-cultural management.

1.3 HR and internationalisation strategy

HR issues will have a key influence on the strategic management of multi-national organisations. The choice of a base of foreign operations, or the decision of whether to set up a foreign subsidiary or enter into a joint venture or strategic alliance with foreign partners, for example, might be influenced by a number of HR factors, including:

(a) Labour costs

(b) Skills available in the local or national labour market: government policy on education and training, available recruitment avenues and media and so on

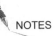
Unit 22: Managing Human Resources Issues

(c) Employment legislation, controlling the employment relationships (eg health and safety regulation, minimum wage)

(d) Industrial relations culture, trade union power

(e) Language, cultural and social differences that would make transfer of HR practices (and/or the use of expatriate staff) difficult to implement

1.4 Human resourcing strategy

Multi-nationals will have to develop specific human resourcing strategies about whether to use 'local' labour, or labour from the 'parent' (head office) country, especially in regard to:

(i) Managerial staff, in order to transfer consistent HR (and business) culture and practices to the international operation

(ii) Technical and professional staff, since equivalent skills or qualifications may not be available in all nations in which the firm wishes to operate.

The range of strategies may be broadly summarised as follows.

Strategy	Advantages	Disadvantages
Key positions are filled with nationals of the 'parent' country. Eg: a US multinational transfers US employees to key positions in foreign subsidiaries.	Facilitates the transfer of the distinctive culture and practices of the parent company to the overseas subsidiary (or project), especially where straight-forward overseas expansion is involved.	• Expatriates find it difficult to adjust to the environment and culture of work/management in the foreign country. • May alienate local employees, because of reward disparity or lack of promotion opportunities.
Key positions are filled by local nationals, although overall control is retained by senior management in the 'parent' country. Eg: a US multinational recruits within Italy to find managers for its Italian subsidiary.	Avoids difficulties of expatriate employment.	• May be cultural/linguistic/priority barriers to co-operation between local and 'parent' country management. • Little genuine cross-cultural experience on either side.
Key positions are filled by the best available people, regardless of nationality. Eg: a US multinational recruits a German to manage a UK subsidiary.	Develops genuine cross-cultural experience.	• Difficult to implement, given 'protectionist' employment policies. • Requires strong corporate culture, communication and co-ordination.

'**Offshoring**' is a major trend of globalisation, whereby organisations in developed countries outsource functions to another group company or third party overseas, in order to take advantage of large, low-cost and increasingly well-educated labour forces in countries such as India and China. This has been traditional in areas such as manufacturing and printing, but has more recently spread to financial services and other service industries: call centres, research and 'back-office' operations are extensively off-shored, using ICT developments such as the Internet to co-ordinate and control operations.

EXAMPLE

As part of workforce restructuring, IBM recently 'offshored' a large number of highly-skilled IT jobs from developed economies – mainly the United States - to Bangalore in India, Shanghai and the north-eastern city of Dalian in China and to Sumare in Brazil.

'Where the IBM initiative differs from what has gone before is that it highlights the fact that developed countries are losing skilled service-sector jobs that have hitherto been seen as offering secure and well-paid employment opportunities. Such services have traditionally been seen as non-tradeable but increasingly more and more jobs in the sector have, thanks largely to the globalising power of the Internet, become internationally mobile. All knowledge-based activities – financial services, communications, health, education, architecture, the law, media – are discovering that the natural protection they have enjoyed in the past is fast diminishing...'

(Walsh, 2004)

Activity 2	(10 minutes)

What are the human resource implications raised by the example given above?

1.5 Human resource development

There may need to be strategies for developing required skills in overseas labour markets where they are currently underdeveloped, for example through the systematic education and training of employees, or the wider sponsorship of education and technical training in the community.

International HRM itself requires the organisation to recruit, retain and/or develop 'cognitively complex self-monitoring managers who have global perspectives and boundary spanning capabilities' (Huczynski & Buchanan, 2001).

- *Cognitively complex*: able to use multiple-solution models rather than 'one best way' approaches

- *Self-monitoring:* personally flexible, sensitive to verbal and non-verbal messages, and able to adjust their behaviour to the social demands of different cultures

- *Global perspectives*: having an understanding of the interrelated and systemic nature of the global community and economy

- *Boundary spanning capabilities:* able to act as interpreters between their own and other cultures

Schneider and Barsoux (1997) suggest that individual background impacts on cross-cultural competence: exposure to different cultures at an early age (via multi-cultural environments, travel or media) develops flexibility. However, these skills can also be enhanced by human resource development strategies which:

(a) Offer diversified work experience in international or multi-cultural settings

(b) Offer relevant awareness and skills training (language learning, cultural briefings, cross-cultural interpersonal skills training)

(c) Encourage networking with professionals of other relevant cultures

(d) Encourage learning through all cross-cultural interactions in the workplace

1.6   Labour mobility issues

Article 48 of the Treaty of Rome protects the free movement of 'workers' (including part-time and economically-active self-employed workers) within the European Economic Area. The general principle is that people coming to the UK for the purposes of employment (excluding short 'business visits') require a **work permit**, but nationals from within the EEA have a right to work anywhere in the EEA *without* permits.

Work permits for non-EEA nationals are tightly controlled, but the Employment Department tends to require less information where the post is a transfer within an international group; is at board level (or equivalent); is in a skill area recognised to be scarce in the EU; or is essential to a project which will bring investment and jobs into the UK.

A combination of new immigration rules and agreements within the EU have complicated the position on UK firms' employment of non-UK nationals. Under the Asylum and Immigration Act 1996, it is a criminal offence to employ someone who is subject to immigration control, unless the person has valid permission to be in the UK which does not prevent them from taking the job.

(a) Employers are required to view a number of official documents provided by a recruit prior to the first day of employment – with additional checking requirements, designed to prevent document fraud, set out in the draft Immigration (Restrictions on Employment) Order 2003. This in itself has been a source of concern to recruiters (particularly in the hospitality, catering and construction industries) who receive large numbers of job applications from candidates who do not have work permits, or who present forged or stolen documents. Employing an illegal worker carries a fine of up to £5,000 per illegal employee

(b) On the other hand, extensive background checks into the immigration or work permit status of foreign recruits 'suspected' of being illegal immigrants lay employers open to claims of discrimination under the Race Relations Act.

FOR DISCUSSION

'The Commission for Racial Equality (CRE) has claimed that Internet job site Monster.co.uk could be acting unlawfully after it deleted the CVs of jobseekers with links to countries that are out of favour with the US.

'According to US legislation, US companies and their subsidiaries are prevented from trading goods, technology and services with Iran, Iraq, Syria, Sudan, Myanmar (Burma),

Cuba, Libya and North Korea. As a result, Monster's European director of communications said, Monster had applied the policy to its UK arm...

'The CRE said that applying the rule to jobs based in the UK could be unlawful under the Race Relations Act 1976. Razia Karim, head of legal policy at the CRE, said: "... As a recruitment agency, Monster may be discriminating in preventing these nationalities from applying for jobs based in Britain." '

(Watkins & Staines, 2003)

What issues does this example raise for international HRM? What kinds of differences does it highlight?

2 THE EUROPEAN EMPLOYMENT ENVIRONMENT

2.1 The European labour market

Some of the key features of the European labour market are as follows.

(a) **General and vocational education**

About 23% of the EU's population is currently in full-time education (comparable to Japan, but slightly lower than in the USA) and 25% of people stay in education after the age of 19.

Vocational Education and Training (VET) varies widely in the extent of specialisation, financing, methods of testing competence and the status and role of VET in the national education system. VET begins at an earlier age in some nations than others, and in some EU countries, vocational qualifications obtained at school offer equal access to higher education as 'academic' qualifications.

Although the proportion of the UK workforce with higher skills (degree or equivalent and above) is similar to France and Germany, the UK compares less well by having a higher proportion of people with low skills and a low proportion with intermediate skills. For example, in 1999 only 20% of the workforce in Germany had low skills, compared to 56 % in the UK, while 65% of the German workforce had intermediate skills, compared to 26% in the UK. (Manocha, 2003)

(b) **Age structure**

As in the UK, the EU workforce is ageing (and shrinking, due to accelerating retirements).

(c) **Non-permanent employment**

Some 15% of all EU workers are estimated to be on part-time contracts, most of them women – although the proportion of working women who are in part-time jobs varies from 10% (Italy, Portugal, Greece) to 80% (Netherlands). Some countries (including France and Germany) have statutory restrictions on the use of temporary employees.

2.2 HR implications of European Union

The implications for European HRM are still being worked out in detail, as EU directives are enacted in the law of member states, and other aspects of European social policy are still subject to negotiation and amendment. However, HR practitioners will need to be aware of the following issues.

(a) **Compliance with EU law** across a wide range of employment issues (as discussed in relevant chapters of this Course Book).

(b) **Differences in specific law and practice** in countries where the organisation may intend to recruit. The Posted Worker Directive provides that any employee posted to a foreign country for more than three months is entitled to the protection of the employment laws of the host country (minimum wage, working hours, notice periods and so on) rather than those of his or her home country, so that organisations cannot cut corners on employment protection by contracting labour from countries where the law is weaker.

(c) **The need for workers to be cross-educated in the languages and cultures of other states**: language is not an area amenable to harmonisation!

(d) **The mobility of labour within the EU**, allowing residence and permit-free working for full-time, part-time and economically active self-employed workers from all member states of the European Economic Area. **The recognition and comparison of qualifications** is a key related issue for recruitment, reward and development: harmonised standards for Higher Educational Diplomas (HEDs) in specific professions and industry-based 'Certificates of Experience' are designed to facilitate mobility of qualified workers.

(e) **Implications of European Monetary Union.** Although the UK has not joined the EMU, the 'euro' has been the accepted currency of business in the EU since 1999, and national currencies have been phased out. A 1998 report *'EMU: Risk or Opportunity'* highlighted: the prospect of pan-European pay bargaining and settlements; the increased importance of European Works Councils for such pay bargaining; the need to reassess corporate structures in view of their potential for mergers and acquisitions, and opportunities for central payroll administrations created by EMU; and the need for employee communication and training to prepare for the change.

(f) **Potential pan-European HRM:** cross-border head-hunting and recruitment advertising, choice of international education and training avenues, management of expatriate management and staff, training in relevant EU markets (and product standards and other differences), management of diversity, welfare for dislocated staff and families, pan-European reward harmonisation and so on.

EXAMPLE

A feature in *People Management* (3 June 1999) described the Eurofighter programme, a four-nation exercise in political, technical, cultural and management integration between British Aerospace, Daimler Chrysler Aerospace (Dasa) of Germany, Alenia Aerospazio of Italy and Construcciones Aeronauticas of Spain, run by a German management company in Germany. Here are some soundbites on the HR issues (as identified by the German HR director) and the techniques used.

> The project's official language is English, and all the teams are multi-national, so fluency is essential. "The southern Europeans feel disadvantaged... The Spanish especially will not admit that they haven't understood something – they simply agree. And you have to be sensitive to varying language skills." Eurofighter has an open learning centre with language facilities...

> But cultural differences go deeper. "The decision-making process is different... The Latins need consensus and aren't empowered to make decisions. The Germans come closer to the Anglo-Saxon model of responsibility, but the Latins need more social contact, which develops trust. It's something we can learn from them"...

There is a handover period for new employees, who are coached by the previous incumbents. They are briefed on local law, including the formalities of registering with the town hall, their entitlement to state benefits, the availability of local services, and – vital to the British contingent, according to [the German HR director] – the fact that cycling drunk in Bavaria is an offence that could cost you your driving licence. Each partner company has a sponsor – a senior manager in Eurofighter – who looks after the welfare of its employees and their families while in Germany…

Managers need extra training to comply with German employment laws such as the rigid agreements on working hours and the role of the works council. "You can't do overtime without authorisation." Through the "right of co-determination" legislation, works councils have the right to negotiate on all terms and conditions. Everyone has to comply, right up to the managing director. Yet it's not a confrontational relationship. "This is a nightmare for British managers, who are used to the union system."

"People here are very experienced. If the organisation is limiting them, they need to be given permission to act. We threw away all the terms of reference from the old days. Job descriptions, for example, were sometimes years old and did not reflect reality… Managers were given responsibility for designing their own jobs, and the works council backed the changes… "Everyone now has a dynamic job description that is updated twice a year. It is job enlargement. This does frighten people, but we try to support them."

Appraisals are a tradition familiar to BAe staff, but other people have had less experience of implementing them successfully. Dasa had an appraisal programme, but it had not provided effective feedback for junior staff. The Spanish had appraisals only for senior managers, while the Italians had no comparable system at all…'

2.3 Harmonisation and divergence between states

The intention of EU policy appears to be the convergence or harmonisation of employment law and practice in member states. However, the protection of common minimum standards and principles does not in itself create a 'pan-European' model for HRM. Member states still vary widely from each other (and from the UK) in:

(a) Their culture (discussed further in Section 6 below), which may dictate different approaches to motivation and reward, employee relations, discrimination issues and so on

(b) The extent of State intervention in employment practices, according to political ideology, and the extent to which regulation, prescription and bureaucratisation is accepted in national culture and systems

(c) Their economic, technical and social development: standard of living, rates of unemployment, pressures on public sector expenditure, communication systems and other infrastructures, taxation incentives and disincentives to particular practices and so on

(d) The specific issues that affect their labour markets: for example, the unification of Germany, the extent of immigration from non-EU countries, their trade agreements with other trading blocs and so on.

(e) Their specific national laws and practices in areas such as: terms and conditions of employment; non-standard work patterns and contracts; family-friendly policies; recruitment procedures; dismissal notices and compensation; anti-discrimination provisions and so on.

FOR DISCUSSION

'A French manager working in a subsidiary of an American corporation that insisted upon an open-door policy may well leave his office door open – thus adjusting to the behavioural requirements of the corporate culture – without any modification whatsoever to his basic concept of managerial authority.' (Laurent, cited by Beardwell & Holden, 1997)

What does this suggest about the 'transferability' of HRM approaches? Do you think there is any possibility of a truly international model of HRM – or is the model too hard to pin down even within one country?

Having already mentioned harmonisation and differences in HR policy and practice within the European Union, we will now go on to look more generally at issues of convergence and divergence in international HRM.

3 CONVERGENCE AND DIVERGENCE IN HRM

As we noted in relation to the European Union, there are attempts to 'harmonise' social and HRM policy for greater consistency and fairness across national borders, and to facilitate the free movement of labour: this process is known as 'convergence'. However, there is also 'divergence': differentiation in response to local conditions and requirements.

Individual trans-national organisations face the same pressures to standardise their HR policies as far as possible in the various countries in which they operate (in order to preserve their distinctive organisation culture, operating style and internal equity) while recognising the need for divergence in the face of environmental differences. The classic challenge is to 'think global, act local': to achieve consistency and equity in core activities and values, while allowing flexibility in non-core activities and values.

3.1 Convergence

It may be argued that the 'activities' of HRM – HR planning, recruitment and selection, appraisal and reward, training and development, welfare, discipline, employee exit and employee relations – are common to organisations everywhere. The need to attract, retain, motivate and develop employees (the 'aims' of HRM) are universal.

The globalisation of business and communications has also encouraged:

- The exchange and sharing of certain technical terms, theories and practices: for example, the widespread adoption of Swedish-style autonomous working groups or Japanese-style quality circles

- The standardisation of certain HR techniques, such as job evaluation and 360° appraisal

- The subordination of national culture and national employment practices to corporate culture and HRM practices, which Boxall (1995) identifies as a tendency of international HRM.

In this sense, there seems to be a convergence of HR policy and practice. Schneider and Barsoux (1997) suggest that alongside the 'convergence myth' of the global village, there is a belief in the convergence of management practice and competence. According to this belief, 'management is management': principles and techniques (such as performance management) can be effective anywhere. With economic, technological and managerial development, business cultures worldwide will be brought into line.

FOR DISCUSSION

'Multinationals could soon be obliged to produce regular reports on their compliance with human rights standards. The UN sub-commission on human rights has adopted a new draft code of conduct that, if approved, could give the UN power to tackle issues among businesses such as bad working conditions. It also wants to censure firms that damage communities by expansion. Under the proposal, the UN could insist that firms regularly report on human rights and are independently monitored. The CIPD welcomed the move, but said reporting should remain voluntary.'

How 'universal' should human rights standards (which affect the treatment of employees by multinational corporations) be? What other areas of HRM (if any) do you think should be subject to globally consistent standards?

Extensive international research does not, however, bear out this idea of a common culture of management (Beardwell & Holden, 1997). While structures and technologies may converge, there is still enough diversity to encourage divergence. The fact is that although everybody 'does' HRM – they seem to do it differently!

3.2 Divergence

Bratton & Gold (2003) point to recent comparative research suggesting that there are significant differences between Asian, European and North American companies with regard to HR strategies. They note that: 'The employment relationship is shaped by national systems of employment legislation and the cultural contexts in which it operates. Thus, as the world of business is becoming more globalised, variations in national regulatory systems, labour markets and institutional and cultural contexts are likely to constrain or shape any tendency towards 'convergence' or a 'universal' model of best HRM practice.'

A number of factors contribute to divergence.

(a) **Cultural factors**, arising from the history, traditions, language, social development and values and religious beliefs of different countries and ethnic groups. Culture amounts to a national way of doing and perceiving things. Cultural factors influence management/worker models, career expectations, perceptions and attitudes to work, education and training needs and so on, and are reflected in the culture of the organisation.

(b) **National legal frameworks.** Specific laws and regulations, and the systems by which they are derived, vary markedly from state to state. The extent of political/legal intervention in employment underscores the cultural dimension.

(c) **Structural factors.** Education and training systems influence the skills available in the labour pool, and therefore HRP, recruitment and development policies. Demographic factors likewise affect the structure of the labour market. Technological and communication infrastructures affect the way in which work is performed and structured, since work organisation and employment policies are different (as the UK experience has shown) in a fast-changing high-tech market than in a low-tech industrial market. Political factors also influence HRM via government intervention.

(d) **Employee relations traditions and ideologies**: the degree of state involvement in industrial conflict and regulation; government support for the unionisation or anti-unionisation of the workforce; collectivisation or individualisation of employment relationships; traditions of co-operation or conflict in industrial relations.

(e)   **National economic development:** unemployment levels, rates of inflation, rate of economic growth, balance of trade: the extent of competition in the local product markets (encouraging HRM for competitive edge) and labour markets (encouraging HRM for attracting and retaining skills).

Activity 3   **(30 minutes)**

Brainstorm a number of cultural dimensions or values on which societies might differ. (Think about all aspects of life that might impact on attitudes in employment.) Suggest examples where possible.

3.3   Comparative HRM

Definition

Comparative HRM is 'a systematic method of investigation relating to two or more countries, which... seeks to explain the patterns and variations encountered in cross-national HRM.' (Bratton & Gold, 2003)

We will now look in some detail at national culture, as one of the key factors in comparative HRM and the management of diversity.

4   CULTURAL DIFFERENCES AND MANAGING DIVERSITY

4.1   What is culture?

Schein (1985) defined culture as 'a set of basic assumptions – shared solutions to universal problems of external adaptation (how to survive) and internal integration (how to stay together) – which have evolved over time and are handed down from one generation to the next'.

Manifestations of culture include:

(a)   **Behaviour:** norms of personal and interpersonal behaviour including forms of address, communication styles, expression of emotion and so on

(b)   **Artefacts:** concrete expressions such as art and architecture, dress codes and symbols

(c)   **Rituals:** patterns of collective behaviour which have customary or symbolic value, such as business formalities and social courtesies

(d)   **Underlying values and beliefs,** which invest the behaviour, artefacts and rituals with meaning. For example, the size of a person's office may imply status and honour, or reflect the importance of privacy within a culture: it 'means' more than the surface suggests.

Activity 4   **(30 minutes)**

Select another culture with which you have had some contact (perhaps working or studying with someone from another culture).

What behaviours have you noticed that are different from the norms of your own culture?

What values do you think might underlie these behaviours?

How easy is it to interpret the cultural values underlying differences in behaviour?

4.2 Globalisation and cultural differences

There is a prevailing sense that 'the world is getting smaller'. Travel, migration, multiculturalism and globalised commerce (especially e-commerce) have eroded national distinctives in what societies wear and eat, what they buy, and how they view themselves in relation to the world. National boundaries are being broken down and global concerns (not just free trade, but social and economic justice and the environment) have gained increasing profile.

Does this mean that cultures are converging? Or, as Guirdham (1999) puts it: 'Are cultural differences disappearing so fast that it is unnecessary to allow for them?' If we look at people wearing jeans, drinking Coke, watching CNN and eating McDonalds in Moscow – or eating sushi in London – we may be tempted to think so. But these are essentially the surface expressions of culture, not the 'deep' culture of worldview and social organisation.

Ethnic separatist movements, ethnic clusters in multicultural cities (eg a 'Chinatown' or 'Little Italy') and anti-globalisation movements testify to the enduring power of cultural distinctives. Moreover, these cultural distinctives have been identified as a source of:

- Competitive advantage or disadvantage in domestic and international markets

- Friction in cross-cultural business relationships and

- Success or failure in reaching cross-cultural markets

EXAMPLE

'More than three-quarters of employees' key work behaviours are dependent on their national culture, delegates at [the 2003] CIPD Psychology at Work conference heard.

'In his keynote speech, Paul Sparrow, Ford professor of international HR management, Manchester Business School, said HR had to accept there was no one solution to best practice in global HRM. Instead, practitioners needed to understand the effect of cultural values on work behaviour and use these "cultural pathways" to reach outcomes, he said.

'Studies undertaken by Sparrow and colleagues in Kenya and Taiwan revealed that by identifying core cultural values, researchers could forecast employees' responses to a range of questions on HR preferences. "We found that by using core cultural values we could predict 75% of answers to questions such as: should the appraisal system focus on measuring outcomes or how you do your job?"

'He said organisations must shy away from "one best way" solutions when designing global HR systems. "Even among HR professionals there are different views about which HR practices deliver competitive advantage, which can have a major impact on global knowledge transfer."

Roberts (2003, (e))

We will look at two influential models of national cultural differences.

4.3 The Hofstede Model

Hofstede (1984, 1991) carried out cross-cultural research at 66 national offices of IBM and formulated one of the most influential models of work-related cultural differences.

The Hofstede model describes four primary dimensions of differences (predominant traits) between national cultures, which impact on all aspects of organisational behaviour: motivation, team working, leadership style, conflict management, HR practices and so on.

Power distance: the extent to which unequal distribution of power is accepted.

High PD cultures accept greater centralisation, a top-down chain of command and closer supervision. Subordinates have little expectation of influencing decisions. White collar jobs are valued more than blue collar jobs.	*Low* PD cultures expect less centralisation and flatter organisational structures. Subordinates expect involvement and participation in decision-making. Clerical and manual jobs are equally valued.

Uncertainty avoidance: the extent to which security, order and control are preferred to ambiguity, uncertainty and change.

High UA cultures respect control, certainty and ritual. They value task structure, written rules and regulations, specialists and experts, and standardisation. There is a strong need for consensus: deviance and dissent are not tolerated. The work ethic is strong. People are risk-averse and experience more stress.	*Low* UA cultures respect flexibility and creativity. They have less task structure and written rules; more generalists and greater variability. There is more tolerance of risk, dissent, conflict and deviance from norms. People take each day as it comes: there is less stress.

Individualism: the extent to which people prefer to live and work in individualist (focusing on the 'I' identity) or collectivist (focusing on the 'we' identity) ways.

High Individualism cultures emphasise autonomy and individual choice and responsibility. They prize individual initiative. The organisation is impersonal and tends to defend business interests: task achievement is more important than relationships. Management is seen in an individual context.	*Low* Individualism (or Collectivist) cultures interdependence, reciprocal obligation and social acceptability. The organisation is seen as a 'family' and tends to defend employees' interests: relationships are more important than task achievement. Management is seen in a team context.

Masculinity: the extent to which social gender roles are distinct. (Note that this is different from the usual sense in which the terms 'masculine' and 'feminine' are used.)

High Masculinity cultures clearly differentiate gender roles. Masculine values of assertiveness, competition, decisiveness and material success are dominant. Feminine values of modesty, tenderness, consensus, focus on relationships and quality of working life are secondary (and confined to women).

Low Masculinity (or Femininity) cultures minimise gender roles. Feminine values are dominant and both men and women are allowed to behave accordingly.

Each of these dimensions is a continuum. Hofstede placed various cultures on the continuum as follows.

Cultural group	Power distance	Uncertainty avoidance	Individualism	Masculinity
I More developed Latin (Belgium, France, Italy, Argentina, Brazil, Spain)	High	High	Medium to high	Medium
II Less developed Latin (Portugal, Mexico, Peru)	High	High	Low	Whole range
III More developed Asian (Japan)	Medium	High	Medium	High
IV Less developed Asian (India, Taiwan, Thailand)	High	Low to medium	Low	Medium
V Near Eastern (Greece, Iran, Turkey)	High	High	Low	Medium
VI Germanic (Germany, Austria, German Swiss)	Low	Medium to high	Medium	Medium to high
VII Anglo (UK, US, Australia, Canada)	Low to medium	Low to medium	High	High
VIII Nordic (Scandinavia, Netherlands)	Low	Low to medium	Medium to high	Low

Activity 5   **(20 minutes)**

According to the Hofstede model, what issues might arise in the following cases?

(a) A Swedish company sets up a subsidiary in Brazil under a Swedish general manager, who wishes to import Scandinavian decision-making styles.

(b) The newly appointed Spanish HR manager of a UK firm asks to see the Rules and Procedures Manual for the HR department.

(c) A US-trained HR manager attempts to implement a system of Management By Objectives in Thailand.

(d) A Dutch HR manager of a US subsidiary in the Netherlands is instructed to implement downsizing measures.

4.4 The Trompenaars Model

Fons Trompenaars (1997) questioned 30,000 managers in 55 countries to identify cultural differences that may affect aspects of organisational behaviour. His findings suggested that certain cultures emphasise some values more than others, on seven key dimensions: cultures do not embody one value *or* another on each dimension, but differ in the amount of emphasis placed on each.

Universalism: behaviour is governed by the standards, rules and norms of the group	**Particularism**: behaviour is governed by one's relationships with a particular individual
Eg: North America, Switzerland, Scandinavia	Eg: Korea, China, Indonesia
Individualism: emphasis is on the individual and individual contribution, the 'I' identity and independence	**Collectivism**: emphasis is on the group/team contribution, the 'we' identity (firm, family) and interdependence
Eg: US, Eastern Europe, Denmark, Nigeria	Eg: Mexico, Indonesia, Japan, India
Affective: Issues are dealt with emotionally; emotions are openly expressed and displayed	**Neutral**: issues are dealt with rationally and unemotionally, with a focus on goals
Eg: Middle East, Southern Europe	Eg: Japan, Germany, UK, China, Korea
Specific: work and non-work roles and relationships are kept separate	**Diffuse**: work and non-work roles and relationships are integrated and merged
Eg: Netherlands, Sweden, US, UK	Eg: China, Singapore, Korea
Achievement: status is based on personal attainments and abilities	**Ascription**: status is based on attributes ascribed to age, gender, background etc.
Eg: North America, Norway, Austria	Eg: Egypt, Indonesia, Korea, Spain, South America
Past/present: the future is seen as growing from the past, history and tradition	**Future**: the future is seen as created fresh from a 'zero base'
Eg: France, Japan, UK	Eg: US, Netherlands

Internal control: individuals are in control of their own lives: they shape events	**External control**: nature and other external forces control much of life: individuals adapt
Eg: North America, UK, Israel, Austria	Eg: Japan, Egypt, China

---

Activity 6 **(no time limit)**

Prepare (and if possible, give) a 'cultural briefing' to someone of another culture, explaining what you think are the important points about your culture in a work/business setting. (You may like to use either the Hofstede or Trompenaars model as a guide.) What are the top 10 things a foreigner would need to know if doing business or working in your country? Describe it as you see it.

If possible, encourage the other person to give you a similar briefing and highlight the differences between his or her culture and your own. Consider any information that surprised you, or the other person: what does this say about cultural assumptions?

4.5 Managing cultural differences

We have already discussed some of the specific HRM policies involved in managing diversity, in Chapter 10. However, it is worth noting that cultural diversity in the workplace also requires:

- **Cultural sensitivity:** the awareness of the potential differences in perception and behaviour that arise from diversity

- **Cultural intentionality**: 'the ability to generate the thoughts, words and behaviours necessary to communicate and work effectively with a variety of diverse groups and individuals' (Ivey *et al*, 1993)

'Rather than knowing *what* to do in country X, or whether national or functional cultures are more important in multicultural teams, what is necessary is to know *how to assess the potential impact* of culture, national or otherwise, on performance.' (Schneider and Barsoux, 1997)

Attention may have to be given to cultural values and norms around:

(a) **Teambuilding**

(i) *Specificity/diffusion.* Forced camaraderie may violate the boundaries between work and non-work relationships

(ii) *Individualism/collectivism.* Team working and rewards may be more congenial to some cultures than to others.

(b) **Communication**

(i) *Language.* Language dominance may create a power or contribution imbalance in a team or negotiation.

(ii) *Communication patterns and styles.* Norms may have to be negotiated within a team or organisation in regard to: the balance of task and social communication; the style and pace of decision-making and negotiation; the nature of conflict and the style of conflict management; preferences for face-to-face or written media; the role of feedback and the style in which it is appropriately given and so on.

(iii) *Inclusive language:* ensuring that barriers to intercultural communication are not created by phrases that exclude or give offence. Biased language may reflect inappropriate or demeaning attitudes or stereotypes.

(iv) *Encouraging, integrating and balancing diverse contributions:* making sure that all members are heard and that their views are properly considered.

(v) *Different cultural values about interaction.* Some people may prefer to raise issues or ideas one-to-one rather than in a group; or in private rather than in public; or in social rather than formal settings.

(c) **Expectations of roles and relationships**

(i) Roles and styles of leadership and team member contribution

(ii) Appropriate degrees of formality and informality

(iii) The role of women, younger people and other (traditionally non-dominant) groups in business contexts

Different expectations can be acknowledged by corporate 'diversity briefings' and awareness training. They should also be brought into the open and negotiated as part of a team 'contract' by line managers and team leaders.

The key aim is to avoid not only discrimination and harassment, but disempowerment of people from different cultures: to ensure that they are able to make a full contribution to the organisation.

Chapter roundup

- International HRM is the process of employing and developing people in international organisations. It means working across national boundaries to formulate and implement strategies, policies and practices which can be applied to an international workforce.

- Key challenges of international HRM include: the complexity of the workforce mix; the management of diversity; the need for communication; and the resourcing of 'world-wide capabilities'.

- Global HR issues will impact on the internationalisation, human resourcing and human resource development strategies of the organisation. Current practical issues affecting HR practitioners include: the trend towards offshoring and the legal ramifications of labour mobility.

- Issues in the European labour market relate to the mobility of labour, European Monetary Union, cultural and linguistic differences and continuing differences in national law and practice for companies exploring the possibilities of pan-European HRM.

- Despite some convergence in (or harmonisation of) the structure, technology and terminology of HRM across the 'global village', there is still enough diversity to support strategies of divergence. Certain aims and activities of HRM are international – but they are 'done' differently.

- Differences in policy and practice may arise from cultural factors, national law and regulation, structural factors (such as education, demographics, infrastructure, politics), employee relations traditions and ideologies, and economic and social development.

- Two influential models of the national cultural differences impacting on the workplace are the Hofstede model and the Trompenaars model.

- Managers need to exercise cultural sensitivity and intentionality, responding flexibly to cultural differences, in order to support organisational diversity policy.

Quick quiz

1 What are the seven key characteristics (7 Cs) of international personnel management?

2 What is 'off-shoring'?

3 How can managers develop cross-cultural skills?

4 Outline the HR implications of European Union.

5 What aspects of HRM can be said to show 'convergence' across national boundaries?

6 What is 'comparative HRM'?

7 What are the manifestations of culture?

8 Explain the terms 'power distance, 'uncertainty avoidance', 'individualism' and 'masculinity' as they are used in the Hofstede model.

9 What are the seven dimensions on which Trompenaars distinguished national culture?

10   What is 'cultural intentionality'?

Answers to quick quiz

1   Cosmopolitan, culture, compensation, communication, co-ordination, competence, consultancy   (see paragraph 1.2)

2   Organisations in developed countries outsourcing functions to another group company or third party overseas.   (para 1.4)

3   Diversified work experience; awareness/skills training; networking; continuous learning through cross-cultural interactions.   (para 1.5)

4   See paragraph 2.2 for a full answer.

5   Basic HR activities (HRP, recruitment, selection, appraisal, training and so on); the broad aims of HRM (attract, retain, motivate, develop); technical terms and techniques (job evaluation, quality circles) (para 3.1)

6   A systematic method of investigation relating to two or more countries, which seeks to explain the patterns and variations encountered in cross-national HRM.   (para 3.3)

7   Behaviour, artefacts, rituals, values and beliefs   (para 4.1)

8   See paragraph 4.3 for a full answer.

9   Universalism-particularism; individualism-collectivism; affective-neutral; specific-diffuse; achievement-ascription; past-present; internal control-external control.   (para 4.4)

10   The ability to generate the thoughts, words and behaviours necessary to communicate and work effectively with a variety of diverse groups and individuals.   (para 4.5)

Answers to activities

1   Barriers to a global labour market include: language; culture (eg the fact that women are discouraged from certain jobs in some cultures); differences in employment law and practice; recognition/equivalency of education/training qualifications; market rates of pay in different currencies (and cost of currency dealings); different expectations of working conditions; personal attachment of workers to family/country of origin.

2   Some of the issues you might have identified include:

   (a)   The requirement to consult with employee representatives on redundancies, together with other redundancy procedures and compensation

   (b)   Likely trade union resistance to the loss of jobs

   (c)   Encouragement of trade union recruiting within the company, and potential loss of morale (because of the erosion of job security) in surviving employees

   (d)   Claims of unfair dismissal by redundant employees, if relocation cannot be shown to be a justifiable 'economic, technical or organisational' reason

   (e)   Impact on employer branding, given likely poor publicity, impacting on future recruitment

   (f)   Poor PR in general, since off-shoring is a highly political issue

3 Here are just some of the many dimensions you may have come up with.

   (a) Attitudes to the balance of work, leisure and family life ('work ethic': traditionally more pronounced in northern/protestant countries of Europe than in Mediterranean cultures)

   (b) The importance attached to the individual vis-à-vis the group or society as a whole (individualistic like the USA; family-oriented like Latino cultures; team/organisation-oriented like Japan)

   (c) Concepts of justice, fairness and ethical dealing (definitions of 'gifts' and 'bribes', for example are fluid in eastern cultures)

   (d) The relative value of different forms of reward and incentive (money is high-value in the US: respect and belonging have high value in Asian cultures)

   (e) Attitudes towards gender roles (women in business are less accepted in Islamic and, to a lesser extent, Asian and 'macho' Latino cultures), age (the seniority culture of Asia or the youth culture of the US and Western Europe), diversity: attitude to disabled, ethnic minorities, sexual orientation, religious beliefs (including specific traditional conflicts eg in Northern Ireland and Islamic states)

   (f) Valued personal attributes and attainments (status attached to education; different styles of education and training)

   (g) Perceptions of continuity/stability/security (Japanese 'commitment' system) v mobility/risk/change (Western 'flexibility' model)

   (h) Styles of interpersonal communication and decision-making (formality, reticence, consensus and hierarchy in Japan: informality, directness, authority in US: differences in eye contact and body language)

   And so on…

4 Whichever specific behaviours you noted in your own experience, you may have found it difficult to interpret the values underpinning them. (Why is it more respectful in a Japanese business context to offer your business card with two hands rather than with one?) The behaviours you noted may have as much to do with the particular *individual's* personality or education or profession/occupation – or the *corporate* culture in which the behaviours were learned, as with his or her national culture.

   The lesson is: beware making assumptions and interpretations. When attempting to manage a diverse workforce, it may be better to *ask* (respectfully) what people find helpful...

5 (a) A low-PD manager is likely to attempt consultative joint decision-making: high PD workers will be inexperienced and uncomfortable with such styles, preferring authoritative instruction.

   (b) A high-UA manager, expecting to find detailed and generally adhered-to rules for everything, may be horrified by the ad hocracy of a low-UA organisation: if (s)he attempts to impose a high-UA culture, there may be resistance from low-UA employees and management.

   (c) A high-individuality manager may implement MBO on the basis of individual performance targets, results and rewards: this may fail to motivate low-individuality workers, for whom group processes and performance is more important.

(d) A low-masculinity manager may try to shelter the workforce from the effects of downsizing, taking time for consultation, retraining, voluntary measures and so on: this may seem unacceptably 'soft' to a high-masculinity parent firm.

6 Your own research.

Assignment 12   (2 hours)

Kaizen Tomorrow Ltd is a large UK manufacturing company. The Production Director approaches you, the HR assistant, and asks your advice about a new idea he has had. He has heard about the success in 'similar' Japanese companies of something called 'quality circles', and he wants to introduce them into KT's factories as soon as possible. 'They're great,' he enthuses. 'You can arrive at decisions for change in product designs and production methods – and get a maximum degree of acceptance from the workers. Quality Circles improve quality, productivity, interdepartmental communication, teamwork and team spirit. They reduce costs and absenteeism. I want them.'

You wonder if you should point out to the Production Director that there is currently very little 'teamworking' as such (although the company sometimes refers to its workers as 'the team'), and even less interdepartmental communication. Worker acceptance of decisions is largely a matter of negotiated compromises between management and the trade unions which represent the various occupational groups involved in production. Previous attempts by management to impose high quality targets were met with suspicion, defensiveness and increased pay claims.

'I'd like to discuss this again,' continues the Production Director 'to hear your suggestions for introducing Quality Circles. I don't foresee any problems – after all, they work fine for the Japanese - but if you think there may be difficulties, you'd better put that in the report as well.'

Your task: Use your research skills to find an article or other account of the experience of a UK company in introducing Japanese management techniques, including Quality Circles.

Make notes in preparation for the meeting. Consider the difficulties of getting this company to work in the way that a Japanese company would, and what could be done to facilitate the process (taking into account current attitudes and structures).

UNIT 23: HUMAN RESOURCES DEVELOPMENT

Chapter 13:
LEARNING AND THE LEARNING ORGANISATION

Introduction

Providing the organisation with the most suitable human resources for the task and environment is an on-going process. It involves not only recruitment and selection, as discussed in Chapters 2-4, but the training and development of employees in order to help them meet the requirements of their current and potential future jobs.

In recent years, there has been a shift in emphasis from **training**, as a separate activity aimed at improving competence in a particular job area, to **learning**, as the process by which individuals develop competence in *any* area, in response to changing requirements. Teaching people how to learn – and supporting their learning at and through their work – enables the organisation to develop human resources more flexibly: by fostering continuous learning to meet changing capability requirements *and* by adapting to the learning preferences and opportunities of individuals. The CIPD's director-general, Geoff Armstrong, was recently quoted as saying: 'There should be a move away from courses where everyone is instructed in the same way on the same thing. We have to become much more customised, and offer continuous learning that creates the capability for organisations to succeed' (*People Management*, 3 April 2003).

In this chapter we examine how people learn, and how learning might be built into organisational culture and practice. In the next chapter, we explore the systematic planning, design, implementation and evaluation of training and development. Finally, in Chapter 15, we survey a range of government-led initiatives aimed at developing skills in the UK.

Your objectives

In this chapter you will learn about the following.

    (a)   Learning theories

    (b)   Different learning styles

    (c)   The impact of the learning curve and transfer of learning

    (d)   Implications of learning theories and styles for planning learning events

    (e)   The learning organisation

    (f)   How training contributes to the achievement of business objectives

    (g)   The role of training and development policy within the organisation

1 LEARNING THEORY

1.1 Three theoretical approaches

It is not possible to put forward a simple definition of learning, because despite intensive scientific and practical work on the subject, there are different ways of understanding how the process works, what it involves, and what we mean when we say that a person 'knows' something (epistemology).

There are three basic theories of how learning works.

(a) **The behaviourist (or stimulus-response) approach**. Behaviourist psychology is based on 'empirical' epistemology (the belief that the human mind operates purely on information gained from the senses by experience) and concentrates on observable behaviour, since 'thought processes' are not amenable to scientific study. It therefore concentrates on the relationship between stimuli (input through the senses) and the organism's responses to those stimuli. The work of Pavlov (on dogs) and Skinner (on rats) suggested that learning is the formation of new connections between stimulus and response on the basis of experience, which they called **conditioning.** According to this theory, we modify our responses to a given stimulus according to whether the feedback on the results of our previous responses was good or bad: an incentive (positive reinforcement) or deterrent (negative reinforcement) to similar behaviour in future. Repetition of the stimulus-response sequence strengthens the conditioning, making us more likely to respond in the same way in future.

(b) **The cognitive (or information-processing) approach.** Cognitive psychology is based on 'rationalist' epistemology (the belief that the human mind imposes organisation and meaning on sensory raw material) and assumes that it is possible to make inferences about those thought processes. According to this theory, our behaviour is 'purposive': we make plans of action in pursuit of goals that we value. Learning is the way in which we process and interpret feedback on the results of past behaviour/experience, and make decisions about whether to maintain successful behaviours or modify unsuccessful behaviours in future, in pursuit of our goals. We do not simply learn new habits (as conditioning theories suggest) but ways of dealing with information and choosing alternative methods of reaching our goals: we learn to learn.

(c) **The social learning approach.** Studies of child development suggest that human beings are designed to learn by imitating other people who are significant to us: our behavioural and role models (who shift over time from our parents and caregivers in childhood, to peers in adolescence, to selected experts and mentors in adulthood). We define our social identity and behaviour by reflection from other people: how they respond to us. We learn to perform actions by 'modelling': watching and analysing the way others do them, and imitating the successful aspects of their performance.

The learning strategies and styles we discuss in this Course Book are essentially based on one or more of these theoretical approaches, incorporating elements of behaviourism (trial and error, repetition and positive/negative reinforcement), cognitive psychology (goal articulation, reflection and interpretation, testing, feedback and adjustment), and social learning (modelling and mentoring).

> **Activity 1** **(10 minutes)**
>
> Before reading what follows, see if you can pick out the aspects of the above theoretical approaches which might be important for the design of training programmes. (Think about the kind of training/learning techniques – which you may have experienced – that occur to you as you read about each theory...)

Implications for training design

Whichever approach it is based on, learning theory offers certain useful propositions for the design of effective training programmes.

(a) The individual should be **motivated** to learn. The purpose and benefits of a learning activity should be made clear, according to the individual's motives or goals: reward, challenge, competence or whatever. Organisational support is critical to the effectiveness of its members' learning.

(b) Clear **goals and objectives** should be set, so that each task has some meaning. This will help trainees in the control process that leads to learning, providing targets against which performance will constantly be measured and adjusted. Motivation to learn will be enhanced if the individual has been involved in setting his or her own learning goals.

(c) Learning should be **structured** and **paced** to allow learning processes to take place effectively and progressively. Each stage of learning should present a challenge (motivation), without overloading trainees so that they lose confidence and the ability to assimilate information/experience.

   (i) Tasks may be broken down, taught and practised stage by stage ('part learning') in order to build up stimulus-response associations, habits or memory: stages are then progressively put together into larger and larger chunks of practice. Alternatively, tasks may be taught or modelled in their entirety ('whole learning') in order to enhance perceived meaning and motivation.

   (ii) Stimulus-response associations and mental processes (especially memory) are subject to pacing effects. The most effective strategy is one which allows for short sessions with frequent rest/assimilation pauses, and which uses repetition (revision/practice) frequently at first and then at increasing intervals.

(d) **Exposure to learning materials** and interactive input (from learning software and/or from coaches or facilitators) enriches the cognitive process and encourages the internalisation of learning. Case-studies, problem solving exercises and so on engage the purposive process of learning. Coaching, mentoring and team learning activities engage social earning.

(e) There should be timely, relevant **feedback** on performance and progress. This will usually be provided by the facilitator, and should be concurrent – or not long delayed. If progress reports or appraisals are given only at the course end, for example, there will be no opportunity for progressive behavioural adjustment.

(f) Positive and negative **reinforcement** should be judiciously used. Recognition and encouragement embeds correct learning and motivates further effort. Constructive criticism of errors is essential for learning, but must be used sensitively: 'punishing' error or slow progress may simply discourage the learner and create a culture of failure. (Even behaviourism notes that negative reinforcement merely conditions people to avoid error and punishment – not to find more constructive behaviours.) 'Failure' should be redefined as 'opportunity for learning'.

(g)   Active **participation** in the learning experience (for example, in action learning or discovery learning) is generally more effective than passive reception (for example, in lectures or reading), because it enhances concentration and conditioning. Practice and repetition can be used to reinforce passive learning, but participation has the added effect of encouraging 'ownership' of the goals and process of change.

1.2   Stages of learning

The 'stages of learning' comprise a simple, intuitive model of the evolution of learned behaviour.

Stage 1.   **Unconscious incompetence**. You aren't aware of what you don't know: you simply act in the way that seems best with the knowledge you have at the time.

Stage 2.   **Conscious incompetence**. You become aware that you don't know. New information, feedback from others, or the results of your behaviour, suggest that there is something missing.

Stage 3.   **Conscious competence**. You work at knowing. You research, analyse, practise, repeat, monitor, adjust. You may be competent – but it requires conscious thought and application.

Stage 4.   **Unconscious competence**. You don't have to think about knowing. You have internalised the knowledge or skill and use it without having to think about it.

Think about the way a baby learns to walk, for example, and you will find that it corresponds to these four stages. The same goes for learning to type or to drive a car (remember how laborious the 'conscious competence' stage seemed?).

Activity 2   **(15 minutes)**

Illustrate the Stages of Learning with another example of learning a work-related skill.

1.3   The learning curve

Definition

A **learning curve** is a graph showing the relationship between the time spent in learning and the level of competence attained. Hence, it describes the progress and variable pace of learning. (It is common for people to say that they are 'on a steep learning curve' when they have to acquire a lot of new knowledge or skills in a short period of time.)

A learning curve may be used:

(a) To suggest *typical patterns* in the acquisition of a given skill or type of skill: the pace of skill acquisition, the standard at which performance 'levels out' (does not improve further); the point at which performance 'plateaus' (levels out for a while and then improves further)

(b) To illustrate the progress of a *given trainee's* learning/proficiency during the training process, in order to monitor the progress and pace of training – and to make allowances for different rates of learning and the 'steepness' of the curve where necessary.

(c) To *plan* the size of the 'chunks' to be taught in one serving or stage of learning, the length of practice/consolidation periods before moving to the next stage and so on.

A 'standard' learning curve is initially steep, levelling out towards proficiency. However, in practice this will depend on the design of the learning programme (allowing for consolidation periods) and the motivation and aptitude of the learner. The curve for the acquisition of skills typically shows one or more plateaus, reflecting the trainee's need to consolidate what (s)he has learned so far, to correct some aspects of performance, to regain motivation and focus after the initial effort, or to establish habitual or unconscious competence in one skill prior to moving on to a new area. Momentum then gathers again, until the trainee reaches proficiency level, where the curve will level off – unless there is an injection of new equipment or methods, or fresh motivation, to lift output again. Such a learning curve is illustrated in Figure 13.1.

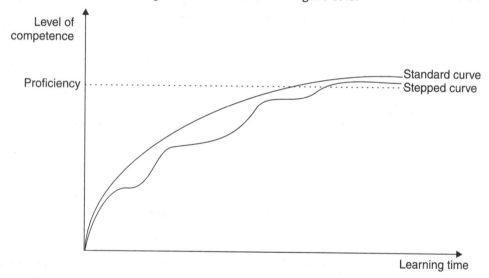

Figure 13.1: Learning curve

Note that learning curves can be quite complex, going down as well as up: for example, if the trainee is unable to practise or apply newly acquired skills and forgets, or refuses to accept new areas of conscious incompetence which emerge in the course of training. An up-and-down 'transition curve' is common in cases where an individual changes jobs or work methods, or makes the transition from a non-managerial to a managerial position.

Activity 3   **(20 minutes)**

Draw a learning curve for:

(a)   An easy task that takes two weeks to learn

(b)   A complex task that takes eight weeks to learn, but for which the training programme has been 'paced' to include consolidation and problem-solving time

---

You may have noticed that the stages of learning and the learning curve appear to be linear or progressive, but in fact form part of an on-going cycle or control system: discovering further areas of conscious incompetence, starting further learning curves in order to adjust performance in response to feedback. This aspect of learning has been formulated as 'the learning cycle'.

1.4   The learning cycle

The best known model is the **experiential learning cycle** devised by David Kolb (1984) and popularised by Honey and Mumford (1992). He suggested that effective learning could start from concrete experience, as well as from abstract concepts. It should not be 'a special activity cut off from the real world and unrelated to one's life', but should integrate concrete (involvement) and abstract (detachment), active (doing) and reflective (observing) elements. This could be conceived as a simple cyclical process, as follows: Figure 13.2.

Figure 13.2: Experiential learning cycle

- *Having an experience:* being fully involved in an action or interaction, utilising your current knowledge and skills.

- *Reviewing the experience:* looking back at what happened, describing it, reflecting on the causes and effects of your behaviour.

- *Concluding from the experience:* forming generalisations, concepts and theories that will enable you to integrate your observations and reflections into your behaviour on future occasions or in other contexts.

- *Planning the next steps:* planning ways in which you can apply and test your conclusions in further action.

Suppose that an employee interviews a customer for the first time (concrete experience). He observes his own performance and the dynamics of the situation (observation) and afterwards, having failed to convince the customer to buy his product, the employee analyses what he did right and wrong (reflection). He comes to the conclusion that he failed to listen to what the customer really wanted and feared, underneath his general reluctance: he realises that the key to communication is active listening (abstraction/ generalisation). He decides to apply active listening techniques in his next interview (application/testing). This provides him with a new experience with which to start the cycle over again.

FOR DISCUSSION

Can you trace the phases of the learning cycle in the way your studies are structured? What phases are well provided for – and which might you require more opportunity for? Do some phases(s) of the cycle naturally appeal to you more than others?

Kolb recognised that people tend to have a preference for a particular phase of the cycle, which he identified as a preferred 'learning style'. We will discuss this aspect of learning theory in Section 2 of this chapter. Meanwhile, we will look at another issue raised by the experiential learning cycle: what is the relationship between theory and practice in learning? If you have read a book on how a car works, should you be able to drive it? If you can drive a car, do you need to be able to explain how it works? And if you have grasped both theory and practice of driving a car, should you also be able to drive a truck? The idea that we can learn something in one context and 'carry it across' to another context is called the transfer of learning.

1.5 Transfer of learning

Definition

> **Transfer of learning** refers to the extent to which newly learned information or skills have been transferred from the learning context to the application of a specific task.

Positive transfer refers to a situation in which learning has been successfully transferred to a task: negative transfer refers to a situation in which learning has not been transferred to the application of a task.

There are two basic approaches to the transfer of learning.

(a) **Transfer by specific correspondence of elements.**

If you were learning French, for example, you might listen to language tapes which feature the repetition and rehearsal of common phrases used in specific contexts: this would facilitate transfer of learning (use of these phrases) when you found yourself in those specific contexts. The workplace equivalent might be hands-on training in a specific administrative or technical procedure used by your employer.

The advantage of this approach, when the correspondences are strong, is that learning can be swiftly and effectively applied in the work context, where it will be further embedded and adapted. The danger with this approach is that if the context, procedure or equipment are not quite the same as the models used in your learning, you might not be able to 'generalise' in order to transfer learning to the new situation. Indeed, the attempt to transfer learning may have a detrimental effect on its application, if the techniques learned in one context are actively 'wrong' in another and have to be unlearned.

BPP PROFESSIONAL EDUCATION

(b) **Transfer by principle.**

If you were learning French, for example, you might use a method which went through the grammatical rules of the language: this might facilitate transfer of learning to a range of situations, since you could simply slot in specific contextual vocabulary as you acquired it. The workplace equivalent would be training which covered:

(i) The desired outcomes of performing a procedure (why it is performed)

(ii) Under what conditions this procedure is likely to be the most appropriate strategy among available alternatives

(iii) How to perform the procedure

(iv) How the stages of the procedure follow and depend on one another and what other variables influence performance

(v) Possible problems during a procedure and how to 'troubleshoot'

(vi) Sources of information and help, should they be required

The advantage of this approach is that it generalises learning and facilitates its transfer across a wider range of contexts. The danger, however, is that it may be too generalised to allow immediate application to a particular work context, and the knowledge may be forgotten if it is not immediately applied.

There is no right or wrong approach to transfer of learning. The nature of the task and the uniqueness or otherwise of the organisation's systems and 'house style' may dictate one or the other. In addition, some people have a preference for learning exactly what they need to do, by doing it: others prefer to work through a conceptual framework and then to apply what they know to a specific context. ('Learning styles' again: we will discuss them below.)

Whichever approach is used, organisations must take into account the transferability of learning if they are not to waste their training efforts and budgets. The range of contexts and variables, and the preferences of trainees, should be taken into account in designing training programmes where possible, to ensure positive transfer. Modern approaches to training (such as competency definition, employability training and attitude and awareness training) are designed to be widely transferable within the organisational context and in the personal lives of trainees.

In addition, practical measures are required to support transfer of learning. The worksite and job context are important in enabling trainees to apply newly-learned skills. They require:

• Appropriate *systems*, *tools* and *resources* to be available to apply their learning on the job, and

• Support from *supervisors*, *peers* and *co-workers* (if whole-team learning had not been used)

Activity 4 **(30 minutes)**

We have already mentioned some situations in which the learning curve levels out or even goes downwards: loss of motivation and negative transfer, for example. Can you think of other factors that might hinder or block learning? (Consider your work or study situation. What factors – cultural, emotional, intellectual, motivational, situational, physical – make it more difficult for you to learn than it needs to be?)

The various theories we have discussed so far encourage a contingency approach to learning: the appropriate strategy and techniques will depend on (among other things) the preferences of the individual for active or reflective, concrete or abstract learning experiences. Several theorists have classified these preferences as distinct 'learning styles': we will discuss them now.

2   LEARNING STYLES

2.1   Honey and Mumford

Kolb (1984) recognised that people tend to have a preference for a particular phase of the cycle, which he identified as a preferred **learning style**.

Honey and Mumford (1992, p. 5) also noted that 'people vary not just in their learning skills but also in their learning styles. Why otherwise might two people, matched for age, intelligence and need, exposed to the *same* learning opportunity, react so differently?' Honey and Mumford formulated a popular classification of learning styles in terms of the attitudes and behaviours which determine an individual's preferred way of learning.

Style	Characteristics	Learning preferences
ACTIVIST *'I'll try anything once'*	Activists involve themselves fully in new experiences. They are open-minded and enthusiastic about new things – but easily bored by long-term implementation and consolidation: act first and think about consequences later. They prefer to tackle problems by brainstorming. They easily get involved with others – but tend to centre activities on themselves.	Learn best from activities which: • present new experiences/ problems • involve short 'here and now' activities • offer excitement, drama and variety • have high visibility/ limelight • allow them to generate ideas without constraints of structure or feasibility • challenge/throw them in at the deep end • involve them with other people • allow them to 'have a go' Learn least from activities which: • involve passive roles and processes

Style	Characteristics	Learning preferences
		• don't allow involvement
		• require the handling of 'messy' data
		• require solitary work
		• involve precise instructions, repetition (practice) and 'theoretical' concepts
		• require follow-up or attention to detail
REFLECTOR *'Look before you leap'*	Reflectors like to stand back to observe and ponder new experiences, preferring to consider all angles and implications, and to analyse all available data, before reaching any conclusions or making any moves. When they do act, it is from awareness of the big picture. They tend to adopt a low profile, taking a back seat in meetings and discussions – though listening and observing others carefully – and tend to have a slightly distant, tolerant, unruffled air.	Learn best from activities which: • encourage observation and reflection • allow them to stand back from events • allow them to think before acting • involve painstaking research • offer an opportunity for review • help them to exchange views with others without risk, with structure • allow them to arrive in their own time Learn least from activities which: • force them into the limelight • require action without warning/planning • give insufficient data • give unanalysed practical instructions • impose time pressures, especially if these necessitate shortcuts
THEORIST *'If it's logical it's good'*	Theorists are keen on basic assumptions, principles, theories, models and systems thinking. They are detached and analytical and like to analyse and synthesise facts and observations into coherent theories. They think problems through systematically and logically. They are interested in maximising certainty, and so tend	Learn best from activities which: • relate to a system, model or theory • allow time to grasp underlying logic • display rationality or logic • have clear purpose and structure

Style	Characteristics	Learning preferences
	to be rigidly perfectionist and uncomfortable with subjectivity, ambiguity, lateral thinking and flippancy.	• allow analysis/generalisation of reasons for success/failure • stretch them intellectually Learn least from activities which: • have no context or apparent purpose • emphasise emotions or feelings • involve ambiguity and uncertainty • require them to act or decide without a basis in policy, principle or concept • skim the surface of the subject • lack theoretical or evidential support • appear shallow or gimmicky • involve them with people with less intellectual styles (eg activists)
PRAGMATIST 'If it works, it's good *(but there is always a better way)*'	Reflectors are eager to try out ideas, theories and techniques to see if they work in practice. They like to get on with things, acting quickly and confidently on ideas that attract them – and tending to be impatient with ruminating and open-ended discussion. They are down to earth: enjoying practical decisions and responding to problems and opportunities 'as a challenge'.	Learn best from activities which: • relate to work problems/ opportunities • offer techniques with obvious practical applications/advantages • allow practise with coaching/feedback from a credible expert • expose them to role models to imitate • allows them to concentrate on practical issues (plans, tips etc) • are followed up with immediate opportunities to implement learning Learn least from activities which: • are not related to immediate needs • are too theoretical or distant from reality

Style	Characteristics	Learning preferences
		• offer no practical guidelines
		• waste time 'going round in circles'
		• offer no apparent benefits or rewards
		• cannot be implemented due to personal or organisational obstacles

Source: compiled from Honey and Mumford (1992)

Training should ideally be designed to accommodate the preferences of all four styles. This can often be overlooked, especially as the majority of training staff are activists!

Activity 5 (15 minutes)

John, Paula, Ringo and Georgette are learning French, as part of their firm's initiative to develop staff in European market.

(a) John reckons that since he does not actually speak to clients, the whole scheme is a waste of time. He claims to be too busy to attend classes.

(b) Paula loves the classes, because they simulate real conversational situations. The trainees have to use whatever vocabulary they have to get their meaning across guided and corrected by the tutor: Paula doesn't like learning grammatical rules, she's happy to pick up the phrases to fit the situations.

(c) Ringo doesn't mind the teaching method either. He doesn't say anything for the first few minutes, though, just picks up what he can, gets it straight (allowing Paula to make the mistakes) and then comes out with a fluent response.

(d) Georgette is lost. She feels frustrated because, although she has learned the phrases for a given situation she is not sure it will apply in other contexts. She takes home a book of grammar at night, to bone up on the general principles and rules.

Who represents which learning style? What style has the course been designed for?

2.2 Kolb's Learning Styles Inventory

Kolb's Learning Styles Inventory is designed to identify the preferences of learners for particular phases of his experiential learning cycle (see Paragraph 1.4 above).

For copyright reasons, the inventory cannot be reproduced here, but the broad categories of preference identified by Kolb are as follows.

(a) The '**converger**' (Abstracting/Generalising and Applying/Testing) prefers applying abstract generalisations in practical and specific ways

(b) The '**diverger**' (Concrete Experience and Reflective Observation) prefers to reflect 'laterally' on specific experience from different points of view

(c) The '**assimilator**' (Abstracting/Generalising and Reflective Observation) is comfortable with concepts and abstract ideas

(d)   The **'accommodator'** (Concrete Experience and Applying/Testing) prefers to learn primarily from doing

Now that we have surveyed some of the theoretical framework of training, let's move on to its organisational framework.

3   THE ROLE OF TRAINING AND DEVELOPMENT

3.1   Outcomes of training and development

We have talked about learning in terms of acquiring the knowledge or ability to do something. In fact, training and development activities may be directed towards a number of different outcomes.

Skill

Definition

> **Skill** may be defined as a learned pattern of operations, or responses to stimuli, which allow the successful, rapid and apparently confident performance of a complex task.

Manual work is often divided into categories according to varying degrees of perceptual-motor skill required: 'skilled' (like electricians and vehicle mechanics), 'semi-skilled' (like machine operators) and 'unskilled' (like road sweepers and canteen assistants). The degree of skill attributed to these jobs is clearly associated with:

(a)   The amount of learning required to master the necessary actions, techniques and methods

(b)   The sophistication of perception and response required (diagnosing a fault and repairing a machine is more skilled work than simply operating it in accordance with learned methods)

Non-manual work involves a wide range of what are classified as 'higher order' thinking skills: cognitive (including information-processing and decision-making), creative, perceptual, linguistic/expressive, social/interpersonal and so on.

Knowledge

Knowledge is a very complex concept, but in the training context may be divided into two areas which are sometimes referred to as 'know-that' and 'know-how'.

(a)   'Know-that' is knowledge **about** something or 'propositional knowledge': awareness of ideas, concepts, theories, methodologies and so on.

(b)   'Know-how' is knowledge **of** something, or the ability to do something: 'practical knowledge'. This may be based on underlying, unverbalised, untaught knowledge ('tacit knowledge'), but is typically acquired through imitation and experience.

Propositional knowledge is commonly associated with formal education, and has traditionally attracted high status in the social hierarchy of skills – while at the same time attracting the suspicion of those with practical knowledge, who see it as divorced from real-world competence. At the end of this course, you may know how HRM 'should' be done – but actually doing it in an organisational setting may be something else again! An organisation clearly needs to acquire and develop both propositional knowledge (understanding of management and technical processes) and practical knowledge (ability to make those processes work in practice).

FOR DISCUSSION

Which is more useful to an organisation: 'know-that' (propositional knowledge) or 'know-how?' (practical knowledge)? Do you agree that 'those who can, do: those who can't, teach'?

Competence

Definition

> **Competence** may be defined as the skill, knowledge and behaviours that need to be applied for effective performance in a work context.

Competence represents one of the 'bundles' of practice which may contribute to the 'fit' or integration of HRM policies in an organisation. (See Chapter 8 if this does not ring a bell.) Competence frameworks may be used in HR planning, recruitment and selection, performance management, reward and training and development. There are two key elements in the concept.

(a) It *integrates knowledge, skills and other attributes* into the notion of overall ability.

(b) It defines and assesses ability *in the context of workplace performance and proficiency.*

Competency definition and testing have become a major element in the design of training and development in the UK: we will return to this theme in Chapter 16, where we trace the history of the competence movement.

Attitudes and awareness

Another recently-recognised area of training is aimed at encouraging trainees to gain insight into their own behaviour and to try to change the negative or restricting attitudes that prevent the individual from attaining more effective performance. Examples of training outcomes include:

(a) Assertiveness (a communication style which asserts one's rights, wishes and opinions in a straightforward, non-passive, yet non-aggressive manner which also respects the rights, wishes and opinions of others)

(b) Insight into the style and effectiveness of interpersonal relations and group dynamics (eg through encounter or 'T' groups)

(c) Insight into the motives underlying undesirable attitudes (racism, sexism, sexual harassment, bullying and so on)

(d) Self-awareness social awareness, social skills and the ability to manage one's emotional responses (collectively called 'emotional intelligence')

> **Activity 6** (10 minutes)
>
> Who do you think would benefit most from assertiveness training, and for what purpose?

Employability

Definition

> **Employability** describes a portfolio of knowledge, skills, competences and attributes that enhances an individual's mobility and power in the labour marketplace. Employability training aims to equip employees with such a portfolio.

Traditionally, training has been seen as a way of improving an employee's performance in a particular job or career path for the benefit of the employing organisation. However, many organisations are no longer in a position to offer long-term job security to their employees. Socially responsible employers wish to classify this new psychological contract and facilitate employees' transition to other jobs by enhancing their employability portfolio – while simultaneously benefiting from the creation of a more flexible multi-skilled labour force.

What benefits can the organisation expect to gain from achieving the above outcomes? This is the first question in evaluating the role of training and development in the organisation.

3.2 Benefits of training and development activity

In so far as training and development activity (or a broader perception of learning) increases competency, skills, versatility, confidence, awareness, knowledge and further learning among employees, it may contribute to the business objectives of the organisation in a number of ways.

(a) Increased efficiency and productivity, through faster, more skilled work and greater labour flexibility (eg through multi-skilling)

(b) Reduction in costs, associated with the above, and with less wastage and fewer errors

(c) Reduction in interpersonal and performance-related problems – both because of enhanced competence and greater confidence

(d) Improved quality of work/service

(e) Fewer accidents and problems with equipment and machinery

(f) Enhanced ability to attract and retain high calibre employees

(g) Improved job satisfaction, motivation and morale among developed employees since skill and career development are key intrinsic rewards which may further increase productivity and quality

(h) Greater communication between employees on job-related issues, with potential for quality improvements and innovations

BPP PROFESSIONAL EDUCATION

(i) Greater potential for increased empowerment and involvement of employees, as they become more aware and more skilled (particularly if training goes beyond technical skills to embrace communication and interpersonal skills, delegation skills for managers, problem-solving and decision-making skills and so on)

(j) The fostering of a culture of continuous learning and improvement, which promotes adaptability to change, organisational flexibility and a positive organisation culture

(k) Compliance with legislation and regulation (where training is given in health and safety measures, non-discrimination and so on)

(l) Better promotion and management succession planning, as employee potential is systematically developed

(m) Fulfilling the future needs of the organisation for skills which may be subject to shortages or fluctuations in the external labour market

(n) Corporate social responsibility (and enhanced employer/recruiter brand) through developing employees – particularly in general employability

We will look at ways in which training and development activities can be evaluated (and justified in terms of their return on investment) in Chapter 14.

EXAMPLE: MOTOROLA

Motorola found themselves trying to compete globally in a market of new technologies and changing demands, with people who, in many cases, had difficulty with reading and basic mathematics. It launched a wide-ranging scheme of education and training (its own 'University') for its employees – and for the employees of suppliers and key customers. Training was designed to develop the person, not just the company and the job. It was aimed at 'creating an environment for learning, a continuous openness to new ideas... We not only teach skills, we try to breathe the very spirit of creativity and flexibility into manufacturing and management.'

(Quoted by Pedler, Burgoyne, Boydell, 1991)

Activity 7   **(20 minutes)**

What might be the benefits of training to the trainee? (Think what you are getting out of doing this course, for example.)

List at least five benefits.

You might by now be thinking that training is obviously such a good thing that an organisation could not go wrong by simply providing some. If performance is poor: do some training! If morale is low: do some training! If empowerment is a foreign concept in your organisation: do some training! Let's get things into perspective ...

Realistic expectations

The personnel function must recognise – and emphasise to line managers – that:

- Training and development can improve performance
  but

- There are many variables in job performance, not all of which may be addressed by training alone
  and

- Even in areas susceptible to training, the training programme must be designed and implemented appropriately for the needs of the organisation and the specific group of trainees – or it will not be effective

3.3 Stakeholders in human resource development

It is worth noting that there are a number of different stakeholders in organisational training and development. (Stakeholders are individuals or groups who have an interest or 'stake' in a given endeavour, because they have contributed to it and/or because they are affected by its outcomes.)

Potential stakeholders in training (in general, or particular training events) include:

(a) The owners and senior mangers of the organisation, who invest in human resource development and determine training policy to reap certain returns on their investment

(b) The line managers of trainees, whose units' performance will be affected by (positive or negative) changes in trainees' competence, behaviour and attitudes

(c) The trainees, who invest time, effort and a range of psychological resources in learning and whose competence, employability and job satisfaction are affected by the organisation's development policies (or lack of them)

(d) The training managers (planners, funders, providers, evaluators) who must develop and deliver successful training in order to meet their own objectives

(e) The instructors, coaches and mentors within the work team, who likewise measure their success by the effectiveness of the learning they deliver and support

(f) Training vendors (course providers, materials publishers, software developers, consultants) whose continued relationship with the firm, and business success, depends on positive evaluation by training managers and trainees

(g) The training community in general, whose reputation, viability and methodology depends on the standard and effectiveness of members' offerings and feedback from customers

The design, planning, delivery and evaluation of learning and training events must take the needs, requirements, preferences and priorities of some or all of these stakeholders into account. As we will see in Chapter 14, most models of training evaluation recognise stakeholder experience and feedback (from at least some constituent groups) as an important measure of success.

FOR DISCUSSION

What do you think are likely to be the key evaluation criteria of each of the stakeholder groups listed above, in measuring the 'success' of a training event or programme? What might be the implications if each of these stakeholder groups were dissatisfied with the experience or outcomes of training?

3.4 The role of training and development policy

Armstrong (2003) suggests that:

> 'The objective of an organisation's policies, processes and programmes for the delivery of learning and training is to achieve its human resource development strategies by ensuring that it has the skilled, knowledgeable and competent people required to meet its present and future needs.'

A human resource development policy will therefore address the following issues.

- Why does the organisation train and develop people: how is human resource development envisaged as contributing to strategic objectives and the HR plan? How does investment in it benefit organisational stakeholders?

- What are the desired outcomes of HRD: skills, knowledge, competence, awareness/attitudes, employability? How do these support business and other HRM strategies?

- How will learning and development needs and objectives be determined? How will they relate individual, team and organisational performance and bottom-line results? What value is placed on employability and 'personal' development?

- Whom does the organisation intend to train and develop? What grades of employee will have access to training, of what type and at what level? What equal opportunity commitments should be made? (This may be part of a wider commitment to encouraging and supporting all members of the organisation to pursue continuous learning opportunities.)

- Who will be responsible for the initiation and control of training: HR specialists, line managers, employees themselves? What value is placed on the concept of 'self-development'?

- When, where and how will training activity take place? What mix of methods, formats and styles will be used?

- How much investment is the organisation prepared to put into training, development and organisational learning?

- How is training and development to be monitored and evaluated?

We will discuss various policy issues in detail in Chapter 14.

3.5 Learning, training and development

It may be worth distinguishing between these terms, although in practice they are often used interchangeably.

- **Learning** is the process whereby people acquire knowledge, capabilities and skills

- **Training** is the use of planned, systematic instruction and other learning events and programmes to promote learning, with the particular aim of enhancing competence in a work role

- **Development** is the growth of people's knowledge and capabilities and the increasing fulfilment of their potential, through a range of learning experiences.

Development is often linked to systems whereby people gain experience within an organisation and are offered increasing opportunities and challenges through lateral or vertical movements in the organisation structure. 'Management development', for example, often implies not only management education and training, but mentorship and career planning, promotion planning and planned managerial succession.

3.6 Management development

Definition

Management development is 'an attempt to improve managerial effectiveness through a planned and deliberate learning process'. (Mumford, 1994)

Much of our discussion of learning and training in Chapter 14 will apply as well to managerial as to non-managerial grades of staff. However, organisations have a significant investment in their managers – and in the quality of their leadership and decisions – and in order to secure and maximise the managerial resource, attention is typically given to:

(a) Some form of management *education and training*. This may range from short skill-based training courses (eg in leadership or interpersonal skills) to on-going learning activities directed towards demonstrating competencies (as defined by in-house or nationally-accredited competency frameworks) to sponsorship/leave for studies towards formal qualifications such as an MBA degree.

(b) Planned *career management*, to enable managers to gain experience of different functions, units or areas of the business, different national cultures (if the organisation is international or internationalising) and increasing levels of responsibility.

(c) *Performance management* to develop and reinforce managerial competencies through on-going goal-setting and continuous improvement.

(d) *Self-managed and experiential learning*, encouraging managers to recognise and seek out opportunities to enhance their skills.

(e) *Guidance and mentoring* by effective motivators, success coaches and power sources in the organisation (usually more senior managers).

Activity 8	(5 minutes)

Suggest three reasons why an organisation should give attention to management training and development.

EXAMPLE: INTERNATIONAL COMPARISONS

- European approaches have traditionally been less concerned with management development as a discrete activity. In France, the making of a manager begins within the higher education institutions and forms part of the development of a historical social elite. In Germany, the approach is more functional: managers tend to stay in functional roles longer, and specialist expertise is pre-developed within the vocational education system. Where there is training, it tends to be highly structured and specified. Despite this 'relatively weak tradition in explicitly focused forms of management', there has been an upsurge of interest in management education since European Union: the emergence of business schools, MBA activity, and EU-led initiatives promoting the exchange of European business and management students between nations.

- The development of managers in Japan (based on a system of commitment and seniority), is long-term, slow-progression, carefully planned and generalist in its scope. 'Whereas Anglo-Saxon models stress individualism and development through short, intensive bursts of training to prepare managers for assignments characterised by challenge and risk, Japanese development programmes are longer and more culturally reflective in focusing on collectivism and group/team effort ... Unlike the US/UK where management development is in the hands of specialists, the Japanese view the relationship between the individual and the boss as a significant factor in developing the manager.'

(Beardwell & Holden, 1997)

So far, we have discussed learning theory mainly in terms of individual learning. We will now look briefly at organisational *learning.*

4 THE LEARNING ORGANISATION

4.1 The learning organisation

Definition

A **learning organisation** is one that facilitates the acquisition and sharing of knowledge, and the learning of all its members, in order continuously and strategically to transform itself in response to a rapidly changing and uncertain environment, and to develop and refine the capabilities required for future success.

A learning organisation values the process of learning – not just its specific outcomes. It learns how to learn: how to be open to new information; how to use feedback to adjust performance; how to view mistakes and failed experiments as opportunities for change; how to make decision-making flexible in order to accommodate learning.

Pedler *et al* (1991) define a learning organisation as one 'which facilitates the learning of all its members and continually transforms itself'.

This implies an underlying vision for organisational learning and flexibility, and the creation of a culture conducive to learning, via an integrated and mutually-reinforcing set of policies, processes and techniques.

4.2 Learning culture

The cultural mechanisms and characteristics of a learning organisation are as follows (Senge, 1990; Garvin, 1993).

(a) Decision-making procedures are continuously modified in the light of experience, avoiding rigid plans and procedures.

(b) Problem-solving is systematic and based on scientific method rather than guesswork: insisting on data rather than assumptions, generating and testing hypotheses.

(c) Experimentation – the systematic search for and testing of new knowledge - is encouraged, in order to generate new insights. Continuous improvement programmes (based on the Japanese concept of 'kaizen') are a feature of learning organisation.

(d) Risk-taking, failures and mistakes are regarded as useful input to the learning process, to avoid problems in future. (This has been called the 'Santayana principle' after the philosopher who said: 'Those who cannot remember the past are condemned to repeat it'.) In any case it is better to experiment with something new than stick with what you know for fear of failure.

(e) Information and feedback is encouraged from all possible sources (notably customers and competitors): opportunities to learn from others should be sought out. This includes the process of benchmarking: identifying best practice in other organisations and transferring appropriately adapted elements of their practice to one's own organisation. (Also known as 'SIS' – 'steal ideas shamelessly'!)

(f) Knowledge is disseminated throughout the organisation by formal communication and informal networking. Everyone operates with the knowledge of environmental changes and challenges and customer demands. Open-channel upward, downward and lateral communication is encouraged.

(g) Everything is open to challenge and questioning: no body of knowledge or procedure becomes 'enshrined' by habitual acceptance. Management actively supports questioning by subordinates.

(h) Selection, training and development, appraisal and reward are based not on existing goals and attainments but on flexibility, continuous improvement, initiative and ability to identify and exploit new areas of activity.

(i) Flexibility of decision-making is supported by self-managed team-working and the role of the manager/supervisor as coach/facilitator.

(j) Training focuses on 'learning how to learn': how to obtain, use and adapt to new information.

Activity 9   **(45 minutes)**

From what you know of how organisational culture is developed and reinforced, and building on the characteristics listed above, what would you expect to be the potential barriers to the creation of a successful learning culture?

4.3 The organisational learning cycle

According to the New Learning for New Work Consortium's report *Managing Learning for Added Value* (as summarised in *People Management*, March 1999) the goal of the new learning paradigm is a workforce capable of taking responsibility for adding value. This amounts to a new learning cycle, which may be illustrated as follows (Figure 13.3)

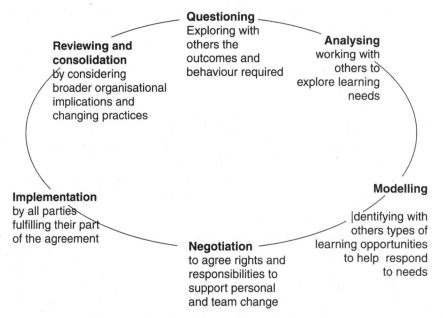

Figure 13.3: A new learning cycle – managing learning to add value

4.4 Individual ownership of organisational learning

Definition

Personal development plans are action plans for individuals' skill and career development which put the onus on the individuals themselves to seek out and organise training and development opportunities.

A 1995 report by the Institute for Employment Studies suggested that the number of large employees implementing PDPs is increasing. 'Organisations no longer feel they can take prime responsibility for the future careers and development of their employees, and the PDP approach clearly places the development ball in the employee's court.'

The most popular PDP schemes take account of people's wider needs and aspirations, rather than focusing on skills required for present job performance.

This trend is also reflected in **employee development programmes** which offer employees a wide range or 'menu' of development opportunities, not necessarily related to the job. The effect of such schemes is to develop a culture in which learning and adaptability is valued, as well as to attract, retain and motivate skilled employees.

EXAMPLES

- A National Health Service development programme for unit general managers includes a budget for each individual to spend – as he or she wishes – on personal development. This can be spent on courses, seminars or books, or on 'buying in' a coach or instructor, or visiting other organisations to observe their methods – whatever. This approach empowers would-be learners, and encourages creative thinking about development needs and opportunities.

- In 1990, the Rover Car Group launched a multi-million pound 'internal business', dedicated to providing learning and development opportunities to all employees: the Rover Learning Business. Employees are encouraged to formulate individual development plans, with the opportunity to learn management skills.

FOR DISCUSSION

Why might an organisation wish to give control of the development agenda to the individual employees? What might the drawbacks be? Who controls your learning objectives and opportunities?

Chapter roundup

- There are three basic theoretical approaches to learning: the behaviourist, cognitive and social learning approaches.

- Learning has been modelled as:

  - Four stages (unconscious incompetence, conscious incompetence, conscious competence, unconscious competence

  - A curve, showing the relationship between learning time and level of competence: training must take account of the steepness of the curve and the need for consolidating plateaux or steps.

  - A cycle, such as the experiential learning cycle of David Kolb (concrete experience, reflective observation, abstract conceptualisation, active experimentation): this can be used as an aid to self-managed learning.

- Transfer of work learning to the work context may be achieved in various ways, depending on the nature of the learning, the motivation and preferences of the learners and the support given by the worksite and work group.

- Honey and Mumford identified four learning styles: theorist, reflector, activist, pragmatist. Learning programmes should take into account the strengths and weaknesses of each style, as well as challenging learners to increase their learning repertoire and flexibility.

- Training may be directed at the acquisition of skill, knowledge, competence, attitudes/awareness or employability.

- The planning, design, implementation and evaluating of learning events and training programmes will have to take into account:

  - The organisation's philosophy and expectations of human resource development, as set out in the HRD policy.

  - The needs, requirements and preferences of various stakeholders in development.

  - The implications of learning theories and styles.

- The learning organisation is one that is skilled at creating, acquiring and transferring knowledge, and at modifying its behaviour to reflect new knowledge and insights.

Quick quiz

1 What is an 'empirical' epistemology and a 'rational' epistemology?

2 What are 'whole' and 'part' learning?

3 Define the four stages of learning.

4 What is a 'plateau' in a learning curve?

5 What are the two approaches to transfer of learning, and what other elements are needed to support transfer to the work context?

6 Which of Honey and Mumford's learning styles shows a preference for the 'generalising/abstracting' stage of the learning cycle?

A   Pragmatist
B   Activist
C   Theorist
D   Reflector

7   Distinguish between skill, 'know-that', 'know-how' and competence.

8   List the potential stakeholders in a training event.

9   Outline an approach to management development.

10   List five methods of creating a learning organisation/culture.

Answers to quick quiz

1   'Empirical': a theory of how people know things based on the belief that the human mind operates purely on information gained from the senses by experience. 'Rational': a theory of how people know things based on the belief that the human mind imposes organisation and meaning on sensory raw material.   (see paragraph 1.1)

2   Whole learning: tasks are taught or modelled in their entirety. Part learning: tasks are broken down and taught and practised stage by stage, building up to the whole task.   (para 1.1)

3   See paragraph 1.2.

4   The point at which progress levels off, due to the trainee's need to consolidate, correct, regain motivation or establish unconscious competence before moving on further.   (para 1.3)

5   Correspondence of elements between the learning situation and applied context **or** transfer by principle, which allows general learning to be transferred to specific contexts. Worksite systems, tools and resources and support from the manager and work group.   (para 1.5)

6   C   (paras 1.4, 2.1)

7   See paragraph 3.1 for a full account.

8   Owners/managers of the firm; line managers of trainees; training managers; instructors/coaches; external training providers; training community.   (para 3.3)

9   See paragraph 3.6.

10   See paragraph 4.2 for a full account.

Answers to activities

1   For a full account of the implications of learning theory for training design, see the text following the exercise.

2   We have used the example of assertiveness training: you may have come up with others.

Stage 1.   You have not heard of assertiveness, so you are not aware that you relate to people in a way that is either aggressive or passive: you simply relate in the way that seems natural to you.

Stage 2.   You read about assertiveness, or someone feeds back to you that your style of relating is unhelpfully unassertive, or you realise that you hardly ever get your needs met without damaging relationships: you realise that your behaviour is unassertive.

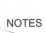

Stage 3.   You research and think about the principles of assertiveness, and remind yourself of them by sticking positive affirmation messages around your home and office. You apply the techniques of assertion consciously, having to remind yourself of the principles, using scripted responses, monitoring their effectiveness.

Stage 4.   You naturally react in an assertive manner, without having to remind yourself or plan to do so.

3   (a)

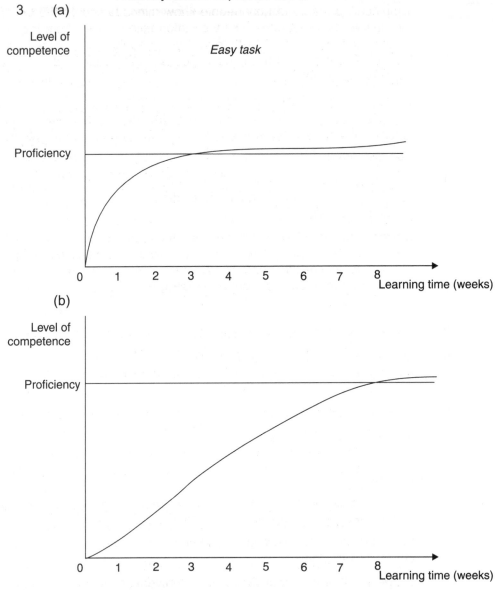

(b)

4   Some of the factors you may have identified include the following.

(a)   Perceptual factors: unconscious incompetence, not seeing that there is a need; not receiving honest feedback from others

(b)   Emotional factors: fear or insecurity about performance (not wanting to be a 'beginner' or 'learner'), fear of being judged, discomfort of conscious incompetence, frustration

(c)   Motivational factors: lack of goals/incentives, unwillingness to take risks or make mistakes, no positive reinforcement for progress, previous bad experience with training

(d) Cultural factors: values about 'not getting above yourself', 'the way we do things here' frustrating application of learning; boss/colleagues/family unsupportive

(e) Physical factors: no suitable space or time to study, practise

(f) Situational factors: lack of training opportunities; poorly designed training courses (negative transfer, unsuited to learning styles of trainees)

(g) Skill factors: poor learning skills (never learned to learn), limited learning styles, poor communication skills

5 John is a pragmatist: Paula an activist: Ringo a reflector: Georgette a theorist. The course seems tailored to activists: reflectors would probably cope, but might not contribute enough to keep the classes going.

6 Assertiveness training is popularly seen as a prime means of remedying under-achievement in women, or of helping women to avoid exploitation at work. It is likely to be part of a 'Women Into Management' programme. The techniques and insights involved are likely to be of benefit to men as well, but it has been recognised that it is primarily women who are disadvantaged in western society by the failure to distinguish between assertion and aggression, submission and conflict-avoidance. Assertiveness training may help women to criticise, confront and direct male subordinates and colleagues non-aggressively. The failure of victims of sexual harassment to come forward may indicate another area in which assertiveness could be of value.

7 (a) It demonstrates that the individual is valued and believed to have potential.

(b) It gives the individual an enhanced sense of security (that he or she is and will be useful to the organisation).

(c) It can enhance a person's portfolio of skills, and hence a person's ability to take responsibility.

(d) It can motivate employees, because they see opportunities for advancement, or to make a difference to quality or innovation.

(e) Training and development sessions enable employees to mix with people from other business functions, and so develop networks and contacts.

(f) Training in areas such as assertiveness, communication or interpersonal skills can enhance personal effectiveness and self-esteem outside the work context.

8 (a) The prime objective of management development is improved performance capacity - both from the managers *and* from those they manage.

(b) Management development secures management succession: a pool of promotable individuals in the organisation.

(c) The organisation's showing an interest in the career development of staff may motivate them and encourage loyalty. (This will be especially important if the firm intends to rely on management succession to fill senior management positions.)

9 Some problems you may have identified include the following.

(a) Inadequate organisation mechanisms for multi-directional communication, training in learning, selection according to flexibility etc: these will have to be established, and old machinery (reporting channels, job descriptions etc) dismantled or adapted

(b) Lack of commitment and example-setting by top management (essential to the development of culture)

(c) Poor communication and/or learning skills in some existing employees: they would need to be developed or the employees would need to be 'weeded out'. (This may happen through 'accelerated wastage', since the learning culture would be highly uncomfortable for them.)

(d) Organisational politics, discouraging the open sharing of information and acceptance of challenge.

(e) Fear/insecurity on the part of managers (required to open their decision-making to challenge) and all employees (fear of risk-taking, never secure in sense of competence under continuous improvement).

(f) Previous management style: punishing mistakes, avoiding risks etc.

(g) Lack of motivation to learn at all levels: inadequate perception of the need to be constantly learning, flexible – when it would be much easier to settle into established routines.

Assignment 13 (2 hours)

Draw up your own 'Personal Development Plan'.

Include:

(a) Areas of knowledge/skill/competence/attitude /awareness that you want to attain;

(b) Qualifications or standards that you wish to attain as evidence of learning;

(c) Potential sources of learning in each of your chosen areas (bearing in mind your own preferred learning style);

(d) Areas of organisational experience that you wish to try (jobs, functions, postings?) Don't forget that, by using the experiential learning cycle, you can turn *any* work task into a developmental activity!

(e) Potential sources of mentorship or guidance within the organisation who could help you attain your learning/experience goals;

(f) An initial timetable or sequence according to which you might aim to acquire the relevant learning/experience.

There is no suggested answer to this Assignment: consult your own goals, aspirations, preferences and organisational opportunities. (Don't be limited to the latter, however: think 'employability' if appropriate.)

If you have studied for Unit 16 of the Business and Management module, the concept of a personal development plan will be very familiar to you.

Chapter 14:

THE SYSTEMATIC APPROACH TO TRAINING AND DEVELOPMENT

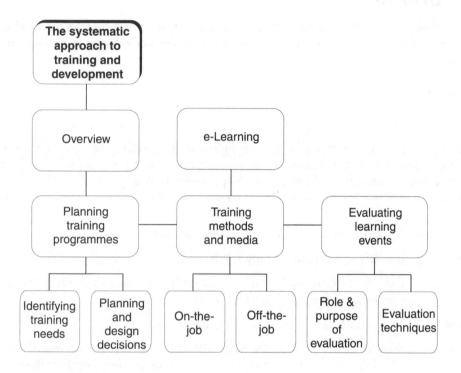

Introduction

In this chapter, we examine the practical application of the principles discussed in Chapter 13, starting with an overview of the systematic approach to training and development.

We discuss the key issues, resources and techniques of each stage of this approach, from the identification of training and development needs to the planning and design of learning events and programmes – and finally, the systematic evaluation of their success and contribution. This is a long chapter: take it at your own pace, and use the activities to consolidate your learning.

Your objectives

In this chapter you will learn about the following.

    (a)   The systematic approach to training

    (b)   The identification of training and development needs

    (c)   The setting of training objectives

    (d)   Planning issues in devising training programmes

    (e)   The advantages and disadvantages of on-the-job and off-the-job training and development methods

(f) The use of a variety of on-the-job and off-the-job methods

(g) The 'what, why, when and who' of evaluating learning events

(h) A range of models and techniques of evaluation

(i) How to investigate a vocational training scheme

(j) Implementation of (training) practice in the UK and one other country

1 OVERVIEW

If training is to make a impact on performance at an individual level, let alone at a strategic level, it must be carefully designed to suit the **need for training** and the **needs of the trainee.**

Definition

> According to the Department of Employment, **training** is 'the systematic development of the attitude/knowledge/skill/behaviour pattern required by an individual in order to perform adequately a given task or job.'

A systematic approach to training encompasses four basic stages.

Stage 1. Identify and define training needs

Stage 2. Design learning and development programmes which meet those needs, selecting relevant methods and media

Stage 3. Implement learning events and programmes

Stage 4. Systematically evaluate training (although this will not necessarily be a one-off, after-the-event exercise, as we will see in Section 4 of this chapter).

We will now look at each of these stages in turn.

2 IDENTIFYING TRAINING NEEDS

2.1 Whose needs and objectives?

Training needs and outcomes should be evaluated in terms of their potential contribution to the key objectives of the organisation, including:

(a) Profitability; by increasing productivity/revenue or reducing costs

(b) The cost-effective provision of services, customer retention, ethical compliance, technical innovation, market standing and other measures of added value

(c) The survival or growth of the business, which may be based on profitability, return on investment for shareholders, retention of market share and so on

(d) Increased employee loyalty (with a knock-on effect in decreased labour turnover and smoother management succession)

(e) Enhanced corporate image (which may impact favourably on consumer attitudes and the ability to attract skilled labour)

(f)   Enhanced potential for quality, innovation, flexibility in the face of change and acceptable risk-taking, through a culture of broad-based competence and support of learning

There is no intrinsic incompatibility between a **business's** strategic goals for training, and the developmental aspirations of **individuals**. The desire for learning, skill development and self-actualisation by the individual have long been recognised (Maslow, Herzberg) as incentives to motivated performance at work, as well as offering personal satisfaction.

Activity 1   **(20 minutes)**

When might fulfilling employee aspirations for training become incompatible with business objectives?

The training needs of individuals and groups vary enormously, according to the nature of the job and particular tasks, and the abilities and experience of the employees.

2.2   Training needs recognition

Some training requirements will be obvious and 'automatic'.

(a)   If a piece of legislation is enacted which affects the organisation's operations, training in its provisions will automatically be indicated. Thus, for example, personnel staff will need to be trained as and when various EU Directives are enacted in UK law.

(b)   The introduction of new technology similarly implies a training need: for relevant employees to learn how to use it.

(c)   An organisation seeking accreditation for its training scheme, or seeking a British Standard or International Standard (say, for quality systems, ISO 9000), will have certain training requirements imposed on it by the approving body.

Other training requirements may emerge in response to **critical incidents**: problems or events which affect a key area of the organisation's activity and effectiveness. A service organisation may, for example, receive bad press coverage because of a number of complaints about the rudeness of its customer service staff on the telephone. This might prompt an investigation which might in turn highlight the need for training in telephone skills, customer care, scheduling (for the team manager, if the rudeness was a result not of lack of skill but pressure of unmanageable workloads) and so on.

Some **qualitative indicators** might be taken as symptoms of a need for training: absenteeism, high labour turnover, grievance and disciplinary actions, crises, conflict, poor motivation and performance. Such factors will need to be investigated to see what the root causes are, and whether training will solve the problem.

Another alternative is **self-assessment** by the employee. This may be highly informal (a list of in-house or sponsored courses is posted on the notice board or intranet and interested employees are invited to apply) or more systematic (employees complete surveys on training needs). An example of a self-administered needs survey for managerial staff (suggested by Kramer *et al*, 1997) is as follows.

Self assessment of training needs

Please indicate in the blanks the extent to which you have a training need in each specific area. Use the following scale

Scale

1 —————— 2 —————— 3 —————— 4 —————— 5

(To no extent)   (To a very large extent)

To what extent do you need training in the following areas?

Basic management skills (organising, planning, delegating, problem-solving)

_____	A	Setting goals and objectives
_____	B	Developing realistic time schedules to meet work requirements
_____	C	Identifying and weighing alternative solutions
_____	D	Organising work activities

Interpersonal skills

_____	A	Resolving interpersonal conflicts
_____	B	Creating a development plan for employees
_____	C	Identifying and understanding individual employee needs
_____	D	Conducting performance appraisal reviews
_____	E	Conducting a disciplinary interview

Administrative skills

_____	A	Maintaining equipment, tools and safety controls
_____	B	Understanding local agreements and shop rules
_____	C	Preparing work flowcharts
_____	D	Developing departmental budgets

Quality control

_____	A	Analysing and interpreting statistical data
_____	B	Constructing and analysing charts, tables and graphs
_____	C	Using statistical software on the computer

The advantage of self-assessment, or self-nomination for training, is that it pre-supposes motivation on the part of the trainee and harnesses employees' knowledge of their own job requirements and skill weaknesses. The drawback, however, is that employees may be reluctant to admit to performance deficiencies.

A further alternative, therefore, is the use of **attitude surveys** and **360° feedback appraisal reports,** since the employee's superiors, subordinates, colleagues and customer contacts will be in a good position to identify performance deficiencies in areas that affect them: this will be particularly important in the case of customers.

Activity 2   **(15 minutes)**

Complete the above self-assessment for yourself. For any areas which are not applicable to your job, put NA (not applicable).

FOR DISCUSSION

What alerted you to a training need, to encourage you to undertake this course? What was the training need: what could you not yet do, or what did you not yet know, that you thought you needed? What help did you get in identifying your training needs? Have you defined them (or had them defined for you) in a helpful way?

Other training requirements may only emerge as a result of systematic learning gap (or training need) analysis.

2.3 Training needs analysis

Definition

> **Training needs** may be defined as the gap between what people should be achieving and what they actually are achieving. In other words:
>
> Required level of competence *minus* present level of competence = training need.

Training needs analysis should be carried out at the *corporate level* as part of the human resource planning process, through:

(a) Analysis of corporate objectives and business plans and their human resource requirements.

(b) Analysis of existing human resource records and appraisals (training evaluations, performance management reports, surveys and so on).

(c) A *human resources audit* or *skills audit* may also be conducted for a more comprehensive accounting of the current level of competence, skill, knowledge (and so on) in the workforce.

At *group/team and individual level*, a similar exercise will be carried out, to identify where the corporate needs can best be met.

The **required level of competence for the job** can be determined by:

(a) **Job analysis,** identifying the elements of the task in terms of key activities and outcomes

(b) **Skills analysis,** identifying the skill elements of the task, such as:

   (i) What senses (vision, touch, hearing etc) are involved?
   (ii) What left-hand/right-hand/foot operations are required?
   (iii) What interactions with other operatives are required?

(c) **Role analysis,** for managerial and administrative jobs requiring a high degree of co-ordination and interaction with others

(d) **Existing records,** such as job specifications and descriptions, person specifications, the organisation chart (depicting roles and relationships) and so on

(e) **Competence analysis** or existing competence frameworks, such as NVQs relevant to the job, to define the skills, knowledge and competencies required to meet performance standards

The **present level of employees' competence** (which includes not only skill and knowledge, but the employee's inclination or willingness to work competently as well) can be measured by an appropriate **pre-training test** of skills, knowledge, performance, attitude and so on. Performance appraisals and past training reports will furnish some of this information. It should be noted that training needs analysis need not have a reactive or problem-solving focus aimed solely at meeting shortfalls in competence in the current job. The *future development needs* of the organisation, team and individuals should also be taken into account, by considering employment, consumer and technological trends (such as the need to increase flexibility, improve e-commerce or customer service skills, or encourage innovation) and employees' potential for promotion, empowerment, multi-skilling and so on. Training and development needs analysis should be part of the pro-active process of performance management, whereby managers and team leaders guide people in setting performance improvement and learning targets for the forthcoming planning period.

The training manager will have to investigate any gap between current and required performance/competence to see whether training might be the solution. (Remember, there are alternative solutions: machinery may need repairing or upgrading, poor motivation might need to be addressed through pay and incentives, and so on.)

If training is identified as the way to close the gap, a *learning or training specification* should be drawn up. This will include specific learning objectives, perhaps with action plans as to:

- methods of learning that may be used

- timescales within which learning should be undertaken and

- methods by which achievement of the objectives will be monitored and measured

2.4 Setting training objectives

Objectives should be clear, specific and related to observable, measurable targets. Ideally, there should be detailed definitions of:

(a) **Knowledge** – what the trainee should understand
(b) **Behaviour** – what the trainee should be able to do
(c) **Standard** – to what level of performance
(d) **Environment** – under what conditions

The advantage of **competency** frameworks is that they typically define competent performance in exactly this specific and quantifiable way.

Objectives are the yardsticks that will allow the trainer (and trainees) to see clearly whether and how far training has been successful. They are usually best expressed in terms of active verbs: at the end of the course the trainee should be able to describe... , or identify... or distinguish X from Y... or calculate... or assemble... and so on.

It is insufficient to define the objectives of training as 'to give trainees a grounding in... or 'to encourage trainees in a better appreciation of...': this offers no target achievement which can be objectively measured. Where possible, a **quantifiable** measure should be added: time taken to perform a task, percentage of questions answered correctly, percentage of errors acceptable, and so on.

Activity 3 (30 minutes)

Translate the following training needs into specific learning objectives. Begin each objective with the words: 'the employee will…'

Training need

(a) To know more about the Data Protection Act
(b) To establish a better rapport with customers
(c) To assemble clocks more quickly

Having defined what a training programme should be able to do, the training manager needs to evaluate different options for how *training is to be delivered, and* how *the desired outcomes are to be achieved. We will outline some of the methods and media available in Sections 4 and 5 below. Here, we will just highlight some of the decisions to be made.*

3 PLANNING AND DESIGN DECISIONS

3.1 Training programmes and learning plans

Once organisational, job/role related and individual learning needs have been established, training managers can plan:

(a) **Training programmes** - a menu or 'core curriculum' of training initiatives which will be offered in the forthcoming planning period, which will be open to relevant categories of staff. Examples (Hargreaves and Jarvis, 2000) include:

- Finance training for project managers

- Management skills for all management staff

- Presentation and interpersonal skills for trainers, interviewers and customer service staff

- Teambuilding and teamworking for all departments

- Basic health and safety training for all staff

- Intra-departmental seminars and in-house discussion groups

It may be necessary to design full-scale formal training programmes, if a suitably-tailored programme is not available 'off the shelf', or if large numbers of staff are regularly involved, making programmes more cost-effective.

Once these have been prioritised, they can be designed and timetabled.

(b) **Learning plans** – individual or team plans for accessing training courses/ resources and/or for taking advantage of learning opportunities at work. These may be more flexibly adapted to individual and team needs. Coaching, mentoring, reading and e-learning, for example, would not require formally designed programmes: learning targets, timescales and monitoring/ evaluation procedures would still need to be planned.

3.2 Type of learning

As we will see in Sections 4 and 5 below, learning experiences may be of different types, which will variously suit particular learning needs.

(a) **Formal and informal learning**

Formal learning often takes place away from the work setting, and involves techniques such as classroom teaching and instruction. It is driven by the teacher or trainer, often to a pre-set curriculum or agenda which may or may not be adapted to all members of the learning group. Transfer of learning may be difficult, although theorists may prefer this method.

Informal learning occurs in the workplace, in response to immediate, job-relevant needs. The learner essentially drives the process by asking questions and accessing opportunities for coaching, advice and instruction. Since it is largely unplanned, it may not systematically meet training needs. However, some learners will find this method more relevant, more suited to their learning style and easier to apply in practice.

(b) **On-the-job and off-the-job learning**

On-the-job or workplace learning may use the workplace as a training environment (eg for briefings, demonstrations or site visits) or may use actual work processes and tasks as learning events. On-the-job training methods include: systematic job instruction; working with experienced colleagues or trainers; coaching or mentoring; and various guided challenges such as project or committee work.

Off-the-job training methods include: formal taught or self-administered courses (eg by computer-based training); outdoor training; research assignments and so on.

We discuss methods – and their advantages and disadvantages – in Sections 4 and 5 below.

(c) **Self-managed learning**

Individuals are encouraged to define their own learning objectives and create action plans (or Personal Development Plans) to meet them. Managers, mentors or trainers may jointly agree learning objectives, in the form of a *learning contract*. They may also guide the learner in accessing resources and learning opportunities, provide coaching, offer feedback as part of the evaluation process and so on.

(d) **Programmed learning**

The trainee works at his or her own pace through a carefully ordered sequence of learning modules and assessments. This is a feature of many distance learning and computer-based training programmes.

(e) **Blended learning**

Blended learning is a recognition that a mix of learning types, styles and technologies may be most effective in order to meet individual needs and learning preferences. This might be applied to a training course or programme: for example, using instruction on basic principles, group exercises for practice, e-learning for consolidation and coaching and mentoring for follow-up back in the workplace. Similarly, an individual's personal development plan might include a blend of reading, e-learning, experiential learning (using mentor feedback), coaching where required, and formal courses for certification.

In an article in *People Management* (14 May 1998), Alan Mumford asks how trainers can decide on the most suitable means of delivering a learning programme. He notes, in particular, that training is all too susceptible to 'flavours of the month': training gurus constantly seem to develop or espouse a 'more modern' or 'more appropriate' method than whatever the training manager has done before.

Mumford suggests that trainers should ask the following questions of any method proposed.

(a) What is the contribution of the method to the development of knowledge, skills and insight?

(b) What is the impact of individual learning-style preferences on the acceptability of the method?

(c) What are the particular features of this method that make it more appropriate than a method I have used previously?

(d) In what way is the method more appropriate than any other method for a particular need?

In addition, there is the need for cost-benefit analysis on any given method: are the outcomes to be gained **worth** the cost involved?

Activity 4 **(20 minutes)**

What methods of learning and training have you encountered in your job? What methods are you using now to study for your qualification? What do *you* think are the advantages and disadvantages of this 'blend' for you as a learner?

3.3 Timing and duration of training

If generic programmes, involving staff from different departments, are being planned, training managers will have to:

(a) Negotiate with line managers the length of time staff can be available for training, when, and how the time could most conveniently be structured (day release, several-day blocks etc).

(b) Consider the availability of training facilities and personnel (especially if external training partners are used): large-scale, specialist programmes may need to be booked up to a year in advance.

(c) Consider the learning curve and learning style preferences of trainees. Programme timetabling will have to take into account the need for icebreakers and participant teambuilding; refreshment and relaxation breaks; variations in 'pace' of learning activity to allow for consolidation, practice, reflection and so on.

There is a noticeable trend (Roberts, 2003 (f)) towards short-course or 'bite size' training, led by the Learning and Skills Council (LSC) Bite Size campaign. Surveys suggest that training courses are increasingly modularised into 1-3 hour blocks – with two days considered a larger training course.

Key advantages of bite-sized learning are cost, time, the speed with which learning can be transferred to the job, and ease of learning. However, this is another area in which *blended* strategies may be required.

EXAMPLE

'There is widespread agreement that much of the demand for bite size is coming from employees. "Our courses are aimed at giving employees a few pragmatic techniques that they can use immediately. This was certainly an area where we found a demand and we knew that our employees were looking for more accessible learning," says [Louise Prashad, capability development manager at drinks company, Diageo].

'She says the training department has found that delivering shorter courses has enabled them to offer a wider range of topics. It has also eased some of the pressures on the training department. "Over 18 months ago we were struggling with the cost of the three-day training courses, as well as trying to get people available for them." ...

'But the experience for the training department wishing to introduce modularisation can be challenging ...

' "One of the biggest challenges is getting the pitch right because of the short duration. There are restrictions on both the topic and the extent to which you can explore it in the short time allocated," [Prashad] told *PM*.

'In addition, it can sometimes be easier to get staff off-site for the whole day rather than an hour. "In some respects it is easier to arrange cover for one day than one hour. In a hospital, the loss of a person for an hour can be very evident in an emergency," says Simon Tisdale, head of training and development, Salford Royal Hospitals NHS Trust. ...'

(Roberts, 2003 (f))

3.4 Training providers

Hargreaves and Jarvis (2000) note the following range of options open to the training department: see Figure 14.1 on the following page.

3.5 Programme administration

A number of administrative matters will occupy the training department, including:

(a) Selecting participants for planned courses, according to preferences for schedule, content, learning style, location and training need priorities identified by line managers.

(b) Negotiating course content, time-tables and costs with external training providers.

(c) Booking external (and internal) training facilities and personnel.

(d) Sourcing relevant training materials and resources.

(e) Compiling calendars of training events, participant information briefings and other supporting materials.

(f) Marketing training programmes within the organisation.

	Advantages	Disadvantages	Factors to be taken into account
In-house options • 'On-the-job' vocational training (eg coaching) • In-house seminars, workshops, mentoring and job exchange for skill development • Participation in national initiatives, eg NVQs or Modern Apprenticeships • Call in a consultant to design and run specialist courses in-house	• May be cost-effective for large trainee numbers • Matching to specific organisational needs • Control over standards, accommodation etc • Ready transfer of learning to work context • Employer brand as corporate trainer	• Distractions from work task/context • Limited space, facilities, expertise? • Training department required to co-ordinate details (catering etc)	• Availability of suitably expert, trained instructors • Number of participants: cost of provision • Other alternatives • External advice and resources available
External options • Contract external training providers to run programmes externally	• Specialist facilities and expertise available • Less distraction from work tasks/ contexts • Greater freedom to raise work problems • Less demands on training department	• Expense • Planning/booking time required • May involve travel/ disruption for participants	• Cost – and resources available • Standard of training facilities • Qualifications, credibility and track record of trainers • Degree of specialism required • Location/travel/ access
Distance-earning options • Published resources • CD-ROM/video resources • Software and web-based (e-learning) resources	• Learner-paced • Can be undertaken in own time/work or home • Cost advantages	• Lack of social interaction and support • Perception of 'own time' v 'work'	• Quality, interactivity and relevance of resources • Learning style preferences of trainees

Figure 14.1: Training and development options
Source: Hargreaves and Jarvis, 2000

FOR DISCUSSION

Beardwell and Holden (1997) quote Fairbairn's 'sad but familiar story of Del the Delegate, who returns from a course full of new ideas, anxious to implement them. He is confronted with scepticism and cynicism from both his bosses and fellow employees. 'The friction set up between Del and his company undermines his enthusiasm and exhausts all his energy. Del's behaviour reverts to what is (and always was) reinforced by the company.''

Is there an alternative ending to this tragic parable?

We will now go back and look at some of the available training methods and media in more detail. We will classify these under on-the-job training (Section 4) and off-the-job training (Section 5), but you should be aware that some methods may be used in either setting.

4 ON-THE-JOB TRAINING AND DEVELOPMENT

There are a number of different approaches to on-the-job training.

4.1 'Sitting with Nellie'

This is the traditional method of skill training. The trainee is placed beside an experienced worker (Nellie) and learns by observing him or her work and by imitating his or her operations and methods under close instruction and supervision, working with the actual materials and equipment that are involved in the job.

Advantages

- High transfer of learning (because learning in context)
- Effective and economical (where task amenable to observation-imitation)
- Immediate feedback and adjustment
- Establishes working relationships as well as skills

Disadvantages

- Ineffective if 'Nellie' uses poor work technique, or skill not amenable to observation

- Ineffective if 'Nellie' lacks training/instruction skills and job requires explanation

- Trainee socialised into shop floor culture of work: not necessarily methods or attitudes desired by management

4.2 Job instruction training

This is a technique which can be added to the 'sitting with Nellie' approach to minimise the disadvantages cited above. It was developed as a guide to systematic on-the-job training.

    (a)   Careful selection and preparation of trainer/'Nellie' and trainee: goals and objectives of learning outlined etc.

    (b)   Full explanation and demonstration of skill/task by the trainer/'Nellie'.

    (c)   Trial on-the-job practice/performance by the trainee.

    (d)   Thorough feedback session between trainer/'Nellie' and trainee to appraise and adjust trainee's performance and set further improvement goals. (Repeat (b) – (d) as required.)

4.3 Coaching

Coaching is one element of the 'sitting with Nellie' approach, but may be used flexibly in a wide range of training situations, and at any time during performance on an on-going basis.

Coaching is on-the-job guidance, advice, correction and teaching with a view to improving performance. A coach should:

(a)   Demonstrate how areas of a job are performed, and guide the trainee's own performance of the same tasks, by advice and correction

(b)   Help the trainee to identify problems or development needs in his or her work

(c)   Seek out or identify opportunities for the trainee to develop, through doing new things at work

(d)   Help the trainee plan the solutions to problems, or approaches to new challenges at work

(e)   Be patient and tolerant of the trainee's initial mistakes, seeing them as necessary learning and problem-solving opportunities

(f)   Encourage the trainee to assess his or her own progress and performance, and to formulate further plans for improvement

Essentially, coaching is a **collaboration** between the coach and the trainee, in which the coach's special role is encouragement and guidance as the trainee develops on the job.

Advantages

- Flexible and interactive: pace and content of learning suited to trainee needs and trainer analysis

- Collaborative: involves trainee in problem-solving

- High transfer of learning (connected to live job performance)

Disadvantage

- Requires coaching skills

4.4   Mentoring

Definition

> A **mentor** is a guide, ideally both more experienced and more powerful in the organisation, whose concern is the trainee's long-term personal development. (S)he may occupy a role as the trainee's teacher/coach, counsellor, role model, protector and/or champion/sponsor in the organisation, spur to action or improvement, critic, encourager and so on, as appropriate to the situation at a given time.

A mentor should:

(a)   Help the trainee to greater self-awareness, by listening to, questioning and challenging his or her ideas, and feeding back on his or her behaviour

(b)   Help the trainee to formulate and clarify his or her needs and ambitions in life, and to identify where events and opportunities at work fit into those plans

(c)   Encourage the trainee to take responsibility for his or her development, while offering support – personally and within the organisation – if required

(d)   Help the trainee to reconcile his or her non-work needs, interests and circumstances with the demands of work (or vice versa)

(e)   Help the trainee to plan specific development and career paths or directions, offering opportunities where appropriate and possible

4.5   Action learning

Action learning was developed by Reg Revans in the 1970s. It is described (Pedler *et al*, 2003) as a method for individual and organisational development in which "working in small groups, people tackle important organisational issues or problems and learn from their attempts to change things".

The key elements of action learning programmes are as follows.

(a)   A small group of four or five people (usually managers) meet together regularly, on a wholly voluntary basis, for the programme period (perhaps several months).

(b)   Each participant brings a managerial or organisational problem they want to deal with.

(c)   Group members support and learn from one another, acting as a mentoring, consulting and problem-solving network. (An external advisor may sit in and facilitate.)

(d)   The group both generates and examines options in response to member issues/problems *and* learns about the interpersonal and managerial processes involved as they do so.

(e)   Group members take action – and the group learns further from feedback on that action (in a learning cycle).

Pedlar *et al* note that many organisational project teams, self-help groups, productivity improvement meetings and quality circles are in fact reflecting action learning processes.

So far we have looked at ways in which employees can acquire and improve skills in a particular job or task through guided imitation and practice. A slightly different approach is to give employees a 'taste' of different jobs and functions.

4.6   Training by switching or 'shadowing' roles

This may be accomplished by a number of methods.

(a)   **Job rotation** or **'shadowing'**: the trainee is given several jobs in succession, to gain experience of a wide range of activities and departments. (Even experienced managers may rotate their jobs to gain wider experience; this method is commonly applied in the Civil Service.)

(b)   **Temporary promotion:** an individual is promoted into a superior's position while the superior is absent. This gives the individual a chance to experience the demands of a more senior position.

(c)   **'Assistant to' positions:** an individual with management potential may be appointed as assistant to a manager. In this way, the individual gains experience of management, without a risky level of responsibility.

(d)   **Project or committee work:** trainees might be included in the membership of a project team or committee, to obtain an understanding of inter-departmental relationships, problem-solving and particular areas of the organisation's activity.

(e)   **Assignments:** trainees may be delegated to a particular task or project by a superior.

Advantages

- Employees gain experience without risking immediate responsibility.

- Task/role variety may increase job satisfaction and awareness of organisational processes.

- Aids career/management/succession planning.

Disadvantages

- May be perceived as perpetual traineeship: not real work
- May be perceived as a 'nuisance' in departments having to 'carry' trainees

4.7   Apprenticeship and traineeship training

Apprenticeships and traineeships involve a combination of on-the-job training (using any of the above methods) and off-the-job training (one or two days a week, or a number of weeks in the year, at a college or university). The trainees earn while they learn, but at a lesser rate than full-time employees of the organisation in which they are placed to gain their work experience.

4.8   Advantages and disadvantages of on-the-job training and development

On-the-job training is very common, especially when the work involved is not complex. It will generally only be successful if:

(a)   **Assignments have a specific purpose** from which the trainee can learn and gain experience; otherwise, it can be unfocused and overwhelming

(b)   **The trainee is a practical type,** who prefers to learn by doing and can tolerate the process of trial and error; (other people might need to get away from the pressures of the workplace to think through issues and understand the underlying principles before applying new techniques)

(c)   **Trainers are themselves trained** in instruction and coaching techniques (as well as modelling efficient and effective work practices)

(d)   **The organisation is tolerant of mistakes.** Mistakes are an inevitable part of on-the-job learning, and if they are punished or frowned on, the trainee will be reluctant to take further risks and will be de-motivated to learn.

There may be real risks involved in throwing people in at the deep-end: the cost of mistakes or inefficiencies may be high and the pressure on learners great. (Would you want to learn medical procedures, or air traffic control procedures, on-the-job?)

An important **advantage** of on-the-job training, however, is that it takes place in the environment of the job itself, and in the context of the work group in which the trainee will have to operate. The style of supervision, personal relations with colleagues, working conditions and pressures, the culture of the office/shop floor and so on will be absorbed as part of the training process.

Activity 5   **(20 minutes)**

If you have had work experience, list the advantages you experienced through on-the-job training. If you have not worked, think about this course and list the disadvantages of the different methods of study you are given.

4.9   Self-development approaches

There are a number of techniques for informal, self-managed experiential learning at work.

- Informal – arising from the job and work context

- Self-managed – planned, implemented and evaluated primarily by the learner

- Experiential – using the learning cycle to turn any work event or action in to a learning opportunity

Methods for self development include:

(a)   **Personal Development Plans** and **learning contracts** formulated with line managers or mentors: formal commitment to work towards specified learning goals, with action plans.

(b)   **Personal Development Journals** or **learning logs**: a structured approach to the learning cycle. The learner selects a critical incident at work which illustrates a learning need: (s)he describes what happened, reflects on the event and its consequences, draws conclusions, and identifies future actions to reinforce successful behaviours and/or change unsuccessful behaviours.

(c)   **Self-development groups**: groups which meet to discuss personal development and work issues, give each other feedback and information and so on – like a flexible action learning group.

Activity 6   **(no time limit)**

Keep a Personal Development Journal for a week.

(a)   Select a particular skill area you want to develop: say, interviewing, presentation, assertiveness or team working.

(b)   Each day, reflect on your day at work. What incidents demonstrate something to you about your competence (good or bad) in your chosen area?

(c)   Describe the incident. What did you and others do or say? How did you feel?

(d)   Reflect on the incident. What could you have done differently to get a better result? (Or what did you do *well,* to get a good result?)

(e)   How can you put your insights into action? Plan to access whatever information, advice, feedback or help you need. (What will you need? Who will you ask? When?) Plan a specific 'next time' to try your better solution.

We will now look briefly at a particular kind of training programme, involving both off- and on-the-job elements: induction.

4.10   Induction training

From his first day in a job, a new recruit must be helped to find his bearings. There are limits to what any person can pick up in a short time, so the process of 'getting one's feet under the table' will be a gradual one. Induction is an ongoing process.

On the first day, a manager or HR officer should welcome the new recruit. The manager might discuss in broad terms what he requires from people at work, working conditions, pay and benefits, training opportunities and career opportunities. He should then introduce the new recruit to the person who will be his immediate supervisor.

The immediate supervisor should then take over the process of induction. Here is a general checklist.

(a) Pinpoint the areas that the recruit will have to learn about in order to start work. Some things (such as detailed technical knowledge) may be identified as areas for later study or training, while others (say, some of the procedures and systems with which the recruit will have to deal) will have to be explained immediately. A list of learning priorities should be drawn up, so that the recruit, and the supervisor, are clear about the rate and direction of progress required.

(b) Explain first of all the nature of the job, and the goals of each task, of the recruit's job and of the department as a whole. This will help the recruit to work to specific targets and to understand how each task relates to the overall objectives of the department - or even the organisation as a whole.

(c) Explain about hours of work and stress the importance of time-keeping. If flexitime is operated, explain how it works. Any other work practices, customs and rules should be explained clearly.

(d) Explain the structure of the department: to whom the recruit will report, to whom (s)he can go with complaints or queries and so on.

(e) Introduce the recruit to people in the workplace. (S)he should meet the departmental manager and all the members of the immediate work team (and perhaps be given the opportunity to get to know them informally). One particular colleague may be assigned to the recruit as a *mentor* for the first few days, to answer routine queries and 'show him (or her) the ropes'. The layout of the premises, procedures for lunch hours or holidays, rules about smoking or eating at work and so on will then be taught informally.

(f) Plan and implement an appropriate training programme for whatever technical or practical knowledge is required. Again, the programme should have a clear schedule and set of goals so that the recruit has a sense of purpose, and so that the programme can be efficiently organised to fit in with the activities of the department.

(g) Coach and/or train the recruit; check regularly on his progress, as demonstrated by performance, reported by the mentor, and/or as perceived by the recruit. Feedback information will be essential to the learning process, correcting any faults at an early stage and building the confidence of the recruit.

(h) Integrate the recruit into the culture of the workplace. Much of this may be done informally: (s)he will pick up the prevailing norms of dress, degree of formality, attitude to customers etc. However, the supervisor should try to 'sell' the values and style of the organisation and should reinforce commitment to those values by rewarding evidence of loyalty, hard work and desired behaviour.

After three months, six months and/or one year the performance of a new recruit should be formally appraised and discussed. This should dovetail into a regular employee appraisal programme.

Activity 7	(5 minutes)

Did you have any form of induction into student life?

Compare your experience to the checklist given above. How effective did you feel your induction was? What difference did it make to your confidence in your studies?'

We will now move on to off-the-job training.

5 OFF-THE-JOB TRAINING

5.1 Training providers

Off-the-job training providers include:

    (a)   Universities and colleges

    (b)   Private-sector colleges and training organisations including assessment centres for group training exercises

    (c)   Training consultancies, which may help the organisation locate or develop courses to meet its needs

    (d)   Publishers of training materials (texts and workbooks, videos, computer-based training packages) or

    (e)   The in-house education and training department of the organisation itself (large organisations)

Internal courses are sometimes run by the training departments of larger organisations. Skills may be taught at a technical level, related to the organisation's particular product and market, or to aspects such as marketing, teambuilding, interviewing or information technology management. Some organisations also encourage the wider development of staff by offering opportunities to learn languages or other skills.

One convenient and popular method of in-house education is computer-based training (CBT) or Interactive Video (IV), using equipment in offices or even trainees' homes. Training programmes may be developed by the organisation or by outside consultants – or bought 'off the shelf': the software (or 'courseware') can then be distributed, so that large numbers of dispersed staff can learn about new products or procedures quickly and simultaneously.

EXAMPLE

'For years universities have been urged to become more businesslike. But the boot, it seems, is on the other foot as a growing number of employers attempt to emulate academia by setting up in-house 'universities'

'Corporate universities take a variety of forms. While some are little more than revamped training departments, others represent ambitious attempts to co-ordinate learning and share knowledge across organisations. A few have even begun to imitate real universities to the extent of investing in academic research. But a common feature of many of these institutions is their use of academic terminology to describe, and raise the status of, corporate training and development activities.

'Lloyds TSB, for example, runs its training function just as if it were a higher education institution, complete with "facilities" covering information technology, operations, management and other areas of the business. It even talks of "corporate governance of the curriculum" and about "the syllabus" – terminology that would not have been used in the past.

'Overseen by a strategy group of senior business leaders, the University for Lloyds TSB, as it is called, aims to align training and development with business strategy while also sending out a clear message to employees that the organisation is prepared to invest in them.

'It has given a strong, tangible focus to all of the learning that's provided, both by courses and multimedia-based distance learning. Our latest round of employee attitude surveys has shown a marked improvement in perceptions of our investment in training and development.'

'Although the University for Lloyds TSB was launched only last year, the corporate university concept is far from new. Pioneered in the US in the 1950s, it was not widely known in this country until the arrival of McDonalds's Hamburger University.

'The fast-food giant has now quietly dropped this title in the UK and these days refers – more accurately – to its nationwide network of "training centres". But the Hamburger University is still going strong on the other side of the Atlantic, where corporate universities are set to outnumber traditional higher educational establishments by the year 2010, according to a report by the US Department of Labor.

'In the UK, the first homegrown corporate university was set up in 1993 by Unipart, followed two years later by Anglian Water's University of Water. But it is only in the past couple of years that the idea has really taken off. According to research by Ray Wild and Colin Carnall of Henley Management College, there are around 200 corporate universities in the UK, and this number is likely to increase over the next few years.'

Anat Arkin, People Management (12 October 2000)

5.2 Training methods

Some methods of off-the-job training include the following.

(a) **Training room instruction.** Similar to on-the-job job instruction training (see Paragraph 4.2 above), but in a dedicated training environment. Instruction is given using presentation techniques and/or a simulation of workplace equipment and methods.

(b) **Lectures** or **taught classes.** These are useful for knowledge or theory/principle-based learning. They may incorporate elements of instruction, case-study, role-play and other techniques to overcome the limitations of passive learning. They suit large numbers of trainees requiring the same basic body of knowledge. Drawbacks include their passivity and the difficulty of absorbing more than three or four key points per session, and their relative inflexibility to individual trainees' learning styles and needs.

(c) **Case study**. Using a description of a real-life scenario or example for analysis, providing insights and opportunities to exercise problem-solving skills, which can be transferred to the work context. Case-studies are a kind of on-paper simulation of work scenarios, allowing experimentation and exploration without risk. They are particularly useful for problem-solving and decision-making in a wide rage of specific contexts.

(d) **Role play.** The simulation of an interpersonal scenario, allowing trainees to experiment with learned behaviours and skills and to observe their effects in interpersonal encounters. This is particularly helpful in training for customer service, interviewing, conflict resolution and so on. It suits small groups, allowing for all-member participation.

(e) **Simulation.** In technical training, this may involve the mocking-up of equipment and environments so that trainees can experiment with technical skills and observe results in a safe, progressively-staged and controlled manner. (Flight simulators for pilots is one example.) In other forms of training, simulation may involve case studies, role plays, assignments of 'in-tray' exercises, which mock up typical tasks and scenarios to test trainees' organisational and problem-solving skills.

(f) **Open** or **distance learning.** Employees access technology-assisted instruction where and when it suits them, using training manuals, workbooks, video (and video conferencing for group sessions), tapes, computer-based packages and so on. Some face-to-face tuition may be used periodically to assess or reinforce learning, or to add more interactive and group work. This can be a highly economical method, especially where trainees are geographically dispersed.

(g) **Discovery learning.** A method by which trainees explore a task or concept for themselves, with relatively little initial instruction or demonstration. Trainees are thus encouraged to find out the key principles, constraints and methods of the task, and to ask the questions that are relevant to them. This is a highly trainee-centred technique which is tailored to the learning styles and needs of the trainees and fosters problem-solving and learning skills alongside specific technical competencies. It is, however, time-, labour- and cost-intensive.

(h) **Programmed learning.** A structure of learning by which a trainee, working at his or her own pace, works through a carefully ordered sequence of units or operations, each with objectives, instruction, testing and consolidation which allow the trainee to master one unit before progressing to the next. This is a feature of many distance learning and computer-based learning programmes.

(i) **Visits and tours.** Trainees are given opportunities to observe other sites, departments, operations and so on. This may be helpful in demonstrating: how skills learned in the classroom are applied in practice; different types of machinery and work organisation; stages of operation before and after that in which the trainee will be involved; application of products/services by customers or end users; and so on.

(j) **Outdoor training.** Physical tasks and activities in challenging environments, designed to help trainees learn about themselves and their motivations, leadership skills, group dynamics and co-operation and so on. This is increasingly used in team-building and leadership training. Another growth area is corporate social responsibility (Allen, 2003), with teams being sent to renovate inner-city residential hostels and similar experiences, to encourage awareness of the wider community's needs. Learning takes place through the process of working out a group solution to a problem or challenge, with a facilitator aiding reflection and analysis afterwards. Outdoor training specialists are increasingly looking to target their offering more accurately, keeping courses short and making sure that they are useful (and clear) metaphors for the workplace.

(k)   **Computer-based training.** Using computer software for instruction and assessment. (This will be discussed further below.)

(l)   **E-learning**: learning or training delivered by electronic technology, particularly ICT developments such as the Internet and company intranets – in support of (rather than instead of) traditional training methods. This is a major development, and we will discuss it separately in Paragraph 5.4 below.

EXAMPLE

'Jaded employees? Perhaps its time to unleash the dogs of motivation. In fact, the Virgin Experience's "Thinking Like Canines" programme is not quite as barking as it sounds. Far from instilling dog-like obedience among staff, the basic aim is to strip bare the essentials of workplace – that occupied by working border collies.

'Professional dog trainer Barbara Sykes, along with her team of canine consultants, takes participants through a variety of sheepdog trials – showing them their own communication foibles and how to get the best from individual team members. There is a strong focus on body language and presenting a clear message. "A dog will only respond to clearly defined body language, so each 'shepherd' learns to use their natural communication in different circumstances, with different recipients and under pressure," says Sykes.

'Within day-long programmes emphasising either leadership or teamwork, participants have to assess different dogs correctly and react to their personalities in order to realise each dog's full potential. Starting off in a training ring, they eventually graduate to the open field, where they are handed a variety of tasks with workplace parallels.

' "The dogs work together in harmony for the good of the pack," Sykes says. "They don't argue about their position and don't waste time scoring points off each other. They accept and respect leadership but use their initiative whenever the need arises." '

(Allen, 2003)

Activity 8   **(20 minutes)**

Suggest a suitable training method for each of the following situations.

(a)   A worker is transferred onto a new machine and needs to learn its operation.

(b)   An accounts clerk wishes to work towards becoming qualified with the relevant professional body.

(c)   An organisation decides that its supervisors would benefit from 'picking up some ideas' on participative management and democratic leadership.

(d)   A new member of staff is about to join the organisation.

(e)   A supervisor allows himself to be intimidated by his workteam and ends up carrying most of the workload himself. Occasionally, he tries to throw his weight around, but this never lasts.

5.3 Training technologies

Three major developments in training technology include the following.

(a) **Video**. Video presentations compare favourably with training films and live lectures in that they are less expensive, easily distributed for individual and group use, and flexible in use (being 'pausable' at any time, to allow for questions or discussion). Video allows the standardisation of training among widely-dispersed staff. (Video training can also be highly entertaining, using sophisticated communication techniques.)

(b) **Interactive video** is a combination of video instruction and programmed learning: presenting a segment of tuition and then inviting response (via computer terminal or class discussion/exercise).

(c) **Computer-based training,** using tailored software to:

    (i) Control and manage the training process (Computer Managed Instruction, or CMI): feeding student records, session logs, test results and progress reports back to the training manager

    (ii) Take the role of instructor/assessor (Computer Aided Instructions or CAI) providing tuition, drill and practice programmes, such as those used to teach typing skills and administer typing tests

    (iii) Facilitate self-learning (Computer Assisted Learning or CAL), by offering simulations, business games, case studies and so on. Integrated computerised 'in tray' exercises, for example, can be used to simulate the business environment and the effect of changing one variable on a series of others.

5.4 E-learning

E-learning is identified as one of the 'topical issues' you might cover in Unit 22. Armstrong (2003) calls it 'perhaps the most important recent development in approaches to the delivery and support of learning'. Surveys suggest that it is showing fast growth world-wide, with the UK becoming a major European market.

The CIPD definition of e-learning (cited by Bratton & Gold, 2003) is: "learning that is delivered, enabled or mediated by electronic technology for the explicit purposes of training in organisations. It does not include stand-alone technology-based training such as the use of CD-ROMs in isolation." This places e-learning firmly in the context of ICT networks, including:

- Networked computers forming a corporate intranet
- The Internet and World Wide Web

E-learning systems

E-learning systems typically include:

(a) Software packages – purchased 'off-the-shelf' from providers, or designed and developed in-house – which provide e-learning programmes and facilities: course content, navigation tools, interactive testing and feedback mechanisms and so on.

(b) Learning support from online tutors and/or 'e-moderators', who track participation, co-ordinate information-sharing and interactions with other learners (discussion boards, chat sessions, web seminars and so on) and provide guidance as appropriate.

In addition, *informal e-learning* may take place through everyday information-sharing and interaction over the Internet or intranet in the course of work.

Advantages and disadvantages of e-learning

Advantages cited for e-learning include:

- Learning at the learner's pace and convenience

- Flexible delivery, with access from home, work, libraries etc

- Reduction in delivery costs

- Potential for collaborative learning in 'virtual learning groups' for employees (and others) spread over wide geographical distances: chat, web conferencing and other technologies allow real time support and interaction

- High degree of interactivity, for immediate feedback (eg test scoring), question and answer and so on

- Potential for multi-media, high-interest presentation of learning material (not just 'e-reading') for enhanced learning motivation

Disadvantages cited include:

- The need for Internet or network connection, which may not be available to all employees – and may be complex and expensive to set up

- The need for culture and attitude change to support e-learning, since it represents (for many people) a radically new way to work and learn

- The poor quality or relevance of some off-the-shelf e-learning programmes

- Limitations in the applications for which e-learning is suited, notably in the area of interpersonal skills. Over-reliance on e-learning alone has led to disappointed expectations

Applications of e-learning

There are several areas in which e-learning might be particularly appropriate, because there are easily identifiable knowledge/learning needs which can be effectively met by electronic means.

(a) *Training in IT skills*. Learners can be led through relevant programmes, shown what to do, given opportunities to practise, tested and given competence feedback and records with little need for interpersonal or face-to-face support. Online support usually takes the form of e-mail contact and response.

(b) *Information/awareness-based learning:* induction briefings, health and safety awareness programmes, job-related information briefings/updates, new product/service information, company policy/rule changes and so on. E-learning does information transfer efficiently and with potential for greater creativity, interest and user-friendliness than oral briefings or printed manuals. Face-to-face methods might be used to follow-up or reinforce learning: emphasising the importance of compliance, say, or getting a team together to discuss the new product they've been informed about.

E-learning is not an optimal stand-alone solution for training needs such as 'soft' people management and interpersonal skills: negotiating, giving presentations, team-building, interviewing, leadership and so on. Instructor-led training, coaching, practice and feedback are required. E-learning may still be used to provide pre-course instruction and orientation, to reduce face-to-face time requirements. It may also be used where necessary to reach geographically dispersed learners: webcasts and video-conferencing can be used to stage virtual meetings and presentations, for example.

However, the limitations of e-learning in these areas gave rise to the concept of blended learning: supporting e-learning with the right mix of face-to-face training methods (and vice versa).

EXAMPLE

'Over 2,500 Royal & Sun Alliance (R&SA) staff will undertake up to 35 hours of e-learning this year developing the IT and people skills that will support their customer facing role. As Katherine Plant, training manager at R&SA, explained: "In the past, with the numbers of people who need training, we would probably have implemented a classroom-based roll-out. My remit, however, has been to look at alternative methods of delivering this training and clearly e-learning is the best solution. We can ensure a consistent, high quality training message every time, wherever our people are located. It's also available to people when they need it and this latest learning technology shows them how much we are investing in their development; it sends the message that as a company we believe in both our people and our customers."

'The first of the three Customer Relationship Management (CRM) training programmes focuses on communication skills and includes the theory of how people communicate. It then looks at the practical skills required to put people at their ease such as how staff can match their pace and their language to that of customers.

'The second e-learning programme considers the rationale behind CRM at R&SA ... This programme recognises that the real experts in the business are its front-line staff and it encourages them to contribute their ideas and make the case for how these ideas could make a difference to their customers.

'The third e-learning programme will educate users on the new single view system which R&SA is implementing and which will underpin all customer contact. This is the system that maps and records all customer enquiries and interactions and ensures that all R&SA's staff have the latest customer details at their fingertips.

'Throughout the programmes R&SA is supporting its people with coaching and role-play exercises. This is the important 'blended solution' aspect of the programme where staff can build their skills, get the objective feedback they need and learn from one another. With such people skills it is seldom a matter of right and wrong; people have their own ways of communicating and they need to develop their own style. The coaching input enables them to build awareness of what they currently do and develop the 'best practice' skills and techniques that they have learned to ensure that their customers get a great service. This is what ongoing coaching and support is really about – helping people to develop their confidence and competence in their role.'

(Clague, 2004)

Effective e-learning

In order for e-learning to be effective, the HR function will need to give attention to the following factors.

(a)   *Strategy.* Sloman (2001) stresses the need to introduce e-learning within the context of an overall HRD plan, with a clear idea of organisational learning needs and the potential benefits of using e-learning to meet all or some of them. Radical use of e-learning involves culture change and requires the support of senior management, new partnerships between the HR and IT functions, and willingness to give employees time and support for e-learning.

(b) *Development and implementation.* Requirements need to be analysed and options (buy-in or develop in-house?) evaluated. Outcomes and accountabilities for delivering e-learning should be specified. The relationship of e-learning with other training methods should be resolved for a planned 'blended' approach. Facilities (computers, connectivity, learning resource centres) and personnel (tutors, e-moderators) will need to be planned. A pilot scheme in a limited area of training (such as IT skills) may be used to test the system. Potential users will have to be made aware of the facilities and the role they will play.

(c) *Learning support.* Learning support is important in the take-up and effectiveness of e-learning, both in the sense of:

    (i) Implementing a change management programme to sell the benefits, overcome resistance and celebrate successes of the new system

    (ii) Supporting the use of e-learning by clarifying how work time and facilities may be used

    (iii) Supporting learning by providing online moderators, access to tutors, and face-to-face instruction components where appropriate

(d) *Design of the learning system.* Pre-purchase evaluation (or development) must ensure that materials:

    (i) Are relevant in their content to the needs of learners

    (ii) Have a user-friendly navigation approach, so users know where they are, how much they have left to complete, where to access different learning tools and so on

    (iii) Have a user-friendly interface design, uncluttered by unnecessary instructions, messages and buttons. Where the interface includes a voice-over, it should be congenial and readily understandable!

    (iv) Have a relatively high information density, so that users to not have to scroll or navigate through large amounts of data to get to relevant items

    (v) Allow for a variety of learning styles and approaches (eg through visual and audio presentations, simulations, assessment exercises, interactive sessions and so on)

(e) *Evaluation.* Monitoring needs to assess the impact of e-learning and employee performance gains, not just system 'traffic': what pages were viewed and how much time was spent online

---

Activity 9 (no time limit)

Check out some e-learning related websites and browse through the links and resources.

www.e-learningcentre.co.uk

www.e-learningnetwork.org

www.smartforce.com

How easy was this information to access and use? What does this say about e-learning?

5.5 Advantages and disadvantages of off-the-job training

Advantages of off-the-job training	Disadvantages of off-the-job training
• It allows exploration and experimentation by inexperienced employees without risking negative consequences for live performance	• If the subject matter of the training course is not felt to relate directly to the individual's job and organisation culture, the learning will not be applied afterwards, and will quickly be forgotten.
• It allows trainees to be away from the work environment where interruptions, distractions and performance pressure may interfere with learning.	• Individuals may feel that courses are, in general, a waste of time. They will not benefit from the training unless they are motivated to learn.
• It allows training to be standardised and distributed across a geographically dispersed workforce (eg via video, CBT or distance learning).	• Immediate and relevant **feedback** on performance and progress may not be available from the learning process, especially if knowledge is tested by unrealistic methods (such as exams) or at wide intervals. This will lower the learner's incentive and sense of direction.
• It allows for self-study at the trainee's own pace (eg via distance learning).	• It does not suit some people, who may not have much experience of (or taste for) classroom learning since school. Some people simply prefer a 'hands-on' type of learning: learning by doing.
• It may have organisational status as a reward or peak: being sent on a course is a sign of potential.	• Some organisational cultures encourage fear and insecurity around training courses, with the perception that a person sent on a course must be performing inadequately.

We will now go on to the 'final' stage of systematic training: evaluation.

6 EVALUATING LEARNING EVENTS

6.1 Purposes of evaluation

Evaluation is the process whereby feedback is gathered on the progress and outcomes of training events or programmes, in order to support further planning and decision-making. It may fulfil a number of purposes.

(a) To **determine the effectiveness of training**: measuring whether each training programme is meeting its intended objectives (in terms of learning outcomes, stakeholder satisfaction, impact on performance and a range of other criteria). Effective evaluation is important to validate training as a business tool for improving organisational performance and profitability.

(b) To **help improve the design of training**: asking 'Are we training the right people in the right things, in the right way, with the right materials, at the right time?'

    (i) Identifying the strengths and weaknesses of specific training approaches, activities, materials and providers, so that programmes can be revised or modified for improved value and benefits.

    (ii) Identifying what types of staff **benefit the most or the least** from a given training approach, in order to adjust and develop future programmes and select appropriate participants

    Effective evaluation enables training designers and providers to make objective comparisons and decisions.

(c) To **support accountability:** determining the cost-benefit ratio or return on investment of each training event (and of training activity as a whole), in order to justify expenditure – and gain the support of management and other training sponsors, in the face of competition for scarce resources.

(d) To gather information on the nature, experience and outcomes of training programmes so that they can be effectively **marketed within the organisation**

(e) To allow **stakeholders** in the training process to express their needs and preferences and to have their feedback heard, in order to improve the relevance and acceptability of training

(f) To provide **management information**: on skills and competences (for human resource planning), training costs, benefits and resources (for HRD planning) and so on

6.2 What should be evaluated?

In one sense, the 'what' of evaluation refers to the **criteria** for measuring training success: what are evaluators looking *for*? There are various models suggesting specific sets of criteria, which we will discuss in Paragraph 6.6. However, the full range of criteria selected for evaluation might include the following.

(a) **Participant reactions**: trainees' satisfaction with the course or activity, its relevance to their work and so on. This can be measured using feedback forms, attitude surveys or 'happy sheets' (and also, as a rough guide, numbers of trainees applying for and attending training events). It is important, because a negative experience may inhibit transfer of learning, cause negative word-of-mouth and impact on future take-up of training opportunities.

(b) **Learning outcomes**: new or enhanced knowledge, skills and attitudes. This can be measured using post-training tests or assessments (and follow-up tests to see how much has been retained after the training is over). The effectiveness of a training event may be measured by the number of participants achieving learning objectives.

(c) **Behaviour change**: new work behaviours which reflect learning outcomes, by applying new skills or awareness on the job. This can be measured using observation and performance monitoring, both before and after training (for comparison). It is important in order to evaluate transfer of learning.

(d) **Performance change**: the outflow of behaviour change into impact on individual, unit and organisational performance. This can be measured using feedback from the performance management system (on key performance indicators), and comparing groups who have and have not been through the training. (Otherwise, it is hard to verify that training has made the difference, rather than a number of other variables.) This is important to make a business case for training.

(e) **Other desired outcomes**: for example, whether training has been effective in encouraging networking and co-operation between participants (particularly if they have been brought together from different units or dispersed teams); or whether training is perceived as a valued benefit or reward (if this is part of the organisation's reward management plans).

(f) **Costs of training**: in order to compare the cost-effectiveness of different approaches and providers, and to provide data for cost-benefit (or return on investment) analysis. The organisation should measure both:

- *Direct* costs, which would not be incurred if the particular training did not take place: the cost of learning resources and materials; external training facilities and trainer/consultant fees; travel expenses and so on *and*

- *Indirect* costs, which would be incurred whether or not the particular programme was held: training department salaries and costs, participant salaries for the duration of the training, in-house training facilities and equipment.

(g) **Efficiency**: the amount of learning achieved relative to the amount of time and effort expended. This is an important element in cost-effectiveness.

(h) **Performance to schedule and specification**: the performance of the training provider in relation to agreed criteria for training completion dates, support services, quality of materials and facilities and so on.

In another sense, the 'what' of evaluation refers to the activities and attributes to be assessed: what are evaluators looking *at*?

Activity 10   **(5 minutes)**

What areas would you look at in order to evaluate the quality and suitability of a training course – both as a learner and as training manager?

6.3 When should evaluation take place?

Evaluation is a decision-making tool. It should lead to decisions about which programmes will be continued or discontinued; which learning methods and activities will be incorporated; which materials and technologies will be used; which course providers and learning facilitators will be used; who should be encouraged to participate and so on. In a sense, therefore, the four 'stages' of systematic training should really be seen as a **cycle** (Bramley, 1986), whereby information from the evaluation stage is fed back into further analysis of training needs, design decisions and programme plans: Figure 14.2.

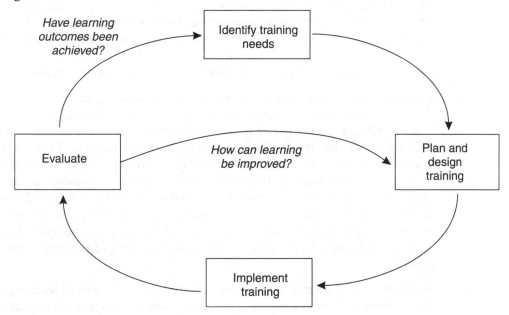

Figure 14.2: Systematic training cycle

There are two basic types of evaluation.

(a) **Formative** (or process) evaluation focuses on appraisal as a source of data which will be fed back into the planning process, in order to refine or improve training. It may be carried out:

- At the development stage, in order to check that the planned approach, activities, content and materials are likely to achieve the desired training outcomes and justify their anticipated costs.

- On an on-going or periodical basis throughout the training programme, in order to highlight any problems or shortcomings which need adjustment.

(b) **Summative** (or product) evaluation focuses on appraisal of the effectiveness of the completed event or programme, at its conclusion. The 'product' or results of the programme are analysed and recommendations made as to whether the programme should be continued and/or modified in future.

Both types of evaluation are necessary. Formative feedback is particularly beneficial because it helps training providers to get things right *this* time – not just next time! This in turn helps to ensure the least possible waste of time and resources.

6.4 Who should evaluate training?

We noted in Chapter 13 that there are a number of stakeholders in training. All of them will want to carry out some level of evaluation in order to justify their particular 'investment' in the training. The roles of key stakeholders in the evaluation process may be summarised as follows.

(a) **Senior management** will undertake a strategic-level evaluation of training as a whole, both formative (in order to approve the human resource development plan and resources) and summative (in order consider the business case for further or adjusted plans). Information about the impact of training on overall organisational performance and culture may only be available at this level.

(b) **Training/development specialists** will have the primary responsibility for evaluating particular training programmes and events, in order to design and manage programmes effectively, justify past and future expenditure, and supply management information for the higher level. Evaluation criteria, methods and schedules should be built into all training plans.

(c) **Trainees** have an important role in evaluating training events in which they have participated: trainee satisfaction is a key criterion, because it supports effective learning and transfer of learning. Trainee feedback *during* training is particularly valuable, as it helps trainers to adapt activities as far as possible to the needs and preferences of the current participants: trainees should be encouraged to co-operate with trainers in improving their experience and outcomes – rather than complaining at the end. In addition, feedback may be sought on the wider perception of training by employees, which will influence its take-up (where voluntary), effectiveness (which depends on learner motivation) and usefulness as part of the total reward package.

(d) **Trainees' line managers** have a strong interest in the transfer of learning to the workplace. Their main role in evaluation will be to assess the impact of training on work behaviour and individual/group performance, as a key criterion of training effectiveness.

(e) **External training providers** will need to evaluate their own performance in relation to desired outcomes: number of courses run, number of students, income, profitability, reputation, client/trainee satisfaction and so on. They should make use of feedback from their customers (both training managers and trainees) and should provide feedback to them (eg trainee test and assessment results, and perhaps also a report on the conduct or motivation of trainees).

6.5 How is evaluation data gathered?

A number of formal and informal evaluation techniques may be used.

Method	Advantages	Limitations
Interviews		
• With participants, line managers, team members • To assess satisfaction, learning, impact on work performance	Flexible focus and style Opportunity for clarification, probing Face-to-face: may encourage personal feedback (eg on aspirations, problems)	Time/labour-intensive Costly May be unstructured Face-to-face: may inhibit honest feedback May 'lead'/influence responses

Method	Advantages	Limitations
Questionnaires • 'Happy Sheets' (reaction or satisfaction focused) • Systematic evaluation instruments (reaction, outcome and improvement focused)	Low cost to administer May be tailored to specific events May allow anonymity, more honest responses Respondents control pace and depth of feedback	If badly designed or managed: poor data quality and return rate Data may be too general Questions may focus on 'likes/dislikes' rather than learning achieved, content relevance and how trainers/materials/facilities supported learning (or not).
Direct observation • Of training (eg by assessors 'sitting in') • Of post-training behaviour	Good way to measure behavioural change Non-intrusive on personal responses	May be disruptive May be subjective: requires trained observers May influence behaviour
Written tests • Knowledge test (eg by multiple choice) • Case study analysis	Low-cost development Ease of administration Ease of processing/scoring (objective testing) Allows wide sampling	May not relate to directly to work: only measures cognitive learning May not reflect learning (eg due to test stress or literacy/language problems)
Performance tests • Competence assessment • Simulation/in-tray exercises/role plays	Relevance to work and performance Includes cognitive and skill-based learning Allows evaluation of 'soft' (interpersonal) skills	Time consuming to create, administer and score May require external development/assessment High cost
Performance data • Individual performance and training records • Archived unit results	Job-based Easy to review Historical: not influenced by evaluation process	Relevant records may not be available Records prepared for other purposes may not contain usable data

FOR DISCUSSION

Have you ever been asked to fill in a feedback or review sheet for training events or materials? How seriously did you take this exercise? What might prevent students or trainees from taking the feedback process seriously (or engaging in it at all)? What kinds of questions could be asked to give planners and providers *meaningful* feedback to help them improve training?

6.6 Evaluation models

There are a number of models of evaluation. The most influential is The Kirkpatrick Model, originally devised in 1959.

The Kirkpatrick Model

Kirkpatrick (1998) sets out four levels of evaluation:

Level	Evaluation of	Measure	Methodology
1	**Reaction**	Trainee satisfaction: 'Were participants pleased with the programme?'	Post-training forms, quantifying reactions as far as possible, and encouraging written comments and suggestions
2	**Learning**	The extent to which learning objectives were met: 'What did participants learn in the programme'?	Pre- and post-training written or performance-based tests of the materials covered in the training
3	**Behaviour**	Transfer of learning to the workplace: 'Did the participants change their behaviour based on what was learned'?	Various: eg observation, work/output sampling, follow-up training audit, competence assessment
4	**Results**	Impact on the organisation: 'Did the change in behaviour positively affect the organisation?'	Monitoring comparable pre- and post-training data: sales or productivity, accidents, customer satisfaction

The Kirkpatrick model is widely known and accepted. It usefully highlights key outcomes of training, the link between them and the need to evaluate all four of them. As Armstrong (2003) notes: 'Training produces reactions, which lead to learning, which leads to changes in job behaviour, which lead to results at unit and organisational level Trainees can react favourably to a course... but learn little or nothing. They might learn something, but be unable or unwilling to apply it. They might apply it but it does no good within their own areas, or it does some good in their function, but does not improve organisational effectiveness'.

However, there are some well-recognised issues in applying this model.

(a) It can be interpreted as focusing on post-training or summative evaluation, rather than formative evaluation, for the purposes of programme design and inter-stage adjustments and improvements. Kaufman (1994), for example, separates Level 1 into 'enabling' (the availability of inputs for the training programme) and 'reaction' (participants' satisfaction).

(b) Many organisations evaluate only at the easiest and least costly Level 1: using 'smiles tests' which are meaningless in terms of justifying training's contribution (Level 4). Nor does enjoyment imply that trainees will apply what they have learned to their jobs: it may be seen as irrelevant, or may not be backed by managerial or resource support. Phillips (1997) adds a useful strand at Level 1 called 'intent to apply'.

(c) Level 4 is particularly difficult in practice: it is not always easy to prove that improved results are attributable to training, let alone to quantify its contribution.

(d)   Evaluation at all levels for all programmes may not be necessary or cost-effective. Training planners may find information Levels 1-2 feedback more useful in designing training events: obtaining information at higher levels of evaluation may appear both more costly and less valuable.

(e)   Despite the widespread neglect of Level 4, the model in some respects falls short. Kaufman (1994) adds a Level 5 which addresses the broader societal outcomes of training (adding the wider community to the list of stakeholders). Phillips (1997) adds a Level 5 for Return on Investment (ROI) assessment, calculating a monetary value for the impact of the instructional programme.

FOR DISCUSSION

'The evaluation of training, like motherhood and apple pie, is inherently a good thing. but, because short-term priorities always crowd out their longer-term competitors, it's typically something we plan to do better next year – after all, we've got away with it so far, so another year won't hurt!' (Shepherd, 2004)

Why does a firm really *need* to evaluate its training programmes?

The CIRO model

The CIRO model (Warr, Bird and Rackham) sets out four evaluation categories.

Context	Identify:

- the performance need/deficiency or desired outcome at which the instructional programme is aimed

- the specific changes in work behaviour that will overcome the deficiency

- the knowledge, skill or attitudes needed to change behaviour

Input	Identify the resources to be used in conducting the programme
Reaction	Measure the participants' satisfaction with the programme
Outcome	Measure the results of the programme in terms of context requirements.

This more formative model uses similar *outcome* measures to the Kirkpatrick model, but broadens the scope of evaluation to include planning *inputs* including need analysis and resourcing. It does not offer an extensive framework for assessment (like the Kirkpatrick model or ROI) but it provides a strong linkage between the objectives of the training programme and its eventual outcomes, creating an objective basis for validation of the programme: did it achieve what it was intended to achieve?

The CIPP model

The CIPP model (Stufflebeam) goes further, collecting extensive process-focused information from a variety of sources, to provide the basis for decision-making and continuous programme improvement. CIPP stands for: Context, Input, Process (learning/teaching processes, trainer skills, group dynamics, methods and media used) and Product (outcomes).

Return on Investment (ROI) model

Definition

> **'Return on investment** (ROI) is a measure of the monetary benefits obtained by an organisation over a specified time period in return for a given investment in a training programme. Looking at it another way, ROI is the extent to which the benefits (outputs) of training exceed the costs (inputs).' (Shepherd, 2004)

Phillips (1997) put forward ROI as a quantitative measurement of training impact, stressing its use in justifying expenditure on a planned training programme (or training activity as a whole) and evaluating the extent to which the planned/desired return was achieved. It is seen as a 'Level 5' evaluation, not a substitute for measuring learner satisfaction, learning outcomes or learning transfer.

ROI is a complex process of data gathering and analysis. Phillips suggested that programmes suitable for ROI evaluation are those which:

(a) Involve large target audiences

(b) Are expected to have a long life cycle

(c) Are important to the strategic objectives of the business

(d) Require significant investment

(e) Have high visibility

(f) Are developed through systematic and comprehensive needs assessment.

A (deceptively simple) approach to calculating ROI (Shepherd, 2004) involves:

(a) Forecasting and/or measuring the **total costs** associated with a training programme (including evaluation costs).

(b) Forecasting and/or measuring the **total financial benefits** of the training programme. This is not easy, as many of the benefits of training are non-quantifiable and difficult to measure, some may take time to emerge to the point where they offer a measurable return on investment: paradigm shifts and cultural changes, employee satisfaction and commitment, increased flexibility and ideas generation and so on. However, quantifiable categories include:

(i) Labour savings

(ii) Productivity increases

(iii) Other cost savings (eg fewer machine breakdowns and accidents, lower staff turnover)

(iv) Other income generation (eg higher sales success rates, new product ideas)

(c) **Calculating return on investment:**

% ROI (over a specified period) = (benefits/costs) × 100

(d) **Calculating the 'packback' period:** how long it will take before the benefits of the training match the costs and the training pays for itself. This is a powerful tool in marketing a training proposal to senior management – as long as the figure is relatively low!

NOTES

Payback period = costs/monthly benefits

Activity 11   **(no time limit)**

Find out how training is evaluated in your own work organisation, or another organisation of your choice. (You may use published sources or personal contacts to obtain this information.) What model of evaluation is used (if any)? How effective is the method perceived to be? What limitations or difficulties are experienced in practice?

Chapter roundup

A systematic approach to training can be illustrated as follows.

Quick quiz

1 How do 'training needs' arise in an organisation and how would you carry out a 'training needs analysis' if required to do so?

2 What is 'blended learning'?

3 List three methods of 'on-the-job' training.

4 What are the advantages and disadvantages of 'on-the job' training methods?

5 What is induction?

6 Training using physical challenges in unfamiliar environments is called 'Action Learning'. True or false?

7 Outline the advantages and disadvantages of e-learning.

8 Suggest three key reasons for evaluating training.

9 What criteria should be evaluated?

10 What do TKM, CIPP, CIRO and ROI stand for?

Answers to quick quiz

1 The answer depends on the job or tasks and the abilities and experience of individuals or groups. Training needs analysis entails finding the difference between the required level of competence and the present level. (see paragraphs 2.2-2.3)

2 Using a mix of learning types, styles and technologies in order to meet needs and preferences of trainees. (para 3.2)

3 Coaching, job rotation, 'assistant to' positions. (paras 4.1-4.7)

4 The main advantage is that it is relevant to the job. It takes place within the job environment, so that the style of supervision, personal relations and working conditions are absorbed. The main disadvantages are pressure and the cost of mistakes. (para 4.8)

5 Introducing new recruits to the job and environment. (para 4.10)

6 False. (paras 4.5, 5.2)

7 See paragraph 5.4 for a full answer.

8 Determining effectiveness, improving design, supporting accountability. (para 6.1)

9 See paragraph 6.2 for a full answer.

10 The Kirkpatrick Model; Context, Input, Process, Product; Context, Input, Reaction, Outcome; Return on Investment. (para 6.6)

Answers to activities

1 Fulfilling such aspirations may become incompatible with business objectives if:

(a) Specific training outcomes become divorced from the strategic aims of the business, and become focused on purely personal development for its own sake

(b) Training outcomes serve to increase employee mobility, by giving them transferable skills and self-confidence

(c)   Training outcomes encourage the employee to 'outgrow' the organisation's culture and leadership style, creating expectations and capabilities that the organisation may not (yet) be in a position to utilise or even tolerate

2   Your own needs assessment: you might make this the basis for Activity 11, later.

3   The answer offered by Torrington and Hall (1991) is as follows.

Training needs	Learning objectives
(a) To know more about the Data Protection Act	The employee will be able to answer four out of every five queries about the Data Protection Act without having to search for details.
(b) To establish a better rapport with customers	The employee will immediately attend to a customer unless already engaged with another customer.
	The employee will greet each customer using the customer's name where known.
	The employee will apologise to every customer who has had to wait to be attended to.
(c) To assemble clocks more quickly	The employee will be able to assemble each clock correctly within thirty minutes.

4   Your own experience. Note particularly how the *blend* of approaches gives you variety, suits your learning style and so on. Disadvantages may include inconsistent messages, extra time/cost and so on.

5   You have probably covered most of the following points.

Advantages include working for a specific purpose, carrying out practical work, the feeling of achievement when a task is completed successfully, knowing you have made a contribution to the organisation's objectives, learning to work with others. If mistakes are made they are rectified and do not affect your overall performance (unless you make too many or keep making the same mistakes).

Disadvantages could include the difficulty of relating exercises or assignments to the 'real work' situation, working mainly on your own and the few practical applications for your studies. Unlike work, you only have one chance to get things right: the marking system means that if you make a mistake there is little you can do once the work is handed in and marked.

6   We highly recommend this exercise: it may become a (very useful) habit!

7   Your own experience (NB: important source of learning!)

8   Training methods for the various workers indicated are as follows.

   (a)   Worker on a new machine: on-the-job training, coaching.

   (b)   Accounts clerk working for professional qualification: external course – evening class or day-release.

   (c)   Supervisors wishing to benefit from participative management and democratic leadership: internal or external seminar, or group training exercise. Careful attention will need to be given to how these 'ideas' will be integrated into practice on the job.

(d)   New staff: induction training.

(e)   Intimidated supervisor: assertiveness training.

9   Note that this activity was in itself an exercise in e-learning!

10   Evaluation would typically cover areas such as: the learning and teaching processes used; course content; materials and teacher aids; credibility and competence of trainers/facilitators; training premises and amenities; flexibility and quality of service; costs; and outcomes of training (according to the criteria discussed earlier).

11   Your research: good evidence of competence in this area!

Assignment 14   **(2 hours)**

Price-U-Like Stores

You are a recently appointed Personnel and Training Manager for Price-U-Like Stores. As a result of the increasing cut throat competition in the retail grocery sector, you launched a new initiative in customer care in the firm, some eight weeks ago.

You arrive at work this morning, to find the following e-mail message waiting for you.

Memo: Personnel and Training Manager

From: A Smith – Chief Executive

Re: 'Customer Care' programme

Despite the publicity and financial backing given to this project, I was very concerned to learn from Public Relations that there has been an increase in complaints from customers about staff; particularly about the ways in which they have been treated by check-out staff and supervisors. Comments range from 'unhelpful' to 'surly', 'rude', 'bloody-minded'. On one occasion a customer referred to obscene gestures from one particular check-out operator.

Whilst I acknowledge that these issues cannot be laid solely at the door of the 'Customer Care' programme, they clearly stand in stark contrast to the objectives of the programme and what we are trying to achieve.

Please put together a training programme for all front line store staff (currently 100 across 10 stores) to put across the message of 'Customer Care' more effectively.

Task:

Produce an outline full-day training programme on Customer Care in Price-U-Like Stores. The programme should indicate current problem areas and a rationale for the Customer Care initiative and why you have chosen to run the programme in the way you decide. Also indicate how you will evaluate the programme.

(e)   Self-limitation to low-skilled product and service markets. The deputy director of SKOPE (Skills, Knowledge and Organisational Performance) has been quoted as saying: 'Employers can happily ignore the government's warning about the effects of globalisation. In today's climate many firms can and do compete successfully on low skills and by producing goods at the low end of product specialisation. There is no impetus for them to change.' (Manocha, 2003)

FOR DISCUSSION

Why do you think UK employers have been so reluctant to develop their people?

EXAMPLE: INTERNATIONAL COMPARISONS

	UK	Germany	US	Japan
Extent of State intervention	Voluntarist (left to employers)	Directed (laws and guidelines require employers to provide training funding and resources)	Voluntarist (anti-federalist, with wide variation)	Voluntarist/directed (voluntary, provision, but strong directives setting and enforcing high-quality training standards)
Orientation to development	Finance (rather than industry) oriented. Individualist development. Development largely extraneous to corporate culture: seen in context of performance improvement or management succession	Industry oriented (eg engineering) Functionally specific	Individualist: trainee aspirations, effort, reward. Excellent training by leading companies – otherwise unco-ordinated.	Collectivist view of development. On-going long-term training within employment: structured development for individual/organis-ation benefit. Development embedded in corporate culture, open to all employees

In the 1980s, recognition of the UK's poor skill base in relation to global competitors, supported by growing business/employer influence, led policy makers and educationalists to seek ways to shift the emphasis in education towards vocational skills. Competence approaches (aimed at defining, developing and assessing competent performance of specific job-related tasks) were introduced along side other aspects of change in education – including the National Curriculum, GCSEs, General National Vocational Qualifications (GNVQs) and the use of problem-based and experiential learning – which focus on learners' development of skills and abilities, rather than on purely theoretical knowledge.

The 1990s saw the development of a broader agenda, responding to the challenges of global competition, developments in ICT and the transition from industrial to knowledge-based economies. The Department for Education and Employment – and its successor, the Department for Education and Skills – engaged in intensive research, strategy and standard development.

A Skills Task Force was set up in 1998 to develop a National Skills Agenda to 'ensure that Britain has the skills needed to sustain high levels of employment, compete in the global marketplace and provide opportunity for all' (National Skills Force, 1998). The Task Force conducted a series of major research reports, case studies and skills surveys. Key findings included:

(a)   Mismatch between skill supply and demand (notably in technical jobs)

(b)   Lack of systematic analysis of future skill requirements

(c)   Lack of training for lower-level and flexible workers, particularly in small organisations

(d)   Lack of qualified adults in the workforce, especially compared with major European competitors such as France and Germany

The government's 2003 White Paper *21st Century Skills: Realising Our Potential* states that despite extensive intervention, the UK still has skills gaps in basic skills (including literacy and numeracy); intermediate skills such as at professional, apprenticeship and technician level; maths; and leadership and management skills.

EXAMPLE

The National Employers Skills Survey 2003

The LSC has published the key findings of the largest survey to be conducted into the scale and impact of skills shortages in England.

Over 72,000 employers working in 27 different sectors of business took part in the National Employers Skills Survey (NESS), which was commissioned by the LSC in partnership with the Learning and Skills Development Agency and the Department for Education and Skills.

The LSC aims to use the findings to plan and fund action to boost employee training in firms and tackle skills gaps that affect the performance of individual firms and the national economy.

LSC Chief Executive Mark Haysom says: 'This survey, the largest of its kind into the skills needs of employers in England, will allow us to better identify those specific areas most in need of investment and continue our work with employers to develop solutions. We need businesses to recognise the issues at stake here and work in partnership with us.'

Key findings include:

(a)   Over one in 10 of the English workforce – 2.4 millions workers – lack the skills needed to do their job

(b)   One third of employers have no training plan to plug workforce skills gaps

(c)   One fifth of job vacancies – 135,000 posts – remain unfilled because of a lack of skilled applicants

(d)   Poor basic skills cost a typical business employing 50 people £165,000 a year

(e)   Employers in London are the least likely to offer their employees training

(Learning and Skills Council, 2004)

1.2 Skills, employment and competitiveness

Low training and skill levels raised concerns about national economic performance, due to:

(a) The potential inability of many UK firms to respond to changing world economic conditions and technological developments

(b) Poor productivity and competitiveness compared with other countries

(c) Self-limitation to competing in relatively low-skilled product and service markets

(d) The social costs of having a rising proportion of the potential labour force condemned to long-term economic inactivity because of inadequate skills (including literacy and numeracy)

Bratton and Gold (2003) note that the economic case for investment in human resource development can be made at different levels.

(a) At the individual level, there is a close relationships between learning (in various forms) and job prospects, especially in terms of minimising unemployment and increasing overall earnings.

(b) At the organisational level, HRD is a central feature of a 'bundle' of HRM practices which have been shown to impact on corporate performance. HRD itself may offer measurable financial returns on investment – and may also contribute less readily quantifiable benefits, such as employee commitment and organisational flexibility.

(c) At the level of the national economy and society as a whole, there is a demonstrable connection between school enrolments, the proportion of the labour force in higher education and the level and growth of the nation's gross domestic product (GDP). Skill levels are argued to be important for future national competitiveness. Low qualifications also prevent entry into the labour market and contribute to the emerging problems of **social exclusion**. *Bridging the Gap*, the 1999 social exclusion unit report, found that 9% of 16-18 year olds were not in education, training or work, creating a mix of educational, health and social welfare problems. This has become a key focus of government policy-making in recent years.

Activity 1   **(20 minutes)**

'Michael Porter, in his recent DTI-sponsored review of UK competitiveness, said that labour force skills continue to be an area of competitive disadvantage for the UK. It has been estimated that poor skills levels account for up to a fifth of the productivity gap. All of which provides compelling support for the official line that the country needs to upskill to boost the economy.

'But do raised skill levels directly equate to increased productivity?' (Manocha, 2003)

From our discussion in this and the previous chapter, suggest two reasons why raising skill *levels* might not directly equate to increased *productivity*.

1.3 Government policy on training and development

Interventionist approaches to HRD seek to influence organisational decision-making in the interests of the economy as a whole. In France, for example, there is a highly-developed concept of 'social partnership' between government and organisations, supported by tax levies on organisations to fund training grants.

Under the UK's voluntarist approach, the role of government (and related agencies) is seen primarily as encouraging and facilitating organisational training.

(a) **Stimulating employer demand** for skills and investment in education and training: researching and promoting the business case for learning and development, and promoting benchmark HRD standards such as Investors in People (discussed in Section 3 below).

(b) **Developing the national training infrastructure**, including:

(i) The establishment of an integrated **framework of vocational qualifications** based on national standards: National Vocational Qualifications (NVQs) in England and Wales, and SVQs (Scottish Vocational Qualifications) in Scotland (discussed in Section 2 of this chapter)

(ii) The establishment of a national **network of regionally-based institutions** to co-ordinate, finance and administer delivery of national training programmes. This was previously the role of Training and Enterprise Councils (TECs) and Local Enterprise Councils (LECs) in Scotland. The regional basis of the network allowed links with local authorities and chambers of commerce, careers services in schools, local Job Centres and so on, fostering business support and community awareness. In the interests of greater clarity and co-ordination, these were replaced in 2001 by the Learning Skills Council (LSC) and its local delivery units (discussed in Section 3 of this chapter).

(c) Providing funding for specific **initiatives to support HRD**, where the market alone fails to maintain sufficient levels of demand and investment. A number of national initiatives are aimed at enhancing the employability of young people and their access to training, including New Deal (formerly Youth Training), Connexions and Modern Apprenticeships (discussed in Section 3 of this chapter.)

(e) Stimulating **demand for learning**. The Green Paper, *The Learning Age: a Renaissance for a New Britain* (DfEE, 1998) set out the government's vision for 'lifelong learning' and the 'learning society'. A key policy goal of the Lifelong Learning agenda is to drive up the demand for learning, of any kind, among individuals. The theory is that if individuals can be encouraged to engage in learning activities, this will improve their employability *and* their openness to further learning within organisations, creating the impetus for continuous improvement that is a key to competitive advantage. This particularly applies to unqualified adults who have previously been excluded from the training market. Initiatives launched to support individual education and learning include the University for Industry (UfI) and learndirect (discussed in Section 3 below).

Activity 2   **(5 minutes)**

What sources of information can you monitor regularly, in order to keep up to date with government policy on skills, training, life-long learning and other aspects of HRD?

We will now look at some of the key areas of training infrastructure discussed above, starting with the development of competence-based training.

2   COMPETENCE-BASED TRAINING

2.1   The competency movement

Historically, the UK has shown an educational bias towards knowledge – and educational institutions and occupations which deal in knowledge – rather than practical skills. The poor performance of British industry and management (as discussed earlier) provided political impetus towards the definition and development of more practical, demonstrable workplace competences.

'The concept of training for competence is that it should be criterion related, directed at developing the ability of trainees to perform specific tasks directly related to the job they are in, or for which they are preparing, expressed in terms of performance outcomes and specific indicators. It is a reaction against the confetti-scattering approach to training as being a good thing in its own right, concerned with the general education of people dealing with general matters.' (Torrington *et al*, 2002)

The idea has been around for some time, having its roots in teacher education in the US, but only gained currency in the UK in the 1980s. The Review of Vocational Qualifications in England and Wales (RVQ) Working Group report in April 1986 recommended the introduction of NVQs, to address weaknesses in the then current system, including (www.qca.org.uk/TheStoryOfNVQ):

- Assessment methods biased towards testing of knowledge rather than skill or competence

- Insufficient recognition of learning gained outside formal education and training

- Many barriers to accessing vocational qualifications and inadequate arrangements for progression and transfer of credit

- Limited take-up of vocational qualifications.

The National Council for Vocational Qualifications (NCVQ) – now the Qualification and Curriculum Authority – was formed to develop a criteria for a clear, coherent and comprehensive system of vocational qualifications. This led to National Vocational Qualifications (NVQs, discussed below) and a wide range of other vocational qualifications (VQs) accredited within the framework.

Competence-based training and assessment has been enthusiastically promoted by the government, proponents of management development (such as the Management Charter Initiative) and professional bodies, as a way of:

(a)   Supporting the career and development aspirations of learners without the historical bias towards formal academic achievement: NVQs, for example, have no formal pre-entry qualifications.

(b) Supporting flexible and job-relevant learning, through on-going training and assessment in the workplace, with no pre-determined time-frame for completion, and potentially minimal inputs from education providers.

(c) Supporting employers' objectives for HRD, by focusing on relevant job skills. Competence frameworks and assessments also support a range of HR planning and performance management applications.

(d) Supporting employees' employability objectives. NVQs, for example, are modularised, so that learning can be transferred freely between providers and elements can be tackled in any order (to suit job- and employer-related priorities).

2.2 The Qualifications and Curriculum Authority

The QCA (ACCAC in Wales and SQA in Scotland) developed the National Qualification Framework, which creates a coherent classification for NVQs. It is the regulatory authority in charge of the formal recognition of all standards and qualifications in education and training, including the National Curriculum, GNVQs, NVQs and technical certificates awarded under Modern Apprenticeship schemes.

The QCA also shares with the Learning and Skills Council (LSC) and the Sector Skills Development Agency (SSDA) a remit to:

- Extend the take-up of vocational qualifications, including their use by more 14-19 year olds

- Develop a more flexible VQ system. A proposed programme of work, with a seven-year workplan, was endorsed in 2003: watch this space!

2.3 National Vocational Qualifications (NVQs)

NVQs and SVQs are part of the National Qualifications Framework in the UK. They are work-related, competence-based qualifications, reflecting the skills and knowledge needed to do a job effectively.

'NVQs are based on national occupational standards: statements of performance that describe what competent people in a particular occupation are expected to be able to do. They cover all the main aspects of an occupation, including current best practice, the ability to adapt to future requirements and the knowledge and understanding that underpin competent performance' (www.qca.org.uk).

Competence frameworks are developed by Standards Setting Bodies made up of representatives of an occupation or profession nationwide. Qualifications are **delivered** through a network of training centres (eg local colleges) which are approved by one of several **awarding** bodies (eg EdExcel, City and Guilds and professional bodies) which in turn must be **accredited** by the Qualifications and Curriculum Authority (or its equivalents).

Standards of competence identify the key roles of a given occupation and break them down into areas or units of competence. These in turn are formulated as statements describing what a competent person should be able to do at different levels, including:

- The specific activities concerned (elements of competence)
- To what standard (performance criteria)
- In what contexts and conditions (listed in a range statement)
- With what underpinning knowledge and understanding.

Activity 3   **(30 minutes)**

Use your existing knowledge (eg of the HNC/HND qualification) or research skills to find out how the 5 Levels of competence for NVQs are defined.

Torrington *et al* (2002) note that NVQs have had a 'rough ride' since the concept was first introduced. There have been reservations in relation to:

(a) **Standards**. Employers inevitably care more about fulfilling their own skill requirements then those of the national employment base – and may find occupational standards too general and/or over-onerous for their own needs. In some areas – such as management – competence frameworks inevitably oversimplify the complexity and need for flexibility of the work.

(b) **Assessment**. The assessment process is time-consuming, particularly in view of the bureaucracy (and specialist terminology) involved. The need to collect acceptable evidence of competence may distract attention from learning, work requirements and other development needs. The quality of assessment also depends heavily on individual assessors: there has been some pressure to re-introduce written examinations in some settings.

(c) **Educational issues**. Since the training agenda is set by the demonstration of job performance, there may be a lack (and future loss) of training in cognitive (thinking) skills. The framework does not address the difficulties of defining higher-level competencies (eg creative conceptual skills) or underlying issues such as the reluctance of UK employers to invest in training.

However, NVQs and SVQs have certainly added to the number of vocational qualifications offered and attained in the UK. According to the DfES website, in Autumn 2003, 49.9% of economically active adults were qualified to at least Level 3 or equivalent: 6.9% higher than in 1997. NVQs are also (as we noted earlier) an important part of the national infrastructure and the basis of training targets.

2.4 The Management Charter Initiative

The MCI was set up in 1988, as the operating arm of the National Forum for Management Education and Development. Its aims were to:

(a) Define generic standards of assessment for management competence

(b) Promote 'best practice' in management education, training and development

(c) Develop ethical and qualification standards with a view to the eventual 'professionalising' of management under a chartered body.

The Management Standards Centre is now the government-recognised Standards Setting Body for management and leadership. This involves overseeing the current occupational standards for management originally developed by the MCI – although a major project is currently under way to develop new standards for management and leadership, currently open to consultation. Watch this space: www.management-standards.org!

Managerial qualifications originally developed by the MCI, as the basis for NVQs and SVQs in Management and Team Leading include: Management (at Level 3 or Level 4), Energy Management (Level 4), Quality Management (Level 4), Environmental Management (Level 4), Operational Management (Level 5) and Strategic Management (Level 5).

The standards cover eight key roles of management performed within an organisation: Managing Activities; Managing Resources; Managing People; Managing Information; Managing Energy; Managing Quality; Managing Projects; Managing Environmental Performance.

The competency-based approach to management development appears to have taken hold in the UK. Some observers, however, note that organisations are beginning to move away from the MCI model (perceived to be bureaucratic, prescriptive and rigid in its standardisation) and towards:

(a) In-house frameworks, reflecting specific organisational culture and context

(b) The use of more 'holistic' forms of development, underpinning specific competencies with a wider skill base, employability training, mentoring, self-managed and experiential learning, learning to learn and so on.

FOR DISCUSSION

How far can managerial work be defined or assessed as competences? For which particular aspects of a manager's job would it be hard to demonstrate 'outputs'? What other approaches to management qualifications would you propose?

2.5 National training targets

The aim of National Targets for Education and Training, according to the DfES's Standards website (www.standards.dfes.gov.uk/otherresources/publications) is:

'To improve the UK's international competitiveness by raising standards and attainment levels in education and training to world class levels through ensuring that:

1. All employers invest in employee development to achieve business success.

2. All individuals have access to education and training opportunities, leading to recognised qualifications, which meet their needs and aspirations.

3. All education and training develops self-reliance, flexibility and breadth, in particular through fostering competence in core skills.'

The targets set by the Learning and Skills Council for 2004 include:

- 80% of 16-18 year olds in structured learning

- 85% of 19 year olds qualified to at least Level 2

- 55% of 19 year olds qualified to at least Level 3

- 52% of economically active adults of working age (and 18 or over) qualified to at least Level 3

- 28% of adults with a Level 4 qualification

- 750,000 adults with improved literacy and numeracy skills (the Skills for Life target)

3 CONTEMPORARY TRAINING INITIATIVES

3.1 Learning and Skills Councils

The Learning and Skills Council was set up in April 2001, bringing various learning providers together under a single funding regime. It is responsible for funding and planning all education and training for over 16-year-olds in England, other than in universities.

The LSC's website states its vision as follows: 'By 2010, young people and adults in England will have knowledge and productive skills matching the best in the world.' Its main tasks are:

- Raising participation in training by young people

- Increasing demand for learning by adults and increasing the supply of flexible, high-quality learning opportunities for adults

- Raising the quality of education and training delivery

- Equalising opportunity by facilitating access to learning

- Developing education-business links

In April 2002, 47 local LSCs were established to deliver outcomes at a regional and sub-regional level, replacing the old Training and Enterprise Councils (TECs). Each local Council includes representatives of employers, trades unions, learning providers and community groups. They work in partnership with each other (Local Strategic Partnerships) to develop shared community strategies, particular in deprived areas. The LSC also seeks to work alongside the Employment Service, the Small Business Service ('Business Link'), Connexions, the University for Industry, and further education and sixth form colleges.

3.2 Modern Apprenticeship schemes

The UK government launched Modern Apprenticeship in 1994 in an attempt to involve industry more closely in the process of vocational training. Apprenticeships (traditionally available in crafts and engineering sectors) are available in childcare, tourism, travel, retail and a range of other industries.

The apprenticeship model combines vocational education (towards NVQ Level 3) including core skills development (literacy, numeracy, communication and so on) with hands-on experience in a sponsoring organisation. Apprentices are attached to a particular employer (as contracted between the administering LSC and the employer) for the purposes of training: there is no guarantee of employment at the end of the training period.

Foundation modern apprenticeships (FMA) normally consist of approximately 180 guided learning hours, equivalent to one-day-a-week of off-the-job learning over a period of one year, or 30 weeks. The NVQ component is at Level 2.

Advanced modern apprenticeships (AMA) normally consist of approximately 360 guided learning hours, equivalent to one-day-a-week of off-the-job learning over a period of two years, or 60 weeks. The NVQ component is at Level 3: technical certificates are mandatory to support the knowledge and understanding required.

Technical certificates are qualifications that support structured off-the-job teaching and assessment of the knowledge and understanding required by an NVQ. They have recently been introduced to modern apprenticeships to improve the quality of the programmes and to form the basis for apprentices to progress, either within the workplace or to further or higher education (www.qca.org.uk/Modernapprenticeship). Sector Skills Councils are responsible for the development of modern apprenticeships in their sectors, working with awarding bodies, providers and employers to identify suitable qualifications for use as technical certificates.

BPP
PROFESSIONAL EDUCATION

EXAMPLE

ASDA announces major workplace training pilot including Modern Apprenticeships: 18/02/04)

'ASDA today announced a workplace training pilot for 1,000 employees following the validation of the company's own in-house training programme. Colleagues will be offered the chance to train toward National Vocational Qualifications (NVQ) in retail and Modern Apprenticeships.

'In a trial commencing in March, 1,000 ASDA employees in eight North London stores will train toward fully transferable retail qualifications. Employees over the age of 25 will work toward NVQ Level 2 qualifications and younger employees, aged 16-24, will work toward Modern Apprenticeships.

'Also commencing in March, 1,000 employees will train toward voluntary, paid, basic skills qualifications, following a successful basic skills pilot in 2003. ASDA expects the pilot and the basic skills implementation to deliver benefits including: increasing productivity, improved staff morale and retention and a higher level of internal promotion.

'The Learning and Skills Council, the organisation responsible for developing skills in England, has contributed over £500,000 to the pilot and the first stage of the basic skills roll out. ASDA's goal is to use the NVQ and Modern Apprenticeship trial to offer company-wide accredited workforce development...

'David Smith, People Director at ASDA, said: 'It's been great to work so closely with the Learning and Skills Council and City & Guilds to extend our adult learning offering, and in the future to create a well thought-out and relevant Retail Modern Apprenticeship for our stores. Their flexibility and can-do approach has meant that over a thousand colleagues will benefit from training programmes that offer a transferable qualification and life-changing basic skills.'

(Learning and Skills Council, 2004 (b))

FOR DISCUSSION

The Adult Learning Inspectorate (ALI) failed 46% of work-based training schemes in inspections throughout 2002/2003, although this was an improvement on the year before (www.ali.gov.uk). The Association of Learning Providers commented (*People Management*, 4 December 2003) that judgements on performance were made on incorrectly defined measures: for example, a person leaving a modern apprenticeship for a better paid, better skilled job constituted a 'failure'.

What do you think is a 'successful' outcome for a Modern Apprenticeship, for all the stakeholders concerned?

3.3 Investors in People

The Investors in People scheme (IiP) was launched in 1991 by the National Training Taskforce, together with the Confederation of British Industry (CBI), Trades Union Congress (TUC), the Institute of Personnel and Development (IPD) and leading national businesses. It was designed to provide a national benchmark standard for investment in employee training and development. IiP is delivered in the UK by local Learning and Skills Councils and 'Business Links' (the Small Business Service), which have targets for the number of organisations committing to the scheme and attaining the standard.

Organisations seeking accreditation must audit their current training practice and provision (with the aid of survey instruments provided) and bring them into line with published standards. They are required to produce evidence of their training objectives and standards, which are assessed by the LSC. The programme is not intended to be a prescriptive set of rules and procedures: organisations are encouraged to develop their own solutions and methods towards benchmark standards. The key principles (as set out on the IiP website) are:

(a) **Commitment** to invest in people to achieve business goals

(b) **Planning** how skills, individuals and teams are to be developed to achieve these goals

(c) **Action** to develop and use necessary skills in a well defined and continuing programme directly tied to business objectives

(d) **Evaluating** outcomes of training and development for individuals' progress towards goals, the value achieved and future needs.

Commitment to IiP requires significant time, effort and investment – potentially including major cultural change. The benefits of IiP status have been debated. Some studies have shown an increase in commitment to HR development, a belief in the value of the process and perceived performance gains, particularly where it was used to assess performance and implement continuous improvement (Alberga *et al*, 1997) The IiP website devotes a whole page to the standard's benefits, and a library of successful case studies.

EXAMPLE

Although the Pontin's name is well known to British holiday makers, the Pontin's of the 21st century is very different from the traditional 'holiday camp' of the past. New managing director Colin Homer is turning a loss-making organisation into a profitable one, using Investors in People to improve the core area of the business... namely its employees.

This is a human resources challenge most managers would baulk at: 300 full-time employees are joined each Spring by 1,600 seasonal workers whose turnover has meant that, in past years, Pontin's has had to employ over 5,000 people during the summer season to fill the 1,600 positions... But as a staunch advocate of the business benefits that Investors in People recognition brings, Colin Homer is already seeing improved employee retention – which will in turn result in greater productivity and reduced costs.

Pontin's can now give employees more and better reasons for staying with the company... Following the guidance of Investors in People, Pontin's is now putting in place a structure whereby every employee will have:

- a personal development file with job descriptions and aims
- access to NVQs
- access to funding for vocational training
- assistance with professional qualifications
- assessment of aims and goals and help in achieving them

Even if someone only stays for a matter of months, they should still have a new qualification to take to their next job.

(Investors in People, 2004)

Other studies, however, suggest that:

(a)   Organisations have difficulties administering the process

(b)   It encourages organisations to underrate the importance of informal development methods

(c)   It does not imply genuine commitment to improving development, since organisations may seek IiP status purely as a rubber stamp for their employer brand

(d)   It is a 'spurious' tool for stimulating the demand for organisational HRD, because many of the organisations achieving the standard were already convinced of its benefits and doing what was required (Bratton and Gold, 2003).

Activity 4   **(no time limit)**

Check out the Investors in People website (www.investorsinpeople.co.uk) and view the Investors in People Standard itself. Use it as a checklist to do a quick appraisal of your own organisation: would it (broadly) qualify as an 'Investor in People'? What areas would have to be brought in line with the standard?

3.4   New Deal

New Deal is delivered by Jobcentre Plus, through its network of Jobcentres. It is a key part of the Government's strategy to:

(a)   Get people off benefits and into work, giving long-term unemployed people the opportunity to develop or upgrade their skills

(b)   Improve the overall skills base and employability of the UK workforce

The **New Deal for Young People** programme is mandatory for jobseekers aged 18 to 24 who have been unemployed for 6 months or more and are claiming Jobseeker's Allowance. The initial part of the programme is a concentrated period of help and advice in order to help them to find work. The government offers subsidies to employers who take on a full-time or part-time New Deal employee, plus a grant towards certified vocational training. Candidates become employees under normal terms and conditions, and training arrangements must be agreed with a New Deal personal adviser.

The **New Deal 25 Plus** programme is also mandatory for those claiming Jobseeker's Allowance for 18 months or more. Jobseekers undertake short courses to refresh existing skills or learn new skills. Employers are given the option of taking candidates on Work Trial. They are also offered subsidies to take candidates on for six months, full-time or part-time, allowing long-term unemployed people to gain work experience and show what they can do.

There are also a number of voluntary programmes, including:

•   New Deal for Lone Parents: advice on childcare, access to training and help with applications for in-work benefits.

•   New Deal 50 Plus: advice and assistance with job search, and access to retraining.

•   New Deal for Disabled People: advice and support from Job Brokers, who can also work with employers to adapt the workplace for disabled people.

The new sector-specific **Ambition Programme** works with business leaders in sectors with skills shortages that would not ordinarily recruit jobless people (IT, retail, construction and energy) to:

(a) Improve placement and retention rates of New Deal participants in jobs with good career potential, not usually accessible to unemployed people

(b) Meet employer HR and skill shortages.

Employers' hiring requirements are used to define training needs and standards of job readiness of New Deal candidates, with a steering group of business leaders from each sector overseeing the programme.

Activity 5 **(5 minutes)**

What would be the potential benefits to employers of taking on people who join New Deal 25 Plus, voluntary programmes or Ambition Programme?

3.5 University for Industry and learndirect

Ufi Ltd. is one of the government's key partners in delivering its workforce development and lifelong learning agendas. It 'aims to drive up demand for learning, help adults improve their employability by acquiring new knowledge and skills, and help businesses become more competitive.' (www.ufi.com)

Ufi works with a broad range of public and private providers in local, employer and sector-based 'hubs', to deliver mainly online courses and information through a network of e-learning centres. One of its priorities is meeting the training needs of small and medium-sized enterprises (SMEs), although it also works with many large employers, including Barclays, Nissan, Tesco and Remploy. Ufi also works with the Adult Basic Skills Strategy Unit and awarding bodies to offer the National Certificate in Adult Literacy and Numeracy, through online tests. Further links with further and higher education establishments should develop further e-learning routes to accredited qualifications, while a pilot scheme is currently working with 14 – 16 year olds who have been excluded from mainstream schooling.

As the world's largest supported e-learning network, Ufi plays a key part in delivering the government's recently-launched e-learning strategy (*Towards a Unified e-Learning*, July 2003): 'E-learning should become a standard feature of learning and teaching for all ages, from school children to pensioners, throughout the education system, in the workplace and beyond.' (UfI, 2003).

learndirect is a government-sponsored network of online learning and information services, developed by Ufi in 2000 to help deliver workforce development and lifelong learning. In particular, it aims to support the government's vision of a 'learning society' where people can access learning opportunities and upgrade their skills throughout their lives, whether they are

- employees seeking to improve their workplace skills
- job seekers wishing to improve their employability
- people who feel excluded from the world of education or IT or
- interest learners

learndirect offers supported flexible learning courses in three main categories: skills for life (literacy, numeracy and ESOL); business and management; and IT skills. Over 80% of courses are online, while others are delivered via workbooks or CD-ROM.

learndirect's free information and advice service (delivered by phone helpline and web site) offers guidance to adults wanting to access learning opportunities.

learndirect can be accessed via over 2,000 e-learning centres located throughout England, Wales and Northern Ireland in high street locations, libraries colleges and workplaces. There are also 'virtual learning centres' run completely online, allowing enrolment and learning from home, libraries or wherever users wish.

Activity 6	(no time limit)

Check out the learndirect website at www.learndirect.co.uk and www.learndirect-advice.co.uk. Also check out www.learndirect.co.uk/personal/freestuff/tasters to experiment with free 'taster' courses.

How might you use learndirect as part of your own self-managed learning?
How might you use it as a Human Resource Developer?

3.6   Connexions

Connexions is the government's support service for young people aged 13 – 19 in England, joining up the work of six government Departments and their agencies, together with private and voluntary sector groups and youth and careers services. Launched in April 2003, it offers practical help with choosing and accessing courses and careers – as well as personal counselling on issues like drug abuse and homelessness. Connexions is delivered through local Partnerships – based on LSC areas, working to national planning guidelines and managed and monitored by local management committees.

'Connexions is the government's ambitious attempt to stop young people bouncing from pillar to post for support during their transition to adulthood. The previous services geared towards young people formed a patchwork of provision, with too many teenagers falling through the gaps and joining the drop-out generation.' (Prasad, 2003)

A 'Connexions Card' encourages young people to stay in learning after the age of 16, by accumulating points for attending school, college or work-based training: points can be redeemed for goods and services, or VIP passes at sports events, concerts and fashion shows.

Personal advisers are deployed in schools, colleges and the community, available on an outreach basis to provide support and guidance on formulating goals and accessing relevant services.

FOR DISCUSSION

How is Connexions relevant to employers?

3.7   Union learning representatives

Increasing employee demand for training and development is a feature of the new psychological contract of employment. Trade unions have for some years worked for the development of their members, developing learning provision and creating demand from sections of the workforce that had little access to employer-provided training: manual workers, part-timers, older and ethnic minority workers and so on.

In 1998, the TUC set up a task group to examine how to improve the role of trade unions in learning. It proposed a network of Union Learning Representatives (ULRs) in workplaces to: analyse members' training needs; provide members with information and advice on learning matters; arrange learning and training and promote its value to members; and consult with the employer on union members' learning and training. The Union Learning Fund provides training for union learning reps and contributes to the costs of developing and co-ordinating learning programmes.

The government has supported ULRs as important contributors to its basic skills, social inclusion and lifelong learning agendas. The network has grown rapidly: The TUC hopes to have 22,000 reps in place by 2010. The Employment Protection Act 2002 (which came into force in April 2003) awarded ULRs paid time off for reps to perform their duties.

The benefit of having union learning representatives (ULRs) in the workplace are said to be as follows.

(a)   They are a trained and inexpensive source of training advice for employers (www.dti.gov.uk.employment)

(b)   They are trusted by, and have access to, workers who might not otherwise engage in learning. This contributes to equal opportunities and inclusion, 'reaching out in particular to people who do not do well in formal education or who need help with English as a second language' (Margolis, 2003)

(c)   They support learning focused on the employees' development needs – not just immediate job training – and this has benefits to employers, through increased openness to learning, continuous improvement, confidence, improvement in basic skills, employability and so on.

(d)   They are advocates for training, ensuring that line managers follow through with agreed time off, resources and so on, against pressures to side-line development activities.

EXAMPLE

Although the law does not provide for paid time off for workers to study, ACAS reckons some companies are already doing this. One example is Sainsbury's, which has encouraged the ULR initiative and allows learning to happen in working time.

It all started in 2001, when a deputy shop steward made an approach to the company to introduce a lifelong learning project. He devised a plan that involved sending learner reps on a 10-day course promoting basic skills awareness. In April 2002, a successful bid was made to the LSC for £100,000 of funding for courses in Sainsbury's depots in Hertfordshire... Sainsbury's now has 73 learner reps. The project has grown so fast that there is a rep in each region... ULRs deliver courses when they are needed to suit shift work. 'In a climate of multi-racial employment, we found huge demand for courses in English as a second language, in particular', [Sarah Lacey, learning rep for the Union of Shop, Distributive and Allied Workers] explains. 'Sainsbury's has done a marvellous job in recognising a basic skills need and allows two hours paid time off a week, she says. 'People do not have to give up their own time to attend. For the company, the benefits have been phenomenal too.'

(Margolis, 2003)

NOTES

FOR DISCUSSION

What does the example above suggest about the impact of HRD on employee relations?

4 WHERE NEXT?

Vocational Education and Training (VET) policy and initiatives are still very much work in progress. The government released a new White Paper *21st Century Skills: Realising Our Potential* in July 2003, aimed at increasing the employability of the workforce and helping individual employers to meet their skills needs, by proposals including:

- Guaranteed free learning for adults to achieve their first Level 2 qualification

- Support for adults to gain Level 3 qualifications in technician and higher craft and trade skills in regions or sectors with skills shortages

- Means-tested £30 weekly grant for adult learners studying full-time further education courses

- Expansion of the Sector Skills Council network to help identify employers' skills needs, with extra LSC funding for skill gaps

- Removal of the 25-year-old threshold for Modern Apprenticeships

- Establishment of ICT skills as a third essential 'skill for life' alongside literacy and numeracy

- Publication of employer training guides on skills

- Launch of a 'Skills Alliance' including representatives from the CBI and TUC, to engage employers in driving the strategy forward.

These proposals are currently the subject of consultation and pilot schemes. Watch this space!

You will need to use your research skills and awareness to keep up-to-date on consultations and reviews, new proposals, body name changes and so on. Some useful information sources include:

- Local colleges, universities and school link officers (and their websites)

- *People Management, Training Journal* and other HRD journals

- The World Wide Web:

www.dfes.gov.uk	The Department for Education and Skills
www.iipuk.co.uk	Investors in People, UK
www.lsc.gov.uk	The Learning and Skills Council
www.learndirect.co.uk	University for Industry learndirect
www.newdeal.gov.uk	New Deal
www.qca.org.uk	The Qualifications and Curriculum Authority

NOTES

Chapter roundup

- Vocational education and training in the UK has traditionally suffered from low levels of employer commitment and investment, leading to skill gaps, lack of competitiveness and social exclusion of people lacking basic skills.

- Government policy on VET has focused on: stimulating employer demand for skills; developing the national qualifications framework (including NVQs); establishing regionally-based institutions to deliver training programmes; initiatives for employability training; and stimulating a demand for life-long learning and basic skill development.

- The competency movement has supported training for competence as a way of focusing attention on transferable, employable, competitive vocational skills. NVQs are based on national occupation standards. Management competences were first developed by the Management Charter Initiative.

- The Learning and Skills Council is responsible for planning and funding all education and training for over-16 year olds in England, other than in universities. The Qualifications and Curriculum Authority is responsible for the formal recognition of all standards and qualifications in education and training.

- A range of training initiatives has been launched to involve industry in education and training (Modern Apprenticeships); define benchmark standards in HRD (Investors in People); improve the employability of unemployed people (New Deal); encourage lifelong, flexible and e-learning (Ufl/learndirect); and support young people in accessing learning (Connexions).

- Union Learning Representatives contribute to the basic skills, social inclusion and lifelong learning agendas by supporting workplace learning.

Quick quiz

1   What are some of the causes of poor investment in training in the UK?

2   What is the theory behind the Lifelong Learning Agenda?

3   What are the advantages and disadvantages of NVQs?

4   What do QCA, MCI and LSC stand for?

5   What is the purpose of national training targets?

6   An Advanced Modern Apprenticeship includes a Level 2 NVQ component. True or false?

7   What are the four principles of Investors in People?

8   Which government programme is mandatory for a 24 year old who has been unemployed for 6 months or more and is claiming Jobseeker's Allowance?

9   The world's largest supported e-learning network is:

    A   Connexions
    B   Ufl
    C   SVQ
    D   The Ambition Programme

10   What are the advantages of having Union Learning Representatives in the workplace?

Answers to quick quiz

1   Philosophies of organisation and management; human capital theory; lack of HRP; voluntarist framework; self limitation to low-skill markets
(para 1.1)

2   Encouraging individuals to engage in learning of any kind improves their employability and openness to learning, creating a culture of continuous improvement.
(para 1.3)

3   See paragraphs 2.1 and 2.3 for a full answer.

4   Qualifications and Curriculum Authority; Management Charter Initiative; Learning and Skills Council
(paras 2.2, 2.4, 3.1)

5   Improve competitiveness; raise education and training standards; improve employer investment in training; broaden individual access to training; increase competence in core skills.
(para 2.5)

6   False: Level 3.
(para 3.2)

7   Commitment, planning, action, evaluation
(para 3.3)

8   New Deal for Young people
(para 3.4)

9   B
(para 3.5)

10   See paragraph 3.7 for a full answer

Answers to activities

1   Manocha himself identifies two problems with the more-training-equals-higher-productivity equation.

(a)   'The UK doesn't simply need higher-level skills: it needs the *right* skills. As many a dinner party conversation has recorded, while the UK pushes for more graduates, we are short of plumbers...' The government is addressing this by matching skills output with industry requirements (as we see later in the chapter).

(b)   'What happens to the higher-skilled people? Many commentators point out that the productivity gap will not be closed by training people and then sending them back to an unreceptive workplace, where new skills are wasted through lack of opportunity.' We noted the need for transfer of learning in Chapter 13.

2   Suggestions include: quality national press; HRM and HRD journals; web sites of relevant organisations (starting with the Department of Education & Skills).

3   As set out at www.dfes.gov.uk/nvq/what (although you could have used a number of other information sources) the five levels are as follows.

Level 1   Competence which involves the application of knowledge in the performance of a range of varied work activities, most of which may be routine and predictable

Level 2   Competence which involves the application of knowledge in a significant range of varied work activities, performed in a variety of context. Some of these activities are complex or non-routine and there is some individual responsibility or autonomy. Collaboration with others, perhaps through membership of a work group or team, may often be a requirement.

Level 3   Competence which involves the application of knowledge in a broad range of varied work activities performed in a wide variety of contexts, most of which are complex and non-routine. There is considerable responsibility and autonomy and control or guidance of others is often required.

Level 4   Competence which involves the application of knowledge in a broad range of complex, technical or professional work activities performed in a variety of contexts and with a substantial degree of personal responsibility and autonomy. Responsibility for the work of others and the allocations of resources is often present.

Level 5   Competence which involves the application of a range of fundamental principles across a wide and often unpredictable variety of contexts. Very substantial personal autonomy and often significant responsibility for the work of others and for the allocation of substantial resources feature strongly, as do personal accountabilities for analysis, diagnosis, design, planning, execution and evaluation.

4   Your own research and application.

5   The key benefit to employers is ease of access to potential employees who may already have the skills and experience required, and who have had guidance in training to meet employer requirements (especially in the Ambition programme). In the case of voluntary programmes, it may also support equal opportunity programmes. The financial incentives should not be the primary benefit – but may help to reduce the risk.

6   Your own research. If you had trouble accessing the information, what does this say about the programme?

Assignment 15   **(no time limit)**

Identify and investigate a vocational training scheme of your choice, relevant to your area of study or work. Compile a dossier or take notes of information you find as to the scheme's:

(a)   Aims and objectives
(b)   Entry/access qualifications and commitments
(c)   Funding assistance for the learner (if any)
(d)   Delivery methods and locations
(e)   Assessment methods and standards
(f)   Managing bodies and accountabilities
(g)   Qualifications offered
(h)   Routes to further qualifications or employment opportunities (if any)

Prepare a set of slides as visual aids for the presentation of this information (eg to a study group or to HRD staff who need briefing). You may use PowerPoint (or similar) or draft slides by hand.

PART D

UNIT 24: EMPLOYEE RELATIONS

Chapter 16:
THE CONTEXT OF EMPLOYEE RELATIONS

Introduction

Thanks largely to its turbulent history and tainting with political colours, industrial relations is an emotive subject which requires careful handling in study and professional contexts: as you read, try to appreciate both sides of the debate.

Traditionally, industrial relations are the dealings and co-operation (or lack of it) between management and workers, usually via their representatives in a trade union or staff association. However, trade unionism has been on the decline in the UK (and USA) and a high proportion of employees do not now belong to unions. Nevertheless, industrial relations still exist in organisations. A shift to the term 'employee relations' reflects a broader orientation towards communication with and involvement of employees, and a more unitarist perspective in which co-operation is regarded as both possible and desirable in order for business' and employees' needs to be met.

In this chapter we will consider the players and ideologies involved in industrial relations and the shift towards 'employee relations'. In Chapters 17 and 18 we will examine more closely some of the processes involved in the management of employee relations.

Your objectives

In this chapter you will learn about the following

(a)   The unitary and pluralistic frames of reference

(b)   The development of trade unions and the nature of industrial relations

(c)   The role of a trade union and its contribution to effective industrial relations

(d)   The ideological framework of industrial relations

(e)   The roles taken by the main actors in employee relations

(f)   The impact of human resource management on employee relations

1 PARTIES IN INDUSTRIAL RELATIONS

1.1 What are industrial relations?

Definition

> **Industrial relations (IR)** comprises 'all the rules, practices and conventions governing interactions between managements and their workforces, normally involving collective employee representation and bargaining.'
>
> (Graham and Bennett, 1998)

Industrial relations policy and practice covers areas such as:

(a) Procedures for setting terms and conditions of work, profit-sharing, training targets, equal opportunities policy and so on

(b) Disciplinary and grievance procedures, both individual and collective, including external arbitration and conciliation. (Individual disciplinary and grievance procedures were discussed in Chapter 6.)

(c) Recognition of trade unions (if applicable) to represent worker interests through the processes of collective bargaining and consultation

(d) Development of added or alternative mechanisms for employee representation and consultation (such as works councils, joint consultation committees and employee forums)

(e) Determination of the structure and scope of consultation and employee involvement in decision-making, within the framework of collective bargaining, partnership agreements, works councils, general HRM policies and so on

1.2 Workers and their organisations

Trade unions

Definitions

> A **trade union** is an organised association of employees who 'consist wholly or mainly of workers of one or more description and whose principal purposes include the regulation of relations between workers and employers' (Trade Unions and Labour Relations (Consolidation) Act.
>
> An **independent trade union** is one which has been certified as being autonomous and financially self-supporting: not dominated by an employer because of the provision or withdrawal of financial or other support.

A single trade union might include members from different organisations in the same industry, and a single organisation might employ workers who belong to a number of different trade unions. Employees may be members of various unions, but the employer is not compelled to deal with a union unless it is 'recognised' for the purposes of collective bargaining or negotiation. Until recently, there was no statutory provision for obtaining or enforcing recognition: that was changed by the Employment Relations Act 1999 (Paragraph 2.6 below).

A firm may recognise a number of different unions in the workplace, to represent different categories of employees. Multi-unionism has significant drawbacks: encouraging demarcation disputes and the proliferation of work rules; competitive and therefore escalating pay settlements; and the cost and complexity of multiple bargaining time and machinery.

Firms desiring to simplify bargaining arrangements and secure greater flexibility and integration will often seek to negotiate a **sole recognition** or **single union agreement**, whereby only one union is recognised for the purpose of collective bargaining: workers who want representation must join this union. Sole recognition – and even more, the de-recognition of one union in favour of another – is, however, fraught with inter-union competition, and may not be perceived as genuinely representative of the interests of all staff. It is frequently achieved by a 'beauty contest approach', which arguably creates a situation in which unions must offer to fulfil the expectations of management in order to be granted recognition (and access to a fresh pool of members) rather than fulfilling the expectations of their members.

The primary functions carried out by a trade union are directly related to its objectives of improving the collective pay, conditions and job security of its members. Trade unions pursue their objectives through the processes of:

(a)   **Collective bargaining** and negotiation (discussed in Chapter 17), which determines minimum standards to be applied to members covered by the resulting agreement

(b)   **Joint consultation**: discussing with representatives of management issues of mutual concern (such as re-organisations, redundancies, health and safety).

(c)   **Member services**: representation in grievance and disciplinary matters; obtaining sickness and accident benefits; advising on, and arranging access to, basic skills and workplace training (through Union Learning Representatives, as discussed in Chapter 15); legal advice and assistance.

Activity 1   **(15 minutes)**

What other activities of unions are you aware of, which are not directly connected to the achievement of its goals, but which might indirectly be effective in protecting members' rights?

The Trades Union Congress (TUC)

The TUC is a voluntary association of unions originally established in 1868. It holds an annual week-long congress or conference, for the purpose of debate, policy formation and the election of its general council. The TUC's purpose is:

(a)   To formulate and express policy for the UK trade union movement as a whole

(b)   To consult with industry and government bodies on issues affecting the trade union movement, and to lobby for relevant legislation

(c)   To manage disputes between affiliated unions (eg over membership 'poaching' or job demarcation) through a Disputes Committee

(d)   To intervene and try to effect a settlement in an industrial dispute, if invited to do so by the union involved

(e)   To investigate complaints that an affiliated union's conduct is against the interest or policy of the congress

The TUC has limited influence over its affiliates, however, through the threat of suspension or expulsion from the Congress. The autonomy of affiliates is still a key value.

We will discuss trade unions in more detail in Section 2 below. However, trade unions are not the only employee representatives with whom management may deal, formally or informally. There has been a trend towards non-unionised forums for consultation and participation. Again, these will be discussed in detail later (in Chapter 18), but we will survey some of the possibilities briefly here.

Staff associations

Staff associations represent the employees (or groups of employees) within a particular organisation. They have been particularly popular among white-collar workers (eg in banking and insurance), for whom trade unionism was less socially acceptable. The main reasons for employees to form a staff association are the desire for collective representation and/or negotiating powers (eg to respond to a specific threat, such as redundancies) – *without* the formality and ideological baggage of a trade union. The majority of staff associations are recognised by employers for the purposes of consultation and negotiation. However, their narrow membership base and lack of funding limits their bargaining power.

Management generally prefer to deal with staff associations because they are less subject to third-party external interests: mutuality of interests may therefore be expected to be easier to achieve, with less external exposure, and staff associations may offer sufficient representation to head off demands for unionisation. Most staff associations, however, are independent of the employer and provide a genuine alternative to trade unions in terms of employee representation.

Professional bodies and associates (eg the British Medical Association) may also represent the interests of their members in negotiation with employers, alongside their role as guardians of professional ethics and standards, educators and certifiers of practitioners and so on.

1.3   Managers and their organisations

Employers' associations and federations

Employers' associations are voluntary private groups of employers founded to facilitate trade, communication and representation in areas of common interest. Some are national bodies covering a whole industry (for example, the Engineering Employers Federation), while others are regional or specialised in their scope.

The largest UK employers' associations include the Engineering Employers' Federation, the Chemical Industries Association, the Road Haulage Association, the Federation of Master Builders, the Newspaper Society and the British Clothing Industry Association.

Employers' associations consist of companies of different sizes and organise themselves in different ways: most are consultative, rather than decision-making, bodies. Some give priority to trade matters, others to employee relations.

They were initially developed on an ad hoc basis in response to specific industrial disputes with the early trade unions, but by the end of the nineteenth century, in response to the growing influence of unionism, adopted the federated approach to organisation at an industry/national level.

The role of the associations has declined with the increasing decentralisation of industrial relations processes: the growth in company- or plant-level bargaining, for example, and the decline of industry-wide agreements. Nevertheless, employers' associations still negotiate agreements at national level, especially in industries (such as electrical contracting and printing) which are dominated by small companies in competitive labour markets: national agreements provide industry frameworks and reduce price competition for skills. Moreover, employers wishing to influence EU policy, must be part of an employers' association, which in turn may be affiliated to one of the EU-wide employer voices recognised by the EU Commission for the purposes of consultation and negotiation.

The main purposes of employers associations are:

(a) To give general help and advice on employee relations issues

(b) To represent members' views to political influencers and decision-making bodies (eg lobbying parliament)

(c) To assist member firms in the resolution of disputes (including representation at Employment Tribunals)

(d) To negotiate sectoral collective agreements (where applicable) with trade unions

The Confederation of British Industry (CBI)

The Confederation of British Industry (CBI) was formed in 1965 as the main national federation of employers' associations in the UK, with the purpose of promoting British industry through political lobbying. Its main function is to influence policy on industry-related issues: it is not directly involved in employee relations processes, although it does maintain working relationships with the TUC, ACAS and other bodies.

1.4   Third parties

Third parties, such as government, arbitrators and judges (now including the European Court of Justice) have an important bearing on industrial relations, because they set a framework for what employers and employees can and cannot do.

The government has established agencies such as the Advisory, Conciliation and Arbitration Service (ACAS) and Employment Tribunals, to assist or act as go-betweens in employment and industrial relations matters.

ACAS

According to the Employment Protection Act 1975, ACAS was designed to 'promote the improvement of industrial relations'. It is an independent body, governed by a Council whose members are appointed after consultation with worker and employer organisations.

ACAS has the ability to intervene at the request of employers and/or trade unions in the event of a possible or actual trade dispute. It may enquire into a complaint by a recognised trade union that insufficient information has been disclosed for collective bargaining purposes. It may also enquire on its own initiative into any industrial relations matter and publish its findings. It prepares and publishes Codes of Practice giving guidance for improving industrial relations (in areas such as disciplinary procedure).

ACAS may also be involved in individual conciliation cases, prior to hearing by tribunal. (It is frequently called in, for example, over equal opportunity and unfair dismissal complaints.)

Activity 2   **(10 minutes)**

Look up some definitions: what is the meaning of (a) conciliation (b) mediation and (c) arbitration. (Add the ways in which ACAS accomplishes these things, briefly, if you know.)

The Central Arbitration Committee

This body acts as arbitrator in disputes referred to it by ACAS. Under the Employment Relations Act 1999, it is called upon to make a ruling in cases where a union and an employer fail to reach agreement on union recognition or on the conduct of collective bargaining or on the establishment and operation of European Works Councils.

Employment Tribunals

Employment Tribunals (formed under the Employment Tribunals Act 1996) deal with most cases brought under employment law. They consist of an independent, legally-qualified chairperson, and two representative members, from the employer and the union. Their constitution is informal, but their decisions are legally binding. Evidence is given on oath, witnesses are called and legal representation is permitted as in a court of law. Appeals may be made (on points of law only) to the Employment Appeals Tribunal: this is a formal court, consisting of a judge and lay members representing both sides of industry, and its decisions establish legal precedent.

Tribunals – and proposed changes to the system – were discussed in Chapter 7.

EXAMPLE: INTERNATIONAL COMPARISONS

In the USA, although the government plays a limited role in influencing collective agreements, third party intervention in negotiation and mediation (eg via the Federal Mediation and Conciliation Service) is widespread.

1.5 Other stakeholders

A recent article in *People Management* (Wild, 2003) suggested that there is increasing public awareness of Corporate Social Responsibility (CSR) in relation to labour-related globalisation issues such as the use of child labour and sweatshops in developing nations, and the widening gap between 'fat cat' managerial pay and that of workers. These issues have been brought to the public's attention not by trade unions, but by pressure groups (non-government organisations, or NGOs) such as Oxfam, Anti-Slavery International and Clean Clothes.

Pressure groups have arguably become lead players in employment-related issues. Industries in sporting goods, and apparel, fashion and food retail are among the targets of widespread PR pressure, consumer protest and boycott in relation to labour practices.

'The challenges for unions and HR practitioners are different. Some unions are starting to form alliances with pressure groups. HR needs to take the initiative to defend its company's interests on employment-related issues as a whole and not to focus too closely on relations with the company's own employees. HR is also best placed to understand the new risks associated with the employment-related behaviour of contractors or companies that form part of the supply chain' (Wild, 2003).

FOR DISCUSSION

Whose 'business' is it how corporations treat their workers?

1.6 The role of the HR department

As in many other areas of HRM, it is often the line managers who have responsibility on a day-to-day basis for the implementation of industrial relations policy in regard to:

(a) Exchanging information with office representatives – say, to discuss changes in work procedures or newly-introduced rules

(b) Conducting disciplinary and grievance measures

(c) Implementing collective agreements on working procedures and conditions

(d) Managing interpersonal and team relations in such a way as to minimise potential conflict and preserve organisational authority in the face of collective labour strength

However, there is a continuing role of HR specialists in developing policies which promote consistent decisions on industrial relations issues, especially since line managers may resist employee relations techniques in the belief that they will hamper their work and limit their flexibility.

FOR DISCUSSION

Clegg (1976) argued that: 'If line managers are left to handle industrial relations issues for themselves, the pressures of production are likely to lead to ad hoc and contradictory decisions ... If a personnel policy is introduced to promote consistent decisions on industrial relations issues, its effectiveness may depend on granting authority to the personnel department to override the natural priorities of the line managers.'

How can the HR function overcome the 'natural priorities' of line managers in the sphere of employee relations?

We will discuss in Section 4 below how HR policy affects industrial relations, and how the HRM approach ('employee relations') differs from the traditional approach ('industrial relations'). Here, we will look in more detail at the major player in traditional industrial relations: the trade unions.

2 TRADE UNIONS

2.1 Types of trade union

Unions are often distinguished as follows.

(a) **Craft and occupational unions**, which recruit employees who perform certain jobs. These include:

  (i)   White collar unions (employees in office work or desk jobs), and
  (ii) Craft unions (manual workers skilled at a particular craft)

  Examples include the British Airline Pilots Association (Balpa) and the National Union of Teachers.

(b) **Industrial unions**, which recruit all grades of employees employed in a particular industry. Examples include the National Union of Mineworkers and the Iron and Steel Trades Confederation.

(c) **General unions**, which organise workers from a variety of different jobs and industries. Examples include the Transport and General Workers Union (T&G) and GMB, the 'general' trade union.

Despite these different types, the UK system is essentially 'job-centred': the job an individual performs largely determines which union (s)he will join.

EXAMPLE: INTERNATIONAL COMPARISONS

- In Germany, trade unions are organised on industrial lines: one trade union represents all organised employees at a workplace, irrespective of their individual occupation. The German Trade Union Federation (DGB) is a non-political affiliation based on industrial unionism.

- In Japan, unions are mostly organised by company or establishment: an enterprise union consists of regular employees of a single firm, both white- and blue-collar. This has traditionally been supported by long-term career stability.

- In France, unions are mostly general unions, organised into five major confederations with broad divisions along politico-religious lines: socialist, communist, social democratic, Christian.

- Job- or occupation-centred unionism is a feature of Anglo-Saxon countries such as the UK, USA and Australasia.

2.2 Trade union representatives

Trade union representatives include:

(a) *Full-time paid officials:* 'organisers' or 'officers', employed by the union at district or regional level to carry out its policies under the direction of its national executive committee; and headquarters staff (financial, legal and administrative, under a 'general secretary').

(b) *Part-time voluntary officials*, elected to be branch officers of the union in a particular area.

(c) *Workplace representatives* (shop stewards or staff representatives) who are employed by the organisation, but act on behalf of their fellow employees as their recognised representative. (Some very large firms with sensitive industrial relations may retain one or two employees on full pay to act in their union capacity full time.) Shop Stewards are the link between the work group, the union officials and management: they require extensive knowledge of the union's service, employment and industrial relations law, ACAS and tribunal machinery, the policies and practices of the organisation, the role of managers and so on.

The structure of a union is democratic: local branch members elect representatives to a district or regional committee, which elect a national committee. The policy of the union is (theoretically) representative of the views of members, not of its leadership. However, the potential divergence between the goals and values of individual members and those of the organisation is just as great for a trade union as for a business. This view was given a political edge by the Conservative government's legislative support for the rights of individual union members (for example, secret balloting on use of union funds and industrial action). Its Industrial Relations Code of Practice stated that it should be the responsibility of the union to ensure that:

(a)   Its members understand the organisation, policy and rules of the union

(b)   Its members understand the powers and duties of the members themselves and those of their union representatives

(c)   Its officials are adequately trained to look after their members' interest in an efficient and responsible way

2.3   The rise, fall and rise of trade unionism

Early development

The UK trade union movement is the oldest in the world. Trade unions developed in the mid-nineteenth century, mainly as organisations of skilled workers in craft-dominated industries seeking to secure employment. In the latter half of the century, labourers and other unskilled workers also organised.

The local craftsman's clubs were initially suppressed by the Combination Acts (1799, 1800), which made illegal any combination of working men for the purpose of improving their work conditions: the government of the day feared the spread of revolutionary ideas from France.

The Acts were repealed in 1824. An outbreak of strikes followed, and a further Act was passed in 1825 allowing trade unions to exist, but limiting their right to strike.

The first attempt to unite skilled and unskilled worker was Robert Owen's Grand National Consolidated Trades Union (1834). This collapsed following the transportation to Australia of the so-called 'Tolpuddle Martyrs': six members of the Friendly Society of Agricultural Labourers of Tolpuddle, Dorset, founded in 1833 to secure fair wages for its members, who were charged with administering unlawful oaths, and became the founding heroes of the trades union movement.

In 1851, the first successful national trade union, the Amalgamated Society of Engineers, was formed, and the Trades Union Congress (TUC) met for the first time in 1868.

Trade unions were finally granted legal status in 1871.

Rise...

Following legal status, more trades unions began to be formed, particularly by unskilled workers. The London dockers successfully struck in 1889 (for a wage of sixpence, ie 2 ½ pence, per hour!), encouraging others.

During the 1890s, the trades union movement supported the formation of the Labour Party, supplying funding (as it continues to do today). The Labour Representation Committee was formed in 1900 and renamed the Labour Party in 1906. In that same year, unions in the UK finally became secure: the Trade Disputes Act (1906) prevented employers form suing unions for damages following a strike.

The Labour Party grew in influence until in 1922 it replaced the divided Liberal party as one of the two major UK parties: in 1924 and 1929/31 it was able to form a minority government (under Ramsay MacDonald).

1926 saw a national strike by workers in Britain's major industries, lasting from 3-12 May: The General Strike. The TUC called out its members in support of the miners, who had refused to accept a reduction in wages. The strike involved over two million workers in transport, iron and steel, building, printing, gas and electricity. However, the government was able to keep essential services going, and the strike was forced to fold. This was a blow to the trades union movement, and the subsequent Trade Disputes Act (1927) made general strikes illegal.

In 1945, however, Labour won a huge majority in the first post-war general election, and was able to introduce a programme of radical policies under Clement Attlee: this included widespread nationalisation of industries, the setting up of the social security system – and the repeal of the Trade Disputes Act.

The unions became increasingly powerful during the Labour term(s) in government. The Industrial Relations Act (1971) was enacted by a Conservative government, introducing strike ballots and cooling-off periods, but this was repealed by the following Labour government in 1974.

In 1975, ACAS was set up to assist in settling industrial disputes.

Trade union membership in the UK reached a peak of 13.29 million in 1979, also the year in which the number, duration and severity of strike actions reached their peak.

And fall...

During the 1980s and early '90s, the power of trade unions in the UK was affected by a number of factors.

(a) Declining membership and the increase in non-unionised organisations. Total union membership, for example, peaked at 13.2 million in 1979 and fell to just below £7.9 million in 2001. This is partly due to the decline in manufacturing, the traditional heartland of unionism, and the growth in the service sector where membership has traditionally been low. Meanwhile, competitive pressures resulted in employers' de-recognising of trade unions in order to end restrictive work rules and collective bargaining. Falling membership creates a vicious circle: weakening union effectiveness, which further depresses membership, and so on.

(b) Union concerns such as collective negotiation, occupational demarcations and work rules were being marginalised by HRM trends such as: negotiation of individual contracts; individual performance management and performance- or merit-related pay awards; multi-skilling and flexible working; direct communication policies; worker empowerment, involvement and participation schemes; the introduction of Japanese management and production techniques (collectivist, participative, low-conflict) and so on. The whole trend towards 'commitment'-based HRM, with a unitary perspective, suggested that the adversarial industrial relations model, associated with unionism, could be by-passed.

(c) The unions' power was intentionally weakened by Conservative governments from 1979 – 1997, through legislation such as:

 (i) The abolition of the 'closed shop', under which membership of a union could be made a condition of employment

 (ii) The requirement for secret balloting of union members when electing voting members of a union's governing body, and when proposing industrial action, which gave support to the more moderate elements of the trade union movement

 (iii) The protection of individual union members' rights (including the right to refuse to participate in or support a strike)

 (iv) The right of employers to dismiss employees taking unofficial strike or other industrial action

 (v) The prevention of the use of union funds to compensate a member for the consequences of unlawful conduct during a strike (eg paying fines)

And rise…?

There has been a significant turnaround in the last few years in the number of union recognition agreements in force in the UK and the number and proportion of workers covered by such agreements.

This has been accelerated by:

(a) New recognition laws (see Paragraph 2.6 below)

(b) The Labour government's support for an industrial relations climate in which employers are less inclined to behave unilaterally, thus legitimising the union role in organisations

(c) Employer recognition that there is a positive business case for dealing with the workforce through unions, as a more efficient, positive and democratic method. Trade unions may be argued to fulfil a number of key managerial functions (Sisson & Storey, 2000).

 (i) An *agency* function, acting on behalf of large numbers of employees in their dealing with management, with benefits for consistency and management time/cost savings.

 (ii) A *feedback* function, voicing the complaints and grievances of employees – which management need to be aware of

 (iii) A *stabilising* function, helping to manage workforce discontent by legitimising procedures and managerial prerogatives

(d) Concerted recruitment drives, often supported by employers who have signed voluntary and partnership agreements with a union. 'At a workplace level, partnership means employers and trade unions working together to achieve common goals such as fairness and competitiveness. This more co-operative attitude on the part of trade unions, it is argued, has made employers more willing to recognise them and have a relationship with them' (Gennard & Judge, 2003).

The picture for unions is not all rosy, however. Many of the sectors showing growth in recognition and membership (eg printing, newspapers, financial services) are these in which unions were de-recognised in the 1980s: unions may merely be recovering lost ground, rather than making inroads into areas where they have traditionally been weak (services, retail, hospitality).

In addition, union leaders are also concerned that the new recognition law has sparked inter-union disputes and competition for single-union recognition deals, wasting union resources and distracting from the key task of recruitment. The TUC conference 2000, for example, highlighted two long-running disputes over single-union deals signed by the Transport and General Workers Union (T&G): at the JVC Kilbride factory, squeezing out the Iron and Steel Trades Confederation (ISTC), and at Eurotunnel, squeezing out the train drivers' union, Aslef.

2.4 The sources of trade union power

The power of a given trade union in bargaining and negotiating with employers will depend on a complex of factors.

(a)   The degree of support for union actions from its members, and its ability to attract and maintain membership. This in turn may depend on a number of factors:

(i)   The conditions pertaining in the industry or organisation, the aspirations of members and hence the perceived advantages of trade union membership.

(ii)   Employment issues such as recessionary downsizing, or the introduction of new technology, which enhance the perceived importance of worker representation.

(iii) Competition for members between unions, or between a union and a staff association.

(b)   The perceived success or failure of the union in obtaining beneficial agreements for its members.

(c)   The bargaining environment, including:

(i)   The employer's HRM policies. If terms and conditions are felt to be fair, good in comparison to market rates and so on, there will be little impetus for bargaining.

(ii)   The local labour market. If there is a local shortage of the skill groups represented by the union, it will have greater bargaining power, but the reverse is also true: in time of high unemployment, the union movement is weakened. 'There is less talk about the quality of working life when there is little work to be had' (Huczynski & Buchanan, 2001).

(d)   The culture of the union, and in particular its willingness to use industrial muscle. This resides primarily in the threat of withdrawal of labour in disputes (discussed in Chapter 17).

Activity 3   **(5 minutes)**

Why do you think size of the union (number of members) has been left out of our account?

2.5 The law on trade union membership and activities

The **closed shop** (whereby an employee had to be a member of a relevant union in order to obtain or retain a job) was stripped of all legal protection under the Employment Acts 1988: dismissal for non-membership of a union was automatically to be deemed unfair, and industrial action to create or maintain closed shop practices lost its legal immunity. On the other hand, further legislation has protected the freedom of individuals to join the union of their choice. No action may be taken to compel people to be members of a union, nor to deter them. Nor can employees be prevented from participation in union activities at an appropriate time: if the union is both independent and recognised by the employer, there is a further right to reasonable time off for union activities.

Individual union members' rights (Employment Act 1988) include:

(a)   The right not to be unjustifiably disciplined by a union (eg by fines, expulsion, withdrawal of benefits or blacklisting) for refusing to strike, for crossing a picket line or for initiating or inciting legal actions against the union

(b)   The right to inspect the union's accounting records

The **Employment Relations Act 1999** reinforced these rights.

*   Individuals not currently included in collective contracts can have these rights extended to them by decision of the Secretary of State for Trade and Industry.

*   Employees covered by a collective workplace agreement cannot be forced to sign an individual contract.

*   Blacklisting of, or discrimination against, trade union members is outlawed.

Activity 4	**(15 minutes)**

Why do you think the closed shop existed, and why was it abolished?

The law on strikes is discussed in Chapter 17. The Employment Relations Act 1999 also introduced major new provisions for statutory trade union recognition, the first time this has been subject to UK law. We will look at the implications for industrial relations.

2.6 Trade union recognition

Under the Employment Relations Act 1999, independent trade unions can apply in writing to an employer to be granted recognition. Recognition may be:

(a)   Voluntary, if a ballot (triggered by 10% union membership within the proposed bargaining unit) returned a 40% 'yes' vote, or

(b)   Automatic, if more than 50% (plus one person) of the bargaining unit are 'full and conscious' members of the union

If the union and the employer fail to reach agreement on recognition or on the conduct of collective bargaining, the Central Arbitration Committee (CAC) can make a ruling.

Initial reports from the CAC suggest that trade unions are using applications for statutory recognition as bargaining tools to win voluntary agreements from employers. Several hundred new recognition deals per year have been signed since 1999. High-profile 'scalps' include Virgin Atlantic, which after many years of refusal entered discussions on recognition with the pilots' union Balpa. The overwhelming majority of trade union agreements have been voluntary agreements for recognition, covering at least pay, hours and holidays.

There are also a small but significant number of non-traditional deals stipulating that bargaining should be conducted through company councils or staff forums, on which there may also be representation for union members. This usually happens where union recognition is added to existing consultation procedures: examples include Monarch Airlines' agreement with the AEEU and Eurotunnel's with the T&G.

> The proposition unions are putting to employers is different from what it was a generation ago. More are approaching companies with an offer that seeks to provide workforce representation in a way that's not necessarily going to make life disruptive for the employer. They are asking: "How can we work with you?" We've been surprised at the extent to which the voluntary approach seems to be the dominant one." *(People Management,* September 2000)

The ERA 1999 has since been reviewed, and changes announced in the Employment Relations Bill (December 2003). If enacted as it stands the bill will:

- Slightly adjust the procedure for obtaining statutory recognition in trade unions' favour (eg by providing better access and information rights)

- Simplify the procedure for industrial action ballots and allow postal votes for absent workers

- Protect employees taking official and lawfully organised industrial action: eg exempting 'lock-out' days from the 8 week protected period during which dismissals are automatically unfair (so that employers cannot simply prevent employees returning to work for 8 weeks).

Watch this space!

Industrial relations can be contentious, with both legitimate differences and ingrained prejudices on either side. We will now look briefly at the ideological framework underlying industrial relations.

3 THE IDEOLOGICAL FRAMEWORK

3.1 Unitary and pluralist frames of reference

Fox (1975) identified three broad ideologies which are involved in industrial relations.

(a) **Unitary ideology.** All members of the organisation, despite their different roles, have common objectives and values which unite their efforts. Workers are loyal, and the prerogative of management is accepted as paternal, and in everyone's best interests. Unions are a useful channel of communication, but are no longer strictly necessary: they can indeed be counterproductive in offering support to potentially disruptive elements.

> Any business must mould a true team and weld individual efforts into a common effort. Each member of the enterprise contributes something different, but they must all contribute towards a common goal. Their efforts must all pull in the same direction, without friction, without unnecessary duplication of effort.'

(Drucker, 1955)

(b) **Pluralist ideology.** Organisations are political coalitions of individuals and groups which have their own interests. Management has to create a workable structure for collaboration, taking into account the objectives of all the various interest groups or stakeholders in the organisation. A mutual survival strategy, involving the control of conflict through compromise, can be made acceptable in varying degrees to all concerned.

(c) **Radical ideology**. This primarily Marxist ideology argues that there is an inequality of power between the controllers of economic resources (shareholders and managers) and those who depend on access to those resources (wage earners). Those in power exploit the others by indoctrinating them to accept the legitimacy of their rights to power, and thus perpetuate the system. Conflict between these strata of society – the proletariat and the bourgeoisie – does not aim for mutual survival, but for revolutionary change: bringing down the system.

> The history of all societies hitherto is the history of class struggles. Freeman and slave, patrician and plebeian, lord and serf, guildmaster and journeyman, in a word, oppressor and oppressed, stood in constant opposition to one another, carried on an uninterrupted, now hidden, now open fight.

> (Marx and Engels, *The Communist Manifesto*, 1888)

3.2 Different stakeholder interests

'Them and us' attitudes have traditionally been ingrained in UK industry, partly because of class-consciousness. You should be aware that they are to an extent inevitable, given the tendency of people to draw boundaries round any group they are in. It should be remembered that there are different interest groups **within** both management and employees as well as **between** them. For example, there may be a clash of interests between HR managers aiming for the stability, quality and flexibility of the workforce, in accordance with ethical HR practice, and production operations managers aiming for immediate efficiency gains through 'lean production'. The interests of white-collar, craft and unskilled workers may clash over differentials, status and demarcation boundaries.

However, the root of union-management conflict, as we have seen, frequently lies in genuine inequities and artificial status distinctions. We have already discussed ways in which less divisive systems (such as single status agreements, salaried status for all grades and Japanese management practices) are available to emphasise a unitary rather than a pluralistic perspective.

According to Gennard and Judge (2003), 'the rationale for employee relations is to solve the problem that in a labour market the buyers (employers) and sellers (employees) have an endemic conflict of interests over the 'prices' at which they wish to exchange their services.' In this view, there is a perpetual trade off between what the employer wants (productivity, quality, functional flexibility, numerical flexibility and/or labour stability according to circumstance and so on) and what the employee wants in return (a certain level of pay and incentives, family-friendly policies, opportunities for development, job security and/or mobility according to circumstances and so on).

Employee relations therefore recognises differences (if not conflicts) of interest. Gennard and Judge quote a Recognition Procedural Agreement involving the Scottish Carpet Workers Union which includes the following general principles.

> The union recognises management's responsibility to plan, organise and manage the company's operation.

> The company recognises the union's responsibility to represent the interests of their [sic] members and to maintain or improve their terms and conditions of employment and work within the constraints imposed on the plant by corporate policy and finance.

3.3 Shared stakeholder interests

Trade unions have a vested interest in the success of the organisation to which their members belong because unless the organisation prospers, the job security, pay and benefits of their members will be compromised. Likewise, employers have a vested interest in the continuing commitment and welfare of employees, in order to maintain the viability of the business through the availability, quality and competitiveness of goods and services.

Sir Ken Jackson (*People Management*, September 2000) writes:

> It is clear that unions need to improve their ability to support their members. Our aim is to secure a better deal for them by adding value to their employers. We want to contribute to the success of the company by applying our representational talents with honesty, passion and industrial knowledge... It is only when managers are given intelligent, coherent criticism that they think through all the implications of their decisions. Equally, on many occasions, an informed union organisation will support managers' decisions and give them added credibility with the workforce.

3.4 Co-operation

According to the radical perspective, co-operation is merely collaboration in perpetuating oppression. According to the pluralist perspective, it is a negotiated process of mutual survival, taking into account the needs of the various stakeholders in the organisation. According to the unitary perspective, it is the natural mode of business relations and achieves greater productivity and satisfaction for all parties than conflict or competition. Whatever your opinion, it is worth bearing in mind the following points.

(a) Co-operation has a rational appeal. It is demonstrable that a suitable number of people co-operating on a task will achieve a better result than one person doing the same task (synergy may enable 2+2 to equal 5) and that groups of co-operating individuals have higher productivity than groups of competing individuals. *However*, it has also been demonstrated that this is not always the case: collaboration can adversely affect individual and group performance, because of group norms, the distraction of group maintenance processes and the tendency of cohesive groups to become blinkered, self-protecting and risky in their decision-making.

(b) Co-operation has an emotional appeal. It incorporates values about unity, teamwork, comradeship and belonging: as such, it is a useful cornerstone to the communication of corporate culture. *However*, Charles Handy (among others) has suggested that organisations are too quick to label and discourage differences, argument and competition as 'conflict': these are not only natural and inevitable (pluralist perspective) but potentially beneficial and fruitful (Handy, 1993).

(c) Co-operation is a common cultural value-cluster: collectivist cultures such as Japan and Sweden emphasise inter-dependence. *However*, individualist cultures such as the UK and USA value independence more highly.

Activity 5   **(15 minutes)**

How might conflict in the form of differences, argument and competition be beneficial and fruitful for an organisation?

4   EMPLOYEE RELATIONS

4.1   HRM and industrial relations

Guest (2001) described four possible orientations to industrial relations strategy as follows.

Figure 16.1: Guest's orientations for industries relations strategy

(a)   **The new realism: high emphasis on HRM and industrial relations**. Companies such as Rover, Nissan and Toshiba have initiated collaborative arrangements, extended consultation processes and moves towards single status, in order to facilitate greater flexibility, more multi-skilling, the removal of demarcations and improvements in quality.

(b)   **Traditional collectivism: emphasis on industrial relations without HRM**. Unions provide useful, well-established channels for communication and the handling of grievance/discipline/safety issues: it is easier to continue to operate a traditional pluralist industrial relations arrangement.

(c)   **Individualised HRM: emphasis on HRM without industrial relations**. This is an 'essentially piecemeal and opportunistic' approach which is only common among North-American firms.

(d)   **The black hole: no industrial relations.** HRM is not considered a policy priority for management, but neither is there seen to be a need for a traditional industrial relations system.

It has been argued that a thorough-going 'HRM' approach – with its unitary perspective and commitment-based strategies - renders the traditional 'industrial relations' approach irrelevant and marginalises the traditional roles of the trade union.

Activity 6   **(15 minutes)**

(a)   What are the features of relations in the 'industrial relations' model and the 'HRM' model (see Chapter 8 if necessary)?

(b)   What kinds of HRM policies, discussed in this Course Book, would reduce the perceived need for trade union representation?

At the TUC's 1994 conference, however, its HRM Taskforce reported that it found no direct relationship between HRM techniques and anti-unionism. In fact, HRM was most prevalent in unionised workplaces. Taskforce chair Bernadette Hillan said: 'If an employer is really trying to improve business performance, is committed to involving workers in the running of the organisation and is seeking to develop a real partnership with recognised trade unions, then HRM and collective bargaining can work in harmony.' She did, however, admit that some employers were using at least the language of HRM as an excuse to de-recognise unions.

The 2000 TUC conference was likewise told by its general secretary, John Monks, that: 'The most successful companies in the UK have the very best management practice, where unions are strong and working in partnership with management.'

FOR DISCUSSION

'One of the unsubstantiated myths in employee relations has been the idea that non-unionism is the panacea for business success, for which organisations such as Marks & Spencer and IBM are put forward as prime examples of the concept. There will always be a debate between those who see trade unions as a negative influence and those, like most of our European partners, who see rights at work (including trade union membership and collective bargaining) as part of an important social dimension to working relationships.

'Although the debate about unionism versus non-unionism continues, the real question tends to be ignored. That is – is it easier to manage with unions or without unions? …

'How many of the companies who yearn for non-union status would be prepared to make the investment in people management that the organisations that they envy have done?'

(Gennard & Judge, 2003)

Debate the issues raised here, justifying your views.

4.2 From 'industrial relations' to 'employee relations'

The Industrial Relations Services have identified four approaches to industrial relations (as cited by Armstrong, 2003).

(a) **Adversarial**: the organisation decides what it wants to do and employees are expected to fit in. Employees only exercise power by refusing to co-operate.

(b) **Traditional**: a good day-to-day working relationship, but management proposes and the workforce reacts through its elected representatives.

(c) **Partnership**: the organisation involves employees in the drawing up and execution of organisation policies, but retains the right to manage.

(d) **Power sharing**: employees are involved in both day-to-day and strategic decision-making.

Definition

Employee relations 'consist of all those areas of HRM that involve general relationships with employees, through collective agreements where trade unions are recognised [industrial relations] **and/or** through commonly applied policies for employee involvement and communications.' (Armstrong, 2000)

According to Armstrong, employee relations strategy will be concerned with how to:

(a) Build **stable and co-operative relationships** with employees that minimise conflict

(b) Achieve **commitment** through employee involvement and communications processes

(c) Develop **mutuality** – a common interest in achieving the organisation's goals through the development of organisational cultures based on shared values between management and employees

He suggests that such strategies will result in the following kinds of policies.

(a) Changing forms of recognition, including single union recognition or de-recognition

(b) New bargaining structures, including decentralisation or single-table bargaining (discussed in Chapter 17)

(c) The achievement of increased levels of commitment through involvement or participation – giving employees a voice

(d) Deliberately by-passing trade union representatives to communicate directly with employees

(e) Increasing the extent to which management controls operations in such areas as flexibility

(f) Generally improving the employee relations climate in order to produce more harmonious and co-operative relationships

(g) Developing a 'partnership' with trade unions (discussed in Chapter 18), recognising that employees are stakeholders and that it is to the advantage of both parties to work together

EXAMPLE 1

Strike Free: New Industrial Relations in Britain by Philip Bassett (1986) illustrated the height of the 'anti-union' phase of HRM in the UK. The following was the experience of the (then) leading-edge computer company, IBM.

Company management attribute the good employee relations to IBM's belief in respect for the individual. One aspect of this philosophy is that IBM does not recognise trade unions for collective bargaining purposes. To do so, they believe, would imply that without trade unions employees' interests would be neglected. Management are convinced that the company's record disproves such a belief.

IBM does not discourage its employees from becoming members of trade unions, but very few of them do so. Even of those who do, a significant minority are against collective bargaining. Pay in IBM is not a collective matter for employees; instead, the company conducts its own confidential survey of comparable companies and determines salary ranges centrally. There is scope for line managers to recommend increases for specific individuals based on merit.

The other traditional function of trade unions at plant level is to assist their members over the hurdles of the employer's grievance system. IBM believe that their own internal complaints procedures, which allow an individual to take a grievance to the very highest levels of management, remove the need for any union involvement.

Other companies, looking at IBM's industrially harmonious, strike-free, non-union record, have asked how they could emulate it. The answer given by a former personnel director of the company is simple: 'You start 30 years ago.'

NOTES

EXAMPLE 2

Canadian-owned Sheerness Steel, Kent, is the first company in its industry to have de-recognised unions, led by the Iron and Steel Trades Confederation (ISTC), as part of a change to a single status company. According to the personnel director: "We have become a single status company with personal contracts, salaries, performance-related pay and no defined jobs – people do whatever they are trained to do. We realised that we no longer had anything to debate or discuss with the unions and that they were no longer necessary."

However, according to the ISTC, the workforce is not happy. Local conditions of high unemployment "had made it difficult for members to withstand company pressure to take personal contracts". The change to salaried work means that employees have lost overtime payments which, according to the ISTC, has severely affected their earnings. On the other hand, many of the old disciplinary problems, such as being late, are no longer a problem: just as well, perhaps, since the unions are no longer even allowed to represent individual members in disciplinary cases…"

(*Personnel Management Plus*, September 1992)

FOR DISCUSSION

Do the examples cited above reflect an HRM approach to employee relations?

Chapter roundup

- Industrial relations comprises all the rules, practices and conventions governing interactions between managements and their workforces, normally involving collective employee representation and bargaining.

- Employee relations consist of all these areas of HRM that involve general relationships with employees, including industrial relations and employee involvement and communication.

- The stakeholders in industrial relations include: management and/or employers' associations, worker representatives (trade unions, staff associations or other forms of representation) and third parties, such as ACAS, Employment Tribunals and a range of non-government organisations.

- Trade unions may be craft/occupational, general or industrial. After a period of declining membership (accelerated by HRM policies, the decline of manufacturing and Conservative government policy) the political climate and statutory recognition laws (Employment Relations Act 1999) have shown an upswing in unionism.

- There are three basic perspectives on industrial relations: unitary, pluralist and radical.

Quick quiz

1 What is an independent trade union?

2 What are the purposes of employers' associations?

3 How might wider society be involved in employee relations in a firm?

4 Distinguish between craft, industrial and general unions.

5 What is a shop steward?

6 Give four reasons for the recent turnaround in the number of workers covered by union recognition agreements.

7 What was the closed shop and what happened to it?

8 Distinguish between the unitary and pluralist frames of reference.

9 In what ways might management and workers be said to have:

(a) Different interests, and
(b) Common interests

10 Outline Guest's four orientations to industrial relations strategy.

Answers to quick quiz

1 One which has been certified as being autonomous and financially self-supporting, not dominated by an employer. (see paragraph 1.2)

2 To give help and advice on employee relations issues; to represent members views to political influencers; to assist in dispute resolution; to negotiate sectoral agreements. (para 1.3)

3 Through pressure groups seeking to oppose exploitative labour relations. In a wider sense, in demanding corporate social responsibility.
(para 1.5)

4 Craft unions recruit employees who perform certain jobs. Industrial unions recruit all grades of employees in a particular industry. General unions organise workers from a variety of different jobs and industries.
(para 2.1)

5 A workplace union representative: the link between the work group, union officials and management. (para 2.2)

6 Statutory recognition (Employment Relations Act 1999); Labour government support for partnership; recognition of unions as a useful and efficient mechanism for employee relations; increasing recruitment, supported by single union and partnership agreements. (para 2.3)

7 An employee had to be a member of a particular union to secure or retain employment. The closed shop was stripped of legal support: dismissal for non-membership was made automatically unfair, selection on membership discriminatory and industrial action in support of a closed shop unlawful. (para 2.5)

8 Unitary: all members of the organisation, despite their different roles, have common interests and objectives which unites their efforts. The management prerogative is recognised as being in everyone's best interests.

Pluralist: organisations are political coalitions of individuals and groups which inevitably have their own interests. Management has to take into account the objectives of all the various stakeholders in the organisation, to develop a strategy of mutual compromise and survival. (para 3.1)

9 Basically, differences arise from the labour market: trading off the objectives of buyers (management) and sellers (workers) of labour. Common interests arise from both sides' vested interest in the survival and prosperity of the organisation.
(See paragraphs 3.2, 3.3 for a full account.)

10 New realism: high emphasis on HRM and industrial relations eg through partnership agreements.

Traditional collectivism: emphasis on industrial relations without HRM eg through collective bargaining.

Individualised HRM: HRM without industrial relations eg through individual contracts.

Black hole: no HRM or industrial relations eg authoritarian management.

(para 4.1)

Answers to activities

1 (a) Lobbying politicians to obtain legislation to improve conditions of work (eg the minimum wage)

   (b) Developing political affiliations with other trade unions, to create a power base for achieving political influence

   (c) Providing financial support for a sympathetic political party (traditionally, the Labour Party)

   (d) Establishing non-negotiatory processes for sharing management decision-making: eg by joint consultative committees or partnership agreements.

   (e) Providing welfare help and support for members: funding during industrial action, say.

2 (a) Conciliation (getting conflicting parties together for informal discussion to resolve a dispute)

   (b) Mediation (providing a mediator or mediation board, which hears arguments and makes proposals and recommendations as a basis for settlement)

   (c) Arbitration (assisting in the appointment of independent arbitrators who make a binding ruling)

3 Size is a variable insignificant in itself: size as a proportion of potential membership may be a more significant factor in determining the credibility of the union. The threat of industrial action even by a large union would be hollow if its membership represented a very small proportion of workers in the relevant organisation or sector. A union which is small in terms of membership numbers may have a very strong negotiating position if its members are of an occupational category which is significant to the organisation or national life (eg nurses, firemen).

4 The closed shop was encouraged by unions as a means of increasing their membership and bargaining power within a company. It was supported by some managements as a way of facilitating single-union agreements. Closed shops were criticised for interfering with individual rights of choice; constraining management decision-making on recruitment and retention; and strengthening the bargaining power of unions to the detriment of industrial relations.

5 (a) Differences allow for diversity of talents, viewpoints, ideas: necessary for innovation, problem-solving, understanding human dynamics, flexibility. Differences reflect the diversity of the customer base: conformity may blinker the organisation to potential needs or problems. Suppression of diversity may cause stress and resentment.

   (b) Argument is useful to clear the air, help divergent viewpoints to emerge, encourage empathy with different viewpoints: extremely helpful in conflict resolution, in change management (bringing resistance into the open), in encouraging emotional intelligence.

(c)   Controlled competition between teams has been demonstrated to increase team cohesion/co-operation and motivation and improve performance. Competition tied to incentives is a powerful energiser of performance (particularly in individualistic cultures).

6   (a)   IR = low trust, collectivist, pluralist. HRM = high trust, individualist, unitarist.

    (b)   Examples include: direct voluntary communication and consultation on matters which will affect employees; worker involvement techniques; fair, consistent and transparent discipline and grievance handling; equitable and non-discriminatory recruitment, selection, appraisal and reward systems; health, safety and welfare policies clearly aimed at problem-solving and worker protection; programmes at improving the work environment; flexible remuneration packages (such as cafeteria benefits) encouraging individual aspirations and priorities.

Assignment 16   **(1½ hours)**

Select an organisation of your choice and use your research skills and/or contacts to access the following information.

(a)   Whether the organisation is represented by an employer's association. If so, which one? What is its function, and what does the organisation's involvement with it consist of? What reports of the employer's association activities are available?

(b)   Whether the organisation recognises one or more trade unions for the purposes of collective bargaining and consultation. What is the nature and scope of this recognition? What are the roles of trade union officials in the organisation and what is the nature of their relationship with (a) HR, (b) senior and (c) line management?

(c)   What other stakeholders (if any) are involved in employee relations processes in the organisation?

(d)   What is the orientation of the organisation to industrial relations? If it is not unionised, how does it go about maintaining communication with employees? How does it handle collective grievances? How does it establish felt-fair pay and conditions? If it is unionised, how does it regard its relationship with unions?

(e)   What potential problems can you identify (if any) in the organisation's industrial relations culture and practice?

Chapter 17:
INDUSTRIAL RELATIONS PROCESSES

Introduction

In this chapter we explore some of the key processes in industrial relations: collective bargaining, and the related strategies and skills of negotiation and the management of industrial disputes.

In each of these areas, we will see signs of the shift towards a unitarist perspective discussed in Chapter 16, while at the same time recognising the differing interests of stakeholders in the organisation. Even industrial conflict must be managed in the context of an on-going relationship. This perspective is typified in the various measures taken to involve employees in decision-making, under the general banner of 'participation' and 'involvement': it will be covered in Chapter 18.

Your objectives

In this chapter you will learn about the following.

    (a)   Different types of collective dispute

    (b)   Dispute procedures and the resolution of conflict

    (c)   The nature and scope of collective bargaining

    (d)   Negotiation processes and strategy

1 INDUSTRIAL CONFLICT

1.1 Types of collective dispute

Individual disputes against employers are covered by disciplinary and grievance procedures (see Chapter 6): note that under the Employment Relations Act 1999, employees are entitled to be accompanied by a colleague or trade union representative in procedures concerning 'serious issues'. A trade union may get involved in an individual case where a principle of workers' rights is involved.

We have already seen in Chapter 16 that there are deep-rooted ideologies of conflict embedded in industrial relations in the UK. Collective disputes typically involve pay, conditions of employment, job security or breach of contracts and negotiated agreements.

According to the Employment Act 1982, a 'lawful trade dispute' is one between workers and their own employers, wholly or mainly about work related matters, and *not:*

- Demarcation and other inter-union disputes
- Disputes between workers and employers other than their own
- Disputes other than those mainly connected with pay and conditions or
- Disputes overseas

1.2 Industrial action

Industrial action in pursuance of a dispute may take a number of forms (discussed below), but are classified on four basic dimensions.

(a) **Official** action is supported by the trade union representatives of the employees in dispute, and conducted according to union procedure, including secret balloting of members.

(b) **Unofficial** action is taken by a part of the workforce without recognition and support from union officials and without balloting and approval procedures.

(c) **Primary** action is aimed at the employer with whom the participating union is in dispute.

(d) **Secondary** action is aimed at employers who trade with firms in dispute, but who are not directly involved in the dispute themselves.

Activity 1   **(15 minutes)**

What do you think might be the purpose of threatening or implementing industrial action?

EXAMPLE

In September 2003, members of the Communication Workers Union (CWU) voted against a national strike against Royal Mail by a narrow majority of 50.9% to 49.1%. Strike action was thought to have been inevitable. Why did the workers vote 'No'?

'The most likely explanation is that, aided by an intensive communications strategy implemented by chairman Allan Leighton and Tony McCarthy, head of human resources, workers decided they could work with the pay deal, which offered a productivity-linked 14.5 per cent pay rise.

'One Royal Mail worker told *PM:* "I think the fact that Royal Mail kept repeating the main points of the deal helped. It drove home to me that it's a fair amount of extra money for just a few minor changes in working practices."

'Importantly, unlike in previous disputes, Leighton and McCarthy focused on involving local management and keeping them fully informed of the pay proposal. Since local managers better understood the situation, they were more inclined – and more able – to convince workers of how the pay deal would benefit them.'

(Roberts, 2003 (g))

[Note: despite the 'No' vote, Royal Mail workers in London subsequently staged a series of 24-hour strikes over the London weighting allowance.]

Definition

> **Strike action** is the withholding of labour in the course of a dispute with management

Various forms of primary industrial action by union members (in order of severity) include the following.

(a)   *Withdrawal of co-operation* by the union (eg refusal to participate in disciplinary procedures).

(b)   *Insistence on formal rights* by the union (eg raising trivial infringements as grievance issues, insistence on taking time off or limiting overtime, where there would normally be informal flexibility).

(c)   A *work-to-rule or go-slow:* employees follow official work procedures and rules to the letter, thereby reducing productivity without doing anything to justify disciplinary action by management. This also highlights the extent to which management take for granted the commitment and voluntary contribution of employees.

(d)   A *ban on overtime* and weekend working to restrict productivity, often highlighting issues of work organisation.

(e)   A *token withdrawal of labour:* for example, a one-day strike by the union membership in the workforce, as a protest against management's unwillingness to make further concessions in negotiation. These may be repeated over a period of time, in order to provide a recurring disruption to the organisation's operations without a complete loss of pay: 24-hour strikes by Royal Mail workers in 2003 is one example.

(f)   *Indefinite strike action* by the entire union membership in the workforce, either at national level, company level or plant level: the 1984 miners' strike is a historic example.

(g)   *Picketing:* striking workers maintain a presence outside the employer's premises (a 'picket line'). The aim of the picket line is to highlight the protest and to inform and solicit the support of workers attempting to enter the workplace. In practice, this often takes the form of active discouragement and intimidation of strike-breakers, replacement workers and others. The Employment Act 1982 protects unions and their members against most civil and criminal actions 'in contemplation or furtherance of a trade dispute', including picketing at or near the place of work with a purpose that is 'peacefully to obtain or communicate information, or peacefully to persuade a person to work or not to work'. Secondary picketing (of organisations not involved in the dispute) is not protected, however.

Activity 2 **(5 minutes)**

What are the corresponding 'industrial sanctions' which might be used by management in furtherance of an industrial dispute? Why might these be used as a 'last resort'?

The *threat* of applying industrial sanctions may be sufficient to make either or both of the parties adjust their position in a dispute, it being in the interests of neither party to incur the heavy costs of such sanctions – particularly if there is unlikely to be a successful outcome.

1.3 Statistics on strikes

Official statistics on the use of industrial sanctions in the UK only cover strikes. They measure:

(a) The frequency (number) of strikes

(b) The size of strikes (that is, the number of workers involved)

(c) The duration of strikes (that is, the number of working days lost) – since this figure on its own may give a distorted impression if there are a few very long strikes. For example, the 1984 miners' strike accounted for 83% of the total number of working days lost to strikes in that year!

All three measures peaked in 1979 (2,125 stoppages in progress, 4.6 million workers involved, and 29.4 million working days lost – of which 54% were accounted for by a strike of engineering workers). All three measures have since been steadily falling.

- In the year 2000, there were 212 stoppages, involving 182,000 workers and a loss of 499,000 lost working days.

- In 2001, there were 194 stoppages, involving 167,000 workers and a loss of 525,000 working days.

(Labour Market Trends)

However:

- In 2002-2003, the number of companies hit by strike action *doubled* to 22%, according to a poll by law firm DLA (*People Management*, 11 September 2003). Key causes of strikes were pay, working conditions and job security, with disputes over pensions on the rise. The survey identified managerial fears of industrial unrest and union militancy. HR practitioners, however, stressed that a more educated and informed workforce should expect greater levels of involvement – and that this is bound to cause some dispute, especially with line managers unaccustomed to consultation.

- As noted earlier there has also been a marked increase in the number of complaints made to Employment Tribunals in the wake of new employment legislation. *Individual* disputes also suggest shortcomings in employee relations!

1.4 The law on strikes

Relevant provisions include the following.

(a) Official industrial action requires the secret balloting of all affected members. Seven days' notice must be given to an employer of a union's intention to ballot its members on industrial action. The Employment Relations Act 1999 makes it harder for employers to challenge strike ballots, by giving the courts greater scope to disregard 'small accidental failures' in the organisation of ballots. It also clarifies the guidelines on balloting and allows the validity of a ballot to be extended by up to four weeks (if the union and employer agree) to give time for negotiations to continue.

(b) In the course of a lawful and duly balloted trade dispute, the trade union, its officials and participants in the dispute are immune from legal action. However, members of the public have the right to apply for a court order restraining a union from taking **unlawful** industrial action.

(c) Picketing carries legal immunity only if the pickets consist of employees who normally work at the premises, former employees (if the dispute concerns their termination), and employees who have no fixed place of work or who cannot picket their own place of work (and who therefore picket the premises from which their work is administered). Picketing solely to obtain or communicate information is not unlawful, but may become so if it involves obstruction of the public highway or breach of the peace. Secondary action of any kind is unlawful.

(d) An individual may not be unjustifiably disciplined by a union (eg by fines, expulsion, withdrawal of benefits or blacklisting) for refusing to strike, refusal to go slow if by so doing (s)he would be in breach of contract, or for crossing a picket line.

(e) It is unlawful to dismiss strikers for the first eight weeks of a strike: dismissal of workers during unofficial strike or other industrial action was previously excluded altogether from the statutory 'unfair dismissal' code.

EXAMPLE

'The 250 British Airways staff who staged an unofficial walkout [in July 2003] certainly achieved the profile they would have wished for.

'The dispute provoked furore among customers left stranded at Heathrow airport, cost BA £40 million and also marked the beginning of days of deadlock in talks between management and staff.

'Many have been unsympathetic to the reason for the strike, which centred around the introduction of an electronic clocking-in system.

'While members of the public remained largely indifferent, some fellow colleagues described it as a 'piffling issue'.

'But analysts and experts have warned the significance of this strike should not be undermined. What is critical, they have said, is that in this era of partnership working and general lack of rebellion, staff reached a point of such desperation they were willing to take the drastic action of staging a strike without their unions' backing. It demonstrates the severity of the breakdown in relations between management and staff. ...

'Mike Emmott, the CIPD's head of employee relations, agrees that this raises questions about people management practices at BA.

' 'Workers do not take such drastic action as to walk out when they feel that they have trust in their management, when they feel listened to and when they feel that their best interests are at heart,' he says.

' 'Management has been saying that the scheme is simply about turning the paper-based system into an electronic one and that the workforce should trust them, but the simple fact is that the workforce doesn't believe them,' he adds.

(Watkins, 2003 (d))

1.5 No strike agreements

The 'right to strike' in enshrined in employment law. However, no-strike agreements may be made by voluntary agreement between employers and unions. The Trade Union and Labour Relations Act 1974 states that a no-strike clause in a collective agreement can only be made part of individual contracts of employment when the agreement provides expressly and in writing for its inclusion, and when the agreement is made reasonably accessible to employees at the workplace.

No-strike clauses effectively deprive union negotiators of the threat of strike action in the event of breakdown in bargaining, and arguably deprive workers of one of their only sources of power in the employment relationship. They therefore tend to be attached to collective agreements which support the managerial prerogative, such as single-union and partnership agreements. They also tend to be accompanied by pendulum arbitration facilities (see above), giving employees some scope for redress.

FOR DISCUSSION

Do you think certain categories of worker should be deprived of the right to strike, in the national interest? If so, which? (Think of times when your own life was disrupted by strike action.)

Having seen how industrial disputes arise, we will now consider how they may be resolved.

2 DISPUTE RESOLUTION PROCEDURES

2.1 Dispute procedures

Detailed procedural agreements on disputes are generally made during collective bargaining or other (non-union) negotiated agreements. A typical dispute procedure would provide for the 'escalating' involvement of more senior representatives of both sides, with a guarantee of new industrial action until all stages have been followed through.

(a) Meeting of union representative and middle management

(b) Meeting of district union officer and senior management

(c) Meeting of regional and then national officials of the union and employers' association (in national disputes)

(d)   Conciliation (if required)

(e)   Mediation (if required)

(f)   Agreement to abide by the decision of an independent arbitrator (as a last resort, since the decision then passes out of the hands of the parties involved)

If dispute procedures fail to re-open negotiation or resolve conflict, the parties may consider calling in ACAS to offer the services of conciliation, mediation and arbitration.

2.2   The role of ACAS

Conciliation is a voluntary process of discussion, facilitated by ACAS conciliators whose role is to make constructive suggestions, provide information and manage the process. At this stage, ACAS has no power to impose or recommend settlements. ACAS will only agree to conciliate where internal dispute resolution procedures have been exhausted without result. The conciliation process typically involves:

(a)   Fact-finding, to explore the reasons for the dispute, often through separate meetings of the conciliator with each side.

(b)   Explanation of each side's position in joint meetings, often facilitated by side meetings between the conciliator and the parties separately, to encourage parties to keep talking and to consider potential areas of movement towards settlement (which parties may not wish to consider openly in full session at first).

(c)   Negotiation towards a mutually acceptable position, finalised in a joint agreement between the two sides.

If a voluntary settlement is not reached through conciliation, ACAS can arrange for *mediation*. This involves the appointment of an independent person or Board of Mediation, who will consider the case of both sides (set out in writing) and then hear both sides' evidence and arguments at a hearing. The mediator makes a formal proposal or recommendation as a basis for settlement of the dispute, but this is not legally binding on either party.

If both parties agree to *arbitration*:

(a)   Terms of reference must be defined, setting limits to the arbitrator's powers and to the issues to be considered: traditional arbitration or pendulum arbitration (see above) may be used.

(b)   Parties may select the independent arbitrator from the ACAS panel, or may let ACAS appoint an arbitrator.

(c)   A date and venue are set for the arbitration hearing. Prior to the hearing, both sides exchange and submit to the arbitrator a written statement of their case and arguments, supporting documents, and a list of those attending (usually the negotiators). The arbitrator may also request a site visit, for example if the dispute concerns the conditions under which work is done or the level of skill required.

(d)   An informal, private and confidential hearing is held, at which the arbitrator hears arguments from both sides. A typical procedure would allow each side an uninterrupted opportunity to state its case and critique the opposing case (as set out in the written submission), prior to questioning by the other side and by the arbitrator. The arbitrator then ensures that both parties have said or asked everything they wish to, and invites closing statements.

(e)   The arbitrator considers the arguments after the hearing and delivers an award via ACAS, usually within two to three weeks.

In 2000/2, the ACAS Annual Report showed 1,226 completed collective conciliations, 5 successful mediations and 55 arbitration hearings.

FOR DISCUSSION

Why might employers and trade unions regard arbitration as a little-used instrument of last resort?

What more effective ways might each seek to resolve disputes?

2.3   Conflict resolution techniques

The rationale behind the collaborative approach is explored in the win-win model of conflict resolution. Cornelius and Faire (1989) suggest that there are three basic ways in which a conflict or disagreement can be worked out.

(a)   *Win-lose*: one party gets what he wants at the expense of the other party. However well justified such a solution is, there is often lingering resentment on the part of the 'losing' party, which may begin to damage working relationships.

(b)   *Lose-lose:* neither party gets what he really wants. Compromise comes into this category. However logical such a solution is, there is often resentment and dissatisfaction on both sides: even positive compromises only result in half-satisfied needs.

(c)   *Win-win:* both parties get as close as possible to what they really want. Whether or not such an outcome is possible, the attempt to find it invariably generates more options, more creative and collaborative problem-solving, more open communication and a greater likelihood of preserved working relationships.

A basic win-win approach may be outlined as follows.

(a)   **Find out why each party *needs* what they say they *want*.** Probing for, and mapping, both party's fears/concerns and needs in the situation facilitates meaningful problem-solving. It also encourages communication, supports other people's values, and separates the problem from the personalities involved.

(b)   **Find out where the differences dovetail.** Diverging needs may seem like the cause of conflict – but they also offer potential for more creative problem-solving, since the different needs may not be mutually exclusive: there may be opportunities for both sets of needs to be satisfied by different means.

(c)   **Design more options,** where everyone gets more of what they need. Techniques for doing this include:

(i)   Brainstorming, which temporarily (and by agreement) allows the generation of options temporarily *uncensored* and *uncriticised* by viewpoints which by definition are limited by the conflict;

(ii)   Chunking (breaking a big problem down into manageable chunks and seeking solutions to each); and

(iii)   Devising usable 'currencies' (suggestions and concessions which are easy or low-cost for both parties, and can be traded in negotiation). The aim is *mutual gain*.

   (d)   **Co-operate**. Treat the other person as a partner in problem-solving, not as an opponent in competition.

The example given (Cornelius and Faire, 1989, p. 19) is of two men fighting because they both want an orange. The win-win approach would ask each man why he *needs* the orange. One may need it to make orange juice, while the other needs only the skin of the orange to make candied peel: the conflict disappears. If both men need the juice, other options will be explored: sharing the juice; getting more oranges; diluting the juice; buying one man some bottled orange juice and so on. Even if compromise is settled on, the outcome will be a win-win, because both parties will have been **appropriately assertive** and **willingly co-operative**, enhancing the relationship between them (which adds to the 'win' outcome).

EXAMPLE

Dispute resolution procedure: the British Airways walkout

18 July	250 BA staff take part in unofficial walkout after BA announces it is to introduce an electronic swipe-card system.
19 July	Staff return after unions announce talks with BA.
23 July	Talks break down, with unions accusing BA of 'failing to move an inch'.
24 July	GMB and Amicus say that they will ballot staff over strike action.
26 July	Talks resume at conciliation service ACAS after BA chief executive Rod Eddington agrees to attend the talks.
28 July	TUC joins the talks in a 'peace broker' role.
31 July	Unions say the dispute has been resolved, after BA agrees to make scheme voluntary until September, and to separate the issue from ongoing pay negotiations.

(Watkins, 2003 (d))

Activity 3   **(30 minutes)**

From the elements, timetable and result listed in the above example, how successful do you think this dispute resolution was?

2.4   Coping with industrial action

While managerial focus is likely to be on avoiding industrial action, through dispute resolution procedures and the threat of sanctions, there should be contingency plans in place to minimise the disruptions caused by industrial action if and when it occurs.

Depending on the nature of the business, and the group of workers involved, key considerations may be:

(a)   *To maintain incoming deliveries* of materials and supplies: eg for a retail organisation, or a factory threatened with picketing.

(b)   *To maintain production output or service levels:* eg by finding suitable alternative labour (transfers of staff from other sites, or jobs, use of short-contract and casual staff), or re-organising and prioritising(using up existing overstocks, transferring stock from other plans, transferring production to other plants, encouraging overtime working prior to strike).

(c)   *To maintain supply of goods and services to the customer:* eg through picket lines, by subcontracting distribution, or encouraging customer self-service.

3   COLLECTIVE BARGAINING

3.1   The nature and scope of collective bargaining

Definition

Collective bargaining is the process whereby employers and employee representatives negotiate agreements by which terms and conditions of employment (and related matters) are determined for groups of represented employees.

Collective bargaining is basically concerned with reaching two types of agreement.

(a)   *Substantive agreements*, which determine the terms and conditions of employment. A substantive agreement between a union and employer might cover areas such as: rates of pay for various categories of worker; premium rates of pay; working hours, breaks and holidays; benefits; access to training programmes and so on.

(b)   *Procedural agreements*, which determine the methods and procedures for:

   (i)   Arriving at substantive agreements. (What negotiating machinery should be set up? Should a particular issue be discussed at national level, company level, local plant/branch level – or not at all?)

   (ii)   Settling any disagreements or disputes which cannot be resolved by normal negotiation. There might be arrangements to refer disputes at plant level to regional or national level, or to arbitration. Procedural rules would determine what the arbitration arrangements should be (eg involving ACAS).

   In practice, there are likely to be a range of procedural arrangements and agreements, in areas such as: employee grievances; disciplinary action; redundancy; health and safety; staff development; pay grading; union recognition and so on. Procedural arrangements and agreements basically provide 'law and order' in the workplace: a definition of fair and reasonable behaviour by employers, and the rights and obligations of employees, in a given set of circumstances.

A '*workforce agreement*' is a new arrangement, under the Working Time Regulations (1998), which allows employers to fix working-time arrangements with workers who do not have collectively-agreed terms or conditions. This allows flexibility in taking account of the needs of local workforces or workgroups in applying the regulations.

Note that non-unionised, as well as unionised, organisations have substantive and procedural arrangements (pay grades, dispute procedures etc) in place: employers may (or may not) have drawn these up in consultation with workers.

Gennard & Judge (2003) note that even the outcome of collective bargaining is not, in practice, confined to union members.

(a) Unionised companies apply collectively-bargained terms and conditions to non-union staff as well.

(b) Non-unionised companies partly determine their terms and conditions with regard to market rates – which take into account collectively-bargained terms elsewhere.

The Workplace Employment Relations Survey (1998) shows that the overall proportion of employees covered by collective bargaining is 41% (63% in the public sector); this represents a large decline from equivalent figures of 54% (80%) in 1990. Over the UK economy as a whole, 30% of employees had their pay determined unilaterally by management, and more than 70% had their pay determined by methods not involving collective bargaining (Gennard & Judge, 2003).

3.2 Levels and parties in collective bargaining

Collective bargaining may take place at different levels.

(a) Some issues are discussed at national (or *multi-employer*) level, between *representatives of employers* for the industry or sector and *national trade union officials*. In France, Holland, Italy, Sweden, Finland, Belgium and Spain, for example, sectoral collective agreements are common. These may provide only a basic outline and floor of conditions (for example, minimum rates of pay, maximum weekly and overtime hours, paid holiday entitlements) which trade unions expect to elaborate and improve through *company-level* agreements.

(b) Other issues will be settled at *company level*, by *representatives of management* and the *unions or staff associations* recognised by the company. Ford, for example, have their own company-wide pay agreements, and do not join in national negotiations with an employers' federation. This allows pay and conditions to be related to the economic and competitive circumstances, and internal equity considerations, of the particular firm.

(c) Other issues will be settled at more local level by 'domestic' (or enterprise) bargaining, involving representatives of *plant or business unit management* and *local shop stewards*. Phillips Electronics in the UK, for example, has abandoned its national bargaining structure in favour of plant by plant negotiations. This reflects the decentralisation of industrial relations (among other HRM functions) within organisations. Enterprise bargaining may be autonomous, or co-ordinated across all plans/unit, by taking place within centrally-set parameters.

Decentralised bargaining has increased in recent years, because it provides greater flexibility than national agreements. This applies both to the employer (allowing for greater labour flexibility by tailoring work rules and pay agreements to the needs of specific plants) and to the employee (reflecting the desire for more direct influence in employment terms and conditions, which has created a further trend towards individualised contracts). It is also more easily changed, if necessary, because there is less (and more accessible) negotiating machinery. This relative flexibility may have drawbacks, however, if it results in fragmented and inequitable pay structures, inflationary 'leapfrogging' of settlements, and freedom to break or re-negotiate agreements at will. It also relies on competent negotiations by plant-level management.

3.3 Single-table bargaining

Definition

> **Single-table bargaining** describes a situation in which the terms and conditions of all represented workers employed by an establishment are determined in a single set of negotiations. This could involve a single union representing different types and grades of employees (manual and non-manual), or several unions which negotiate a bargaining position amongst themselves prior to negotiating with management as a single bargaining unit.

> **Activity 4** **(45 minutes)**
>
> What would you anticipate to be the advantages and disadvantages of single-table bargaining?

Beardwell and Holden (1997) argue that the significance of single-table bargaining is not primarily its advantages in simplifying and integrating bargaining processes, but the opportunity to extend consultation beyond the basic negotiation forum, to include matters which affect all employees: training and development, fringe benefits, the future direction of the business, change management and so on.

We will be covering employee consultation in Chapter 18, but you should be aware that trade unions recognised for the purpose of collective bargaining are entitled to certain information.

3.4 Disclosure of information

An employer must provide information in response to a written request by a union representative, as long as:

(a) It relates to his (or an associated employer's) undertaking

(b) It is in his possession

(c) It is in accordance with good practice (as laid down in an ACAS Code of Practice)

(d) Lack of the information would materially impede the representative in collective bargaining

The ACAS Code of Practice recommends that information should be disclosed on pay and benefits, conditions of service, human resources, performance (eg productivity, sales/order forecasts) and financial matters. It suggests that unions should define and request the information before negotiations begin, stating why they consider it relevant. A union may apply to the Central Arbitration Committee if it believes disclosable information has been withheld. If an employer refuses to comply with a Committee declaration that information should be disclosed, the CAC may make an enforceable award of terms and conditions, at the request of the trade union.

There is no obligation to give information relating to:

(a)   Information given in confidence

(b)   Information relating to particular individuals

(c)   Information which – in any context other than collective bargaining – would cause injury to the undertaking

(d)   Information protected by statute (say, in the interests of national security) or subject to legal proceedings

3.5   Attitudes to collective bargaining

Chamberlain and Kuhn (1965) traced a historical development in attitudes towards collective bargaining.

(a)   At first, there was a **marketing theory**, in which collective bargaining was seen as pay bargaining for the supply of labour. Rates of pay would be settled on the basis of supply and demand.

(b)   Later, a **governmental (or control) theory** developed. Collective bargaining was seen as a way of making rules of conduct and enforcing those rules in addition to pay bargaining.

(c)   Finally, a **managerial theory** emerged, on the basis that decisions about matters in which both management and employees have a vital interest should be discussed and decided by collective negotiation.

A greater range of matters theoretically now come within the sphere of collective bargaining arrangements. Negotiations might cover not only pay, conditions of employment (holidays, hours of work etc) and demarcation lines, but also promotion and training opportunities, fringe benefits, health and safety, equal opportunities and so on. In practice, the Workplace Employee Relations surveys suggest that the number of non-pay items subject to collective bargaining has actually fallen in the private sector.

As we saw in Chapter 16 on union recognition, a managerial approach to collective bargaining is arguably a systematic, efficient, relationship-building and equitable method of conducting industrial relations. It encourages a collectivist orientation which is suited to some cultures of employment and may encourage teamworking and identification with the organisation in others.

Activity 5   **(20 minutes)**

There has been a decline in collective bargaining in recent decades. From what you know of the development of trade unionism during this period, why might this be so?

3.6   The status of collective agreements

In most democratic societies, collective agreements are legally binding: if either party breaks the terms of the agreement, the other can pursue its rights through the courts. This is not the case in the UK! UK collective agreements are only binding in 'honour'. This means that agreements are generally not as comprehensive or precise as legal contracts; they are often reviewed and renegotiated annually. It is, however, important to have rigorous procedural arrangements in place, to define acceptable behaviour and dispute/appeal mechanisms.

4   NEGOTIATION

Definition

> **Negotiation** is a process whereby two parties come together to confer with a view to concluding a jointly acceptable agreement.

4.1   The purpose of negotiation

The general purpose of such a process is for interest groups to attempt to resolve differences between and within themselves, in order to *maintain co-operation* in the pursuit of shared or superordinate goals. Such an approach may be applied in a number of different situations, including collective (and individual) bargaining, conflict resolution and group decision making. Negotiation is basically a *problem-solving technique*, enabling parties to meet their own needs (as far as possible) without breaking the relationship or co-operation between them. This is obviously essential where management and workers are concerned!

Gennard & Judge (2003) suggest that this process requires:

- **Purposeful persuasion**: whereby each party attempts to persuade the other to accept its case by marshalling arguments, backed by factual information and analysis.

- **Constructive compromise**: whereby both parties accept the need to move closer towards each other's position, identifying the parameters of common ground within and between their positions, where there is room for concessions to be made while still meeting the needs of both parties.

Fisher *et al* (1999) suggest three criteria for effective negotiation:

- It should produce a wise agreement: 'one which meets the legitimate interests of each side to the extent possible, resolves conflicting interests fairly, is durable and takes community interests into account'.

- It should be efficient.

- It should improve (or at least not damage) the relationship between the parties.

FOR DISCUSSION

How important is the assumption of on-going relationship in your dealings with other people at work (or in your studies)? What does this encourage you to do, and what does it *prevent* you from doing, in the informal 'negotiations' you conduct every day?

4.2   Approaches to negotiation

There are two basic approaches to negotiation.

(a)   **Distributive bargaining**, where negotiation is about the distribution of finite resources. One party's gain is another's loss: a 'win-lose' or 'zero sum' equation. If a pay increase of, say, 10% is gained, where the management budget was 5%, the extra has to be funded from elsewhere – profits, investments, other groups (such as shareholders), increased prices, increased productivity, cuts in training or whatever.

(b) **Integrative bargaining,** based on joint problem-solving, where negotiations aim to find a mutually satisfying solution to problems. This has emerged in recent years in a technique called the 'win-win' approach, a process of exploring and defining the needs and fears of all parties with a view not just to getting the best outcome for one's own party ('win-lose') or even compromise ('lose-lose') but to fulfilling the needs of all parties: a 'win-win' solution may not be available, but the process makes it possible. 'Win-win' negotiation is based on the desire to preserve a constructive relationship between the negotiating parties. 'Win-lose' outcomes can cause resentment or under-motivated performance by the 'losing' party, and perpetuates underlying conflict.

We will be outlining a negotiation process based on concessions and the attempt to find 'middle ground'. However, you should be aware of an alternative approach to collective bargaining, called 'pendulum arbitration'.

Definition

> **Pendulum arbitration is** a system whereby a third party will arbitrate on behalf of the two principals in collective bargaining, should they fail to reach agreement, by awarding the final position of one side or the other: either the employer's final offer or the employees' final claim.

Traditional arbitration draws from both sides of the negotiation in an attempt to find 'middle ground', and this may encourage principals to exaggerate their demands, knowing that they will eventually have to compromise or 'split the difference'. Pendulum arbitration encourages principals to moderate their final positions and to attempt to settle in good faith, knowing that an extreme position will rebound on them if the decision goes to the other side. It avoids the drawing out of the negotiation process by each side holding back from their final position during bargaining.

In practice, however, it is a difficult process, since disputes may involve complex multiple issues, and the final positions of each side on each issue may not be clear.

FOR DISCUSSION

What kind of industrial relations atmosphere is created by a concept such as 'pendulum arbitration'?

Do you think that a 'win-win' solution is possible in collective bargaining?

4.3 The negotiating process

The following (Figure 17.1) is a general overview of the negotiation process. Any negotiation will involve the stages illustrated, although the duration and approach of each will vary according to the particular situation.

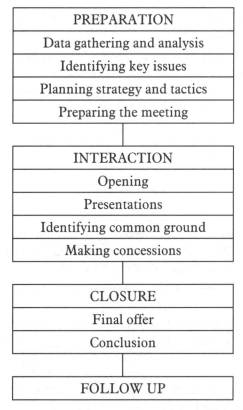

Figure 17.1 The negotiation process

4.4 Preparing a negotiation and negotiation strategy

Formal negotiations, as opposed to informal 'arrangements', should follow broad guidelines.

(a) **Set objectives, parameters and priorities** which are achievable and consistent with industrial relations policy. These are likely to be couched in optimum, most likely and fall-back terms (see (e) below).

(b) **Research the background** of issues over which negotiations are to be conducted: trends in union responses, market pay rates, case studies from similar organisations/sectors, relevant legislation and court decisions and so on.

(c) **Recognise potential for conflict.** In an integrative framework, each side accepts that the objectives and perspectives of the other side are as genuine and legitimate as their own. Even in a distributive framework, it must be recognised that the outcome will have to be 'sold' to all parties, and the consequences of resistance, resentment and lost relationship managed. Recognition of the needs, wants and fears of the other party helps in managing expectations and in the process of devising a workable trade-off between divergent interests.

(d) **Identify tradable items and bargaining power.**

Each party identifies the key issues or items likely to be on the bargaining agenda, and decides on which of these it will be willing to trade or make concessions. It also tries to anticipate the items on which the other party will be willing to trade or make concessions. Some items will be non-tradable: others may be amenable to movement on both sides, especially if some items are identified as being relatively 'cheap' for one party to give up and relatively valuable for the other party to receive.

Each party may also attempt to evaluate its bargaining power, relative to the other party. A frequently used formula for this is:

$$\text{Bargaining power of A} = \frac{\text{Costs to B of disagreement with A's terms}}{\text{Costs to A of disagreement with B's terms}}$$

If the cost of disagreeing is greater than the cost of agreeing, the bargaining power lies with the other side.

Activity 6   (10 minutes)

This bargaining power model provides a quantitative measure of relative bargaining power. What other, more qualitative factors are there that might enhance or detract from the bargaining power of one side or the other?

(e)   **Determine negotiating strategy**. Given a fair idea of what the other side's position and bargaining power are likely to be, the party in question should be able to predict any demands the other side will make, or what kind of offer is likely to be accepted. Each side should look for potential counter-arguments to its own case, without underestimating the potential gap between the parties.

There are basically three possible outcomes for either side:

(i)   If we were to achieve all our objectives, what would be the *ideal settlement* or outcome?

(ii) If we were to make progress, but being realistic about the power of the other side, what is a *realistic settlement* or outcome?

(iii) If we were to concede, what is an acceptable *fall-back position*: the least favourable outcome that can be accepted without failing to meet our objectives?

A position for each side should be estimated for each of the above situations, and areas of agreement concentrated on, as potential *middle ground*.

John Sawbridge (*People Management* 14 September 2000) suggests that:

The union will move only if it believes that:
- there is no other option
- its members will benefit
- it will be painful not to do so.

(f)   **Determine the agenda** ('terms of reference') of the meeting. The agenda for negotiation should be accepted (or acceptable) in advance by both sides. The order of items may have tactical significance: imposing time pressures for agreement on issues raised late in the day, say, or gaining momentum on related issues by placing them after a major point of agreement.

(g)   **Issue prior information**. This may be done:

(i)   As pre-conditioning: for example, advance announcement of poor trading results and intense competition as a prelude to negotiating pay awards, redundancies or productivity agreements.

(ii)   As a matter of legal obligation. Information relevant to collective bargaining must be disclosed to trade union representatives (see above).

(iii) To allow all parties to do their homework, for better quality decision-making, (unless there is any assumed advantage in surprise disclosures).

(h)   **Select participants.** Representatives of management must be articulate, persuasive, acceptable to employee representatives and authoritative enough to implement agreed decisions. Face-to-face negotiations require particular skills in persuasion, personal rapport, reading of verbal and non-verbal signals and so on.

4.5   Conduct of negotiation

During the conduct of the negotiations themselves, participants should consider the following.

(a)   *Opening presentation:* a broad statement of each side's ideal position or opening offer, explaining the rationale (and strength of feeling) behind the proposals and supporting them with relevant data. This will be a clue to strategy – and may also be an opportunity for broad general agreement. It is recommended that the party seeking change be invited to state its case first.

(b)   *Fact-finding:* each party should use the other party's presentation as an opportunity for fact-finding, rather than point scoring or unconsidered ('knee-jerk') opposition. Active listening should be used to clarify or expand on proposals, or to probe for supporting data. During the fact-finding process, the negotiator should gain a better understanding of the other party's ideal position or proposal *and* its strengths and weaknesses (Dobler *et al*, 1990). At the end of this session, there may be a recess or adjournment to allow negotiators to reassess their positions and strategies.

(c)   *Identifying common ground:* having established each others' ideal positions (potentially polarised differences) the emphasis switches to exploring the territory *within* the bargaining range in which agreement might be reached; the room for manoeuvre offered by both parties' (possibly dovetailed) realistic and fall-back positions should be explored.

(d)   *Use of the negotiating strategy and bargaining power.* Items should be linked and packaged to achieve two-way momentum, so that no party gives away anything without getting something in return. Be firm on principles and flexible on details, so that there is room to move without compromising strategic priorities.

(e)   *Making concessions.* A concession is 'a revision of a position you have held previously and justified publicly' (Guirdham, 1995). Concessions are not easy to make without undermining credibility – but *must* be made in order to bring both parties progressively closer together. They should be made only in response to pressure – or to offers-in-exchange from the other party – and in small increments. *Reciprocal concessions* can be promoted by negatively reinforcing the other side's present position (eg emphasising that it will not work) and positively reinforcing movement (eg offering options for them to move without losing face).

The meeting should be facilitated by an experienced chairperson, who will ensure that the meeting is conducted in a courteous and effective manner: sticking to the point of the agenda reached; giving alternating opportunities to speak (rather than a 'free for all'); and so on.

Activity 7   **(30 minutes)**

From your study or awareness of communication and persuasion techniques, suggest some techniques which you might use in negotiation.

Adjournments may be used to give parties time to review progress, consider proposals, enter informal 'off-the-table' discussions which might help break an impasse, or just 'cool off' when negotiation reaches a heated stage.

All relevant details of the discussion should be recorded by a minute-taker, stenographer or sound recorder, in order to furnish minutes which can be used in formulating final agreements.

4.6 Settlement and follow-up

At the conclusion of negotiations, both parties must be satisfied that all issues have been discussed and that they understand exactly what has been agreed: the proceedings should be summarised and agreements 'played back' for confirmation by both sides. If there is any misunderstanding or ambiguity which raises objections, negotiations should recommence.

Once there is oral agreement, the points should be written up as a signed 'draft agreement', stating:

(a) Who made the agreement and on what date

(b) Who is to be covered by the agreement (groups and grades of employee, for example)

(c) When the agreement is to take effect, how long it is to run, and whether and how it may be amended or terminated prior to this date

(d) The contents (or 'clauses') of the agreement and any exceptions that may apply

(e) How disagreements and appeals will be dealt with once the negotiated settlement is implemented

The draft agreement should be circulated and checked by both sides, and clauses initialled once their wording is accepted. When all clauses have been approved by both sides, the agreement can be printed, formally signed and communicated to those affected by its provisions.

Activity 8 **(1 hour)**

In an example cited by Gennard and Judge (2003), the annual pay negotiations between a trade union and a manufacturing company started with the following sets of demands.

- Substantial increase on all basic rates of pay

- Wage increase of 1.5%

- Holiday pay to be improved, to include all earnings in the 12 weeks prior to the holiday period

- No changes to the basis of calculation of holiday pay

- Shift premiums payable at weekends to be raised to double-time and for nightwork to time-and-a-third

- No changes to shift premiums

- Overtime payments to be time-and-a-half (standard) and double-time plus time in lieu (customary holidays)

- No changes to overtime payments

- Drivers' overnight allowance increased to £20 per occasion

- Drivers' overnight allowance increased to £18 per occasion

- Any additional costs of the settlement to be recovered in full by efficiency and productivity improvements at plant levels

Consider which items are most important, and which most tradable, for each side. (If possible, role play a negotiation with a fellow student.) Come up with a 'trade' of terms that you think might be acceptable to both parties.

Chapter roundup

- A lawful trade dispute is one between workers and their own employers, wholly or mainly about work-related matters. Various forms of sanctions are available to workers in pursuance of an industrial dispute, including strikes. Strike action has been strictly controlled by legislation and has correspondingly declined in severity and frequency.

- Collective bargaining is the process whereby employee and employer representatives negotiate agreements on terms and conditions of employment (and related matters) for groups of represented employees. There has been a tendency to decentralise bargaining to plant level, in order to retain flexibility.

- Negotiating is a bargaining process through which commitments and compromises are reached, using the relative power of the parties involved.

Quick quiz

1 Distinguish between primary and secondary industrial action.

2 List five areas of industrial action that are subject to UK legislation.

3 Outline the process of arbitration of a trade dispute and the role of ACAS.

4 What are procedural agreements in collective bargaining?

5 What is single-table bargaining?

6 What does the ACAS Code of Practice recommend on the disclosure of information for collective bargaining?

7 What is pendulum arbitration?

8 What three outcomes of negotiation should negotiators plan in advance, as the basis of negotiating strategy?

9 What is the 'win-win' approach?

10 Draw an overview of the process of negotiation.

Answers to quick quiz

1 Primary: aimed at the employer with whom the participating union is in dispute. Secondary (unlawful): aimed at employers who trade with firms in dispute. (para 1.2)

2 Balloting of members; legal immunity for lawful dispute; outlawing of secondary action; individual member rights not to participate; unlawful dismissal of strikers in first eight weeks of dispute. (para 1.4)

3 See paragraph 2.2 for a full answer.

4 Agreements which determine methods and procedures for arriving at substantive agreements (on pay, conditions and so on) and for settling disputes. (para 3.1)

5 Terms and conditions of all workers (manual and non-manual) are determined in a single negotiation. This may be achieved by multiple unions pre-negotiating a bargaining proposal prior to collective bargaining with management. (para 3.3)

6 Information should be disclosed on pay and benefits, conditions of service, human resources, performance (productivity, sales, orders) and financial matters. Unions should define and request specific information before negotiations begin. (para 3.4)

7 Instead of the arbitrator finding 'middle ground' between the final offer/claim of each side, (s)he awards for one side's final position over the other: **either** the employer's final offer **or** the employees' final claim. (para 4.2)

8 Ideal settlement, realistic settlement, fall-back position. (para 4.4)

9 An approach to conflict resolution and distributive bargaining/negotiation which seeks to meet the needs of both parties as far as possible. (paras 2.3, 4.2)

10 See paragraph 4.3 (Figure 17.1).

Answers to activities

1   Industrial action may be used as:

(a)   A demonstration of bargaining strength, by the threatened or actual withdrawal of labour and/or restriction of productivity, aimed at forcing management to enter negotiations or make concessions, or

(b)   A gesture of protest to highlight a grievance issue, aimed at management, government and other influential bodies, or at the general public. (For example, a literal 'go-slow' was staged by a transport union in Sydney, Australia in November 2000. Bus drivers drove at a crawl during the rush hour to highlight the failure of state government and policy to enforce city-centre bus lane rules, exposing drivers to stress, risk and commuter frustration: passengers and the media were handed leaflets explaining the purpose of the action and urged to support the protest.)

2   The main industrial sanctions available to the *employer* are:

- Locking out some, or all, of the workforce from the worksite
- Closing the worksite and/or relocating operations elsewhere
- Dismissing employees who participate in industrial action

The main reasons why these are 'last resort measures' is because:

(a)   They are costly, involving lost production/service. Unless alternative arrangements can be made (see paragraph 1.7) this may mean lost orders and lost customers.

(b)   They risk escalating the conflict, hardening attitudes on both sides.

(c)   They risk long-term damage to the loyalty and commitment of staff after the particular dispute is over.

(d)   They need to be carefully checked for legality, with regard to detail (eg if it is unlawful to dismiss within the first 8 weeks of a strike).

3   The dispute was effectively resolved within two weeks.

The unions successfully got together to bring staff to the discussion table with BA initially, and persuaded them to return to work on this basis.

First-round talks appear not to have been successful. However, this may have been a bargaining strategy by BA, determined not to give way initially, given the unofficial nature of the original worker action. Positive use is made of third-party conciliation, both through ACAS and the TUC.

The involvement of the chief executive is a positive gesture of willingness by BA to come to the table seriously.

The outcome is relatively satisfactory to both sides. It appears that the swipe-card system may in itself be not the prime cause of the dispute, but worker fears about the erosion of their flexible working arrangements (work-life balance), lack of managerial trust and so on. The procedure will only have been truly successful insofar as these matters were brought into the open and discussed.

4   **Advantages**

(a)   Less time and resources spent on negotiations than with multiple bargaining.

(b)   Takes account of more viewpoints, more representative: enhances likelihood of acceptance of decisions. (Particularly helpful for change management affecting multiple groups of employees.)

(c)   Encourages resolution of inter-union disputes as part of preparation for negotiation: saves wasted time and energy in harmonising separate agreements.

(d)   May help avoid demarcations and inflexible work rules, with overall bargaining perspective (needs for flexibility, quality etc).

Disadvantages

(a)   Agenda may be overcrowded by concerns of multiple groups.

(b)   Requires higher levels of negotiating and relationship management skills.

(c)   Inflexibility: management may be less able to differentiate and change agreements with different segments of the workforce.

(d)   Inter-union disputes may not be resolved prior to negotiation.

(e)   May hamper individual union attempts to recruit members.

5   Decline in collective bargaining, due to:

(a)   The decline in union membership, and therefore the number of workers covered by collective bargaining

(b)   The rise of individual- and team-based systems, with new emphasis on employees' responsibility for self-management and self-development: individual contracts, learning plans and career mobility; team-centred performance management, performance-related pay and so on

(c)   The rise of workforce flexibility, with the erosion of job descriptions, occupational demarcations and associated work rules

(d)   The decentralisation of employee relations (and other HRM) processes to line managers

(e)   The introduction of non-negotiatory consultation and involvement techniques

As we saw in Chapter 16, however, union recognition in the UK may be on the upturn: watch this space!

6   Quantitative elements of bargaining power include:

- The intrinsic merit of each party's case or argument (the stronger your case, the better the prospect of achieving agreement on your terms)

- The skill and ability of the negotiator

- The potential for coercion (the power of underlying sanctions or 'threat' eg to close a plant, or initiate industrial action)

Note that bargaining power may be actual or 'real' and/or perceived, and that the one may be much higher or lower than the other…

7   (a)   Gain agreements or commitments from the other side that can be used as a stepping stone for the logical progression of your argument.

(b)   Summarise periodically, especially to highlight common ground and consolidate progress.

(c)   Sell the benefits of your proposals to the other side: allow them to agree with you, without loss of face, whenever possible.

(d) Preserve a tone of commitment, belief, even emotion: make your cause human.

(e) Use questions. Positive, joint-problem-solving questions: 'What would it take to make this work?'. Probing, challenging questions: 'Where would the money for that proposal come from?' Push for answers where necessary.

(f) Release information with a tactical awareness of its affects on negotiating position.

(g) Use all interpersonal and communication skills: listening, empathy, accessible language, giving non-verbal cues (eg confident body-language) and interpreting non-verbal cues (eg signs of hesitation, tentative phrasing, suggestions of readiness to move).

8 In the example cited, the agreed settlement was as follows.

Company conceded	*Company gained*
• Wage increase of 1.5%	• No changes to holiday pay
• Increase in drivers' overnight allowance to £20 per occasion	• No change to weekend shift premiums
• Shiftwork premiums (nightwork) increased to time-and-a-third	• No change to overtime premiums
	• Additional costs of the agreement fully covered by efficiency/productivity improvements

---

Assignment 17   **(1 hour)**

You are the HR manager of a firm (in a sector of your choice). Your firm recognises the relevant union(s) for its sector for the purposes of collective bargaining, and at least one of these has shown itself to be militant in its approach to the use of sanction (industrial action) in the pursuit of claims for better pay and conditions. Management has made concessions over the years, but is unable to continue to do so without threatening the firm's viability. This argument is unlikely to impress the union. Line managers are saying that a major stoppage is on the cards again – although they do not know when, or on what issue, it will occur.

Devise a contingency plan for dealing with strike action if or when it occurs.

Chapter 18:
EMPLOYEE PARTICIPATION AND INVOLVEMENT

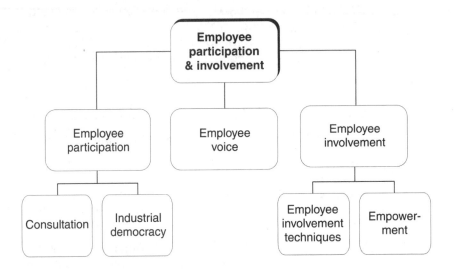

Introduction

The concept of 'employee voice' embraces 'a whole variety of processes and structures which enable, and sometimes empower employees, directly and indirectly, to contribute to decision-making in the firm' (Boxall & Purcell, 2003). The term has come to embrace a wide range of mechanisms for:

- *Employee involvement:* informing and consulting employees about aspects of decision making

- *Employee participation:* involving employees (often via their representatives) in the decision making machinery of the organisation

In this chapter, we look at both of these key aspects of employee relations, drawing together coverage in other chapters (especially Chapters 8 and 15) of the role of HRM and line management in shifting focus from 'industrial relations' to 'employee relations', and from a unitarist towards a pluralist frame of reference.

Your objectives

In this chapter you will learn about the following.

(a) Different forms of employee consultation and participation

(b) Industrial democracy and its European roots

(c) Employee involvement techniques

(d) Empowerment

(e) Employee voice (Unit 22)

1   EMPLOYEE VOICE

1.1   What is employee voice?

Armstrong (2003) summarises 'employee voice' as 'the say employees have in matters of concern to them in their organisation'. He suggests that this is closer to *participation* ('ensuring that employees are given the opportunity to influence management decisions and to contribute to the improvement of organisations performance') than to *involvement* (where 'management allows employees to discuss with it issues that affect them but management retains the right to manage'). However, employee voice may be seen as a framework for both processes.

Employee voice is both an individual concept and a collective concept: it includes, for example, individual grievances and suggestions as well as collective bargaining and industrial democracy agreements made with trade unions and/or other employee representatives.

Marchington *et al* (2001) model the territory of employee voice as follows: Figure 18.1.

- Involvement may be *direct* (where management deal with individuals/teams) or *indirect* (where management deal with trade unions or other representative groups)

- Involvement may be based on a *shared agenda* (directed at improving organisational performance and the quality of working life) or on a *contested agenda* (directed at addressing areas of conflict, dissatisfaction or competition)

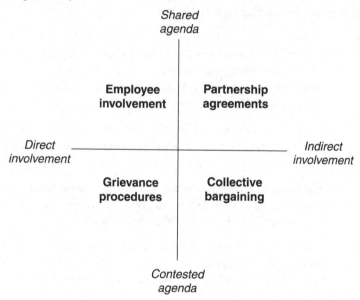

Figure 18.1: Employee voice matrix

In practice, an organisation's approach will be a mixture of direct and indirect, and focus on both shared and contested agendas (weighted according to whether HRM policies take a pluralistic or unitarist viewpoint, as discussed in Chapter 16). If there is an anti-union culture of management, the balance will shift towards direct involvement. If there is a co-operative or unitarist culture of management, the balance will shift towards shared agenda.

1.2 Purposes of employee voice

Marchington *et al* (2001) suggest that employee voice offers:

- The ability for individual employees to express dissatisfaction, solve problems with management and preserve working relationships

- The ability for employees collectively to express their needs and wishes in matters that affect them, providing a counterbalance to managerial power

- The ability for employees to contribute to management decisions, allowing the organisation to harness the expertise and commitment of workers to improve quality, productivity and work organisation

- The ability for employers and employees to demonstrate their intention to focus on shared goals, mutual interests and co-operative working relations, for the long-term benefit of the organisation and its people

Employee voice thus involves both 'soft' HRM elements (fairness, relationship, mutual commitment) and 'hard' HRM elements (problem-solving, conflict/grievance management and performance improvement).

1.3 Mechanisms of employee voice

Marchington *et al* (1992, 2001) classify the main approaches to implementing employee voice as 'representative participation' (which we call 'participation' in this chapter) and 'upward problem-solving' (which we include among techniques for 'involvement').

(a) *Representative participation* includes:

- *Collective representation:* grievance procedures, collective bargaining, collective dispute resolution and other settings in which trade unions, staff associations or elected employee representatives represent the interests of individual employees or groups of employees (as discussed in Chapters 16-17).

- *Joint consultation:* formal non-negotiatory meetings between management and employee representatives to discuss matters of shared interest or concern (discussed in Section 2 below).

- *European Works councils:* joint consultation machinery for organisations with sites in two or more member states of the European Union (discussed in Section 2 below).

- *Partnership schemes:* formal agreements between management and employee representatives to work together for mutual benefit, in a non-adversarial climate (discussed in Section 2 below).

(b) *Upward problem-solving* includes:

- *Two-way communication:* encouraging upward communication (from staff to management) as well as downward, eg through briefing groups, team meetings and corporate intranets.

- *Upward communication:* seeking staff feedback, opinions and suggestions, eg through attitude surveys, suggestion schemes and employee intranet discussion groups.

- *Project teams:* getting staff and management together to solve problems, discuss issues or generate ideas (eg quality circles, customer care task forces).

FOR DISCUSSION

'What institution embodying the employee voice might be appropriate. Is it a trade union? A works council? Or should employee voice not be viewed any longer in terms of collective representation?' (Gennard & Judge, 2003).

What do you think?

We will now go on to look at some of the mechanisms of employee voice in more detail.

2 EMPLOYEE PARTICIPATION AND CONSULTATION

2.1 What is participation?

Definition

> **Employee participation** 'concerns the extent to which employees, often via their representatives, are involved in the decision-making machinery of the organisation. This includes joint consultation, collective bargaining and worker representation on the board'. (Gennard & Judge, 2003)

As noted in Section 1 above, there are different degrees and methods of participation, reflecting the extent to which organisations wish to involve employees in decision-making.

> **Activity 1** (30 minutes)
>
> Outline four general reasons why an organisation may consider it desirable or necessary to work towards employee participation.

2.2 Information and consultation

We have already encountered some of the circumstances in which recognised trade unions (or other employee representatives) are legally entitled to information and consultation, including:

- *Redundancy,* where more than 20 people are affected (see Chapter 7)
- *Health and safety* (see Chapter 11)
- *Collective bargaining* (see Chapter 17)

FOR DISCUSSION

The general secretary of the GMB told the 2000 TUC conference: 'We need better rights to consultation and information. I look forward to the day when British workers hear about the changes in their employment from the lips of their managers and not from the pages of the *Financial Times* or the early morning news bulletins of the BBC'.

Do workers have a 'right' to information and consultation in a moral sense?

Consultation, from a legal point of view, means talking formally to employee representatives on a matter which will affect employees or their work, with a view to seeking agreement. There is no obligation on employees to negotiate or take employee views into account in any specific way – but there must be dialogue entered into 'in good faith'.

Under the Companies Act 1989, an organisation employing more than 250 employees is required to include a statement in its Directors' Report describing the action taken in the previous financial year to introduce, maintain or develop arrangements for:

(a) Information/consultation of employees on matters affecting their employment

(b) Consultation with employee representatives to canvass their views on matters affecting them

(c) Financial participation of employees in the company's performance

(d) Extending employees' awareness of financial and economic factors affecting the company's performance

Activity 2 (no time limit)

Get hold of the Directors' Report (found as part of the Annual Report and Accounts) of any public limited company of your choice. Examine the statements made in regard to the above matters. Do they reflect genuine involvement or participation, from what you can gather?

2.3 Joint consultation and works councils

Definition

Joint consultation is a process by which management and employee representatives jointly examine and discuss issues of mutual concern.

Joint consultation is the main form of representative participation in the UK. Gennard and Judge (2003) distinguish between 'employee communication' (similarly concerned with the interchange of information and ideas within an organisation) and 'consultation', which involves managers actively seeking and taking account of the views of employees before making a decision. Consultation 'affects the process through which decisions are made in so far as it commits management first to the disclosure of information at an early stage in the decision-making process and second to take into account the collective views of the employees.'

Joint Consultative Committees (JCCs) – sometimes called 'Works Councils' – are composed of managers and employee representatives who come together on a regular basis to discuss matters of mutual interest. Members should include senior managers (in order to demonstrate commitment and mobilise authority where required) and representatives of all significant employee groups (in order to be regarded as genuinely representative). Committees usually have a well defined constitution and terms of reference.

Like any committee or group meeting, a JCC meeting will need a skilled Chairperson to facilitate and control discussion, and a clear and manageable agenda, circulated in advance for member preparation. Minutes will need to be taken for feeding back to the parties represented (via briefing groups, noticeboards, intranet and so on). Management needs to demonstrate its commitment to genuine consultation by giving appropriate facilities, time off and training to committee members. In unionised organisations, issues such as pay bargaining are generally left to collective bargaining, so JCCs must also be given something of perceived importance to deal with if they are not to be marginalised as ineffectual 'talk shops'.

Activity 3   **(No time limit)**

What are the structures for joint consultation in your work organisation (or one you know well or can find out about). What issues are consultations designed to cover? What influence do they have on organisational policy? How are they regarded by employees in general?

Bratton & Gold (2003) suggest that there are arguments both for *integrating* consultative machinery with negotiating (collective bargaining) machinery in an organisation and for *separating* the two activities.

Arguments for integration	Arguments for separation
• Communicating, consulting and negotiation are interlinked processes	• May reduce organisational complexity
• Union reps must be involved in consultation anyway	• Collective bargaining deals with substantive/procedural matters: consultation addresses other matters
• As collective bargaining's scope expands, remaining issues are less important	• Regular JCC meetings ensure that consultation is (and is seen to be) a managerial commitment

The most recent Workplace Employee Relations Survey (1998) shows that 23% of workplaces (with more than 25 employees) have a functioning JCC: 20% in the private sector, 32% in the public sector. Larger organisations are more likely to have both workplace committees and higher-level committees (for consultation on a multi-site or organisation-wide basis).

2.4 European Works Councils

While JCCs are voluntary works councils, the term 'European Works Council' is specifically used to describe mandatory meetings between management and elected employee representatives (independent of trade unions) under the 1994 European Works Council Directive, which became law in the UK in 1999.

A European Works Council must be set up in all organisations with more than 1,000 employees in Member States and employing more than 150 people in each of two or more of these. A Pan-European Works Council (or alternative) has to be agreed between central management and a Special Negotiating Body of employee representatives from the countries involved.

If no agreement is reached, a fallback system requires the establishment of a **European Works Council** of employee representatives with the right to meet central management at least once a year for information and consultation about the progress and prospects of the company. It may also request further or special meetings on transnational ('community scale') issues of concern, defined as 'measures significantly affecting employees' interests': large scale redundancies, for example.

EXAMPLE

Electrics giant Panasonic decided in 1994 to adopt a proactive view of the European Works Council Directive and to conclude a voluntary agreement with employee representatives, resulting in the establishment of:

(a) A 'Panasonic European Congress' (PEC), meeting yearly for consultation on transnational issues. The congress involves representatives from different nations; different types of operations (sales, manufacturing, R & D) and both unionised and non-unionised companies.

(b) Two representative committees: an Employee Representative Committee and a Management Representative Committee, which meet three or four times a year to discuss the agenda for the annual meeting, agree the minutes and be informed and consulted on transnational issues.

(c) A Panasonic UK Consultative Committee (PUCC), with 11 employee representatives from the different divisions of Panasonic UK Ltd. (The UK company was non-union and non-works-council, so there was no existing formal structure for information and consultation with elected employee representatives.) The PUCC meets with company directors every two months to discuss company performance, sales figures, health and safety, canteen and sports facilities, technological and structural changes and training and education.

Note that EWCs do not represent industrial democracy or co-determination such as operates in countries such as Germany or Sweden (discussed later in this section). They are only for the purposes of consultation.

(a) Councils have the right to be informed and consulted about 'any measure likely to have a considerable effect on employees' interests'.

(b) Matters for discussion must be transnational or 'community scale': this is not an alternative forum to discuss matters affecting a single group of employees.

The European Commission is now reviewing the operation of the original EWC Directive: watch this space!

FOR DISCUSSION

Running costs for an EWC have been reported (*People Management*, 6 November 2003) as running as high as £150,000 a year, because of training, travel and transportation costs, and the entitlement to 'assistance' from an expert paid for by the employer.

How might developments in Information and Communications Technology (ICT) be used to reduce the cost of meetings – and/or keep the wider employee body better informed?

2.5 Draft Information and Consultation of Employees Regulations 2005

The EU parliament adopted the Information and Consultation Directive in 2002. Draft regulations for the UK underwent consultation in the second half of 2003, and will come into force from March 2005 (for organisations with 150 employees or more) to March 2008 (for organisations with 50 employees or more).

Under the draft regulations, an employer must set up a works council if requested to do so by a written petition from at least 10% of its workforce (or 250 of them, whichever is lower). The employer must:

(a) Inform representatives about recent and foreseeable developments concerning the enterprise's activity and economic and financial situation

(b) Consult representatives on any restructuring of employment (particularly, threat to jobs) with a view to exchanging views

(c) Consult representatives on decisions that are likely to lead to substantial changes in work organisation and contractual relations (eg collective redundancies or business transfers) 'with a view to reaching agreement'

The practical arrangements used for this process must be agreed by the workforce. If current structures do not meet the requirements of the Regulations, management will have to negotiate new machinery with employee representatives. This is likely to occupy lots of attention in HR departments over the next few years: watch this space!

EXAMPLE

In two weeks, 13 people from all walks of life and all levels of Marks & Spencer will participate in the first meeting of its national business involvement group (Big), the company's body for information and consultation. Their role will be to debate business decisions and HR policies face-to-face with their chief executive, Roger Holmes.

These types of staff council are being established in companies across the UK in response to the European directive on information and consultation, which comes into force in March 2005. But for M&S, the new group is the culmination of a series of measures aimed at improving employee communications.

There have been discussion groups in the stores for some years. But during the firm's financial difficulties in 1999, staff were involved in a consultative process called Clearview, which moved communications up a gear. It involved brainstorming sessions between employees and managers to consider what was wrong with the structure, processes and culture of the business.

M&S recognised the contribution that such a process made to the organisation's recovery. A review of the staff focus groups in Spring 2001 indicated that they wanted a structure that enabled issues to be represented at a more senior level and wanted managers and staff to sit in a combined forum. This led to the creation of Bigs at a local and area level in September 2001.

Local Bigs were set up in 309 shops, head office locations, the financial services unit and its distribution centres. Area Bigs provided a forum for issues that affected more than one store or business area. The company also had a European council, established in 1995 in line with EU legislation. But discussions were confined to issues affecting more than two countries. This was despite the closure of continental European stores in 2001, leaving the European council with members from only the UK and the Republic of Ireland. A review in March last year highlighted the need for a national forum.

(Higginbottom, 2003 (c))

Unit 24: Employee Relations

2.6 Partnership agreements

Definition

> **Partnership agreements** are negotiated arrangements 'in which both parties (management and the trade union) agree to work together to their mutual advantage and to achieve a climate of more co-operative and therefore less adversarial industrial relations.' (Armstrong, 2003)

Partnership agreements generally include undertakings from both sides, linking job security, pay awards or participation (in the control of management) to productivity gains or greater flexibility in work organisation (in the control of unions).

Gennard & Judge (2003) identify six key principles underpinning partnership agreements in the workplace.

	Principle	Comment
1	Commitment to success of the enterprise	Partnership depends on shared understanding and commitment in regard to the business goals of the organisation
2	Recognising legitimate interests	A recognition that interests and priorities will not always coincide: parties must respect each others' responsibility to do their best for their stakeholders
3	Commitment to employment security	Measures to maximise employment security (eg limit redundancies) and improve staff employability (eg through transferable skills training)
4	Focus on the quality of working life	Recognition of the need to develop employees and create opportunities for personal growth
5	Transparency	Real sharing of information and early discussion of plans for the future
6	Adding value	Partnership should access and deploy commitment/resources not available through previous employees relations machinery

> **Activity 4** **(30 minutes)**
> What advantages might parties in a partnership agreement be aiming for?

Note that partnership also has its critics!

> There are critics who see partnership as an illusory concept. Those on the left of the political spectrum... fear that unions, far from gaining influence, will be co-opted by management into their projects, effectively neutralising any chance of opposition. Critics from the right would argue that partnership hampers management's ability to manage, or, as the president of the CBI... believes, that it may even provide a "Trojan horse" through which unions could gain more influence.
>
> *(People Management,* 14 September 2000)

EXAMPLE

Legal & General agreed a partnership deal with the MSF in 1997, an experience reported as follows in *People Management* (September 2000).

'The objectives of the agreement are:

- To work together to further the success of the business by enabling a flexible approach in a time of rapid and continuous change

- To work together in a spirit of mutual confidence, partnership and co-operation, both formally and informally

- To work together to achieve fairness and equality in the treatment of staff, including transparent pay systems, contractual provisions that encourage equal treatment regardless of age, creed, disability, race or sex, and access to good vocational training and career development.

'The parties set out to recognise both their differences and their shared interests. They committed themselves to avoiding conflict that would damage the business. MSF accepted management's right to manage. Legal & General acknowledged the union's right to represent its members both collectively and on individual matters of grievance or discipline.

'Collective bargaining machinery was replaced by a Joint Employment Policy Forum (JEPF) meeting that would take place every six months. The JEPF was given wide scope to discuss business strategy, training and development, health and safety, reward and equal opportunities. Both sides preferred joint communication and informal methods of dispute resolution where possible, with the intention 'to talk at the earliest possible stage on all matters of mutual interest'. The agreement also committed management to give representatives training that would enable them to perform their union functions properly.

In April 2000, Legal and General and the MSF reviewed the agreement. Key concerns were that:

(a) Not all managers seemed to understand what partnership meant. This issued in failure to involve union representatives in employment matters, to give representatives time off for their duties or to encourage union membership.

(b) Union representatives were insufficiently trained and experienced to meet the demands of the partnership role, and the inequality in expertise between them and managers undermined the relationship.

(c) Employees were ambivalent about the deal. On the one hand, MSF didn't like the idea of 'freeloaders' (non-members who enjoyed the benefits of the agreement without paying union subscriptions). On the other, employees complained that the union had grown too close to management and lacked 'bite' in negotiations.

'Further training, and greater promotion of the partnership concept, were two ways forward.'

We will now look briefly at European models of employee participation, which are closer to 'industrial democracy'.

3 EMPLOYEE PARTICIPATION AND INDUSTRIAL DEMOCRACY

3.1 Social dimensions of the European Union

The European Union was partly developed as a 'Single Market' or trading bloc, removing barriers to trade and competitive bias, standardising technical regulations and creating a convergence of conditions between European markets. However, it also has a socio-political dimension which embraces employment issues, since it is believed that the success of the Single Market depends on the united efforts of employers and labour.

The main statement of European social policy is the 'Community Charter of the Fundamental Social Rights of Workers'– commonly known as the 'Social Charter' – which was ratified by 11 of the (then) 12 member states: the UK opted out. The Charter is based on the desire to improve living and working conditions and to ensure effective use of human resources across the EU. It is a statement of intent to guarantee individual rights in areas such as: freedom of movement; fair remuneration; improvement of living and working conditions (including working time); freedom of association and collective bargaining (the right to join, or not to join, a trade union; the right to negotiate and conclude collective agreements and the right to collective action such as strikes); access to vocational training; equal treatment for men and women; health and safety in the workplace; and the protection of children, adolescents and the disabled in the workplace.

Additional rights are guaranteed in respect of the information, consultation and participation of workers. Changes that affect the workforce such as new technology, working practices, mergers, restructuring and collective redundancy should involve prior consultation with employees.

All members of the EU have since agreed that the Social Charter be implemented by directive: member states will be bound to legislate and 'mobilise all the resources necessary' to implement its provisions. Some have already been covered by EU Directives, while others are still subject to negotiation and amendment.

3.2 The European Company Statute

The European Company Statute (2001) gives companies the option of forming a European company which can operate on a Europe-wide basis and be governed by Community law. An accompanying Directive requires employee involvement arrangements in all such companies, including:

(a) Collective bargaining on decisions or

(b) A two-tier board structure, with elected worker representatives on the senior or 'supervisory' board to which the management or 'executive' board is responsible, or

(c) A unitary board structure with worker representatives as non-executive directors, or

(d) A sub-board level company council, solely comprised of worker representation

3.3 National cultural differences in regard to participation

In Germany, the concept of consultation and participation is based on a system called co-determination, formally involving employees and their representatives in nearly all decisions relating to personnel and other aspects of company policy. Co-determination is supported by specific legislation. There are three methods by which workers can participate: by Works Councils, Supervisory Boards and Management Boards.

(a) In workplaces with more than five employees, the workforce elects a **works council** consisting solely of workers' representatives. This council has the right:

   (i) To receive information on health and safety, work organisation, jobs, work environment, the hiring of executives and planned changes which could adversely affect employees

   (ii) To make suggestions during the formulation and implementation of HR plans, and specifically regarding vocational training (eg apprenticeships) and other training and development opportunities

   The views and suggestions of the council must be considered, although they are not binding on managerial decision-making.

(b) In companies employing more than 500 people, elected worker representatives sit on the **supervisory board** which meets four times a year. Worker representatives make up one-third to one-half of this policy-making body (depending on size), with other board members elected by the shareholders, under a 'neutral' chairperson. The supervisory board is responsible for deciding the overall direction of the enterprise; matters concerning corporate finance and structure (including mergers and takeovers); and the appointment, dismissal and remuneration of members of the executive or management board.

(c) The executive or **management board** is the full-time body responsible for the day-to-day running of operations.

Sweden also operates a co-determination system based on consultation with employees and the participation of representatives in decision making at both board and shop floor levels. Industrial democracy was developed early in Sweden, and techniques such as job enrichment, autonomous working groups and 'quality of working life' programmes were developed by companies such as Volvo back in the 1970s. The Swedish model is more highly unionised that the German model, with union membership over 80%.

Belgium, France, Italy, Spain and the Netherlands also have works councils supported by legislation, but the range of issues open to employee approval is smaller than in the German or Swedish co-determination models. Belgium and the Netherlands have an additional legal requirement for large companies to operate a two-tier (supervisory and executive) board of directors.

In **Japan**, employee involvement practices are deeply embedded in the collectivist and commitment-based culture of employment, in techniques such as quality circles, teamworking, consensus decision-making and long-term employee development. There is a unitarist assumption of the value of participation, supported by the training of group leaders and workers in the skills of participative working. However, observers note that employee involvement techniques are not primarily used as decision-making mechanisms or channels of communication (as in Europe) but as a cultural mechanism reinforcing identification with shared aims and goals.

Activity 5   **(5 minutes)**

From your knowledge of national cultural differences (Chapter 12) what characteristics would you expect to be most relevant to a country's acceptance of industrial democracy?

We will now look at employee involvement. We have already covered many employee involvement techniques in other contexts (such as reward, quality management, flexibility and development), and have discussed issues of involvement and empowerment of employees in our exploration of the HRM approach in Chapter 8. As you review such topics, bear in mind that they are part of the overall relationship of employees and management in the organisation.

4 EMPLOYEE INVOLVEMENT TECHNIQUES

4.1 Employee involvement

Definition

> **Employee involvement** describes a wide range of policies and techniques for 'informing and consulting employees about, or associating them with, one or more aspects of running an organisation.' (Gennard & Judge, 2003)

Employee involvement concentrates mainly on individual employees and the degree to which they can be encouraged to identify with the goals of the organisation. It can be distinguished from employee participation (discussed earlier), which concerns the extent to which employees are involved (via their representatives) in management decision-making.

The aims of involvement may be:

(a) To generate commitment to the organisation

(b) To help the organisation improve performance, especially in the face of change

(c) To enable the organisation to better meet changing customer requirements

(d) To improve the challenge and satisfaction of the work experience

(e) To aid the organisation in attracting and retaining skilled labour

(f) To develop the business awareness of labour at all levels

(g) To increase employee incentives and accountabilities through tying reward to company performance and profitability, and/or

(h) To marginalise trade unions

Guest (2001) describes five ways to get employees involved.

- By improving the provision of information to employees

- By improving the provision of information from employees

- By changing the structure and arrangement of work

- By changing the incentives

- By changing relationships, through more participative leadership and informality

> **Activity 6** (15 minutes)
>
> Suggest three techniques (already encountered in this *Course Book*) by which each of the above could be implemented.

Marchington *et al* (1992) similarly divide employee involvement schemes into four categories.

(a) **Downwards communications:** from managers to other employees and so on. This includes house journals, employee reports and briefings.

(b) **Upwards problem-solving forms:** designed to tap into individual and team knowledge and expertise. This includes suggestion schemes, attitude surveys, quality circles, customer care programmes and so on.

(c) **Financial participation:** linking rewards of individuals to the performance of the unit or business. This includes profit sharing, employee share ownership and factory-wide or value added bonus schemes (discussed in Chapter 5).

(d) **Representative participation:** employees are involved in decision-making through their representatives on JCCs, advisory councils, works councils, or collective bargaining. (This may operate at different levels of involvement, from consultation and dialogue to co-determination and even to control, eg in worker-managed teams or co-operatives.)

In addition, involvement may be encouraged by:

(a) **Empowerment:** the devolving of control and responsibility to individuals or teams at the workplace or 'front line' customer-service level. Empowerment may be 'soft' (providing enhanced opportunities for involvement in decision-making, fewer status barriers, more open communication, greater flexibility) or 'hard' (devolution of responsibility and accountability: standards and targets, monitoring and control)

(b) **Inclusion in the cultural and strategic priorities of the business.** Employees are invited and encouraged to share in commitment to quality, customer care, continuous improvement, learning and so on. This is frequently linked to empowerment as a set of guiding values and objectives within which teams can be more or less self-managing.

We will look at some of these techniques in more detail, where they have not been covered elsewhere in this Course Book.

4.2 Downward communication

Downward communication is usually well established in an organisation in the form of instructions, job briefings, rules and policies and announcement of plans by managers to staff.

There may, however, be potential for more empowering downward information flow about a wider range of matters, including: company strategy and future plans; positive performance feedback, celebrating individual, team and company achievements; competitor and other environmental factors that may influence work (or stimulating problem-solving); and so on.

Examples of mechanisms for downward communication of this type include:

(a) *In-house journals,* bulletins and newsheets (and their electronic equivalents by e-mail or *intranet* pages). This is commonly used to foster a sense of involvement and belonging, but may be made a tool for greater participation by including various mechanisms for feedback and interaction: suggestion schemes, 'letter' pages, discussion forums, noticeboards and so on.

(b) *Team briefings,* where management pass information face-to-face to team members, on a regular basis. This enables people to feel that they know what is going on, and have access to the information required to do their work. Briefing meetings can also be used for interactive question-and-answer and problem-solving, however, for a more participative element.

(c) *Management by Walking Around.* The managerial culture of some organisations will need to be changed in order to increase information flow to employees. The hoarding of information as a source of power by managers, or the withholding of information on a 'need to know' basis are a feature of command-and-control cultures rather than facilitate-and-empower organisations.

FOR DISCUSSION

Is there too much information flowing around organisations – or does keeping employees 'in the loop' meaningfully contribute to employee relations?

4.3 Upward communication

Upward communication is rarer than downward – but vital to many modern organisations in:

(a) Providing feedback on progress and performance, so that plans can be adjusted where necessary

(b) Harnessing the experience and know-how of employees for innovation, problem-solving and decision-making

(c) Giving management insight into employees' needs, interests and problems, to help them manage better

(d) Demonstrating the value management places on employees, establishing the mutual trust and commitment that underpins constructive employee relations.

Mechanisms for upward communication include the following.

Attitude surveys

Surveys of employee opinions are a useful source of feedback (especially if there are no other direct avenues for employees to express their satisfactions and dissatisfactions). Attitude surveys may be carried out via:

(a) *Questionnaires,* whether standardised or tailored to the particular organisation or issue concerned. These may be paper-based or (increasingly) posted online on a company intranet. Questionnaires have the advantage of being quick and relatively cost-effective to administer, although they must be carefully designed if they are to elicit honest, meaningful and comparable responses.

(b) *Interviews*, either completely free-flowing or structured to a specific agenda of issues. Interviews are time-consuming and costly, but may also be more revealing, allowing a skilled interviewer to probe.

(c) *Focus groups*, allowing a structured response to interview questions by a representative sample of employees on specific issues

The IPD have produced the following checklist for conducting an employee attitude survey.

(a) Gain the commitment of senior management, clarify objectives and define areas where the company is prepared to take action.

(b) Decide between a census of employees - probably paper-based - and a random sample - maybe face-to-face interviews.

(c) Conduct a pilot survey.

(d) Design a questionnaire - this needs experienced help.

(e) Tell employees what is being done: the more internal publicity, the greater the chances of success.

(f) Guarantee confidentiality.

(g) Consider measures to improve the response rate, for example by holding supervised completion sessions in company time.

(h) If the survey involves face-to-face interviews, conduct them with one or two employees at a time. Avoid group discussions - it is difficult to maintain confidentiality in groups and to enable everyone to have a say.

(i) Produce the final report. Distil the evidence, reach conclusions and put forward recommendations. Present the report to top management.

(j) Report back to employees with a summary of the main findings.

(k) An individual or a group should be made responsible for action following the survey findings; progress should be monitored.

Activity 7 **(15 minutes)**

How would you respond to the following objections from a management traditionalist to employee surveys?

(a) Good managers already know their staff's opinions.

(b) Surveys are superficial, impersonal and bureaucratic.

(c) Surveys open cans of worms and raise false hopes.

(d) Surveys contain built in bias because of the unknown opinions of the many who do not respond.

Suggestion schemes

Suggestion schemes were discussed in Chapter 5 as a way of offering performance rewards and incentives. However, they are also an important mechanisms for upward communication.

Quality circles

Definition

> **Quality circles** are groups of six to ten employees from different levels and/or disciplines within an organisation, who meet regularly to discuss problems of quality, quality control, customer care or related issues in their area of work.

Quality circles emerged first in the US but were most enthusiastically adopted in Japan. They are still used to get employees involved in organisational quality values, but some commentators suggest that they have been superseded by other team-based working methods and a wider orientation to quality in organisations (such as a Total Quality Management orientation).

The circle is facilitated by a leader who directs the discussion and helps to orient and develop members (as required) in quality control and problem-solving techniques. It is important that the group is made up of volunteers, in order to harness genuine commitment and enthusiasm.

Quality circles do not generally have responsibility for making, implementing or following up recommendations. Even as discussion groups, however, they may have significant benefits, as members return to their departments as ambassadors for quality, customer care and employee involvement.

FOR DISCUSSION

Why might values such as quality or customer care be a powerful focus for attempts to involve employees?

4.4 Empowerment

Empowerment has two key aspects. It involves giving workers discretion to make decisions about how to organise work in order to achieve task goals *and* making workers responsible for achieving production and quality targets. (The French word for empowerment is 'responsibilisation'.)

The purpose of empowerment is:

(a) To free employees from rigorous control by instructions and orders, which contributes to job satisfaction *and* learning and flexibility

(b) To give employees opportunities for growth and job satisfaction through taking responsibility for their ideas and actions

(c) To release and develop resources in the workforce that would otherwise remain inaccessible, including creativity and initiative

(d) To harness employee commitment by allowing them to share in the process of target-setting and work organisation

(e) To decentralise decision-making and problem-solving initiative to 'front line' customer-facing roles, to enhance the flexibility and responsiveness of customer service

Empowerment goes hand in hand with:

(a) *Delayering,* or a cut in the number of levels in the organisation hierarchy: responsibility previously held by managers is, in effect, being given to operational workers

(b) *Flexibility,* since giving responsibility to the people closest to the product or customer encourages responsiveness

(c) *New technology,* since skilled knowledge workers need less supervision, being better equipped to identify and control the means to clearly understood ends

(d) *Employee development,* since the personal and interpersonal skills needed to meet the challenges of responsibility and participation in decision-making need to be developed

(e) *Unitarist employee relations,* since empowerment rests on the belief that employees will recognise and commit themselves to the business goals of their unit and organisation.

Empowerment implies a shift in the role of both *line managers* (who effectively become 'coaches' and 'facilitators' in team decision-making processes, setting parameters and providing information and guidance where required) and *HR practitioners* (who increasingly share responsibility for delivering HR policy outcomes not only with line managers but with employees themselves).

EXAMPLE

The validity of this view and its relevance to modern trends appears to be borne out by the approach to empowerment adopted by Harvester restaurants, as described in *Personnel Management.* The management structure comprises a branch manager and a 'coach', while everyone else is a team member. Everyone within a team has one or more 'accountabilities' (these include recruitment, drawing up rotas, keeping track of sales targets and so on) which are shared out by the team members at their weekly team meetings. All the team members at different times act as 'co-ordinator' - the person responsible for taking the snap decisions that are frequently necessary in a busy restaurant. Apparently, all the staff involved agree that empowerment has made their jobs more interesting and had hugely increased their motivation and sense of involvement.

We will look briefly at two approaches to empowerment: self-managed teamworking and total quality management (TQM).

4.5   Self-managed teams

Self-managed teams are the most highly-developed form of team working. They are permanent structures in which team members collaboratively decide all the major issues affecting their work: work processes and schedules, task allocation, the selection and development of team members, the distribution of rewards and the management of group processes (problem-solving, conflict management, internal discipline and so on). The team leader is a member of the team, acting in the role of coach and facilitator: leadership roles may be shared or rotated as appropriate.

Self managed teams generally have the following features (Harrington-Mackin, 1994).

(a) They contract with management to assume various degrees of **managerial responsibility** for planning, organising, directing and monitoring (which may increase as the team develops). Team members learn and share the jobs usually performed by a manager: no 'visible' immediate manager is present. They often report to 'absentee' managers with broad responsibilities for several functions, whose role is to act as integrators/facilitators.

(b) They perform **day-to-day planning and control functions**: scheduling and co-ordinating the daily and occasional tasks of the team and individuals; setting performance goals and standards; formulating and adopting budgets; collecting performance data and reviewing results.

(c) They perform **internal people management functions**: screening and interviewing candidates to join the team, and contributing to selection/hiring decisions; providing orientation for new members; coaching and providing feedback on member performance; designing and conducting cross-training on all tasks.

(d) Team members cross-train in all the tasks necessary for a particular process, and members rotate flexibly from job to job.

(e) Weekly team meetings are used to identify, analyse and solve task and relationship problems within the team: reviewing team working and progress; getting team members to research and present team issues and so on.

Activity 8   **(20 minutes)**

What do you think are likely to be the advantages of self-managed teamworking for the organisation?

4.6 Total quality management (TQM)

TQM is a Japanese-inspired orientation to quality in which quality values and aspirations are applied to the management of *all* resources and relationships within the firm and throughout the value chain (from suppliers to distributors), in order to seek continuous improvement and excellence in all aspects of performance.

Mullins (1999) synthesises various definitions of TQM as expressing: 'a way of life for an organisation as an whole, committed to total customer satisfaction through a continuous process of improvement, and the contribution and involvement of people'.

Two key aspects of TQM are:

- *Quality chains*. The quality chain extends from suppliers through to customers, via the 'internal customers' of each department within the organisation. The chain may be broken at any point where people or processes fail to fulfil the quality requirements of their immediate customer.

- *Total involvement*. Quality requires the commitment of all staff, and needs to be modelled from the top by senior management. It needs to be supported and reinforced by HRM policies for recruitment, training, appraisal, reward and development. It also emphasises the importance of people: communication, awareness and problem-solving are more important than mere systems.

NOTES

FOR DISCUSSION

On a scale from 'no voice' through involvement and participation to full empowerment or democracy, where would you place the orgnisation you currently work for, or one you know well?

Chapter roundup

- Employee voice embraces 'a whole variety of processes and structures which enable, and sometimes empower employees, directly and indirectly, to contribute to decision-making in the firm.

- Employee participation concerns the extent to which employees, often via their representatives, are involved with management in the decision-making machinery of the organisation. It includes joint consultation, works councils, European Works Councils and worker representation on the board.

- Employee involvement is the process of informing and consulting employees about, or associating them with, one or more aspects of running an organisation. It may be accomplished by two-way communication, financial participation, representative participation, empowerment and inclusion in cultural programmes such as quality management and organisational learning

Quick quiz

1. Distinguish between the terms 'employee voice', 'employee participation' and 'employee involvement'.

2. Draw Marchington *et al*'s matrix model of employee voice.

3. Give three examples of 'representative participation'.

4. What is joint consultation?

5. What is an EWC and when is it compulsory to have one?

6. A partnership agreement reflects a pluralist approach to employee relations. True or false?

7. Outline the German model of co-determination.

8. Give five examples of employee involvement techniques.

9. What is TQM?

10. What are the purposes of empowerment?

Answers to quick quiz

1. Employee voice covers the range of possibilities from no voice through to full participation. Involvement is consultation/communication where management retains the right to manage. Participation allows employees to influence organisational decisions. (para 1.1)

2. See figure 18.1.

3. Collective representation, joint consultation, European Works Council, partnership agreements. (para 1.3)

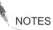

4   Formal non-negotiatory meetings between management and employee representatives to discuss matters of shared interest.   (para 2.3)

5   A Pan-European body of employee representatives with the right to meet central management at least once a year for information and consultation about the progress and prospects of the company. All organisations with more than 1,000 employees in the EU member states, with more than 150 people in each of two or more states, must establish some form of Europe-wide consultational system: an EWC is the fallback system if unions and employee negotiators fail to agree on an alternative.

                                                                        (para 2.4)

6   False: unitarist.   (para 2.6)

7   See paragraph 3.3 for a full answer.

8   Communication (eg briefings, journals)

     Up-down communication (eg suggestion schemes, quality circles)

     Financial participation (eg profit-sharing, share ownership)

     Representative participation (eg joint consultation, works councils)

     Empowerment (eg self-managed teamworking, delegation)

     Cultural programmes (eg TQM, customer care, learning organisation)
                                                                        (para 4.1)

9   Total Quality Management: a whole-organisation approach to managing quality through the application of quality values, continuous improvement and total involvement.   (para 4.3)

10   See paragraph 4.4 for a full answer.

Answers to activities

1   Participation may be desirable or necessary because of the following factors.

     (a) **Commitment**: the perceived need to obtain a higher level of identification with organisational goals and a higher degree of acceptance and support of strategies for change.

     (b) **Quality of decision-making**: the perceived need to involve employees with 'front-line' knowledge, experience and influence in areas such as quality management and customer care. Quality circles and empowered teams are developed on this basis.

     (c) **Trade union pressure.** Collective bargaining has been extended into areas traditionally considered as management concerns: human resource levels, training and so on. Joint consultation is another prevalent form of worker participation, where management discuss matters of concern regularly with union representatives, on Joint Consultative Committees (JCCs) or non-negotiatory staff forums. A more radical approach is the formation of partnership agreements with worker representatives.

     (d) **Legal requirements**. Participation and consultation have occupied a high profile in employment protection and – most recently – in the social policy of the European Union, with provision for employee representation in decision-sharing structures such as Works Councils and Supervisory Boards.

2   Your own research.

3   Your own research (and opinion).

4   Some advantages (identified by Legal & General and MSF in their partnership agreement) include:

    (a)   Increased flexibility, honesty and trust in relationships

    (b)   Better quality, faster decision-making, with decisions that were more likely to be readily accepted within the company

    (c)   Positive public relations for the company – and for the union ('rebranded' to attract new members)

    (d)   Having the right people focused on the right issues

    (e)   The development of an 'adult' relationship in which company and union could move in the same direction

5   Low power-distance and collectivist cultures are particularly likely to accept employee participation at a deep level.

6   (a)   Briefing groups and meetings, Joint Consultation Committees or works councils, open direct communication from managers, encouraging informal networking, 360° feedback, consultation policy, noticeboards/memos etc.

    (b)   Suggestion schemes, quality circles, upward appraisal, JCCs or works councils, attitude surveys

    (c)   Increased delegation (empowerment), self-managed and/or multi-skilled teamworking, horizontal structures focused on the customer, job design based on whole meaningful tasks

    (d)   Financial participation through profit-related pay, employee share ownership schemes; cafeteria benefits; learning/development opportunities

    (e)   Participative management style; single status agreements; culture of informality (Management By Walking Around); role of supervisor as coach/facilitator.

7   Nigel Nicholson (*Financial Times*, January 1993) gives the following answers (briefly summarised).

    (a)   How do managers know if their reading of opinions is correct?

    (b)   Yes, they are no substitute for good personal communications, but 'Thanks for asking us' is a common response.

    (c)   Cans of worms probably should be opened. 'Management's commitment, clearly communicated at the outset, should be not only to take action where feasible, but also to be frank about reasons for not acting when this would be unreasonably difficult, contentious or costly.

    (d)   Bias is modest when return rates of over 50% are achieved, and a well-designed and carefully introduced survey can expect returns of 65% or more.

8   Self-managed teamworking is said to have advantages in:

- Saving in managerial costs

- Gains in quality and productivity, by harnessing the commitment of those who perform work

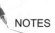

- Encouraging individual initiative and responsibility, enhancing organisational responsiveness (particularly in front-line customer service units)

- Gains in efficiency, through multi-skilling, the involvement of fewer functions in decision-making and co-ordinating work, and (often) the streamlining of working methods by groups

However, self-managed teams are a comparatively recent (and rare) phenomenon, and require skilled leadership and culture change (particularly in former 'command and control' organisations) in order to be effective.

Assignment 18 (1½ hours)

Semco is a Brazilian company which makes pumps, dishwashers and cooking units. The company attracted enormous media and business interest in the early to mid 1990s. Here's why.

(a) All managers are rated by their subordinates every six months, on a scale of 1 to 100. Those managers who consistently under-perform are squeezed out.

(b) Workers elect their own bosses: 'In a plant where everyone has a financial stake in its success, the idea of asking subordinates to choose bosses seems an eminently sensible way to stop accidents before they are promoted.'

(c) Workers set their own salaries – but they know they might price themselves out of the department's budget if they aim too high.

(d) The workers decide how much of the profits to share and how much to re-invest in the business.

(e) Workers are encouraged to work from home.

(f) Everyone 'from the cleaner upwards' has access to the company's books.

Semco's boss, Ricardo Semler, believes that democracy has been introduced to the work place: this is a radical departure from 'classical' organisation theory, but at a time when firms like IBM are being overtaken by smaller, more flexible competitors, his ideas are gaining currency. 'The trouble is that the corporate world is run by people not exactly busting keen to lose their parking lots, let alone to subject themselves to monthly scrutiny by people whom, currently, he can hire and fire. Even corporate turkeys don't vote for Christmas.' (Victor Keegan, *The Guardian*, 1993).

Compare Semco (as sketched in the above portrait) to a 'classical organisation' with a traditional 'industrial relations' approach.

ANSWERS TO ASSIGNMENTS

Answer to Assignment 1

Class One Insurance Services

Matters for urgent attention might include:

    (a)   Recruitment of staff for replacement and growth

    (b)   Harmonisation of terms and conditions between sites and grades

    (c)   Develop grievance procedure to deal with perceived inequities

    (d)   Deal with miscellaneous but long-standing problems

    (e)   Set up regular visits to all sites

    (f)   Produce standardised procedures and policies for all divisions

    (g)   Collate salary information to get internal and external equity

    (h)   Examine pay strategy for sales staff

    (i)   Meet with trade union representatives on a regular, on-going basis

    (j)   Check health and safety procedures

Matters for longer term attention might include:

    (a)   Relocation of all staff to one site

    (b)   Reduction in numbers of administrative staff (especially at headquarters)

    (c)   Analysis of training needs

    (d)   Motivating long-serving staff

    (e)   Draw up age profiles to check future succession problems

    (f)   Conduct an attitude survey to test staff morale

    (g)   Establish a computerised records and pay system

    (h)   Check business plan and build personnel strategies around it

    (i)   Establish a system of performance appraisal

    (j)   Communicate business results to all staff

Answer to Assignment 2

Human Resource Planning at Quick-Send Ltd

1   (a)   A bar chart would provide the best illustration of the age profile.

    (b)   The most striking point shown by the age profile is that 94 staff (43%) are over 50 years old. Quick-Send therefore have an ageing workforce. While such workers tend to have good attendance records and low absenteeism, the company will have to plan for replacements when they retire. The company should also have a clearly thought-out retirement policy.

            A second factor is the number of young staff: 62 (28%) are under 30. The training requirements of such staff need to be considered.

2   (a)

Year	Total number of staff
X	217
X + 1	190
X + 2	160
X + 3	200
X + 4	231
X + 5	237

NOTES

(b)

Year	Total number of staff needed	Shortage/surplus (before labour turnover)		Labour turnover	Shortage/surplus taking into account labour turnover	
		Shortage	*Surplus*	*turnover*	*Shortage*	*Surplus*
X	217					
X + 1	190		27	9		18
X + 2	160		30	8		22
X + 3	200	40		10	50	
X + 4	231	31		12	43	
X + 5	237	6		12	18	

3   The figures show that for the next two years the warehouse and packing department will have a surplus of staff. After that there is a predicted shortage for each of the following three years.

Given that 20 of the current staff are currently over 60, it would not appear that the firm will have a problem for the first year faced with a predicted surplus of 18 staff.

Similarly, in the following year, the company could consider offering staff early retirement to overcome the predicted surplus of 22 staff. Voluntary redundancy could also be considered on a very limited basis.

The picture changes very much in the third year. If the predicted increase in orders and the stabilisation of the ratios is correct, the firm will be faced with a shortage of employees. Given the current ageing workforce, plans should be laid for recruitment and training of staff for these years, or the possibility of relocation from other areas of the organisation considered. Space and facilities for the increase in staff numbers is another consideration.

Answer to Assignment 3

Rottenborough District Hospital

The first point to note is that the three Rs are different (although they do overlap). There would be little point, for example, in developing a targeted recruitment policy if you made no efforts to keep your women returnees motivated and satisfied once working for you. You should also acknowledge the value of women workers and the problems you can expect as an organisation if they are under-represented.

Alternative ways in which you can attract, keep and encourage back your target group might include:

(a)   Staff banks
(b)   Term-time working
(c)   Homeworking
(d)   Jobshare and flexi-time
(e)   Nursery and childcare vouchers

These are all relatively easy to implement. Longer term considerations might include:

(a)   Reprofiling of jobs to create career pathways for non-professionals

(b)   Analysing criteria for success at higher levels

(c)   Improving the organisational image for recruitment

(d)   Targeting women returnees more specifically in your recruitment campaigns

(e)   Train all staff involved in recruitment and selection

(f)   Review your job requirements to make essential skills specific

(g)   Standardise and control questions asked of interview candidates

Once more, don't forget that the answer has to be in the form of a report to your Director of Human Resources.

Answer to Assignment 4

This was designed to be an active and inter-active learning exercise: there is no suggested answer.

For guidance, if needed, use some of the frameworks given in the text, as follows.

Task 1.   Paragraph 6.3, Chapter 3

Task 2.   Section 2, Chapter 4 (Paragraph 6.4, Chapter 3)

Task 3.   Paragraphs 2.2-2.3, Chapter 4

Task 4.   Paragraph 2.3-2.4, Chapter 4. (Also see Paragraph 1.3 on discrimination and privacy, and Paragraph 1.4 to select options for further selection techniques.)

Answer to Assignment 5

Ad Hoc Ltd

(a)   See the table of Paragraph 2.2 Chapter 5, to remind you of the advantages and disadvantages.

(b)   **Overcoming weaknesses**

Some of the above weaknesses are such that they cannot be overcome in practice - they are inherent in the objectives of the technique. Their effects can be minimised, however, by choice of the particular method, the way in which the system is implemented and by building on the strengths of the technique. To a great extent the particular weaknesses of job evaluation, and ways in which they can be minimised, will vary according to the method used, the method of implementation, the training of the evaluator, and the attitudes of workers and management. In general terms, however, the value of the method can be enhanced as follows.

(i)   Whichever method is used, evaluations must be kept up to date, with periodic reviews.

(ii)   The process should (time, resources and expertise permitting) be as scientific as possible. A more qualitative approach, such as factor comparison or points rating, should be adopted, and the factors to be studied, the weightings and scores should be systematically determined. There must still be some element of subjectivity, but a visible attempt at objectivity is being made.

(iii)   Job analysts and evaluators must be trained in the use of the appropriate techniques, must have access to job documentation and to job holders (for observation and interview), and their evaluations should be monitored or reviewed to ensure that they are keeping up with changes in the organisation and applying techniques correctly.

(iv)   It should be recognised by management, and by job holders, that job evaluation is only part of the pay/reward setting process. Job evaluation alone allows for no incentive level of reward: bonuses and increments for merit or performance will need to be added to the salary structure if there is not to be a demotivating effect. Moreover, job evaluation may be seen to be a threatening - or simply irrelevant - basis for salary structures, if it is not recognised that there are factors unrelated to job content which affect the value of jobs, such as equity ('felt fair' rewards), market rates of pay, negotiated pay scales, age and experience and so on.

(v) Problems of acceptance by staff - since job evaluation is a highly political exercise - can be minimised by implementing the system in an open, sensitive way. The purpose, objectives and potential benefits will need to be 'sold' to staff in advance: it will in particular have to be made clear that it is the job, not the job-holder, which is being evaluated. The role of collective bargaining may have to be discussed with unions. Appeal and revision procedures will have to be built into the system, and employees must be allowed to voice any uncertainties, suspicions and objections they may have about the affect of job grading on earnings, confidentiality, promotion and so on.

Answer to Assignment 6

Biotherm PLC

The overall purpose of the appraisal interview should be to encourage Alan Heath to become more a part of the personnel team (after all he has specialist knowledge which cannot be replaced). You cannot ignore his sickness record because it impacts on performance. However, you should attempt to understand the reasons behind his poor attendance rather than tackling it at this stage (this is best left for a separate occasion). You should ensure at all costs that the appraisal interview does not become a disciplinary one.

Your plan should include the following:

(a) Discussion on achievement of past objectives

(b) Reasons behind failure to achieve objectives

(c) Problems and successes in current performance (you should have consulted in advance with the main people Alan interacts with, eg line managers, colleagues, external clients)

(d) Attempts to understand Alan's personal needs (he may be motivated by his 'expertise' for example, rather than any additional pay award)

(e) A discussion of Alan's job aspirations this will follow on from the previous point but you should have done your homework in advance on the requirements of the job immediately senior to his

(f) A commitment not to duck difficult issues but to explore you may find out some very good reasons behind his refusal to work beyond contracted hours, for example

(g) An attempt to agree a set of SMART objectives

Your approach to this interview should be 'problem-solving', rather than 'tell and sell' or 'tell and listen'.

Answer to Assignment 7

Q and R Ferries PLC

The dismissal of Roger Price is potentially fair, but the punishment is likely to be viewed by a tribunal as being too severe. They are therefore likely to rule unfair dismissal. Mary Gardner's case is likely to be viewed as fair dismissal, due to capability. However, Q and R Ferries are likely to be criticised by a tribunal for lack of consultation with the employee. Thus the areas of severity and consultation are likely to be the main points a tribunal will take into account.

You will shortly be interviewing the relevant department managers as part of your preparation for the tribunal cases. You should ask the following questions:

Roger Price's manager;

(a) were all relevant procedures followed? (eg sick reporting)

(b) did Roger Price know about the procedures?

(c) did you follow the disciplinary procedures? If so, was dismissal the right level or should you have issued a warning?

Mary Gardner's manager;

(a) were there any alternatives to dismissal? (eg career break)

(b) were Mary Gardner's health problems known on appointment?

(c) why didn't anyone talk to Mary Gardner?

Overall questions might challenge the wisdom of passing authority right down the line without overseeing it, and a possible recommendation of health screening on appointment.

Answer to Assignment 8

The basic points can be found in Chapter 8, Sections 1 and 2. You may have chosen to use diagrams such as the Harvard map of HR territory to illustrate soft-hard approaches (perhaps drawing the employee life-cycle of the Michigan model); the 27-points-of-difference table is already well-suited to presentation.

In terms of format and style, you were given lots of leeway. Be as creative and professional as you can: the results may act as evidence of competence under Assessment Criteria 22. Remember to be concise (this is a summary): it will help you to sort out in your own mind what is important about the two 'theories' under discussion.

Answer to Assignment 9

Flex Consult

(a) The seaside holiday hotel will be able to anticipate peaks in demand on Bank Holiday weekends and during the summer holiday season. It will require a mix of unskilled and semi-skilled staff to cover extra demand. A typical solution would be to obtain skilled agency and/or seasonally contracted staff (perhaps annual regulars) with the addition of casual labour if required for general duties. There may also be a continual daily fluctuation of demand at the hotel, centred around housekeeping in the mornings, and around the bar/restaurant (if any) in the evenings: the employment of permanent part-time staff may be the solution here.

(b) The domestic appliance manufacturer might be able to anticipate peaks in demand in the fourth quarter of the year, with Christmas and January sales purchases. Such a regular seasonal fluctuation could be dealt with by securing extra hours of work through overtime or adding shifts, or by annual hours contracts stipulating a core period of labour before and during the peak period. These methods would have the advantage of utilising the existing skilled workforce, rather than obtaining outside labour who would require time and resources to 'get up to speed' with the product and production methods.

(c) The firm of management consultants needs to respond more flexibly to more or less random demands from new clients. It also requires access to highly-skilled professional people, without sufficient lead times to train them to meet immediate short-term demands. The firm will probably therefore rely on freelance consultants with whom it has a relationship of trust: possibly past employees who have set up on their own, or who have experienced training or collaboration with the firm and therefore know its 'house style' and methods. The firm should keep a group of 'associate consultants' on its books, and include them in consultant briefings and training programmes where possible.

Answer to Assignment 10

Glamour Products

You face a number of problems in this case study:

(a) Line manager and supervisor resentment

(b) Managing director's dismissive attitude to equal opportunities

(c) Adverse publicity for Glamour Products

(d) Impending IT case on unfair dismissal on grounds of race

(e) Uneasy relations with trade union

(f) Managing director's belief that training alone can deal with a complex problem

(g) Lack of any equal opportunities policy

You must attempt to deal with these, in particular the last two. Equal opportunities is a philosophy which should be embraced wholesale by an organisation if it is adopted. It is not something which can be packaged and delivered in a one-day training course. You should, therefore, undertake to do the following:

(a) Investigate the grounds for unfair dismissal of Mr Patel

(b) Draw up an equal opportunities policy, having involved all interested parties (managers, staff, union representatives)

(c) Make it explicit that racist language will not be tolerated

(d) Attempt a long term education programme on equal opportunities: there is no point in simply ensuring compliance with the law: this will not make the problem go away and may serve to exacerbate existing negative attitudes

(e) Analyse other areas to ensure that equal opportunities are being observed for example, what is the representation of ethnic minority employees across different levels and functions in the organisation? Does your recruitment procedure support equal opportunities or work against it?

Don't forget to write your answer in the form of a faxed memo back to the Managing Director (as the question asks), pointing out the reasons why you feel a day conference isn't the right approach.

Answer to Assignment 11

Duntoiling Nursing Homes

To deal with this difficult situation effectively you need to do the following:

(a) Introduce a disciplinary procedure if none currently exists

(b) Consider the Health and Safety at Work legislation, particularly the employer's obligations of duty and care towards staff

(c) Define constructive dismissal (this means where an organisation has changed terms and conditions of employment to such an extent that the employees feel they have no other option but to resign)

(d) Consider the wisdom of unilateral changes in terms and conditions without notice (ie Cheeseman imposing these changes without any consultation)

(e) Consider reinstating the employee with possible concessions (eg counselling to give up smoking)

(f) Prepare your ideal and 'fall-back' positions when negotiating

(g) Question why the policy was introduced in the first place

(h) Ask why there was no involvement from the personnel function in implementing the smoking policy

(i) Develop a 'best practice' model showing how to introduce a smoking policy and do it again (remember the employer's duty to protect employees from the effects of passive smoking). The model should include:

   (i) A consultation period (say 3 months)
   (ii) Establishing a consultative committee
   (iii) Conducting a staff attitude survey
   (iv) Making provision for special cases
   (v) Make formal changes to terms and conditions
   (vi) Retrain line managers in disciplinary matters
   (vii) Review and monitor the policy

Again remember that the question asks for your answer to be in the form of a brief to Mr Cheeseman.

Answer to Assignment 12

Kaizen Tomorrow Ltd

Limits to quality circles

The production director should be advised that the nature of the changes recommended by the quality circle will depend on the range of skills and experience of the circle members. The wider their skills are, and the broader their experience, the more significant and far-reaching will be the changes they might suggest. Groups of workers with similar skills are more likely to make suggestions for limited changes within the sphere of their own work experience. What range of skills should the circles have? How will unions demarcation lines (and the associated culture of inflexibility) be overcome?

The 'terms of reference' of the circles should be made clear. Are they to **recommend** changes to senior management, or will they have the authority to **decide** changes, and make them? Management does not currently enlist or invite worker input (unlike Japanese style): how will this be overcome?

Need for co-operation

Since the purpose of quality circles is to encourage innovation, the co-operation of employees will be crucial. The plans for setting up quality circles should therefore be discussed with the employees who will provide membership of the circles. How to create a culture of participation and consensus? Need for shared culture values/mechanisms to promote:

(a)   Identification with the organisation

(b)   Quality awareness/Japanese continuous improvement orientation)

Problems with quality circles

Possible problems with the introduction of quality circles might be:

(a)   Not enough support from top management

(b)   No co-operation from middle management

(c)   Discouragement because of unrealistic expectations of what the circles can do

(d)   Lack of support from trade unions

(e)   Poor choice of circle leaders – not experienced in facilitation of open discussion, seeking consensus

(f)   Insufficient training of circle members – not experienced in collective decision-making

(g)   Unwillingness to participate among employees – lack of identification with quality goals

(h)   Individual egos won't join in the circle 'team' spirit

Successful introduction of quality circles

The keys to a successful programme are:

(a)   Creating a proper atmosphere in which to launch them – a positive approach and good publicity

(b)   Giving circle members adequate training in quality circle techniques

(c)   Introducing circles slowly, one or two at a time, instead of setting up too many all at once; learning from experience; getting employees to accept the value of circles from their experience and observations over time

(d)   Full support from top management

(e)   An enthusiastic 'facilitator' – a manager in charge of making the circles a success

(f)   Setting up a good system for following up and evaluating proposals for change

(g)   Giving recognition to circle members – for instance, rewards for successful changes

Answer to Assignment 13

No suggested answer: your Personal Development Plan is personal!

Answer to Assignment 14

Price-U-Like Stores

The first thing to note is that you should not draw up this training programme in isolation, but should seek the input of key managers and staff. The course should go through a 'pilot run' to iron out any problems which can then be changed. Importantly, the programme should be designed as a package which is capable of being transferred and delivered by other trainers (this is particularly important for multi-site organisations such as Price-U-Like Stores).

The style of the programme should be broad and mixed, allowing delegates to experience Customer Care first hand, then allowing them to reflect on what they have learnt and whether they can apply it to real situations they face. The programme should have clearly stated aims and objectives.

Indicative content of the programme might include:

- (a) Icebreaker exercise
- (b) Why have a Customer Care initiative?
- (c) The importance of front-line staff to Customer Care
- (d) Internal and external customers
- (e) Listening skills, empathy, body language
- (f) Why people complain

Delivery techniques might include discussion, role-play, brainstorming, videos, group problem solving, case studies, scenarios, lectures. Since this is likely to be a large-scale, strategic-level initiative, you may want to evaluate it at more than one level (using Kirkpatrick's model). You may even choose to attempt a 'fifth level' evaluation of impact on the community (since society should benefit from customer focus) and/or ROI. You could at least identify costs and benefits in your answer (if not put a monetary value to them).

Answer to Assignment 15

Your own research. (You may have an opportunity to give this presentation as demonstration of competence in this area.)

Answer to Assignment 16

Your own research.

Answer to Assignment 17

Your strike contingency plan should contain some of the following elements.

- (a) Monitor employee and union attitudes, in the course of all formal and informal communications: ascertain likely duration, scope and severity of strike.

- (b) Prepare strategies for negotiation, dispute handling, conciliation: lay out realistic and fall-back options. (Best scenario: union agreement to delay claims, relate claims to productivity guarantees/increases, engage in profit-sharing.) Prepare analysis of costs of various options.

- (c) Communicate direct with workforce in attempt to avert strike. (Letters sent to employees homes, or with pay slips.) Emphasise need to work together, tighten belt in order to preserve firm/jobs in the face of external recession, competition. Lead by example on productivity, pay constraints.

(d) Public/financial relations exercise. Emphasise pressures on business, concern for jobs etc through editorial coverage in local (national?) press, broadcast, financial media. (Paid advertising as a last resort.)

(e) Take steps for protection of the firm's property and interests (security doors, check and secure keys, block access to confidential files, employ security guards if required).

(f) Take steps to ensure that materials and supplies can come in and orders go out freely (anticipate picket arrangements – notify police of potential for obstruction; arrange for transport/unloading/storage staff if affected by strike).

(g) Re-organise to minimise disruption by striking workers, maintain output or level of service sufficient to satisfy demand: schedule stock-take, equipment servicing during strike period to utilise down time; re-allocate tasks among workers not involved in strike action (supply cross-training if required); engage alternative sources of labour (temporary/casual); offer added incentives to non-striking workers to increase overtime and/or productivity.

(h) Stop pay of individuals on strike. Issue formal disciplinary warnings to strikers, with clear consequences for breach of contract. (NB If dismiss any strikers, must dismiss all.)

(i) Appoint Management Task Force to co-ordinate firm's response; provide on-going information to media; support non-striking workers.

(j) Brief legal advisers and take advice on actions available and consequences of options.

Answer to Assignment 18

Some of the issues you may have raised are as follows.

Under a classical organisation/control/industrial relations system:

(a) Managers would be appraised by their managers (top-down): the idea of upward appraisal contravenes ideas of managerial status and authority. (Would not be possible in an elitist management culture, such as France or a high power-distance culture.)

(b) Managers would be appointed by the board or more senior managers. 'Leadership' by election (formal or informal) has always been acceptable – but 'management' traditionally implies authority delegated or conferred by position in the organisation. The idea of elected managers changes the whole culture of employee relations, blurring the lines between 'us' and 'them', while therefore increasing support for subsequent managerial decisions. It also affects the culture of the organisation, which traditionally reflects top-down managerial vision and values, as a form of control.

(c)(d) Salary levels would be set by top management, based on a rational structure of equity, differentials, market rates, cost-minimisation and so on, in line with the HR plan. Self-nominated salary places emphasis on the perceived value of a fair day's work for a fair day's pay – and the link between higher pay and more/harder/better work – to the employees themselves. This is effectively self-motivation. Financial participation in the form of work-nominated profit-sharing requires business/economic awareness and responsibility on the part of employees, including awareness of shared interest in the continuing competitiveness of the business, and the dynamics of the labour market.

(e) Working from home is a commitment rather than control-based system (HRM rather than IR), encouraging flexibility, reducing direct supervision and so on. This is perhaps the least radical of the measures for increasing employee discretion, but it reflects a culture of trust and assumed mutual interest that is typical of the new unitarist HR perspective.

(f) In the traditional IR framework, trade unions officials may be given access to this information prior to collective bargaining on wages. On-going, open access to financial information ('transparency') increases the accountability of management – but since workers share this responsibility, it is likely to increase both the sense of partnership and the quality of worker-manager decision-making (especially on financial matters).

INDEX

NOTES

NOTES

PROFESSIONAL EDUCATION

NOTES

BIBLIOGRAPHY

Adair, J & Allen, M (1999) *Time Management and Personal Development*. London: Hawksmere

Adams, J S (1963), 'Toward an understanding of inequity' *Journal of Abnormal & Social Psychology* 64/4.

Alberga, T, Tyson, S & Parsons, D (1997) 'An evaluation of the Investors in People Standard', *Human Resource Management Journal* 7 (2)

Albrecht, K & Albrecht, S (1993) 'Added Value Negotiating', *Training*, April pp 26-29

Armstrong, M (2000) *Strategic Human Resource Management: A Guide to Action* (2nd edition). London: Kogan Page

Allen, A (2003) 'Out of the ordinary', *People Management*, 4 December

Armstrong, M (2003) *A Handbook of Human Resource Management Practice* (9th edition). London: Kogan Page

Arnold, J, Copper, C & Robertson, I (1995) *Work Psychology: Understanding Human Behaviour in the Workplace* (2nd edition). London: Pitman

Atkinson, J (1984) 'Manpower strategies for flexible organisations' *Personnel Management*, August

Atkinson, J & Meager, N (1986) *Changing patterns of Work*. London: IMS/OECD

Barnes, P (1997) 'Teleworking'. *Chartered Secretary*, May

Beardwell, I & Holden, L (1997) *Human Resource Management* (2nd edition). London: Pitman

Beer, M, Spector B, Laurence P, Quinn Mills, D & Walton, K (1984) *Managing Human Assets*. New York: Free Press

Beer, M & Spector, B (1985) 'Corporate transformations in human resource management', *HRM Trends and Challenges* (ed Walton & Lawrence). Boston, Mass: Harvard University Press

Blyth, A (2003) 'The art of survival', *People Management*, 1 May

Blyton, P & Turnbull, P (1992) *Reassessing HRM*. London: Sage

Bolton, T (1997) *Human Resource Management: An Introduction*. Oxford: Blackwell

Bond, S (2003) 'How to effect changes in working hours', *People Management*, 10 July

Bottomley, C (1998) in *People Management*, 9 September

Boxall, P F (1995) 'Building the theory of comparative HRM', *HRM Journal*, 5 (5)

Boxall, P F & Purcell, J (2003) *Strategy and Human Resource Management*. Basingstoke: Palgrave Macmillan

Bramley, P (1986) *Evaluation of Training: A practical guide*. London: BASIE

Bratton, J & Gold, J (2003) *Human Resource Management: Theory and Practice* (3rd edition). Basingstoke: Palgrave Macmillan

Brewster, C (1999) 'Strategic HRM: the value of different paradigms', *Strategic Human Resource Management* (ed Schuler, Jackson). Oxford: Blackwell

Bridges, W (1994) *Jobshift: How to Prosper in a Workplace Without Jobs*. London: Allen & Unwin

Bronstein, M (2003), 'A life less ordinary', *People Management*, 17 April

Brown, D & Baron, A (2003) 'A capital idea' *People Management*, 26 June

Burgoyne, J (1999) *Developing Yourself, Your Career and Your Organisation*. London: Lemos & Crane

Burns, J M (1978) *Leadership*. London: Harper & Row

Business Basics (1997) *Human Resource Management* (3rd edition). London: BPP Publishing

Cartright, A (2003) 'How to deal with requests for flexible working', *People Management*, 6 November

Chamberlain, N W & Kuhn, J (1965) *Collective Bargaining*. New York: McGraw Hill

CIPD (1994) *Statement on Counselling in the Workplace*. London: CIPD

Clague, I (2004) 'Soft touch strategies', posted at www.learningtechnologies.co/article on 02/03/04.

Clarke, K (2003) 'Show me the money' *People Management*, 1 May

Clegg, H (1976) *The System of Industrial Relations in Great Britain*. Oxford: Blackwell

Clutterbuck, D (1991) *Everyone Needs a Mentor: How to Foster Talent Within the Organisation* (2nd edition). London: IPM

Connock, S (1991) *HR Vision: Managing a Quality Workforce*. London: IPM

Constable, R & McCormick, R J (1987) *The Making of British Managers*. London: BIM

Cooper, C (2003) 'Minority report', *People Management*, 4 December

Cornelius & Faire, S (1989) *Everyone Can Win: How to Resolve Conflict*. Sydney: Simon & Schuster Australia

Critchley, R (1996). 'New paradigms for "sustainable employability"', *HR Monthly*, April, pp 22-23

Cuming, M W (1993) *The Theory and Practice of Personnel Management*. London: Butterworth Heinemann.

Cushway, B & Lodge, D (1994) *Human Resource Management*. Nichols

Dalgamo, D & Davies, P (2003) 'How to consult on collective redundancies', *People Management*, 11 September

Department for Education and Employment (1998) *The Learning Age: a renaissance for a new Britain*. Sheffield: DfEE

Department for Education and Employment (1999) *Learning to Succeed: a new framework for post-16 education*. Sheffield: DfEE

Department for Education and Employment (2000) *Labour Market and Skill Trends*. Sheffield: DfEE

Dobler, D W, Burt D N & Lee, L (1990) *Purchasing and Materials Management*. (5th edition) New York: McGraw Hill

Drucker, P (1955). *The Practice of Management*. London: Heinemann

Equal Opportunities Commission (2000) *Good Practice Guide: Job evaluation schemes free of sex bias.* Manchester: EOC.

Evans, J (2003) 'DTI official hints at tougher law', *People Management,* 10 July

Fisher, R, Ury, W & Patton, B (1999) *Getting to Yes: Negotiating an Agreement Without Giving In* (2nd edition). London: Random House

Fombrun, C J, Tichy, N M & Devanno, M A (1984) *Strategic Human Resource Management.* New York: Wiley.

Fox, A (1975) *Industrial Relations and a Wider Society: Aspects of Interaction.* London: Faber & Faber

Gardenswartz, L & Rowe, A (1993) *Managing Diversity: A Complete Desk Reference and Planning Guide.* Homewood, IL: Irwin

Garvin, M (1993) 'Building a Learning Organisation', *Harvard Business Review,* July-August

Gennard, J and Judge, G *Employee Relations* (3rd edition) London: CIPD

Goldthorpe, J H, Lockwood, D C, Bechofer, F & Platt, J (1968) *The Affluent Worker: Industrial Attitudes and Behaviour.* Cambridge: CUP

Goss, D (1994) *Principles of Human Resource Management.* London: International Thomson Business Press

Graham, H T & Bennett, R (1998) *Human Resources Management* (9th edition). London: Pitman

Gratton, L, Haily, V H, Stile, P & Truss, C (1999) *Strategic HRM.* Oxford: OUP

Guest, D E (1989) 'Personnel & HRM: Can you tell the difference?' *Personnel Management,* January pp 48-51

Guest, D E (1991) 'Personnel management: the end of orthodoxy', *British Journal of Industrial Relations* 29 (2)

Guest, D E (1999) 'Human Resource Management: the workers' verdict', *Human Resource Management Journal* 9 (2)

Guest, D E (2001) 'Industrial relations and HRM', *Human Resource Management: A Critical Text* (2nd edition) (ed Storey). London: Thomson

Guest, D E, Michie, J, Sheehan, M & Conway, N (2000) *Employment Relations, HRM & Business Performance.* London: CIPD

Guirdham, M (1999) *Communicating Across Cultures.* Basingstoke: Palgrave

Handy, C B (1989) *The Age of Unreason.* London: Business Books

Handy, C B (1993) *Understanding Organisations.* Harmondsworth: Penguin

Hargreaves, P & Jarvis, P (2000) *The Human Resource Development Handbook* (revised edition). London: Kogan Page

NOTES

Hersey, P & Blanchard, K H (1988) *Management of Organisational Behaviour: Utilising Human Resources* (5th edition). New Jersey: Prentice Hall

Herzberg, F W (1966) *Work and the Nature of Man*. New York: Staples

Higginbottom, K (2003 (a)) 'More than lip service' *People Management*, 4 December

Higginbottom, K (2003 (b)) 'HR in the spotlight' *People Management*, 20 November

Higginbottom, K (2003 (c)) 'Mind your own business', *People Management*, 1 May

Hofstede, G (1989) *Cultures Consequences*. Beverley Hills, CA: Sage

Hofstede, G (1991) *Cultures and Organisations*. London: McGraw Hill

Holmstrom, R (2003) 'Time well spent', *People Management*, 28 August

Honey, P & Mumford, A (1990) *The Opportunist Learner*. Maidenhead: Peter Honey.

Honey, P & Mumford, A (1992) *A Manual of Learning Styles* (3rd edition). Maidenhead: Peter Honey

Huczynski, A & Buchanan, D (2001) *Organisational Behaviour: An Introductory Text*. Harlow, Essex: FT Prentice Hall.

Hunt, J (1982) *Managing People in Organisations*. NY: McGraw Hill

Huthwaite Inc (2000) *Behaviour of Successful Negotiators*. Percellville, VI: Huthwaite Inc.

Ingham, J (2003) 'How to implement a diversity policy', *People Management*, 24 July

Investors in People (2004) posted at www.investorsinpeople.co.uk/IIP/...CaseStudies, 12.02.04

IPD (1998) *The IPD Guide to Outsourcing*. London: IPD

IPM (1992) *Statement on Counselling in the Workplace*. London: IPM

Ivey, A, Ivey, M & Simek Morgan, L (1993) *Counselling and Psychotherapy: a Multicultural Perspective* (3rd edition). Boston, Mass: Allyn & Bacon

Johns, E (1994) *Perfect Customer Care*. London: Random House

Jones, B (1982) *Sleepers, Wake!: Technology and the Future of Work*. Oxford: OUP

Kane & Stanton (1994) *Human Resource Planning in a Changing Environment*.

Katz, R (ed) *Career Issues in Human Resource Management*. New Jersey: Prentice Hall

Kaufman, R & Keller, J M (1994) 'Levels of Evaluation: Beyond Kirkpatrick', *HRP Quarterly* (5)

Kirkpatrick, D L (1998) *Evaluating Training Programmes: the Four Levels*. San Francisco: Berrett-Koehler

Kohn, A (1993) 'Why incentive plans cannot work', *Harvard Business Review*, Sep-Oct p 54-63

Kolb, D (1984) *Experiential Learning*. New York: Prentice Hall

Kramar, R, McGraw, P & Schuler, R (1997), *Human Resource Management in Australia* (3rd edition). Melbourne: Addison Wesley Longman

Legge, K (1989) 'Human Resource Management: a critical analysis', *New Perspectives in HRM* (ed Storey). London: Routledge

Legge, K (1998) 'The morality of HRM', *Experiencing HRM* (ed Mabey, Skinner & Clark). Cambridge

Liff, S (2000) 'Manpower or HR planning: what's in a name?' *Personnel Management* (3rd edition) ed Bach & Sisson. Oxford: Blackwell

Livy, B (1988) *Corporate Personnel Management.* London: Pitman

Lockett, J (1992) *Effective Performance Management.* Kogan Page

LSC (2004 (a)), posted at www.lsc.gov.uk/National/media/News/Nationalemployersurvey on 02/02/04

LSC (2004 (b)), posted at www.lsc.gov.uk/National/media/PressReleases/ASDAMA on 18.02.04

Lupton, T (1974) *Wages and Salaries.* London: Penguin

Maier, N (1958) *The Appraisal Interview.* New York: Wiley

Manocha, R (2003) 'Catch 22', *People Management,* 9 October

Marchington, M, Goodman, J, Wilkinson, A & Ackers, P (1992) *New Developments in Employee Involvement.* London: HMSO

Marchington, M, Wilkinson, A, Ackers, P & Dundon, A (2001) *Management Choice and Employee Voice.* London: CIPD

Margolis, A (2003) 'Licenced to skill', *People Management,* 26 June

Martin, A O (1967) *Welfare at Work.* London: Batsford

Maslow, A (1954). *Motivation and Personality.* New York: Harper & Row

McGregor, D (1987) *The Human Side of Enterprise.* London: Penguin

Mowdray, R, Porter, L & Steers, R (1982) *Employee-Organisation Linkages* London: Academic Press

Moxon, G R (1958) *Functions of a Personnel Department.* London: IPM

Mullins, L (1985) 'The personnel function: a shared responsibility' *The Administrator,* May.

Mullins, L (1999) *Management and Organisational Behaviour* (5th edition). Harlow, Essex: FT Prentice Hall

Mumford, A (1994) *Management Development: Strategies for Action.* London: IPM

Munro Fraser, J (1971) *Psychology: General, Industrial, Social.* London: Pitman.

National Skills Task Force (1998) *Towards a National Skills Agenda.* London: DfEE

National Skills Task Force (2000) *Skills for All: research report from the NSTK.* London: DfEE

Ouchi, W (1981) *Theory Z.* Reading, Mass: Addison Wesley

Overman, S (2003) 'HR drives change at Levis', *People Management*, 6 November

Oxford Institute of International Finance (2002) *Managing Self Development*. London: OITF

Parsloe, E & Wray, M (2000). *Coaching and Mentoring: Practical Methods to Improve Learning*. London: Kogan Page

Pedler, M Burgoyne, J & Boydell, T (1991) *The Learning Company*. Maidenhead: McGraw Hill

Pedler, M, Burgoyne, J & Boydell, T (2001) *A Manager's Guide to Self Development* (4th edition). Maidenhead: McGraw Hill.

Pedler, M, Brook, C & Burgoyne, J (2003) 'Motion Pictures', *People Management*, 17 April

Persaud, J (2003) 'Fitness First', *People Management*, 11 September

Personnel Standards Lead Body (1993) *A Perspective on Personnel*. London: PSLB

Peters, T J & Waterman, R (1982) *In Search of Excellence*. New York: Harper & Row

Peters, T J (1989) *Thriving on Chaos*. New York: Pan

Peters, T J (1994) *Liberation Management*. New York: Pan

Phillips, J (1997) *Return on Investment in Training and Performance Improvement Programs*. Houston, TX: Gulf.

Pickard, J (2003) 'Joint effort', *People Management*, 24 July

Plumbley, P (1991) *Recruitment and Selection* (5th edition). Hyperion

Prasad, R (2003) Connexions Special Supplement, *The Guardian*, January 29

Purcell, J, Kinnie, N & Hutchinson, S (2003) 'Inside the black box' *People Management*, 15 May

Ream, B (1984) *Personnel Administration*. London: ICSA

Rees, W D (1996) *The Skills of Management* (4th edition). London: Thomson Business Press

Roberts, Z (2003 (a)) 'Barclays banks on older staff', *People Management*, 29 May

Roberts, Z (2003 (b)) 'The last taboo' *People Management*, 1 May

Roberts, Z (2003 (c)) 'Royal Mail admits racism', *People Management*, 10 July

Roberts, Z (2003 (d)) 'BT drive for top women', *People Management*, 11 September

Roberts, Z (2003 (e)) 'Culture key to global HRM', *People Management*, 18 December

Roberts, Z (2003 (f)) 'Fast-track learning', *People Management*, 10 July

Roberts, Z (2003 (g)) 'What's going on at Royal Mail?', *People Management*, 23 October

Rodger, A (1970) *The Seven Point Plan* (3rd edition) London: NFER

Rosenberg, M (2003) 'Best laid plans', *People Management*, 3 April

Schein, E H (1985) *Organisational Culture and Leadership*. San Francisco: Jossey Bass

Schneider, S & Barsoux, J (1997) *Managing Across Cultures*. Harlow, Essex: FT Prentice Hall

Schuler, R S (1995) *Managing Human Resources*. St Paul, Minn: West Publishing

Senge, P (1990) *The Fifth Discipline: the Art and Practice of the Learning Organisation*. New York: Random Century

Shepherd, C (2004) 'Assessing the ROI of training', www.fastrak-consulting.co.uk/tactix/features on 02/03/2004

Sisson, K & Storey, J (2000) *The Realities of HRM: Managing the employment relationship*. Buckingham: OUP

Sloman, M (2001) *The e-Learning Revolution*. London: CIPD

Sloman, M (2003) 'Learning Curve', *People Management*, 25 September

Solomon, C M (2001) 'Managing Virtual Teams', *Workforce*, June

Stone, F M (1999) *Coaching, Counselling and Mentoring*. New York: AMACOM

Storey, J (1989) 'From personnel management to human resource management', *New Perspective on HRM* (ed Storey). London: Routledge

Storey, J (1992) *New Developments in the Management of Human Resources*. London: Routledge

Taylor, S (1998) *Employee Resourcing*. London: IPD

Torrington, D (1994) *International Personnel Management*. Englewood Cliffs, NJ: Prentice Hall

Torrington, D & Hall, L (1991) *Personnel Management: A New Approach*. Englewood Cliffs, NJ: Prentice Hall

Torrington, D, Hall, L, Taylor, S (2002) *Human Resource Management* (5th edition). London: Pearson Education

Townsend, R (1985) *Further up the organisation*. London: Hodder & Stoughton

Trades Union Congress (2000) *Qualifying for Racism*. London: TUC

Trompenaars, F (1993) *Riding the Waves of Culture*. London: Nicholas Brealey

Tulip, S (2003 (a)) 'Just rewards', *People Management*, 25 September

Tulip, S (2003 (b)) 'Flexible trend', *People Management*, 20 November

Tyson, S & Fell, A (1986) *Evaluating the Personnel Function*. London: Hutchinson

University for Industry (2003) 'UfI/learndirect well placed to deliver Government's e-learning vision', posted at www.ufi.com/press/releases on 08/07/03

Upton, R (2003) 'Star gazers', *People Management*, 26 June

Vroom, V (1964) *Work and motivation*. New York: Wiley

NOTES

Walsh, M (2004) 'Ill winds offshore', *The Bulletin*, February 3

Watkins, J (2003 (a)) 'Staff turnover hits four-year low', *People Management*, 4 December

Watkins, J (2003 (b)) 'Tests cut EA turnover', *People Management*, 25 September

Watkins, J (2003 (c)) 'Stress busters', *People Management*, 25 September

Watkins, J (2003 (d)) 'Serious turbulence', *People Management*, 7 August

Watkins, J & Staines, K (2003) 'Job firm risks discrimination', *People Management*, 15 May

Welch, J (2003) 'In the hiring line', *People Management*, 26 June

Whetten, D, & Cameron, K (2002) *Developing Management Skills* (5th edition). New Jersey: Prentice Hall

Whetten, D, Cameron, K & Woods, M (2000) *Developing Management Skills for Europe* (2nd edition). Harlow, Essex: FT Prentice Hall

Wild, A (2003) 'Pressure point', *People Management*, 10 July

Wood, R and Payne, T (1998) *Competency-based Recruitment and Selection*. Chichester: Wiley

Woodruffe, C (1992) 'What is meant by a competency?' *Designing and Achieving Competency* (ed Boam & Sparrow). Maidenhead: McGraw Hill

Woolnough, R (2003) 'Child benefits', *People Management*, 4 December

See overleaf for information on other
BPP products and how to order

HND/HNC Order

To BPP Professional Education, Aldine Place, London W12 8AW
Tel: 020 8740 2211. Fax: 020 8740 1184
E-mail: Publishing@bpp.com Web:www.bpp.com

Mr/Mrs/Ms (Full name)
_____

Daytime delivery address
_____
Postcode _____

Daytime Tel
_____
E-mail _____

5/04

Course Books

MANDATORY (£9.95 each)

Unit 1 Marketing ☐

Unit 2 Managing Financial Resources and Decisions ☐

Unit 3 Organisations and Behaviour ☐

Unit 4 Business Environment ☐

Unit 5 Common Law I ☐

Unit 6 Business Decision Making ☐

Unit 7 Business Strategy ☐

Unit 8 Research Project ☐

Special offer: Buy all 8 Mandatory Texts for £70 ☐

ENDORSED TITLE ROUTES (£14.95 each)

Units 9-12 Finance ☐

Units 13-16 Management ☐

Units 17-20 Marketing ☐

Units 21-24 Human Resource Management ☐

Units 25-28 Law ☐

Special offer: Buy any 2 Endorsed Title Routes for £25 ☐

SUBTOTAL £ _____

TOTAL FOR PRODUCTS £ _____

POSTAGE & PACKING

Texts	First	Each extra	Online	
UK	£5.00	£2.00	£2.00	£ ___
Europe*	£6.00	£4.00	£4.00	£ ___
Rest of world	£20.00	£10.00	£10.00	£ ___

TOTAL FOR POSTAGE & PACKING £ _____

Grand Total (Cheques to *BPP Professional Education*)

I enclose a cheque for (incl. Postage) £ _____

Or charge to Access/Visa/Switch

Card Number ☐☐☐☐ ☐☐☐☐ ☐☐☐☐ ☐☐☐☐   CV2 No ☐☐☐ last 3 digits on signature strip

Expiry date _____   Start Date _____

Issue Number (Switch Only) _____

Signature _____

We aim to deliver to all UK addresses inside 5 working days; a signature will be required. Orders to all EU addresses should be delivered within 6 working days. All other orders to overseas addresses should be delivered within 8 working days. * Europe includes the Republic of Ireland and the Channel Islands.

Review Form & Free Prize Draw – HND Specialist Units 21 to 24 (5/04)

All original review forms from the entire BPP range, completed with genuine comments, will be entered into one of two draws on 31 January 2005 and 31 July 2005. The names on the first four forms picked out on each occasion will be sent a cheque for £50.

Name: _____   Address: _____

_____

_____

How have you used this Course Book?
(Tick one box only)

☐ Home study (book only)

☐ On a course: college _____

☐ Other _____

During the past six months do you recall seeing/receiving any of the following?
(Tick as many boxes as are relevant)

☐ Our advertisement

☐ Our brochure with a letter through the post

Why did you decide to purchase this Course book? *(Tick one box only)*

☐ Have used BPP Texts in the past

☐ Recommendation by friend/colleague

☐ Recommendation by a lecturer at college

☐ Saw advertising

☐ Other _____

Your ratings, comments and suggestions would be appreciated on the following areas

	Very useful	Useful	Not useful
Introductory pages	☐	☐	☐
Topic coverage	☐	☐	☐
Summary diagrams	☐	☐	☐
Chapter roundups	☐	☐	☐
Quick quizzes	☐	☐	☐
Activities	☐	☐	☐
Discussion points	☐	☐	☐

	Excellent	Good	Adequate	Poor
Overall opinion of this Course book	☐	☐	☐	☐

Do you intend to continue using BPP HND/HNC Course books?   ☐ Yes   ☐ No

Please note any further comments and suggestions/errors on the reverse of this page.

The BPP author of this edition can be e-mailed at: pippariley@bpp.com

Please return this form to: Pippa Riley, BPP Professional Education, FREEPOST, London, W12 8BR

Review Form & Free Prize Draw (continued)

Please note any further comments and suggestions/errors below

The Learning Centre
SOUTH TRAFFORD COLLEGE
Manchester Road
West Timperley
Altrincham
Cheshire
WA14 5PQ

Free Prize Draw Rules

1   Closing date for 31 January 2005 draw is 31 December 2004. Closing date for 31 July 2005 draw is 30 June 2005.

2   Restricted to entries with UK and Eire addresses only. BPP employees, their families and business associates are excluded.

3   No purchase necessary. Entry forms are available upon request from BPP Professional Education. No more than one entry per title, per person. Draw restricted to persons aged 16 and over.

4   Winners will be notified by post and receive their cheques not later than 6 weeks after the relevant draw date.

5   The decision of the promoter in all matters is final and binding. No correspondence will be entered into.